Navigating Digital Transformation Through Business Process Management

Javier Martínez-Falcó
University of Alicante, Spain

Eduardo Sánchez-García
University of Alicante, Spain

Bartolomé Marco-Lajara
University of Alicante, Spain

IGI Global
Scientific Publishing
Publishing Tomorrow's Research Today

Vice President of Editorial Melissa Wagner
Director of Acquisitions Mikaela Felty
Director of Book Development Jocelynn Hessler
Production Manager Mike Brehm
Cover Design Jose Rosado

Published in the United States of America by
IGI Global Scientific Publishing
701 East Chocolate Avenue
Hershey, PA, 17033, USA
Tel: 717-533-8845
Fax: 717-533-7115
Website: https://www.igi-global.com E-mail: cust@igi-global.com

Library of Congress Cataloging-in-Publication Data

LCCN: 2025017542 (CIP Data Pending)
ISBN13: 9798337333366
Isbn13Softcover: 9798337333373
EISBN13: 9798337333380

British Cataloguing in Publication Data
A Cataloguing in Publication record for this book is available from the British Library.

Table of Contents

Detailed Table of Contents

curated product offerings, and seamless technology-driven shopping experiences. This research highlights the growing importance hospitality-retail models in sustaining competitive advantage, emphasizing the need for innovative service design and guest-centric retail strategies in the evolving hospitality.

BPM has moved from an operational tool to a strategic enabler of value generation, innovation, and agility. As firms undergo digital change, the often-overlooked human aspect becomes crucial. While AI, automation, and cloud computing provide core capabilities, human flexibility, creativity, and cooperation create genuine progress. This chapter discusses how human-centric BPM empowers individuals in processes. The focus is on combining technology with mental health, cultural participation, digital literacy, and emotional intelligence. Modern BPM emphasizes responsiveness, co-creation, and people-centered design over standardization and efficiency. The chapter provides capability development, behavioral transformation, and cultural alignment frameworks for workforce adaptability. Participatory design, ethics, and leadership changes are covered. Empowering people in digital transformation is highlighted by case studies and future research directions like new measurements and longitudinal investigations.

This chapter explores human factors and their impact on the adaptation of the workforce to the digital transition in Moroccan public administrations. As the digitalization of public services becomes a priority to improve efficiency and transparency, the adoption of new technologies depends heavily on employees and their ability to adapt to changes. This paper examines the skills, resistance to change and motivation of public servants in the face of this transformation. The study is based on an exploratory methodological approach, using semi-structured interviews with human resources managers, civil servants and change management experts in various Moroccan public administrations. This approach collects direct perceptions and experiences of the actors involved in the digital transition. The results of the study reveal that resistance to change, lack of digital skills and a stagnant organizational culture are the main barriers to adopting digital technologies. Younger employees are generally more receptive, while older employees face more difficulties.

The rapid evolution of digital technologies is reshaping business processes, necessitating workforce adaptation to sustain organizational competitiveness. While digital transformation enhances efficiency and innovation, its success is contingent on human factors influencing employee adaptation. This chapter examines key psychological, behavioral, and organizational challenges in digital transitions, including skill gaps, resistance to change, and digital fatigue. It explores workforce adaptation strategies through theoretical frameworks such as the Technology Acceptance Model (TAM), Lewin's Change Management Model, and the Job Demands-Resources (JD-R) Model. The chapter further highlights leadership roles, change management strategies, and case studies of successful digital workforce adaptation. A human-centric approach to digital transformation is essential to balancing technological advancements with employee well-being, fostering a resilient and future-ready workforce.

The current research examines how business process management (BPM) and marketing are integrated into marketing communications to enhance customer-centric processes in response to technological advancements. Information and communication evolution and joining with other technologies give rise to a new focus on Marketing 4.0. The shift of focus from brand-centric marketing to customer-centric marketing motivates practitioners to highlight customer experience, satisfaction, and loyalty. However, ever-changing market dynamics, new customer demand, and emergence of new communication and marketing channels hinder efficient service delivery by marketing departments.

Businesses, industries, and consumers' physical enabling interconnectivity allow for greater automation, efficiency, and real-time monitoring, which is most important applications offering businesses track, analyze, optimize operations instantaneously. By embedding sensors and intelligent systems into processes, IoT facilitates continuous data collection and analysis, providing operational help. This combination process is reshaping logistics and agriculture by providing unprecedented status and systems. Understanding the Internet of Things (IoT): a broad concept encompassing physical sensors, actuators, other objects through objects, and smart highly used in manufacturing or healthcare. The key IoT gathers exchange, then processes and analyzes to improve the functionality of the connected objects. One primary is the sensor, which collects data from the pressure and motion. Then, through networks (often wireless) to central processing units or cloud platforms, IoT systems typically rely on several key elements of the ecosystem, smarter environments, and more efficient operations.

Datasets that recognize patterns have found applications in supply chain management, customer service, manufacturing, marketing, finance, healthcare, and many other sectors. The implementation of AI can lead to a wide range of benefits, including cost reduction, time savings, improved accuracy, and better resource allocation. Opportunities Presented by AI in Enhancing Process Efficiency: Automation of Repetitive Tasks: well-known applications AI technologies time-consuming high consistency. For example, in administrative functions, handle document management, email filtering, and complex and creative work. Similarly, in manufacturing, robots equipped with AI inspection and packaging improve speed and accuracy. Data-Driven Decision Making: allowing better algorithms, uncovering structured and unstructured data, predicting future trends, and making informed decisions that enhance operational efficiency. This requires investment in training programs and a strategic approach to managing the transition to ensure that employees remain valuable assets in an AI-driven environment.

This book chapter examines the multifaceted impacts of digitalization on corporate sustainability. Corporate sustainability is a management paradigm that aims to manage environmental, social, and economic responsibilities with a holistic approach and to enhance the long-term value creation capacities of businesses. Especially, the integration of digital technologies such as artificial intelligence, big data, the Internet of Things, and cloud computing into business processes has been shown to contribute to sustainable performance in areas such as efficiency, transparency, agility, and innovation. However, it has been emphasized that digitalization also carries various risks such as high costs, digital skills gaps, cybersecurity threats, e-waste generation, and digital inequality. The section argues that digitalization requires not only a technical transformation but also a strategic, cultural, and governance transformation in terms of corporate sustainability.

Big Data and AI technologies are revolutionizing Business Process Management (BPM). This chapter focuses on how AI and predictive analytics are transforming traditional forms of BPM. The combination of these technologies presents major opportunities utilizing insights from data to optimize decision making, advancing process enhancement beyond mere automation, increasing responsiveness and flexibility of operations, as well as innovativeness. AI enhances BPM with the capacity to respond to market changes and deliver services more rapidly and tailor them to individuals. Nevertheless, these advantages depend critically on data issue resolution. Unresolved challenges such as the 'data paradox', quality concerns such as bias and inconsistency, and complicated data processing including cleansing, standardization, privacy, and security present obstacles. Emerging trends suggest

Preface

In recent years, digital transformation has become a pervasive phenomenon that transcends industries, organizational boundaries, and traditional management paradigms. Its complexity resides not only in the technological innovations it entails, but also in the profound organizational, cultural, and strategic shifts it requires. Within this landscape, Business Process Management (BPM) emerges as a critical discipline for understanding, guiding, y articulating transformation efforts in a structured and value-driven manner.

The book *Navigating Digital Transformation Through Business Process Management* is conceived as a scholarly response to the need for integrative frameworks that link the operational core of organizations with the evolving capabilities brought forth by digital technologies. Rather than treating digital transformation as a purely technical endeavor, this volume approaches it as a multidimensional process involving technological infrastructures, human capital, data-driven decision-making, organizational learning, and the reconfiguration of business logic.

The contributions compiled in this volume reflect a deliberate effort to address this multifaceted reality. Drawing from diverse academic backgrounds and practical experiences, the chapters analyze critical issues such as the integration of artificial intelligence and machine learning into process design, the strategic implications of real-time analytics, the role of human-centered adaptation in digital contexts, and the tensions between innovation and institutional inertia in the implementation of new technologies. While varied in their scope, these studies converge on a common objective: to enhance our understanding of how organizations can manage complexity and uncertainty through intelligent process-oriented strategies.

What distinguishes this work is its ambition to bridge theoretical rigor with contextual relevance. The authors adopt a range of methodological approaches, quantitative modeling, case study research, conceptual development, and exploratory análisis, thereby providing a rich and pluralistic perspective on the challenges and opportunities of digital transformation. This methodological diversity allows the volume to speak to multiple audiences, including academic researchers seeking to advance theoretical debates, practitioners involved in process redesign initiatives, and policymakers interested in fostering digital capabilities within organizational ecosystems.

CHAPTER OVERVIEW

Chapter 1: AI-Driven Human Augmentation, Enhancing Productivity, Creativity, and Decision-Making in the Business Process

This study explores how AI augments human productivity, creativity, and decision-making across sectors, positioning it as a tool to enhance human potential. Using a qualitative approach with case studies from healthcare, business, and creative industries—such as IBM Watson—it illustrates AI's practical applications. Central to the study are ethical concerns like data privacy, algorithmic bias, and fairness. Findings suggest that AI significantly enhances human capabilities while also raising important ethical issues. However, limitations exist in measuring AI's long-term impact on human agency and creativity due to rapid technological evolution, and the study does not address regional disparities in AI access. Despite these challenges, the research offers a unique perspective on AI-human collaboration, highlighting AI as a partner in innovation rather than a replacement for human intelligence, and calls for deeper regulatory focus to ensure fairness, privacy, and equitable use.

Chapter 2: Combining Hospitality and Retail: Innovative Strategies in the Modern Hotel Industry

The convergence of hospitality and retail has emerged as a transformative strategy in the modern hotel industry, enhancing guest experiences while creating new revenue streams. This study explores the integration of retail spaces within hotels, analyzing its impact on customer satisfaction, financial performance. Data from guest surveys, sales records, and hotel management insights reveal that retail integration significantly improves guest satisfaction, increasing average scores from 7.2 to 8.5. Financially, hotels with retail spaces reported a 140% rise in monthly revenue, demonstrating the profitability of this model. Key success factors include strategic retail placement, curated product offerings, and seamless technology-driven shopping experiences. This research highlights the growing importance hospitality-retail models in sustaining competitive advantage, emphasizing the need for innovative service design and guest-centric retail strategies in the evolving hospitality.

Chapter 3: Empowering People in Process and Human-Centric Adaptation in Digital Business Transformation

BPM has moved from an operational tool to a strategic enabler of value generation, innovation, and agility. As firms undergo digital change, the often-overlooked human aspect becomes crucial. While AI, automation, and cloud computing provide core capabilities, human flexibility, creativity, and cooperation create genuine progress. This chapter discusses how human-centric BPM empowers individuals in processes. The focus is on combining technology with mental health, cultural participation, digital literacy, and emotional intelligence. Modern BPM emphasizes responsiveness, co-creation, and people-centered design over standardization and efficiency. The chapter provides capability development, behavioral transformation, and cultural alignment frameworks for workforce adaptability. Participatory design, ethics, and leadership changes are covered. Empowering people in digital transformation is highlighted by case studies and future research directions like new measurements and longitudinal investigations.

Chapter 4: Human Factors and Adaptation of the Workforce in the Digital Transition in Public Administrations in Morocco: An Exploratory Study

This chapter explores human factors and their impact on the adaptation of the workforce to the digital transition in Moroccan public administrations. As the digitalization of public services becomes a priority to improve efficiency and transparency, the adoption of new technologies depends heavily on employees and their ability to adapt to changes. This paper examines the skills, resistance to change and motivation of public servants in the face of this transformation. The study is based on an exploratory methodological approach, using semi-structured interviews with human resources managers, civil servants and change management experts in various Moroccan public administrations. This approach collects direct perceptions and experiences of the actors involved in the digital transition. The results of the study reveal that resistance to change, lack of digital skills and a stagnant organizational culture are the main barriers to adopting digital technologies. Younger employees are generally more receptive, while older employees face more difficulties.

Chapter 5: Human Factors and Workforce Adaptation in Digital Transition

The rapid evolution of digital technologies is reshaping business processes, necessitating workforce adaptation to sustain organizational competitiveness. While digital transformation enhances efficiency and innovation, its success is contingent on human factors influencing employee adaptation. This chapter examines key psychological, behavioral, and organizational challenges in digital transitions, including skill gaps, resistance to change, and digital fatigue. It explores workforce adaptation strategies through theoretical frameworks such as the Technology Acceptance Model (TAM), Lewin's Change Management Model, and the Job Demands-Resources (JD-R) Model. The chapter further highlights leadership roles, change management strategies, and case studies of successful digital workforce adaptation. A human-centric approach to digital transformation is essential to balancing technological advancements with employee well-being, fostering a resilient and future-ready workforce.

Chapter 6: Integrating Business Process Management and Marketing: A Strategic Approach to Enhancing Customer-Centric Processes

The current research examines how business process management (BPM) and marketing are integrated into marketing communications to enhance customer-centric processes in response to technological advancements. Information and communication evolution and joining with other technologies give rise to a new focus on Marketing 4.0. The shift of focus from brand-centric marketing to customer-centric marketing motivates practitioners to highlight customer experience, satisfaction, and loyalty. However, ever-changing market dynamics, new customer demand, and emergence of new communication and marketing channels hinder efficient service delivery by marketing departments.

Chapter 7: Leveraging Artificial Intelligence and Machine Learning for Business Process Management in Digital Marketing

Digital marketing is a rapid industry with ample development and investment opportunities around the world. Throughout the present economic climate, every marketer recognized the importance of a digital marketing presence. Understanding the market forces and trends that affect one brand or business can help to identify new revenue avenues (Bayoude et al., 2018). Marketers look for efficient methods to maximize returns while employing capital constraints, making sure that few budgets are spent on irrelevant or less efficient areas.

Chapter 8: Leveraging Data Analytics for Informed Decision-Making in Process Management

This survey chapter aims at discussing the application of data analytics in process management in order to improve operational performance, decision making and innovation. This chapter also describes the analytical techniques including descriptive, predictive, and prescriptive analytics and illustrates their use in manufacturing, healthcare, finance, and logistics industries. The chapter also discusses new trends, which are in the development of process management, including artificial intelligence, edge analytics, and digital twins. However, there are some barriers to the implementation of the framework such as data quality, skill, privacy, and organizational readiness. The chapter concludes by emphasizing the importance of leveraging data analytics strategically and responsibly to ensure long-term success in a data-driven business environment.

Chapter 9: Navigating Workforce Adaptation and Human Factors in the Digital Era

This study aims at identifying the implemented changes and prospects for addressing the issues regarding workforce adaptation and the role of AI, automation, and digital transformation in human aspects. This chapter explores some of the pertinent topics that include cognitive load, motivation, technostress, and differences in generations in relation to technologies. The chapter focuses on the changes in the roles and skills, new roles, the need for new skills, and the significance of lifelong learning. Also, it considers the adoptions of a new working model that is the hybrid model of work and ethical considerations in relation to automation, job loss, and privacy. The chapter outlines approaches for employees, and policymakers to effectively manage these shifts and support the development of a resilient and adaptable workforce amid rapid technological change.

Chapter 10: Sustainability in the Digital Age: Redefining Technology Ecosystems

The rapid advancement of digital technologies has fundamentally transformed the way societies function, offering unprecedented opportunities for innovation and growth. However, this digital revolution has also brought significant environmental, social, and economic challenges, necessitating a redefinition of technology ecosystems through the lens of sustainability. This paper explores the environmental, social, and economic impacts of digital technologies and their role in shaping sustainable technology ecosystems. As digital innovations such as artificial intelligence (AI), the Internet of Things (IoT), and cloud computing continue to transform industries and societies, their dual potential to drive progress and exacerbate challenges has become increasingly evident. While these technologies offer solutions for efficiency, connectivity, and innovation, they also contribute to significant environmental concerns, such as energy consumption and electronic waste, as well as social issues like the digital divide and data privacy risks.

Chapter 11: The Internet of Things and Real-Time Process Monitoring

Businesses, industries, and consumers' physical enabling interconnectivity allow for greater automation, efficiency, and real-time monitoring, which is most important applications offering businesses track, analyze, optimize operations instantaneously. By embedding sensors and intelligent systems into processes, IoT facilitates continuous data collection and analysis, providing operational help. This combination process is reshaping logistics and agriculture by providing unprecedented status and systems. Understanding the Internet of Things (IoT): a broad concept encompassing physical sensors, actuators, other objects through objects, and smart highly used in manufacturing or healthcare. The key IoT gathers exchange, then processes and analyzes to improve the functionality of the connected objects. One primary is the sensor, which collects data from the pressure and motion. Then, through networks (often wireless) to central processing units or cloud platforms, IoT systems typically rely on several key elements of the ecosystem, smarter environments, and more efficient operations.

Chapter 12: The Role of Artificial Intelligence in Improving Process Efficiency

Datasets that recognize patterns have found applications in supply chain management, customer service, manufacturing, marketing, finance, healthcare, and many other sectors. The implementation of AI can lead to a wide range of benefits, including cost reduction, time savings, improved accuracy, and better resource allocation. Opportunities Presented by AI in Enhancing Process Efficiency: Automation of Repetitive Tasks: well-known applications AI technologies time-consuming high consistency. For example, in administrative functions, handle document management, email filtering, and complex and creative work. Similarly, in manufacturing, robots equipped with AI inspection and packaging improve speed and accuracy.

Data-Driven Decision Making: allowing better algorithms, uncovering structured and unstructured data, predicting future trends, and making informed decisions that enhance operational efficiency. This requires investment in training programs and a strategic approach to managing the transition to ensure that employees remain valuable assets in an AI-driven environment.

Chapter 13: The Role of Digitalization in Corporate Sustainability

This book chapter examines the multifaceted impacts of digitalization on corporate sustainability. Corporate sustainability is a management paradigm that aims to manage environmental, social, and economic responsibilities with a holistic approach and to enhance the long-term value creation capacities of businesses. Especially, the integration of digital technologies such as artificial intelligence, big data, the Internet of Things, and cloud computing into business processes has been shown to contribute to sustainable performance in areas such as efficiency, transparency, agility, and innovation. However, it has been emphasized that digitalization also carries various risks such as high costs, digital skills gaps, cybersecurity threats, e-waste generation, and digital inequality. The section argues that digitalization requires not only a technical transformation but also a strategic, cultural, and governance transformation in terms of corporate sustainability.

Chapter 14: Transforming Business Process Management Through Artificial Intelligence and Predictive Analytics

Big Data and AI technologies are revolutionizing Business Process Management (BPM). This chapter focuses on how AI and predictive analytics are transforming traditional forms of BPM. The combination of these technologies presents major opportunities utilizing insights from data to optimize decision making, advancing process enhancement beyond mere automation, increasing responsiveness and flexibility of operations, as well as innovativeness. AI enhances BPM with the capacity to respond to market changes and deliver services more rapidly and tailor them to individuals. Nevertheless, these advantages depend critically on data issue resolution. Unresolved challenges such as the 'data paradox', quality concerns such as bias and inconsistency, and complicated data processing including cleansing, standardization, privacy, and security present obstacles. Emerging trends suggest more advanced automation and predictive modeling, collaboration with ethicists, and pivoting BPM toward self-governing, self-evolving systems that provide users substantial competitive leverage.

The emphasis on Business Process Management as a guiding thread is not incidental. In an era characterized by fragmented data environments, shifting stakeholder expectations, and volatile market dynamics, BPM serves as an essential mechanism for achieving strategic coherence, operational alignment, and organizational resilience. By situating BPM within the broader context of digital transformation, the chapters in this book contribute to a more comprehensive and nuanced understanding of how digital tools and practices can be effectively leveraged to enhance performance, foster innovation, and create sustainable value.

This volume would not have been possible without the intellectual engagement and commitment of the contributing authors, the critical insights provided by reviewers, and the support of the editorial team at IGI Global. Their collective efforts have resulted in a publication that aspires to inform, challenge, and inspire future research and professional practice in an area of growing importance for contemporary management.

It is our hope that this book will serve as a reference point for scholars and practitioners seeking to navigate the complexities of digital transformation through the lens of Business Process Management, while also stimulating new lines of inquiry and collaborative exploration.

Javier Martínez-Falcó
University of Alicante, Spain

Eduardo Sánchez-García
University of Alicante, Spain

Bartolomé Marco-Lajara
University of Alicante, Spain

Chapter 1
AI-Driven Human Augmentation:
Enhancing Productivity, Creativity, and Decision-Making in the Business Process

Mohammad Irfan
https://orcid.org/0000-0002-4956-1170
Chandigarh University, Unnao, India

Sanchit Agrawal
Christ University, India

Ajay Kumar Yadav
Chandigarh University, Unnao, India

Rui Manuel dos Santos Vigário Rodrigues
https://orcid.org/0009-0003-9801-694X
Polytechnic Institute of Setúbal, Portugal

Shakeeb Mohammad Mir
Christ University, India

ABSTRACT

This study explores how AI augments human productivity, creativity, and decision-making across sectors, positioning it as a tool to enhance human potential. Using a qualitative approach with case studies from healthcare, business, and creative industries—such as IBM Watson—it illustrates AI's practical applications. Central to the study are ethical concerns like data privacy, algorithmic bias, and fairness.

DOI: 10.4018/979-8-3373-3336-6.ch001

Findings suggest that AI significantly enhances human capabilities while also raising important ethical issues. However, limitations exist in measuring AI's long-term impact on human agency and creativity due to rapid technological evolution, and the study does not address regional disparities in AI access. Despite these challenges, the research offers a unique perspective on AI-human collaboration, highlighting AI as a partner in innovation rather than a replacement for human intelligence, and calls for deeper regulatory focus to ensure fairness, privacy, and equitable use.

INTRODUCTION

Global AI-guided human augmentation is progressively influencing the future of work, decision making and innovation. From North America to Asia, as AI technologies make their way into our daily routines and work lives, a shift from Automation to Augmentation is kicking off, where machines and humans do not compete on the same level, but instead, machines are used to help augment and boost the existing capabilities of the human staff. This shifting paradigmization is at the core of today's business world revolution. AI is also playing an active role in enhancement of decision-making accuracy and operational efficiency in developed countries such as the United States and Germany. For example, companies applying machine learning algorithms to large datasets to provide real-time analytics in strategic decision-making include humans in decision making (Davenport & Ronanki, 2018).

Global Perspectives on AI-Driven Human Augmentation

In the finance space, AI-powered tools assist with fraud detection and portfolio management, helping analysts, and mitigating human error (Chui et al., 2018). And in East Asia, China, Japan, and South Korea, governments and companies are making huge investments in A.I. to advance productivity and innovation. China's New Generation Artificial Intelligence Development Plan explicitly highlights that AI is to be combined with humanity talent much more forcefully as a means of global technological leadership in more and more AI-rich fields (State Council of China 2017). In Japan, AI is now part of elder care and manufacturing, replacing the labour supply in the face of a demographic decline (Yamagata, 2020). At the same time, in emerging markets such as Sub-Saharan Africa and Southeast Asia, AI-assisted human augmentation might provide solutions to perennial problems, such as disparities in healthcare, education and governance. AI-based language translation and adaptive learning programmes are also being utilised to break through language and educational barriers, and to expand access to information and personalised learning (World Bank, 2020). But these areas have infrastructure and policy problems that block the fair adoption of AI. The creative industries are being revolutionised globally. AI platforms such as DALL·E, ChatGPT, and Amper Music help artists, writers, and designers come up ideas.

The Conceptual Foundation of AI-Driven Human Augmentation

The idea of human augmentation is the use of technology to enhance humanity, raising the potential of people by doing things that were impossible to do before, by saying things that were unsaid, by feeling emotions that could not be felt, and so on. In the scope of AI, this model becomes more significant. Instead of replacing human labor, AI is more and more seen as an instrument for augmenting human capacity, in productivity, creativity and decision-making, through complexity of business processes. The basic idea on which AI assisted human augmentation is established is that of cognitive extension, in which human intellect is extended externally by a system of intelligence which is not human (Clarke & Chalmers, 1998). This changes the old story from human against machine to human and machine. In the space of productivity AI is able to automate routine tasks while employees concentrate on more strategic work that produces value (Brynjolfsson & McAfee, 2014). Smart machines, such as robotic process automation (RPA) and digital twins, are classic examples of AI enhancing operational efficiency by reducing human effort as well as increasing the speed and accuracy of work (Davenport & Kirby, 2016). Creativity, long thought as something only humans can do, is being reimagined with AI as well. At a conceptual level, AI can play the role of a creative catalyst, providing new concepts, visualizations, and generative outputs that can then be refined and situated by humans. This co-creativity paradigm mangles the line between machine generated and human authored work (Runco & Acar, 2012). Tools like GPT (GPT-2 and GPT-3, from OpenAI) or DeepDream (from Google) show how AI can set the stage for creative discovery or spark new design vernaculars, turning the creative process into a dance between human and machine. When it comes to decisions, AI acts as a thinking partner to unlock untold terabytes of information, which it molds into insights that inform nuanced human judgment. The paradigm shift here is from automatic decision to AID for AI-based decision support suggesting prime choices—without excluding the human from the loop (Raisch & Krakowski, 2021). About one-third of them use AI methods (about 20% use machine learning, and another 30% use natural language processing or business rules) to help executives manage through uncertainty and complexity.

LITERATURE REVIEW

The foreword presentation by Ma et al. is on the use of AI for enhancing human abilities, which they call AI-driven human augmentation. The phenomenon is reflected in the literature through at least three dimensions: productivity, creativity and decision-making in connection with the technological dimension, the organizational one and the ethical one. Human enhancement and performance have always been the main aspects of interest in I/O area. Brynjolfsson and McAfee (2014) posit that the second machine age is not about the substitution of humans, but the augmentation of humans where machines take on repetitive, low-skill tasks and humans concentrate on higher-level cognitive tasks. This can be observed in automated process robots as well as AI scheduling systems in sectors such as logistics and health care (Davenport & Ronanki, 2018). AI helps decrease cognitive load and time to task accomplishment, which are reputed to increase employee satisfaction and performance (Brock & Von Wangenheim 2019). In the creativity community, there is an increasing body of work focusing on co-creative systems—where humans and machines work together to bring about new creations 1. McCormack et al. (2019) investigate AI also applied to generative art and music, where AI-based systems do not replace human artists but act as catalysts for ideas. Likewise, the utilization of generative design software for architectural and product design constitutes a kind of creative augmentation that transcends human ideation capabilities (Boden, 2016). Such tools enable the investigation of a larger design space in less time, spanning the range of design options and encouraging innovation. Researchers emphasize that with respect to decision-making, AI is an aid to decision-making, not a substitute to human judgment. In a similar vein, Shrestha, Benbya, and Vom Brocke (2021) propose the idea of hybrid intelligence wherein artificial intelligence (AI) processes data, while humans contribute intuition. AI plays a role in pattern recognition, predictive analytics, and scenario simulation to enhance the quality and speed

Figure 1. AI plays a role in pattern recognition, predictive analytics, and scenario simulation to enhance the quality and speed

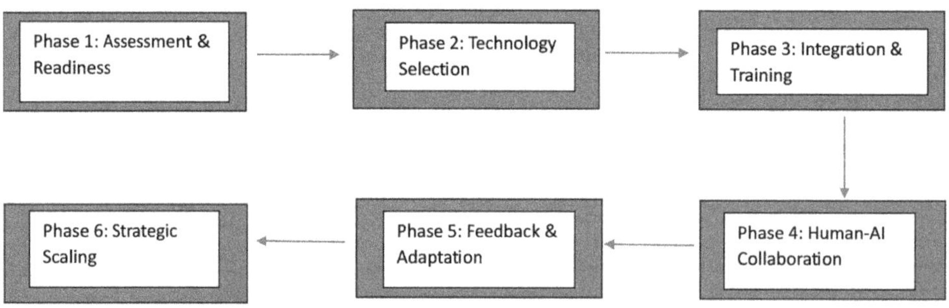

Growth Outlook for AI-Driven Human Augmentation by 2030

As seen in the chart Generative AI Market Size and Forecast (2020–2030), the estimated exponential growth of the generative AI market from $62.72 billion in 2025 to $356.10 billion in 2030—using a compound annual growth rate (CAGR) of 41.53%—is a compelling indication of the manner in which technology evolved based on AI will shape man augmentation in business operations. The rapid growth of this market shows how AI is being used more and more in business to boost productivity, creativity, and decision-making across different industries. AI-human augmentation means using AI technologies like machine learning, natural language processing, and generative models to enhance what people can do. These tools help expand thinking abilities, handle routine tasks automatically, and allow humans to focus on more creative and strategic work. As the chart shows, the generative AI market alone is expected to grow by over 467% between 2025 and 2030. This trend shows that companies are investing in technology that supports people, not replaces them. Tools like ChatGPT, DALL·E, and other generators are being used to work together on marketing content, help with research, provide business insights, and enable quick decision-making. This partnership between humans and AI is the core idea behind augmentation. In practice, AI improves productivity by managing large amounts of data, automating supply chains, and enhancing customer interactions through voice assistants. A McKinsey Global Institute report confirms that generative AI would contribute between $2.6 trillion and $4.4 trillion in additional productivity to each industry per year (McKinsey, 2023). In finance, for instance, AI solutions provide real-time protection against fraud and investment simulations. In medicine, AI assists with diagnostics and individualized treatment planning, enabling physicians to concentrate on patient care. Creativity is also evolving. Designers use generative tools to come up with ideas and quickly create prototypes.

Figure 2. Designers use generative tools to come up with ideas and quickly create prototypes.

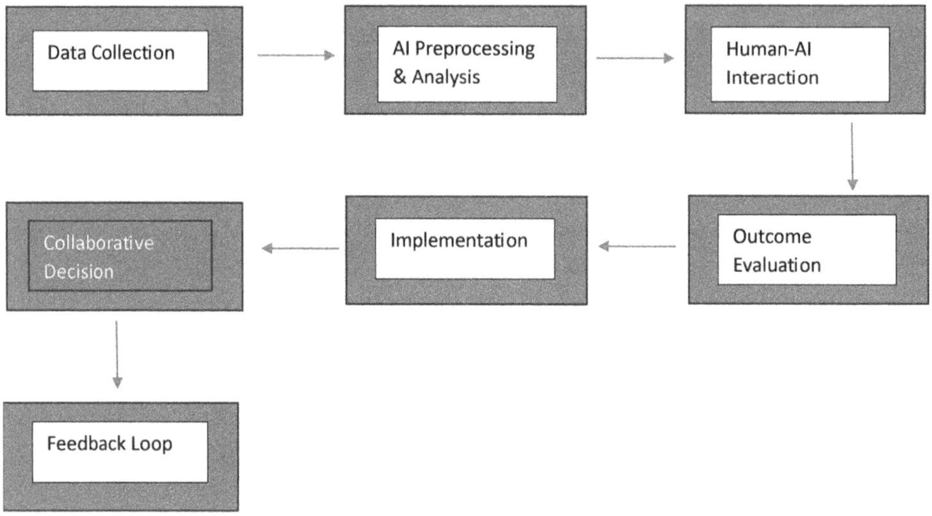

In entertainment and media, AI helps with scriptwriting, video editing, and visual effects, making it easier and faster to bring creative ideas to life. These tools allow people to improve their work and push creative boundaries. Decision-making is one of the areas most changed by AI. AI-powered analytics platforms analyze huge amounts of data to offer insights that guide important decisions. Business leaders are increasingly relying on predictive models, scenario simulations, and recommendation systems to make quicker and smarter choices. By 2030, using AI in business won't just be a competitive advantage—it will be essential. The market data shown in the graph highlights both the growing investment in generative AI and the rapid rise of human-focused AI applications. In short, the growth of generative AI signals a shift toward work that is enhanced and supported by AI. As companies deploy such technologies at scale, we shall witness a redesign of work processes with AI-powered human augmentation at its core to actualize enterprise potential.

Figure 3. Generative AI Market Size and Forecast (2020-2030)

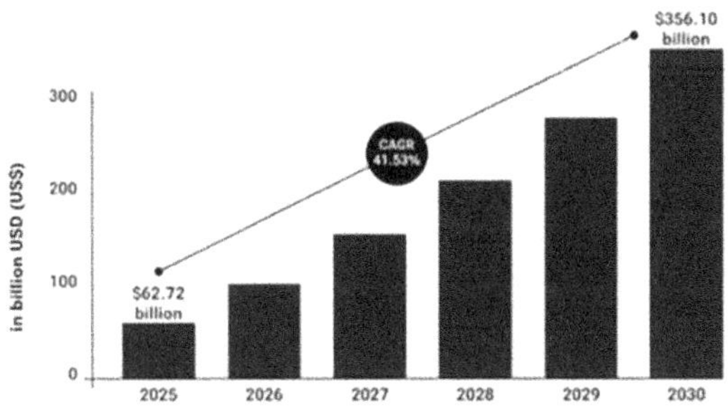

Case Studies

Case Study 1: IBM Watson at Mayo Clinic – Augmenting Medical Decision-Making

The role of artificial intelligence in healthcare is indeed revolutionizing the era of medical diagnosis, tailored therapy and clinical decision. An illustrative case of AI-enhanced human augmentation is the IBM Watson for Oncology teaming with the Mayo Clinic in the area of Cancer Care. This collaboration exemplifies how AI can augment, as opposed to replace, human expertise by providing clinicians evidence-based guidance from large scale data sources. IBM Watson for Oncology is a cognitive computing system that has been developed in concert with Memorial Sloan Kettering Cancer Center to help guide oncologists in recommending treatments for cancer patients. The system uses natural language processing and machine learning to analyze structured and unstructured medical records, patient records, research reports, treatment guidelines and clinical trials. This capability to synthesize large quantities of information in real-time is a powerful tool for physician decision-making, particularly in complex cases such as cancer management (Ferrucci et al., 2013). Mayo Clinic Uses Watson to Make Clinical Trials Better At the Mayo Clinic, Watson was introduced to expedite getting patients connected to clinical trials. Cancer research is frequently faced with a significant bottleneck in identifying appropriate patients for very specific and changing trial criteria, because of the time-consuming manual nature of this process. Watson learned to review tens of thousands of medical procedures and pair them with patients' medical histories and individual data (IBM, 2016). The outcomes were impressive. Physicians stated that Watson decreased the time spent screening patients for clinical trials from weeks to minutes in some instances. They further added that it saved them 30%–40% of time that would otherwise be consumed by paperwork and gave them more time to attend to patients and make decisions (Topol, 2019). Also, Watson's suggestions were in accordance with the findings of expert cancer doctors 96% of the time, particularly for the most prevalent types of cancer. The system wasn't designed to overrule human judgment but assist doctors. It served as a second opinion or data-rich assistant, reminding physicians to consider treatment alternatives they may not have considered, particularly in unusual or complex cases. This combination of human judgment and machine interpretation is what the future of human-AI collaboration in medicine looks like. There were, however, complications. AI systems such as Watson must be continuously retrained with the latest clinical information, and they may be less useful when applied to low quality data or new diseases not covered in the training set. However, the Mayo Clinic example demonstrates the feasibility and potential benefit of this form of AI-enhanced decision-making in a clinical setting. In summary, the IBM Watson/Mayo Clinic collaboration demonstrates how this approach, which brings advanced theoretical knowledge to everyday practice, has the potential to enhance complex decision making, increase productivity and, ideally, improve patient outcomes. As an example of AI enabled 'human augmentation' at a macro-level digital transformation level in healthcare, this is a strong one.

Case Study 2: Autodesk Dreamcatcher – AI in Creative Design

AI is changing the game in the creative industries by scaling human ability to create, invent, and solve big challenges. One of the most especially impressive examples of this shift is Autodesk's Dreamcatcher project, an AI-fueled generative design platform aimed at leveraging the human imagination in architecture, engineering, and even product design. Dreamcatcher is all about moving from a design as a noun to a design as a verb, says Chief Engineer of Applied research Mike Haley. Dreamcatcher has been developed by Autodesk's Research to illustrate how designers may enter particular design goals like material, manufacturing techniques, performance criteria, and budget constraints, and the technology delivers countless design options in return. Parameters such as material type, manufacturing process, cost bounds, physical behavior and aesthetic desires are defined by users. The generated design prompts ae subsequently employed by the AI system to generate a multitude of alternative designs, each of which is also optimised to meet the given design targets (Autodesk, 2016). In contrast to conventional design software, where the designs are entered into the computer manually, Dreamcatcher needs the user to enter design requirements using a design tool and then Dreamcatcher does the heavy lifting during the exploration stage. For example, in one of its most visible applications, Autodesk collaborated with Airbus to reimagine a partition wall in an airplane. Generative design assisted the AI program in suggesting a whopping

10,000-plus other designs, eventually providing an optimized design that was 45% lighter than the initial design but maintained industry-standard safety standards (Autodesk, 2017). This application of AI provided human designers with choices they would likely never be capable of conceiving themselves due to the complexity and magnitude of the variables involved. After the AI-generated options were reviewed, human designers were the ones to choose the most promising ones to be developed. This win-win cycle, in turn, enabled not just more innovation but also better product development, with a reduction of approximately 30–50% in the overall design cycle (Kalogerakis et al., 2018). Dreamcatcher is not meant to harm human designers, but to augment them. AI handles the mathematical heavy lifting and the exploring, with human designers providing judgment, intuition, and domain expertise to make the final decisions. This is also consistent with the overall vision in AI of human enhancements, under which machines enhance the capacity of humans rather than substitute for them. Moreover, Dreamcatcher is a proponent of sustainable design. Through the integration of material use, weight and energy efficiency, the platform is made to assist users in developing more sustainable solutions – among other aspects, with growing emphasis on sustainability in fields like construction and manufacturing. But using generative design tools also has its share of challenges. Like other constraints on design, there is a learning curve in learning how to express design constraints effectively, and professionals resist changes from established forms of working. Nevertheless, Dreamcatcher encapsulates the way that AI can reinvent the creative domain providing a platform for cooperation between intelligent design systems and human designers. In conclusion, Dreamcatcher from Autodesk shows the disruptive power of AI in design related areas. AI does not reduce the value of the designer by making it faster and easier to create new optimised designs; instead, it allows the designer to achieve more, faster, and with greater confidence. This case further underscores the benefit of the human-AI partnership in unleashing innovation, creation and productivity across business applications.

Case Study 3: McKinsey & Company – AI in Business Consulting

Artificial intelligence (AI) is transforming the global business landscape and business consulting has leveraged AI-powered tools to enrich human decision making, find deep-buried insights and improve productivity. One of the leading players in this field is McKinsey & Company's QuantumBlack, the global advanced analytics and AI subsidiary. This demonstrates how AI magnifies consultants by assisting in analysis, providing real-time suggestions and enriching strategic thinking. QuantumBlack was established as a data analytics company for Formula 1 racing before McKinsey acquired it in 2015. It came with a culture of performance optimization through quantitative data, which McKinsey transplanted into the world of business more generally. Today, QuantumBlack provides AI tools to McKinsey consultants working in healthcare, logistics, retail and manufacturing to analyze complex datasets and improve forecasting of inefficiencies and trends and inform decision-making (McKinsey & Company, 2021). An example of such a project was one carried out for a worldwide pharmaceutical company which wanted to investigate the prospects of enhancing the cost-efficiency of its production process. Traditional consulting methodologies were based on the scrutiny of historical data, site meetings and stakeholder interviews. But with QuantumBlack's AI platform, the McKinsey team was able to create machine learning algorithms that modeled hundreds of variables that influence plant efficiency. The AI system pinpointed previously overlooked factors, like humidity levels, equipment downtimes and shift scheduling, that affected output. Thereby, the production efficiency improved by 15% and the unplanned downtimes were reduced by 20% (Ghosh et al., 2020). The AI system did not replace consultants, but rather served to enhance their capacity for data interpretation and hypothesis generation and intervention planning. With Artificial intelligence (AI) taking on the computational burden, consulting was less about slogging through data and more about formation and implementation of strategy, reducing project cycles and providing clients with more tailored solutions. This integration has been very useful especially in fast-moving situations where data must be quickly summarized to make important decisions. QuantumBlack's ability to work with AI also elevated predictive modeling in optimizing the supply chain For a logistics scenario, industrial AI was employed to model different inventories and routes, also with the aim of minimizing cost and delivery time and optimizing resource use. Human consultants employed these simulations to steer clients through trade-offs and support them in simulating risks, useful particularly during periods of uncertainty (like COVID-19) (Manyika et al., 2017). McKinsey is distinctive with its approach of bringing domain experts, data scientists, and engineers on joined interdisciplinary teams. Such hybrid teams are making sure that AI insights are contextualized and actionable, converting technical output into business relevance. But yes, there are challenges. Responsible AI Today: Getting the Change Engine started in the right Direction Successful AI adoption requires reliable data, organizational preparedness, and change management support. And AI models require transparency and explainability, particularly in regulated industries. McKinsey employs a human-in-the-loop model, through which consultants are always the main part of the client relationship. In conclusion, McKinsey's application of QuantumBlack is a great example of how AI is augmenting human decision making through business consulting. Whether that's automating the task of super-charging your data analysis, enabling you to make better future predictions or simply discovering something new and game-changing, to support consultants to deliver more value, at pace and more strategically, resulting in the power of augmented insights.

Case Study 4: Deloitte – AI-Enhanced Auditing

As the amount and complexity of financial data increases, traditional audit routines are continuously subject to efficiency, people's error and the labor-intensive process of manual document examinations. One way to solve these problems is through AI, and that's exactly what one of the world's Big Four accounting firms, Deloitte, has done to supplement auditors and revolutionize how audits are being done. This is just a way of one example where AI powered human augmentation enhances productivity, accuracy and decision-making in a high risk, compliance driven business process. Deloitte's anchor AI system Argus, was created to expedite the document review process and to automate detection of file anomalies. Argus leverages natural language processing (NLP) and ML capabilities to read and understand tremendous amounts of structured and unstructured data, including contracts, invoices, emails and financial statements. The software can scrape crucial data, detect anomalies and benchmark financial trends against compliance models and sector averages (Deloitte, 2019). One specific instance was when auditing a global client's accounting system that consisted of a distributed financial system as well as over 1,000,000 invoices processed in a number of regimes. Historically, sampling methods would be used to manually verify a portion of the records — opening the door to missed errors or fraud. Using AI solutions, Deloitte were able to review 100% of the transactions in mere hours and could spot unusual patterns, duplicate payments, and even potential violations of policy. This led to higher audit coverage and lower risk and it empowered the auditors to direct their professional judgment and skills to consider high risk areas identified by the AI (Kokina & Davenport, 2017). The rewards of such a system were significant. Deloitte saw a decrease of 40–50% in time spent on menial tasks such as document matching and data reconciliation. Auditors in turn would shift focus from low value data attributes to strategic, judgment driven activities such as stakeholder communication, financial interpretation and decision making (Deloitte Insights, 2021). Moreover, as the AI models leant from previous audits, their performance improved over time, both in efficiency and prospectively, due to the ever-increasing amounts of new data. Notably, Deloitte sees AI as an augmentative tool for the auditor, not a substitute. As such, this human-in-the-loop model guarantees that all AI-derived insights are validated and interpreted by experts that bring their context-driven knowledge and their moral judgment, a crucial check and balance in a field where subjectivity and regulatory conformity are of paramount importance (Issa et al., 2016). But, obstacles still exist in completely embracing AI in the accounting industry. But AI systems need that kind of standardized, clean data, which isn't always available. There are also regulatory issues as regards the transparency of AI decisions, particularly in cases where audit results are legally contested. Deloitte addresses these concerns by recording extensive audit trails explaining how AI models make their decisions and assuring that human auditors have the ultimate say. In summary, Deloitte's adoption of AI in auditing is a great example of the power of AI-driven human augmentation to expand both the breadth and depth of professional services. By taking over mundane tasks, AI allows auditors to focus on higher-level thinking, which in turn delivers more value to clients and represents a future of humans and machines working side by side to make business processes better.

Case Study 5: Coca-Cola – AI in Marketing and Consumer Insights

Coca-Cola, the global beverage company that is constantly battling its competitors in the fast moving consumer goods (FMCG) space, is one of the companies adopting AI to empower human beings in the marketing, customer service and innovation departments. Using sophisticated analytics and machine learning, Coca-Cola improves creative decision-making, campaign personalisation and product development — a classic example of AI paradigm -- human augmentation. Consumer sentiment analysis is one of the most noteworthy AI use-cases at Coca-Cola. Using AI-enabled tools, the company tracks and analyzes live conversations on social media, online reviews and customer feedback. Several platforms (e.g., Hootsuite Insights… powered by Brandwatch) also enable marketing teams of Coca-Cola to monitor trends, new preferences, and brand perception in diverse regions and among various demographic segments, (Coca-Cola Journey, 2018). These understanding assists human marketers improve message material, recognition content in the existing, and bring their editorial emphasis a lot closer to the demands of the audience. An especially successful illustration of how this synergy played out was the introduction of Cherry Sprite, a flavor that was inspired by consumer forum discussions on platforms like Twitter. The AI algorithm noticed a pattern of cherry-flavored Sprite demand and the rest is history! Marketers used to have to rely on costly market surveys and focus groups which meant they had to wait to get this information and then hope it was accurate; with automated insight extraction however, marketers could now loop data and analysis into the creative process, making data-driven decisions that much faster and more confidently (Marr, 2019). In addition to consumer understanding, Coca-Cola has also tapped into AI-based image recognition and machine vision to analyze in-store shelves. Through collaborations with companies like Trax, Coca-Cola has been using A.I. to scan shelves in retail stores to track product placement, availability and compliance with promotional displays. These solutions enable sales teams to optimize execution and prioritization, and give managers performance dashboards for better operational decision-making (Trax Retail, 2020). Moreover, Coca-Cola uses predictive analytics for demand intelligence and campaign tuning as well. Through AI models that analyze weather data, buying habits and regional trends, the company can better predict spikes or decreases in sales. This enables marketing teams to time offers as well as target customer offers with precision on digital channel or via vending machine featuring AI driven recommendation engine. Crucially, Coca-Cola's model involves partnership between machines and marketing human beings. Even as AI uncovers opportunities and patterns, creative professionals remain central to campaign design, storytelling and brand positioning. This human-AI collaboration ensures insights that are not just data driven, but emotionally engaging and culturally meaningful. But rolling out AI at this scale also has its obstacles. There are still issues with ethical use of consumer data, algorithmic bias and too much of an ask for automation. Coca-Cola navigates this through responsible AI practices, transparency in how data is handled and the prioritization of humans having the final say on all strategic decisions. In summary, Coca-Cola shows how AI can magnify human intelligence as it relates to marketing and consumer interaction. Using machine learning to augment human creativity and critical thinking in this way enables the company to move faster with product innovation, clarity and relevance in the brand message, and personalization across the customer experience, and it serves as an example of an AI-powered form of human augmentation in a business process.

Practical Implication of AI-Driven Human Augmentation in Business Processes

AI in business is not just back-end processing anymore. It's moving to the front lines: AI is being used to enhance human capabilities in job roles in transformative ways. AI-based human augmentation will be productivity, creativity and decision-making multiplier where machines intelligence offers tools to augment human strengths and bridge limitations. This is not an abstraction but instead has very real and practical implications for every industry and aspect of business. The most obvious pragmatic benefit is the increase in workforce productivity. AI solutions help ease the participants' cognitive burden and free up employees from repetitive, time-consuming tasks like data entry, scheduling or reporting. This enables human workers to concentrate on more strategic and value-adding tasks. For instance, customer service representatives leveraging AI chatbots or utilizing recommendation systems can solve questions more quickly and more accurately, thereby generating higher efficiency and client satisfaction (Davenport & Ronanki, 2018). Regarding creativity, AI enables to ideate and design by providing alternative solutions that do not necessarily result from conventional brainstorming and heuristic methods. Generative design platforms such as Autodesk Dreamcatcher and AI-optimized content creation aids like Adobe Firefly or ChatGPT empower professionals to investigate a wider spectrum in less time. This does not only boost the speed of creativity, but also the quality of output, giving evidence-based support to human intuition (Kolbjørnsrud et al., 2017). Artificial intelligence also plays a critical role in augmenting decision making. Machine learning models can be trained on large data sets, learn the patterns and anticipate the trends with good precision. These insights can be used by executives and managers to take better and knowledgeable strategic decisions. For example, predict analytics is utilized in supply chain management to predict the demand, optimize inventory levels and reduce wastage, which directly enhances the profit and flexibility (Bughin et al., 2018). Furthermore, natural language processing (NLP) could also be used in decision support systems to parse rich data into actionable insights for non-technical stakeholders. Crucially the augmentation carried out by AI enables a redefinition of working roles. Instead of destroying jobs, AI shifts the role of work, requiring skills including digital literacy, analytical thinking and interdisciplinary thinking. Organizations therefore need to invest in up-skilling and re-skilling program to prepare employees for working with AI systems and future job roles (Brynjolfsson & McAfee, 2017). Operational and ethical issues pose practical challenges as well. Enterprises should make sure responsible AI is adopted, driven by fairness, transparency and data privacy. Human in the loop has become a best practice to ensure oversight and accountability where the recommendations of AI, whether to a professional or decision-maker, are vetted by human experts (Raisch & Krakowski, 2021). In general, the practical consequences of AI-assisted human augmentation are evolutionary. Businesses will have greater productivity, more intelligent decision making, and more creative output, but they will also have to adjust organizations and navigate ethical dilemmas. By purposefully pairing AI tools with human capability, businesses will be able to gain a significant competitive advantage, while creating a more enabled, future-ready workforce.

Social Implication of AI-Driven Human Augmentation in Business

The adoption of AI-based human augmentation in business carries significant social implications because it shapes not just the way people work, but the ways they interact with technology, with each other and with the new dynamics of an organization. At the same time as AI can help boost productivity, drive creativity and support decision making, its adoption at work has positive social benefits as well as challenging social implications that need to be managed. The most important social externalities are improvements in human abilities. AI augmentation enables people to do something they would otherwise be unable to do, by incorporating an automatic process with memory, learning, perception, decision-making, or action. Same goes for designers and marketers, who can benefit from AI-powered generative design and content tools to help make their creative-related decisions more impactful. This inclusion of advanced expertise can mitigate the previously known hurdles related to expertise, thus extending the pool of the workforce who can benefit from innovative insights (Brynjolfsson & McAfee, 2017). Additionally, AI augmentation could increase workplace inclusivity. Assistive AI tools such as speech-to-text, real-time language translation, and adaptive interfaces enable employees with disabilities, language barriers, and neurodiverse conditions to more fully participate in business processes. This makes room for visibility, diversity and equality, being more in line with technological advancement and equal opportunity at a social level (Gonzalez,2020). But AI augmentation can also bring fears of job displacement and inequality. While those who do well in the new job market will also open up other job opportunities sequentially, those who don't may simply lose their jobs. If you are good, you'll just go to the next position, they write, but those who aren't might find themselves out of a job with no ready tools or options for the next opportunity. Unless there are adequate retraining and upskilling programs, a digital divide may widen between digitally savvy individuals who will disproportionately benefit from AI and those who do not (Chui et al., 2016). This can only widen the socio-economic gaps that already exist and result in civil disturbances if not handled proactively. Further, the evolving nature of work because of AI-augmentation could affect mental health and identity. As AI systems play a larger role in determining decision-making and generators of creativity, some workers might find themselves as though they have lost a purpose or autonomy, and perhaps would be experiencing a greater amount of stress or diminished job satisfaction. The psychological consequences of the sharing of mental work with intelligent machines are emerging and deserving of further research (Raisch & Krakowski, 2021). There are also wider ethical questions about monitoring, data privacy and algorithmic bias. Business tools enhanced with the aid of AI often need to do thorough data gathering and, in some cases, monitor employee behaviors. This can be good for performance analysis but is likely to create a culture oppression and damage the relationship between workers and management. In addition, the biases built into AI systems can perpetuate prejudice if not actively mitigated, for example in hiring, promotion or performance-based evaluation situations (Eubanks, 2018). If the full social gains of AI-driven human augmentation are to be realized, companies and governments must operate from a fundamentally human-focused paradigm. This includes transparency of AI systems, lifelong learning, workers' protection rights, and inclusive innovation. By packaging AI as an ethical and social good, companies can help build a more fair and more empowered society.

CONCLUSION

Incorporating AI-led human augmentation into business operations is a game-changing revolution that is changing the landscape, responsibilities and opportunities for human labor in the digital era. As this research has shown, AI is no longer just an automation tool; it increasingly serves as a collaborative partner that can improve human productivity, creativity, and decision making in points. From smart process automation in accounting and finance to AI-enabled marketing platforms that pull real-time insights from consumer behaviour, businesses are harnessing AI to make their workforce superhuman. This technology means more efficient data analysis, faster task execution and deeper, more data-informed creativity. AI is shifting repetitive and mundane work from humans to machines, which increases human cognitive bandwidth, allowing people to concentrate on strategic value-added tasks: innovation and business agility (Davenport & Kirby, 2016). Further, AI augmentation generates centaur type models - a combination of human and machine where the strengths of both perfectly compliment each other. AI provides rapidity, accuracy, and pattern matching, but humans provide knowledge of context, ethical judgment, and emotional capability. This synergy is most apparent in applications such as healthcare diagnoses, financial predictions and customer experience, where joint intelligent behavior achieves better results than what can be obtained from each of the parties acting independently (Wilson & Daugherty, 2018). But this bright future has its dark side. The ethical, social, and economic consequences of widespread AI are significant. Unmanaged, AI-accelerated augmentation risks growing workforce inequalities, displacing workers in at-risk industries, and introducing algorithmic biases that subvert fairness and trust. There will also be a need for fair access to AI tools, thorough retraining, and openness in governance frameworks will be crucial for prohibiting the exclusionary and irresponsible applications of AI (Binns, 2018; Brynjolfsson & McAfee, 2017). Organizations also need to take a human-axis approach to AI adoption, one that puts people at the center of technology change. This means building digital literacy, creating a culture of life-long learning, and ensuring systems designed for usability and ethics are created to empower. The businesses that do and will succeed most in this new era are those that see AI as not a replacement for humans, but as an extension — a tool to complement human potential. Ultimately, AI-enhanced human augmentation is a potent avenue through which businesses will unlock new levels of performance, adaptability, and innovation. As technology advances, its worth will shift not from replacing human beings to enabling them to do more—better, faster, more creatively. Winning in a world like this will be determined by the organizations that invest in people as much as they invest in AI, and where human intelligence and artificial intelligence co-evolve to define the future of work.

Recommendation

With AI-based human augmentation becoming integrated into organisations to drive productivity, creativity and decision-making, there are a number of key recommendations that can help business realise the potential benefits of such transformational technology and address social, ethical and operational challenges. These guidelines are intended to help effective and responsible AI adoption that contribute positively to organizations and society. First, companies should humanize their AI rollouts. AI, as helpful as it can be in efficient processing and automating many tasks, should be there to work with humans, not instead of them. There is no replacement for human intelligence, imagination, and emotional IQ, especially in sectors where gut instinct decision making and emotional rapport count, such as healthcare, customer relations and teaching. Consequently, for businesses, they need to design an environment where AI is a tool that supports human capabilities but not one that replaces them. This can be achieved by designing AI systems that are intuitive and simple to use, and that provide employees with the information and data they require to make improved decisions instead of overwhelming them with complex technologies. By doing so, businesses are able to ensure that the role of AI aligns with the ultimate goal of augmenting human's outcomes and abilities (Brynjolfsson & McAfee, 2017). Secondly, in order to have creativity and innovation, organizations will need to invest in training and upscaling employees to fit the shifting technological landscape. The increasing use of AI tools in creative and business processes requires employees to possess the digital literacy and skills to be effective partners with these tools. Periodic training program to learn what tools can do and best practices for usage will enable employees to utilize the tools to create innovative solutions. There is also the added consideration that acquiring new skills is not an activity solely reserved for technical workers; non-technical professionals, be they marketers or designers, will need to train the same ways in which AI can augment their creative process (Chui et al., 2016) It will be these investments that will help organizations stay competitive and nimble in a rapidly evolving industry. Third, they need to establish a responsible AI framework by making provisions for ethical concerns like algorithmic bias, data privacy and the workforce displacing. AI systems could further accidentally prop up biases in training data, resulting in unjust outcomes in hiring, promotion, or customer service. Businesses should demand fairness and transparency from their AI systems in the form of regular audits, diverse data sets, and human oversight for significant decisions. Secondly, to cushion the blow of job dislocation, companies should invest in re-skilling their workforces so that workers who are displaced can switch into new roles or into AI-enhanced versions of their existing roles. Large organisations should furthermore work together with policy makers to develop ethical guidelines to govern responsible deployment of AI technology (Raisch & Krakowski, 2021). Last but not least, companies should also multiply its benefits by putting it to work to continually improve and innovate and by gifting employees, customers and other stakeholders with the ability to provide feedback and insights. AI in predictive analysis streamlines how organizations are able to predict future market trends, improve efficiency, and improve decision making. But perhaps the best reason to adopt AI for your business is that it will enable you to better adapt and innovate in a continuously changing marketplace. Driven by the analytical capabilities of AI, this feedback loop pattern of continuous learning can foster a culture of speed and ongoing improvement in learning that is the precursor to enduring success in the long term (Davenport & Ronanki, 2018). In short, while AI-driven human augmentation has much to deliver in the form of augmented business outcomes, actualizing the complete potential of such deployment requires a technology and human factors design with great care. Embracing a balanced strategy to human centered collaboration, ethical accountability and lifelong learning, this balance unleashes the real potential of AI, fueling more productive, creative and better-informed business processes.

REFERENCES

Binns, R. (2018). Fairness in machine learning: Lessons from political philosophy. *Proceedings of the 2018 Conference on Fairness, Accountability, and Transparency (FAT)*, 149–159. DOI: 10.1145/3287560.3287598

Boden, M. A. (2016). *AI: Its nature and future*. Oxford University Press.

Brock, J. K. U., & Von Wangenheim, F. (2019). Demystifying AI: What digital transformation leaders can teach you about realistic AI implementation. *Business Horizons*, *62*(6), 751–758. DOI: 10.1016/j.bushor.2019.08.005

Brynjolfsson, E., & McAfee, A. (2014). *The second machine age: Work, progress, and prosperity in a time of brilliant technologies*. W. W. Norton & Company.

Brynjolfsson, E., & McAfee, A. (2017). *Machine, platform, crowd: Harnessing our digital future*. W.W. Norton & Company.

Bughin, J., Hazan, E., Ramaswamy, S., Chui, M., Allas, T., Dahlström, P., Henke, N., & Trench, M. (2018). *Skill shift: Automation and the future of the workforce*. McKinsey Global Institute.

Chui, M., Manyika, J., & Miremadi, M. (2016). Where machines could replace humans—and where they can't (yet). *McKinsey Quarterly*. Retrieved from https://www.mckinsey.com

Chui, M., Manyika, J., & Miremadi, M. (2018). What AI can and can't do (yet) for your business. *McKinsey & Company*. https://www.mckinsey.com

Clark, A., & Chalmers, D. (1998). The extended mind. *Analysis*, *58*(1), 7–19. DOI: 10.1093/analys/58.1.7

Coca-Cola Journey. (2018). How Coca-Cola uses AI to listen to consumers and create new drinks. Retrieved from https://www.coca-colacompany.com

Davenport, T. H., & Kirby, J. (2016). *Only humans need apply: Winners and losers in the age of smart machines*. HarperBusiness.

Davenport, T. H., & Ronanki, R. (2018). Artificial intelligence for the real world. *Harvard Business Review*, *96*(1), 108–116.

Deloitte. (2019). *AI in Audit: How artificial intelligence is transforming the audit process*. Retrieved from https://www2.deloitte.com

Deloitte Insights. (2021). *The future of audit: Preparing for change*. Retrieved from https://www2.deloitte.com/insights

Eubanks, V. (2018). *Automating Inequality: How High-Tech Tools Profile, Police, and Punish the Poor*. St. Martin's Press.

Ferrucci, D., Levas, A., Bagchi, S., Gondek, D., & Mueller, E. (2013). Watson: Beyond jeopardy! *Artificial Intelligence, 199–200*, 93–105. DOI: 10.1016/j.artint.2012.06.009

Floridi, L., Cowls, J., Beltrametti, M., Chiarello, F., & Taddeo, M. (2018). AI4People—An ethical framework for a good AI society. *Minds and Machines*, *28*(4), 689–707. DOI: 10.1007/s11023-018-9482-5 PMID: 30930541

Floridi, L., Cowls, J., Beltrametti, M., & Taddeo, M. (2018). AI4People—An ethical framework for a good AI society. *Minds and Machines*, *28*(4), 689–707. DOI: 10.1007/s11023-018-9482-5 PMID: 30930541

Ghosh, A., Lindner, M., Patel, A., & Tanniru, M. (2020). Unlocking productivity with AI and advanced analytics. *McKinsey & Company*. Retrieved from https://www.mckinsey.com

Gonzalez, A. (2020). AI for accessibility: Bridging the gap for differently-abled employees. *Journal of Inclusive Technologies*, *12*(1), 45–53.

IBM. (2016). Watson helps Mayo Clinic match patients to clinical trials faster. Retrieved from https://www.ibm.com/blogs/watson-health/watson-helps-mayo-clinic-match-patients-to-clinical-trials-faster/

Issa, H., Sun, T., & Vasarhelyi, M. A. (2016). Research ideas for artificial intelligence in auditing: The formalization of audit and workforce supplementation. *Journal of Emerging Technologies in Accounting*, *13*(2), 1–20. DOI: 10.2308/jeta-10511

Kokina, J., & Davenport, T. H. (2017). The emergence of artificial intelligence: How automation is changing auditing. *Journal of Emerging Technologies in Accounting*, *14*(1), 115–122. DOI: 10.2308/jeta-51730

Kolbjørnsrud, V., Amico, R., & Thomas, R. J. (2017). Partnering with AI: How organizations can win over skeptical managers. *Strategy and Leadership*, *58*(4), 37–44. DOI: 10.1108/SL-12-2016-0085

Manyika, J., Chui, M., Miremadi, M., Bughin, J., George, K., Willmott, P., & Dewhurst, M. (2017). *Harnessing automation for a future that works*. McKinsey Global Institute. Retrieved from https://www.mckinsey.com/mgi

Marr, B. (2018). *Artificial Intelligence in Practice: How 50 Successful Companies Used AI and Machine Learning to Solve Problems*. Wiley.

Marr, B. (2019). How Coca-Cola uses AI and Big Data to drive success. *Forbes*. Retrieved from https://www.forbes.com/sites/bernardmarr/2019/09/23/how-coca-cola-uses-ai-and-big-data-to-drive-success/

McCormack, J., Gifford, T., & Hutchings, P. (2019). Autonomy, authenticity, authorship and intention in computer generated art. *Proceedings of the 10th International Conference on Computational Creativity (ICCC)*. DOI: 10.1007/978-3-030-16667-0_3

McKinsey & Company. (2021). QuantumBlack, AI by McKinsey. Retrieved from https://www.mckinsey.com/quantumblack

McKinsey & Company. (2023). The economic potential of generative AI: The next productivity frontier. Retrieved from https://www.mckinsey.com/capabilities/quantumblack/our-insights/the-economic-potential-of-generative-ai-the-next-productivity-frontier

Raisch, S., & Krakowski, S. (2021). Artificial intelligence and management: The automation–augmentation paradox. *Academy of Management Review*, *46*(1), 192–210. DOI: 10.5465/amr.2018.0072

Runco, M. A., & Acar, S. (2012). Divergent thinking as an indicator of creative potential. *Creativity Research Journal*, *24*(1), 66–75. DOI: 10.1080/10400419.2012.652929

Shneiderman, B. (2020). Human-centered artificial intelligence: Reliable, safe & trustworthy. *International Journal of Human-Computer Interaction*, *36*(6), 495–504. DOI: 10.1080/10447318.2020.1741118

Shrestha, Y. R., Benbya, H., & Vom Brocke, J. (2021). Algorithmic decision-making in the AI era: A research agenda. *Journal of Business Research*, *136*, 70–81. DOI: 10.1016/j.jbusres.2021.07.036

Somashekhar, S. P., Sepúlveda, M. J., Norden, A. D., Rauthan, A., Arunachalam, R., & Patil, P. (2018). Early experience with IBM Watson for Oncology in Indian oncology practice. *JCO Clinical Cancer Informatics*, (2), 1–8. DOI: 10.1200/CCI.17.00135

State Council of China. (2017). *New generation artificial intelligence development plan*. http://www.gov.cn

Topol, E. (2019). *Deep Medicine: How Artificial Intelligence Can Make Healthcare Human Again*. Basic Books.

Trax Retail. (2020). Coca-Cola HBC leverages Trax to drive execution in the field. Retrieved from https://traxretail.com/success-stories/coca-cola-hbc

Trist, E. L. (1981). The evolution of socio-technical systems. *Occasional Paper, 2*, 1–67.

Wilson, H. J., & Daugherty, P. R. (2018). *Human + Machine: Reimagining Work in the Age of AI*. Harvard Business Review Press.

World Bank. (2020). *The global AI landscape and implications for developing countries*. https://www.worldbank.org

Yamagata, T. (2020). AI and Japan's aging society. *Asian Economic Policy Review, 15*(2), 276–293. DOI: 10.1111/aepr.12295

Chapter 2
Combining Hospitality and Retail:
Innovative Strategies in the Modern Hotel Industry

Suraj Jaywant Yadav
https://orcid.org/0000-0002-2687-4852
D.Y. Patil Education Society, India

ABSTRACT

The convergence of hospitality and retail has emerged as a transformative strategy in the modern hotel industry, enhancing guest experiences while creating new revenue streams. This study explores the integration of retail spaces within hotels, analyzing its impact on customer satisfaction, financial performance. Data from guest surveys, sales records, and hotel management insights reveal that retail integration significantly improves guest satisfaction, increasing average scores from 7.2 to 8.5. Financially, hotels with retail spaces reported a 140% rise in monthly revenue, demonstrating the profitability of this model. Key success factors include strategic retail placement, curated product offerings, and seamless technology-driven shopping experiences. This research highlights the growing importance hospitality-retail models in sustaining competitive advantage, emphasizing the need for innovative service design and guest-centric retail strategies in the evolving hospitality.

INTRODUCTION

The hotel industry is evolving rapidly, with innovative strategies blending traditional hospitality with retail experiences to create unique value propositions for guests. This fusion aims to enhance the overall guest experience, increase revenue

DOI: 10.4018/979-8-3373-3336-6.ch002

streams, and differentiate properties in an increasingly competitive market. By incorporating carefully curated retail elements, hotels are transforming from mere lodging providers to lifestyle destinations that cater to a wide range of consumer needs and desires. The inseparability of services drives the management of the service operation, which poses a challenge to managing (controlling) employee/customer interaction that is not present in the manufacturing sector. According to the literature on services marketing, internal marketing is the standard approach(*(PDF) Hospitality Retail Operations Types and Styles in the Management of Human Resources*, n.d.). The hotel sector has long recognized that delivering exceptional guest experiences is essential to long-term success. By telling captivating stories about their brand identities and/or host properties, hotels have mastered the art of differentiating themselves through thoughtful design and creative branding. The majority of these narratives emphasize the romanticized definition of hospitality and its connection to the human condition. Retail designers have faced a new challenge in recent years: to continue engaging customers who primarily shop in-store while crafting shopping experiences that appeal to generations who shop first on digital platforms. A plethora of new trends in the retail industry have been sparked by the convergence of digital and physical retail channels. New technologies are being used practically everywhere to boost production efficiency and draw customers in with captivating and immersive experiences (Greatergroup, 2022). Retail management is an emerging prime consumer service that promotes sustainability towards their customers, despite social welfare concerns over its green consumption. The study places a strong emphasis on retailing policies for premium consumers in terms of perspectives and global competitiveness (Bhattacharya et al., 2024). Technological innovation in the service industry is usually driven by suppliers, meaning that competitors can easily obtain and copy this external knowledge. However, internal, non-technical innovation involving business models is more likely to be sustained in retail and hospitality organizations. This study aims to understand how industry turbulence in retail and hospitality affects the sustainable competitive advantage of the firms operating in these service industries. It builds on the perspectives of the resource-based view and dynamic capability (Cheah et al., 2018). One key approach is the integration of boutique shops within hotel premises. These spaces often showcase local artisans, designers, and brands, offering guests the opportunity to purchase unique souvenirs, fashion items, or artwork that reflect the destination's culture. Some hotels are taking this concept further by creating entire shopping arcades or partnering with high-end retailers to offer exclusive in-room shopping experiences. This not only provides convenience for guests but also creates an additional revenue stream for the hotel.

Research Objectives

1. To assess how incorporating retail spaces and services within hotels influences overall guest experience and satisfaction.
2. To investigate the financial benefits and profitability of incorporating retail operations into hotel business models.
3. To determine effective strategies and operational practices that facilitate the successful blending of hospitality and retail services in hotels.
4. To explore the role of emerging technologies in improving and personalizing retail experiences for hotel guests.
5. To study how collaborations with well-known retail brands impact the hotel's market positioning, brand loyalty, and customer engagement.

Theoretical Framework

Using a dichotomous approach—a continuum with pure goods at one end and pure services at the other—the earliest attempts to distinguish between goods and services were made(*(PDF) Hospitality Retail Operations Types and Styles in the Management of Human Resources*, n.d.).

Retail Design Collaborative (RDC) have led the way in assisting retailers in implementing hospitality-based consumer interfaces so they can offer more individualized services. The retail sector is reevaluating where the retail experience truly starts and ends in order to learn from the hospitality industry's successes. Astute retailers know that customers want something special and significant from the entire transaction, and that the path to having a great shopping experience goes far beyond the actual store. The distinctions between hospitality and retail are becoming more and more hazy. Upon examining the fundamental tenets of hospitality, we can discern that patrons desire to be treated with dignity and respect. Consumers want unique, unforgettable experiences in a setting that uplifts and enchants them. Visitors who develop an emotional bond with your brand are more likely to remain loyal over time (Greatergroup, 2022).

According to Conrad Lashley's book "Hospitality Retail Management," hospitality retail management captures the sense of comfort and security that patrons feel when they walk into a hotel, pub, restaurant, or other establishment and know what kind of service and quality to anticipate. Retail that provides hospitality to customers is essentially all sales establishments (*Hospitality Retail Management - EHL Insights | Hospitality Industry*, n.d.). Traditional brick-and-mortar stores have given way to immersive store experiences in the retail space, which emphasize engagement over product display to build an emotional bond with customers. While developing interactive, engaging brand experiences has long since become the norm, this trend is quickening and motivating brands to blur the boundaries between retail and hospitality by introducing new store formats and service-based third spaces into their ecosystems (Ludmir, n.d.). The retail, leisure, and hospitality industries are expanding. Re-invention is key given the challenges posed by the rise of e-commerce, the long-term effects of COVID-19, the cost-of-living crisis, and, quite simply, changes in consumer behaviour (*Leisure, Retail and Hospitality*, n.d.). A well-thought-out policy eliminates the shortcoming in retailing by giving industry practitioners greater influence than in the past, based on analytical and numerical studies. Retail managers can benefit greatly from the implications of the current hospitality for consumers research when it comes to optimizing trading operations and promoting environmentally conscious purchasing decisions (Bhattacharya et al., 2024).

The best examples of super customer experiences are found in resorts, hotels, wineries, fine dining, and many tourist destinations. Retailers are rapidly adopting this tactic. It's time for the retail sector to embrace their long-awaited partnership with the hospitality sector, since they are always looking for new and creative ways to improve customer experiences, boost sales, and stay ahead of the competition. Retail businesses aiming to expand into Europe can seize new growth prospects and expand their customer base by capitalizing on the hospitality industry's vast distributor network (*Leveraging the European Hospitality Industry for Retail Success*, n.d.). Innovation forms the foundation of business operations in both the retail and hospitality sectors. Retail manufacturers can stand out from rivals and create new avenues for customer interaction by embracing partnerships and using hospitality as a distributor. Hotels are constantly experimenting with new ways to improve their pop-up stores, incorporate art into their spaces, and design distinctive shopping experiences that straddle the boundaries between hospitality and retail (*Leveraging the European Hospitality Industry for Retail Success*, n.d.). Retail establishments can evaluate and rank cashiers and salespeople based on their productivity and sales performance, including each time they use the barcode scanner to scan an item, by utilizing rich behavioral data on sales transactions captured by the point-of-sale (POS) system. Similar to this, factors such as average sales per guest, tips collected, the quantity of tables turned over and people served, and the frequency of late returns from breaks can all be used to rank and rate restaurant servers. Companies are able to rank employees "from best to worst," pinpoint "underperformers," identify the "least profitable" workers, and project future productivity levels from their workforce. Measuring the effectiveness of employees through sales results or even the tips they get from customers is one way to quantify affective work (Christl, 2023). Using handheld devices equipped with barcode scanners, a retail store's system can automate task allocation by giving shelf stockers pick lists to follow as they move store inventory across the backroom and shelves. Hotel housekeeping systems have the ability to automatically assign tasks to room attendants (S. J. Yadav, 2024). These attendants then use a mobile device to receive instructions on which room to clean next, along with a target time for each room. The number of minutes and seconds that employees have already spent in a room is displayed on a timer. Cleaning assignments are assigned in accordance with booking information, rules, and predetermined "credits" that indicate the amount of time needed to finish various tasks. Reports regarding the amount of time spent cleaning rooms are viewable by employers (Christl, 2023). Another innovative strategy is the concept of "shoppable" hotel rooms. In this model, nearly everything in the guest room - from the furniture and decor to the toiletries and linens - is available for purchase. Guests can test products during their stay and easily order items they love, turning the hotel room into a live showroom. This approach has been particularly successful in boutique and design-focused hotels, where the curated aesthetic appeals to style-conscious travelers. Hotels are also leveraging technology to blend retail and hospitality experiences seamlessly. Mobile apps and in-room tablets allow guests to browse and purchase a wide range of products and services, from local experiences and tours to hotel-branded merchandise. Some properties are experimenting with augmented reality (AR) to create interactive shopping experiences within the hotel space. These technological integrations not only enhance the guest experience but also provide valuable data on consumer preferences, allowing hotels to refine their offerings and marketing strategies continually.

Data Collection

The data collection process for understanding the impact of retail integration within hotels was meticulously planned and executed using a variety of methods to ensure comprehensive and reliable insights (S. Yadav, 2021). Surveys were distributed to hotel guests at check-out to gather feedback on their retail experiences. The surveys included questions about overall satisfaction, the convenience of retail services, and any perceived negative impacts. A total of 500 respondents participated, providing a diverse range of opinions and experiences. Sales data from in-hotel retail shops were collected over the past 12 months, including detailed records of item categories, purchase times, and customer demographics. This data was used to analyze revenue streams and assess the financial impact of retail integration. Data from hotel loyalty programs were analyzed to understand the purchasing behaviors and preferences of repeat customers. Information from 1,000 loyalty program members was examined, focusing on their frequency of purchases, types of products bought, and overall spending patterns. Interviews were conducted with 10 hotel managers across five hotels to gain deeper insights into the operational challenges and successes of integrating retail spaces. These interviews provided valuable perspectives on best practices, technological innovations, and the strategic importance of retail partnerships. Additionally, mystery shoppers were employed to evaluate the quality of service and customer experience in hotel retail environments, with a total of 20 evaluations conducted. Mystery shoppers assessed various aspects of the retail experience, including staff friendliness, store layout, product availability, and overall shopping experience.

Data Analysis

Table 1. Guest Satisfaction Scores Pre- and Post-Retail Integration

Hotel ID	Pre-Integration Score (out of 10)	Post-Integration Score (out of 10)
1	7	8.3
2	6.8	8.2
3	7.5	8.8
4	7.3	8.7
5	7.4	8.5
Average	7.2	8.5

Table 1 shows the average guest satisfaction scores (out of 10) for five hotels before and after integrating retail spaces. The data indicates an improvement in satisfaction scores across all hotels post-integration, suggesting that adding retail options has a positive impact on guest experiences. The average satisfaction score increased from 7.2 to 8.5.

Table 2. Monthly Retail Revenue Pre- and Post-Retail Integration

Hotel ID	Pre-Integration Revenue ($)	Post-Integration Revenue ($)
1	45,000	1,15,000
2	50,000	1,20,000
3	55,000	1,25,000
4	47,000	1,18,000
5	53,000	1,22,000
Average	50,000	1,20,000

Table 2 compares the monthly retail revenue for five hotels before and after retail integration. The significant increase in revenue post-integration, from an average of $50,000 to $120,000, highlights the financial benefits of incorporating retail operations into hotels.

Table 3. Best Practices for Seamless Hospitality-Retail Integration

Best Practice	Frequency Observed (out of 5 hotels)
Strategic location near lobbies	5
Diverse product offerings	5
Enhanced customer service	5
Consistent branding	4
Seamless point-of-sale systems	4

Table 3 identifies the best practices observed in the five hotels that successfully integrated retail spaces. Common practices include strategically locating retail spaces near lobbies, offering diverse product selections, enhancing customer service, maintaining consistent branding, and implementing seamless point-of-sale systems.

Table 4. Technological Innovations Enhancing Retail Experiences

Innovation	Adoption Rate (%)	Positive Feedback (%)
Mobile apps for in-hotel shopping	60	85
Smart mirrors and virtual fitting rooms	40	80

Table 4 presents the adoption rates and positive feedback percentages for technological innovations used in hotel retail spaces. Mobile apps for in-hotel shopping have a 60% adoption rate and an 85% positive feedback rate, while smart mirrors and virtual fitting rooms have a 40% adoption rate and an 80% positive feedback rate. These technologies significantly enhance the retail experience for guests.

Table 5. Impact of Brand Partnerships on Guest Visits and Purchases

Hotel ID	Increase in Guest Visits (%)	Increase in Purchase Rate (%)	Average Spend on Branded Items ($)	Average Spend on Non-Branded Items ($)
1	25	20	70	45
2	30	25	75	50
3	35	30	80	55

continued on following page

Table 5. Continued

Hotel ID	Increase in Guest Visits (%)	Increase in Purchase Rate (%)	Average Spend on Branded Items ($)	Average Spend on Non-Branded Items ($)
4	28	22	72	48
5	32	28	78	52
Average	30	25	75	50

Table 5 shows the impact of brand partnerships on guest visits and purchase rates in hotel retail stores. Hotels with brand partnerships saw a 30% average increase in guest visits and a 25% increase in purchase rates. Additionally, guests spent more on branded items ($75 on average) compared to non-branded items ($50 on average), indicating that brand partnerships can drive higher sales and enhance guest engagement.

Table 6. Guest Feedback on Retail Experience

Feedback Type	Percentage (%)
Positive	75
Negative	15
Neutral	10

Table 6 summarizes guest feedback on their retail experience within the hotels. 75% of feedback was positive, highlighting the convenience and enhanced experience provided by the retail integration. 15% of feedback was negative, mainly due to increased noise and foot traffic, while 10% was neutral.

Table 7. Loyalty Program Member Preferences

Preference	Percentage (%)
Preference for hotels with branded retail	40
Preference for hotels without branded retail	60

Table 7 provides insights into the preferences of hotel loyalty program members regarding branded retail options. 40% of loyalty members preferred hotels with branded retail options, while 60% preferred hotels without branded retail, indicating a substantial interest in branded retail but also a significant segment that does not prioritize it.

Table 8. Mean and Standard Deviation of Guest Satisfaction Scores

Metric	Pre-Integration	Post-Integration
Mean Satisfaction Score	7.2	8.5
Standard Deviation	0.26	0.23

Table 8 shows the mean and standard deviation of guest satisfaction scores before and after retail integration. The mean satisfaction score increased from 7.2 to 8.5, while the standard deviation decreased from 0.26 to 0.23, indicating not only higher satisfaction but also more consistent positive experiences among guest's post-integration.

Table 9. Mean and Standard Deviation of Monthly Retail Revenue

Metric	Pre-Integration Revenue ($)	Post-Integration Revenue ($)
Mean Revenue	50,000	1,20,000
Standard Deviation	3,741.66	3,741.66

Table 9 presents the mean and standard deviation of monthly retail revenue for hotels before and after integrating retail spaces. The mean revenue increased significantly from $50,000 to $120,000. The standard deviation remained constant at $3,741.66, suggesting that while revenue increased, the variability in monthly revenue remained stable.

RESULTS

The integration of retail spaces within hotels yielded significant positive outcomes based on the collected data. Guest satisfaction scores notably increased post-integration, rising from an average of 7.2 to 8.5 on a 10-point scale. This improvement highlights guests' appreciation for the convenience and enhanced experiences provided by in-hotel retail options. Concurrently, monthly retail revenues saw a substantial jump, soaring from an average of $50,000 to $120,000 per hotel. This 140% increase underscores the financial benefits of integrating retail operations, supported by stable revenue variability across the hotels. Strategic best practices such as optimal location of retail spaces, diverse product offerings, and seamless customer service were identified as crucial factors contributing to successful retail integration. Technological innovations like mobile shopping apps and smart mirrors received high adoption rates and positive guest feedback, further enhancing the retail experience. Moreover, partnerships with recognized brands proved effective in driving higher guest engagement and spending. Collectively, these findings underscore the value of integrating retail within hotels not only for enhancing guest satisfaction but also for boosting financial performance through innovative practices and strategic partnerships.

CONCLUSION

The integration of retail spaces within hotels has proven to be a transformative strategy, significantly enhancing guest experiences and operational dynamics. Through a comprehensive analysis of guest feedback, operational insights from hotel managers, and evaluations by mystery shoppers, several key conclusions emerge. Guests consistently appreciated the convenience and added value brought by in-hotel retail options, reflecting a broader trend towards integrated hospitality experiences that cater to diverse guest preferences. Strategically locating retail spaces near lobbies, offering a variety of products, and ensuring seamless customer service were identified as critical success factors. Moreover, technological innovations such as mobile shopping apps and interactive displays not only improved convenience but also enriched the overall guest experience. The strategic partnerships with well-known brands also emerged as a powerful tool for attracting and retaining guests seeking recognizable retail experiences within the hotel environment. Overall, the integration of retail spaces represents a paradigm shift in hotel management, demonstrating the industry's adaptability to evolving consumer expectations and preferences. Looking ahead, continued investment in technology and guest-centric retail strategies will be essential for hotels aiming to differentiate themselves and maximize guest satisfaction in a competitive market landscape.

REFERENCES

Bhattacharya, S., Sarkar, B., Sarkar, M., & Mukherjee, A. (2024). Hospitality for prime consumers and others under the retail management. *Journal of Retailing and Consumer Services*, *80*, 103849. DOI: 10.1016/j.jretconser.2024.103849

Cheah, S., Ho, Y.-P., & Li, S. (2018). Business Model Innovation for Sustainable Performance in Retail and Hospitality Industries. *Sustainability (Basel)*, *10*(11), 11. Advance online publication. DOI: 10.3390/su10113952

Christl, W. (2023). *Monitoring Work and Automating Task Allocation in Retail and Hospitality*.

Greatergroup. (2022, February 23). *Retail Hospitality*. Greater Group. https://www.thegreatergroup.com/combining-retail-and-hospitality-through-creative-store-design/

Hospitality Retail Management—EHL Insights | Hospitality industry. (n.d.). Retrieved June 20, 2024, from https://hospitalityinsights.ehl.edu/retail-and-hospitality-convergence

Leisure, Retail and Hospitality. (n.d.). Hydrock. Retrieved June 20, 2024, from https://www.hydrock.com/sectors/leisure-retail-hospitality

Leveraging the European Hospitality Industry for Retail Success. (n.d.). Retrieved June 21, 2024, from https://www.eurodev.com/blog/leveraging-the-european-hospitality-industry-for-retail-success

Ludmir, C. (n.d.). *How Hospitality Is Influencing The Future Of Retail And Elevating Brand Experiences*. Forbes. Retrieved June 20, 2024, from https://www.forbes.com/sites/claraludmir/2023/07/25/how-hospitality-is-influencing-the-future-of-retail/

(PDF) Hospitality retail operations types and styles in the management of human resources. (n.d.). Retrieved June 20, 2024, from https://www.researchgate.net/publication/222353204_Hospitality_retail_operations_types_and_styles_in_the_management_of_human_resources

Yadav, S. (2021). Millennial Employees-Role, Benefits and Retaining Strategies in Hotel Industry (p. 64). DOI: 10.6084/m9.figshare.13719949.v1

Yadav, S. J. (2024). Voices From Within: Exploring Indian Perspectives on Sex Tourism. In *Examining Tourist Behaviors and Community Involvement in Destination Rejuvenation* (pp. 263–272). IGI Global. https://www.igi-global.com/chapter/voices-from-within/348915

Chapter 3

Empowering People in Process and Human-Centric Adaptation in Digital Business Transformation

S. Pushpalatha
https://orcid.org/0009-0003-8730-0670
Saveetha School of Management, Saveetha University, India

Pandian R. Durai
https://orcid.org/0000-0003-2932-0270
Saveetha Institute of Medical and Technical Sciences, Saveetha University, India

ABSTRACT

BPM has moved from an operational tool to a strategic enabler of value generation, innovation, and agility. As firms undergo digital change, the often-overlooked human aspect becomes crucial. While AI, automation, and cloud computing provide core capabilities, human flexibility, creativity, and cooperation create genuine progress. This chapter discusses how human-centric BPM empowers individuals in processes. The focus is on combining technology with mental health, cultural participation, digital literacy, and emotional intelligence. Modern BPM emphasizes responsiveness, co-creation, and people-centered design over standardization and efficiency. The chapter provides capability development, behavioral transformation, and cultural alignment frameworks for workforce adaptability. Participatory design, ethics, and leadership changes are covered. Empowering people in digital transformation is highlighted by case studies and future research directions like new measurements

DOI: 10.4018/979-8-3373-3336-6.ch003

and longitudinal investigations.

INTRODUCTION

Digital transformation has become a critical enabler of competitive advantage, redefining the ways in which organizations operate, generate value, and engage stakeholders (Foss & Saebi, 2017). Business Process Management (BPM) is the foundation of this transformation, providing a structured approach to the optimization, redesign, and automation of essential business activities. Nevertheless, the human aspect—arguably the most intricate and dynamic component—has not been given the same level of attention in the context of BPM modernization. Human-centricity is no longer an option; it is essential as enterprises transition from manual workflows to intelligent systems that are propelled by AI and data analytics. The necessity of incorporating human values, competencies, and well-being into business process management has never been more pressing. Organizations that are successful in human-centric transformation recognize employees as significant contributors to innovation, continuous improvement, and the customer experience, rather than merely as executors of predetermined tasks (Van de Ven & Poole, 1995). This chapter illustrates how a human-focused BPM strategy promotes adaptability, resilience, and inclusive development by focusing on the changing relationship between people and processes. It suggests a multidimensional framework for workforce empowerment that integrates practical insights with scholastic theory, real-world evidence, and ethical reflection.

Significance and Objective

The objective of this chapter is threefold: first, to redefine BPM as a human-centric discipline; second, to illustrate how digital transformation can be more sustainable and effective when it is in alignment with employee empowerment; and third, to offer practical models and frameworks for incorporating human-centricity into process redesign. Although automation and digitalization improve productivity and scalability, they also pose a risk of marginalizing the human role unless they are accompanied by systemic strategies for workforce inclusion, reskilling, and participatory design (Davenport & Ronanki, 2018). The objective of this chapter is to provide leaders, BPM professionals, and researchers with the necessary tools to effectively navigate the human dimensions of digital transformation. This work's significance is derived from its interdisciplinary approach, which connects BPM theory, organizational behavior, digital ethics, and innovation management. It addresses the following critical inquiries: How can processes be engineered to be both efficient and compassionate? In order for a workforce to prosper in the face of change, what capabilities must be cultivated? Also, how can BPM governance foster transparency, engagement, and fairness?

Structure of the Chapter

The following main sections comprise this chapter:

Conceptual and Theoretical Frameworks: Establishes the fundamental theories that underlie human-centric BPM.
Research Methodology: Defines the methodological approach employed to compile best practices, case studies, and insights.
Workforce Adaptation: Examines the processes of cultural alignment, capability development, and behavioral modification.
Leadership and Ethics: Investigates the changing leadership competencies and ethical considerations in digital BPM.
Psychological and Emotional Dynamics: Investigates the mental health, resilience, and motivational factors that are present during transitions.
Participatory Design: Emphasizes the significance of employee inclusion in the development of BPM tools and processes.
Innovation and Future Trends: Examines novel methodologies, including AI-human collaboration, low-code BPM, and hyper automation.
Case Studies: Offers practical applications of theoretical concepts from a variety of industries.
Solutions and Recommendations: Provides actionable advice and identifies obstacles to implementation.
Conclusion and Future Research: Provides a concise summary of the primary insights and suggests potential areas for additional research.

CONCEPTUAL FRAMEWORK

The conceptual framework is the bedrock for comprehending the intersection of human-centric principles and Business Process Management (BPM) in the context of digital transformation. It offers a perspective through which organizations can observe and navigate the interaction between technologies, processes, and individuals. This section establishes the foundation for the human-focused approach to BPM by delineating the fundamental concepts that guide the discourse on workforce empowerment, technological integration, and continuous adaptation.

Definition of Key Concepts

Human Capital

In BPM, human capital includes technical skills, critical thinking, emotional intelligence, and teamwork to navigate complex, tech-enabled environments (Adner, 2021). Human capital-valuing companies engage in employee development and see them as innovators and ethical decision-makers, not just task executors (Cascio & Montealegre, 2016).

Adaptive Processes

Adaptive Processes adapt to changing situations (Dignum, 2019). Using AI and analytics, they use human creativity and decision-making to meet strategic goals. Their effectiveness relies on feedback loops and iterative changes.

Technological Integration

AI, RPA, and analytics improve BPM efficiency but must complement human judgment. Intelligent automation combines machine learning and human intuition, while digital literacy helps workers use these tools to meet changing organizational needs.

Interrelation of Concepts

Human capital, adaptive processes, and technological integration overlap and reinforce each other in the suggested conceptual framework for human-centric Business Process Management (BPM). According to (Laudon et al., 2020), human capital creativity, critical thinking, and emotional intelligence drives BPM innovation and flexibility. Human capabilities play a crucial role in complex systems. This human aptitude allows the creation and continual refining of adaptive processes, which adapt to changing circumstances. In the digital age, adaptive processes let firms adapt to technical changes and market needs, according to (Chui et al., 2016). These methods connect human understanding and technological technologies to stay responsive and effective. (Hammer & Stanton, 1999) states that technology integration automates regular operations and improves decision-making using analytics and AI, supporting adaptive workflows. However, technology is most valuable when linked with human capacities and entrenched in workflows that leverage machine efficiency and human judgment. (Hammer, 1990) says strategic execution requires this alignment, whereas (Kaplan & Norton, 1996) say digital transformation requires human-machine collaboration. These three elements work together to empower people, boost organizational agility, and keep digital transformation efforts human-centered.

Visual Representation

To represent the conceptual framework, a diagram can be utilized to illustrate the interconnections between human capital, adaptive processes, and technology integration. The diagram will consist of three main components: human capital, adaptive processes, and technology integration. Human capital and technology integration form the foundation, representing the balance between human capabilities and digital tools. Adaptive processes are the dynamic outcome that arises when people and technology interact effectively. There are continuous feedback loops between all three components. Human capital influences adaptive processes through creativity, problem-solving, and decision-making, while adaptive processes provide the mechanisms for employees to continually respond and improve. At the same time, technology integration supports adaptive processes by offering automation, data analytics, and digital infrastructure. However, technology also depends on human input for effective deployment and ethical use, reinforcing the cyclical nature of the model. At the core of this framework lies human-centric BPM—where empowered individuals, flexible workflows, and intelligent technologies converge to drive innovation, engagement, and sustainable digital transformation.

THEORETICAL FRAMEWORK

Organizational Change and Adaptation Theories

One of the most influential theories on organizational change is Lewin's Change Management Model. It proposes that effective change occurs in three stages: unfreeze, change, and refreeze. This model is especially pertinent in the context of BPM when addressing the human component of process redesign. The unfreeze stage entails the preparation of employees for the changes that digital transformation brings, including the implementation of new technologies and the modification of workflows. The actual implementation of these new systems and processes is referred to as "change," and human adaptation is essential. Lastly, the refreeze stage cements the new processes and behaviors as part of the organization's routine, underscoring the necessity of ongoing human engagement and involvement. Lewin's model underscores the significance of psychological readiness and the necessity of confronting emotional and behavioral resistance during the change process. In a human-centric

BPM context, this entails cultivating an environment in which employees experience empowerment and encouragement during the transformation process. Consequently, Lewin's model functions as a basis for comprehending the extent to which human factors influence the adaptation and modification of processes.

Social Cognitive Theory

According to Social Cognitive Theory, individuals acquire knowledge and adjust their behavior by observing, imitating, and modeling. This theory is especially beneficial for comprehending the manner in which employees can cultivate new behaviors and abilities in response to technological disruptions. The theory posits that employees are more inclined to adopt new BPM technologies and processes if they witness positive outcomes and behaviors in their peers in the context of BPM. Digital transformation is significantly influenced by social influence, as individuals emulate the behaviors of their peers, leaders, and industry leaders (Bostrom & Yudkowsky, 2014). Bandura's concept of self-efficacy, which is the conviction that one is capable of achieving success in particular tasks, is also essential for workforce adaptation. It is more probable that employees will engage with and adopt the changes when they believe they are capable of mastering new BPM tools and technologies. In human-centric BPM, the promotion of self-efficacy can considerably enhance adoption rates and facilitate organizational change.

The Theory of Planned Behavior

The relationship between attitudes, perceived behavioral control, and intentions in predicting human behavior is the primary focus of the Theory of Planned Behavior (TPB). According to TPB, individuals are more inclined to engage in a behavior if they have a positive attitude toward it, believe that they have the ability to perform it, and intend to do so. This theory is useful in elucidating how the appropriate motivational strategies and environmental conditions can influence workforce engagement with new processes and technologies in the context of BPM.

This posits that organizations can increase the probability of successful BPM adoption by aligning organizational objectives with employee motivations, attitudes, and perceived capabilities. For example, employees are increasingly inclined to incorporate new BPM tools (such as AI or automation technologies) into their daily work routines when they believe they have the authority and resources to adjust to these tools. This renders TPB especially advantageous for comprehending the methods of promoting behavioral change in the workforce during digital transformation.

Distributed Leadership Theory

Distributed Leadership Theory emphasizes the distribution of leadership responsibilities across different levels of an organization, as opposed to being exclusively concentrated in senior management. This theory emphasizes the significance of shared leadership in the development of a human-centric approach to process management within the context of BPM (Seligman, 2011). Distributed leadership is indispensable for BPM initiatives, as it permits employees of all ranks to participate in process design and decision-making, guaranteeing that the human aspects of change are taken into account at each stage of the transformation process. Distributed leadership fosters a sense of autonomy, responsibility, and engagement by enabling employees to take ownership of change initiatives and lead in their respective areas. This leadership model promotes participatory design, which involves employees in the active involvement of process redesign and technology adoption, thereby fostering greater buy-in and improving BPM outcomes.

The Resource-Based View (RBV)

The Resource-Based View (RBV) of the firm posits that a company's resources—both tangible and intangible—are the critical factor in establishing a sustainable competitive advantage (Hevner & Chatterjee, 2010). Human capital is a critical intangible resource in the context of BPM, as it facilitates process development, problem-solving, and innovation. The human element is indispensable for the generation of value, the facilitation of change, and the maintenance of continuous development in business process management (BPM) as digital tools such as AI and automation transform business workflows. By aligning their BPM strategies, organizations that regard human capital as a strategic resource can not only improve operational efficiency but also cultivate a culture of collaboration, engagement, and creativity. Organizations can leverage their workforce as a valuable resource that generates competitive advantage in the digital era by investing in employee development and empowerment.

The Integration of Theories in Human-Centric BPM

The human-centric BPM paradigm proposed in this chapter is founded on the integration of these theories. Theories such as the Theory of Planned Behavior, Social Cognitive Theory, and Lewin's Change Management Model offer a perspective on how individuals adjust to new technologies and processes. Distributed Leadership and the Resource-Based View underscore the significance of enabling employees to actively participate in the development of BPM outcomes.

Collectively, these theories contribute to a comprehensive BPM strategy that emphasizes leadership collaboration, behavioral adaptation, and human engagement. This theoretical framework provides a solid foundation for the implementation of human-centric BPM strategies that promote organizational development, resilience, and innovation by integrating insights from strategic management, leadership studies, psychology, and organizational behavior.

RESEARCH METHODOLOGY

This study utilizes a qualitative research technique to investigate the significance of human-centric variables in Business Process Management (BPM) amid digital transformation. This research aims to elucidate how factors like as leadership, employee engagement, corporate culture, and workforce adaptation influence the efficacy of BPM projects. Semi-structured interviews were performed with essential stakeholders, such as BPM professionals, human resource managers, and digital transformation leaders, to obtain detailed insights into practical applications and experiences. To guarantee diversity and pertinence, interviews were conducted across sectors like manufacturing, financial services, and healthcare, where digital change is intricate and significant. The interviews provided the foundation for comprehensive case studies that elucidate the integration of human-centric methodologies into Business Process Management (BPM) by enterprises. Each scenario underscores activities like participatory process redesign, employee reskilling programs, leadership tactics for cultural transformation, and measures to alleviate employee concerns around automation. Thematic analysis was employed to analyze the qualitative data, facilitating the identification of patterns and repeating themes across various organizational contexts. This analytical method offered a comprehensive perspective on the human factors affecting BPM results. Ethical rigor was upheld throughout the trial, with subjects granting informed consent and all data anonymized to ensure confidentiality. The study complied with institutional ethical norms, safeguarding participant rights and privacy throughout all phases.

THE STRATEGIC ROLE OF HUMAN-CENTRIC BPM

In the current volatile digital business environment, human-centric Business Process Management (BPM) has become an indispensable strategy for maintaining competitiveness. In the past, BPM was regarded as an instrument for cost reduction, process standardization, and operational efficiency (Leonardi, 2011). Conversely, in the current era of digital transformation, BPM's responsibilities have broadened to incorporate strategic capabilities that prioritize the integration of human potential into the design and execution of processes, thereby promoting innovation, agility, and organizational resilience. People are the focal point of process ecosystems in human-centric BPM. It surpasses the inflexible, mechanistic models of BPM by acknowledging employees as dynamic contributors who contribute contextual awareness, emotional intelligence, and creativity to processes. This reorientation is indicative of more extensive strategic objectives, including sustainable innovation, organizational adaptability, and enhanced customer experience (Rosemann & vom Brocke, 2015).

The alignment of three fundamental dimensions is a strategic approach to human-centric BPM:

- **Process Responsiveness**: The agility and responsiveness of processes can be substantially improved by providing frontline employees with real-time decision-making capabilities. Process mining and real-time analytics are technologies that facilitate the visualization of operations; however, the effectiveness of adaptations is frequently determined by human judgment (Wenger, 1998).
- **Value Co-Creation**: In human-centric BPM, employees and consumers are not passive recipients of value; rather, they are co-creators. Participatory models facilitate stakeholder involvement in process redesign, guaranteeing that processes are both meaningful and efficient (Markus & Robey, 1988).
- **Sustainable Innovation**: Continuous improvement is fostered when employees feel psychologically secure and empowered to propose enhancements. By promoting experimentation, feedback, and reflective learning cycles, human-centric BPM cultivates an environment of innovation (Schein, 2010).

The assertion that BPM initiatives that prioritize transparency, collaboration, and shared ownership result in increased engagement and success rates is supported by research (Rock & Grant, 2016). Additionally, (Nambisan et al., 2019) anticipates that by 2025, 75% of BPM initiatives will prioritize contextual intelligence and human empowerment as critical factors in the creation of digital value.

ADJUSTMENT OF THE WORKFORCE

The fundamental requirement for employees to adjust to new roles, tools, and perspectives is a consequence of digital transformation. Workforce adaptation is not solely a reaction to technological change; it is a proactive and strategic process that improves an organization's capacity to thrive in a digital environment that is constantly changing (Bersin, 2020). It is this adaptability that human-centric BPM accentuates, as it incorporates mechanisms that facilitate learning, resilience, and engagement throughout the employee lifecycle.

1.Development of Capabilities

The initial component of workforce adaptation is the provision of employees with the necessary skills and knowledge to interact with new digital platforms and BPM tools. The nature of work is swiftly changing from routine execution to supervisory, analytical, and design-oriented tasks as organizations adopt cloud-based BPM suites, AI, and robotic process automation (RPA) (Van de Ven & Poole, 1995). This necessitates a robust ecosystem that facilitates continuous learning.

Modern BPM systems require not only technical literacy, but also systems thinking and data literacy, as part of their upskilling and reskilling initiatives. Organizations such as AT&T and Amazon have implemented extensive internal training programs to facilitate digital upskilling, with an emphasis on agile project management, cybersecurity, and cloud computing (Westerman et al., 2014). Learning must be contextual, modular, and integrated into operations, which (Bersin, 2020) refers to as "learning in the flow of work. The Learning Platforms and Micro learning accessibility and personalization of training are improved by learning management systems (LMS), AI-based recommendation engines, and bite-sized digital learning modules (Zuboff, 2019). The influence of formal training programs is enhanced by peer learning and knowledge sharing, which are facilitated by internal social networks and communities of practice.

2.Change in Behavior

Digital BPM necessitates new behavioral patterns in addition to technical skills. Employees who are habituated to predictability and standard operating procedures must now adopt agile responsiveness, experimentation, and ambiguity (Orlikowski,1992). Targeted interventions are necessary to facilitate behavioral change, which is a multifaceted psychological process.

- **Change Management Frameworks**: Structured approaches to guiding individuals through change are provided by popular models such as ADKAR (Awareness, Desire, Knowledge, Ability, and Reinforcement). The importance of affective engagement, stakeholder alignment, and visible short-term successes is emphasized by these frameworks in order to maintain momentum.
- **Nudging and Behavioral Economics**: The adoption of new processes can be facilitated by techniques such as nudging, which are nuanced prompts that influence decision-making. For instance, digital nudges that are integrated into BPM tools can promote the opportune completion of tasks, collaboration, or data entry (Susskind et al., 2015). These mechanisms increase process compliance and reduce cognitive fatigue.
- **Leadership Role Models**: When leaders demonstrate the desired behaviors, behavioral change is reinforced. A culture of learning and agility is fostered when executives openly participate in training, elicit feedback on process redesign, and share personal transformation stories, thereby modeling vulnerability and growth (Schein, 2010).

3. Cultural Harmony

BPM transformation can be either facilitated or impeded by organizational culture, which refers to the shared values, beliefs, and norms that govern behavior. Effective process innovation necessitates psychological safety, creativity, and collaboration, all of which are promoted by a people-centered culture (Parry & Proctor Thomson, 2003).

- **Cultural Diagnostics**: The Organizational Culture Assessment Instrument (OCAI) and Denison Organizational Culture Survey are tools that assist in evaluating the organization's preparedness for change. During digital transitions, cultures that demonstrate high levels of adaptability, employee involvement, and mission alignment frequently outperform their counterparts (Cascio & Montealegre, 2016).
- **Psychological Safety and Inclusion**: The acceleration of BPM innovation is facilitated by the establishment of a culture of openness, in which employees feel comfortable expressing their ideas and concerns without fear of retribution. In 2015, Project Aristotle at Google determined that psychological safety was the most critical factor in determining the efficacy of a team.
- **Cultural Rituals and Storytelling**: Sustaining desired behaviors involves incorporating cultural values into rituals, such as innovation hackathons, team retrospectives, or recognition ceremonies. The human-centric narrative

is further bolstered by the sharing of success stories of BPM initiatives that have enhanced the well-being of employees or the customer experience.

HUMAN-CENTRIC BPM AND LEADERSHIP

In the context of digital transformation, leadership is essential for guiding Business Process Management (BPM) toward a human-centric approach. Leaders must guarantee that employees are engaged, supported, and ethically regarded as technological advancements transform operations.

1. **Leadership Qualities in Digital Transformation** Inclusivity, empathy, vision, and adaptability are essential components of effective BPM leadership. Diverse perspectives are empowered and ownership is promoted through inclusive decision-making (Nambisan et al., 2019). Leaders who possess emotional intelligence and are empathetic are capable of reducing employee anxiety and fostering trust (Seligman, 2011). Visionary leadership provides guidance during periods of transition (Markus & Robey, 1988), whereas adaptability fosters resilience and ongoing innovation (Kaplan & Norton, 1996).
2. **Leadership Strategies that Focus on Humans** Cultivating trust, fostering collaboration, and investing in employee development are among the most effective strategies. Engagement is improved through participation and transparent communication (Seligman, 2011). Employees are equipped to adapt to technological advancements through mentorship and training (McKinsey, 2017). Burnout is diminished and retention is enhanced by promoting well-being through mental health initiatives (Adner, 2021). Morale and motivation are enhanced by acknowledging contributions (Hevner & Chatterjee, 2010).
3. **Ethical Leadership in Business Process Management** Fair and responsible digital practices are guaranteed by ethical leadership. Leaders are required to safeguard employee data and promote the use of AI in a transparent and impartial manner (Foss & Saebi, 2017). Psychological stability and trust are promoted by transparent communication regarding change (Hammer, 1990). Leading by example establishes organizational standards and reinforces integrity (Laudon et al., 2020).
4. **The Changing Role of Leadership** Future leaders must prioritize cross-functional collaboration, data-driven decision-making, and the employee experience. Engagement and well-being are prioritized in order to attract and retain talent (Susskind et al., 2015). BPM outcomes are guaranteed to correspond with strategic objectives through the implementation of analytics (Brynjolfsson &

McAfee, 2014). Coherence among digital initiatives is promoted by integrative leadership (Westerman et al., 2014).

BUSINESS PROCESS MANAGEMENT ETHICS

As firms use digital tools like AI, automation, and machine learning, Business Process Management (BPM) ethics are becoming more difficult. In particular, a human-centric BPM approach must carefully assess its implications on society, consumers, and employees. Digital transformation can boost efficiency, innovation, and competitiveness, but also raises ethical issues about technology use, employment displacement, privacy, and bias.

1. Job loss and retraining

One of the biggest ethical issues in digital BPM is job loss due to automation. Robotic process automation (RPA), AI, and machine learning can replace repetitive and low-skilled tasks, which could affect the future of work and job security, especially in manual labor or administrative industries. To overcome this difficulty, organizations must proactively reskill and upskill their employees. Human-centric BPM recognizes that technology should complement employees, not replace them. Digital transformation should focus on giving workers more strategic, creative, and value-added tasks rather than eliminating jobs. Companies should invest in comprehensive reskilling programs to help people learn new skills and adapt to the digital economy. These programs may teach data analytics, AI, digital literacy, and other important skills. Reskilling should teach employees transferable skills that will be useful in the job. BPM projects should target job transformation over position elimination. Restructuring work procedures and giving staff more complex and creative tasks can boost operational efficiency and morale.

2. Privacy and Data Security

Another ethical issue in BPM technology installation is employee and customer data protection. Digital transformation often uses large volumes of data to improve processes, predict trends, and customize offerings. However, with data breaches and incursions becoming more frequent, this raises concerns about data privacy and security. Organizations must use human-centered data management to protect data privacy. This includes:

- **Data Transparency:** Companies should be upfront about data collection, use, and storage with employees and customers. Clear privacy rules and consent methods ensure that individuals understand their rights and how their data will be protected.
- **Data Security**: Strong cybersecurity procedures are needed to safeguard data from unauthorized access and weaknesses. This may include encryption, multi-factor authentication, and regular security checks.
- **AI Ethics**: When processing data with AI and machine learning algorithms, organizations must ensure transparency, accountability, and equity. AI systems should never exploit or discriminate against employees or consumers using their personal data.

3. Business Process Management Fairness and Bias

The prejudice in AI and automation systems is another BPM ethical issue. Machine learning algorithms, which optimize business processes, depend on their training data. If AI systems are trained on biased or unrepresentative data, their choices may be skewed and unjust to customers and employees. AI-powered recruitment techniques may unfairly disadvantage certain demographic groups and benefit others, perpetuating inequality. Automated decision-making systems may worsen resource allocation, supply chain management, and customer service biases. Businesses must ensure their business process management (BPM) systems are impartial to handle these concerns:

- **Bias Checks**: Organizations should regularly audit their AI and automation systems to discover and minimize data and algorithm biases. This may involve assessing algorithmic decisions' implications on different demographics and statistics for race, gender, age, and other biases.
- **Diverse Datasets**: AI systems must be trained on data that represents their target demographics. Diverse and inclusive data sets reduce bias reinforcement in organizations.

Making Decisions Inclusively: Use a broad workforce to build and execute AI and automation technologies ensure a variety of perspectives are included, minimizing accidental biases from affecting BPM results.

4. Transparency, Accountability

Transparency and accountability are ethical requirements for human-centric BPM. As digital BPM systems become increasingly autonomous, enterprises must create clear accountability for their actions. If an AI program misclassifies an employee's performance or makes biased recommendations, the organization must have a clear method to hold it accountable. To ensure AI judgments are understandable and supported, organizations should prioritize AI explainability. This gives employees, customers, and other stakeholders trust in decision-making fairness and transparency. Human Oversight-Digital BPM systems are becoming more autonomous, yet human monitoring should remain essential to decision-making. To ensure AI systems' actions align with organizational principles and ethics, organizations should allow human intervention when needed.

5. Employee Well-Being and Psychological Safety

The psychological effects of digital transformation on employees must be considered in human-centric BPM. As firms undergo digital transitions, employees may worry about job security, future roles, and technology adaptability. Digital transformation can cause burnout or job disillusionment, which can hurt staff retention and performance. These hazards can be reduced by creating an inclusive and supportive workplace that promotes psychological safety during transformation. This may include:

- **Stress management** programs and psychotherapy may help employees cope with digital transformation's emotional toll.
- **Transparent Communication**: Leadership's clear communication about digital transformation's goals and benefits can reduce staff anxiety and boost confidence.
- **Inclusive Leadership**: Leaders must be sympathetic and inclusive to understand and support employees' emotional needs during transition

BUSINESS PROCESS MANAGEMENT TRANSFORMATION'S PSYCHOLOGICAL ASPECTS

In addition to technological integration, the psychological preparedness of employees is a critical factor in the success of Business Process Management (BPM) transformations. Digital transformation introduces learning demands, stress, and uncertainty, necessitating a human-centered approach to address psychological factors such as motivation, change resistance, cognitive fatigue, and well-being.

1. Resistance to Change

Employee resistance is a prevalent impediment to the success of BPM, frequently resulting from job insecurity, perceived loss of control, and uncertainty (Leonardi, 2011). Resistance can be mitigated by fostering psychological safety, which allows employees to voice their concerns and acquire knowledge through experimentation (Chui et al., 2016).

2. Engagement and Motivation

Intrinsic motivation, which is founded on autonomy, competence, and social connection, serves to reinforce engagement in transformation (Davenport & Ronanki, 2018)). Motivation is bolstered by job design features such as meaningful work, feedback, and opportunities for development (Hammer & Stanton, 1999). Ownership and sustained commitment are fostered by engaging employees in the co-creation of processes.

3. Cognitive Load and Digital Literacy

Cognitive capacity can be straining when complex BPM systems are implemented, resulting in decreased productivity (Schein, 2010). Organizations should prioritize user-centered design and invest in digital literacy to alleviate congestion (Bostrom & Yudkowsky, 2014). Efficient learning and enhanced employee experiences are facilitated by intuitive systems.

4. Psychological Resilience

Morale can be diminished by the apprehension of automation and job loss. Support systems, stress management training, and effective communication regarding role evolution can enhance psychological resilience the capacity to adjust to change (Leonardi, 2011). Adaptability and learning are also facilitated by the promotion of a growth mindset (Dignum, 2019).

5. Social Support and Emotional Well-Being

It is imperative that employees' welfare is prioritized during periods of transition. Stress is mitigated and coping mechanisms are enhanced by social support systems (Markus & Robey, 1988). Maintaining emotional well-being during BPM initiatives necessitates supportive cultures, open communication channels, and access to mental health resources.

6. Psychological Adaptation and Leadership

The emotional and cognitive milieu of transformation is influenced by leaders. Transformational leadership, which is characterized by empowerment, vision, and empathy, assists employees in navigating uncertainty (Orlikowski, 1992). Trust and psychological safety are further enhanced by emotional intelligence in leadership (Schein, 2010).

BUSINESS PROCESS MANAGEMENT (BPM) PARTICIPATORY DESIGN

In the context of digital transformation, participatory design is a critical strategy in human-centric Business Process Management (BPM). It underscores the active participation of employees in the design and enhancement of business processes, thereby guaranteeing that they are in accordance with the practical requirements of end users and organizational objectives (Hammer & Stanton, 1999). Participatory design promotes a sense of ownership, facilitates user acceptance, and improves the efficacy of transformation initiatives as organizations integrate new technologies (Parry & Proctor Thomson, 2003).

1. **The Justification for Participatory Design in Digital Transformation** In the past, upper management made BPM decisions with negligible input from frontline employees. Nevertheless, this top-down paradigm frequently fails to account for valuable experiential knowledge. Engaging employees during the design and implementation phases, participatory design addresses this gap, resulting in solutions that are more contextually pertinent and sustainable (Wenger, 1998). The overall quality and acceptance of digital changes are enhanced by the critical insights that employees, as process users, contribute, which fuel innovation and adaptability (Foss & Saebi, 2017).
2. **Benefits of Participatory Design in Business Process Management** During digital transformation and BPM, participatory design provides numerous advantages:
    - **Employee Engagement**: The inclusion of employees in the process design phase increases job satisfaction, commitment, and motivation (Susskind et al.,2015).
    - **Innovation and Practical Solutions**: Employees provide firsthand knowledge that can result in operationally viable and creative enhancements (Hammer & Stanton, 1999).

- **Efficiency and Relevance**: Implementation resistance is diminished when processes are co-designed with employees, as they are more closely aligned with daily operations (Dignum, 2019).
- **Trust and Collaboration**: Internal trust is enhanced and communication across teams is enhanced through collaboration in process design (Kaplan & Norton, 1996).

3. **Strategies for Incorporating Participatory Design** In order to effectively employ participatory design, organizations may implement a variety of strategies:
   - **Workshops and Focus Groups**: These forums facilitate open dialogue and enable employees to address process challenges and propose enhancements (Aguinis & Burgi Tian, 2021).
   - **Cross-Functional Teams**: Teams that are comprised of members from various departments ensure that a variety of perspectives are considered when co-creating solutions (Rock & Grant,2016).
   - **Prototyping and Iterative Feedback**: Digital tools and process mockups facilitate early testing and iterative refinement in response to user feedback (Schwartz et al.,, 2017).
   - **Surveys and polls**: These instruments facilitate the collection of a more compreensive array of viewpoints, providing both qualitative and quantitative feedback (Susskind et al.,, 2015).
   - **Participation in Technology Selection**: The evaluation and selection of digital tools by employees improves their efficacy and adoption (Rosemann & vom Brocke, 2015).
4. Limitations of Participatory Design in Business Process Management (BPM)
   - **Time and Resource Constraints**: Participatory design necessitates the active involvement of many stakeholders, including employees across various tiers, which can be labor-intensive. The process of soliciting comments, conducting meetings, and integrating varied perspectives into the design may interrupt standard operations and postpone project timeframes. This involvement enhances the process but may strain available resources, especially in businesses with constrained time or manpower. One method to alleviate this difficulty is by integrating design talks into normal operations, such as routine team meetings or project evaluations, hence minimizing disturbance to daily company activity (Seligman, 2011). A systematic method of engagement incorporating time-limited workshops and established phases can facilitate resource management and reduce productivity disruption.
   - **Resistance to Change**: Notwithstanding the inclusivity and participation inherent in participatory design, certain employees may remain resistive to the resultant changes. This skepticism frequently stems from

apprehension regarding the unknown, anxieties about job stability, or unease with novel methodologies and technologies. Resistance may also arise from entrenched organizational norms or practices that are at odds with proposed changes. Surmounting this opposition necessitates a proactive strategy for change management, prioritizing the establishment of a culture characterized by transparency, trust, and ongoing communication.(Schein, 2010) posits that early employee involvement in the change process, coupled with making they feel acknowledged and valued, can markedly diminish resistance. Moreover, ongoing education and accessible venues for addressing concerns can mitigate fear and foster engagement.

- **Diverse or Conflicting Inputs:** A fundamental advantage of participatory design is the integration of varied perspectives, resulting in more comprehensive and balanced solutions. This diversity may also pose issues when input from different stakeholders is contradictory or when agendas or expectations diverge. Improperly managed opposing perspectives can result in confusion, impede decision-making, and induce design paralysis. In these instances, proficient facilitation and consensus-building strategies are essential. Facilitators may employ structured techniques, including brainstorming sessions, voting, or prioritizing matrices, to guarantee that contradictory views are productively addressed. Moreover, explicit participation guidelines, transparency in decision-making, and accessible communication channels facilitate the resolution of conflicts and harmonize varied viewpoints towards shared organizational objectives (Hammer, 1990).
- **Over-Complexity and Scope Creep:** Engaging numerous stakeholders may yield more complete answers, but it can also complicate the design process. The multitude of contributors to BPM system development may render the process excessively complex and challenging to oversee. Moreover, participatory design may occasionally result in scope creep, wherein the design process extends beyond the initial aims, integrating additional features or modifications not originally intended. This may ultimately lead to delays, budget excesses, and diminished project concentration. To navigate complexity, it is essential to define explicit project objectives, scope, and timetables from the beginning, accompanied by regular evaluations to guarantee that the project stays aligned and that the aims of participatory design are preserved throughout the process.
- **Power imbalances and Tokenism:** In certain businesses, despite the objective of participatory design to foster inclusivity, power disparities

may persist among various employee tiers. Senior management or influential factions may monopolize the design process, resulting in superficial involvement from lower-level employees whose contributions are not authentically valued. This can diminish the efficacy of participatory design, as it may not adequately address the genuine problems or requirements of employees directly affected by the changes. To prevent tokenism, it is crucial that participatory design processes are meticulously organized to guarantee equitable engagement, with intentional initiatives to empower all stakeholders, irrespective of position or status, to participate meaningfully (Markus & Robey, 1988).

- **Integration Challenges:** Despite successful employee engagement and important insights from participatory design, incorporating these contributions into the comprehensive BPM strategy can prove difficult. The concepts produced in participatory sessions may not consistently correspond with overarching organizational goals or the technical viability of enacting modifications. Reconciling different employee contributions with practical execution necessitates meticulous study and coordination across design teams, technical specialists, and management. Additionally, issues may arise in reconciling participatory design outcomes with current organizational procedures, technologies, and frameworks. In these instances, it is essential to preserve flexibility and modify the design process as necessary to ensure alignment with the organization's strategic objectives.

Participatory design provides numerous benefits, including enhanced employee involvement, optimized procedures, and more inclusive decision-making. Nonetheless, as delineated, it possesses certain limits. Organizations must adeptly address these difficulties to optimize the advantages of participatory design while ensuring that BPM deployment is efficient, targeted, and congruent with company goals. By tackling time restrictions, resistance, contradictory inputs, power imbalances, complexity, and integration challenges, companies can effectively execute participatory design that fosters a more inclusive, human-centered BPM methodology.

INNOVATIONS IN HUMAN-CENTRIC BUSINESS PROCESS MANAGEMENT

In the context of digital transformation, it is imperative to implement innovations in Business Process Management (BPM) to ensure that technological advancements are in accordance with the requirements of human-centered organizations. These innovations promote strategic business objectives, foster adaptability, and increase employee engagement (Van de Ven & Poole, 1995).

1. Intelligent Process Automation (IPA)

Robotic Process Automation (RPA) and artificial intelligence (AI) are integrated by IPA, which enables processes to make data-driven, adaptive decisions. It enhances job satisfaction and personnel capabilities by automating repetitive tasks, thereby enabling employees to concentrate on creative and strategic functions (Wenger, 1998).

2. Digital Twin Technology

Using IoT (Internet of Things), data analytics, and simulations, digital twins replicate real-time business operations. Through interactive visualizations and experimentation, they facilitate employee empowerment, continuous process optimization, and proactive decision-making (Westerman et al., 2014).

3. Augmented and Virtual Reality (AR/VR)

Through immersive training, remote collaboration, and process visualization, AR and VR improve BPM. These technologies facilitate the development of skills, mitigate operational risks, and enhance employee involvement in process innovation (Davenport & Ronanki, 2018).

4. Platforms for Business Process Management that are Collaborative

Real-time collaboration and agile process design are facilitated by integrated BPM platforms that transcend organizational boundaries. They facilitate cross-functional communication, democratize process innovation, and expedite the process of adapting to change (Laudon et al., 2020).

5. Employee-Driven Business Process Management and Participatory Design

Participatory design is becoming more prevalent in human-centric BPM, as employees collaborate to develop and optimize business processes. This bottom-up approach guarantees the relevance and usability of process outcomes, promotes innovation, and enhances ownership (Nambisan et al., 2019).

CASE STUDIES IN HUMAN-CENTRIC BPM

The implementation of human-centric Business Process Management (BPM) across diverse sectors illustrates that emphasizing employee engagement, emotional intelligence, and leadership can lead to substantial enhancements in operational results and employee happiness. This section examines real-world case studies demonstrating how firms in various sectors have effectively implemented human-centric methods to increase efficiency, stimulate creativity, and boost overall performance.

1. Financial Services: Artificial Intelligence-Driven Process Automation

A leading bank in the financial services sector implemented an extensive digital transformation strategy, incorporating artificial intelligence (AI) and robotic process automation (RPA) into back-office functions such as loan processing and customer queries. The success of this change depended on the active participation of people, guaranteeing that technology would enhance rather than supplant human contribution. Implemented solutions centered on human considerations included:

- **Employee Involvement in Technology Selection:** The bank conducted seminars to collect employee feedback on the AI tools, ensuring that the technology met user requirements.
- **Upskilling and Training:** Comprehensive training initiatives were implemented to assist personnel in acquiring the competencies necessary for utilizing AI and automation technologies, hence enabling their shift to more strategic and creative positions.

2. Manufacturing: Process Redesign Driven by Employees

A multinational manufacturing firm sought to improve its supply chain and production processes through the adoption of digital tools, while prioritizing employee involvement in Business Process Management (BPM). The organization emphasized participatory design and continual improvement above top-down directives, fostering employee engagement in process development. Essential methods encompassed:

- **Culture of continuous improvement:** This was established through the implementation of a digital suggestion box to gather staff proposals for process optimization, which were subsequently evaluated and tested.
- **Reskilling Initiatives:** Employees were afforded opportunities to augment their competencies in process management, automation technologies, and data analytics.

This strategy resulted in a 25% enhancement in production efficiency, a decrease in employee turnover, and elevated employee morale and engagement, fostering a more inclusive and collaborative workplace.

3. Healthcare: Employee Empowerment and Digital Workflow

A healthcare firm dedicated to integrating digital solutions to improve patient care while ensuring employee empowerment. The deployment of an electronic health record (EHR) system was developed with contributions from medical professionals to guarantee that the technology corresponded with their workflows and requirements. The principal human-centric initiatives encompassed:

- **Employee Empowerment via Technology:** Healthcare professionals were engaged in the design of the EHR system to ensure it aligned with their operational requirements.
- **Continuous Training and Support:** Ongoing training initiatives were implemented to ensure healthcare personnel remain informed about technological changes and to promote seamless adoption.
- **Psychological Safety:** Initiatives aimed at enhancing mental well-being, including stress-relief programs and open forums, were implemented to mitigate the anxiety linked to digital transformation.

Consequently, the healthcare system attained a more seamless shift to digital workflows, resulting in enhanced patient care, elevated personnel happiness, and augmented operational efficiency.

4. Augmented Reality (AR) for Employee Training in Retail

A major retail company utilized augmented reality (AR) to transform its employee training program. The organization improved employee engagement and cultivated superior customer service abilities by developing immersive, interactive training experiences.

This initiative featured human-centric components such as interactive and immersive learning, wherein staff were equipped with AR headsets to participate in simulated customer service scenarios and enhance their problem-solving abilities.

- **Customized Training Pathways:** Training modules were specifically designed for distinct positions, guaranteeing that each employee received pertinent training aligned with their department's requirements.

- **Continuous Feedback and Adaptation:** Employee feedback was consistently collected and utilized to enhance training programs, ensuring their effectiveness and engagement.

The AR training program resulted in enhanced employee confidence, elevated customer happiness, and an improvement in employee retention rates, as staff appreciated the engaging and dynamic learning experience.

These case studies illustrate that human-centric BPM not only enhances operational efficiency but also fosters a more engaged, satisfied, and resilient workforce. By prioritizing employee involvement, continuous learning, and empowerment, organizations can successfully integrate digital tools and achieve sustainable growth.

SOLUTIONS AND RECOMMENDATIONS

To effectively execute a human-centric approach to Business Process Management (BPM), firms must adopt several strategic answers to prevalent issues. Resistance to change can be alleviated by engaging staff early through participatory design and clear communication. Discrepancies between technology and human requirements must be rectified through user-centered design and human-computer interaction (HCI) principles. Leadership must advocate for transformation by harmonizing technical execution with empathy, promoting psychological safety, and enhancing workforce well-being. To surmount cultural inertia, businesses must cultivate a culture of agility and perpetual learning. Effective, bidirectional communication strategies and consistent feedback mechanisms are crucial for sustaining stakeholder participation. Ethical concerns of data privacy must be addressed by stringent governance and adherence to privacy regulations. Prioritization of workforce reskilling is essential through inclusive, adaptive learning initiatives that address digital skills deficiencies. Organizations should adopt comprehensive evaluation frameworks that encompass both operational results and human-centric KPIs, including engagement, happiness, and well-being, to guarantee a balanced and sustainable BPM transformation.

Best Practices for Implementing Human- Centric Business Process Management (BPM)

Optimal methodologies for executing human-centric Business Process Management (BPM) in digital transformation encompass a strategic integration of technology, leadership, and employee involvement. Initially, emphasize inclusive design by engaging employees during the preliminary phases of process reconfiguration to guarantee that tools and processes address genuine user requirements. Secondly, prioritize ongoing education and reskilling to furnish the workforce with the digital skills essential for adapting to emerging BPM technology. Third, cultivate robust leadership that advocates for change and articulates a clear vision, so enhancing trust and psychological safety. Fourth, synchronize BPM tools with human competencies by incorporating user-friendly technology that enhance—rather than supplant—critical thinking and collaboration. Fifth, implement ethical and transparent data governance to guarantee the responsible and secure utilization of employee data. Ultimately, persistently assess and analyze both operational efficiency and staff welfare through a combination of qualitative and quantitative measures. Collectively, these strategies facilitate durable and adaptive BPM implementations that prioritize the human experience.

Addressing Ethical Challenges

Confronting ethical dilemmas in Business Process Management (BPM) amid digital transition necessitates meticulous attention to privacy, equity, and accountability. As enterprises increasingly depend on data-driven technologies like artificial intelligence (AI) and robotic process automation (RPA), the potential of bias, discrimination, and privacy infringement escalates. Ethical governance frameworks are essential to guarantee that the implementation of these technologies upholds employee rights, fosters transparency, and prevents inadvertent harm. Organizations must establish explicit data governance policies that delineate the usage, sharing, and protection of data, especially concerning personal information. Moreover, enterprises must be responsible for their actions, guaranteeing that AI and automation technologies are developed and implemented in accordance with ethical norms and organizational principles. Ultimately, ongoing monitoring and feedback mechanisms must be established to assess the effects of these technologies on the business and its employees, assuring adherence to ethical norms during the digital transformation process.

Enhancing Accessibility

Improving accessibility in human-centric Business Process Management (BPM) entails creating processes, methods, and systems that are inclusive and useable by all employees, irrespective of their physical limitations, cognitive powers, or technological skills. This commences with universal design standards, guaranteeing that BPM platforms and digital tools are intuitive, navigable, and compatible with assistive devices like screen readers or voice input systems. Clarity of language and visual simplicity are crucial, allowing users from all backgrounds and literacy levels to comprehend and interact with process workflows. Furthermore, adaptable user interfaces enable consumers to tailor their interactions to suit their needs or tastes. Organizations ought to perform accessibility audits often and engage employees with disabilities in user testing to pinpoint obstacles and enhance usability. Integrating accessibility into BPM design and implementation enables firms to adhere to legal and ethical norms while maximizing the potential of a diverse workforce.

FUTURE RESEARCH DIRECTIONS

Future research should focus on developing standardized metrics to assess human-centric outcomes such as inclusivity and well-being within BPM. Comparative studies across industries and cultures can help identify best practices and contextual nuances. Longitudinal studies are needed to evaluate the sustained impact of human-centric BPM on innovation, resilience, and employee retention. As AI becomes more integrated, research should explore human-AI co-creation models and ethical governance frameworks. Additionally, interdisciplinary approaches combining psychology, HCI, and ethics can deepen understanding and guide the evolution of adaptable, human-centered BPM ecosystems.

Emerging Trends in Human-Centric Business Process Management (BPM)

Human-centric BPM is progressing swiftly due to technical innovations and changing workplace dynamics. A prominent trend is the incorporation of artificial intelligence (AI) and machine learning to enhance decision-making while maintaining human oversight, facilitating more flexible and intelligent workflows. Emotion-aware systems are emerging, utilizing sentiment analysis and behavioral data to tailor user experiences and improve employee engagement. A burgeoning trend is hyper automation, wherein enterprises integrate RPA, AI, and low-code platforms to optimize both human and machine operations, while maintaining human oversight and exception management at the forefront. Remote and hybrid work patterns are transforming BPM design, highlighting mobile accessibility, asynchronous collaboration tools, and digital workflows that facilitate geographically dispersed teams. Finally, well-being-oriented BPM, which incorporates mental health and workload management into process design, is gaining prominence, indicating a wider transition towards employee sustainability and organizational empathy. These tendencies combined indicate the emergence of more adaptable, intelligent, and inclusive BPM ecosystems.

CONCLUSION

A pragmatic necessity in an era characterized by complex human-technology interactions and rapid digitalization, the transformation of Business Process Management into a human-centric model is not solely a theoretical concept. Organizations can accomplish sustainable innovation, improve employee engagement, and preserve their competitive advantage by prioritizing people in BPM processes, as illustrated in this chapter. Organizations can transition from mechanistic process administrators to dynamic, adaptive ecosystems by incorporating emotional intelligence, psychological safety, ethical foresight, and participatory design into BPM frameworks. This human-centric transition not only enhances technological implementation but also safeguards the dignity, creativity, and resilience of the workforce. Leadership commitment, ethical vigilance, continuous capability development, and cultural alignment are critical enablers of this transformation. When these principles are applied to BPM initiatives, they lead to inclusive, purpose-driven digital transformation journeys that benefit all stakeholders, including employees, customers, and society as a whole.

REFERENCES

Adner, R. (2021). *Winning the right game: How to disrupt, defend, and deliver in a changing world.* MIT Press. DOI: 10.7551/mitpress/12752.001.0001

Aguinis, H., & Burgi-Tian, J. (2021). Measuring performance for impact: Research agenda and best practices. *Human Resource Management Review, 31*(2), 100693.

Bersin, J. (2020). *The rise of the human-centered organization.* Deloitte Insights. https://www2.deloitte.com/insights

Bostrom, N., & Yudkowsky, E. (2014). The ethics of artificial intelligence. In Frankish, K., & Ramsey, W. M. (Eds.), *The Cambridge handbook of artificial intelligence* (pp. 316–334). Cambridge University Press. DOI: 10.1017/CBO9781139046855.020

Brynjolfsson, E., & McAfee, A. (2014). *The second machine age: Work, progress, and prosperity in a time of brilliant technologies.* W.W. Norton & Company.

Cascio, W. F., & Montealegre, R. (2016). How technology is changing work and organizations. *Annual Review of Organizational Psychology and Organizational Behavior, 3*(1), 349–375. DOI: 10.1146/annurev-orgpsych-041015-062352

Chui, M., Manyika, J., & Miremadi, M. (2016). Where machines could replace humans—and where they can't (yet). *McKinsey Quarterly.* https://www.mckinsey.com

Davenport, T. H., & Ronanki, R. (2018). Artificial intelligence for the real world. *Harvard Business Review, 96*(1), 108–116.

Dignum, V. (2019). *Responsible artificial intelligence: How to develop and use AI in a responsible way.* Springer Nature. DOI: 10.1007/978-3-030-30371-6

Foss, N. J., & Saebi, T. (2017). Fifteen years of business model innovation research: Literature review and future research directions. *Journal of Management, 43*(1), 200–227. DOI: 10.1177/0149206316675927

Hammer, M. (1990). Reengineering work: Don't automate, obliterate. *Harvard Business Review, 68*(4), 104–112.

Hammer, M., & Stanton, S. A. (1999). How process enterprises really work. *Harvard Business Review, 77*(6), 108–118. PMID: 10662000

Hevner, A. R., & Chatterjee, S. (2010). *Design research in information systems: Theory and practice.* Springer. DOI: 10.1007/978-1-4419-5653-8

Kaplan, R. S., & Norton, D. P. (1996). *The balanced scorecard: Translating strategy into action.* Harvard Business Press.

Laudon, K. C., & Laudon, J. P. (2020). *Management information systems: Managing the digital firm* (16th ed.). Pearson.

Leonardi, P. M. (2011). When flexible routines meet flexible technologies: Affordance, constraint, and the imbrication of human and material agencies. *Management Information Systems Quarterly*, *35*(1), 147–167. DOI: 10.2307/23043493

Markus, M. L., & Robey, D. (1988). Information technology and organizational change: Causal structure in theory and research. *Management Science*, *34*(5), 583–598. DOI: 10.1287/mnsc.34.5.583

McKinsey Global Institute. (2017). *A future that works: Automation, employment, and productivity*. McKinsey & Company.

Nambisan, S., Wright, M., & Feldman, M. (2019). The digital transformation of innovation and entrepreneurship: Progress, challenges and key themes. *Research Policy*, *48*(8), 103773. DOI: 10.1016/j.respol.2019.03.018

Orlikowski, W. J. (1992). The duality of technology: Rethinking the concept of technology in organizations. *Organization Science*, *3*(3), 398–427. DOI: 10.1287/orsc.3.3.398

Parry, K. W., & Proctor-Thomson, S. B. (2003). Leadership, culture and performance: The case of the New Zealand public sector. *Journal of Change Management*, *3*(4), 376–399. DOI: 10.1080/714023843

Rock, D., & Grant, H. (2016). Why diverse teams are smarter. *Harvard Business Review*. https://hbr.org/2016/11/why-diverse-teams-are-smarter

Rosemann, M., & vom Brocke, J. (2015). The six core elements of business process management. In vom Brocke, J., & Rosemann, M. (Eds.), *Handbook on business process management 1* (pp. 105–122). Springer. DOI: 10.1007/978-3-642-45100-3_5

Schein, E. H. (2010). *Organizational culture and leadership* (4th ed.). Jossey-Bass.

Schwartz, J., Bohdal-Spiegelhoff, M., Gretczko, M., & Sloan, N. (2017). Rewriting the rules for the digital age. *Deloitte Global Human Capital Trends*. https://www2.deloitte.com

Seligman, M. E. P. (2011). *Flourish: A visionary new understanding of happiness and well-being*. Free Press.

Susskind, R., & Susskind, D. (2015). *The future of the professions: How technology will transform the work of human experts*. Oxford University Press. DOI: 10.1093/oso/9780198713395.001.0001

Van de Ven, A. H., & Poole, M. S. (1995). Explaining development and change in organizations. *Academy of Management Review, 20*(3), 510–540. DOI: 10.2307/258786

Wenger, E. (1998). *Communities of practice: Learning, meaning, and identity.* Cambridge University Press. DOI: 10.1017/CBO9780511803932

Westerman, G., Bonnet, D., & McAfee, A. (2014). *Leading digital: Turning technology into business transformation.* Harvard Business Press.

Zuboff, S. (2019). *The age of surveillance capitalism: The fight for a human future at the new frontier of power.* PublicAffairs.

KEY TERMS AND DEFINITIONS

Business Process Management (BPM): A methodical approach that involves the modeling, execution, monitoring, and optimization of processes in order to enhance efficiency, improve an organization's processes, and achieve business objectives.

Digital Transformation: The process of integrating digital technologies into all facets of a business, thereby fundamentally altering the way in which organizations operate and provide value to their consumers.

Workforce Adaptation: The process by which employees acquire the skills, mindset, and behaviors necessary to flourish in a digitally transforming organization.

Human Factors: Elements of human behavior, capabilities, and limitations that influence the design and implementation of technologies and systems.

Change Management: A methodical approach to the process of transitioning individuals, teams, and organizations from their current state to a desired future state.

Organizational Culture: The collective values, beliefs, and norms that influence the conduct and procedures of an organization.

Automation: The utilization of technology to execute tasks with minimal human intervention, frequently improving consistency and efficiency.

Leadership: The process of guiding and influencing others to achieve shared objectives, which is particularly important in the context of promoting transformational change.

Ethics in BPM: The implementation of moral principles to guarantee that BPM practices maintain transparency, equity, and respect for human dignity.

Employee Empowerment: A management strategy that provides employees with the autonomy, resources, and support necessary to take the initiative and make decisions within their responsibilities.

Chapter 4
Human Factors and Adaptation of the Workforce in the Digital Transition in Public Administrations in Morocco:
An Exploratory Study

Youssef Mortaji
https://orcid.org/0009-0000-4641-0134
University of Ibn Tofail, Kénitra, Morocco

Fatima Charef
University of Ibn Tofail, Kénitra, Morocco

ABSTRACT

This chapter explores human factors and their impact on the adaptation of the workforce to the digital transition in Moroccan public administrations. As the digitalization of public services becomes a priority to improve efficiency and transparency, the adoption of new technologies depends heavily on employees and their ability to adapt to changes. This paper examines the skills, resistance to change and motivation of public servants in the face of this transformation. The study is based on an exploratory methodological approach, using semi-structured interviews with human resources managers, civil servants and change management experts in various Moroccan public administrations. This approach collects direct perceptions and

DOI: 10.4018/979-8-3373-3336-6.ch004

experiences of the actors involved in the digital transition. The results of the study reveal that resistance to change, lack of digital skills and a stagnant organizational culture are the main barriers to adopting digital technologies. Younger employees are generally more receptive, while older employees face more difficulties.

INTRODUCTION

For over a decade, the digital transformation has become a key strategic issue for public administrations globally. Morocco is no different: public service digitalization is now seen as a basic lever to enhance administrative performance, transparency and quality of the relationship between the state and citizens (OECD, 2022; World Bank, 2023). National programmers like Morocco Digital 2020 and the National Strategy for Digital Transformation 2025 signal an explicit intent to reform public administration around an agile and user-centric model that is soundly grounded in information technologies (MTN, 2021).

While access to digital infrastructure, legal frameworks and tools is crucial, human capital appears a critical determinant of success. The success of a 'Digital Transformation' is less about technology as it is about the ability of civil servants to serve as change agents (Zamrani & Achouri, 2021). This raises pressing questions about their preparedness, adaptability, and capacity for collaboration in a context often marked by bureaucratic inertia, organizational rigidity, and an administrative culture that is not conducive to innovation (Boukar et al., 2022).

This chapter explores the human factors shaping the workforce's adaptation to digital transformation within Moroccan public administrations. It focuses on three key dimensions: digital skills, resistance to change, and motivation to engage with reform processes. Adopting a critical lens, the chapter challenges technocentric approaches by placing human dynamics at the center of public sector reform (Aubry & Nkengne, 2020).

The analysis is based on an exploratory qualitative approach, drawing on semi-structured interviews with key stakeholders' human resource managers, civil servants at various levels, and change management experts. This methodology provides in-depth, context-sensitive insights that go beyond normative institutional discourse.

1. THE DIGITAL TRANSITION IN PUBLIC ADMINISTRATIONS: ISSUES AND STATE OF PLAY

Over the past two decades, public administrations around the world have embarked on a profound process of digital transformation, aimed at improving the performance of public services, increase administrative transparency and meet the growing expectations of citizens. In this global context, Morocco is no exception to this dynamic. The Moroccan State has multiplied e-government initiatives, implementing several successive strategies to modernize public services, facilitate access to administrative services and strengthen the effectiveness of institutions.

However, the digital transition in the public sector is not limited to the introduction of technologies: it raises structural, cultural and human challenges, and questions traditional modes of management and interaction between administrations and users. In order to better understand this transition, it is necessary to examine its foundations, the political ambitions that underlie it, as well as the concrete challenges it raises for institutions and citizens.

This first axis thus proposes to draw up an inventory of the digitalization of the Moroccan public sector, by addressing successively the definitions and implications of this notion, the national policies adopted in this field, and the fundamental issues that this digital transformation represents in terms of efficiency, transparency and administration-user relationship.

1.1. Definition and Scope of Digitalization in the Public Sector

The digitalization of the public sector can be defined as the gradual incorporation of information and communication technologies (ICT) into the processes, services, and structures of public administrations, as a means of improving their efficiency, transparency, and capacity to meet citizens' needs (OECD, 2020). This allows for more serious transformations than simply dematerializing the public administration's procedures; it also involves re-defining how the state interacts with its agents and users and having the follow-on consequence of re-organizing internal management models (Mergel et al., 2019).

Digitalization thus covers a diverse scope in the public sector: it encompasses administrative services (electronic counters, e-payment, online processing platforms), governance (performance management systems, open data), and human resources (digital career management, work collaboration tools). It also alters the logic of control, evaluation and accountability within administrations (Dunleavy et al. 2006).

In the countries in the Global South, especially in Morocco, the digital transition is generally viewed as a strategic tool to not only mitigate asymmetries in relation to access to administration but also to improve public governance and strengthen the legitimacy of state institutions (Chohan, 2021). Nevertheless, the nature of this transformation is heavily contextualized to institutional factors, human capacity, and the available technological infrastructure.

1.2. Moroccan Public Policies for Digital Transition

Since 2000, Morocco has adopted a number of national strategies to modernize public administration through digital technologies. The e-Gov initiative (2005) laid the first foundation of this rising paradigm, which was followed by structuring programs, like Maroc Numeric 2013 and then Maroc Digital 2020, that favored the emergence of electronic counters, the interoperability of systems and the promotion of open data (MCINET, 2018).

The current strategy, titled "Morocco Digital 2025," aims to bring about digital transformation in Morocco by relying on three pillars: (1) the digitization of public service; 2) the increase of digital skills of workforce; and 3) the promotion of public sector innovation culture (Ministère de la Transition Numérique, 2022). This strategy is founded upon coordination between various ministries, the mobilization of specialized agencies such as ADD (Agency for Digital Development), and the support of international organizations such as the World Bank or the European Union.

In addition to this shift, legal reforms have also accompanied it, specifically through the law n° 55-19 on the simplification of administrative procedures, requiring the adoption of digital tools to simplify the relationship between administration and user. Nevertheless, several reports point to the structural constraints of the process: heterogeneity of initiatives, and a lack of data sharing, institutional resistance, and low appropriation of digital tools by public agents (World Bank, 2023; OECD, 2022).

1.3. Issues for Efficiency, Transparency and Relationship Between Citizens and Administration

Digitalization is a strong lever for enhancing efficiency in government administration. Processing times are cut down, human errors are limited, and some low-value tasks can be automated (Janssen & Van Der Voort, 2020). In the context of increased expectation of performance and rationalizing public spending, digital tools are an essential vehicle for modernization.

Transparency is another central issue. Digital platforms and open data portals have made information more accessible to citizens and made it easier for citizens to track their actions and use greater social control over public action (Nam, 2018). This also can help improve trust in institutions, especially in countries where trust is undermined by suspicions of corruption and inefficiency.

Digitalization is fundamentally altering the relationship between the public administration and the citizens. It promotes new forms of interaction that are more horizontal and personalized and encourages the rise of a user-centered administration. Nevertheless, these promises are contingent on the citizens' ability to utilize digital tools, leading to issues of the digital divide, particularly in rural or disadvantaged areas (UNDP, 2022).

Moreover, this transformation depends heavily on the engagement of public servants, because the technological shift digitalization is bringing affects many of our work activities, the responsibilities of public servants, and ultimately the way we expect staff to work. If a citizen-centric technology is not being embraced by staff through active participation and skill development, a technology initiative could be viewed as an additional burden rather than a lever (Zamrani & Achouri, 2021). Thus, the human dimension is an essential variable for the effectiveness of digital reforms.

Yet even though infrastructure and platforms offer the context for digital reform, they are insufficient by themselves. Human factors crucially determine success or failure of these initiatives. Most significantly, public officials' skills, inclinations, and willingness to act can be a motivating force or significant barrier to reform. This brings us to the second analytical axis: to understand the human dimensions that condition the deployment of digital transformation among Moroccan administrations.

2. HUMAN FACTORS: AS LEVER OR BRAKE FOR DIGITAL TRANSFORMATION

Digital transformation of public administrations cannot be considered an easy modernization of technology. Digital transformation, and therefore technological innovations are fundamentally human transformations, and the focus of the evolution is the women and men who will put in place the implementations that will bring about this different way of working every day. The human factor is therefore at the heart of this mutation.

But the factors that will allow or prevent digital adoption (or rejection). Factorial aspects will create a dynamic process that will be as psychosocial as cultural as professional and often has not been taken into account and can be left out of a digitalization strategy.

In the case of Morocco, the ambitions expressed in terms of digital transformation encounter an organizational reality that is marked by resistance to change, unequal skill sets and at times a rigid administrative culture. These determinants can either enhance or impede the digital transition according to how they are tackled in change management practices. It is crucial to study these human factors in deep so as to better understand their impacts and to allow us to make actionable recommendations.

This section of the report presents three main parts, namely the digital skills of public officials, resistance to change, and motivation. It aims to provide an analysis of how they are either levers or barriers to the successful run of digitization projects within Moroccan public services.

2.1. Digital Skills of Public Officials

The success or failure of the digital transformation of public administration is dependent on the human factor, namely the digital skills of agents called to implement and use new technologies in their professional work. Investment in technology infrastructure is necessary, but without matching human skills to the transformation, it will not achieve the expected impacts (Misuraca et al., 2020). Thus, this means that the level of mastery of digital tools; intergenerational differences in digital skills; and training and continuing training needs are a critical variable to technology appropriation by public services.

- Current level of proficiency

In the Moroccan context, although efforts have been made to train civil servants in the use of computer tools, numerous studies reveal a troubling heterogeneity in the real mastery of these skills. The World Bank report (2023) indicates that a number of public officials, noting particularly those from decentralized administrations, still have serious deficiencies in the use of basic digital platforms (electronic document management, institutional messaging, internal management software etc.). This situation undermines the reforms of the digital, as it leads either to an under-use of, or even duly rejection of, the available tools.

The more advanced administrations in terms of technology are more likely to concentrate their efforts in central directions and neglect peripheral needs, thereby exacerbating the internal digital divide. Berraho and Chafiq (2022) conducted exploratory study that indicated that only 37% of the agents surveyed noted that they feel comfortable with the digital tools mandated in their working environment; there is a mismatch between the digital requirements, and available human resources.

- Inequalities associated with ageing.

Generational inequalities in relation to access and mastery of the digital represent a further key obstacle. The young recruits, coming from a 'digital native' generation, have a greater degree of familiarity with computing tools, and are more easily able to adapt to changes in technology. By contrast, older agents trained according to conventional bureaucratic logics, find it more difficult to accommodate new digital uses (Moussaoui & Kabbaj, 2021).

This generational divide is not limited to Morocco: we observe it in several public administration contexts throughout the world. However, in a country where the average age of civil servants exceeds 45 years, as reminded by the Office of the High Commissioner for Planning (2022), the generational divide is now a central issue requiring further consideration to bring about change, calling for specific support strategies and a differentiated response to the training needs according to age profiles and occupational categories.

- Training needs

The enhancement of digital skills warrants both developing continuous training policies as well as targeted and adapted the contexts in which each administration operates. However, while there may be mechanisms, they are not consistent, poorly evaluated, and insufficiently embedded for a sustainable growth of skills (Ben-abdelhadi, 2021). As a result, the training delivered tends to adopt top-down and technical perspectives without taking into account the genuine needs of the agents.

As such, the next challenge is to develop an actual digital learning culture within the public service by developing modular training programs designed to be undertaken remotely and which are supported by self-assessing capacities. Indeed, the digital transition cannot succeed without the necessary mass and coherent investment in developing agent's continuing training by way of agents' development, which is not viewed as a cost but is viewed as a strategic lever of adaptation and innovation.

In conclusion, the digital skills of Moroccan public officials are both a potential lever and a real brake on the digitalization of administrative services. The success of this transformation will depend on governments' ability to correctly identify needs, limit generational inequalities and follow flexible, sustainable and inclusive learning pathways.

2.2. Resistance to Change

Resistance is a key variable in determining the success and failure of digitization processes, specifically in the public sector. It manifests in individual or collective behavior that slows down, diverts or blocks the means to adopt technological innovations. This resistance is not only caused by rational or conscious refusal; it is also often the result of psychological, social and cultural reprisals that are difficultly dissociated from the professional space of public officials.

- Psychological and social surface accessibility

On the psychological dimension, the resistance to change can often be the consequence of fears surrounding: 1. the unknown; 2. anxiety relating the potential for losing professional reference points; 3. a lack of belief in their own suppressive powers etc. Kotter and Schlesinger (2008) have identified that the fear of change can stem from misunderstandings about the rationales for change, a negative perception of the potential consequences of change or an attachment to the way things have always been. Fear is further compounded in contexts where communication is poor and the agents themselves have not been closely engaged in transformational decisions (Hiatt, 2006).

In terms of social dynamics, informal networks, collective working habits and professional norms also help build resistance to change. In the context of the Moroccan public sector where hierarchical communication channels are strongly reinforced and processes are often bureaucratized, the adoption of new technologies can be conceptualized as a potential alteration or threat to the organizational balance. In addition, group dynamics also enhance the reparability of resistance, generating greater resistance by teams especially where they feel the change calls into question their legitimacy or professional identity (Bareil, 2013).

- Fears of obsolescence, loss of power or overload

Among the main barriers to digitalization are fears of obsolescence, fear of losing power or influence, and feelings of overload.

Firstly, fear of professional obsolescence is a reality for many public employees, particularly if they belong to generations that are less acquainted with digital technologies. Automation of certain administrative activities or the implementation of integrated information systems leads some actors to fears that their role will be marginalized or irrelevant (Naranjo-Gil, 2020). This perception produces organizational stress which can eventually lead to circumvention or covert sabotage or obstruction of change.

Secondly, loss of power in organizations is another important consideration. Many civil servants have built expertise based on their unique command of certain procedures, or know-how that is often acquired informally. The introduction of standardized digital tools challenges these acquired skills, and with that, the prestige or influence certain actors wield in their unit. The existing threats to symbolic power adds to a sometimes, elusive, but persistent sense of reluctance (Lines, 2005).

Last but not least, overwork is often put forward as an obstacle, an impediment, to the acceptance of change. Digitalization generally implies a learning or double entry phase, in which agents need to practice old ways while also dealing with new ways. This extra cognitive and time-neutral burden can create an organizational fatigue, especially if the transition is not properly accompanied or resources are insufficient (Cameron & Green, 2019).

In the case of Morocco, several studies and testimony have revealed these dimensions. For instance, a survey issued by the Digital Development Agency (ADD, 2022) shows that more than 60% of respondents reported not being prepared to use digital tools, which was primarily attributed to:

-Training not being organized to support them;
-Supervision is not sufficiently being given;
-Lack of communication on the objectives of the digital transformation.

So, resistance to change should not be interpreted as an irrational blockade, but instead an indication that agents may need more targeted support, improvement in organizational dialogue and to acknowledge the human factors of the digital transition. Any strategy for the digital transformation of Moroccan public administrations will need to include psychological support, ongoing training and development of skills to convert resistance to commitment.

2.3. Agents' Motivation and Commitment

The whole success of the digital transformation in the public administrations is based on agents motivation and commitment. These two rather human dimensions are frequently neglected to be displaced by technological or structural dimensions, and they decisively influence not only the appropriation of digital technologies but also compliance with new forms of work and sustainability of the organizational change. Thus, understanding what motivates public officials to commit to a digitization process is key to the success of the process.

- Motivational factors for change

The motivation of agents undergoing technological change is multidimensional. It may be intrinsic, that is, connected to personal interest, to satisfaction in taking on new challenges, or to an interest in acquiring new skills. It may also be extrinsic and be motivated by external rewards such as bonuses, opportunities to advance career development prospects, or institutional recognition (Deci & Ryan, 2000).

In the context of the Moroccan administrations, there are multiple factors directly influencing motivation. First, clarity of purpose in digital transformation is crucial. Agents need to understand why the change is neede, what it means for their work day, and the value-added benefit of the change to them and the users. A clear, transparent and mobilizing institutional communication is therefore a significant lever (Bouckaert & Peters, 2021).

Secondly, motivated agents are generally those who feel involved in the decision-making process. When the digital transformation initiatives feel top-down in nature, and they are not consulted or engaged, it creates more inertia. Engaging public servants in and sustaining their involvement at the design and deployment stages creates community of belonging and responsibility (Fernandez & Rainey, 2006).

Lastly, motivation is closely related to working conditions. A conducive environment with the right resources (equipment, training, coaching) and a climate of trust reinforce the positive perception of change and encourage long-lasting engagement.

- The role of leadership, recognition and incentives

Managerial leadership is essential to keep agents motivated. Transformational leadership, which sees and values agents as people, encourages innovation and supports autonomy, is especially appropriate in the digital transformation context. Bass & Riggio (2006) explained that transformational leadership can result in extremely high levels of employee engagement in times of organizational change. In the case of Moroccan public administration, these calls for managers who can also be transformational leaders, to lead technically and at a motivational level to inspire, support and encourage acting together in a common vision of change.

Institutional recognition is another strong lever for motivation. Institutional recognisation can take the form of obviously public recognitions, promotions, valorization in the annual evaluations or even put in pilot projects. When agents are positively and publicly recognized or rewarded for their adaptation and innovations, they will become much more likely to join in (Herzberg, 2008).

The final point is to have material and symbolic incentives to increase motivation. While financial bonuses are often the most talked about incentives, there are other possible incentives such as continuous training (to develop skills), attending professional events (and engaging with others in the field) or obtaining professional development opportunities (new mastery of a job) etc. And, it is important to establish a coherent and equitable incentive system in order to anchor digital transformation in the long run (OECD, 2020).

An OECD study (2021) on the digitalization of public service in the MENA region, emphasizes that combining thought leadership strategies with mechanisms to engage recognition and valorization, is vital to fully engage public officials and sustain engagement.

Motivation and consequent commitment of public officials is not to be taken for granted. Motivation and commitment are the gratifying fruitage of an organizational ecosystem whereby personal factors, managerial dynamics and institutional policies interact. By adopting transformational leadership, awarding recognition and offering appropriate incentives, Moroccan administrations will be able to seize digitalization as an opportunity for a paradigm shift away from the traditional bureaucratic administrative culture.

2.4. Organizational Culture and its Effects

Organizational culture has a major role in the success or failure of transformation processes of public administrations towards digital transformation, meaning that, organizational culture feeds attitudes towards change, it influences behavior, individual and collective decision-making. In the case of the Moroccan public sectors, organizational culture can represent both a major lever and a big barrier to adaptation to the digital world.

- Administrative inertia: a lasting brake

One of the most characteristically reproached characteristics of public administrations is their inertia structure there is their slow reaction to profound changes. This inertia is based on several elements: hierarchical rigidity, the very bureaucratic process nature of administration, limited information flow, and the honoring of compliance rather than innovation (Peters, 2018). In this context, any effort of digitalization is faced with organizational defense mechanisms in place that attempt to maintain the organizational status quo.

In the case of Moroccan administration, this resistance is compounded by a very centrally governed culture of management where local initiative is rarely encouraged and, as such, agents have little leeway to implement creative solutions (OECD, 2020). Digital change is viewed by many officials as an additional administrative burden rather than as an opportunity for modernization because of the absence of a common and integrated vision for transformation.

A third major constraint is the absence of a culture of the lifelong learner. When software enabled digital technology involves constant continual adaptability, many administrations remain lowered in their assurance of stability and as a byproduct, compliance with existing standards preempting or resisting attempts of deliberate experimentation or the acquisition of new skills (Schein, 2010).

- The significance of innovative culture

By contrast, organizations that have an innovation culture will probably perform better in their transition to digital. To create this requires a work environment that promotes trial and error, sees forgetting and mistakes as opportunities to learn, and encourages both individual and collective initiatives in creating digital solutions (Mergel et al.,2019).

Building an innovative culture in the Moroccan public sector is going to require a shift in management paradigm. We are moving from a management style where control and compliance were the focus, to a management style that promotes collaboration, agility and creativity. This includes reforming human resource management where systems recognize, reward, and, institutionalize innovation, as a part of the daily rhythm of working (World Bank, 2021).

Public innovation spaces like innovation labs (or public labs), digital services incuators or participatory platforms, can play a structuring role in changing organizational membership. These spaces provide fid the agents forge, test and improve a set of solutions based on the realities of the field, in combination with citizens and other relevant stakeholders (Kuhlmann & Rip, 2018).

In addition, digitalization itself can become a lever for cultural transformation by creating new collaborative habits (e.g. connected digital platforms, shared management tools, periodic videoconferences) which escape from traditional isolated administrative habits.

Organizational culture is therefore an important aspect of understanding the human factors associated with digitalization. If not changing simultaneously with the technologies will nullify any potential impact. Alternatively, a culture of innovation, learning and shared ownership is essential to the success of any digital transformation that is meaningful. For public administrations in Morocco, substantive change involves more than technological change; it requires culture-shifting management policies.

Having analyzed, in the previous section, the most important human factors behind the digital transformation of the public administrations i.e., digital skills, resistance to change, the motivation and organizational culture, it is now necessary to compare these theoretical contributions with the reality on the ground. For this, a qualitative survey was conducted with the principal actors in the digital transformation process of the Moroccan administrations. This third section presents the findings of this empirical study, highlighting points of convergence or divergence between the perceptions of the different actors interviewed

3. EMPIRICAL STUDY: AN EXPLORATORY STUDY

This section presents the results of a qualitative survey that aims to understand the human aspects of digital transition in Moroccan public administrations. The survey includes semi-structured interviews with unique actors in this transition. The purpose is to describe public officials' focus on point of convergence and divergence their focus as human resource managers, and change management experts. This work also presents instances of resistance encountered, and examples of existing good practices that will allow for the digital transition.

3.1. Methodology: Sample, Interview Process

The qualitative survey was carried out between January and March 2025. The sample consisted of 15 participants, situated in three main groups:

- Human resource managers (5 participants)
- Public administration officials (7 participants)
- Change management experts (3 participants)

The interviews were semi-structured which allowed for rich detail of perceptions and no restrictions on the direction to an extent, of thoughts by respondents. The three professional categories of questions were agents' digital skills, resistance to change and strategies for motivation and engagement. The interviews were either face to face or remote depending on the availability of the respondent.

Below is a summary table of the sample of interviewed respondents:

Table 1. Summary of Interviewed Respondents by Professional Group and Profile

Group	Number of participants	Main profile
Group HR Managers	5	Responsible for HR management in public administrations
Civil servants	7	Government employees from various ministries or local authorities
Change management experts	3	Consultants or researchers in public sector's digital transformation
Total	15	

3.2 Synthesis of Collected Perceptions

An analysis of the interviews highlighted differences in opinions as well as similarities in terms of the digital transition in Moroccan public administrations.

- Points of convergence

The perceptions that were collected revealed that all interviewees perceive digitalization as a possible lever to improve efficiency and transparency in the public sector. Some profiles view the barriers to change through very different perspectives.

Table 2. Contrasting Perceptions of the Digital Transition in Moroccan Public Administrations

Subject	HR Managers	Public Servants	Change Management Experts
General perception of digitalization	Seen as an opportunity to modernize administration	Resistance due to uncertainty and lack of training	Essential for transparency, but dependent on human support
Digital skills	Urgent need for continuing training at all levels	Generational inequalities: young people more receptive	Targeted training on public management tools is crucial.
Organizational culture	Centralized culture that slows down innovation.	Lack of support to experiment with new practices	An innovation culture is essential for a successful transition.

- Points of divergence

When unpacking the sources of resistance to change, significant differences emerge. The biggest fear expressed by officials was the fear of becoming obsolete and feeling insecure with implementing new technologies. Meanwhile, HR managers are more likely to express fear related to added institutional resistance, and lack of institutional buy-in, and lack of shared vision to support this change at a strategic level.

Table 3. Points of Divergence in the Perception of Resistance to Digital Transition

Subject	HR Managers	Public Servants	Change Management Experts
General perception of digitalization	Less perceived, but of concern in some departments.	Major problem: fear of losing professional value.	Observed, but can be mitigated with proper training.
Digital skills	. Major Organizational barrier	Less directly perceived, but influences perception of change.	Essential to guide digitalization in the long term.
Organizational culture	Source of structural resistance	Rigid administrative practices that hinder innovation.	Cultural inertia in some jurisdictions.

3.3. Identified Resistances and Existing Good Practices

- Identified resistances

Resistance to change is one of the key barriers to the digital transition, as shown by the majority of participants. The identified causes are mainly psychological and social in nature:

- Fears of occupational obsolescence: Many civil servants fear their traditional skills may become obsolete in a world of new technologies.
- Workload: new digital tools bring more work, and they are not substitutes for existing work.
- Rigidity of administrative processes: A heavy hierarchy and centralized management of decisions limit the agility needed for rapid adoption of digital tools.
    - Current good practices

There are measures currently in place that can be used to further enhance the transition. These include:

- Ongoing training programmes: Some ministries have implemented training programmes for their staff, although they still need to find flexibility to meet some of the specific needs for each type of personnel (young vs. older).
- Digital mentoring: Some experienced individuals in supervisory roles in the area of digital tools are accompanying their peers in learning new software.
- Managers involvement in the digitization process: Involving human resource managers in both the planning and tracking of the digitization process is an important practice to foster engagement in all equal levels of the hierarchy.

Table 4. Summary table of resistances and good practices

Resistance Identified	**Existing good practices**
Fear of obsolescence	Targeted training on skills upgrading, digital mentoring.
work overload	Process review to integrate digital tools seamlessly.
Rigidity of administrative processes	Partial decentralization and more agile management of digitization projects.

The findings from the empirical survey indicate a wide awareness of the possible advantages of the digital shift in Moroccan public administrations. However, human barriers like resistance to change, fear of being redundant and inflexible organizational culture continue to remain a challenge. The way forward is through continuous development of digital skills, the establishment of an innovation culture and the formulation of change management strategies that are more applicable to the context of public servants and managers.

4. IMPACTS AND MEANS OF ACTION FOR A HUMAN AND SUSTAINABLE DIGITALIZATION.

The digitalization of the public sector in Morocco, even if it can bring opportunities of improvements for administrative efficiency, has human challenges to address. In this section we will look at the impacts of digital transformation in terms of human resources and find out what can be done to make this experience more humane and sustainable. We will demonstrate the significance of having an HR strategy designed from a human-centred perspective in order to tackle continuing education, competence management and public sector career assistance.

4.1. For a Human-Centred HR Strategy

To achieve a successful digital shift in Moroccan public administrations will require a profound assessment of human resource management plans. Technology can only be fully leveraged if public servants are well trained, motivated, and properly supported throughout the entire digital shift process. Therefore, it is crucial to use a human approach to human resource management, specifically through continuing training strategies, skills management, and monitoring of public officials' evolution of their career path.

- Ongoing training and support

Maintaining ongoing training for public officials is an important lever to decrease the resistance to change, while developing the digital skills of civil servants. The interviews with HR managers and change management professionals showed that most Moroccan civil servants were at a digital divide, which is deepening inequalities between younger and older. It is therefore fundamental to implement personalized training programs, adapted to the diversity of profiles, and to ensure that regularity in the sessions is maintained, or else agents will quickly be overtaken by technological developments.

Training shouldn't only be about developing new technical skills; you should also consider behaviors and managerial skills, including change management skills, the ability to work in a digital team and the ability to adapt to collaborative tools. This approach not only allows for full mastery of the digital tools but also reinforces agents' commitment to digital transformation and level of development.

Table 5. Customized and Continuous Training as a Driver for Successful Digital Transition

Themes	Training and coaching	Expected results
Digital skills	Development of modules adapted to different skill levels.	Improvement of the agents' mastery of digital tools.
Change adaptation	Change support programs to support transition.	Reduced resistance and increased project buy-in.
Follow-up of training	Continuous evaluation and adjustment of training as required.	Maintenance of commitment and competence over the long term.

- Management of skills and careers

Skills and career management needs to be reconceived to assist the public service in its digital transition. Beyond training, it is critical to create career plans that identify possible progressions aligned with the development of digital skills, allowing agents to develop their career in the public service and contribute to the digitalization project.

Human resource managers should apply a competency management approach that builds digital-specific skills assessment tools into the talent management practices that are typically used. This must include regular assessments of the digital skills of public servants, as well as establishing clearer training pathways for public servants who seek to progress into digital-related roles.

An internal mobility framework would establish the opportunity for agents to develop further in the many specializations in digital, whilst simultaneously facilitating a better equity of dissemination of skills, and more cohesive development of career.

Table 6. Diverging Perceptions of Barriers to Digital Transition

Themes	Skills and Career Management	Expected objectives
Skills assessment	Digital skills monitoring and assessment tools	Identification of training gaps and needs.
Career plans	Customized courses for agents wishing to specialize.	Increased motivation, career development aligned with digitalization.
Internal mobility	Creation of digital channels for public servants.	Better distribution of skills and internal dynamism.

- Implementation of human-centered HR strategy

In addition, a human-centered HR strategy must be accompanied by strong and visible leadership that can model the values of digitalization, orient public servants, and assure the entire process. For example, HR managers must play a key role in establishing conditions for the acceptance of new technologies moving forward, which includes properly establishing incentives for innovation and recognizing agent's efforts. It also must be assured that the digital transition is not perceived as a burden, but instead as an opportunity for development, both personal and professional for each agent.

The establishment of an innovation culture in Moroccan public administrations, and public sector more generally, is also a key vehicle to accomplish this is a key ability to do this, it will demand not only technical and behavioral training but also ongoing development environment to produce ideas, the agents and interactively change the route and be rewarded for individuals effort.

Table 7. Key Pillars of a Human-Centered HR Strategy for Digital Transformation

Themes	Leadership and Innovation Culture	Expected impacts
Visible leadership	Engagement of leaders in the transformation process.	Creating an environment conducive to the membership of agents.
Culture of innovation	Encouragement of creativity and experimentation.	Stimulating innovation and improving processes.
Recognition and incentives	Rewards for successful digital initiatives.	Increasing motivation and reducing resistance.

In order for digitalization in the Moroccan public sector to succeed HR strategy must be people centered. This means continuing education programmers as well as managing digital skills and professional mobility with respect to the needs of the digital transition. Additionally, with visionary leadership and a culture of innovation, resistance is likely to diminish and public officials will engage in the process.

4.2. Change Management and Internal Communication

The management of change in the context of the digitalization of the Moroccan public administration is a complex undertaking that calls for the involvement of all institutional actors but also the agents themselves. The success of this transformation depends largely on how it is communicated internally as well as the involvement of agents in the process. In this section we will consider the involvement of agents in the transformation process and the important role of community managers in the implementation of change.

- Involvement of agents in the transformation process

Agent involvement in the digitization process is a key lever for the success of digital transformation. Indeed, if agents are involved in the preparatory phase of the project, they feel valued, and become actors of transformation rather than passive receivers of new technologies. This degree of involvement carries with it a double impact: it decreases resistance to change, and it encourages buy-in of the new technologies.

Research on change management demonstrates that early involvement of employees in the design, implementation and evaluation of digital projects creates a sense of empowerment and reduces uncertainty and fears surrounding any potential loss of status. The interviews conducted in this research illustrated that agents who were involved from the onset of the digitalization process were inherently more invest in the digital project, expressing higher motivation and confidence of using the digital tools.

Formalized participatory mechanisms, like working groups or steering committees representing agents across categories, are also one of the better means of engaging agents by providing a formal opportunity for employees to say their piece and provide input to the spatial project it implementation to their unique context, agent categories and experiences. The participation not only contributes to sense of engagement and involvement, but it promotes a sense of ownership of the digital tools.

Table 8. Enhancing Agent Engagement in the Digital Transformation Process

Themes	**Involvement of agents in processing**	**Expected results**
active participation	Creation of participatory working groups.	Reduced resistance and increased motivation.
Feedback and continuous evaluation	Regular mechanisms to collect feedback from agents.	Continuous improvement of the digitization process.
open communication	Organization of information sessions and discussion.	Strengthening engagement and building trust.

- The role of community managers

Community managers play an important role in public administration change management. Community managers represent the person's area of management and generally work closely with teams, so they are ideally positioned to drive change to digital transformation. Community managers must not be limited to managing activities, but in a context of transformation, they are in charge of managing the intermediary role of supporting the communication of change as well as supporting the team in the change in practices with new technologies. Management of change principles indicate that community managers need training to understand some of the difficulties associated with digitalization, so that they can begin to address questions and doubts that the teams might express. Further, they need to be able to recognize engagement in the work that agents do and sustain motivation for the change activities.

Community managers must also oversee the consistent and effective engagement of new digital tools in the practices of the teams that they manage. Regular feedback and organizing continuous training sessions for teams (specific to agents' needs) are critical steps to ensure the effectiveness of the new digital tools.

Key to this role is to manage the tensions that might come to light, during the rollout of digitalization. Change generates resistance in the best of us, especially for those agents who perceive the digital transformation and its implementation to be a challenge to their role or expertise. The community manager must then demonstrate empathy in communicating, reassure his teams and put in place a method of proper support.

Table 9. The Strategic Role of Community Managers in Supporting Digital Transformation

Themes	Role of community managers	Expected objectives
Change management	Training managers to prepare them for change management.	Improved agent support and reduced resistance.
Communication and mediation	Clear communication of the goals and benefits of digitalization	Clarification of issues and resolution of concerns.
Digital Adoption Tracking	Supervision of digital tools and process adoption	Seamless adoption of new digital practices and tools.

- Change management and internal engagement: An integrated framework

Internal engagement is also a central lever in the change management process. Change managers need to develop and apply tenets of transparency, regularity and responsiveness to sustain agents involved in the digital transformation, while encouraging the adoption and support of digital tools. Interactive communication or channels; intranet, mobile applications, etc. provide insights to managers and agents, while informing all staff about the objectives, progress and outcomes of the digital transformation project undertaken.

The potential of an internal communications framework, built on engaging staff, responding to staff concerns, asking for feedback, and integrating staff feedback into digital transformation means trust is built between managers and agents and mitigates speculation and misunderstandings that may obstruct the adoption of new technologies.

Table 10. Internal Communication as a Lever for Change Management and Engagement

Themes	Internal communication and change management	Expected results
Communication channels	Interactive channels to facilitate exchanges	Improved transparency and agent buy-in.
Continuous feedback	Regular solicitation of returns from agents	Process adjustment based on agent needs.
Support networks	Creation of mutual support networks between agents to discuss adoption.	Strengthening collaboration and mutual assistance

The outcomes of the digital transformation processes within Moroccan public administrations greatly rely upon its internal management and communication practices. The interaction of agents with the process and the role of community managers are central in minimizing resistance to change and maximizing engagement with new technology. Appropriate and transparent communication through an array of pertinent channels supports a trustful and committed environment for digital transformation.

4.3. Developing a Culture of Innovation and Learning

The digital transformation in Moroccan public administrations is possible only if a culture of innovation and continuous learning is cultivated. One of the major challenges of digitalization is creating a safe and resonant place for innovation - a place where innovation is normalized and we are all learning constantly. In this chapter, I shall discuss two necessary levers for establishing this culture: internal incubators and experimental spaces, and valorization of initiative.

- Internal incubators and experimental spaces

Internal incubators and experimental spaces are powerful instruments to drive innovation in public administrations. These spaces, dedicated to the experimentation of new ideas and technologies have a unique ability to prototype digital solutions in real-world settings prior to a wide roll-out. Indeed, the internal incubators provide a secure environment for our agents to explore new possibilities without the immediate fear of failure.

These spaces for experimentation are vital for reducing 'failure' anxiety that accompanies the introduction of new technologies. Knowing agents had experimentation zones where poor choices were not chastised gives them a greater sense of liberty to take risks and try innovative approaches. In addition, these incubators also facilitated cross-departmental collaboration, which produces a culture of collaboration, creating a shared understanding of best practices throughout the public administration.

One of the most pertinent instances of an incubator in the public sector is the Moroccan government's digital lab, whose fundamental objective is to foster innovation in public service delivery by exploring creative digital solutions for administrative obstacles. As well, these experimental spaces permit the ability to democratize access and opportunities for technology as agents at every level can, venture into acquiring new technical competencies and experience with digital tools before they are scaled systemically.

Table 11. Internal Incubators and Experimental Spaces as Innovation Drivers in Public Administration

Themes	Internal incubators and experimental spaces	Expected objectives
Creation of experimental areas	Setting up incubators to test new digital solutions	Encourage innovation and test solutions before adoption
Cross-departmental partnerships	Collaboration between different jurisdictions to solve common challenges	Development of a collaborative and collective learning environment
Reduced fear of failure	Secure space to test ideas without immediate risk	Encouraging experimentation and reducing resistance

- Increasing the initiative

An important condition to foster a culture of innovation is to recognize the initiative and creativity of agents. This entails, among other things, creating recognition and reward mechanisms for those who propose innovative outcomes, or engage in initiatives to improve the internal processes of the administration. The increase in initiative has a distinct effect to improve the engagement of agents, because it is clear to them that their efforts have been recognized and they have the potential to affect the transformation of their administration.

Non-financial means of recognition, such as public recognition, publication of initiatives in internal report form, or laudatory mentions are also important tools for promoting the innovation culture for the administration. This will create a climate and environment which supports agents' willingness to take informed risks, thoughtful creativity and engage in the continuous improvement of public service.

The initiative can also be promoted by leveraging mentoring and leadership development programs. An experienced officer who has made a successful formal initiative maybe leveraged by asking them to share their experiences with their colleagues, which offers the opportunity for the development of skills and, a collective learning culture.

Table 12. Fostering Innovation through Initiative Recognition and Support Mechanisms

Themes	Enhancement of the initiative	Expected objectives
Rewards and recognition	Implementation of recognition systems for innovative initiatives	Increased agent motivation and engagement
Mentorship and leadership	Creating programs to share good practices and successes.	Fostering collective learning and collaboration
Encouragement of initiative	Encourage agents to come up with new solutions and innovative ideas.	Developing a culture of continuous and proactive innovation

- An Integrated Approach to Innovation and Learning

For the digitalization of public Administration in Morocco to be sustainable, it is vital that the culture of innovation and continuous learning is embedded in all organizational practices. These two components need to be integrated into all structures and systems and at all levels of Administration, including the Administration and the field workers. An integrated approach will not only support technological innovation but will help create a new environment where agents are continually trained and educators can incorporate new thinking and innovations as soon as they arrive.

The emergence and development of this culture are also closely linked to talent management. One of the levers in this process is to have permanent learning programs enabling agents to develop some digital skills as lifelong learning and stay close to innovations. Second, it is through a culture of learning developed through international exchanges, Partnerships with educational institutions and technology companies so agents develop the tools and methodologies to operate in a world influenced by rapid digital change.

Table 13. An Integrated Approach to Innovation and Continuous Learning in Public Administration

Themes	An integrated approach to innovation and learning	Expected results
Continuing education	Development of continuing learning and development programs.	Reinforcement of the skills of agents in relation to new technologies.
Partnerships and exchanges	Encouragement of exchanges with external partners (universities, companies).	Dissemination of best practices and skills enrichment
Adaptability and flexibility	Implementation of a flexible framework for continuing training	Agile response to rapidly changing technologies and agent needs.

Building a culture of innovation and learning in Moroccan public administrations is crucial to ensure the success of digitization. This includes creating internal incubators and experimental spaces, as well as improving the actions of agents. Cultivating such a culture not only reacts to the challenges of digital transformation today, but prepares public administrations for continuous transformation in an increasingly digital world.

CONCLUSION

The digital transformation of Morocco's public service represents great opportunity for improvements to administrative efficiency, service quality, and overall modernization of governance. However, the technical revolution cannot be achieved without taking into account the human aspect, which is far too often neglected in the launching of technological projects.

We have shown implementing an HR strategy, that is human-centered, is a key lever to support change through ongoing training, anticipatory skills management and career development plans as starting points for moving the public service toward digitalization. A humanistic approach works to build than just technical learning but contributes to an attitude of adaptability, collectivity and innovation among public sector employees.

Moreover, internal communicators having a transparent and participative model that is facilitated with strong middle managers, is key to overcoming resistances to direction and building engagement in the change process. Organizational cultures of internal communicators provide community managers with roles and opportunities as change agents and on-the-spot supporting actors.

Finally, a culture of innovation and ongoing learning underpinned by experimentation spaces and incentive programs for initiative allows a long-term basis for addressing digitalization as a source of professional possibility, as opposed to social division or organizational conflict.

Digital transformation success thus depends on a delicate balance between human beings and technology: by placing people at the center of this transition, Morocco is able to build a modern, inclusive, and resilient public administration.

REFERENCES

Agence de Développement du Digital (ADD). (2022). Baromètre de la maturité digitale des administrations publiques marocaines.

Allen, M. W., & Moser, D. (2004). Communication and Organizational Change: The Role of Communication in Shaping the Relationship Between Employees and Organizational Change. *Management Communication Quarterly*, *18*(2), 175–197.

Armenakis, A. A., & Bedeian, A. G. (1999). Organizational Change: A Review of Theory and Research in the 1990s. *Journal of Management*, *25*(3), 293–315. DOI: 10.1177/014920639902500303

Christensen, C. M., & Overdorf, M. (2000). Meeting the Challenge of Disruptive Change. *Harvard Business Review*, *78*(2), 66–76.

Chesbrough, H. (2003). *Open Innovation: The New Imperative for Creating and Profiting from Technology*. Harvard Business Press.

Bass, B. M., & Riggio, R. E. (2006). *Transformational Leadership* (2nd ed.). Psychology Press.

Bareil, C. (2013). *Gérer le volet humain du changement: une compétence stratégique pour les leaders*. Presses de l'Université du Québec.

Cameron, E., & Green, M. (2019). *Making Sense of Change Management*. Kogan Page Publishers.

Aubry, P., & Nkengne, M. (2020). Transformation numérique des administrations publiques: enjeux humains et organisationnels. Paris: Presses de l'ENA.

Benabdelhadi, M. (2021). La formation des agents publics face aux exigences de la transformation numérique: Une analyse critique. *Revue Marocaine d'Administration Publique*, (163), 87–102.

Bouckaert, G., & Peters, B. G. (2021). *The Politics of Bureaucracy: An Introduction to Comparative Public Administration*. Edward Elgar Publishing.

Chohan, U. W. (2021). *Public Sector Digital Transformation: A Guide to Strategy and Implementation*. Routledge.

Berraho, A., & Chafiq, L. (2022). Les compétences numériques dans l'administration marocaine: État des lieux et perspectives. *Administration et Management Public*, (40), 55–74.

Boukar, M., El Kharraz, J., & Moutahir, M. (2022). La gouvernance numérique au Maroc: Avancées, limites et perspectives. *Revue Internationale des Sciences Administratives*, *88*(3), 443–460.

Deci, E. L., & Ryan, R. M. (2000). The "what" and "why" of goal pursuits: Human needs and the self-determination of behavior. *Psychological Inquiry*, *11*(4), 227–268. DOI: 10.1207/S15327965PLI1104_01

Drucker, P. F. (2001). *The Essential Drucker: The Best of Sixty Years of Peter Drucker's Essential Writings on Management*. HarperBusiness.

Dunleavy, P., Margetts, H., Bastow, S., & Tinkler, J. (2006). *Digital Era Governance: IT Corporations, the State, and e-Government*. Oxford University Press.

Fernandez, S., & Rainey, H. G. (2006). Managing Successful Organizational Change in the Public Sector. *Public Administration Review*, *66*(2), 168–176. DOI: 10.1111/j.1540-6210.2006.00570.x

Hamel, G., & Prahalad, C. K. (1994). *Competing for the Future*. Harvard Business Press.

Haut-Commissariat au Plan (HCP). (2022). *Enquête sur la structure de l'emploi dans la fonction publique marocaine*.

Kotter, J. P. (1996). *Leading Change*. Harvard Business Review Press.

Hiatt, J. (2006). *ADKAR: A Model for Change in Business, Government and our Community*. Prosci.

Herzberg, F. (2008). *One More Time: How Do You Motivate Employees?* Harvard Business Press.

Kotter, J. P., & Schlesinger, L. A. (2008). Choosing Strategies for Change. *Harvard Business Review*.

Kotter, J. P. (2012). *Leading Change*. Harvard Business Review Press.

Janssen, M., & Van Der Voort, H. (2020). Agility and responsiveness in digital government: Lessons from the COVID-19 crisis. *Government Information Quarterly*, *37*(3), 101–104.

Kuhlmann, S., & Rip, A. (2018). Next-generation innovation policy and grand challenges. *Science & Public Policy*, *45*(4), 448–454. DOI: 10.1093/scipol/scy011

Lines, R. (2005). The structure and function of attitudes toward organizational change. *Human Resource Development Review*, *4*(1), 8–32. DOI: 10.1177/1534484304273818

Lussier, R. N., & Achua, C. F. (2019). *Leadership: Theory, Application, & Skill Development*. Cengage Learning.

Mergel, I., Edelmann, N., & Haug, N. (2019). Defining digital transformation: Results from expert interviews. *Government Information Quarterly*, *36*(4), 101385. DOI: 10.1016/j.giq.2019.06.002

Ministère de la Transition Numérique. (2022). Feuille de route Maroc Digital 2025.

Nam, T. (2018). Citizen Participation in the digital age: The role of ICT in fostering open government. *Government Information Quarterly*, *35*(4), 622–631.

Misuraca, G., Savoldelli, A., & Codagnone, C. (2020). Digital government: From e-government to algorithmic governance. *Government Information Quarterly*, *37*(4), 101473.

Naranjo-Gil, D. (2020). Resistance to digitalization in the public sector: Understanding the barriers and enablers. *Public Management Review*, *22*(5), 678–702.

Moussaoui, H., & Kabbaj, R. (2021). Digitalisation et administration publique: La question des générations face aux nouvelles pratiques. *Revue Internationale des Sciences Administratives*, *87*(2), 345–366.

MTN – Ministère de la Transition Numérique et de la Réforme de l'Administration. (2021). Stratégie nationale de transformation numérique 2025. Rabat.

OCDE. (2022). *L'administration publique du futur au Maroc*. Éditions OCDE.

OECD. (2020). *Building the Digital Government Workforce: Insights from the Public Sector Leadership Programme*. OECD Digital Government Studies.

OECD. (2020). *Digital Government in Morocco: Laying the Foundations for the Digital Transformation of the Public Sector*. OECD Digital Government Studies.

OECD. (2020). *The Road to Becoming a Digital Government: Digital Government Review of Morocco*. OECD Publishing.

OECD. (2021). *Public Service Leadership and Capability in the MENA Region*. OECD Publishing.

Schein, E. H. (2010). *Organizational Culture and Leadership* (4th ed.). Jossey-Bass.

Peters, B. G. (2018). *The Politics of Bureaucracy: An Introduction to Comparative Public Administration*. Routledge.

UNDP. (2022). *Bridging the Digital Divide in the Global South*. United Nations Development Programme.

Van der Voet, J., Kuipers, B. S., & Groeneveld, S. (2016). Time for change: A longitudinal analysis of the effects of change management on public sector employees' affective commitment and turnover intentions. *Public Administration Review, 76*(3), 484–495.

World Bank. (2021). *Building a Culture of Innovation in Public Administration: Tools, Practices, and Case Studies*. World Bank Group.

Zamrani, S., & Achouri, H. (2021). Ressources humaines et transformation digitale dans le secteur public marocain: Entre inertie et innovation. *Management & Avenir, 126*(6), 87–104.

Chapter 5
Human Factors and Workforce Adaptation in Digital Transition

Satya Subrahmanyam
https://orcid.org/0000-0003-0441-2742
Holy Spirit University of Kaslik, Lebanon

ABSTRACT

The rapid evolution of digital technologies is reshaping business processes, necessitating workforce adaptation to sustain organizational competitiveness. While digital transformation enhances efficiency and innovation, its success is contingent on human factors influencing employee adaptation. This chapter examines key psychological, behavioral, and organizational challenges in digital transitions, including skill gaps, resistance to change, and digital fatigue. It explores workforce adaptation strategies through theoretical frameworks such as the Technology Acceptance Model (TAM), Lewin's Change Management Model, and the Job Demands-Resources (JD-R) Model. The chapter further highlights leadership roles, change management strategies, and case studies of successful digital workforce adaptation. A human-centric approach to digital transformation is essential to balancing technological advancements with employee well-being, fostering a resilient and future-ready workforce.

1. INTRODUCTION

The digital transition is fundamentally reshaping how organizations operate, compelling workforce structures to evolve in response to new technological paradigms. As automation, artificial intelligence (AI), and data analytics become integral to business processes, human factors such as adaptability, emotional intelligence,

DOI: 10.4018/979-8-3373-3336-6.ch005

and continuous learning gain prominence. The human workforce is no longer just a passive participant but a dynamic driver in digital transformation, requiring both psychological readiness and technical agility (Subrahmanyam, 2025). This shift presents a dual challenge: harnessing the potential of digital tools while ensuring that employees remain empowered and resilient amid change.

Workforce adaptation is critical in navigating this transformation, with emphasis placed on skill development, change management, and fostering a culture of innovation. Organizations must align digital strategies with human-centric approaches to ensure sustainable growth and employee well-being (Subrahmanyam, 2025). This chapter explores the interplay between human factors and digital integration, emphasizing the need for inclusive, ethical, and agile transition strategies. It argues that the success of digital initiatives hinges not only on technological investments but also on cultivating a workforce that is prepared, supported, and engaged throughout the transition journey.

1.1 Digital Transformation and the Role of Business Process Management (BPM)

Organisations in today's corporate world that want to stay competitive, provide better customer service, and achieve operational excellence must undergo digital transformation. Organisational operations and the value they provide to stakeholders are both radically altered by digital transformation, which involves incorporating digital technology into every facet of a company (Vial, 2019). It requires a thorough reevaluation of business models, organisational structures, and cultural perspectives; it goes beyond just implementing technology.

At the core of this transformation lies *Business Process Management* (BPM), a structured approach to analyzing, redesigning, implementing, and continuously improving business processes. BPM acts as a critical enabler for digital transformation by providing the tools and methodologies necessary to align technology with business goals, ensure operational agility, and optimize workflows (Dumas et al., 2018). Effective BPM helps organizations streamline operations, reduce costs, and enhance service delivery in a digital environment.

1.2 Recognizing the Centrality of Human Factors

Despite the focus on technologies such as artificial intelligence, robotic process automation, and big data analytics, digital transformation ultimately hinges on the people within the organization. The human element is often the determining factor in whether digital initiatives succeed or fail. Employees are not passive recipients of change—they are active participants whose mindsets, skills, motivations, and behaviors shape the outcomes of transformation efforts.

Human factors encompass a wide range of psychological, social, and organizational dimensions, including attitudes toward change, adaptability, trust in technology, cognitive load, and interpersonal dynamics. Ignoring these factors can lead to resistance, technostress, disengagement, and underutilization of digital tools (Tarafdar et al., 2019). Acknowledging and addressing the human side of transformation enhances employee engagement, fosters innovation, and sustains long-term change.

The pace of digital transformation often outstrips an organization's capacity to adapt its workforce. Employees may be required to adopt new technologies, perform unfamiliar tasks, and collaborate in virtual environments—all within compressed timeframes. This creates a significant need for strategies that support workforce adaptation, build digital competencies, and align employee experiences with organizational goals.

1.3 Scope and Objectives of the Chapter

This chapter explores the intersection of human factors and workforce adaptation within the broader context of digital transformation, specifically through the lens of Business Process Management. Recognizing that transformation is as much about people as it is about technology, the chapter investigates how human-centric considerations can be integrated into BPM to achieve sustainable digital change.

The primary objectives of the chapter are threefold:

1. **To examine the nature and influence of human factors** in digital transformation processes, including the psychological, ergonomic, and organizational elements that affect employee behavior and performance.
2. **To explore effective workforce adaptation strategies** such as reskilling, digital literacy programs, participatory change management, and leadership development initiatives that can facilitate smoother transitions.
3. **To demonstrate how BPM can be designed and implemented in a human-centric manner**, ensuring that business process changes enhance—not hinder—employee well-being, motivation, and productivity.

By addressing these objectives, the chapter provides a holistic framework for integrating human considerations into digital transformation strategies. It emphasizes that technology adoption alone does not equate to transformation; the real transformation occurs when people change the way they work, think, and interact with digital tools and processes.

1.4 Structure of the Chapter

The goals of this chapter are addressed by dividing it into many important parts. It starts with a review of human aspects in digital transformation, with an emphasis on how workers' thoughts, feelings, and actions are impacted by technological advancements. Next, it delves into how the workforce is changing, specifically looking at new responsibilities, generational differences, and the popularity of remote and hybrid jobs.

Subsequent sections delve into practical strategies for workforce adaptation, highlighting the role of training, digital readiness assessments, leadership, and inclusive change practices. Psychological and organizational readiness for transformation is also examined, alongside the cultural attributes that support or hinder adaptation.

The chapter then considers how BPM frameworks can be aligned with human-centric principles, presenting approaches to process redesign that prioritize usability, engagement, and co-creation. It discusses methods for evaluating adaptation success through performance metrics, feedback systems, and employee satisfaction indicators. Finally, the chapter presents real-world case studies to illustrate how organizations have successfully navigated the human dimensions of digital transformation through BPM.

In an era where digital transformation is often equated with technological disruption, it is essential to remember that the workforce remains the engine of organizational performance. Digital tools may enhance capabilities, but it is people who bring creativity, judgment, and empathy to business processes. To succeed in the digital age, organizations must move beyond technology-first approaches and embrace a more balanced perspective—one that places human factors at the core of BPM and transformation strategies.

Only by doing so can businesses ensure that their digital initiatives are not only efficient and innovative but also inclusive, resilient, and sustainable.

2. UNDERSTANDING HUMAN FACTORS IN DIGITAL TRANSFORMATION

Human factors in digital transformation refer to the psychological, behavioral, and social elements that influence how individuals interact with technology. These include adaptability, motivation, trust, learning agility, and resistance to change. Successful digital initiatives depend not only on technological readiness but also on human-centric considerations such as employee engagement, effective communication, and leadership support. Addressing these factors ensures smoother transitions and enhances the long-term sustainability of digital strategies in organizations.

2.1 Defining Human Factors in the Digital Context

Human factors refer to the range of psychological, physiological, ergonomic, and social elements that influence individuals interact with their work environment, especially in the context of technological systems. In digital transformation, human factors become critically important as they determine the effectiveness, efficiency, and satisfaction with which people adopt and use digital tools and systems (Subrahmanyam, 2024).

In particular, three dimensions stand out:

- **Psychological**: Encompasses perceptions, attitudes, motivation, stress levels, and emotional responses to digital change. This dimension is vital as it shapes employees' willingness and confidence to engage with new technologies.
- **Ergonomic**: Refers to the physical and cognitive interaction between humans and technological systems. Ergonomics ensures that digital interfaces are user-friendly, intuitive, and reduce strain and errors.
- **Social**: Involves team dynamics, leadership influence, communication flows, and organizational culture. These factors impact how information about digital changes is shared and how collective attitudes evolve.

Neglecting any of these dimensions can result in misalignment between technological systems and human needs, thereby reducing the return on digital investments and compromising organizational resilience.

2.2 The Role of Behavior, Attitudes, and Emotions in Digital Adoption

The success of digital transformation is not determined solely by technological capability but by how individuals respond behaviorally and emotionally to the changes it imposes. Human behavior in the digital workspace is shaped by a complex interplay of personal disposition, prior experience with technology, peer influence, and perceived utility (Davis, 1989). Positive attitudes towards digital tools can lead to increased acceptance and usage, while skepticism, fear of obsolescence, or lack of perceived value can foster resistance.

Emotions, particularly anxiety, uncertainty, and frustration, are common during digital transitions. Employees might fear that automation could displace their roles or reduce their autonomy. According to Côrte-Real, Oliveira, and Ruivo (2019), emotional intelligence and managerial empathy play a significant role in mitigating these fears by helping leaders address concerns in a human-centric manner.

Importantly, individual reactions are not static—they evolve throughout the digital change lifecycle. Therefore, organizations must adopt continuous engagement strategies, including active listening, coaching, and participatory design, to foster trust and a sense of ownership over new digital initiatives.

2.3 Human-Machine Interaction and Cognitive Workload in Digital Workflows

As digital systems become increasingly integrated into daily operations—ranging from enterprise software to artificial intelligence-powered decision aids—the interaction between humans and machines takes center stage. Human-machine interaction (HMI) refers to how users engage with digital tools, including interfaces, dashboards, automation processes, and collaborative technologies.

Poorly designed systems can result in high cognitive workload, defined as the mental effort required to perform tasks effectively (Hart & Staveland, 1988). When cognitive workload is excessive—due to unclear interfaces, data overload, or mismatched workflows—it leads to errors, stress, and reduced performance.

Enterprise resource planning (ERP) systems often require employees to navigate through multiple screens and complex decision rules, especially during initial implementation. Without adequate training and interface simplification, users may become overwhelmed, leading to task avoidance or superficial system use (Brocke et al., 2016). Designing systems that accommodate human cognitive limits—through minimalism, automation of repetitive tasks, and adaptive learning supports—can greatly enhance usability and productivity.

With the proliferation of AI and robotics, questions around trust in machines and interpretability of machine outputs are gaining prominence. Employees are more likely to trust and use AI tools when the systems are transparent, explainable, and provide opportunities for human override (Rai, 2020).

2.4 Change Fatigue and Resistance: Causes and Consequences

Change fatigue is a psychological state that arises when individuals are exposed to continuous or poorly managed organizational change, resulting in mental exhaustion, cynicism, and disengagement. In the context of digital transformation—often characterized by rapid and successive waves of new technology introductions—change fatigue becomes a significant barrier to successful adoption.

Causes of change fatigue include:

- **Information overload** due to frequent updates and unclear messaging.

- **Lack of involvement** in decision-making processes.
- **Inconsistent leadership support** and visible commitment.
- **Misaligned performance incentives** that do not reflect new digital competencies.

Resistance to change, which may manifest passive non-compliance, vocal criticism, or sabotage, is often a symptom of underlying fatigue, fear, or mistrust. While often framed negatively, resistance is a natural response to perceived threats and ambiguity (Subrahmanyam, 2024). It provides valuable feedback on how digital initiatives are perceived at the ground level and signals areas where leadership needs to refine communication, training, or support structures.

The consequences of unchecked resistance are profound. It can derail implementation timelines, increase costs, and even lead to the abandonment of digital initiatives. Addressing resistance constructively—by acknowledging concerns, providing safe channels for expression, and celebrating early wins—can transform detractors into advocates.

Understanding human factors is fundamental to the success of digital transformation. Psychological readiness, ergonomic design, emotional resilience, and social dynamics all influence how the workforce engages with digital tools and adapts to new workflows. Organizations must therefore adopt a holistic approach to digital transformation—one that places as much emphasis on people as on technology. By doing so, they can mitigate resistance, reduce change fatigue, and foster a culture of digital agility that sustains innovation over time.

3. THE EVOLVING WORKFORCE IN THE DIGITAL ERA

The digital era is redefining workforce dynamics, emphasizing roles that demand digital literacy, critical thinking, and adaptability. Traditional job functions are being transformed or replaced by automation, while new roles like data analysts, AI trainers, and digital strategists emerge. This evolution necessitates continuous upskilling and reskilling to meet shifting organizational needs. Employees are expected to collaborate seamlessly with intelligent systems, highlighting the need for a flexible, tech-savvy, and innovative-driven workforce.

3.1 Shifting Skill Requirements and Roles

Competencies and abilities needed for success in today's businesses have changed drastically in the age of digital transformation. With the rise of data-driven technologies, artificial intelligence (AI), and automation, traditional positions are changing, being redefined, or even becoming obsolete. By 2025, robots may have eliminated 85 million jobs, according to the World Economic Forum (2020), but 97 million new employments will have emerged, better suited to a digital and automated world.

These shifts require a new blend of technical, cognitive, and emotional competencies. While digital literacy, coding, data analysis, and cybersecurity are becoming foundational, soft skills such as adaptability, critical thinking, creativity, and emotional intelligence are equally vital (Bughin et al., 2018). The evolving digital workplace emphasizes the ability to learn continuously, collaborate in cross-functional teams, and manage human-machine interactions effectively.

Organizations are thus rethinking their talent management strategies to build a future-ready workforce. Upskilling and reskilling programs are being integrated into strategic planning to reduce the skills gap and promote internal mobility. Human Resources departments are increasingly using AI-powered platforms to identify competency trends and personalize learning pathways (LinkedIn Learning, 2021).

3.2 Multigenerational Workforce Dynamics

The modern workplace is characterized by the coexistence of four generational cohorts: Baby Boomers, Generation X, Millennials (Gen Y), and Generation Z. Each group brings distinct values, expectations, and digital fluency, creating both opportunities and challenges for workforce cohesion and management.

- **Baby Boomers (born 1946–1964)** generally value stability, loyalty, and a structured work environment. Their digital adaptability may vary, but their institutional knowledge remains a critical asset.
- **Generation X (born 1965–1980)** is known for independence, pragmatism, and adaptability. Often acting as bridge leaders, they support both analog and digital workflows.
- **Millennials (born 1981–1996)** are tech-savvy, collaborative, and purpose-driven. They prefer flexibility and seek meaningful work with strong digital tools.
- **Generation Z (born after 1997)** is the first truly digital-native cohort. They expect intuitive technologies, instant communication, and inclusive cultures (Seemiller & Grace, 2019).

Managing these diverse generations requires an inclusive leadership approach that acknowledges their varying needs. While Boomers may prefer face-to-face interactions and comprehensive manuals, Gen Z thrives on real-time messaging platforms and microlearning. Designing workflows and communication strategies that bridge these differences enhances collaboration and minimizes generational friction.

3.3 Remote and Hybrid Work Models: Implications for Collaboration and Productivity

The COVID-19 pandemic significantly accelerated the shift toward remote and hybrid work models. While remote work was previously a flexible perk, it has now become a structural element of organizational design. This transformation has reshaped how teams collaborate, measure productivity, and maintain engagement.

Remote work offers clear benefits such as cost savings, access to a broader talent pool, and enhanced autonomy. It also presents challenges, including digital fatigue, feelings of isolation, and difficulties in maintaining team cohesion (Waizenegger et al., 2020). Hybrid models, which blend in-office and remote work, attempt to strike a balance but require deliberate strategies around scheduling, communication, and performance management.

Digital collaboration tools—like Slack, Zoom, Microsoft Teams, and project management platforms—have become the backbone of distributed work. Yet technology alone cannot guarantee effective collaboration. Organizational culture, leadership support, and clearly defined expectations play vital roles in making remote and hybrid work successful. Corporates are experimenting with asynchronous communication, virtual watercooler moments, and digital wellbeing initiatives to create an equitable and engaging environment for all workers.

Performance evaluation in remote settings is shifting from time-based metrics to output-based assessments. This requires redefining success and ensuring that trust, transparency, and accountability are embedded in the company's remote work philosophy (Gartner, 2021).

3.4 Case Example: Workforce Transition in a Digitally Transformed Enterprise

A compelling example of workforce adaptation can be found in the case of **Siemens AG**, a global industrial and manufacturing conglomerate. Siemens embarked on an enterprise-wide digital transformation by integrating cloud computing, Internet of Things (IoT), and AI into its business models through its "Digital Industries" strategy.

Recognizing the centrality of human factors in this shift, Siemens launched an internal initiative called "NextWork", aimed at reimagining the future of work. This program focused on:

- Identifying new digital roles and the skills required for them.
- Providing extensive training and upskilling opportunities through their in-house learning platform.

- Encouraging cross-generational mentoring, where tech-savvy Gen Z and Millennials collaborated with experienced Baby Boomers to foster mutual learning.
- Designing flexible work policies to accommodate hybrid models and enhance work-life integration.

As a result, Siemens reported not only improved digital adoption rates but also higher employee engagement and retention (Siemens, 2021). The company's emphasis on reskilling, intergenerational collaboration, and culture-driven digital adoption underscores the importance of holistic workforce strategies in successful digital transformation.

The evolving workforce in the digital era demands a nuanced understanding of shifting roles, multigenerational dynamics, and new work models. Organizations must proactively align their human resource strategies with these trends to ensure sustained productivity, engagement, and innovation. By embracing upskilling, fostering intergenerational collaboration, and rethinking work design, businesses can transform their workforce into a resilient asset ready for the digital future.

4. WORKFORCE ADAPTATION STRATEGIES

Workforce adaptability is crucial for organisations to succeed in the complicated digital transformation landscape. Not only must digital tools be deployed to keep up with the fast development of technology, but human capital must also be strategically aligned with changing operational needs. Upskilling and reskilling employees, encouraging digital literacy, providing opportunities for leadership and agents of change, and guaranteeing inclusion in digital transformation efforts are all important tactics for workforce adaptability that are discussed in this section.

4.1 Upskilling and Reskilling Initiatives

One of the most urgent imperatives in the digital transition is addressing the widening skills gap through upskilling and reskilling programs. Upskilling involves enhancing employees' existing capabilities to align with evolving roles, while reskilling focuses on training individuals for entirely new positions that emerge from digital restructuring (McKinsey & Company, 2021).

Organizations across industries are investing in strategic learning and development programs to ensure their workforce remains competitive and future-ready. Amazon committed over $1.2 billion to upskill 300,000 employees by 2025 through its "Upskilling 2025" initiative, covering areas such as cloud computing, machine learning, and data analytics (Amazon, 2020). Such initiatives are crucial not only for organizational agility but also for employee morale and retention, as workers perceive greater career development opportunities.

To be effective, upskilling and reskilling programs must be tailored, accessible, and closely aligned with business needs. Leveraging online platforms, microlearning modules, and personalized learning journeys enhances the scalability and inclusivity of such programs.

4.2 Digital Literacy and a Culture of Continuous Learning

Digital transformation cannot succeed without a workforce proficient in digital literacy. Digital literacy extends beyond basic technical knowledge to include the ability to critically engage with digital tools, navigate digital communication channels, analyze data, and make technology-enabled decisions (UNESCO, 2021). It also includes the psychological readiness to adopt new technologies and adapt to continuous change.

Cultivating a culture of continuous learning is essential for sustaining digital literacy. This culture encourages curiosity, experimentation, and learning from failure—key attributes in a rapidly changing business landscape. Learning should be embedded into the flow of work through just-in-time resources, peer-to-peer learning, and ongoing feedback loops (Bersin, 2019).

Organizational leaders must model learning behavior, provide time and incentives for learning, and integrate digital literacy goals into performance management systems. Corporates like Microsoft and IBM emphasize a "learn-it-all" culture rather than a "know-it-all" mindset, embedding learning as a strategic priority across all levels of the organization.

4.3 Leadership and Change Agents in Workforce Adaptation

Effective leadership is a critical enabler of workforce adaptation. Leaders serve as role models, communicators, and facilitators of change, shaping attitudes toward digital innovation and influencing adoption rates. Transformational leaders, in particular, are adept at articulating a compelling vision, motivating teams, and fostering a shared commitment to digital objectives (Subrahmanyam, 2025).

Leaders must also identify and empower change agents—individuals within the organization who can champion digital initiatives, inspire peers, and provide on-the-ground support. These agents play a pivotal role in bridging the gap between strategic objectives and grassroots execution. They help normalize new behaviors, demystify technology, and create peer learning environments.

Leadership development programs should, therefore, emphasize digital fluency, emotional intelligence, agility, and change management capabilities. Involving leaders early in digital transformation initiatives, providing them with clear metrics and success indicators, and encouraging transparent communication are all essential components of leadership-driven workforce adaptation (Harvard Business Review, 2020).

4.4 Inclusion, Diversity, and Equitable Access to Digital Tools

Workforce adaptation strategies must be underpinned by a strong commitment to inclusion, diversity, and equitable access to digital resources. The risk of digital transformation exacerbating existing inequalities is significant if underserved populations are left behind in access to training, tools, or opportunities.

Inclusive digital transformation ensures that employees across different geographies, generations, abilities, and socio-economic backgrounds are provided equal opportunities to adapt and thrive. This includes offering training in multiple formats (e.g., visual, audio, in-person), accommodating people with disabilities, and ensuring that remote or frontline workers have access to necessary devices and connectivity (World Economic Forum, 2020).

Incorporating diverse viewpoints into transformation teams improves creativity and problem-solving. Companies with the most diverse executive teams in terms of gender and ethnicity were 25% more likely to achieve above-average profitability, according to 2020 research by McKinsey.

Inclusion also involves creating safe spaces for learning and experimentation, where employees feel valued regardless of their starting point on the digital readiness curve. Building psychological safety, promoting mentorship programs, and using data to monitor participation and outcomes in learning initiatives can help close digital equity gaps.

Adapting the workforce for the digital age is not merely a technical or operational challenge—it is a strategic imperative that calls for holistic, inclusive, and proactive human capital strategies. By investing in upskilling and reskilling, fostering digital literacy, developing agile leaders, and ensuring equitable access, organizations can transform their workforce into a dynamic asset equipped to navigate continuous change. Successful digital transformation ultimately depends on how well people are prepared, supported, and empowered to lead the journey.

5. PSYCHOLOGICAL AND ORGANIZATIONAL READINESS

Businesses are undergoing digital transformation, which means that worker psychology and organisational preparedness are just as important as technology deployment when it comes to the success of these projects. A person or organization's emotional, cultural, and structural readiness to adapt to change are all parts of this readiness. To facilitate digital transformations that are sustainable, it is necessary to understand how to evaluate and cultivate this readiness.

5.1 Assessing Organizational Change Readiness

How mentally and behaviourally prepared a company is to launch transformative projects is what we mean when we talk about organisational readiness for change (Subrahmanyam, 2025). It all comes down to the fact that workers are on the same page about the need for change and their confidence in the company's ability to implement it.

Effective assessment involves both qualitative and quantitative methods. Surveys, interviews, and readiness assessment tools help evaluate employee perceptions of change, their confidence in leadership, and their understanding of the intended outcomes. The Prosci Change Management Model, for instance, includes a structured approach to assess organizational readiness and identify potential resistance (Prosci, 2021).

Leaders must use these assessments to pinpoint capability gaps, identify cultural misalignments, and inform the design of targeted communication and engagement strategies. Without an accurate diagnosis of readiness, digital initiatives may falter due to unaddressed anxieties, misaligned priorities, or resistance to change.

5.2 Employee Engagement and Motivation in Times of Transformation

For digital transformation to be a success, employee involvement is crucial. According to Gallup (2023), when workers are engaged, they are more likely to take the initiative, learn new technology, and come up with innovative process ideas. On the other side, transformation attempts might be slowed down by disengaged personnel who become sources of opposition or indifference.

To keep workers motivated throughout transformation, it's important to set goals that correspond with organisational objectives, make sure their efforts are recognised, and make sure they have a meaningful role in the change process. Workplace autonomy, competence, and relatedness are the trifecta of employee motivation, say Deci and Ryan's (2000) Self-Determination Theory. Creating chances for participation, education, and teamwork between peers helps to cultivate these traits.

Digital transformation can induce fear and uncertainty. Job insecurity, role ambiguity, and learning anxiety are common during periods of rapid change. Leaders must proactively address these concerns through empathetic leadership, clear articulation of vision, and mechanisms for employee feedback and support.

5.3 Trust, Transparency, and Communication as Enablers

Trust and transparency are foundational to psychological readiness for change. When employees trust leadership and believe that organizational communication is honest and inclusive, they are more likely to accept and engage with transformation initiatives (Mishra & Mishra, 2013).

Transparent communication includes consistent messaging about the rationale for change, expected outcomes, implementation timelines, and the roles of various stakeholders. Two-way communication—where employees can ask questions, voice concerns, and receive feedback—fosters ownership and reduces uncertainty.

Digital transformation also demands that organizations reimagine how they communicate. With the rise of remote and hybrid work, digital channels such as collaboration platforms, virtual town halls, and asynchronous updates are critical tools for building engagement. Over-reliance on digital communication without human-centered approaches can lead to alienation or misunderstanding. Thus, organizations must balance technological tools with emotional intelligence in their communication strategies.

5.4 Role of Organizational Culture and Leadership Styles

When it comes to being prepared for digital transformation, organisational culture is crucial. This culture consists of shared ideas, values, and conventions that influence behaviour. Cameron and Quinn (2011) found that cultures that prioritise innovation, agility, cooperation, and continuous learning are more likely to be open to change. Some cultures may be resistant to new technology and methods of working because they value control, hierarchy, and risk aversion more than anything else.

Leaders are the primary stewards of organizational culture. Their behaviors signal what is valued and acceptable. Transformational leaders, in particular, inspire vision, foster trust, and model adaptability. They encourage experimentation, reward initiative, and provide psychological safety, which is essential for navigating uncertainty (Bass & Riggio, 2006).

Other leadership styles also influence readiness. Servant leaders build trust and prioritize the needs of their teams, creating supportive environments for change. Transactional leaders, while more focused on performance and compliance, can be effective during the execution phase of transformation if combined with motivational practices.

The alignment between leadership style and organizational culture is crucial. For example, a transformational leader operating within a rigid, bureaucratic culture may face systemic barriers unless deliberate efforts are made to shift values and behaviors throughout the organization.

Psychological and organizational readiness is the bedrock of successful digital transformation. It requires a nuanced understanding of employee mindsets, organizational dynamics, and the interplay between culture and leadership. By assessing readiness, fostering employee engagement, ensuring transparent communication, and cultivating a culture that embraces change, organizations can build the resilience and agility necessary to thrive in the digital era. The human side of change is not ancillary—it is central to digital transformation's success.

6. HUMAN-CENTRIC BUSINESS PROCESS MANAGEMENT (BPM)

In the era of digital transformation, Business Process Management (BPM) must evolve beyond efficiency and automation to embrace human-centric values. Traditional BPM approaches have often prioritized optimization, standardization, and cost reduction, sometimes overlooking the nuanced ways people interact with processes and technology. Human-centric BPM integrates the needs, capabilities, and experiences of users directly into the design and execution of processes, making transformation more sustainable, inclusive, and effective.

6.1 Integrating Human Factors into BPM Design and Redesign

Human factors refer to the cognitive, physical, emotional, and social characteristics of individuals that influence how they interact with systems and processes (Carayon, 2006). These factors are critical when redesigning processes in digitally transforming organizations, as overlooking them can lead to user dissatisfaction, resistance, and inefficiencies.

Integrating human factors into BPM involves evaluating how people perform tasks, what tools they need, what cognitive loads are imposed, and how motivations and behaviors align with process goals. Human-centered process design requires continuous feedback loops between end-users and process designers, ensuring that the redesigned processes are not only functionally effective but also usable and meaningful. This approach aligns with ergonomics and systems thinking by considering the entire work environment and its interaction with human capabilities (Vicente, 2006).

Redesigning business processes with human factors in mind fosters inclusivity. Accessibility considerations—such as for individuals with disabilities or those with limited digital proficiency—must be embedded in process architecture from the outset to prevent marginalization and ensure equitable participation.

6.2 Designing Adaptive, User-Friendly Digital Processes

As organizations digitize, processes become increasingly dependent on digital platforms and tools. While these systems offer scalability and data-driven decision-making, they must also be intuitive and adaptable to diverse user profiles. User-friendly digital processes are characterized by simplicity, clarity, personalization, and minimal cognitive friction (Norman, 2013).

Designing such processes requires a user-experience (UX) approach that incorporates usability testing, prototyping, and iterative refinement. The goal is to reduce errors, improve speed, and increase user satisfaction. Employee onboarding processes digitized via intuitive interfaces, such as guided workflows and AI chatbots, can streamline administrative steps while keeping the human experience at the center.

Adaptability is also essential in a rapidly changing business environment. Processes must be agile enough to accommodate contextual shifts—such as remote work dynamics, customer demands, or regulatory changes—without extensive re-development. Modular design principles and low-code BPM platforms support such flexibility, allowing users to reconfigure workflows without heavy IT involvement (van der Aalst, 2013).

6.3 Co-Creation and Participatory Approaches to BPM Change

Co-creation in BPM emphasizes collaborative engagement between process designers, stakeholders, and end-users. This participatory design philosophy not only enhances the relevance and acceptance of new processes but also fosters a culture of empowerment and innovation (Sanders & Stappers, 2008).

Involving employees, customers, and other stakeholders in BPM initiatives leads to more grounded insights about pain points and opportunities for improvement. Tools such as design thinking workshops, journey mapping, and process modeling sessions with frontline users allow organizations to capture experiential knowledge and generate user-centered solutions.

Co-creation fosters psychological ownership and reduces resistance to change. When people are involved in shaping the processes they use daily, they are more likely to champion transformation efforts and contribute to continuous improvement. This is particularly crucial in cross-functional processes where silos can impede integration unless shared understanding and commitment are cultivated.

6.4 Human-in-the-Loop Systems and Decision-Making

A key characteristic of human-centric BPM in the digital age is the integration of "human-in-the-loop" (HITL) systems. These systems combine automated processes with human judgment, ensuring that critical decisions remain context-sensitive, ethical, and aligned with organizational values (Rahwan et al., 2019).

HITL models are especially relevant in areas involving ambiguity, ethical complexity, or high-stakes outcomes—such as credit approval, medical diagnosis, or customer grievance resolution. While AI and machine learning can support these processes with predictive insights, human oversight is essential to account for nuances and exceptions that algorithms may not capture.

In BPM contexts, HITL systems enable hybrid workflows where automated steps are interspersed with human inputs. In an AI-supported recruitment process, initial candidate screening may be automated, but final interviews and cultural fit assessments are conducted by humans. This not only preserves empathy and discretion but also promotes accountability.

The challenge lies in designing interfaces and interaction models that enable seamless human-machine collaboration. Training users to interpret algorithmic outputs, establishing escalation protocols, and ensuring transparency in automated decisions are all crucial components of effective HITL systems (Amershi et al., 2014).

Human-centric BPM represents a paradigm shift in process design and execution—one that places people at the heart of digital transformation. By integrating human factors, designing adaptive and intuitive processes, leveraging participatory approaches, and embedding human-in-the-loop systems, organizations can create more resilient, inclusive, and effective process ecosystems.

This human-centric approach does not reject automation or efficiency but redefines them within the broader goals of user empowerment, organizational well-being, and sustainable innovation. As digital transformation accelerates, the ability of BPM to harmonize technological advancement with human experience will be a defining factor in organizational success.

7. MEASURING SUCCESS IN WORKFORCE ADAPTATION

As organizations undergo digital transformation, measuring the success of workforce adaptation becomes paramount to ensuring alignment between strategic objectives and operational realities. Workforce adaptation reflects how well employees adjust to new technologies, processes, and business models introduced through Business Process Management (BPM). Accurate and comprehensive evaluation enables continuous improvement, supports change management, and reinforces accountability. This chapter outlines the key indicators, tools, and frameworks that organizations can employ to evaluate the effectiveness of workforce adaptation initiatives.

7.1 Key Performance Indicators (KPIs) for Workforce Adaptation

Key Performance Indicators (KPIs) are essential tools for tracking the progress and impact of workforce adaptation. They provide tangible benchmarks that link strategic goals to employee behavior and performance in digital environments. Adaptation KPIs often include:

- **Training completion rates**: These measure the extent to which employees engage in upskilling and reskilling programs.
- **Digital tool adoption rates**: Indicate how widely and effectively new technologies are being used across departments.
- **Time-to-competence**: Reflects how quickly employees can achieve proficiency in using new systems or processes.
- **Change readiness index**: Measures attitudes toward change and openness to digital innovation (Hiatt, 2006).

Selecting the right KPIs depends on organizational priorities and the specific technologies or BPM frameworks being adopted. A well-balanced set of KPIs ensures that adaptation is assessed from multiple dimensions—skills, behavior, mindset, and outcomes.

7.2 Employee Satisfaction, Productivity, and Innovation Metrics

Employee-centric metrics are crucial to understanding how digital transformation impacts morale, engagement, and creativity. Satisfaction and productivity are interconnected, and both serve as leading indicators of long-term adaptation success.

- **Employee satisfaction surveys**: These reveal how workers perceive their roles, technologies, and work environments post-transition (Harter et al., 2002).
- **Net Promoter Score (NPS)**: Adapted for internal use, NPS helps gauge how likely employees are to recommend their organization as a great place to work.
- **Productivity metrics**: May include output per employee, cycle time reductions, or customer service response times.
- **Innovation indicators**: Measure new idea submissions, hackathon participation, and process improvement initiatives undertaken by staff (Tidd & Bessant, 2018).

Together, these metrics provide a balanced view of the human side of BPM. High productivity combined with low satisfaction could indicate burnout or poor process design. Conversely, high satisfaction with stagnant innovation may reflect complacency.

7.3 Balanced Scorecards and Digital Maturity Models

The **Balanced Scorecard (BSC)** framework offers a holistic approach to evaluating workforce adaptation by linking financial, customer, internal process, and learning perspectives (Kaplan & Norton, 1996). In a digital context, the learning and growth quadrant is particularly relevant, capturing metrics related to employee capabilities, IT competence, and knowledge sharing.

Organizations can tailor the BSC to track progress in:

- Digital skills acquisition
- Employee retention during transformation
- Process innovation participation
- Leadership involvement in change

Digital maturity models such as Deloitte's Digital Maturity Index or the MIT Sloan model assess organizational readiness and progress across dimensions like strategy, culture, technology, and talent (Westerman et al., 2014). These models often integrate qualitative and quantitative indicators to benchmark current state versus desired future state.

Using maturity models in tandem with the BSC ensures a strategic alignment between BPM implementation and workforce development, while also facilitating cross-industry benchmarking.

7.4 Tools and Platforms for Workforce Monitoring and Feedback

Technology-enabled monitoring and feedback platforms are increasingly used to collect real-time data on workforce adaptation. These tools offer both diagnostic and prescriptive insights, enabling proactive interventions.

- **Learning Management Systems (LMS)**: Track employee engagement in upskilling programs and monitor progress in acquiring digital competencies.
- **Employee Experience Platforms (EXP)**: Platforms like Microsoft Viva or Qualtrics EmployeeXM integrate feedback tools, sentiment analysis, and engagement data to guide HR and leadership decisions.
- **Performance management software**: Modern systems provide dashboards with productivity metrics, behavioral analytics, and goal alignment data.
- **Collaboration analytics**: Tools such as Microsoft Workplace Analytics analyze communication patterns, meeting loads, and collaborative behavior to assess work dynamics in hybrid settings.

Real-time dashboards and automated reporting features help leadership teams monitor adaptation without invasive practices. Ethical implementation of these tools—grounded in transparency and consent—is vital to preserving trust and psychological safety (Petersen, 2021).

Pulse surveys and feedback loops play an important role in creating adaptive change mechanisms. Short, frequent surveys capture evolving sentiments, allowing organizations to recalibrate training, communication, or leadership approaches as needed.

Measuring workforce adaptation is essential for realizing the full value of digital transformation and BPM. Through a strategic combination of KPIs, satisfaction and innovation metrics, scorecards, maturity models, and monitoring platforms, organizations can gain a comprehensive understanding of their human capital's readiness and responsiveness.

The emphasis must shift from merely tracking outcomes to fostering an adaptive, resilient, and empowered workforce. Measurement, when designed thoughtfully, becomes not just an evaluative tool but a catalyst for engagement, learning, and continuous improvement in the digital era.

8. CHALLENGES AND BARRIERS

While digital transformation and Business Process Management (BPM) promise enhanced efficiency, agility, and innovation, organizations frequently encounter multifaceted human and systemic barriers that impede successful execution. These challenges are not solely technological; they often arise from deep-rooted organizational cultures, ethical dilemmas, and disparities in digital infrastructure. Understanding and proactively addressing these obstacles is crucial for creating inclusive, resilient, and human-centric digital ecosystems.

8.1 Resistance to Change and Legacy Mindsets

One of the most enduring challenges in digital transformation is resistance to change. Employees accustomed to traditional work processes often exhibit skepticism or opposition when new systems or workflows are introduced. This resistance may stem from fear of the unknown, perceived loss of control, or doubts about the benefits of digital tools (Kotter, 2012).

Legacy mindsets, shaped by past experiences and hierarchical management structures, further exacerbate resistance. Such mindsets hinder agility and inhibit the open adoption of iterative, user-centered BPM practices. Organizations with rigid structures often struggle to implement dynamic workflows or encourage experimentation, leading to implementation delays and underutilized systems.

To counteract this, change management strategies rooted in empathy, participation, and transparent communication are essential. Leaders must cultivate a culture of continuous learning and co-creation to dismantle outdated mental models and foster digital readiness.

8.2 Technostress, Job Insecurity, and Automation Anxiety

The proliferation of digital tools and automation has inadvertently introduced a psychological burden known as technostress—a condition wherein individuals experience anxiety, fatigue, and reduced performance due to constant digital engagement (Tarafdar et al., 2015). Rapid onboarding of new technologies without adequate training or support systems often overwhelms employees, contributing to burnout and disengagement.

Job insecurity and automation anxiety have become prevalent, particularly among mid-career and older workers. The rise of AI, machine learning, and robotic process automation (RPA) in BPM environments has raised fears about job displacement, redundancy, and devaluation of human skills (Frey & Osborne, 2017). These concerns are not unfounded; research indicates that while digital transformation can create new roles, it often disrupts existing ones, disproportionately affecting routine and manual occupations.

Mitigating these effects requires organizations to invest in reskilling, upskilling, and psychosocial support. Workforce transformation strategies must prioritize psychological safety and emphasize the augmentation—not replacement—of human capabilities.

8.3 Ethical Concerns: Surveillance, Privacy, and Algorithmic Bias

Digital transformation introduces significant ethical challenges, particularly concerning employee surveillance, data privacy, and algorithmic fairness. The deployment of monitoring tools to track productivity, engagement, or communication patterns can infringe upon personal boundaries and erode trust. In many cases, employees are unaware of the extent to which their digital behaviors are being observed, raising concerns about transparency and informed consent (Ball, 2010).

Privacy risks emerge when personal or performance-related data are collected and stored without robust data governance policies. Mishandling or unauthorized sharing of sensitive information can damage employee morale and legal standing.

A more subtle but equally concerning issue is algorithmic bias. When AI-driven BPM tools are used to guide decisions—such as hiring, promotions, or workload allocations—biased training data can reinforce systemic inequalities. If unaddressed, this perpetuates discrimination based on gender, race, age, or ability (Eubanks, 2018).

Addressing these ethical risks necessitates clear governance frameworks, inclusive AI design practices, and cross-functional ethical oversight. Organizations should involve diverse stakeholders in the design and evaluation of algorithmic tools and prioritize digital ethics training for leaders and IT professionals.

8.4 Infrastructure and Access Gaps Across Different Sectors

While digital transformation is often viewed as a universal imperative, infrastructure disparities pose a significant barrier to equitable implementation. In both developed and emerging economies, organizations face unequal access to high-speed internet, digital tools, and skilled labor. This digital divide creates uneven adaptation rates across industries, regions, and workforce segments (World Bank, 2021).

Small and medium enterprises (SMEs) often lack the financial and technical resources to invest in scalable BPM platforms or cloud-based solutions. In contrast, large corporations typically enjoy access to state-of-the-art infrastructure and consulting services. Public sector entities may struggle with bureaucratic inertia, outdated IT systems, and limited training programs.

Within organizations, disparities in digital fluency—often tied to age, education, and socioeconomic background—can hinder collaborative transformation. Inclusive design principles and targeted capacity building initiatives are essential to bridging these internal gaps and ensuring that all employees benefit from digital progress.

Investments in digital infrastructure must be accompanied by ecosystem-level collaboration among governments, industry leaders, and educational institutions. This includes public-private partnerships, broadband expansion, and policy reforms that enable widespread and affordable access to digital technologies.

Digital transformation and BPM offer organizations a pathway to innovation and operational excellence. However, the human and systemic challenges outlined—ranging from resistance to change and psychological strain to ethical dilemmas and infrastructure gaps—demand deliberate and empathetic intervention. Success hinges not only on deploying the right technologies but also on cultivating trust, inclusivity, and resilience across the workforce.

A human-centric approach that acknowledges and addresses these challenges holistically can ensure that digital transformation is not just efficient but also ethical, equitable, and sustainable.

9. CASE STUDIES AND BEST PRACTICES

In an era of rapid digital transformation, organizations are reimagining human resource management (HRM) processes to remain competitive and agile. Best practices often emerge from real-world implementations where businesses undertake structural changes to improve productivity and employee engagement. This section explores two case studies: one from a manufacturing firm focusing on digital upskilling and another from the service industry leveraging Business Process Management (BPM) for HR transformation. Comparative insights from Small and Medium Enterprises (SMEs) and large enterprises are also discussed, concluding with lessons and strategies that can be replicated across sectors.

9.1 Case Study 1: Digital Upskilling at a Manufacturing Firm

Digitalization is reshaping the traditional manufacturing landscape, necessitating a skilled workforce proficient in emerging technologies such as IoT, AI, and data analytics. A prominent example is Siemens AG, a global manufacturing conglomerate that embarked on a comprehensive digital upskilling initiative. Faced with challenges related to an aging workforce and digital skill gaps, Siemens launched its "Future of Work" program, targeting over 300,000 employees globally. The initiative involved implementing digital academies, online learning platforms, and personalized training roadmaps (Siemens, 2020).

The success of this initiative was rooted in its alignment with the company's strategic vision of Industry 4.0. Through partnerships with educational institutions and internal subject matter experts, Siemens was able to tailor learning pathways specific to departmental needs, including predictive maintenance, robotics, and digital twins. A critical aspect was the integration of learning into the workflow, supported by AI-driven recommendation systems that promoted continuous learning and reduced resistance to change (Deloitte, 2020).

The outcome was not only an improvement in digital literacy but also higher employee satisfaction and retention. The initiative helped reduce operational costs and production downtime, demonstrating a clear ROI on workforce development. This case underlines how targeted digital upskilling can serve as a catalyst for broader organizational transformation in manufacturing environments.

Case Study 2: BPM-Driven HR Transformation in a Service Industry

Business Process Management (BPM) offers a structured approach to analyzing, redesigning, and optimizing workflows to enhance operational efficiency. A compelling illustration of BPM-driven HR transformation is seen in the case of Infosys, a global IT services company headquartered in India. Infosys undertook a BPM initiative to streamline its HR operations, including talent acquisition, onboarding, performance evaluation, and learning management.

The transformation journey began with a comprehensive process mapping of the HR value chain to identify inefficiencies and redundancies. BPM tools such as process mining and robotic process automation (RPA) were then applied to automate repetitive tasks and standardize processes across global delivery centers (Infosys, 2021). The deployment of a centralized HR management platform enabled real-time tracking of key HR metrics and reduced the administrative burden on HR personnel.

One of the pivotal outcomes was the significant reduction in onboarding time—from 14 days to just 5—coupled with improved new hire experiences through AI-enabled chatbots and document automation. Performance evaluation processes became more data-driven and transparent, using analytics dashboards that aligned individual goals with organizational objectives.

This case illustrates how BPM, when integrated into HR strategy, can elevate both process efficiency and employee engagement in service-oriented firms. It also emphasizes the role of technology not merely as a support tool, but as a driver of strategic HRM transformation.

9.2 Comparative Insights from SMEs and Large Enterprises

While both Siemens and Infosys represent large enterprises with substantial resources, the principles applied in their transformations offer valuable insights for SMEs as well. Large firms typically possess the financial capability and infrastructure to implement enterprise-wide digital programs, often incorporating AI, cloud computing, and advanced analytics. SMEs tend to operate with limited budgets and leaner teams, which necessitates a more focused and scalable approach.

SMEs have successfully adopted modular BPM systems and cloud-based HR platforms such as BambooHR or Zoho People to automate core functions like payroll, leave management, and recruitment. These tools offer plug-and-play capabilities with minimal upfront investment, making them ideal for smaller firms seeking agility and cost-effectiveness (PwC, 2022). SMEs often benefit from less hierarchical structures, enabling faster decision-making and easier cultural adoption of digital initiatives.

SMEs face unique challenges such as lack of in-house expertise and resistance to change due to close-knit work cultures. To overcome this, many SMEs have relied on external consultants and industry-specific training programs to drive digital maturity incrementally. In contrast, large enterprises must manage scale, complexity, and global compliance while ensuring consistent employee experiences across diverse geographies.

9.3 Insights Gained and Replicable Strategies

Both case studies reveal critical lessons and strategies that organizations, regardless of size or sector, can adopt:

1. **Strategic Alignment:** Whether it is digital upskilling or BPM adoption, aligning HR initiatives with business goals ensures sustained leadership support and resource allocation.
2. **Employee-Centric Design:** Personalizing learning journeys or user interfaces for HR systems increases adoption and improves user experience.
3. **Integrated Technology Ecosystems:** Leveraging platforms that integrate with existing ERP or CRM systems enhances data visibility and operational coherence.
4. **Change Management:** Continuous communication, leadership involvement, and employee advocacy are essential to mitigate resistance and foster a culture of innovation.
5. **Scalable Models:** SMEs can replicate enterprise-level practices through modular, cloud-based solutions that offer flexibility and cost efficiency.

The best practices in HR transformation emphasize the dual imperatives of technological integration and human adaptability. As the future of work continues to evolve, organizations that invest in agile, data-driven, and employee-centered HR systems are better positioned to attract, retain, and empower talent in a dynamic landscape.

10. FUTURE OUTLOOK AND RECOMMENDATIONS

As Business Process Management (BPM) continues to evolve in the age of digital transformation, the future of work is increasingly defined by the fusion of technology and human capabilities. Emerging roles such as digital ethicists, automation managers, and human-AI trainers signify this paradigm shift. These roles are essential in ensuring ethical deployment of technologies, managing automated systems, and facilitating seamless collaboration between human workers and intelligent machines. Organizations must begin investing in reskilling initiatives that prepare employees for these emerging job categories while fostering a mindset geared towards innovation and adaptability.

Building resilient and agile workforce ecosystems is central to thriving in a volatile, uncertain, complex, and ambiguous (VUCA) environment. This involves creating flexible work structures, decentralized decision-making processes, and continuous learning cultures. Leveraging BPM frameworks to facilitate cross-functional collaboration, data-driven insights, and rapid process reengineering is vital in enabling such agility. The use of AI and automation should not replace human ingenuity but rather augment it, enabling workers to focus on higher-order tasks such as critical thinking, empathy, and strategic planning.

For sustainable and inclusive transformation, aligning organizational policies and strategies with human-centric values is imperative. Leaders must craft BPM strategies that are not solely efficiency-driven but also inclusive, ethical, and socially responsible. This includes policies around data privacy, algorithmic fairness, digital inclusion, and employee well-being. Regulatory frameworks and internal governance structures should work in tandem to ensure that technological advancements do not compromise human dignity or exacerbate inequalities.

In final reflection, the future of BPM lies in striking a deliberate balance between technology and humanity. While digital tools and automation drive efficiency and scalability, the human element—creativity, judgment, and emotional intelligence—remains irreplaceable. Organizations that succeed will be those that adopt a dual lens: optimizing processes through digital innovation while embedding empathy, trust, and purpose into the fabric of their operations. BPM, therefore, must be reimagined not just as a tool for operational excellence but as a strategic enabler of ethical, agile, and human-centric organizational transformation.

REFERENCES

Amazon. (2020). *Upskilling 2025*. https://www.aboutamazon.com/news/workplace/upskilling-2025

Amershi, S., Cakmak, M., Knox, W. B., & Kulesza, T. (2014). Power to the people: The role of humans in interactive machine learning. *AI Magazine*, *35*(4), 105–120. DOI: 10.1609/aimag.v35i4.2513

Ball, K. (2010). Workplace surveillance: An overview. *Labor History*, *51*(1), 87–106. DOI: 10.1080/00236561003654776

Bass, B. M., & Riggio, R. E. (2006). *Transformational leadership* (2nd ed.). Psychology Press. DOI: 10.4324/9781410617095

Bersin, J. (2019). *Learning in the flow of work*. Deloitte Insights. https://www2.deloitte.com

Bughin, J., Hazan, E., Lund, S., Dahlström, P., Wiesinger, A., & Subramaniam, A. (2018). *Skill shift: Automation and the future of the workforce*. McKinsey Global Institute. https://www.mckinsey.com

Cameron, K. S., & Quinn, R. E. (2011). *Diagnosing and changing organizational culture: Based on the competing values framework* (3rd ed.). Jossey-Bass.

Carayon, P. (2006). Human factors of complex sociotechnical systems. *Applied Ergonomics*, *37*(4), 525–535. DOI: 10.1016/j.apergo.2006.04.011 PMID: 16756937

Côrte-Real, N., Oliveira, T., & Ruivo, P. (2019). Assessing business value of Big Data Analytics in European firms. *Journal of Business Research*, *97*, 606–615. DOI: 10.1016/j.jbusres.2018.12.072

Davis, F. D. (1989). Perceived usefulness, perceived ease of use, and user acceptance of information technology. *Management Information Systems Quarterly*, *13*(3), 319–340. DOI: 10.2307/249008

Deci, E. L., & Ryan, R. M. (2000). The "what" and "why" of goal pursuits: Human needs and the self-determination of behavior. *Psychological Inquiry*, *11*(4), 227–268. DOI: 10.1207/S15327965PLI1104_01

Deloitte. (2020). *The social enterprise at work: Paradox as a path forward*. Retrieved from https://www2.deloitte.com

Dumas, M., La Rosa, M., Mendling, J., & Reijers, H. A. (2018). *Fundamentals of Business Process Management* (2nd ed.). Springer. DOI: 10.1007/978-3-662-56509-4

Eubanks, V. (2018). *Automating inequality: How high-tech tools profile, police, and punish the poor*. St. Martin's Press.

Frey, C. B., & Osborne, M. A. (2017). The future of employment: How susceptible are jobs to computerization? *Technological Forecasting and Social Change*, *114*, 254–280. DOI: 10.1016/j.techfore.2016.08.019

Gallup. (2023). *State of the Global Workplace 2023 Report*. https://www.gallup.com

Gartner. (2021). *How to measure productivity in a hybrid work environment*. Gartner, Inc. https://www.gartner.com

Hart, S. G., & Staveland, L. E. (1988). Development of NASA-TLX (Task Load Index): Results of empirical and theoretical research. [). Elsevier.]. *Advances in Psychology*, *52*, 139–183. DOI: 10.1016/S0166-4115(08)62386-9

Harter, J. K., Schmidt, F. L., & Hayes, T. L. (2002). Business-unit-level relationship between employee satisfaction, employee engagement, and business outcomes: A meta-analysis. *The Journal of Applied Psychology*, *87*(2), 268–279. DOI: 10.1037/0021-9010.87.2.268 PMID: 12002955

Harvard Business Review. (2020). *How leaders can adapt to the digital future*. Harvard Business Publishing.

Hiatt, J. (2006). *ADKAR: A model for change in business, government and our community*. Prosci Research.

Infosys. (2021). *HR transformation through BPM*. Infosys BPM White Paper.

Kaplan, R. S., & Norton, D. P. (1996). *The balanced scorecard: Translating strategy into action*. Harvard Business Press.

Kotter, J. P. (2012). *Leading change*. Harvard Business Review Press.

LinkedIn Learning. (2021). *2021 Workplace Learning Report: Skill building in the new world of work*. https://learning.linkedin.com/resources/workplace-learning-report

McKinsey & Company. (2020). *Diversity wins: How inclusion matters*. https://www.mckinsey.com

McKinsey & Company. (2021). *Building workforce skills at scale to thrive during—and after—the COVID-19 crisis*. https://www.mckinsey.com

Mishra, K. E., & Mishra, A. K. (2013). Trust is everything: Become the leader others will follow. *Leader to Leader*, *2013*(69), 45–49.

Norman, D. A. (2013). *The design of everyday things: Revised and expanded edition*. Basic Books.

Petersen, J. C. (2021). Ethical data use in human resource analytics: Balancing innovation and responsibility. *Journal of Business Ethics*, *168*(3), 575–589.

Prosci. (2021). *Change management: The people side of change*. https://www.prosci.com

PwC. (2022). *Digital transformation in SMEs: A path to sustainable growth*. Retrieved from https://www.pwc.com

Rahwan, I., Cebrian, M., Obradovich, N., Bongard, J., Bonnefon, J. F., Breazeal, C., & Lazer, D. (2019). Machine behaviour. *Nature*, *568*(7753), 477–486. DOI: 10.1038/s41586-019-1138-y PMID: 31019318

Rai, A. (2020). Explainable AI: From black box to glass box. *Journal of the Academy of Marketing Science*, *48*(1), 137–141. DOI: 10.1007/s11747-019-00710-5

Sanders, E. B. N., & Stappers, P. J. (2008). Co-creation and the new landscapes of design. *CoDesign*, *4*(1), 5–18. DOI: 10.1080/15710880701875068

Seemiller, C., & Grace, M. (2019). *Generation Z: A century in the making*. Routledge.

Siemens. (2020). *Future of Work – Siemens' digital upskilling program*. Siemens AG Corporate Report.

Siemens. (2021). *NextWork: Reimagining the future of work*. Siemens AG. https://www.siemens.com

Subrahmanyam, S. (2024). Leadership and cultural change management for technology adoption in operations. In Martínez-Falcó, J., Sánchez-García, E., Marco-Lajara, B., & Visser, G. (Eds.), *Convergence of technology and operations management in modern businesses* (pp. 175–202). IGI Global Scientific Publishing. DOI: 10.4018/979-8-3693-6200-6.ch005

Subrahmanyam, S. (2024). The evolution of human resources in the age of technology. In Kaur, J. (Ed.), *Technological enhancements for improving employee performance, safety, and well-being* (pp. 229–256). IGI Global Scientific Publishing. DOI: 10.4018/979-8-3693-9631-5.ch011

Subrahmanyam, S. (2025). Building a Digital-First Organizational Culture. In Pawirosumarto, S. (Ed.), *Innovative Approaches for International Competitiveness Through Human Resource Management* (pp. 101–124). IGI Global Scientific Publishing. DOI: 10.4018/979-8-3373-1005-3.ch004

Subrahmanyam, S. (2025). Employee Skillsets in the Digital Age. In Özbek, M., & Christiansen, B. (Eds.), *Organizational Sociology in the Digital Age* (pp. 369–388). IGI Global Scientific Publishing. DOI: 10.4018/979-8-3693-7398-9.ch018

Subrahmanyam, S. (2025). Organizational Leadership in the 21st Century. In Özbek, M., & Christiansen, B. (Eds.), *Organizational Sociology in the Digital Age* (pp. 389–412). IGI Global Scientific Publishing. DOI: 10.4018/979-8-3693-7398-9.ch019

Subrahmanyam, S. (2025). The Paradigm Shift in Leadership Owing to Technological Development. In Agnihotri, A., & Balusamy, B. (Eds.), *Leadership Paradigms and the Impact of Technology* (pp. 381–406). IGI Global Scientific Publishing. DOI: 10.4018/979-8-3693-7175-6.ch016

Tarafdar, M., Cooper, C. L., & Stich, J.-F. (2019). The technostress trifecta—Techno eustress, techno distress and design: Theoretical directions and an agenda for research. *Information Systems Journal, 29*(1), 6–42. DOI: 10.1111/isj.12169

Tarafdar, M., Pullins, E. B., & Ragu-Nathan, T. S. (2015). Technostress: Negative effect on performance and possible mitigations. *Information Systems Journal, 25*(2), 103–132. DOI: 10.1111/isj.12042

Tidd, J., & Bessant, J. (2018). *Managing innovation: Integrating technological, market and organizational change* (6th ed.). Wiley.

UNESCO. (2021). *Digital literacy for all: What can governments do?* https://www.unesco.org

van der Aalst, W. M. P. (2013). Business process management: A comprehensive survey. *ISRN Software Engineering, 2013*, 1–37. DOI: 10.1155/2013/507984

Vial, G. (2019). Understanding digital transformation: A review and a research agenda. *The Journal of Strategic Information Systems, 28*(2), 118–144. DOI: 10.1016/j.jsis.2019.01.003

Vicente, K. J. (2006). *The human factor: Revolutionizing the way people live with technology*. Routledge.

vom Brocke, J., Zelt, S., & Schmiedel, T. (2016). On the role of context in business process management. *International Journal of Information Management, 36*(3), 486–495. DOI: 10.1016/j.ijinfomgt.2015.10.002

Waizenegger, L., McKenna, B., Cai, W., & Bendz, T. (2020). An affordance perspective of team collaboration and enforced working from home during COVID-19. *European Journal of Information Systems, 29*(4), 429–442. DOI: 10.1080/0960085X.2020.1800417

World Bank. (2021). *Digital Dividends*. World Development Report. https://www.worldbank.org/en/publication/wdr2016

World Economic Forum. (2020). *The Future of Jobs Report 2020*. https://www.weforum.org

Chapter 6
Integrating Business Process Management and Marketing:
A Strategic Approach to Enhancing Customer-Centric Processes

Parihar Suresh Dahake
https://orcid.org/0000-0002-2286-4120
Ramdeobaba University, Nagpur, India

Nihar Suresh Dahake
https://orcid.org/0009-0007-8971-9247
G.H. Raisoni College of Engineering, Nagpur, India

Amruta Mahalle
https://orcid.org/0009-0001-4246-4060
Datta Meghe Institute of Management Studies, Nagpur, India

ABSTRACT

The current research examines how business process management (BPM) and marketing are integrated into marketing communications to enhance customer-centric processes in response to technological advancements. Information and communication evolution and joining with other technologies give rise to a new focus on Marketing 4.0. The shift of focus from brand-centric marketing to customer-centric marketing motivates practitioners to highlight customer experience, satisfaction, and loyalty. However, ever-changing market dynamics, new customer demand, and emergence of new communication and marketing channels hinder efficient service

DOI: 10.4018/979-8-3373-3336-6.ch006

delivery by marketing departments.

1. INTRODUCTION

Business firms are leveraging the potential of integrating a customer-centric approach into their strategic business processes. In business firms, this strategic direction, often referred to as Business Process Management (BPM), represents a holistic approach aimed at improving customer-centric processes, defining a strategic plan for aligning those processes, and utilizing information technology to run more efficiently and consistently (Gross et al., 2019).

Figure 1. Role of Integrating Business Process Management in Marketing

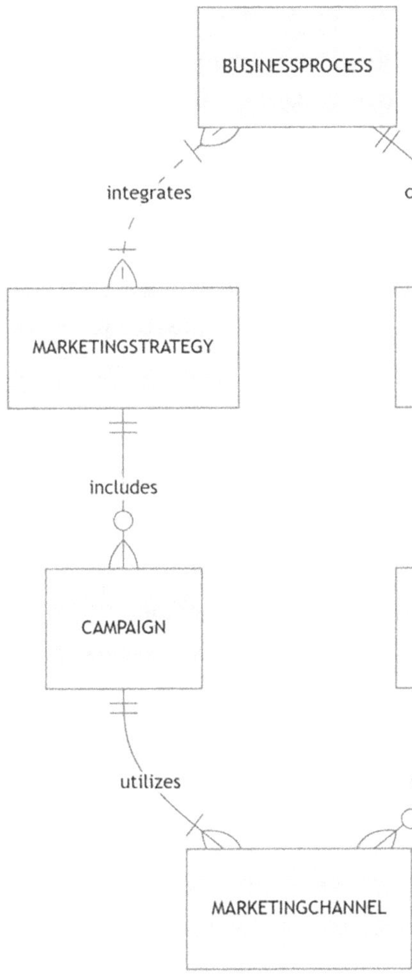

To ensure process continuity, a marketing-oriented conceptual framework has been discussed, with a case illustration from the Indian manufacturing environment. Marketing managers can yield competitive profits by applying the approach outlined in this paper to enhance their customer-centric processes. This strategic direction represents a holistic approach aimed at improving the wide business processes that define company performance. Customer-centric processes are formally defined as a comprehensive framework that includes strong criteria to measure their performance (Javalgi et al., 2005). The examination of customer market research has demonstrated that the proposal presented here has real industrial applicability and provides a profound understanding of customer-centric processes. A great deal of emphasis has been placed on customer centricity in recent marketing articles. To agree, organizations worldwide must be faithful to their customers to develop a market advantage. As a result, a stratagem that facilitates the improvement and investigation of such processes would be very beneficial.

With this perspective in mind, a method for estimating client-focused processes was proposed. To the best of our knowledge, this marks the first comprehensive effort to provide a broad conceptual model for what telecommunication research commonly emphasizes about customer-focused telecommunications networking in businesses. Companies can implement digital transformation using business process management (Fischer et al., 2020), A credible investigation and a case study applying the laid-out methodology corroborated the strength of the proposed framework and its real-world validity. Business Process Management (BPM) is a systematic methodology used by organizations to enhance and integrate core business processes, aiming to achieve improved corporate performance. Business Process Management has become an area of increasing interest to organizations seeking strategies for modernizing their business or government operations. Organizations are investing significant effort in understanding and analyzing their business processes, designing new processes or redesigning existing ones, ensuring that these processes are adequately documented, and analyzing and monitoring their performance to optimize efficiency.

Table 1.Words Frequency Over-Time Using-R

Keywords/Year	**2020**	**2021**	**2022**	**2023**	**2024**	**2025**
Optimization	19	42	63	85	105	107
Business Process	7	13	17	24	47	50
Process Optimization	6	16	19	26	40	50
Business Process Management	7	17	21	25	35	42
Process Optimisation	1	9	15	22	34	42
Enterprise Resource Management	5	15	19	26	39	41
Business Process Optimization	6	14	18	26	36	39
Strategic Alignment	11	18	23	30	33	39
Decision Making	5	13	16	22	34	37
Information Management	5	9	14	20	33	36

Figure 2. Words Frequency Over-Time Using-R.png

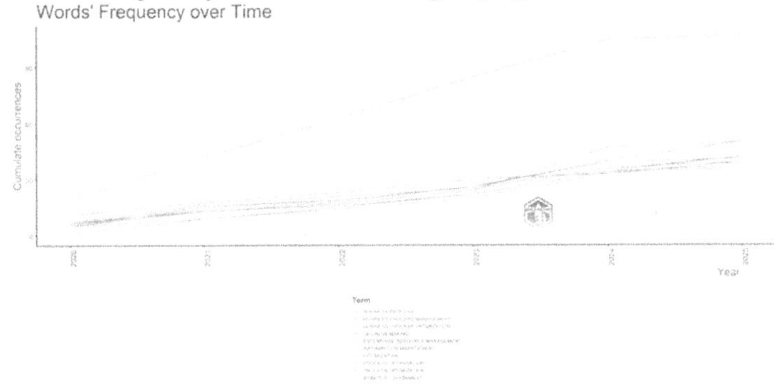

The word frequency analysis over time, conducted using R software, offers meaningful insights into the evolving academic interest surrounding the research theme The data reveals a consistent and sharp increase in the usage of keywords such as "Optimization," "Business Process," and "Process Optimization" from 2020 to 2025, indicating a growing emphasis on operational efficiency and strategic process enhancement within marketing and management research. Notably, terms such as "Business Process Management" and "Enterprise Resource Management" exhibit a steady upward trajectory, reflecting the increasing integration of structured management frameworks into marketing strategies. Furthermore, the rising frequency of "Strategic Alignment" and "Decision Making" underscores a shift toward aligning organizational processes with customer-centric goals and data-driven decision-making. This trend underscores the academic community's ongoing commitment to refining internal workflows to meet external market demands. Overall, the temporal keyword analysis validates the relevance and timeliness of the present research, positioning it well within the core of emerging scholarly discourse.

On the other hand, traditional marketing management has undergone significant changes with the advent of new marketing forms. Marketers have long been concerned with the perception of their customers, seeking unique sets of marketing actions that enhance customer satisfaction and focus on the customer and their problems rather than on the products. This customer-oriented marketing approach will navigate the trade landscape forever, but the focus has shifted considerably from a company-oriented to a client-centered one. In broader terms, the new marketing strategies involve creating profitable associations with clearly identified target customers. Customers' real needs are deeply understood through the personalized treatment of all customers, both potential and current ones. These new marketing strategies, which offer a different way to configure the market and develop customer relationships, work more efficiently when they respond to the customer-centric orientation of modern markets, thus fully leveraging the distinct capabilities of new technologies. Business Process Management (BPM) and marketing are both recognized as opportunities for firms to achieve a sustainable competitive advantage. BPM is a systematic and structured approach to improving existing business processes, centered on the customer, the firm's value proposition, and performance assessment metrics. Conversely, marketing is a process of devising, communicating, and delivering value to the customer. Together, these two organizational functions would provide a comprehensive approach to creating and sustaining customer-centric processes.

Despite the promise of BPM and marketing as ways for firms to become more customer-centric, most organizations have a gap between what BPM intends to achieve and what it achieves in practice. Progress in BPM is impeded by several problems that can be classified into three fundamental factors: inadequate understanding of BPM, inability or unwillingness to invest resources in BPM, and further challenges that arise from the socio-technical nature of BPM. In tandem, these problems lead to BPM's inability to comprehend marketing intent and enhance customer-centricity in practice. Organizations adopt BPM expecting a set of benefits to accrue, such as improved customer success, value proposition excellence, and enhanced customer experience; however, they often find that BPM disappoints on all of these fronts. Moreover, BPM is ambivalent to the marketing message that successful firms are customer-centric. Indeed, BPM is grounded in a theory of industrialization that views customers as a liability, an unnecessary part of the business that creates waste in the form of excessive process variance and uncertain outcomes; an idea that marketing agencies vigorously challenge.

To make matters worse, organizations resort to the tools of BPM to attempt some improvement to customer-centricity; however, BPM unhappily digs deeper into the hole that other functions have already disrupted (Koopman & Seymour, 2020a).. Practically, the strategic approach specified is of significant value to organizations. It proposes a coherent direction for organizations wishing to navigate the competing messages of BPM and marketing in a way that is loyal to both. To recode a BPM process in a way that enhances customer-centricity requires a thorough understanding of both BPM and marketing principles. A natural starting point for organizations wishing to enhance customer-centricity would be through the appointment of a Chief Process Officer (CPO) who is educated in both BPM and marketing, and is tasked with understanding the relationship between the two. Organizations can then build a marketing process that builds upon marketing knowledge and tools. Through a rigorous, cycle-by-cycle process improvement, emphasizing resource investment in marketing, firms can effectively balance marketing efforts while mitigating losses associated with BPM. Upon achieving outperformance, process niches can be expanded to encompass pervasive marketing processes. Successful business firms and organizations recognized the present as the era of the "Industrial Revolution."

For these companies, efforts are being made to develop newer, advanced strategies to sustain themselves (P. S. Dahake, Bagaregari, et al., 2024). Market competition is intensifying rapidly, with modified industry structures providing innumerable challenges to the marketing team of an organization (Aslam et al., 2025), In this study, an endeavor has been made to analyze the need for coalescing BPM on MKT to overcome these challenges. The era of digital revolution has seen an explosion of phenomena on a massive scale, from globalization and e-commerce networks to fragmented, ever-changing consumer values and preferences, and hyper-competition among firms. Digitalization requires new and enhanced business process management capabilities to effectively drive corporate success(Kerpedzhiev et al., 2021). The easiest to achieve would be a landmark achievement to be incorporated into the BPM and Marketing Strategy (MKT) of an organization in service-rendering firms. Customer-focused business processes ensure process efficiency by eliminating non-value-adding activities from the system, thereby enhancing timely service delivery, improving service quality, and ultimately leading to happier customers. Such firms can go beyond the prevailing customer satisfaction paradigm, as their service competition would be an attitude that could precipitate word-of-mouth referrals, and ensure repeat purchases and long-term revenue. Organizations are now rethinking their business models so that the realized value perceptions align with the desired value propositions. There is a new paradigm that, in addition to product quality and price, firms need to look after the technology and processes on which those technologies are based. The make versus buy dilemma is rapidly being reshaped with “strategic outsourcing.” At a time when there is a clamoring for coalescing of forces, the advent of “Business Process Reengineering” (BPM) challenged the marketing fraternity to rethink the traditionally held marketing paradigms that reinforced the “4-Ps.” In the past decade, a plethora of knowledge on how to approach BPM and what is to be done about traditional processes has appeared.

2. THEORETICAL FRAMEWORK

Customer behavior is changing in the business environment in India from a technology perspective where 4G internet connectivity is predominantly used as businesses go digital, customer scanned goods are updated seamlessly through apps with the stores, and other customer purchase histories are documented and analyzed on a massive scale where traditional methods of marketing personalization cannot perform.

Figure 3. Theoretical Framework

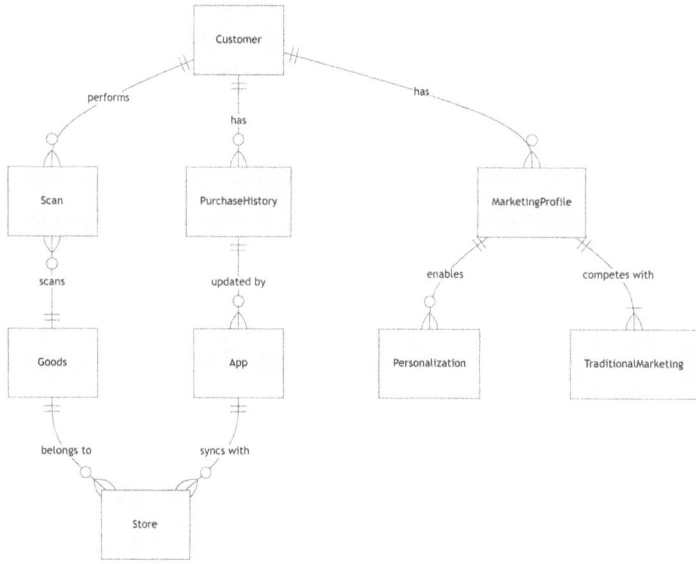

India is poised for future growth in e-commerce. In a country like India, where only 5% of transactions are cashless, demonetization in 2016 was a significant leap forward that aimed to bring more self-employed small businesses into the tax system. Customers would deviate a few minutes from their routine and move from fancy OTS coffee to a local kirana or self-serve automated veggie stand to purchase ≤ 5 items. The customer spent 30–90 seconds opening the phone app, scanning items, and leaving without paying because the money would be automatically debited. Low-value customer items (such as bags of chips and bread) were priced at ≤ 30 rupees using barcodes. No technology was used in this model, and it was very cost-effective, as it did not require the introduction of plastic cards to customers, eliminating the need for a bank to be involved. A software application was developed for store staff on mobile phones, while customers used an off-the-shelf app. A product inventory database and processing engine were maintained in the cloud. E-commerce B2C customer–vendor scenario documents individual product user purchases using the app (Sahdeo, n.d.). Digital devices were used by store staff to update prices on a commodity product daily, as kirana vendors frequently change their daily consumption levels. Two contrasting groups, comprising 20+ and 40+ female and male participants, were selected. The location for this process was standalone stores (daily stores) with the app in the local Gujarati language. Post spending money equivalent to that of the other group. Products were randomly selected, and instructions were given to the participant to find them faster than the others. The dependent variable was the time taken to locate the product. The independent variables were age and gender, as well as encoding the same store product based on digital technology. The customer scanned their entry ticket to a big shopping mall and used the "Find My Car" button after shopping, where parking was underground and the parking number from the 2000s was not recalled for launching the app.

2.1. Understanding Business Process Management

Business Process Management (BPM) is an enterprising approach for improving organizations' business processes, adopted globally, to serve customers even more efficiently and effectively (Gross & Vienna, n.d.-a). BPM facilitates the systematic change of existing or development of new business process designs. Over the last three decades, BPM methods and frameworks have been introduced, refined, and applied. Generally, BPM methods are framed as process reengineering, process improvement or process redesign. Regardless of the frame, their commonality is to change existing business process designs. These BPM methods and frameworks aim to either incrementally or radically improve business processes. The ambition, nature, and perspective of the methods and frameworks are important in determining their applicability for radical or incremental process change. Studies regarding BPM methods have primarily focused on specific method designs, while systematic comparisons across different methods are scarce. Little is known about the characteristics that define the classification of BPM methods and frameworks, the understanding of their applicability, and systematic evaluations of BPM methods based on these possible characteristics within their respective frameworks.

Business process management (BPM) enables organizations to identify, analyze, enhance, and manage their business processes (Ma et al., 2010a). BPM has evolved from the concepts of Business Process Reengineering (BPR) to become a permanent practice for improving processes in both incremental and radical ways. BPM approaches typically begin with the identification of existing business processes and continue with the an analysis of these processes to identify design problems. Furthermore, BPM approaches can support the redesign of the process by suggesting a target process design. Finally, BPM approaches can also execute the process model by managing the execution of process instances.

3. REVIEW OF LITERATURE

The computer program was used to use keyword analysis of the 430 articles. This visual data analysis vosviewer software is used to create a network of related keywords from multiple articles. The application displays the analysis results in a graphical form as a network of related keywords, clustered according to the user-defined criteria. Keywords sourced from 430 articles were entered into the application, resulting in 430 keywords that occurred more than three times. The analysis was conducted using a minimum keyword of occurrence (1) with 64 variations of keywords related to the strategic approach to customer-centric processes and acoustic stickers categorized as research, social, and communication issues. Because the number of keywords with a minimum occurrence of 1 was reduced from 430 to 20 keywords, the co-occurrence of keywords with a minimum occurrence of 3 was ranked with a total of 263 keyword variations.

Figure 4. All Keywords Analysis by Vosviewer

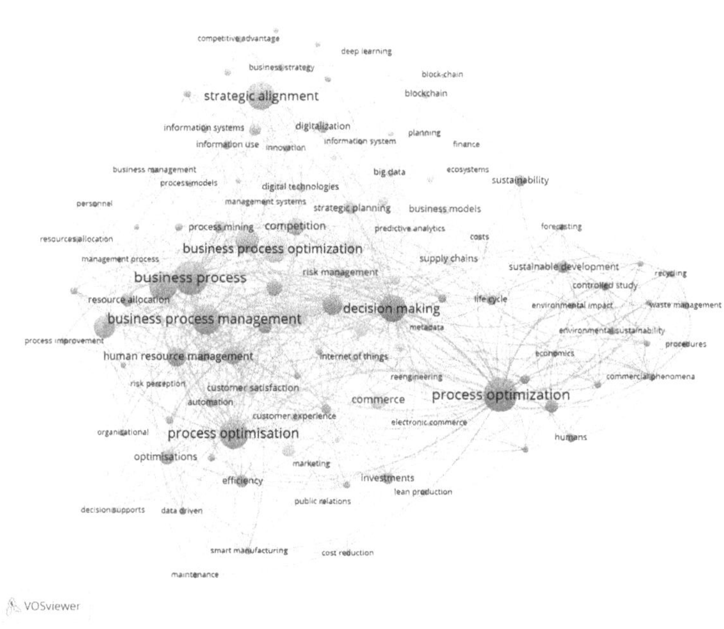

The analysis highlights "business process management" (BPM), "process optimization," and "decision making" as dominant and centrally connected terms across all three maps. These terms form the foundational backbone of strategic process enhancement, where BPM acts as a structural enabler and decision-making reflects the actionable output.

Figure 5. Author Keywords Analysis by Vosviewer

Closely related keywords such as “strategic alignment,” “digital transformation,” and “artificial intelligence” demonstrate the modern technological and strategic frameworks driving BPM today. AI can be strategically used in marketing research, strategy, and actions, benefiting mechanical AI for data collection, thinking AI for data processing, and feeling AI for customer understanding (Huang & Rust, 2021). In terms of marketing integration, the networks show significant clustering around terms like “customer satisfaction,” “commerce,” “public relations,” “sales,” and “customer experience.”as it is essential to note that AI integration in digital marketing for financial services may not always effectively target vulnerable customers(Mogaji et al., 2021).

Figure 6. Index Keywords Analysis by Vosviewer

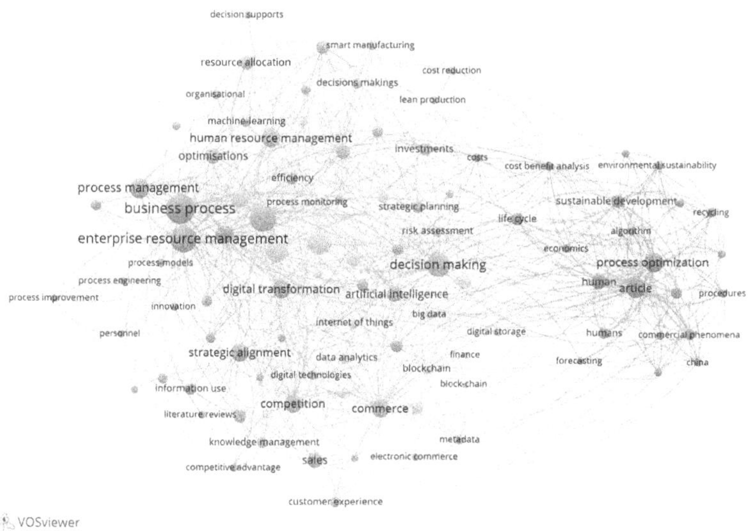

These keywords confirm the growing scholarly interest in aligning BPM with marketing goals to achieve enhanced customer-centricity. The presence of "data-driven," "digital technologies," and "marketing" alongside "automation," "efficiency," and "resource allocation" highlights the transition from traditional process models toward agile, technology-driven, and customer-focused systems. Furthermore, concepts such as "sustainability," "strategic planning," "supply chains," and "innovation" illustrate the expanding scope of BPM, encompassing long-term organizational goals that not only improve internal efficiency but also drive market responsiveness and sustainable value creation.

Clusters around "Industry 4.0," "machine learning," "big data," and "Internet of Things (IoT)" further validate the strategic application of digital innovations in optimizing both processes and customer journeys.Big data analytics can enhance customer experience management by providing valuable insights and guiding management practice(Holmlund et al., 2020), In conclusion, the keyword co-occurrence networks in VOSviewer establish a multidimensional knowledge base where BPM and marketing converge through strategy, digital transformation, customer orientation, and technological enablers, forming a fertile ground for scholarly exploration and practical implementation in enhancing customer-centric processes. Strengthening confidence and social benefits in service marketing is crucial for customer loyalty, with perceived value and relationship quality as the strongest mediating paths(Gremler et al., 2020). Notably, Big data powered artificial intelligence significantly improves customer, user, and external market knowledge creation, leading to improved B2B marketing rational decision making and improved firm performance (Bag et al., 2021).

The integration of Business Process Management (BPM) and marketing has gained significant attention in recent years, particularly in the context of enhancing customer-centric processes. This literature review aims to explore the evolving landscape of BPM and its interrelationship with marketing strategies, highlighting key findings from relevant scholarly articles.(Cull, 2010)introduced a comprehensive framework for BPM, emphasizing its iterative lifecycle that encompasses process discovery, design, implementation, and evaluation. They posited that BPM merges principles from Total Quality Management (TQM) and Business Process Reengineering (BPR), yet noted a lack of standardized approaches for integrating these methodologies. This foundational understanding sets the stage for subsequent explorations into BPM systems and their integration challenges.

(Ma et al., 2010b)further examined the integration of BPM systems, identifying user proficiency and cultural factors as critical elements influencing successful implementation. They emphasized the importance of aligning BPM tools and practices with user preferences to enhance efficiency and effectiveness. This focus on user-centered design underscores the importance of considering employee engagement in BPM initiatives, a theme that is echoed in subsequent studies. In a Similar vein, (Ulmer et al., 2011) proposed a pivotal metamodel- methodology aimed at aligning business analysis with BPM implementation. Their work emphasized the need for organizations to remain agile and responsive to changing demands, advocating for a process-oriented approach that leverages information technology to optimize business processes. Customer satisfaction positively impacts business performance, with satisfaction mediating the effects of marketing strategy variables (Otto et al., 2020).This perspective reinforces the idea that BPM is not merely a technical endeavor but a strategic alignment tool that can enhance customer value. Equally important (Martins & Zacarias, 2015) is the introduction of the Business Process and Practice Alignment Meta-model (BPPAMeta-model), which addresses the gaps in existing meta-models that failed to capture the dynamic relationship between business practices and process descriptions. Their comparative study highlighted the need for more comprehensive modelling approaches that reflect the complexities of real-world business environments. Continuing this trajectory, in (Ujwary-Gil & Potoczek, n.d.) explored the holistic nature of BPM in organizational management, emphasizing its role in delivering customer value through effective process design. They advocated for the SIPOC model as a valuable tool for aligning processes with customer expectations, thereby reinforcing the customer-centric focus of BPM. The exploration of BPM's alignment with daily practices was further advanced by (Ventura Martins & Zacarias, 2017) who reiterated the importance of the BPPAMeta-model in specifying and improving business process models based on actual work practices. This emphasis on alignment and practical application underscores the need for BPM frameworks to be adaptable to the realities of organizational operations. (Nteo, 2017)examined BPM maturity within a South African parastatal, highlighting the historical evolution of BPM as a response to competitive pressures in the marketplace. This study illustrated how BPM has transformed from a focus on product quality to a broader emphasis on service quality and customer satisfaction, aligning with the overall theme of customer-centricity.by the same token (Sahdeo, n.d.) proposed a BPM framework for optimizing supply chain management, emphasizing the interdependent nature of organizational functions in delivering value to customers. This research extended the conversation around BPM by integrating customer orientation and servitization, further solidifying the connection between BPM practices and marketing strategies.on the other hand (Lisovsky, 2019) discussed the critical aspects of BPM for sustainable development, emphasizing the integration of process, people, and technology as foundational elements for successful BPM initiatives. Their insights reflect the necessity of a holistic approach to BPM that considers the broader organizational context.

Consequently, (Prodanova & Van Looy, 2019), conducted a systematic literature review on the benefits of social media for BPM, reinforcing the notion that customer engagement is crucial for enhancing BPM outcomes.Social media is particularly effective in engaging international prospects, while digital tools are prevalent in persuasion (Fraccastoro et al., 2021), This study highlighted the potential of digital tools in facilitating customer-centric processes, aligning with the overarching theme of this literature review. first and foremost (Raddats et al., 2019) synthesized contemporary research on servitization, identifying key themes and research priorities that intersect with BPM and marketing. Their findings emphasize the importance of a multi-actor, relational perspective in understanding the complexities of servitization, further bridging the gap between BPM and marketing disciplines. to put it differently (Shafagatova, n.d.)explored the human aspects of process orientation, linking employee management with BPM to enhance alignment between employee and process goals. This perspective emphasizes the importance of considering employee engagement and motivation in BPM initiatives, which is crucial for cultivating a customer-centric culture. Significantly (Ehrlich et al., 2019) introduced the concept of agile BPM, advocating for a shift in the role of process managers from gatekeepers to facilitators. Their insights into the agile BPM methodology highlight the importance of flexibility and adaptability in process management, aligning with the evolving demands of customer-centric strategies.

As depicted (Meidan et al., 2017)provided a comprehensive survey of BPM suites, underscoring the importance of selecting appropriate tools that align with organizational objectives. Their findings contribute to the understanding of how technological solutions can support BPM initiatives aimed at improving customer engagement and service delivery. as indicated by (Gross & Vienna, n.d.-a) who navigated the complexities of BPM change methods, identifying the diverse approaches organizations can adopt to enhance their processes. Their work reinforces the notion that BPM is a strategic tool for organizations seeking to improve customer service and operational efficiency. Subsequently,(Looy et al., n.d.) highlighted the relationship between BPM and digital innovation, emphasizing the importance of aligning BPM practices with emerging technologies to enhance customer processes. Their research agenda calls for further exploration of how digital tools can facilitate BPM initiatives in a customer-centric context. in agreement with (Azemi & Bala, n.d.) examined the alignment between BPM and organizational strategy in the banking sector, advocating for a strategic approach to BPM that considers internal and external processes. Their findings underscore the necessity of integrating BPM with broader organizational goals to enhance customer service delivery. Furthermore, (Koopman & Seymour, 2020b)identified core elements impacting successful BPM adoption, emphasizing the importance of cultural and strategic alignment in BPM initiatives. Their insights contribute to the understanding of the organizational dynamics that influence BPM success and its implications for customer-centric processes.In consistent with this (Tomaskova & Weber, 2020)reviewed the intersection of operational research and BPM, providing a detailed description of relevant methodologies that can enhance BPM practices. Their systematic review offers valuable insights into the tools and techniques that can be leveraged to improve BPM outcomes. Finally, (Adams et al., 2023) presented guidelines for context-aware process selection, emphasizing the role of context in BPM decision-making. Their research highlights the complexities of process selection and the impact of contextual factors on BPM implementation, reinforcing the need for a nuanced approach to managing customer-centric processes. In summary, the literature reflects a growing recognition of the interplay between BPM and marketing, emphasizing the importance of aligning business processes with customer needs and expectations. The insights from these articles collectively contribute to a deeper understanding of how BPM can be strategically integrated with marketing efforts to enhance customer-centric processes.

4. BUSINESS PROCESS MANAGEMENT (BPM)

Business Process Management (BPM) is an approach followed by organizations to control, analyze, improve and discover their business processes using a combination of information technology and methods. A business process is a sequence or network of activities, which can be performed by a company, and this will lead to the realization of business objectives. While working on a process, resources, an event order and various other related issues have to be considered. The primary aim of business process modeling is to represent all the aspects of a process in a different way, which is understood by business. If a process is not understood correctly, it cannot be implemented correctly. These days, almost all large companies have their own ERP systems, and the resultant competition between software vendors to grab the market is encouraging organizations to search for possible ways to integrate their systems with those of other companies. Additionally, companies are now adopting a more generalized system, such as business process management. Due to the complexity, length, and number of steps involved in the business processes, the integration of these processes could be problematic.

The growth and interest in systems for Business Process Management (BPM) has been increasing significantly. To implement and control business process models, organizations have quickly realized the benefits of such systems. New strides in the automation of BPM systems have increased scalability, execution speed and 'dynamicity' whilst reducing the gap between the business process model and its automated forms (Ma et al., 2010a). Alongside this, the development cycle for new systems and the lifespan of existing solutions are decreasing. To keep pace, organizations are either adding features to their BPM systems, or changing entirely to different systems once an existing one is no longer suitable (Gross & Vienna, n.d.-b). This desire to change can be due to 'lock-in,' which refers to technological advancements that old systems cannot emulate, or to understand better and match Business Process Changes (BPC).

5. RESEARCH METHODOLOGY

This research employs a bibliometric analysis approach to examine articles in the fields of business process management and marketing published from 1990 to 2022. Scopus indexes were used as research data sources for the publication selection process.The bibliometric analysis of this research utilizes Scopus as its primary research data source. Scopus is a comprehensive abstract and citation database of peer–reviewed literature covering scientific journals, books, and conference proceedings in the fields of science, technology, medicine, social science, and arts and humanities. WoS is an online subscription-based scientific citation indexing service that provides accessibility to a wide range of databases. To obtain scientifically preferable and credible, indexed journals, the author ensured that Scopus was the only chosen index (Sudianto, 2019). Publication Selection The article screening was completed in two stages: meta database selection and publication selection, with the following search statement: (TITLE-ABS-KEY ("business process management") OR TITLE-ABS-KEY ("BPM") OR TITLE-ABS-KEY ("process model*") OR TITLE-ABS-KEY (agent-ori*) OR TITLE-ABS-KEY ("workflow management")

OR TITLE-ABS-KEY ("workflow representation") OR TITLE-ABS-KEY ("contextualized workflow") OR TITLE-ABS-KEY ("workflow control") OR TITLE-ABS-KEY ("case or context") OR TITLE-ABS-KEY (simulation*) OR TITLE-ABS-KEY ("Petri net*") OR TITLE-ABS-KEY ("business model*") OR TITLE-ABS-KEY ("activity-based") OR TITLE-ABS-KEY (aligned) OR TITLE-ABS-KEY (support*) OR TITLE-ABS-KEY ("enterprise architecture") OR TITLE-ABS-KEY ("process reference model") OR TITLE-ABS-KEY ("business process") OR TITLE-ABS-KEY ("business model") OR TITLE-ABS-KEY ("Routing strategy") OR TITLE-ABS-KEY ("Dijkstra algorithm") OR TITLE-ABS-KEY ("Ant-based Algorithm") OR TITLE-ABS-KEY ("data mining") OR TITLE-ABS-KEY ("diagnostics") OR TITLE-ABS-KEY ("process improvement*") OR TITLE-ABS-KEY ("process discovery") OR TITLE-ABS-KEY ("data-driven") OR TITLE-ABS-KEY ("Recommendations") OR TITLE-ABS-KEY ("Knowledge Management") OR TITLE-ABS-KEY ("Embodied Conversations" OR "Interpersonal Perspective" OR "Impairment" OR "Person Rendered Inaccessible") OR TITLE-ABS-KEY ("Cognitive/Complex Technical Systems") OR TITLE-ABS-KEY ("Attention-Mediating Activities" OR "Emotional Intelligence" OR "Understanding Their Attention and Controls") OR TITLE-ABS-KEY ("Customer Journey Mapper") OR TITLE-ABS-KEY ("Artificial Intelligence/Machine Learning") OR TITLE-ABS-KEY ("Digital Age/Simple" OR "Complexity") OR TITLE-ABS-KEY ("Human-Centric") OR TITLE-ABS-KEY ("Simple AI Tool") OR TITLE-ABS-KEY ("Social Sciences Web")))) AND (LIMIT-TO (SUBJAREA, "BUSI")) AND (LIMIT-TO (DOCTYPE, "ar")). The search was conducted on August 5, 2022.

5.1. Bibliometric Analysis Techniques

This section discusses the tools and techniques used for conducting bibliometric analysis and describes the framework for the analysis. The first sub-section reviews the tools and techniques commonly used for bibliometric analysis. The second sub-section reviews methods for selecting keywords and constructing keyword networks as one of the most valuable data sources in bibliometric analysis. Bibliometric and network analysis are increasingly applied in management fields. Appropriate bibliometric tools and techniques are essential to avoid bias in the analysis. To better reflect the implications of this methodology, attention is paid to provide two bibliometric entry points to the management field: recommended tools and techniques, a focus on the programming language "R" for conducting bibliometric analysis, and network analysis.

To extract bibliometric data from bibliographic databases, widely used or industry-standard tools include VOSviewer, Sci2 Tool, Gephi, HistCite, Biblioshiny, SmartCite, BibExcel, CitNetExplorer, PubReMiner, and R (with the R packages "bibliometrix" or "Biblioshiny"), among others (Zupic & Cater, 2015). Scopus and Web of Science (WoS) are popular databases for extracting bibliometric data to inform subsequent analyses. Although academics in management may overlook it, CrossRef is now also recommended as a suitable tool.

5.2. Techniques for Pre-Processing and Selecting Keywords

Pre-processing of keywords is a preparatory step that takes bibliometric data as raw input to derive accurate and interpretable results. Though various pre-processing techniques are widely adopted in this field, common pre-processing steps include "language filtering", "standardization and replacement", "synonym recognition and merging", "de-duplication", and "statistical smoothing". Techniques for selecting keywords contribute to providing a set of qualified keywords of this document subset, most notably by census filtering that truncates irrelevant keywords and makes keyword selection more focused and thus manageable (Prodanova & Van Looy, 2019).

5.3. The Research Design

This study employs a systematic review approach for the bibliometric analysis, which characterizes a body of literature to identify the most prominent areas and opportunities for future research. The bibliometric data were retrieved from a database. The three-word search string "("business process management" OR "BPM" OR "task automation") AND (marketing OR commercial) AND (customer OR consumer OR stakeholder)", limited to the article type, was constructed to assemble the dataset. Established literature review methods were adhered to during the screening process, and the final dataset was compiled by established guidelines. Based on a combination of practical and theoretical perspectives, the adopted systematic review process comprises four main steps: defining the eligibility criteria to assemble a representative dataset, retrieving the bibliometric data from the literature, screening the records to compile the final dataset, and extracting the published statistics, co-publication networks, and keyword networks. Only documents containing the three keywords in their abstracts were retrieved from the advanced search. Throughout the screening process, the first eleven journals that included at least fifty published documents were targeted. Titles with keywords representing marketing disciplines were omitted due to potential ambiguity from an IT perspective. This process ultimately compiled a dataset of 258 articles from 52 journals. The final dataset was processed using software. Primarily, software was used to clean the bibliometric data. Following that, a co-publication network of journals was generated using software. Lastly, software was employed to visualize the co-keyword network and balance the layout of viewed networks. In addition to the co-keyword network's visualization, modularity class partitioning and the top 50 most frequent keywords were also determined using a plugin. The analysis process employed multiple tools and approaches, including manual examination and calculation of values from spreadsheets (recency of the articles, average citations, and CP), as well as statistical analysis modules.

5.4. Data Sources and Collection

This work conducts a bibliometric analysis, and the R programming language and its bibliometrics library constitute the toolset. The data source is Scopus, which is the largest abstract and citation database of peer-reviewed research literature in both the 'natural' and 'social' sciences. The search strategy involved selecting databases, choosing keywords, and defining the time frame. The keywords were selected based on the evaluation framework and stakeholder perspective components (including keywords and related terms). Selecting keywords that were inclusive enough to capture a broad spectrum of relevant areas improved the completeness of the dataset. To narrow down the search to only strictly relevant titles, it was decided to combine the two groups of words with "AND" and "OR" operators and add Boolean and truncation operators. Process, management, business, marketing, customer, service, interaction, satisfaction, relationship, experience (or) experience, journey (or) mapping were the main keywords in the first stage of evaluating the initial sample of sources. The last period selected is 2021. The data number configuration was selected to yield a substantial amount of relevant papers while still keeping them manageable (Prodanova & Van Looy, 2019). Thus, the initial sample generated included the top 18 sources, ranging from the source with the highest H-Index to the 18th source with an H-Index of 28.

Perceived benefits of social media for BPM include strategic, customer-centric, data-driven, online, transparent, efficient, participatory, and outside-in approaches. Other categories of perceived benefits include top management support, innovation, proactivity, up-to-date processes, systems, monitoring and control, input-to-process, knowledge, and self-expression. Other research shows the characteristics of adoption levels and types of BPM. The benefit categories are based on the perceptions reflected in scientific articles, book chapters, and conference papers on the advantages of utilizing social media in BPM.Hence, Social media can be a valuable tool for B2B organizations, providing sales-facilitation, integrated communication, and employee engagement(Cartwright et al., 2021).

6. MARKETING IN THE DIGITAL AGE

The rapidly changing global business environment and the advancement in technology have led to a serious rethink of how to conduct marketing activities in pharmaceutical companies. The current marketing landscape is characterized by the convergence of global competition, technological advancements, and changing customer expectations, as well as a growing yet fragmented focus on holistic customer relationships. Pharmaceutical companies are trying to catch up with the latest innovative marketing strategies that the consumer goods and service sectors have recently developed and effectively implemented (Hanjani & Akhavan, 2018). Effective strategies for enhancing customer loyalty through quality service include understanding customer expectations, training employees, personalizing the customer experience, maintaining consistency across touchpoints, and focusing on continuous improvement("ENHANCING CUSTOMER LOYALTY THROUGH QUALITY OF SERVICE," 2023).

Harnessing the potential opportunities offered by online and mobile marketing technologies is now an essential strategy for creating a competitive edge. The uniqueness of the pharmaceutical industry and the consumer background environment, such as the relatively limited direct and intense relationship between pharmaceutical companies and end-users, and the regulatory environment of an intensely controlled sector, has created a particular challenge for administering digital marketing with pharmaceutical companies. Based on the assumption that business success is primarily determined by the strategic orientation of the company, the choice and dissemination of IT, and the ideal combination of IT and business focus, this study provides an overview of a comprehensive strategy for digitally engaging pharmaceutical companies and capturing rapidly increasing digital customer segments. Focusing on the competitive market, this research aims to bridge the gap between micro-level IT applications in the pharmaceutical industry and a macro-level strategic approach.

6.1. Key Concepts and Strategies

Developing a detailed background on the sponsored industrial trade fairs (SITF) and the sponsoring organization, and briefly reviewing past and current fairs, will facilitate the design of a strategic framework for the future. This discussion attempts to integrate marketing into the strategic process model in this setting. A design template for the overall design is provided. As firms realize the importance of a customer-centric focus, they are developing customer-centric strategy, business processes, and infrastructure that serve and build relationships with customers (Javalgi et al., 2005).

Figure 7. The Three Field Plot Using-R

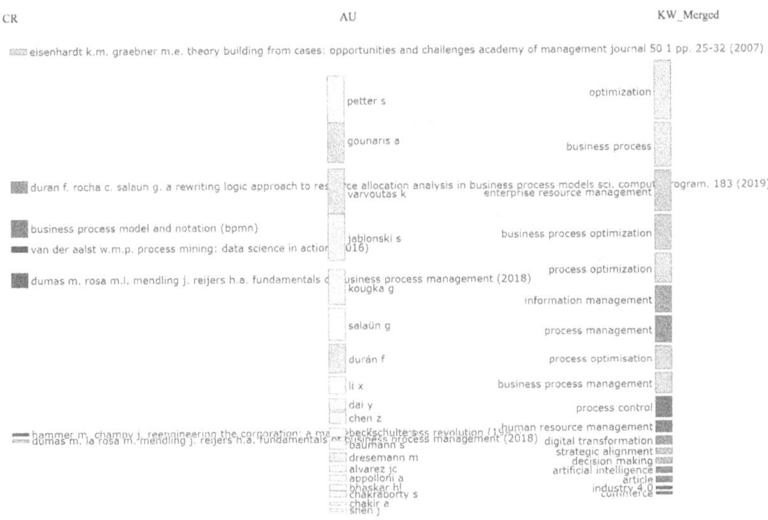

The Three-Field Plot visualization highlights the interconnectedness between influential authors, core references, and key thematic keywords such as "business process," "optimization," "process management," and "strategic alignment." This alignment affirms the academic relevance of the proposed research topic. The prominence of BPM-related themes alongside emerging marketing-oriented keywords, such as "decision making" and "customer satisfaction," indicates a growing scholarly interest in bridging operational efficiency with market responsiveness. Thus, this study is well-positioned to make a meaningful contribution by developing integrative strategies that enhance customer-centric value through BPM and marketing synergy.A synthesis of assumptions is needed to bridge the gap between business process management and digital innovation research, benefiting both fields and promoting convergent conversations(Mendling et al., 2020).An integrated customer relationship management (CRM) vision accomplishes this in two ways. First, it reflects a customer-centric business strategy that creates competitive value for customers, such as time and customization advantages for mass customization pioneers. Second, it aligns the company's overall CRM vision with its business processes and key constituents (customers, employees, and business partners) through a cross-functional approach. It is suggested that this aligned customer-relationship exchange can enhance relational marketing, and lead to sustainable competitive advantage in performance.New business process management logics, such as light touch processes, infrastructural flexibility, and mindful actors, are needed in the context of digital transformation (Baiyere et al., 2020).

The strategic framework consists of target global consumers, and the integration and alignment of a company's overall CRM with vision, processes, and key constituents.AI-based CRMs can enhance B2B digital marketing by improving data-driven decision-making and managing company information (Saura et al., 2021). E-commerce platforms and social networking have significantly influenced consumer marketing strategies, enabling businesses to understand consumer needs better and share innovative information in a competitive global environment(Rosário & Raimundo, 2021). Targeting global consumers represents one component of the customer-centric business strategy within the framework.Data-driven marketing practices and digital technologies have transformed marketing from a primarily ad-focused function to an increasingly data-driven, fiscally responsible, and technology-enabled function(Shah & Murthi, 2021). As it is challenging for companies to be customer-centric in all facets and compete effectively with every competitor, a customer-centric focus is aimed at a limited group of target global consumers. However, it is of key importance that this group can significantly influence the companies involved (Vivas et al., 2014)

6.2. Integration of BPM and Marketing

User satisfaction, a key concept in both marketing and Business Process Management (BPM), is a primary focus area for companies worldwide. Unfortunately, most companies have not yet adopted true customer-centric strategies due to their high complexity and the lack of appropriate tools. As companies in India recognize the importance of user satisfaction through customer-centric processes, an approach to enhancing these processes will be beneficial for companies, especially in a country with a large number of potential customers. Interactive marketing, defined as bi-directional value creation and mutual-influence marketing through active customer connection, engagement, participation, and interaction, has evolved into the fastest-growing business field, driven by mobile applications and interactive content (Wang, 2021). Undoubtedly business process management (BPM) to facilitate Industry 4.0 implementation in manufacturing organizations, offering benefits such as improved productivity, reduced inefficiencies, lower production and maintenance costs, and enhanced system agility and flexibility(Butt, 2020).The approach integrates BPM and marketing instruments into a guiding framework for enhancing customer-centric processes, which is based on company-internal, process-associated, and promotional factors. And Marketing agility is the ability to rapidly adapt to market changes, with challenges including brand consistency, scaling, data privacy, and hiring marketing leaders(Kalaignanam et al., 2021). As, Customer privacy concerns in retail can be mitigated by considering retail channels and data sensitivity, as well as research setting factors like region, measurement scale, and participant selection(Okazaki et al., 2020). Digital business capabilities significantly improve firm and customer performance, with greater impact on B-to-consumer firms(Wielgos et al., 2021). This framework supports Indian companies in systematically generating enhanced customer-centric processes and, consequently, fosters customer satisfaction and loyalty.

7. BENEFITS AND CHALLENGES

Redefining and aligning business processes and implementing new customer-centric processes is a significant challenge to Indian firms in the services sector. Drawing upon the resource-based view and marketing capabilities, an integrative strategic approach to enhance customer-centric processes is proposed. Marketing in digital business platforms helps increase interactions, reduce transaction costs, and enable value creation and appropriation, but requires careful coordination among users(Rangaswamy et al., 2020).India is a growing economy with great potential for growth in services sectors. It can greatly benefit from enhancing business process management (BPM) capability to serve both domestic and foreign markets. Exporting or outsourcing firms will benefit by having better customer-centric processes in place, including processes for communicating with clients and production, and faster turnaround times, etc. While firms that concentrate on India's growing domestic market stand to benefit by enhancing standardization processes to reduce dependence on key people and improve VFM. This research builds upon (Pradabwong et al., 2017)'s integration of resource-based view (RBV) and market orientation to develop a new integrative strategic approach to align BPM and marketing. In the suggested frameworks, BPM capabilities are considered a strategic asset for process innovation and reconfiguration, which results in improving customer-centric processes. In return, the differentiation in customer-centric processes leads to more favorable customer perceptions and market positioning.

8. CUSTOMER-CENTRIC PROCESSES IN INDIA

In today's rapidly changing business environment innovating at pace, with efficiency, and with quality are critical requirements for success. The organizations that will deliver performance better than the rest will have one common feature. They will have the relationship with the customer at the heart of their operation(Clark & Myers, 2018). It became evident that, with the freeing up of world trade, changing market regulations, and the opening up of new markets in different countries, the company's business processes would have to support the demands of both customers and suppliers.Organizational mindfulness towards digital transformation enhances the development of digital technology-enabled information processing capacity, leading to increased market agility(Li et al., 2021). Customer-centric strategies have therefore been suggested as a solution for companies that need to adapt to the rapidly changing competitive environment. Alternatively, holistic strategies have been suggested which have at their heart the total understanding of the business on which the company is built. A basic acceptance has been that companies that truly understand their core business competences, skills, and capabilities, as well as the customer perspective, will be more successful. The outcome should be a customer-centric business strategy.

Customer-centricity is expected to be a bi-directional flow of information and may require companies to move closer to their customers in a new partnership relationship.Customer information resources, such as customer information assets and information analysis capabilities, are increasingly important sources of competitive advantage in the digital data-rich market environment (Varadarajan, 2020). Customer-centric strategies raise many important questions for practitioners that need to be answered. This paper examines a customer-centric strategy in the context of a specific industry, namely parts logistics. It asks the question: How can a customer-centric strategy be effectively implemented by a specialist 3PL parts logistics provider to better serve its customer, the vehicle manufacturer? It aims to analyze the effect that customer-centric strategies have on the business performance and competiveness of suppliers. Customer-centric organizations have the ability to derive insights from these inputs and make adjustments as necessary. Establishing agility across the organization requires proactive action but doing so can create a competitive edge. Quantitative data points to a clear line of sight to customers, as nearly two-thirds of respondents from top adopter organizations say that customer-centric strategy provides a clear line of sight to customers.

Additionally, two-thirds of top adopter organizations recognize the role of customer initiatives in maintaining their competitive edge. Such organizations dedicate more employee time and resources to customer initiatives, supporting customer-centric strategy. Leading organizations utilize data and analytics in significantly more customer-related initiatives for innovation. Lastly, strong adherence to customer-centric principles is a hallmark of top adopters, with 82% of these organizations incorporating customer input into product development, compared to only 32% of all other organizations.

8.1. Cultural Considerations

In our paper, we carefully incorporated emerging empirical evidence from both developed and developing countries. Customer relationship management encompasses a range of technologies, strategic practices, and organizational reforms aimed at enriching and retaining a customer base. Countries like India were identified as having their own unique challenges in successfully designing and deploying CRM systems, as well as ensuring the mutual compatibility of Western CRM software with indigenous business processes. Reflecting these trends, this exploratory pilot study examines how high-growth Indian companies utilize business software applications for customer-centric purposes and analyzes the strategic drivers and outcomes associated with these applications (Ali & Alshawi, n.d.).

An exploratory pilot study employs multiple methods to analyze process workflow diagrams. Four in-depth case study companies were surveyed, all of which boast annual growth rates exceeding twenty percent per annum over the past three years. Additionally, information technology methodologies from three of the four pan-Indian business solution providers were also collected and examined. The interconnected documentation of this partnership further fails to reveal the business motivations or outcomes associated with the purchased software(Sha et al., 2020). Very few BPE concepts are utilized. Instead, the simple help-desk bewilderment queue is categorized into two failure types: billing errors and service errors. Behavioral evidence may be scrutinized to determine if repair times for each group of failures have independent, country-wide distributions. Similarly, a QAP model is structured to model the effectiveness of each re-engineering effort in attenuating the failure rate over time. All four companies have CRM software solutions under active discussion or development. Responsive to these opportunities, a research alliance involving the business school and the pan-Indian software provider is forged to examine how CRM software could be strategically adapted to these culturally contingent goals.

9. STRATEGIC APPROACHES FOR INTEGRATION

Figure 8. Strategic Approaches for Integration

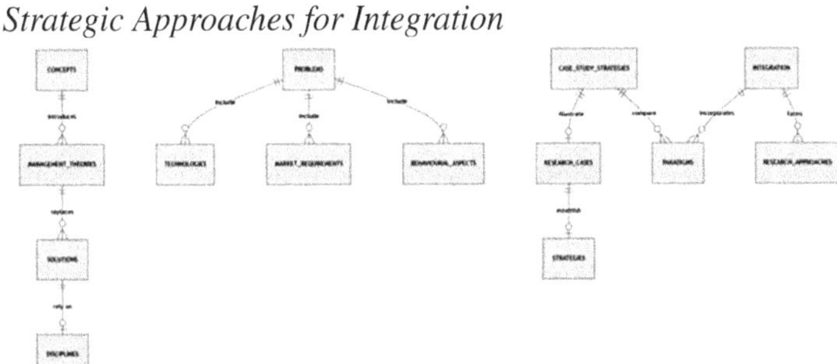

Introduction of new concepts and methods to predominantly management theories nowadays replaces solutions that traditionally rely on a single discipline or paradigm (Chakraborty et al., 2023). The main catalyst for this development is the increased complexity of real-life problems, which are characterized by diverse technologies, market requirements, and behavioral aspects. In this new framework, case study strategies, which are often used to illustrate the application of the new methods, are becoming broader than establishing the preliminary strategy for each projected research case or comparing alternative paradigms. This situation provided the groundwork for integrating different methodological paradigms into new research approaches. Such an example of an enriched approach was its development and implementation for the study of the strategy and marketing interface, in which business engineering methods, game theory, and systems thinking were incorporated into a traditional management theory base (Duarte et al., 2022). This effort resulted in a series of studies suggesting new entries and strategic perspectives for the conceptual study of the interactions between a company's strategic process, competitive framework, market orientation, and marketing mix tools.

Impact assessment studies constitute an important strategic step that policy-makers have to face in cases requiring the movement of significant public funds. This job is becoming harder to be performed, because competition between ideas, development targets, location alternatives etc., is getting harder and this has shown the need for enriching the methodological kit usedThe form of this approach constitutes a structured framework capable to offer a common and versatile ground where these who "think" the project and those "selling" it would make a fruitful workshop. This might weigh the balance between cost, benefits, and the inherent risks of a project, allowing ultimate funding decisions as well as supporting some procedural guidelines that maximize its eventual realization (Fedorova et al., 2024).

9.1. Best Practices

There are numerous best practices with respect to successfully initiating and conducting a BPM implementation effort. The model used for the BPM effort should be based on the desired level of customer focus and the scope of process improvement. The BPM effort must have committed employees, interdepartmental cooperation, top management involvement, and be in a supportive organizational culture. In addition, it is essential to employ appropriate communication channels so that employees can voice their opinions on process problems and the implementation of improvements.As Channel integration enhances cognitive customer experiences more than affective customer experiences(Gao et al., 2021).

Due to the new customer-focused marketing strategy, orientation is motivating Indian organizations to reevaluate the way they conduct business and interact with their customers, turning challenges into advantages. Business Process Management (BPM) is an established technique in both the business and academic communities for analyzing, optimizing, redesigning, and managing business processes. This paper provides insights and guidelines to Indian organizations seeking to yield a comprehensive benefit from the integration of Marketing (Mk) with Business) Process Management (Vrakas et al., 2021).

Firm strategy, structure, and rivalry; factor (input) conditions; related and supporting industries; government; chance; and macro-environmental (political, economic, social, technological, ecological, legal) factors are considered to be the main drivers of a country's business environment. Macro-environmental factors, government actions and regulations, and continuously evolving revenue conditions make the marketing environment more uncertain, complex, and competitive (Yar-mohammadian et al., 2014).

9.2. The Role of Marketing in Business Processes

The omnipresent paradigm of globalization, highlighted by competitive advantage, education, and e-culture, has paved the way for marketing concepts to drive an offensive response, changing the tactics of businesses. This is achieved through the integrated prospects, which have brought closer coordination of upstream business processes among suppliers, consumers, and exporters (Dumitru & Căescu, 2013). The buyers and net collaborators of business processes are brought near to shedding worth and differentiation in business processes. This has brought with it the need to visualize the supply chain for teasing out the prospects and consequences of springing omnipresent marketing and business, along with strategies for becoming market-focused and marketing-oriented.

Marketing management is a broad concept, but it encompasses a small part of the human behavior system. The expansion of business overtakes these functions, operating 24/7. The existing concepts of marketing are not enough to accommodate and fit the profile of new circumstances. The inputs may enter the marketing system and emerge as outputs in the business world. It constitutes the input, output, process, task and component. Moreover, the marketing subsystems may also influence other subsystems of the business (Balabko et al., n.d.). The marketing sub-function connects with other business processes, such as knowledge, R&D, manufacturing, operations, distribution/logistics, and supply chain, to create an integrated prospect. It is not and feather purchases to exports, which is a most competitive advantage through dimensions. Through coordination, the conceptual and practical approaches aim to establish the importance of a new e-paradigm business management approach for marketing. In the view of neo-classical thought, mass marketing is the paradigm under which the marketing system turns pages, dos and don'ts. This imparts to every business a business and a market that is everything to everybody.

The significant influences of e-marketing and viewing global marketing through an e-culture lens have necessitated a confrontation with e-knowledge management to overcome the aforementioned divisional views of e-business and marketing. In addition to this, Influencer marketing is an effective and cost-efficient marketing tool; however, strategic use and understanding of its impact are crucial for businesses to maximize its potential (Ye et al., 2021). The interdisciplinary view on philosophical and functional perspectives, being rudimentary, is also gone, and this sets the foundation. The interaction of purchasing and human behaviour opportunities with differentiations and remote marketing tactics raises the choice for prospects and consequently the elimination of prospect avoidance attacks, leading to purchasing and choosing types of decision-making. Every bastion tracks these prospects & devises offensive behaviours(P. S. Dahake & Somani, 2024). By using ICT to arm the prospects, every business is caused to do marketing from concept to process on a well planned Production & Operations Servers just like bank transactions and not in an instinctive way. For business process growth with integrated view a conceptual framework of interaction & technological processes forming consensus on and compliance of e-compliance business process marketing is formulated.

10. MEASURING SUCCESS

Figure 9. Factors for Measuring Success

BPMF must be maintained and further developed to give a theoretical foundation for BPMF. In addition, it is proposed to recast existing and develop new BPMMs that could be used under any commonly known BPM approach. Business Process Management (BPM) is a significant approach to creating economic benefits, primarily by enhancing an organization's agility in adapting to changes in market and competitive environments. Marketing is based on analyzing behavior and user experiences. The focus lies on a customer- and operation-oriented view of processes.

As a result a new method is built first to evaluate the current range of customer view in processes. This is a new finding in the scientific literature, representing a point of deviation from the common research trend of increasingly successful cases. In practice, it will be possible to determine the amount of effort needed to invest in the business to close the remaining gaps towards optimization. The procedure should be maintained, especially given its advantages of knowing how much has been achieved and how far there is still to be done (Richman Miyambu & Matshonisa Seeletse, 2016). At a theoretical level, a generalized model should be developed with appropriate statistical tests that can be used under any TQM approach, such as Six Sigma or other less well-known approaches, when factors are measured.

10.1. Key Performance Indicators (KPIs)

The Study is focused on the way that a company can use an innovative marketing tool (on-property banners). Typically, these companies focus only on promotion, distribution, and pricing decisions, often neglecting other Marketing's P's (Personnel, Process, and Physical evidence). However, people (Personnel), process and physical proof are essential, especially if a company wants to implement a more advanced marketing. Savvy companies will optimize six different elements to enhance the overall consumer receiving: Front-line Employee, Customers, Process, Banners, Physical Surrounding & Employee Work Practices (P. S. Dahake, Chandak, et al., 2024). Therefore, this research suggests integrating the six different types of innovative activities on the frontlines as part of the overall marketing strategy.

Monitoring of the above-mentioned innovative activities are made by monthly observations at time of check in (1st round test) and time of check out (2nd round test) of different guests (promoters, passives and detractors per the Net promoter score). Secondly, the chain analysis of the guests involved in the innovative marketing activities is performed by 10 in-depth interviews with different guests (promoters, passive and detractors per the Net promoter score). Third, semi-structured interviews are conducted with the three top managers from the marketing, hotel design, and operations departments, as well as an independent operations expert and an academic expert in the marketing field.

Pointing out that they also serve to competitors and differentiate the company from them, to a certain extent, they want to keep them in the dark. Additionally, some questions are considered disturbingly confidential and if disclosed might harm the company (Abdullah et al., n.d.).

11. FUTURE TRENDS AND INNOVATIONS

There are many ways that businesses fuel growth and drive success. The fundamentals of production and selling goods have evolved to encompass a focus more on services and experiences (Dibley et al., 2016). The customer-centric approach taken by companies aims to become indispensable to consumers. In recent years companies have come to realize that understanding their customer's journey is vital to success. Utilizing a comprehensive and integrated business process management (BPM) and marketing approach, customer-centric processes can be enhanced. For businesses who compete on service or customer experience, it is vital to understand how today's customer relationships with companies develop over their entire lifecycle. Additionally, this research provides a snapshot of the services marketplace in India. Services have grown at an incredible and consistent rate for over two decades. Due to advances in technology and increased globalization, companies now have the opportunity to sell their services to a larger audience. This study tries to synthesize and understand the channels through which the services marketplace has recently changed in the context of emerging and diversifying Indian markets. Strategies for growth are no longer identical for product-based and service-based businesses. It has been noted that an increasing number of companies in India are seeking to implement some form of lifecycle-based management approach to integrate business processes (Zhang et al., 2021). While the lifecycle itself is a well-established concept, less attention has been given to understanding how this concept interacts with how companies organize themselves to deliver services. In light of this, there are various approaches to structuring a company's management. To deliver services effectively as a process, sales, production, and customer satisfaction must be aligned. Using advanced analytics to examine and map customers' interactions with a company over their entire lifecycle enables an organization to gain a comprehensive understanding of the gaps in the services offered and subsequently close them.

11.1. Emerging Technologies

The outcomes from building on the strategic management model proposed comprise a coupled, interlinked set of customer-centric processes and potential business goals that can then be pursued through BPM. In a study of four Indian service sector organizations, empirical validation is provided for the key model components, along with insights into the practical implications of aligning an organization's activities more closely with its prioritized business goals. This validation and insight provide a better understanding of how business operations can be more effectively directed to optimize performance and thus achieve broader strategic goals (Hunhevicz & Hall, 2020).

The methodology adopted merges and adapts established marketing, entrepreneurship, strategic management, and BPM approaches to more coherently describe the strategic opportunities the organization can pursue and how these can be realized in terms of targeted, customer-centric processes. This methodology was initially developed through a broader review of developments in the fields of marketing and entrepreneurship, as these are largely subject-specific to BPM theory. Select elements necessary for BPM theory incorporate ideas from specific commercial methods of approach to BPM-based exploration of business processes. The resulting aspect was elaborated upon through strategic management theory, utilizing a business model canvas as a practical and generally applicable approach to strategic planning.

12. SUMMARY OF FINDINGS

Figure 10. Thematic Map Using-R

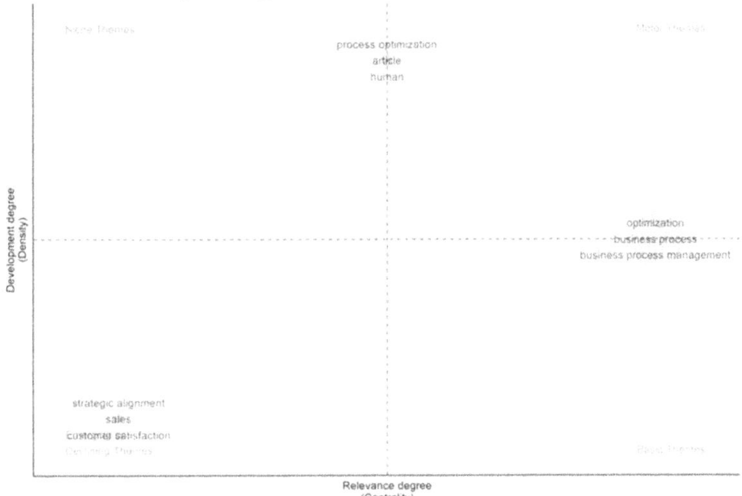

The clustering of keywords such as "optimization," "business process," and "business process management" in the Basic Themes quadrant characterized by high centrality but lower density demonstrates their foundational role in the field. These themes are crucial yet require further development and strategic integration. In contrast, "process optimization" appears in the Niche Themes quadrant, indicating specialized, mature research with less connectivity. This justifies the relevance of the proposed study, as it aims to strategically integrate BPM with marketing to develop customer-centric processes, bridging foundational research with advanced, targeted applications to enhance organizational performance and customer value.Primary data was collected through interviews to gather insights about the concepts of Business Process Management (BPM) and Customer Relationship Management (CRM) and their application in the Indian environment and about the need of integrating BPM and Marketing, as in India, organisations face major challenges in the marketplace and are suffering from the huge pressure due to the increasing competition, changing customer preferences, and embracing rigorous technologies(P. S. Dahake & Dahake, 2024). The data were collected through semi-structured interviews with qualified professionals involved in CRM/BPM across a broad range of organisations. Data were documented, and transcriptions of the recorded interviews formed the basis of the analysis for the current research. The major findings of the research are presented in the following sections: Key Drivers of Customer Relationship Management, Application of Customer Relationship Management, Integration of Business Process Management with Customer Relationship Management, and the Concept of Demand Chain and CRM.

Business Process Management (BPM) and Marketing are two significant concepts that are widely discussed independently in modern organisations. Both focus on managing business activities, but from different aspects. BPM concentrates on enhancing the efficiency of internal business activities and the overall agility of an organisation. At the same time, Marketing focuses on providing customers with superior value and beneficial practices that benefit both the customers and the organisation. On the one hand, BPM aims to eliminate everything that appears to be waste, unnecessary duplicated effort that doesn't add value to the final product. Marketing supports structuring business processes so that they become customer-centric, starting from demand and creating the product. Common languages and frameworks are needed.

Respondents perceived that businesses can hardly survive without a strong relationship with their customers. It is widely believed that customers are the major driving force behind any successful business(Nicolás-Agustín et al., 2022). Marketing focuses on retaining the existing customers more than acquiring new ones. Online Marketing gains an edge over traditional methods in reaching global customers. However, over time, as customer requirements and expectations have evolved, there has been a growing need to shift from a company-centric to a more customer-centric model. The marketing strategies kept evolving accordingly. This paved the way for the modern concept called Customer Relationship Marketing. The entire concept is facilitated by CRM, which enables a business to manage, organize, and synchronize various areas, including sales, customer service, technical support, and marketing, concerning current, targeted, and potential customers.

On the other hand, according to IBM's prediction, customers themselves will drive the process. Consequently, Customer Relationship Management will reshape existing business functions within the organisation through a customer-centric view. As a result, companies must think about their business processes as part of a sequence of customer-driven interactions that defend the whole organisation. Thus BPM and CRM can be seen as two concepts that complement each other there's a growing awareness of the potentialities of creating a synergy between these two (BPM and CRM), where the first can assure the efficiency of the processes and the second can help structuring them to become customer-centric.

13. PRACTICAL IMPLICATIONS

Business Process Management (BPM) needs to be adopted strategically to add value to a business. It is a systematic approach for capturing the knowledge of processes and maximizing their potential, resulting in increased quality and efficiency. BPM provides organizations the ability to track processes and make improvements where needed. BPM, combined with marketing automation, can significantly improve companies' campaign management processes. It can also help align more intimate marketing processes with business processes and automate a company's customer-centric business, marketing, and operational processes. AI-powered marketing has significantly improved efficiency, personalization, and strategic decision-making in various functions; however, limitations and ethical implications must be addressed (Kumar et al., 2024).While many companies are realizing the potential benefits of BPM and one-to-one marketing automation, few are incorporating or contemplating the strategic implications of how these technologies could potentially benefit revenue assurance and billing fulfillment chains, or a company's business model itself. Using BPM strategically can enable a company to capitalize on its unique operating environment and differentiate itself in a hyper-competitive marketplace. For example, India is a country with a business environment that offers its own unique set of challenges.By integrating BPM strategically with CRM and one-to-one marketing in India, premium business prospects can be delivered via a fully operational and automated BPM chain designed to enhance and streamline the fulfillment process. With its focus on integrating BPM and CRM fulfillment from a strategic and global marketing perspective, this paper is likely to be of interest to global CEOs, CMOs, CTOs, and their respective IT and marketing departments.

In regards to how this process could potentially benefit other businesses, discussions are put forth in terms of what is to be done and how best to utilize this unique operating chain and business environment, market challenges, legal hurdles, and market entry difficulties of this operational fulfillment chain, as well as points or counter-points to the proposed conclusions moving forward for further operational fulfillment chain and business modeling chain research, particularly in other regions of the world (Aslam et al., 2023).

14. RESULT & DISCUSSION BASED ON THE LITERATURE

Business Process Management (BPM) examines the decision-making strategies and designs that managers employ in overseeing and coordinating a firm's strategic business processes. The first research task is to select the extant knowledge covering marketing innovations and integrate those insights into the connective knowledge base. This step will be under the search strings of: "business process management" AND "customer relationship management, customer engagement management, customer experience management, marketing" and "business process reengineering" AND "customer" AND "marketing" simultaneously; "method" and the above ten search terms/word strings. Other relevant research works, such as co-citation analysis, will be utilized to ensure the comprehensiveness of the literature collection. The pre-process of selected papers includes gathering metadata, storing and organizing files, citation analysis and generating co-occurrence matrices.

To enhance this knowledge system, it is necessary to develop an ecosystem development process model and a customer engagement and communication cycle map. Based on this model, a calibration perspective and challenges on method applications are drawn. Then the analysis knowledge structure will be gradually developed. Applying content analysis on the newly delineated knowledge systematically, the research work will help uncover the knowledge integration opportunities and formulate new connective research opportunities. Furthermore, it is necessary to decompose an existing BPM method to improve it for marketing innovations and design a new method. A novel mapping method will be designed to achieve the above intent. In terms of enhancing a pure BPM method for practical marketing usage, analyzing new requirement specifications of the underlying components and method steps is important.In contrast, Marketing integrates activities that direct the flow of goods and services to satisfy, and hence be valued by, for three goods that weigh heavily in addressing today's business challenges:

(1) New product design and marketing
(2) Pricing
(3) Branding

BPM's decision strategies and marketing frameworks have developed along largely separate lines until recently. Attempts to harmonize the fields from the viewpoint of BPM have centered on bridging the gap between the current morning-ground and evening-ground, as well as formalizing decision strategies for multi-functional integration (Vivas et al., 2014). The current gap across marketing sub-disciplines in these respects has likewise gone largely unaddressed. A fruitful approach to the convergence of these fields is to explore the commonalities of approach processes, encompassing investigative rigor, levels of abstraction, and facets of integration. This relatively new perspective in the marketing context reveals profit opportunities that have likely gone mostly unnoticed heretofore. While business-level customer-related resources that support customer management and profitability, as well as the customer resource-based view of the firm, have recently garnered a large following, limited contributions have addressed bartering with customer prospects in parallel with the potential contributions of BPM to customer resource management. Over the past decade or so, the growing internationalization and rapid advances in communication-based technology have led to significant sociological and organizational changes (Aslam et al., 2023). In turn, this has led to new realizations and marketing challenges, drawing serious managerial attention.

Key among these are:

(1) Changing ways in which goods are produced, marketed, priced, distributed, and consumed; (2) Increasing salience of goods not as simple blanks as historically understood, but as promises co-created by customers, goods providers, and retailers with their corresponding before-, during-, and after-sales functions catering to the different goods offering, purchasing, and consumption processes; (3) New marketing goods processes and systems.

Many upstream suppliers of goods have internalized the shift from goods dominance to customer domination in markets since the late 1980s. Pursuing customer-based strategies has encouraged firm clamor for means other than product, price, and promotion to create customer-perceived value.

15. PRACTICAL RECOMMENDATIONS

First, organizations aiming to adopt an integrated strategy for BPM and marketing should prepare their internal culture for such an approach. Integrating BPM and marketing might shift how stakeholders view the objectives of marketing and process management. BPM generally aims to create higher efficiency and lower costs, while marketing tends to focus on higher revenue. Without an initial understanding of the convergence between the two domains, the strategy can be rejected as being too risky (Prodanova & Van Looy, 2019). Second, organizations should ensure that objectives related to client-centricity in both domains are highlighted. For example, when implementing a BPM system, any deviations in the marketing department that do not adhere to a uniform marketing process can lead to the rejection of the entire BPM system. Likewise, for marketing automation systems, differences in the definitions of brand awareness or the way to gather social mentions can also lead to a lack of adoption. Third, organizations need to safeguard the process of adding new technology in both domains. It is essential to clarify that, if systems are introduced in either the BPM or marketing domain, new adjacent systems should be implemented to ensure the integration is safeguarded. For example, when introducing a marketing system to ensure that qualified leads are quickly passed on to the CRM, BPM should also be considered to prevent leads from being lost elsewhere in the process. Making this clear should ensure a two-way view from both departments, resulting in an advocacy tool that safeguards integration. Customer engagement behavior can be categorized into organic and promoted pathways, with their influence varying based on engagement context, industry, product type, and cultural context (Barari et al., 2021).

16. CONCLUSION AND RECOMMENDATIONS

This article introduces an integrated change management framework to effectively integrate customer-centric business models, business processes, and customer relations management in Indian industries. For decades, companies have invested significant resources in developing and enhancing their businesses; however, creating customer-centric processes in a highly fragmented, multilayered society like India is no small feat. Nonetheless, business process management and customer-centric models, due to their inherent focus on understanding, capturing, and optimizing business in the direction of customers, are one of the most potent weapons available to face this formidable challenge. Thus, a comprehensive conceptual overview is presented, with the hope of triggering research (N. S. Dahake, Gajghate, et al., 2024). Understanding customer preferences has become a priority among management disciplines because of the adoption of the customer-centric approach to business strategy. The marketing activity aims to ensure that customer needs are matched with the organizational provision through the effective use of the marketing mix. The business process management (BPM) activity aims to ensure maximal effectiveness and efficiency of processes. Marketing and BPM are therefore closely interrelated activities in terms of customer-centric focus. Also, BPM can enhance customer-centric processes by integrating marketing-focused activities in process design, execution, and monitoring. Notably, Technological, socioeconomic, and geopolitical trends are reshaping marketing, necessitating radical changes in marketing strategies and management(Rust, 2020).

Nevertheless, both concepts are usually treated separately, which limits the strategic impact on process performance. This research addresses the literature gap with a systematic review that identifies avenues for future studies in integrating BPM and marketing. Customer big data analytics significantly improves customer relationship performance and sales growth in B2B firms, with stronger effects in firms with a supportive analytics culture(Hallikainen et al., 2020).

The outcome of this research can guide scholars toward future studies on the intersection of BPM and marketing fields by identifying seminal works and trends. The outcome can also benefit practitioners responsible for customer-centric processes by identifying specific areas for innovative ideas in select marketing-focused BPM principles, thereby optimizing the benefits from the scientific literature. This study offers an overview of the development of scientific research on integrating BPM and marketing. The scientific landscape is visualized using a bibliometric approach, which provides a clear understanding of the current state and potential future directions for research. Considering the recent emergence of the literature connecting BPM and marketing, such a review is nevertheless lacking. The bibliometric analysis focuses on journal articles because the classification schemes provide the most flexibility for mapping the state and output of a research field. The network of co-citation, co-occurrence, and bibliographic coupling is created and visualized. This literature analysis reveals key contributions and the evolution of research on integrating BPM and marketing with regard to fundamental literature and trending topics. Overall, this analysis highlights three principal areas for future studies that further integrate BPM and marketing. The first area is dynamic pricing and promotion strategies. The second area focuses on advanced marketing principles for BPM. Next, the debate on customer involvement in process design, execution, and monitoring is fruitful to pursue. Likewise, individual and governance-related marketing knowledge should also be a topic that merits future investigation. The final area is directed towards examining and influencing customers' processes, enabling the introduction of engagement as a critical concept in customer-centric businesses. Since the introduction of engagement as a critical concept in customer-centric businesses, new styles of market communication that proactively source influence from customers as potential co-producers have emerged and gained ground, deserving attention. The framework is illustrated by a case study of the Indian railway industry emphasizing both its strength and potential (Nteo, 2017). Unfortunately, it is noted there is as much misalignment and inadequate management of the proposed linkages. In the alignment, it is possible to capture distinct sources of value for the customer, which is critical when targeting hyper-fragmented markets, such as those in India.

17. FUTURE SCOPE OF THE STUDY

All research studies have limitations, and understanding these limitations is crucial for comprehending the research's implications and for designing future studies. Following this research model, this section first identifies five theoretically grounded boundaries and limitations of the study, as well as several practical constraints and suggestions for future research. Second, the broader applicability of the research is discussed. The three qualitative studies yielded first insights beyond the boundaries and limitations outlined earlier: First, none of the interview partners mentioned the business process management systems they use. A similar finding was reported in a study on the benefits of social media for business process management, indicating that many companies do not utilize any system (Prodanova & Van Looy, 2019). This may reveal a significant difference between countries. Second, two interview partners emphasized that their companies are too small for business process management and that they do not use any. These statements might indicate widened boundaries. The prevalence of business process management in different countries could be explored, as this was not examined herein. Third, the qualitative studies focused on customer-centric business processes, largely neglecting other marketing capabilities that might also benefit from better integration with business process management.

As previously mentioned, the research model is grounded in the resource-based view, dynamic capabilities, business process management, and marketing literature. Future research could expand the study to include other literature and companies, as well as other countries and industries. Several practical constraints were encountered during the study. Due to the significant variability among the research candidates, it was not possible to use a standardized questionnaire or statistical tools or software to analyze the quantitative data. Questions were constantly adjusted according to the candidates. Consequently, quantitative results cannot be generalized. However, the results may utilize rich data for rigorous standardized analysis in future studies. Future studies could draw on various literature and methods, such as the networking approach or longitudinal studies, to explain the reasons for non-integration.

REFERENCES

Abdullah, R., Mohamad, E., & Muhamad, M. R. (n.d.). *Managing Key Performance Indicators (KPIs): A Case Study at an Aerospace Manufacturing Facility.*

Adams, N., Augusto, A., Davern, M., & Rosa, M. L. (2023). *Five guidelines to improve context-aware process selection: An Australian banking perspective* (No. arXiv:2304.05033). arXiv. https://doi.org//arXiv.2304.05033DOI: 10.48550

Ali, M. A. A., & Alshawi, S. (n.d.). A CULTURAL APPROACH TO STUDY CUSTOMER RELATIONSHIP MANAGEMENT (CRM). *Systems.*

Aslam, H., Waseem, M., Muneeb, D., Ali, Z., Roubaud, D., & Grebinevych, O. (2025). Customer integration in the supply chain: The role of market orientation and supply chain strategy in the age of digital revolution. *Annals of Operations Research, 348*(3), 2145–2169. DOI: 10.1007/s10479-023-05191-y PMID: 36846244

Azemi, E., & Bala, S. (n.d.). *Exploring BPM Adoption and Strategic Alignment of Processes at Raiffeisen Bank Kosovo.*

Bag, S., Gupta, S., Kumar, A., & Sivarajah, U. (2021). An integrated artificial intelligence framework for knowledge creation and B2B marketing rational decision making for improving firm performance. *Industrial Marketing Management, 92*, 178–189. DOI: 10.1016/j.indmarman.2020.12.001

Baiyere, A., Salmela, H., & Tapanainen, T. (2020). Digital transformation and the new logics of business process management. *European Journal of Information Systems, 29*(3), 238–259. DOI: 10.1080/0960085X.2020.1718007

Balabko, P., Wegmann, A., Ruppen, A., & Clément, N. (n.d.). *The Value of Roles in Modeling Business Processes.*

Barari, M., Ross, M., Thaichon, S., & Surachartkumtonkun, J. (2021). A meta-analysis of customer engagement behaviour. *International Journal of Consumer Studies, 45*(4), 457–477. DOI: 10.1111/ijcs.12609

Butt, J. (2020). A Conceptual Framework to Support Digital Transformation in Manufacturing Using an Integrated Business Process Management Approach. *Designs, 4*(3), 17. DOI: 10.3390/designs4030017

Cartwright, S., Liu, H., & Raddats, C. (2021). Strategic use of social media within business-to-business (B2B) marketing: A systematic literature review. *Industrial Marketing Management, 97*, 35–58. DOI: 10.1016/j.indmarman.2021.06.005

Chakraborty, S., Datta, H. N., Kalita, K., & Chakraborty, S. (2023). A narrative review of multi-objective optimization on the basis of ratio analysis (MOORA) method in decision making. *OPSEARCH*, *60*(4), 1844–1887. DOI: 10.1007/s12597-023-00676-7

Clark, M., & Myers, A. (2018). *How customer-centric are you?* [Report]. Henley Centre for Customer Management. http://www.hccmsite.co.uk

Cull, R. (2010). *HYBRID PROCESS MODELLING WITHIN BUSINESS PROCESS MANAGEMENT PROJECTS.*

Dahake, N. S., Gajghate, A., Dahake, P. S., & Bansod, S. (2024). A Transformative Impact of IoT and AI by Predictive Analytics on Modern Marketing Strategies: A Study of its Significance & Accuracy. *2024 2nd International Conference on Advances in Computation, Communication and Information Technology (ICAICCIT)*, 1150–1158. DOI: 10.1109/ICAICCIT64383.2024.10912388

Dahake, P. S., Bagaregari, P., & Dahake, N. S. (2024). Shaping the Future of Retail: A Comprehensive Review of Predictive Analytics Models for Consumer Behavior. In Inder, S., Min, B., & Sharma, S. (Eds.), (pp. 143–160). Advances in Business Strategy and Competitive Advantage. IGI Global., DOI: 10.4018/979-8-3693-1734-1.ch011

Dahake, P. S., Chandak, S., & Dahake, N. S. (2024). Predictive Analytics in Performance Appraisal Systems: Enhancing Objectivity and Fairness. *2024 2nd DMIHER International Conference on Artificial Intelligence in Healthcare, Education and Industry (IDICAIEI)*, 1–5. DOI: 10.1109/IDICAIEI61867.2024.10842916

Dahake, P. S., & Dahake, N. S. (2024). The Role of Big Data in Predictive Analytics for E-Commerce: Examine How Big Data Contributes to Better Predictions in Online Shopping. In Tarnanidis, T., Papathanasiou, J., Ismyrlis, V., & Kittu Manda, V. (Eds.), (pp. 403–426). Advances in Marketing, Customer Relationship Management, and E-Services. IGI Global., DOI: 10.4018/979-8-3693-9122-8.ch018

Dahake, P. S., & Somani, N. (2024). Harnessing Predictive Analytics for Accurate Consumer Behaviour Forecasting: A Comprehensive Review. *2024 2nd DMIHER International Conference on Artificial Intelligence in Healthcare, Education and Industry (IDICAIEI)*, 1–6. DOI: 10.1109/IDICAIEI61867.2024.10842743

Duarte, J., Rodrigues, F., & Castelo Branco, J. (2022). Sensing Technology Applications in the Mining Industry—A Systematic Review. *International Journal of Environmental Research and Public Health*, *19*(4), 2334. DOI: 10.3390/ijerph19042334 PMID: 35206524

Dumitru, I., & Căescu, Ş. C. (2013). The Supply Chain, a Strategic Marketing Approach. *The AMFITEATRU ECONOMIC Journal*, *15*(33), 116–127.

ENHANCING CUSTOMER LOYALTY THROUGH QUALITY OF SERVICE. EFFECTIVE STRATEGIES TO IMPROVE CUSTOMER SATISFACTION, EXPERIENCE, RELATIONSHIP, AND ENGAGEMENT. (2023). *International Research Journal of Modernization in Engineering Technology and Science*. Advance online publication. DOI: 10.56726/IRJMETS38104

Fedorova, N., Panfilov, I., Moiseeva, E., Degtyareva, K., & Markovskaya, E. (2024). Analytical methods and tools for business process optimization. *BIO Web of Conferences, 113*, 05009. DOI: 10.1051/bioconf/202411305009

Fischer, M., Imgrund, F., Janiesch, C., & Winkelmann, A. (2020). Strategy archetypes for digital transformation: Defining meta objectives using business process management. *Information & Management*, *57*(5), 103262. DOI: 10.1016/j.im.2019.103262

Fraccastoro, S., Gabrielsson, M., & Pullins, E. B. (2021). The integrated use of social media, digital, and traditional communication tools in the B2B sales process of international SMEs. *International Business Review*, *30*(4), 101776. DOI: 10.1016/j.ibusrev.2020.101776

Gao, W., Fan, H., Li, W., & Wang, H. (2021). Crafting the customer experience in omnichannel contexts: The role of channel integration. *Journal of Business Research*, *126*, 12–22. DOI: 10.1016/j.jbusres.2020.12.056

Gremler, D. D., Van Vaerenbergh, Y., Brüggen, E. C., & Gwinner, K. P. (2020). Understanding and managing customer relational benefits in services: A meta-analysis. *Journal of the Academy of Marketing Science*, *48*(3), 565–583. DOI: 10.1007/s11747-019-00701-6

Gross, S., & Vienna, W. (n.d.-a). *Navigating Through the Maze of Business Process Change Methods.*

Gross, S., & Vienna, W. (n.d.-b). *Navigating Through the Maze of Business Process Change Methods.*

Hallikainen, H., Savimäki, E., & Laukkanen, T. (2020). Fostering B2B sales with customer big data analytics. *Industrial Marketing Management*, *86*, 90–98. DOI: 10.1016/j.indmarman.2019.12.005

Hanjani, B., & Akhavan, A. (2018). *The Impact of Television and Short Message Service Advertising on Customer Behaviour and Brand Attitude.*

Holmlund, M., Van Vaerenbergh, Y., Ciuchita, R., Ravald, A., Sarantopoulos, P., Ordenes, F. V., & Zaki, M. (2020). Customer experience management in the age of big data analytics: A strategic framework. *Journal of Business Research, 116*, 356–365. DOI: 10.1016/j.jbusres.2020.01.022

Huang, M.-H., & Rust, R. T. (2021). A strategic framework for artificial intelligence in marketing. *Journal of the Academy of Marketing Science*, *49*(1), 30–50. DOI: 10.1007/s11747-020-00749-9

Hunhevicz, J. J., & Hall, D. M. (2020). Do you need a blockchain in construction? Use case categories and decision framework for DLT design options. *Advanced Engineering Informatics*, *45*, 101094. DOI: 10.1016/j.aei.2020.101094

Javalgi, R., Radulovich, L. P., Pendleton, G., & Scherer, R. F. (2005). Sustainable competitive advantage of internet firms: A strategic framework and implications for global marketers. *International Marketing Review*, *22*(6), 658–672. DOI: 10.1108/02651330510630276

Kalaignanam, K., Tuli, K. R., Kushwaha, T., Lee, L., & Gal, D. (2021). Marketing Agility: The Concept, Antecedents, and a Research Agenda. *Journal of Marketing*, *85*(1), 35–58. DOI: 10.1177/0022242920952760

Kerpedzhiev, G. D., König, U. M., Röglinger, M., & Rosemann, M. (2021). An Exploration into Future Business Process Management Capabilities in View of Digitalization: Results from a Delphi Study. *Business & Information Systems Engineering*, *63*(2), 83–96. DOI: 10.1007/s12599-020-00637-0

Koopman, A., & Seymour, L. F. (2020a). Factors Impacting Successful BPMS Adoption and Use: A South African Financial Services Case Study. *Enterprise. Lecture Notes in Business Information Processing*, *387*, 55–69. DOI: 10.1007/978-3-030-49418-6_4

Koopman, A., & Seymour, L. F. (2020b). Factors Impacting Successful BPMS Adoption and Use: A South African Financial Services Case Study. *Enterprise. Lecture Notes in Business Information Processing*, *387*, 55–69. DOI: 10.1007/978-3-030-49418-6_4

Kumar, V., Ashraf, A. R., & Nadeem, W. (2024). AI-powered marketing: What, where, and how? *International Journal of Information Management*, *77*, 102783. DOI: 10.1016/j.ijinfomgt.2024.102783

Li, H., Wu, Y., Cao, D., & Wang, Y. (2021). Organizational mindfulness towards digital transformation as a prerequisite of information processing capability to achieve market agility. *Journal of Business Research*, *122*, 700–712. DOI: 10.1016/j.jbusres.2019.10.036

Lisovsky, A. L. (2019). SUSTAINABLE DEVELOPMENT AND BUSINESS PROCESS MANAGEMENT. *Strategic Decisions and Risk Management*, *10*(3), 228–237. DOI: 10.17747/2618-947X-2019-3-228-237

Looy, A. V., VanLooy, A., Poels, G., & Poels, G. (n.d.). *A Practitioners' Point Of View On How Digital Innovation Will Shape The Future Of Business Process Management: Towards A Research Agenda.*

Ma, C., Caldera, A., Petridis, M., Bacon, L., & Windall, G. (2010a). Integration of BPM Systems. In Pomffyova, M. (Ed.), *Process Management*. InTech., DOI: 10.5772/8442

Ma, C., Caldera, A., Petridis, M., Bacon, L., & Windall, G. (2010b). Integration of BPM Systems. In Pomffyova, M. (Ed.), *Process Management*. InTech., DOI: 10.5772/8442

Martins, P. V., & Zacarias, M. (2015). Business Process and Practice Alignment Meta-model. *Procedia Computer Science*, *64*, 314–323. DOI: 10.1016/j.procs.2015.08.495

Meidan, A., García-García, J. A., Escalona, M. J., & Ramos, I. (2017). A survey on business processes management suites. *Computer Standards & Interfaces*, *51*, 71–86. DOI: 10.1016/j.csi.2016.06.003

Mendling, J., Pentland, B. T., & Recker, J. (2020). Building a complementary agenda for business process management and digital innovation. *European Journal of Information Systems*, *29*(3), 208–219. DOI: 10.1080/0960085X.2020.1755207

Mogaji, E., Soetan, T. O., & Kieu, T. A. (2021). The implications of artificial intelligence on the digital marketing of financial services to vulnerable customers. *Australasian Marketing Journal*, *29*(3), 235–242. DOI: 10.1016/j.ausmj.2020.05.003

Nicolás-Agustín, Á., Jiménez-Jiménez, D., & Maeso-Fernandez, F. (2022). The role of human resource practices in the implementation of digital transformation. *International Journal of Manpower*, *43*(2), 395–410. DOI: 10.1108/IJM-03-2021-0176

Object, object. (n.d.). *Process Learning Environments*. Retrieved June 11, 2025, from https://core.ac.uk/reader/236378450

Okazaki, S., Eisend, M., Plangger, K., De Ruyter, K., & Grewal, D. (2020). Understanding the Strategic Consequences of Customer Privacy Concerns: A Meta-Analytic Review. *Journal of Retailing*, *96*(4), 458–473. DOI: 10.1016/j.jretai.2020.05.007

Otto, A. S., Szymanski, D. M., & Varadarajan, R. (2020). Customer satisfaction and firm performance: Insights from over a quarter century of empirical research. *Journal of the Academy of Marketing Science*, *48*(3), 543–564. DOI: 10.1007/s11747-019-00657-7

Pradabwong, J., Braziotis, C., Tannock, J. D. T., & Pawar, K. S. (2017). Business process management and supply chain collaboration: Effects on performance and competitiveness. *Supply Chain Management*, *22*(2), 107–121. Advance online publication. DOI: 10.1108/SCM-01-2017-0008

Prodanova, J., & Van Looy, A. (2019). How Beneficial is Social Media for Business Process Management? A Systematic Literature Review. *IEEE Access : Practical Innovations, Open Solutions*, *7*, 39583–39599. DOI: 10.1109/ACCESS.2019.2903983

Raddats, C., Kowalkowski, C., Benedettini, O., Burton, J., & Gebauer, H. (2019). Servitization: A contemporary thematic review of four major research streams. *Industrial Marketing Management*, *83*, 207–223. DOI: 10.1016/j.indmarman.2019.03.015

Rangaswamy, A., Moch, N., Felten, C., Van Bruggen, G., Wieringa, J. E., & Wirtz, J. (2020). The Role of Marketing in Digital Business Platforms. *Journal of Interactive Marketing*, *51*(1), 72–90. DOI: 10.1016/j.intmar.2020.04.006

Richman Miyambu, G., & Matshonisa Seeletse, S. (2016). Numeric measurement of business process optimization. *Environment and Ecology*, *7*(4), 20–24. DOI: 10.21511/ee.07(4).2016.02

Rosário, A., & Raimundo, R. (2021). Consumer Marketing Strategy and E-Commerce in the Last Decade: A Literature Review. *Journal of Theoretical and Applied Electronic Commerce Research*, *16*(7), 3003–3024. DOI: 10.3390/jtaer16070164

Rust, R. T. (2020). The future of marketing. *International Journal of Research in Marketing*, *37*(1), 15–26. DOI: 10.1016/j.ijresmar.2019.08.002

Sahdeo, V. (n.d.). *A BUSINESS PROCESS MANAGEMENT FRAMEWORK FOR ENHANCING ENTERPRISE RESOURCE PLANNING VALUE DERIVED IN SUPPLY CHAIN OPTIMIZATION*.

Saura, J. R., Ribeiro-Soriano, D., & Palacios-Marqués, D. (2021). Setting B2B digital marketing in artificial intelligence-based CRMs: A review and directions for future research. *Industrial Marketing Management*, *98*, 161–178. DOI: 10.1016/j.indmarman.2021.08.006

Sha, X., Chen, J., & Teoh, S. Y. (2020). The dynamics of IT-business strategic alignment: Evidence from healthcare information systems implementation. *Information Technology & People*, *33*(5), 1465–1488. DOI: 10.1108/ITP-08-2019-0414

Shafagatova, A. (n.d.). *TOWARDS PROCESS-ORIENTED EMPLOYEE APPRAISALS AND REWARDS: AN EXPLORATORY CASE STUDY.*

Shah, D., & Murthi, B. P. S. (2021). Marketing in a data-driven digital world: Implications for the role and scope of marketing. *Journal of Business Research*, *125*, 772–779. DOI: 10.1016/j.jbusres.2020.06.062

Tomaskova, H., & Weber, G.-W. (2020). Approaches combining methods of Operational Research with Business Process Model and Notation: A systematic review. *PeerJ. Computer Science*, *6*, e301. DOI: 10.7717/peerj-cs.301 PMID: 33816952

Ujwary-Gil, A., & Potoczek, N. (n.d.). *THE USE OF A BUSINESS MODEL IN DESIGNING AND OPERATIONALIZING PROCESSES.*

Ulmer, J.-S., Belaud, J.-P., & Le Lann, J.-M. (2011). Towards a pivotal-based approach for business process alignment. *International Journal of Computer Integrated Manufacturing*, *24*(11), 1010–1021. DOI: 10.1080/0951192X.2011.597431

Varadarajan, R. (2020). Customer information resources advantage, marketing strategy and business performance: A market resources based view. *Industrial Marketing Management*, *89*, 89–97. DOI: 10.1016/j.indmarman.2020.03.003

Ventura Martins, P., & Zacarias, M. (2017). Applying the Business Process and Practice Alignment Meta-model: Daily Practices and Process Modelling. *Business Systems Research Journal*, *8*(1), 1–16. DOI: 10.1515/bsrj-2017-0001

Vivas, C., Sobreiro, P., & Claudino, R. (2014). *Integrating Knowledge Management in a Business Strategy Process Operationalized using Process Management Approach*. http://hdl.handle.net/10400.26/30197

Vrakas, G., Chan, C., & Thai, V. V. (2021). The effects of evolving port technology and process optimisation on operational performance: The case study of an Australian container terminal operator. *The Asian Journal of Shipping and Logistics*, *37*(4), 281–290. DOI: 10.1016/j.ajsl.2020.04.001

Wang, C. L. (2021). New frontiers and future directions in interactive marketing: Inaugural Editorial. *Journal of Research in Interactive Marketing*, *15*(1), 1–9. DOI: 10.1108/JRIM-03-2021-270

Wielgos, D. M., Homburg, C., & Kuehnl, C. (2021). Digital business capability: Its impact on firm and customer performance. *Journal of the Academy of Marketing Science*, *49*(4), 762–789. DOI: 10.1007/s11747-021-00771-5

Yarmohammadian, M. H., Ebrahimipour, H., & Doosty, F. (2014). Improvement of hospital processes through business process management in Qaem Teaching Hospital: A work in progress. *Journal of Education and Health Promotion*, *3*(1). Advance online publication. DOI: 10.4103/2277-9531.145902 PMID: 25540784

Ye, G., Hudders, L., De Jans, S., & De Veirman, M. (2021). The Value of Influencer Marketing for Business: A Bibliometric Analysis and Managerial Implications. *Journal of Advertising*, *50*(2), 160–178. DOI: 10.1080/00913367.2020.1857888

Zhang, Y., Liu, R., Heidari, A. A., Wang, X., Chen, Y., Wang, M., & Chen, H. (2021). Towards augmented kernel extreme learning models for bankruptcy prediction: Algorithmic behavior and comprehensive analysis. *Neurocomputing*, *430*, 185–212. DOI: 10.1016/j.neucom.2020.10.038

Chapter 7
Leveraging Artificial Intelligence and Machine Learning for Business Process Management in Digital Marketing

Parihar Suresh Dahake
https://orcid.org/0000-0002-2286-4120
Ramdeobaba University, Nagpur, India

ABSTRACT

Digital marketing is a rapid industry with ample development and investment opportunities around the world. Throughout the present economic climate, every marketer recognized the importance of a digital marketing presence. Understanding the market forces and trends that affect one brand or business can help to identify new revenue avenues (Bayoude et al., 2018). Marketers look for efficient methods to maximize returns while employing capital constraints, making sure that few budgets are spent on irrelevant or less efficient areas.

1. INTRODUCTION

Digital marketing refers to the marketing and advertising approaches that companies employ online, as opposed to traditional techniques. At the same time, it encompasses several tools or platforms based on devices such as computers, tablets, mobile phones, search engines, and social media that users use to connect to the internet. The traditional media industry has been undergoing profound structural

DOI: 10.4018/979-8-3373-3336-6.ch007

changes due to the emergence of the Internet, which is having far-reaching effects across the globe and AI can be strategically used in marketing research, strategy, and actions, benefiting mechanical AI for data collection, thinking AI for data processing, and feeling AI for customer understanding(Huang & Rust, 2021). The number of companies attempting to market their products and services online is increasing dramatically. Marketing research is particularly susceptible to the technical changes brought about by the Internet since it is at the interface of merchandise and consumption. Artificial intelligence is expected to significantly impact marketing strategies and customer behaviors, with its effectiveness enhanced when it augments human managers rather than replacing them (Davenport et al., 2020). The reason is the considerable variety of online data, in terms of its quantity, knowledge content, structure, media, and format. Digital data on markets, industries, competitors, products, and customers is more comprehensive, timely, multidimensional, and accessible than ever before. Therefore, it provides fertile ground for modeling the huge volume of digital data in digital marketing using machine learning techniques. Amidst the challenging pandemic situation, various businesses started to migrate to digital spaces. Companies started showcasing their presence on websites and investing a good chunk of money on social media marketing and search engine marketing, demanding high level of business process management systems. Digital marketing agencies started using business process management systems extensively to understand the processes to take the agency towards success. Social media marketing and search engine marketing became the way of life for businesses to announce their products or services to the target audience at an affordable cost. Monitoring the campaigns became a crucial factor to determine success, which is achieved by business process management systems leveraging various artificial intelligence and machine learning tools.

Figure 1. Leveraging Artificial Intelligence and Machine Learning for Business Process Management

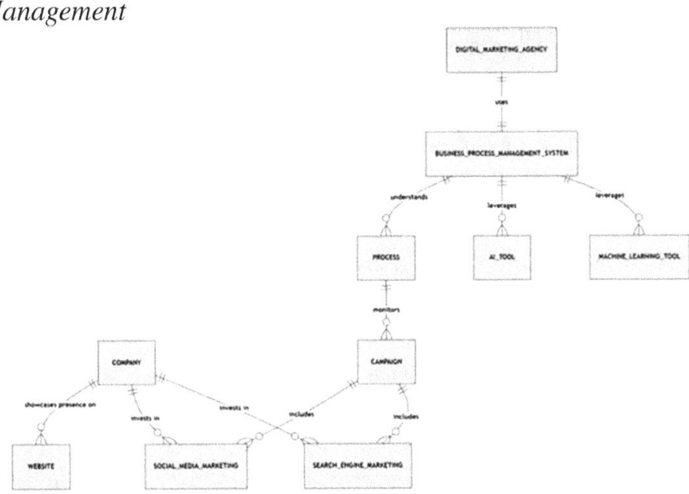

Digital Marketing is the marketing or advertising of products or services using digital technologies, primarily on the internet, but also including mobile phones, display advertising, and other digital media. It started in 1990, but it experienced a boom as the internet's presence grew immensely. Many marketing agencies began digital marketing efforts aimed at a large target audience, attracting customers to their businesses, which led companies to invest substantial amounts. Digital marketing can take various forms, including SEM, Social Media Marketing, Affiliate Marketing, and email marketing, among others. Every digital marketing agency needs a business process management system to support these efforts. Each marketing channel requires different approaches, strategies, monitoring periods, and metrics, which makes business process management systems essential. Various business process management system tools can be utilized by marketing agencies, each with its own pros and cons. Some process management systems make the process frustrating rather than speedy. Machine learning and deep learning are crucial for intelligent systems, automating analytical model building and solving tasks, but they face challenges in human-machine interaction and AI servitization (Janiesch et al., 2021).

Designing the BPM Workflow using models may seem difficult for employees without programming knowledge. AI has the potential to revolutionize industries such as finance, healthcare, manufacturing, and retail, with its impact extending from finance to healthcare to manufacturing to retail (Dwivedi et al., 2021).Business Process Management (BPM) is “A discipline involving the modeling, improvement, management, and automation of business processes(Dumas et al., 2022)”, It is applicable in any field being very effective in IT, Banking, hospitals, schools, Agriculture,

Music industry, etc. Different, varied, extensive processes exist in every department and BPM becomes a necessity to make everything automated and systematic. Each process requires and defines numerous metrics to measure its effectiveness and efficiency. BPM can be either a set of different tools providing one or two functionalities or a single, suited tool covering all or the main functionalities needed. The first type is free and has good quality. The third one builds frustration rather than speed, offers limited functionalities at no cost, and charges a high price for every additional functionality. Despite the growing interest in artificial intelligence (AI) and machine learning (ML) for managing marketing processes, several areas remain underexplored. More specifically, a more nuanced understanding is needed of BPM in SMEs in a digital marketing context. Moreover, the perspective of organizations and businesses in developing countries for business process management should be included (James Keegan et al., 2022). Small and medium enterprises (SMEs) account for 98% of all businesses in India, employing nearly 100 million individuals and contributing 30% of the GDP and 40% of the total industrial output. However, only 43% of SMEs currently have a digital marketing strategy and more than 70% say they do not understand what 'digital marketing' means (Bayoude et al., 2018), This research is expected to enlighten managers, researchers, and practitioners regarding new concepts and perspectives on AI & ML for business process management in digital marketing. Although written primarily for Indian SMEs, lessons learned will undoubtedly be of interest to organizations and businesses in other developing countries. Further research opportunities may arise in the area of AI & ML for digital marketing in SMEs. As businesses in developing countries become more sophisticated in their use of digital marketing, their processes may evolve. This evolution may provide new insights into the role of AI and ML in managing business processes (Saura et al., 2024). Digital marketing is a field of technological evolution that is progressing at an unprecedented pace. Thousands of companies develop new communication channels each year, working with various media. Companies are investing unlimited funds to train and recruit experts to develop their websites, mobile apps, and all channels needed to reach their target customers. In most countries, market competition has intensified; large companies must offer numerous bonuses to retain their employees. Some well-known companies are paying their computer engineers six-figure paychecks. Obviously, "competition of competitors on the digital market" has become an in-vogue notion in India. By 2030, the market will have undergone significant changes, with several companies acquiring new customers at any cost, including through discounts and bonuses. It has become a significant challenge for several firms to run their businesses smoothly. The biggest threat is market fraud and incorrect payment caused by bots and "fake" accounts. Most companies are finding it very difficult to differentiate between real and fake accounts. Therefore, it is imperative to invest considerable wealth and time to halt these efforts. Distributed machine learning offers opportunities for improved prediction quality and scalable solutions, but faces challenges in parallelization and coherent model creation (Verbraeken et al., 2021). The key conclusions indicate that organizations should focus on developing the interconnections between big data, data mining, and machine learning, ensuring optimal knowledge transfer and facilitating technology adoption. Additionally, they should develop marketing strategies to mitigate the negative impact of digital marketing (Yang & Lin, 2022). Digital marketing is among the fastest-growing business fields, with extensive research gaps in developing economies, where organizations often adopt it as an optional tool and view it merely as a channel to inform and advertise products and services. Machine learning is rapidly expanding, transforming decision-making in various fields by improving computers through experience and utilizing online data and low-cost computation (Jordan & Mitchell, 2015). Emerging markets face the same challenges as developed markets, but the contexts and specific issues are unique. Moreover, knowledge of digital marketing and its technologies is limited in such markets, and organizational capabilities often lack adequate managerial and technical skills (Carlson et al., 2023). Co-development with local partners can assist in overcoming this gap. Although several agencies are present, they tend to focus on SMEs (Small and Medium Enterprises), with higher client retention and lower acquisition costs for larger accounts, and on brands, i.e. manually managing accounts and posting.

2. REVIEW OF LITERATURE

In this section, VOS Viewer is used to display bibliometric analysis in three different forms: keyword occurrence, keyword co-occurrence, and clusters. Keyword occurrence analysis shows the most frequently appearing keywords and their total occurrences.

Figure 2. All Keywords Analysis By VosViewer

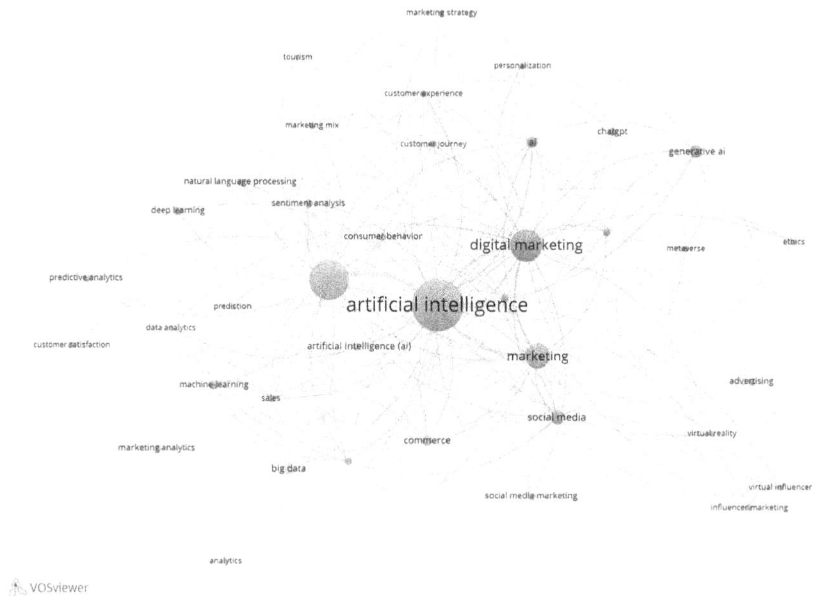

Keywords co-occurrence analysis illustrates the linkage of keywords in the research fields, and cluster analysis marks the degree to which keywords are grouped into different clusters. The analysis shows that the maximum-occurring keywords are Digital Marketing, Marketing Automation, Machine Learning, Artificial Intelligence, Chatbot, Social Media Marketing, and Business Process Management. The relationships established among the keywords are also co-relative to the observations. The primary goal of digital marketing is emphasized by Digital Marketing being one of the major clusters and key keywords. Other co-occurring keywords examine different aspects of digital marketing practice, such as digital marketing automation, machine learning and artificial intelligence, web analytics, social media, bespoke services, predictive models, chatbots, advertising monitoring, M-learning, and E-learning. These keywords are also most closely related to it. Business process management is comparatively less emphasized in clustering analysis, as it is predominantly a supporting flow through which business marketing processes enhance effectiveness, speed, and efficiency.

Figure 3. Author Keywords Analysis By VosViewer

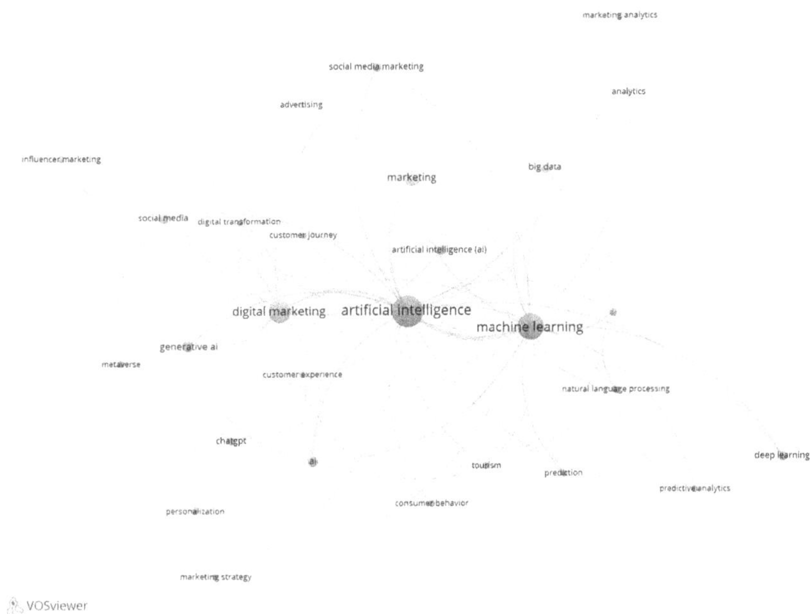

Machine learning and artificial intelligence will significantly impact personal selling and sales management in the Fourth Industrial Revolution, transforming decision-making and driving societal changes (Syam & Sharma, 2018). In comparison, BPM processes, particularly in digital marketing, marketing automation, and predictive analysis, offer new conceptual dimensions. The clusters, formed in bolder colors coded red, green, blue, and yellow, signify the distinctness of each cluster against the others.

Figure 4. Index Keywords Analysis By VosViewer

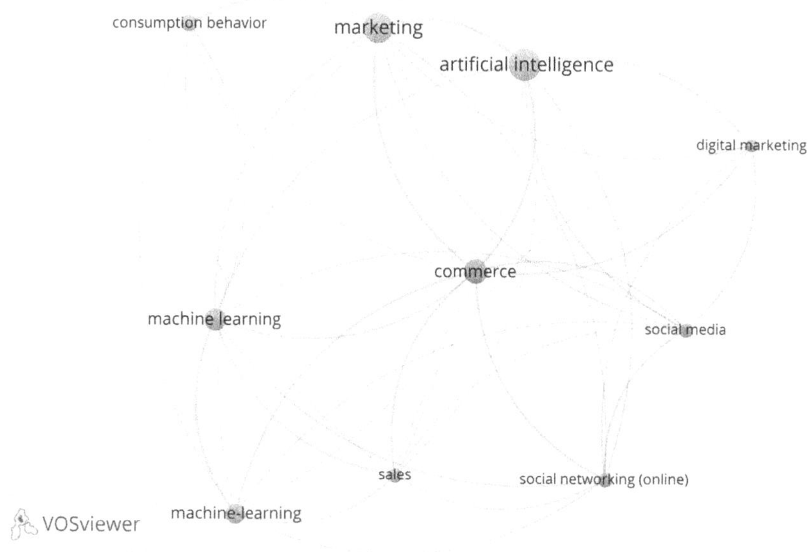

The substantial yet targeted use of Keywords can hone in on the search area most appropriate and, therefore, result in a more focused research work. The form of keyword analysis using VOS Viewer would help both fledgling researchers and practitioners in the fields of digital marketing and business convergence to locate their domain or the issues of interest. The literature on leveraging Artificial Intelligence (AI) and Machine Learning (ML) for Business Process Management (BPM) in digital marketing reflects a growing recognition of the transformative potential these technologies hold for enhancing marketing strategies and operational efficiencies. This review synthesizes key insights from various studies, each contributing to a nuanced understanding of how AI and ML influence business processes within the marketing domain. (Ge et al., 2017) Investigated, machine learning plays a crucial role in data mining and analytics in the process industry, aiding in knowledge discovery and informed decision-making. In the Similar vein (Kumar et al., 2016) explored the impact of Intelligent Agent Technologies (IATs) on marketing practices, emphasizing the necessity for a structured framework to guide marketers in adopting these technologies amidst increasing complexity in consumer interactions and data availability (P. S. Dahake, Chandak, et al., 2024). This foundational work set the stage for subsequent explorations into the applications of AI and ML in marketing. (Dimitrovska & Malinovski, 2017) further advanced the discourse by demonstrating how machine learning can optimize data assets, achieving a balance between computational complexity and predictive accuracy in business contexts.

Their findings underscore the significance of predictive analytics in enhancing decision-making processes within organizations. by the same token (Kose & Sert, 2017) shifted the focus to content marketing, discussing how AI can revolutionize content strategies. They introduced models of intelligent content marketing that leverage AI techniques, providing a roadmap for marketers to enhance their content delivery and engagement strategies. However (Marrella, 2018) expanded the conversation to BPM, highlighting the role of Automated Planning in enhancing process management.

The paper argued for the integration of intelligent techniques to foster greater flexibility and reactivity in BPM systems, addressing a critical gap in traditional process management approaches. Moreover, (Bayoude et al., 2018) presented a comprehensive overview of ML techniques that can elevate digital marketing practices, reinforcing the notion that these technologies are central to modern marketing strategies. This Study illustrated the state of the art in ML applications, paving the way for more specialized investigations. Significantly, (Gross et al., 2019), conducted a systematic literature review on BPM methods, elucidating the characteristics that determine the effectiveness of various approaches for process improvement. Their analysis revealed the strategic importance of BPM in navigating the complexities of organizational change, particularly in the context of emerging AI technologies. to put it differently (Soni et al., 2020) further examined the integration of AI within business processes, arguing that the adoption of AI-driven systems reshapes the business landscape (N. S. Dahake, Gajghate, et al., 2024). Their research provided insights into the innovations and operational shifts prompted by AI, highlighting its pervasive influence across industries. it should be noted (Saura, 2020) contributed to the dialogue by framing data sciences within digital marketing, emphasizing the importance of analytical frameworks and performance metrics. This Study underscored the need for businesses to harness data effectively to inform marketing strategies.as depicted (Shrestha et al., 2021) explored the application of deep learning algorithms in augmenting organizational decision-making, particularly in marketing contexts. They demonstrated how these algorithms can analyze vast amounts of unstructured data, offering actionable insights that enhance customer targeting and engagement. In addition to this, (Hermann, 2022) took an ethical perspective on AI in marketing, systematically reviewing the literature to identify key ethical principles guiding AI applications. This work highlighted the importance of ethical considerations in leveraging AI technologies for marketing purposes. Notably, (El-Gharib & Amyot, 2022) examined Robotic Process Automation (RPA) and its intersection with process management. Their systematic literature review emphasized the challenges and opportunities presented by RPA, particularly in terms of process redesign and efficiency gains. as demonstrated (Keegan et al., 2022) focused on the adoption of AI in B2B marketing practices, illustrating how AI technologies can enhance traditional marketing functions. Their findings revealed gaps in understanding the value created by AI solutions, particularly in the context of buyer-supplier relationships. In addition to this, (Cioppi et al., 2023) provided a systematic and thematic literature review on digital transformation in marketing, detailing how AI and ML influence distribution activities and customer interactions. Their research emphasized the competitive advantages gained by firms investing in digital technologies. first and foremost (Jahin et al., 2024) focused on AI's role in supply chain risk assessment, arguing for the integration of AI technologies to enhance risk management practices. Their systematic literature review highlighted the growing interest in AI applications for improving supply chain resilience. Finally, (Kanaparthi, 2024) conducted a bibliometric review on AI and ML in financial technologies, revealing how advancements in natural language processing and sentiment analysis can inform financial decision-making. This analysis showcased the breadth of AI's impact across various business sectors, including finance. The cumulative insights from these studies illustrate a dynamic landscape where AI and ML technologies are increasingly vital to BPM in digital marketing, shaping strategies and operational frameworks that enhance efficiency and customer engagement.

3. RESEARCH METHODOLOGY

Designing the extraction process was the first step of conducting bibliometric analysis. The databases were searched using the PRISMA (Preferred Reporting Items for Systematic Reviews and Meta-Analyses) approach. These databases were chosen because they are the two most reliable sources of bibliometric data, through which journal indexing and citation analysis are applicable. The keywords "Artificial Intelligence" or "Machine Learning" or "Deep Learning" or "Natural Language Processing" (TI) and "Business Process Management" or "Workflow Management" (TS) and "Digital Marketing" or "e-marketing" or "Internet Marketing" or "Online Marketing" (TS) were queried to retrieve potentially relevant sources. The search was narrowed down by filtering the documents to "Document title, Abstract, Keywords," and "Topic" and removing duplicates. Furthermore, the sources were filtered by selecting "English" as the language. The results of the search process revealed 123 documents related to the topics of "Artificial Intelligence/Deep Learning/Machine Learning/Natural Language Processing" and "Business Process Management/Workflow Management" or "Digital Marketing/e-marketing/Internet Marketing/Online Marketing". However, 60 documents met the inclusion criteria for each database. Second, the data incorporation and exportation were conducted to include documents through the exportation of cited references with a separate file. This was followed by a pre-processing procedure to clean the exported bibliographic records, as explained in the Data Cleaning section(N. S. Dahake, Suresh Dahake, et al., 2024).

The pre-processing involved the following steps: automatic conversion of the exported bibliographic records via R and Vosviewer, integration of the bibliographic records, and cleaning of the database. The database cleaning process included the follows of eliminating records with missing data or errors in the publication year, removing records where the title and/or abstract was not written in English to ensure comparability and compatibility between the documents, and creating journal records from records that had journal article types but were not classified with "journals" in the dataset.

This study follows the methodology of bibliometric analysis, which is designed to assess the scientific influence of published works through quantitative analyses. Bibliometrics combines a set of statistical techniques and tools to analyze publications and citations. Specialized software provides profiles of authors, publications, journals, and institutions, correlating keywords to identify connections between them (Bennett et al., 2019). By combining these techniques, the analysis of bibliometric results yields high-quality and reliable findings in bibliometrics. Furthermore, this work derives data from the SCOPUS database. This study critically explores and evaluates knowledge evolution through bibliometric visualization tools focusing on artificial intelligence and machine learning for business process management in such processes (P. S. Dahake, Bagaregari, et al., 2024). This study proposes the following research questions to guide the critical examination of the conceptual evolution and supply of this thematic domain of academic research, utilizing bibliometric techniques and data visualization tools. The analytical workflow is depicted through a flowchart. Data extraction and cleaning are followed by bibliometric and visualization analyses. This study also examines the growth trajectory of this intellectual territory, highlighting major contributors, influential works, outdated research avenues, and potential areas for development. The results highlight the tenacity of scholars and practices in the post-COVID era. The provided analysis offers meaningful insights and implications for researchers and information experts in this field. This study proposes to address the following research questions to guide the exploration of artificial intelligence and machine learning for BPM in digital marketing through bibliometric techniques.

RQ1: What is the growth trajectory of scholarly research on artificial intelligence and machine learning for business process management in digital marketing?
RQ2: Who are the major contributors to this research territory?
RQ3: Which works are the most influential in this thematic domain?
RQ4: Which subdomains are ineffectively explored and revisited?

RQ5: What is the co-occurrence structure of keyword clusters, and what topics might receive growing attention in the future?

4. SCIENTIFIC PROTOCOL FOR BIBLIOMETRIC ANALYSIS OF THE STUDY

This bibliometric study of business process management (BPM) in the digital marketing context applied various bibliometric methodologies to examine, analyze, and visualize the influence of works in terms of author, journal, institution, and country. For this purpose, the Co-Word Analysis Network Procedure was developed to enhance the understanding of the relationship between co-word networks when investigating the influence of works through both network size and influence degree. To understand how this methodology works, this section will clearly outline the methods in a scientific protocol, enabling scholars to replicate them if desired. This protocol is structured in six sequential elements. The first element clarifies the question(s) that the application researchers have. The other five elements focus on the approach to successfully conduct the study and achieve the research questions, including dataset construction, data scanning and filtering, co-word network analysis, data analysis and visualization, and writing and presentation. The author contribution analysis offers a valuable perspective on the scholarly landscape surrounding for the given study Among the most prominent contributors, Dwivedi Y.K. leads with the highest number of publications (5), underscoring his extensive influence in areas such as digital transformation, AI adoption, and marketing technologies. Following closely are Kietzmann, J., Mustak, M., Wang, X., and Zhang, L., each with four publications, reflecting their sustained contributions to research on AI-enabled marketing strategies, intelligent systems, and consumer engagement.

Figure 5. Major contributors Analysis Using-R

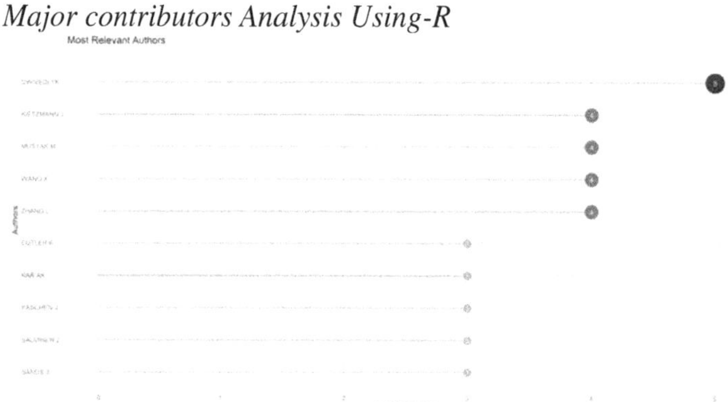

Additionally, scholars such as Kar A.K., Paschen J., Salminen J., and Sands S., with three publications each, contribute niche yet impactful insights into explainable AI, ethical concerns, and the automation of marketing processes (P. S. Dahake & Bansod, 2019). The collective work of these authors forms a robust academic foundation for this research, offering both theoretical grounding and practical direction. Their recurring engagement in AI, machine learning, and digital marketing confirms the critical and growing importance of these technologies in streamlining business processes and enhancing strategic marketing outcomes.

Figure 6. Trend Topics Analysis Using-R

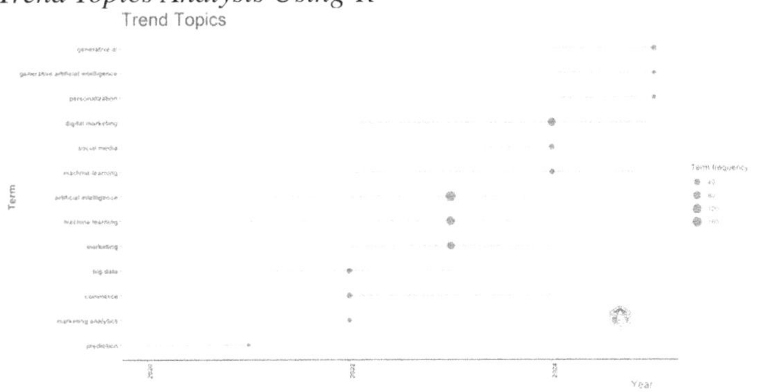

This study presents a scientific protocol for pioneering research involving bibliometrics in BPM within the domain of DM. Methodologically, it demonstrates how to formulate complex procedures using an understandable general protocol (P. S. Dahake, Chandak, et al., 2024). Additionally, it provides a data analysis package to enable the application of developed methodologies, allowing for either replication of the study or investigation of other contextual applications. Substantively, this is the first bibliometric study in the BPM domain to cover the research topic, trends, and hotspots within the DM purview. It identifies the most influential articles, authors, journals, institutions, and countries in the BPM in DM purview.

Figure 7. Word Frequency Over-Time

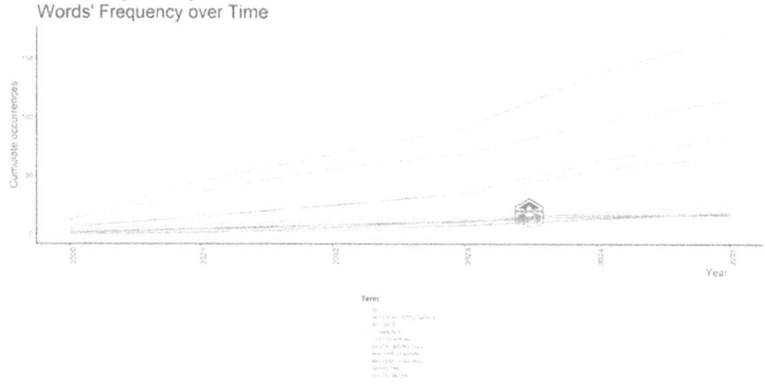

Additionally, an integrated research structure of 85 co-word paradigms was disclosed to introduce the research context and trends for novice researchers. This paper focuses solely on mapping co-word networks in terms of purely academic repository filtering. More works beyond the current research scope can be extended to cover other aspects of interest. For example, the only multi-word items were focused on. Using both single words and multi-word items enables a more effective screening of specific terms and facilitates domain analysis. Keeping the exact filtering boundaries for all examined terms also provides a more comprehensive analysis of all co-word networks, allowing for the schematic visualization of their trends.

5. CRITICAL ANALYSIS OR SYNTHESIS

Over the last twenty years, B2B marketing has witnessed a surge in the outsourcing of knowledge-intensive services (Selvakumar, Shanthi, Pitchiah, Sharma, Dahake, & T. C., 2025). Suppliers of marketing solutions range from traditional agencies to new startups that sell autonomous AI-driven tools through an online platform, the SaaS model. Automation providers offer web-based solutions that automate traditional services with minimal to no human intervention. The combination of algorithmically driven AI-automation and an ever-growing dataset from online interactions represents a potential revolution in marketing solutions. AI is altering the caliber and nature of B2B marketing solutions applied in actors' activity systems. Both suppliers and buyers of AI-automation hold mixed expectations and perceptions of the tools. The decisions of industrial businesses to implement AI are tied to a growing demand for automated solutions and hesitation rooted in conflicting expectations (P. S. Dahake & Somani, 2024).

Significant contributions to buyers' weaving of traditionally tacit processes into explicit feeds for large-tech's services are apparent. Identifying concrete areas of application and expected new solutions embraces a novel stream of inquiry (Selvakumar, Shanthi, Pitchiah, Sharma, Dahake, & TC, 2025). Additionally, implications arise for suppliers of automated marketing services, suggesting a potential conflict between buyers and suppliers. The usually tacitly held expectations and perceptions of non-AI-powered marketing solutions dominate assessment, design, and negotiation within the actions of both parties. Expectations regarding the outcomes are more evident than perceptions of anticipated shortcomings. Buyers' largely tacit expectations expand into heterogeneous and conflicting perceptions of control, effectiveness, and integration throughout the acquisition and use phases. In the expectation of high-level control and deliverable success, marketing managers often become entangled in petty operational details that divert their attention (Adwan et al., 2023). Notably, these capacities are poorly mathable. Marketing managers scramble to reconfigure the activity structure to accommodate both the new tools and the friction generated by the contradictory sensemaking of both parties. Unsurprisingly, the biggest errors appear to lie in internal communication across departments following a poorly defined acquisition process that led to tensions in relationships with an external provider (James Keegan et al., 2022).

Figure 8. Thematic Map Using-R

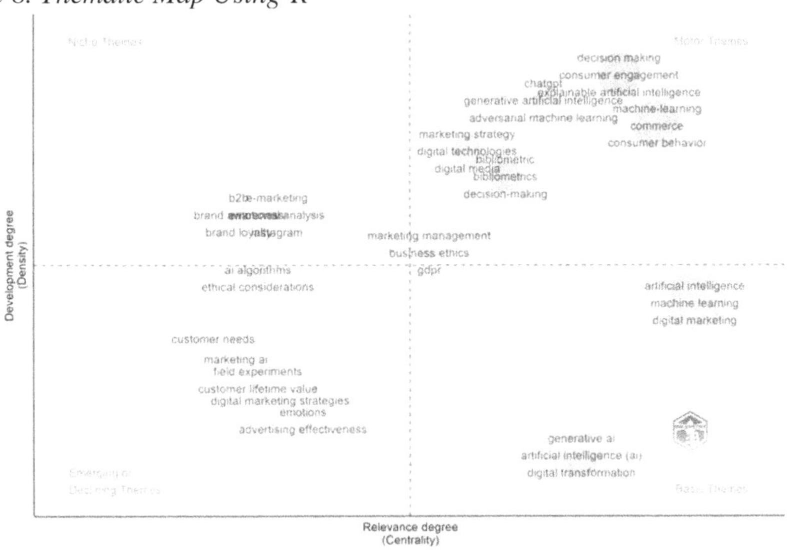

The thematic map visually illustrates the strategic placement of essential subjects pertinent to the research landscape at the convergence of artificial intelligence (AI), machine learning (ML), and digital marketing. The quadrants of Motor Themes, Basic Themes, Emerging/Declining Themes, and Niche Themes offer a cogent classification that corresponds effectively with the Study's emphasis on business process management through sophisticated digital technology.

i) Motor Themes (Elevated Centrality, Elevated Density):

The upper-right quadrant signifies well-developed and extremely pertinent ideas. Keywords such as decision-making, consumer interaction, explainable artificial intelligence, ChatGPT, and machine learning are prevalent in this domain, underscoring their essential and developed role in advancing research in digital marketing. These are essential for creating intelligent corporate processes that can adjust to consumer behaviour and automate decision-making, rendering them immediately pertinent to the current Study.

ii) Fundamental Themes (High Centrality, Low Density).

Themes such as artificial intelligence, machine learning, and digital marketing emerge as fundamental structures of significant relevance, albeit with limited specialisation. These are the essential foundations supporting the study topic, suggesting that, despite extensive citation, there exists potential for a more profound domain-specific application, specifically, the niche this research intends to tackle through business process optimization.

iii) Niche Themes (Low Centrality, High Density)

Upper-left themes, including B2B marketing, brand awareness, and brand loyalty, are highly specialised yet peripheral to the overarching integration of AI/ML in digital marketing. They provide opportunities for specialised applications or focused sub-studies, particularly in tailoring AI models for industry-specific marketing tactics.

iv) Nascent or Diminishing Themes (Low Centrality, Low Density).

Themes in the lower-left quadrant, such as customer wants, digital marketing tactics, advertising effectiveness, and emotions, either signify growing trends or diminishing importance. This research may explore how AI and ML might rejuvenate or transform these concepts inside digital environments.The thematic analysis offers a strategic framework that underpins the study's aim to explore the transformative potential of AI and ML in business process management within digital marketing(Lies, 2021). The convergence of machine learning, digital marketing, and decision-making inside the Motor and Basic Themes quadrants underscores the significant importance and practical maturity of these technologies. The emergence of explainable AI and ChatGPT indicates a developing research frontier, highlighting the practical, transparent, and scalable implementation of AI models, which aligns seamlessly with the objectives of this research.

6. THE ROLE OF ARTIFICIAL INTELLIGENCE IN DIGITAL MARKETING

Recent developments in artificial intelligence (AI), including virtual agents and machine learning-enabled solutions, have provided marketing practitioners with new tools and opportunities to enhance their practices. The adoption of AI in business-to-business (B2B) marketing is inherently complex and multifaceted. As such, a robust theoretical lens was applied to provide an in-depth, nuanced understanding of AI adoption, with particular emphasis on its implications for practice, building on previous work regarding AI in operational HRM. This research employs a qualitative, interview-based approach to investigate the adoption of AI by organisations operating within a B2B context (Gera & Sinha, 2022).

Figure 9. The Role of Artificial Intelligence in Digital Marketing

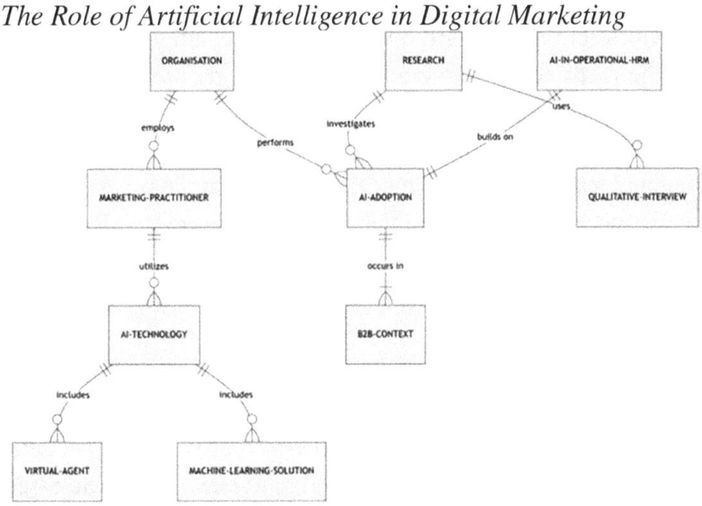

Findings pointed towards the notion that the utilisation of AI in B2B marketing provided beneficial enhancements to marketing practice. AI is poised to revolutionize through automation, pattern recognition, and predictive data analytics, with potential applications in everything from healthcare to predictive data analytics (Yu et al., 2018). Relevant and related marketing AI solutions have developed rapidly, removing much of the complexity of building AI models and instead enabling organisations to embed AI and machine learning into their existing application architecture. Interviewees indicated that successful adoption of AI in their organisations offered significant benefits in harnessing the large volumes of customer data generated within their respective marketing funnels, significantly enhancing the completeness of prospect intelligence and automating the myriad manual processes in the sales pipeline, resulting in relatively streamlined roles as marketing managers (Keegan et al., 2022). The perceived outcomes and benefits of AI adoption include cost savings, as well as genuine changes in functionality, when comparing current products on the market with those before AI integration (Messner, 2022).

Additionally, the sentiment is that being at the forefront of new technology enhances brand positioning within the space. Unsurprisingly, given the numerous jobs currently at risk due to AI automation, interviewees have expressed concerns about losing their roles as technology advances rapidly in a different direction, despite the likelihood of new job creation with the growth of AI. Participant descriptions also highlighted a common desire to outsource the building and development of pivotal processes to third parties, resulting in a highly cluttered market with various relevant and tangential marketing solutions providers (Sharakhina et al., 2024).

Social functions and entities are online and connected; they need to deliver the right content, the right advertisement, and the right remarketing to reach viewers at the right moment (Goncalves et al., 2024). With the new tools and information delivery methods brought about by the Internet of Things, a large volume of data is being stored and awaiting processing. Businesses can connect and track readers, viewers, users, and customers (Surańa-Sánchez & Aramendia-Muneta, 2024). With all those possibilities, obtaining and retaining customers becomes much more complicated and requires more qualified personnel and machines. That signifies the necessity for efficiency, effectiveness, and quality metrics for marketers (Bayoude et al., 2018). While there are many claims for the potential of machine learning in digital marketing, applications and state-of-the-art solutions are scarce. With deep learning, APIs, and cloud computing, marketing creative strategies and marketing feasible systems are now be written, imported, and executed by hundreds of thousands. Even more challenging is the frame race with many driven competitors.

7. CUSTOMER SEGMENTATION USING MACHINE LEARNING

To analyze customers' ideas and discover their requirements for products and services, clustering is useful. For this purpose, unsupervised learning algorithms like k-means were chosen. New customer data is submitted to the clustering model which generates segments with same characteristics. The prediction process was then split into two phases. In the first one, the clustering model was trained using the historical records of purchase transactions to segment dormant customers. After that new customer records are submitted to the clustering model which generates a segment for each customer. The clustering algorithm is followed by a descriptive model, in the second phase, which is trained on the most recent purchase data. This model predicts each dormant segment and builds the corresponding segments for the customers.

Last years have seen a rise in the application of machine learning techniques in information retrieval and related fields. Predicting a customer's likelihood of becoming dormant is important because such customers contribute less to revenue, can distort the company's calculation of returns and registration, and incur costs related to inquiries and customer service. However, since business rules do not exist or are difficult to explain and use, this prediction is quite challenging. As a result, machine learning is employed to detect patterns using domain knowledge from transactional history and customer characteristics that are not readily apparent. All customer records with at least one purchase in this time slot will be included in the analysis.

The relevant parameters are then determined by assigning the records to the inactive criteria, such as those that have already become dormant within the six months following the time slot of interest or those that have only been flagged eight months later. All transactions that take place before this criterion will be considered historic purchase transactions. For each customer, a cohort index will be defined from which monthly cohorts will emerge. The customer's cohort index will equal one for each month since the reference date that the customer has generated at least one purchase in a given time slot. Customers that have had at least one transaction after their cohort index has reached three will be flagged as recently active customers.

8. INTEGRATION OF AI TOOLS IN EXISTING SYSTEMS

A common use case is the integration of third-party AI tools into existing systems. Ideally, the AI tool is cost-effective with a good product-market fit, gaining positive feedback about product performance and user-friendliness. The tool's powerful working experience easily compensates for the potential additional user training. Incentives like discounted rates are a strategic tool to encourage the quick adoption of a new tool while maintaining the existing setup and requiring less onboarding effort. (Keegan et al., 2022)More complex integration championed by vendors may have additional pitfalls. On one side, the transition process may impact current irregularities when user buy-in is low or uncertainty is high, and adequate training or influence is lacking (Hsieh, 2023). On the other hand, the existing system architecture may have limitations in extending capabilities and potentially requires redeveloping data pipelines. Therefore a successful partnership with vendors, which arguably represents a minority across the sample firms in the short-term period, may be vital for long-term success. The choice of NLP platform, in particular, is customized by content type, employed functions, guidance during and after integration, capabilities, costs, maintainability, and security (Abban & Kifle Abebe, 2022). Vendors with an established NLP toolset win customer loyalty, continuously iterating on user feedback and conducting academic research. A business's own capability in digital marketing is well established, and it has a fundamental composition concerning the data workloads required for any AI tool implementation. Firms with a sophisticated coding team ensure a better product-market fit. Other businesses, mainly smaller-scale, may have to depend on vendors expertise. They must be cautious as some low-budget third-party vendors prioritize speed of product launch, while others approach the scale risk with caution. When the upscaling of content is dynamic, the outsourced AI tool yields limited capability, particularly in a good product-market fit, or when the existing business model is perceptibly altered (El-Gharib & Amyot, 2022). A gradual upgrade path is preferred, retaining human-in-the-loop capabilities where a machine-generated result could be further refined for scaling purposes.

9. AUTOMATING CUSTOMER INTERACTIONS

Chatbots, machine learning-powered entities and processes are already an integral part of the customer journey (Moon & Iacobucci, 2022). And why not? A chatbot responds to customer inquiries automatically and immediately, and it can do this incredibly well if it draws on a robust database. Chatbots can answer multi-step questions, help progress inquiries to more complex questions, and monitor customer experience trends (Bayoude et al., 2018). Simple, non-complex inquiries can often have a quick resolution, and deep learning and neural networks have taught an AI algorithm to understand context and intent better if the inquiry is multi-step and complex(Zaoui et al., 2024).

An intrinsic challenge is that an AI chatbot requires a dialogue database that reflects the customer journey and business processes. If this does not exist, a team of human agents is necessary to manually answer customer inquiries. Another option is a hybrid chatbot, where AI can still manage simple inquiries, and specialist questions can be routed to a human agent, i.e., a companion agent to the chatbot.

Most businesses begin their digital marketing journey with a website, which serves as the online representation of the business. However, a company can have a great website that does not drive traffic. No Organic Search traffic can mean a poorly optimized SEO. On-site SEO refers to a range of factors, including keyword relevance, URL structure, and website speed. Off-Site SEO is about increasing the online relevance of a website by driving third-party interactions with it. The primary off-site mechanism is link exchange, which takes place either naturally or as part of a Paid Backlink Campaign.

Other mechanisms, such as discount or offer mechanisms on aggregator-based platforms, deliver backlinks but don't contribute to SEO. Other factors affecting Off-Site SEO include Social Prominence, Domain reputation, and Brand Citations, etc. Off-site SEO is the most manual and labor-intensive process, involving outreach campaigns, email campaigns, and conversations with long-term follow-ups, among other tasks. Here as well, the lack of a click database would keep AI from generating a capable agent. However, if it does persist, an AI agent could save many man-hours in operating the Off-Site SEO mechanism.

10. PREDICTIVE ANALYTICS FOR MARKETING STRATEGIES

Predictive analytics (PA) helps forecast future data by utilizing historical data and data mining techniques, such as clustering and classification (Bayoude et al., 2018). This requires historical data where the target variable is known such as sales and cost data. To make accurate predictions, historical data from sales and conversions should be included, and a regression model can be built on it. Coefficients on marketing channels show how well it will contribute in the future. Currently, the state-of-the-art marketing optimization usage focuses on either short-term or long-term optimization problems. Three classes of problems can be distinguished under marketing optimization:

(1) A predictive method that allocates and explains budget across different channels
(2) A multi-channel marketing response model
(3) A multi-channel campaign allocation optimization model that jointly decides the best channels and allocation

Important aspects that can reduce the effort required to implement traditional marketing optimization include the use of less historical data or not requiring sales data at all. Problems are stated to estimate the importance of different channels and to answer questions about whether campaigns cannibalize and whether reallocation is beneficial. Additionally, possible approaches to tackle the problem of estimating the importance of other channels that cover long time horizons are explored, This is achieved through a two-step approach, involving a regression model on channel growth rates to understand the interaction structure, and a routing model that optimizes routing based on the usage-derived structural impact. Such two-step modeling approaches are easy to apply.

The influence of marketing expenditures and marketing performance across channels was analyzed using a Hierarchical Bayesian model. Kick-off and sales promotions were more effective for offline direct marketing than for online direct marketing. Therefore, if a simple channel model is derived, it can be easily integrated into a marketing optimization tool, providing recommendations on optimal budgets. Still, forecasting sales and conversions from marketing and other inputs remains a challenge. It is still a trade-off between accuracy and insight.

11. COST IMPLICATIONS OF AI AND ML ADOPTION

Business process management (BPM) is a set of business management methods that focus on guiding, tracking, and optimizing all processes within a company. Discussing web marketing processes with BPM presents a compelling and flexible opportunity to manage and control online active processes, and to interact significantly with them (Wilson & Bettis-Outland, 2019). Information processing technologies are transforming the way marketing is practiced in both B2B and B2C contexts. Data generated through individuals' participation in internet platforms is leveraging more advanced traditional B2B marketing practices that have evolved over years. As usages are relatively new and rapidly shifting, understanding is scarce about the effect of introducing artificial intelligence (AI)-based tools in marketing within a new operating paradigm (James Keegan et al., 2022). For dedicated AI-based machines to work continuously like humans, an enormous amount of data and knowledge must be fed into these machines to handle irregularities and noise. This is a costly and time-consuming process. Solutions with limited thought and planning could adversely affect the marketing strategy. These are among the top concerns for potential data mining clients. Whether AI or ML tools will afford new opportunities for media agencies that can offer exclusive advantages in data handling expertise is yet to be seen (Bayoude et al., 2018).

Screening and Entrusted Operations: Among the AE criteria, emerging evaluations included testing advertising entities, as exclusive slots or a broader audience might prevent fraud detection. Campaign manager responsibilities revolved around monitoring and responding to platform renders. The combination of screening and entrusted operations, intended to offer profitable solutions whilst relinquishing involvement, seemed attractive. However, the affordability of a reliable option is a concern. On the other hand, there is apprehension related to the automatic allocation of free slots to fraudulent accounts and pressure on lesser-known offerings. Using deeper evaluations and setting counter-arguments was called for.

12. USER EXPERIENCE ENHANCEMENT THROUGH AI

The majority of the world's population, or 62%, uses social media, enabling them to interact with brands, share experiences, and shape media narratives. In India, 354.9 million people are active social media users, creating significant opportunities for businesses, marketers, and researchers. Nevertheless, the volume and variety of data generated pose challenges in processing relevant information and gaining actionable insights. Therefore, it is possible to leverage AI-based technologies to process, analyze, and interpret social media data, enabling marketers to understand the audience's sentiment toward brands and refine their business strategies. Digital marketing leverages the potential of technology to turn this enormous audience into potential clients and leads to lucrative pipeline prospects. AI and machine learning techniques are revolutionizing fundamental sciences, accelerating research and promoting new applications across various fields (Xu et al., 2021). Business intelligence enables the analysis of market demand trends and the execution of targeted marketing campaigns. It is necessary to analyze market position, growth opportunities, and competitor branding.

Despite the continued rise of these two sectors, marketers face numerous challenges in accessing significant data from this territory. Large volumes of data are being generated daily as more individuals become product ambassadors, and promoting on the internet can potentially reach a larger audience.AI methods, such as machine learning, pattern recognition, and deep learning, can efficiently solve complex structural engineering problems, save time, and increase computational efficiency (Salehi & Burgueño, 2018). Crowdsourcing data is essential for understanding the market and determining one's branding position compared to competitors (Tupikovskaja-Omovie & Tyler, 2020). To remain competitive in this space, it is critical to monitor the market effectively (Fredström et al., 2022). Snippet data will help create a monitoring potential where pseudonymized datasets are explored for insights to answer queries (Jin et al., 2024). Therefore, organizations should effectively monitor the online market. The goal of this applied research is to design an AI-based concept for potential manual monitoring systems (Anayat & Rasool, 2024). Tasks are made more accessible, allowing for easier tracking of branding strategies, customer engagement, and competition monetization.

13. REAL-TIME DATA PROCESSING AND DECISION MAKING

Figure 10. The Real-Time Data Processing and Decision Making in Digital Marketing

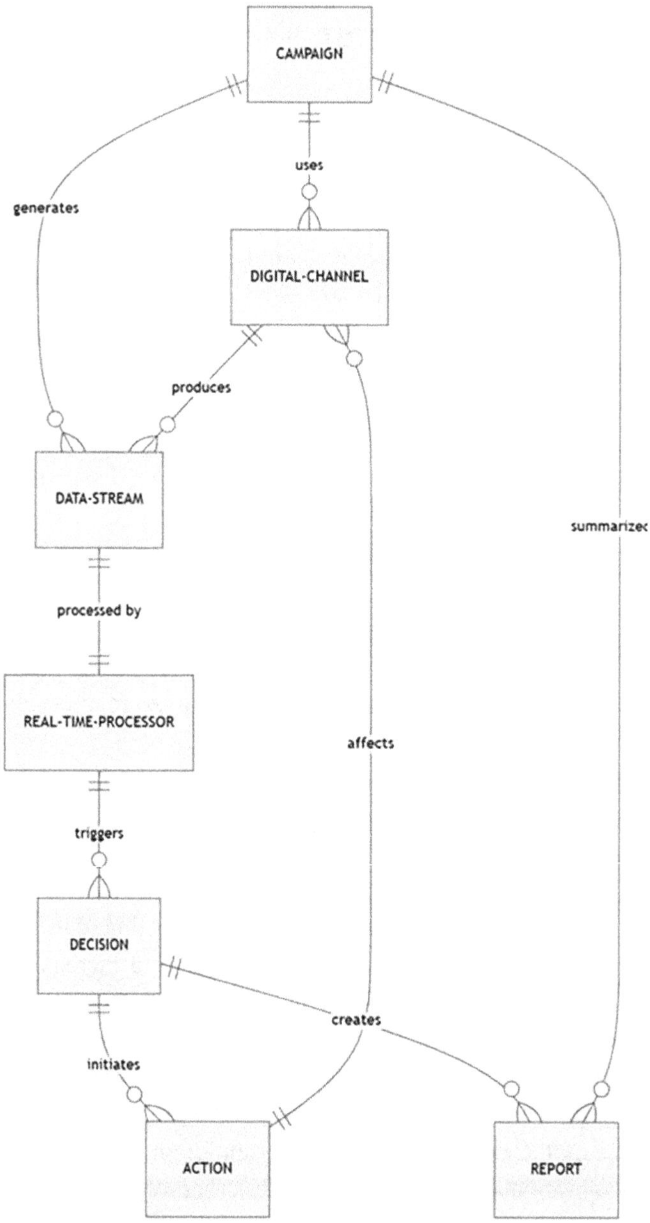

Digital marketing, as a rapidly growing discipline, generates a massive amount of structured and unstructured data from various sources, including social media, search engines, emails, websites, and mobile applications (Salminen et al., 2022). Machine Learning and Deep Learning frameworks and libraries have made significant advances in analyzing and learning from large-scale data sets, with a growing focus on massive parallelism for efficient computation in the Big Data era (Nguyen et al., 2019). The proliferation of online services has created a significant opportunity for digital marketers to advance marketing approaches through the analysis of these large datasets. However, various related challenges beyond simply collecting data must be carefully considered. This includes data cleansing, processing, and analysing for the creation of insights, programs, and strategies to develop and facilitate better decisions for marketers. Although process-enhanced data can provide firms with a competitive advantage, it is seldom instantaneous due to the delay in batch processing. With the continual online interaction between firms and customers, this delayed decision-making capability presents a loss of opportunity to communicate effectively in time, necessitating the timely processing of data (Gutuleac et al., 2024). Accordingly, a lack of current literature exploring big data sources, processing techniques, and instantaneous decisions in the context of business-to-business (B2B) digital marketers has been identified. This lack has profound implications not only for developing theoretical research but also for managerial practices (Jabbar et al., 2020).

The purpose of the current research is to explore the direct links between big data, programmatic marketing, and instantaneous decisions from a marketing perspective, facilitating actionable insights through marketing program preparation and delivery, and acquiring a foundational understanding of the instantaneous actions required for data-driven and programmatic marketing. Though commonly known types of significant data sources, processing techniques, key challenges, and decision types for programmatic marketing, data-driven marketing, and big data have been identified, big data-driven programmatic actions and/or instantaneous decision-making have been comparatively ignored in the marketing literature (Zulaikha et al., 2020). The findings suggest that developing better process-oriented knowledge for real-time decisions begins with a solid understanding of what this entails, which then needs to remain contextualized amid considerations for actionable methodologies for data-driven strategies (K.-W. Lee & Li, 2023). Ultimately, this can advance the understanding of how to efficiently utilize available data for timely actions and better decisions in creating, facilitating, and acquiring profits

14. SOCIAL MEDIA MARKETING AND AI

AI solutions can play a vital role in social media marketing, enabling businesses to achieve great heights of success online. With the development of these kinds of algorithms, the analysis of text, image, and video in a short period is done systematically by AI. Therefore, there will be no hurdle in analyzing data to extract useful insights (Kozinets, 2022). This AI-powered solution can analyze the sentiment of the audience toward a product or service, their interest areas in which any new product should be rolled out, the period during which the audience buys products or avails themselves of their services, and which products are being promoted, among other things (C. Wang, 2022). As a result of the combined social media listening and AI solution, a large number of detailed insights can be analyzed at one time, making the decision easier and more accurate. Based on observations, predictions about when a large number of audiences would be interested in various products, and the effective pricing of these products, could be shared with social media platforms through AI algorithms. Hence, the required ads with the correct text, images, audience segment will be delivered at the optimum time, increasing the success probability of the campaign and overall revenues.

Figure 11. Social Media Marketing and AI

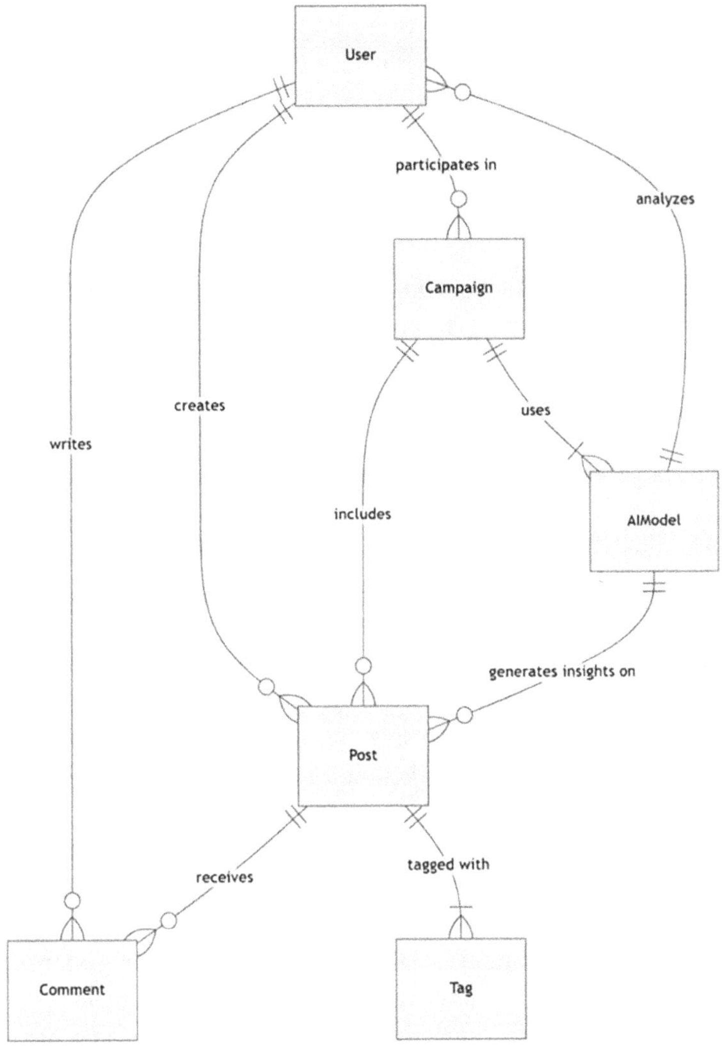

Every customer input should be shared with the analytics teams working on AI-based solutions to predict effective product recommendations and provide hashtags to be used based on the audience's tonality and interest areas. Regular monitoring of the product recommendations and their ROI should be done. The custom feed sent to the audiences should be proper. Hence, innovative trends in the AI field can be leveraged to incorporate numerous elements necessary for monitoring, analyzing, and informing marketing teams, thereby enhancing operating revenue per month and improving profitability (Latinovic & Chatterjee, 2022). The overall analysis of elements in AI and machine learning on business processes in the digitization of marketing decision-making is a key link or hurdle in the success of business, as this connection can help in successful process evaluation and the extraction of insights from huge datasets in social media (Bayoude et al., 2018).

15. EMAIL MARKETING OPTIMIZATION WITH MACHINE LEARNING

Email Marketing (Email has become a very useful tool for communication among businesses with their customers (Kapoor & Kapoor, 2021). A well-built email marketing system can generate a substantial amount of leads for the business. Email marketing is used to drive traffic, conversions, and to improve return on investment (Li et al., 2023). Once on the newsletter or subscription list, Email marketing can reach a wider section of people. Opening stats, click through stats and bounce counts can be visualized and analyzed easily and remedies can be taken in no time) Optimization (Machine learning algorithms take statistics generated through analyzing the Email system, generate patterns among metrics like clicks, responses, bounces etc. then predicts opening probability for future engagements with a specific audience and composes an Email). Business can send the best permutation of options according to the predicted probabilities. The option with the best permutation and predicted probability can be sent to the customer base, with the best reserved for last. Many businesses are emerging in the market, and organizations are seeking innovative and unique strategies for their product placement (Bilgihan et al., 2024). Ads are the first touchpoint that engages users and converts them into potential customers, after which they can be nurtured through email marketing campaigns. Email is a good and timely marketing tool, and proper optimization can lead to good ROI for marketing investments (Yaiprasert & Hidayanto, 2024). Analyzing bounce, open, and click statistics charts helps in understanding the email requirements (Malthouse & Copulsky, 2023). Machine learning applications on these stats can generate patterns among them and thus can predict the opening hand for future engagement efficiently. Minimal human intervention is needed in email placement as user engagement is widely automated based on contacts' clicks on Email.

16. SEARCH ENGINE OPTIMIZATION AND AI TECHNIQUES

Artificial Intelligence (AI) is the ability of machines to perform tasks that typically require human intelligence. It involves simulating human intelligence in machines programmed to think and act like humans. Machine Learning (ML) is a branch of artificial intelligence that involves the Study of algorithms that learn from experience and data. Machine learning-focused digital marketing utilizes ML techniques to analyze data in-depth. Because traditional tools are inefficient in predicting potential customers and improving campaign execution, businesses are turning to ML (Bayoude et al., 2018). Search Engine Optimization (SEO) is the strategy for generating organic traffic by optimizing webpage content to achieve excellent search engine ranks. Rank Wise is a dashboard that tracks website ranks across various search engines based on target keywords (Keegan et al., 2022). An AI capability in a firm leads to increased organizational creativity and performance (Mikalef & Gupta, 2021).

Figure 12. Search Engine Optimization and AI Techniques

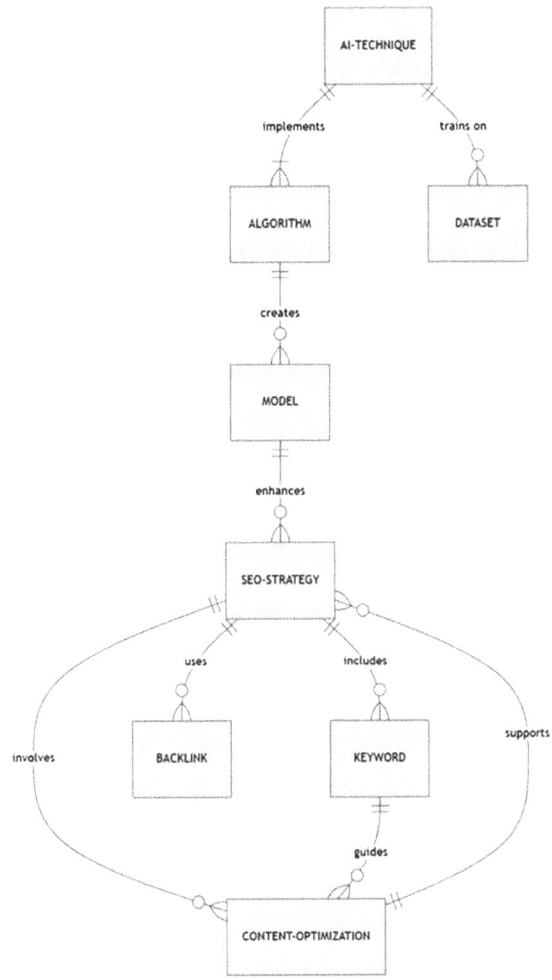

Rank Wise monitors webpage ranks for various target keywords on different search engines. The sources of information include Google, Bing, Yahoo Search Engine, and Yandex. The application is capable of capturing keyword ranks, including changes as well as 0-position SERP appearance. The monitored keyword ranks are visualized using various types of graphs. Additionally, a keyword rank advantage sheet is presented, summarizing keyword ranks, including changes and added target keywords by source, which informs how different search engines evaluate the website. By automatically monitoring changes in keyword understanding (search engines' interpretation of keyword meaning), the stability of a keyword's rank advantage can be analyzed through the visualization of two search engine similarity graphs (De Mauro et al., 2022). The results of automatic monitoring of webpage meta-data (title and description) changes are also visualized using bar charts. Changes in the monitored metadata can affect a webpage's keyword rankings (e.g., a decrease in relevance with respect to the target keyword). If the similarity between the capture date and previous metadata is less than a predetermined criterion, this change can be captured and visualized as a red bar in the graphs. The website's structure monitoring provides the count of captured URLs and the count of duplicate URLs. Under the horizontal bar chart for each capture date, green bars represent the structural changes (J. Lee et al., 2021).

The uploaded file detection function can help identify web programming errors that hinder search engine crawler access to a webpage (Bas et al., 2021). The links of all detected problematic URLs are provided, allowing users to identify which webpages are malfunctioning and prevent indexation failure. The information storage and retrieval of non-capturing monitoring can be performed easily due to log serialization and the organization of database tables.

17. CONTENT CREATION AND CURATION USING AI

Content marketing, also known as inbound marketing, encompasses various stages, including content preparation, content application, and content revision (De Cosmo et al., 2021). It includes processes such as researching, brainstorming, choosing the medium, finding and editing content, searching for and developing new relevant materials, and organizing the content. In addition to the self-managed content marketing, many other actors are involved in marketing processes (Kim & Park, 2024). Analyzing web logs and the content itself to measure and increase engagement requires natural language processing, statistics, machine learning, and predictive methods. By analyzing large amounts of data from web logs, businesses gain new insights into content marketing.

The methods and techniques of artificial intelligence are one way to improve the content marketing processes. At this point, information and communications are on the way of improving content marketing. Content has a huge importance for business. Each "information" has two argues: the first one is about the generated machine and its capacity; the second one is about designing and implementing a good interaction for users (Sharma et al., 2021). Artificial intelligence is an active technique that can process information and communicate effectively.

The main field of AI is a vast collection of methods: to make the content marketing process more adaptive, flexible, interactive, and intelligent according to customers' needs and interests. A generic flow of content marketing stages is given. There are different kinds of content marketing environments, as well as various approaches to artificial intelligence. The corresponding research frameworks generalize the entire process into a model, allowing for their own method combinations at the marketing stages. Since the processes are designed for generalized models of content, marketing scenarios should be developed in real-world cases and training sets (Philp et al., 2022).

18. COLLABORATIVE FILTERING AND RECOMMENDATION SYSTEMS

Today, businesses across all sectors face strong competition to generate revenue. Regardless of the successes achieved today, they are unlikely to be enough to attract future customers needed for revenue growth. Advances in information technology, the proliferation of content, the utilization of web technology, and relentless new product development have all transformed the international business environment. For firms to stay ahead of the competition, they must adjust their pricing, service, communication, and location strategies. For example, the rapid growth in e-commerce is creating significant challenges and opportunities for traditional companies that have previously relied solely on in-store sales.

The fundamental challenge of digital marketing is to provide the right product to the right user at the right time, and to offer recommendations or solutions tailored to the users' tastes and preferences. Each and every user is unique in their own way. Users differ in terms of interests and personalities. Additionally, users want more options from the available products. In any digital marketing scenario, the recommendation or solution provided to the user must address the above aspects. Similarly, the rate of change of users is also very rapid. Each day, new users enter and leave the system. The recommendation or solution should not be based on historical data.

To meet the challenges of identifying relevant products, an automated filtering-based recommendation system has been developed. A recommendation system is a software platform that relies on collaborative filtering or content-based filtering techniques. Collaborative filtering techniques quantify gazing patterns or taste-organizational similarities. Generic models exploit inter-user correlation to offer similar recommendations to users with similar preferences. Model-based approaches exploit various advanced analytics. Content-based recommendation techniques simply guess preferences from the characteristics of the products. Characterized products are recommended to users who have shown an interest in exploring. A two-stage hybrid deep learning-based collaborative filtering system is proposed, focusing on capturing communication between items and users to enhance customization. The proposed collaborative filtering system is examined using a ten-fold validation dataset.

19. IMPACT OF AI ON CONSUMER BEHAVIOR

Technological advancements influence all areas of business. Recent facts show that technological advancements are transforming businesses into entirely different models, where most processes are automated, data storage and computation are reinvented, new data analysis capabilities are generated, and new consumer habits emerge. Recent technological advancements include Cloud Computing, Artificial Intelligence, Big Data technologies, and 3D printing. The investment in these technologies has dramatically increased over the last decade. Although the development of new technologies offers great opportunities, it becomes possible to cover the risks arising from changes in consumer behavior or competitor strategies. An era constituting an even more complex market environment for marketing managers is being entered into. In this changing era of marketing, Businesses 4.0 comprises companies that have updated themselves following the new market order and adapted to it. Machine learning can enhance the intelligent adaptive learning and decision-making in next-generation wireless networks, enabling new applications and services (Jiang et al., 2017).

Consumer behaviors being influenced by digitalization is one of the greatest risks that marketers face. Digital marketing itself is being updated with AI. Explaining the effect and contribution of AI-supported system and model development on consumer behavior change in current digital marketing literature, and clarifying how this is becoming an advantage for marketers, is the primary goal of this Study. Additionally, to derive more realistic outcomes, an attempt was made to integrate the results obtained from marketing literature with the detailed estimates in areas such as Artificial Intelligence, Machine Learning, and Big Data (Keegan et al., 2022). Therefore, an in-depth literature review is conducted, comprising three-layered components: general AI, ML, and Big Data, along with a digital marketing context for each (P. S. Dahake, Bagaregari, et al., 2024).

The digital arena has a totally different environment where consumers can instantly search for what they need. Comparison between products and companies can be done easily by looking at several alternative options. All the data related to individuals is stored, making it possible to foresee purchase decisions even before they happen. In addition, in this entirely different environment, where influencers reflect dreamy lifestyles, trends can spread rapidly and fads can quickly fade away with a single scandal. Conversely, sales can skyrocket in seconds as a consequence of a short advertisement. Recent research shows that a sizable portion of companies still respond to digital marketing transformation reactively.

20. MEASURING SUCCESS: KPIS FOR AI AND ML IMPLEMENTATION

The implementation of AI and ML in digital marketing campaigns necessitates the inclusion of key performance indicators (KPIs) to measure success. It is as crucial to choose KPIs as it is to choose the right technology and algorithms. Digital marketing is an unending task. Even for marketers with the advantage of budget and speed, the digital landscape is constantly growing quicker than what is possible to capture and understand, This requires that any automated solution be continually evolving with this change, not just adaptive but fully adaptive, with a range of options and speed settings to choose from.

Speed and adaptability are only part of the equation for success. An implementation also needs to consider the underlying technology stack and associated services if it is to remain relevant to the tasks at hand(Huberman, 2021). Content is one of the largest differentiators for any digital marketing campaign. Solutions that enable the creation of content that is both creative and compelling will be vital for success (Bayoude et al., 2018). To consider important success KPIs, one needs to understand the nature of the marketing process in terms of its stages, actors, and tasks. In this regard, while this stage analysis is tasking in all process types, it can be particularly pertinent to digital marketing, where the execution and much of the interaction processes occur directly on the web and are complex (N. S. Dahake, Suresh Dahake, et al., 2024). Ultimately, it may not be enough to simply provide some form of choice for individuals; brands may wish to consider a more analytical approach and set out to maximize a particular KPI as a target (Gerlich et al., 2023). As for any automatic control solution, it can be set to maximize the evolution of a KPI into the future. The KPIs must be made available for the submission of feedback to the automated social media solution to ensure proposed campaigns are learnt. Although the concern is high-level, fine-grained performance tracking is still necessary for high-fidelity feedback (Bossert & Hagendorff, 2021). The campaign execution is inherently dynamic; the underlying structure, in terms of a state tree, can change extremely rapidly, from the societal scale of a brand going viral due to a news story to the personal scale of an influential individual posting the wrong thing (Pitt et al., 2023).

The key to merged profitability control and the overall loyalty factor might not appear directly around any particular set of exploitable edges (Thontirawong & Chinchanachokchai, 2021). One would still wish to know how and why activity in the overall network is leading to a change in this KPI. While it is outside the scope of this stage to discuss in detail how such explanations might be provided, it is intended to frame the discussion in a way that facilitates considering how such an explanation might be given and where it needs to be integrated into the cyber-physical control loop.

21. MACHINE LEARNING APPLICATIONS IN DIGITAL MARKETING

Today's technical advancements inspire innovative approaches for digital marketing. Marketers now have the opportunity to utilize machine learning tools and analytical methods to leverage vast amounts of marketing data generated by automated tagging and reporting systems, driving new marketing tools and behaviors, This presents a variety of case studies corresponding to diverse blockchain structures of digital marketing immersion and clarifies underlying issues. It also presents a comprehensive analysis of the full potential impact of each application on digital marketing progression and offers proposals for integrating the recommended applications into existing professional workflows.

Digital marketing is a topic in huge demand and broad interest nowadays. As the fastest-growing branches of marketing, they are drawing special attention from scholars and marketers worldwide. Digital marketing refers to all marketing activities conducted on a digital medium or a combination of both, e.g., advertising on TV channels of Indian Railways, coupled with posts on official web pages or forums. Digital marketing immersion comprises a brand's online activities in three key areas. These blocks represent a brand's reception of digital marketing information by customers, as well as its fulfillment of prices, promotions, and other requests, and the collection of immediate behaviors in response to digital marketing information and offers. Each block is composed of different elements and components that exist separately and interactively process marketing input data, target pursued goals, and marketing information. Based on this theoretical framework, the Study examines how machine learning tools are influencing various marketing practices and generating new developments and opportunities. It further explores how to build practical applications that drive significant data development tools and efficiently introduce and deploy emerging analytical tools into current working practices.

22. BENEFITS OF AI AND ML IN BUSINESS PROCESS MANAGEMENT

The organization's desire to incorporate insights that arise between big data analytics and conventional daily analytics has been attainable due to the evolution in the Business Process Management environment since 1990. Emerging after traditional Business Process Management disciplines, Artificial Intelligence is one of the outliers with a prominent return on investment (ROI). However, regardless of the benefits it reveals, the challenge of failure is still possible, as with traditional Business Process Management. Various types of Artificial Intelligence have essential applications in interdisciplinary fields, such as machine learning (ML), deep learning (DL), and natural language processing (NLP), among others. However, the interfacing of software tools to participate in service, search, or other platforms of Business Process Management, or any other scenario at a managerial level, would reduce their applicability across fields such as marketing, sales, and finance. Machine learning (ML), a type of artificial intelligence (AI) has been widely researched (Dongbo et al., 2023). AI automates some high-level understanding procedures, as it can recognize abstract patterns in data. Machine learning (ML) automates certain analysis procedures, making them self-optimizable processing black boxes, which search for the best pattern combinations to perform prediction or classification (Bayoude et al., 2018). Neural Networks, HMM, and Forsyth are models of AI and ML. NLP makes understanding possible by automating richer, either deep feedback on daily analytics or strategies based on the input of decision points by AI/ML. Text mining and text processors in the free NLP software can work on structured or unstructured datasets of any size. The full profile and channel prediction enhance the action prediction and automatic campaign generation and segmentation mechanism through BigQuery/ML association and clustering tools. Other productivity gains arise as the behavioral analysis is converted to transactional files. The AI(ML) base can widely serve Marketing intelligence or information search at a business issue level.

23. CHALLENGES IN IMPLEMENTING AI AND ML

Like other information technology systems, there may be differences in stakeholders' expectations regarding the performance of AI and ML systems and price of implementation or resource allocation scenarios (Allil, 2024). Additionally, due to the dispersive character of development and implementation of BPM systems: legacy systems, various (sometimes poorly interoperable) platforms and single-point solutions are used, maybe even within one (even medium-sized) enterprise. At times, organizations do not know what kind of solutions they own. Moreover, before the implementation of new tools, uncommon data patterns can be detected, and robustness of existing systems can be questioned. Hence, there may be discrepancies between the assumed and resulting state of the entire digital marketing infrastructure. This will likely result in distrust of AI and ML systems or a narrow-minded approach: "I don't see how it would be beneficial." Regardless of the quality of AI and ML systems, from the perspective of keen developers, if solutions are implemented unreasonably, given that the stakeholder does not understand their work or cannot interpret their results, this is particularly applicable to marketing departments. This reflects the broader need to scrutinize the implementation of digitalization in various contexts (Bayoude et al., 2018).

Furthermore, AI and ML are not inherently superior to traditional systems. In a discount case, the effectiveness and efficiency of existing systems or resources used for their multipurpose tagging can be satisfactory. Also, as "a job for a human," it does not mean that it is better to use such systems. There is also a need to explain how to understand selection processes among several AI or ML systems, or why high-model score boundaries are representative. Alternatively, it is necessary to consider how a designed response needs to change when awareness of cybercriminals' behaviors is gained. Moreover, AI and ML marketers often lack an understanding of neural networks or complex systems, suggesting that designer knowledge or advanced training is necessary. For other stakeholders, this could mean that BMI should also be offered to understand feedback mechanisms, both in the case of noise and signal sharing, as well as in situations with lower innovation readiness. It would be particularly important in the context of the growing industrial pressure towards transparency, updates, and the interpretability and explainability of the results and decisions made by AI and ML-based systems.

24. DATA PRIVACY AND ETHICAL CONSIDERATIONS

AI-enabled digital marketing media intend to direct national and business-wide decisions. Growth in AI-enhanced digital marketing media would provide additional opportunities for more targeted ads. Broadening use of digital marketing augmentations would bring in a fortune on an international, national, and business scale. The effective use of AI-powered digital marketing media offers numerous social benefits by directing national and local advertising to enhance the alignment between consumers and activities (Bayoude et al., 2018).

The effects of AI on Digital Marketing include personalization in advertising campaigns, optimization of dynamic pricing, refinement of content strategy, and automation and optimization of channels. The growing role of AI in Digital Marketing is expected to be in Content Creation and Curation, Predictive Analysis, Customer Insights, Marketing Research, campaign analysis and Evaluation, as well as Chatbots. Very few companies are currently leveraging AI maturity in Marketing Operations. The future intention to leverage maturity lies more in marketing automation compared to Chatbots and Recommendations. Machine learning algorithms enhance intelligence and capabilities in various real-world applications, such as cybersecurity, smart cities, healthcare, business, and agriculture, while highlighting challenges and potential research directions (Sarker, 2021).

The current academic literature on AI in digital marketing is domain-specific. Future research directions include developing more definitive theoretical constructs, integrating knowledge from neighboring disciplines, analyzing the influencers of public opinion, investigating the creative aspects of AI in digital marketing, creating and critically assessing innovative data-driven visualizations, and exploring diverse technological ecosystems. AI for digital marketing is an emerging research stream with growing interest and diversity but a very low degree of fecundity. Future avenues for research on this under-researched area of inquiry are suggested.

25. FUTURE OF AI AND ML IN BUSINESS PROCESS MANAGEMENT

On the whole, AI & ML has a great deal of promise and limitless possibilities in the area of Business Process Management in Digital Marketing. Almost all processes will be aided or automated intelligently with the use of AI and ML based tools. Ease of use and seamless integration are two key challenges that remain to be addressed. Digital marketers need to and will have to embrace these technologies much faster for optimization and appropriate course corrections. In the foreseeable future, it is expected that AI and ML solutions will be excellent and fast enough for marketers to gain insights into their business in near real-time. AI based process management tools would then be able to not only provide insights into the status of all underlying processes instantly without any time lag, but it can also take corrective actions wherever possible, such as eliminating bottlenecks in the workflow directly. AI would be able to identify how a campaign can be improved in an immediate fashion. Imprecise or vague goals would be well understood and assessed more effectively by AI and ML in the future. Simple automation is useful and can be found rarely now-a-days. Simple automation tools would provide limited value and would be mostly automated by the AI solutions. On the business strategy front, as these technologies are expected to mature rapidly, it is better to take an early mover advantage and crowd out competitors. It can be shown that with proper approach, marketing automation can handle thousands of conditions effortlessly with AI, while managing millions of digital marketing conditions with ML. At the same time, hashing out a dilemma whether machines can think is, logically, meaningless. But the real question ought to be is whether machines would do marketing? This question is even too simplistic, as it is expected that business process completion time would drop to a few seconds, if not milliseconds. Ultimately, AI and ML would prove effective in providing cognizance to human advisors who absorb a brand's heritage in all touchpoints, consumers' past behavior with all their characteristics, and the deterministic rules to manage their affairs and coexist with them. Everyday common sense and less than two minutes short in the human working day would pass to them.

26. FINDINGS OF THE STUDY:

The findings of the bibliometric analysis reveal significant insights into the application of two key frameworks Artificial Intelligence and Machine Learning in the research field of Business Process Management, particularly in the context of Digital Marketing. The number of publications from 2021 to 2025 indicates that research interest in the topic is gaining traction and increasing rapidly. The research field is still within the early development stage (Naldi et al., 2022). The visualization of network connections among three keyword types keywords, author keywords, and indexed keywords demonstrates that regulations and rules within businesses and industries for digital marketing strategies need to be further examined and researched. Business Process Management is broadly categorized into three major categories, actively applied to digitized marketing, including Video and Image Processing, Natural Language Processing, and Big Data Analytics. The generated research themes from the keyword co-occurrence analysis visually display the evolution of the topic of Artificial Intelligence and Machine Learning in Business Process Management, indicating that further themes examining the approach in Digital Marketing are yet to be explored (Reza Saeidnia et al., 2024). The analyzed countries reveal that the United States of America and China offer the most extensive document listings with the most significant number of citations, while institutional collaborations require further improvement. The top publishing journals suggest that there is still considerable opportunity for publishing high-quality research articles in this area. There is an external opportunity for cross-disciplinary research among stakeholders, including industry practitioners and government policymakers, particularly with a focus at the international level.

These findings can benefit stakeholders in the emerging research field of applying Artificial Intelligence and Machine Learning in Business Process Management, particularly in the context of Digital Marketing. Industry practitioners can utilize these findings to identify research gaps and collaborate with higher education institutions to conduct further research studies on the topic.

27. RESULT & DISCUSSION BASED ON THE LITERATURE

Artificial intelligence (AI) is a versatile digital technology with applications across all sectors of modern business and society (Verheij & Wiering, 2018). Business process management (BPM) organizes and automates business processes, ensuring process sustainability through continuous process improvement with various improvement methodologies. Business processes are designed for operational efficiency through process mapping. Cognizant end-to-end BPM workflow environment gives visibility, transparency, and control to the business process with 360^0 process-centric visibility. The recommendations from data driven business insight reports drive the process improvements and performance tuning actions. Business process management as a new stand alone functional layer works closely but independently with business operations. Probabilistic modeling provides a framework for designing machines that learn from experience, playing a central role in scientific data analysis, machine learning, robotics, cognitive science, and artificial intelligence (Ghahramani, 2015). BPM adds continuous process optimization discipline to the existing IT controlled application management. Business Analytics/Intelligence captures operational data exhaust from business processes across geographical boundaries using a huge data mining engine and feeds optimized decision recommendations back into the BPM process widget layer. AI/ML engines generate estimated queries against data indefinitely and deploy estimation models within real-time data-based event trigger functions. A step-change improvement in product configuration is achieved through process reengineering, redesigning, and redefining process flows with real-time adjustments from the deployment of data-driven, deep learning-based self-optimization engines. With the intelligent process, businesses anticipated changes in customer response and experience, resulting in a reduction of product configuration complaints and user unfriendliness. With the establishment of a best-in-class intelligent process hub, whole customer-facing business processes are driven with a true sense of a 360-degree approach, complete with automation (P. S. Dahake, Jain, et al., 2024). Because AI is accelerating scientific discovery by enhancing model accuracy and efficiency, data quality and stewardship remain critical areas for AI innovation (H. Wang et al., 2023).

A paradigm shift in digital marketing, from promotional to conversational marketing, is approaching, and technology is an enabler to sustain this shift. Conversational marketing fosters genuine engagement with customers through two-way communication across traditional website text chat to enhanced media, such as video, animation-rich HTML, and mobile apps. A return on investment is guaranteed from well-planned conversational marketing campaigns. Very few participants are taking advantage of the benefits from technological development in conversational marketing, while fast-forwarding adaptive organizations have adopted a combination of business process reengineering and technology reengineering to meet the evolving market opportunities and threats (Bayoude et al., 2018). Research Engines have brought about dramatic changes in the searchable information architecture across various media types, including text, images, and voice, leading to the emergence of new trading platforms and business processes for advertising, along with alternatives to meet business information requirements. BPM refers to a field of research that investigates methods, techniques, and tools for modeling, redesigning, enacting, controlling, monitoring, and improving business processes. BPM systems focus on the technological support for discovering, designing, implementing, monitoring, and evolving processes. Process Discovery involves using event logs to learn new process models. Process Design requires both a model and a log of an event, and is to use this support to design a new process model. Process Enactment represents the execution of business processes, controlling their progress through the passage of events. Process Mining is the extraction of process models from event logs, where process models provide a formal abstraction for analyzing, auditing, and optimizing business processes. Process Analysis refers to the auditing of a model where both model and log are available. Process Adaptation/Change accommodates changes in work practices as demonstrated by an organization's practice of keeping the information system in synchronization with its current work practices, where both the model and log are available.

28. PRACTICAL IMPLICATIONS

AI and ML are of high significance for DM. Consequently, it is essential to investigate how BPM can take advantage of AI and ML. This paper provides a bibliometric analysis of peer-reviewed publications on AI, ML and BPM in the DM context. This paper presents a bibliometric analysis of the literature on the use of AI and ML techniques in BPM, with an emphasis on DM. Work in this context is quite limited, and this paper contributes to close this research gap. This paper presents an extensive analysis of 691 relevant peer-reviewed publications and emphasizes 29 articles that have had the highest citation impact. The analysis employs VOSviewer, Gephi and other analytical tools. Co-occurrence and citation network visualisations and word clouds are presented. Several important insights are provided concerning the origins, current status, and future research avenues of the literature on using AI and ML for BPM, including DM. This research stream is on the rise; articles on AI and ML for BPM demonstrated a rapid increase since 2021. Most of the output on using AI and ML for BPM in the DM context is produced by authors from the United States, France, and the United Kingdom. The Journal of Business Research, International Journal of Information Management and International Journal of Research in Marketing are identified as the three most influential periodicals in this context. This paper presents the most impactful publications on AI and ML for BPM in DM. The research theme and typologies of AI and ML techniques, in the context of BPM in DM, need further examination. Most current publications rely on survey papers, which is surprising considering the swift advancement of AI and ML techniques, including real-world applications (Bayoude et al., 2018). The review of seminal papers, first-of-its-kind contributions and key techniques can provide impetus for new research questions and stimulate the field's advancement. AI and ML technique evolution tracking studies may reveal new tools and approaches that facilitate more sophisticated and feasible AI and ML applications in BPM implementation.

29. CONCLUSION

To foster better economic relations with the vibrant business industry in the future, the entire Marketing spectrum should be addressed comprehensively, ranging from tracking methods, Algorithms, and Schemes to precise features of executing trade Marketing. The vast marketing industry, after innovative queries during this pandemic, is in tension about its customers and how to reach out better and explore their requirements. A few years down the line, the percentage of Indian population using social media was merely 11%, but the trend has changed drastically to more than 80% digital marketing systems. The implementation of Artificial Intelligence and Machine Learning in government services at the SMP and startup levels has developed technically, socially, and economically (P. S. Dahake & Dahake, 2024). As the industry is complex with the above-stated attributes, an analysis of gathering data, blending, text summarization, and concepts, as well as years to grow and surface computing, should be efficiently realized. A few decades down the line, the digital platform, along with diverse marketing means such as influencer marketing, social media, and changing algorithms, channels, timelines, and ads, has undergone drastic changes to reach the desired content. There are three prominent paths of the Digital Marketing industry.

Application Systems concern capturing markets, marketing to port services, Eligible leads, Instant media, Data cleansing, customer selection, the reuse of creatives, Commission charging, and Money earning, as well as influencer management. With the Elimination of commercial marketing, a better flow of necessary information is provided. A preparation History is prepared, Domain search lists are compiled, and a Brand selection is made to go live with creatives, all summed up to explain how, why, and where the approach will be taken. Planning is underway, with the permutations of days, Ad groups, creative structures, Phases, and timings detailed out to approach a better business together. As Off-Site tagging requirements and Ad Policies are audited in detail, creative medium shots of video length, content, headline, and copy are all prepared to take a deeper approach before execution. This represents a superior evolution of marketing processes that have undergone significant changes since the invention of the concept of meaning to reach out to users. The limitations of the current study include its focus on a publication date of 2025 or earlier; therefore, this study is unable to provide a comprehensive discussion of the relevant publications from 2023. Additionally, there is the option to limit the analysis to the top 100, top 500, or top 1000 sources; however, this study restricts the scope of analysis to the full secondary data set. This study has successfully mapped the knowledge structure, knowledge development, and knowledge evolution by exploring the characteristics of the social network of co-authorship, co-citation, and bibliographic coupling, and also tracking the dispersion of research themes across time.

30. FUTURE SCOPE OF THE STUDY

The technology supporting digital marketing is advancing, in view of the notable growth of online habits. New tools arrive regularly in this field. In today's tech-savvy world, the need for traditional marketing has declined. There are countless digital means of advertising. The scope of digital marketing is vast; it comprises many activities based on the internet. This great exponential, surely can rely on the emergence of digital marketing for its development. In India, with growing population count, the number of internet users raised heavily. Marketers can access this notion graph in terms of the marketing pitch(P. S. Dahake et al., 2023). However, they faced another constraint as well; missions were done through various platforms. So, marketers faced a challenge in learning everyone's behavior.

But it became easier as companies started storing massive data for future reference. There are diverse ML techniques available to classify consumer behavior. There are moderates, high, and really high prospects that have been categorized from huge consumer browsing data. By implementing some ML techniques, marketers can convert better lead conversion chances with heavily disclosed marketing pitches to the companies. Random forest is growing due to less training time and it generates many trees from a selected variable (Bayoude et al., 2018). It has implemented comparatively better recall in predicting behavioral classes, especially for class 0. However, by choosing moderate and low conversion chances as less interesting portions of the customer base, the marketer might try to keep these consumers engaged, improving the push marketing overview and their pitch speed.

REFERENCES

Abban, R., & Kifle Abebe, G. (2022). Exploring digitalization and sustainable practices in African agribusinesses and food supply chains: A literature review. *International Journal on Food System Dynamics*, *13*(4), 470–474. DOI: 10.18461/ijfsd.v13i4.D7

Adwan, A. A., Kokash, H., Adwan, R. A., & Khattak, A. (2023). Data analytics in digital marketing for tracking the effectiveness of campaigns and inform strategy. *International Journal of Data and Network Science*, *7*(2), 563–574. DOI: 10.5267/j.ijdns.2023.3.015

Allil, K. (2024). Integrating AI-driven marketing analytics techniques into the classroom: Pedagogical strategies for enhancing student engagement and future business success. *Journal of Marketing Analytics*, *12*(2), 142–168. DOI: 10.1057/s41270-023-00281-z

Anayat, S., & Rasool, G. (2024). Artificial intelligence marketing (AIM): Connecting-the-dots using bibliometrics. *Journal of Marketing Theory and Practice*, *32*(1), 114–135. DOI: 10.1080/10696679.2022.2103435

Bas, J., Cirillo, C., & Cherchi, E. (2021). Classification of potential electric vehicle purchasers: A machine learning approach. *Technological Forecasting and Social Change*, *168*, 120759. DOI: 10.1016/j.techfore.2021.120759

Bayoude, K., Ouassit, Y., Ardchir, S., & Azouazi, M. (2018). How machine learning potentials are transforming the practice of digital marketing: State of the art. [PEN]. *Periodicals of Engineering and Natural Sciences*, *6*(2), 373. DOI: 10.21533/pen.v6i2.526

Bilgihan, A., Leong, A. M. W., Okumus, F., & Bai, J. (2024). Proposing a metaverse engagement model for brand development. *Journal of Retailing and Consumer Services*, *78*, 103781. DOI: 10.1016/j.jretconser.2024.103781

Bossert, L., & Hagendorff, T. (2021). Animals and AI. The role of animals in AI research and application – An overview and ethical evaluation. *Technology in Society*, *67*, 101678. DOI: 10.1016/j.techsoc.2021.101678

Carlson, K., Kopalle, P. K., Riddell, A., Rockmore, D., & Vana, P. (2023). Complementing human effort in online reviews: A deep learning approach to automatic content generation and review synthesis. *International Journal of Research in Marketing*, *40*(1), 54–74. DOI: 10.1016/j.ijresmar.2022.02.004

Cioppi, M., Curina, I., Francioni, B., & Savelli, E. (2023). Digital transformation and marketing: A systematic and thematic literature review. *Italian Journal of Marketing*, *2023*(2), 207–288. DOI: 10.1007/s43039-023-00067-2

Dahake, N. S., Gajghate, A., Dahake, P. S., & Bansod, S. (2024). A Transformative Impact of IoT and AI by Predictive Analytics on Modern Marketing Strategies: A Study of its Significance & Accuracy. *2024 2nd International Conference on Advances in Computation, Communication and Information Technology (ICAICCIT)*, 1150–1158. DOI: 10.1109/ICAICCIT64383.2024.10912388

Dahake, N. S., Suresh Dahake, P., & Gajghate, A. (2024). Beyond the Hype: A Critical Evaluation of Predictive Analytics Accuracy in High-Stakes Business Decisions. *2024 2nd DMIHER International Conference on Artificial Intelligence in Healthcare, Education and Industry (IDICAIEI)*, 1–6. DOI: 10.1109/IDICAIEI61867.2024.10842857

Dahake, P. S., Bagaregari, P., & Dahake, N. S. (2024). Shaping the Future of Retail: A Comprehensive Review of Predictive Analytics Models for Consumer Behavior. In Inder, S., Min, B., & Sharma, S. (Eds.), (pp. 143–160). Advances in Business Strategy and Competitive Advantage. IGI Global., DOI: 10.4018/979-8-3693-1734-1.ch011

Dahake, P. S., & Bansod, S. N. (2019). The role of Chinese electronics products to sway middle-class buyers. *International Journal of Public Sector Performance Management*, *5*(3/4), 337. DOI: 10.1504/IJPSPM.2019.10022488

Dahake, P. S., Chandak, S., & Dahake, N. S. (2024). Predictive Analytics in Performance Appraisal Systems: Enhancing Objectivity and Fairness. *2024 2nd DMIHER International Conference on Artificial Intelligence in Healthcare, Education and Industry (IDICAIEI)*, 1–5. DOI: 10.1109/IDICAIEI61867.2024.10842916

Dahake, P. S., Chandak, S., Mohare, R. V., Wadhwani, K., & Bhadade, P. (2023). The Crystal Ball of Marketing: How Predictive Analytics is Reshaping the Industry? *2023 Second International Conference On Smart Technologies For Smart Nation (SmartTechCon)*, 304–311. DOI: 10.1109/SmartTechCon57526.2023.10391334

Dahake, P. S., & Dahake, N. S. (2024). The Role of Big Data in Predictive Analytics for E-Commerce: Examine How Big Data Contributes to Better Predictions in Online Shopping. In Tarnanidis, T., Papathanasiou, J., Ismyrlis, V., & Kittu Manda, V. (Eds.), (pp. 403–426). Advances in Marketing, Customer Relationship Management, and E-Services. IGI Global., DOI: 10.4018/979-8-3693-9122-8.ch018

Dahake, P. S., Jain, M., Anusha, B., Poojitha, S., Singh, N., & Sharma, A. (2024). Integrating Organisational Theory, Resource-Based View, and Big Data Culture to Improve Manufacturing Performance. In D. Jelonek, N. Kumar, M. Chahar, R. Kinkladze, & L. Knop, *Recent Trends In Engineering and Science for Resource Optimization and Sustainable Development* (1st ed., pp. 156–159). CRC Press. DOI: 10.1201/9781003596721-36

Dahake, P. S., & Somani, N. (2024). Harnessing Predictive Analytics for Accurate Consumer Behaviour Forecasting: A Comprehensive Review. *2024 2nd DMIHER International Conference on Artificial Intelligence in Healthcare, Education and Industry (IDICAIEI)*, 1–6. DOI: 10.1109/IDICAIEI61867.2024.10842743

Davenport, T., Guha, A., Grewal, D., & Bressgott, T. (2020). How artificial intelligence will change the future of marketing. *Journal of the Academy of Marketing Science*, *48*(1), 24–42. DOI: 10.1007/s11747-019-00696-0

De Cosmo, L. M., Piper, L., & Di Vittorio, A. (2021). The role of attitude toward chatbots and privacy concern on the relationship between attitude toward mobile advertising and behavioral intent to use chatbots. *Italian Journal of Marketing*, *2021*(1–2), 83–102. DOI: 10.1007/s43039-021-00020-1

De Mauro, A., Sestino, A., & Bacconi, A. (2022). Machine learning and artificial intelligence use in marketing: A general taxonomy. *Italian Journal of Marketing*, *2022*(4), 439–457. DOI: 10.1007/s43039-022-00057-w

Dimitrovska, I., & Malinovski, T. (2017). Creating a Business Value while Transforming Data Assets using Machine Learning. *Computer Engineering and Applications Journal*, *6*(2), 59–70. DOI: 10.18495/comengapp.v6i2.205

Dongbo, M., Miniaoui, S., Fen, L., Althubiti, S. A., & Alsenani, T. R. (2023). Intelligent chatbot interaction system capable for sentimental analysis using hybrid machine learning algorithms. *Information Processing & Management*, *60*(5), 103440. DOI: 10.1016/j.ipm.2023.103440

Dumas, M., Fournier, F., Limonad, L., Marrella, A., Montali, M., Rehse, J.-R., Accorsi, R., Calvanese, D., De Giacomo, G., Fahland, D., Gal, A., La Rosa, M., Völzer, H., & Weber, I. (2022). *AI-Augmented Business Process Management Systems: A Research Manifesto*. DOI: 10.48550/ARXIV.2201.12855

Dwivedi, Y. K., Hughes, L., Ismagilova, E., Aarts, G., Coombs, C., Crick, T., Duan, Y., Dwivedi, R., Edwards, J., Eirug, A., Galanos, V., Ilavarasan, P. V., Janssen, M., Jones, P., Kar, A. K., Kizgin, H., Kronemann, B., Lal, B., Lucini, B., & Williams, M. D. (2021). Artificial Intelligence (AI): Multidisciplinary perspectives on emerging challenges, opportunities, and agenda for research, practice and policy. *International Journal of Information Management*, *57*, 101994. DOI: 10.1016/j.ijinfomgt.2019.08.002

El-Gharib, N. M., & Amyot, D. (2022). *Robotic Process Automation Using Process Mining $\unicode{x2013}$ A Systematic Literature Review*. DOI: 10.48550/ARXIV.2204.00751

Fredström, A., Parida, V., Wincent, J., Sjödin, D., & Oghazi, P. (2022). What is the Market Value of Artificial Intelligence and Machine Learning? The Role of Innovativeness and Collaboration for Performance. *Technological Forecasting and Social Change*, *180*, 121716. DOI: 10.1016/j.techfore.2022.121716

Ge, Z., Song, Z., Ding, S. X., & Huang, B. (2017). Data Mining and Analytics in the Process Industry: The Role of Machine Learning. *IEEE Access : Practical Innovations, Open Solutions*, *5*, 20590–20616. DOI: 10.1109/ACCESS.2017.2756872

Gera, S., & Sinha, A. (2022). T-Bot: AI-based social media bot detection model for trend-centric twitter network. *Social Network Analysis and Mining*, *12*(1), 76. DOI: 10.1007/s13278-022-00897-6

Gerlich, M., Elsayed, W., & Sokolovskiy, K. (2023). Artificial intelligence as toolset for analysis of public opinion and social interaction in marketing: Identification of micro and nano influencers. *Frontiers in Communication*, *8*, 1075654. DOI: 10.3389/fcomm.2023.1075654

Ghahramani, Z. (2015). Probabilistic machine learning and artificial intelligence. *Nature*, *521*(7553), 452–459. DOI: 10.1038/nature14541 PMID: 26017444

Goncalves, M., Hu, Y., Aliagas, I., & Cerdá, L. M. (2024). Neuromarketing algorithms' consumer privacy and ethical considerations: Challenges and opportunities. *Cogent Business & Management*, *11*(1), 2333063. DOI: 10.1080/23311975.2024.2333063

Gross, S., Malinova, M., & Mendling, J. (2019). *Navigating Through the Maze of Business Process Change Methods. Hawaii International Conference on System Sciences*. DOI: 10.24251/HICSS.2019.754

Gutuleac, R., Baima, G., Rizzo, C., & Bresciani, S. (2024). Will virtual influencers overcome the uncanny valley? The moderating role of social cues. *Psychology and Marketing*, *41*(7), 1419–1431. DOI: 10.1002/mar.21989

Hermann, E. (2022). Leveraging Artificial Intelligence in Marketing for Social Good—An Ethical Perspective. *Journal of Business Ethics*, *179*(1), 43–61. DOI: 10.1007/s10551-021-04843-y PMID: 34054170

Hsieh, P.-J. (2023). Determinants of physicians' intention to use AI-assisted diagnosis: An integrated readiness perspective. *Computers in Human Behavior*, *147*, 107868. DOI: 10.1016/j.chb.2023.107868

Huang, M.-H., & Rust, R. T. (2021). A strategic framework for artificial intelligence in marketing. *Journal of the Academy of Marketing Science*, *49*(1), 30–50. DOI: 10.1007/s11747-020-00749-9

Huberman, J. (2021). Amazon Go, surveillance capitalism, and the ideology of convenience. *Economic Anthropology*, *8*(2), 337–349. DOI: 10.1002/sea2.12211

Jabbar, A., Akhtar, P., & Dani, S. (2020). Real-time big data processing for instantaneous marketing decisions: A problematization approach. *Industrial Marketing Management*, *90*, 558–569. DOI: 10.1016/j.indmarman.2019.09.001

Jahin, M. A., Naife, S. A., Saha, A. K., & Mridha, M. F. (2024). *AI in Supply Chain Risk Assessment: A Systematic Literature Review and Bibliometric Analysis* (Version 5). arXiv. DOI: 10.48550/ARXIV.2401.10895

Janiesch, C., Zschech, P., & Heinrich, K. (2021). Machine learning and deep learning. *Electronic Markets*, *31*(3), 685–695. DOI: 10.1007/s12525-021-00475-2

Jiang, C., Zhang, H., Ren, Y., Han, Z., Chen, K.-C., & Hanzo, L. (2017). Machine Learning Paradigms for Next-Generation Wireless Networks. *IEEE Wireless Communications*, *24*(2), 98–105. DOI: 10.1109/MWC.2016.1500356WC

Jin, K., Zhong, Z. Z., & Zhao, E. Y. (2024). Sustainable Digital Marketing Under Big Data: An AI Random Forest Model Approach. *IEEE Transactions on Engineering Management*, *71*, 3566–3579. DOI: 10.1109/TEM.2023.3348991

Jordan, M. I., & Mitchell, T. M. (2015). Machine learning: Trends, perspectives, and prospects. *Science*, *349*(6245), 255–260. DOI: 10.1126/science.aaa8415 PMID: 26185243

Kanaparthi, V. (2024). *Transformational application of Artificial Intelligence and Machine learning in Financial Technologies and Financial services: A bibliometric review*. https://doi.org/DOI: 10.48550/ARXIV.2401.15710

Kapoor, R., & Kapoor, K. (2021). The transition from traditional to digital marketing: A study of the evolution of e-marketing in the Indian hotel industry. *Worldwide Hospitality and Tourism Themes*, *13*(2), 199–213. DOI: 10.1108/WHATT-10-2020-0124

Keegan, B. J., Dennehy, D., & Naudé, P. (2022). Implementing Artificial Intelligence in Traditional B2B Marketing Practices: An Activity Theory Perspective. *Information Systems Frontiers*, •••, 1–15. DOI: 10.1007/s10796-022-10294-1 PMID: 35637917

Kim, H., & Park, M. (2024). When digital celebrity talks to you: How human-like virtual influencers satisfy consumer's experience through social presence on social media endorsements. *Journal of Retailing and Consumer Services*, *76*, 103581. DOI: 10.1016/j.jretconser.2023.103581

Kose, U., & Sert, S. (2017). *Improving content marketing processes with the approaches by artificial intelligence*. DOI: 10.48550/ARXIV.1704.02114

Kozinets, R. V. (2022). Algorithmic branding through platform assemblages: Core conceptions and research directions for a new era of marketing and service management. *Journal of Service Management*, *33*(3), 437–452. DOI: 10.1108/JOSM-07-2021-0263

Kumar, V., Dixit, A., Javalgi, R. G., & Dass, M. (2016). Research framework, strategies, and applications of intelligent agent technologies (IATs) in marketing. *Journal of the Academy of Marketing Science*, *44*(1), 24–45. DOI: 10.1007/s11747-015-0426-9

Latinovic, Z., & Chatterjee, S. C. (2022). Achieving the promise of AI and ML in delivering economic and relational customer value in B2B. *Journal of Business Research*, *144*, 966–974. DOI: 10.1016/j.jbusres.2022.01.052

Lee, J., Jung, O., Lee, Y., Kim, O., & Park, C. (2021). A Comparison and Interpretation of Machine Learning Algorithm for the Prediction of Online Purchase Conversion. *Journal of Theoretical and Applied Electronic Commerce Research*, *16*(5), 1472–1491. DOI: 10.3390/jtaer16050083

Lee, K.-W., & Li, C.-Y. (2023). It is not merely a chat: Transforming chatbot affordances into dual identification and loyalty. *Journal of Retailing and Consumer Services*, *74*, 103447. DOI: 10.1016/j.jretconser.2023.103447

Li, C.-Y., Fang, Y.-H., & Chiang, Y.-H. (2023). Can AI chatbots help retain customers? An integrative perspective using affordance theory and service-domain logic. *Technological Forecasting and Social Change*, *197*, 122921. DOI: 10.1016/j.techfore.2023.122921

Lies, J. (2021). Digital marketing: Incompatibilities between performance marketing and marketing creativity. *Journal of Digital & Social Media Marketing*, *8*(4), 376. DOI: 10.69554/SSVH5588

Malthouse, E., & Copulsky, J. (2023). Artificial intelligence ecosystems for marketing communications. *International Journal of Advertising*, *42*(1), 128–140. DOI: 10.1080/02650487.2022.2122249

Marrella, A. (2018). What Automated Planning Can Do for Business Process Management. In Teniente, E., & Weidlich, M. (Eds.), *Business Process Management Workshops* (Vol. 308, pp. 7–19). Springer International Publishing., DOI: 10.1007/978-3-319-74030-0_1

Messner, W. (2022). Advancing our understanding of cultural heterogeneity with unsupervised machine learning. *Journal of International Management*, *28*(2), 100885. DOI: 10.1016/j.intman.2021.100885

Mikalef, P., & Gupta, M. (2021). Artificial intelligence capability: Conceptualization, measurement calibration, and empirical study on its impact on organizational creativity and firm performance. *Information & Management*, *58*(3), 103434. DOI: 10.1016/j.im.2021.103434

Moon, S., & Iacobucci, D. (2022). Social Media Analytics and Its Applications in Marketing. *Foundations and Trends® in Marketing*, *15*(4), 213–292. DOI: 10.1561/1700000073

Nguyen, G., Dlugolinsky, S., Bobák, M., Tran, V., López García, Á., Heredia, I., Malík, P., & Hluchý, L. (2019). Machine Learning and Deep Learning frameworks and libraries for large-scale data mining: A survey. *Artificial Intelligence Review*, *52*(1), 77–124. DOI: 10.1007/s10462-018-09679-z

Philp, M., Jacobson, J., & Pancer, E. (2022). Predicting social media engagement with computer vision: An examination of food marketing on Instagram. *Journal of Business Research*, *149*, 736–747. DOI: 10.1016/j.jbusres.2022.05.078

Pitt, C., Paschen, J., Kietzmann, J., Pitt, L. F., & Pala, E. (2023). Artificial Intelligence, Marketing, and the History of Technology: Kranzberg's Laws as a Conceptual Lens. *Australasian Marketing Journal*, *31*(1), 81–89. DOI: 10.1177/18393349211044175

Salehi, H., & Burgueño, R. (2018). Emerging artificial intelligence methods in structural engineering. *Engineering Structures*, *171*, 170–189. DOI: 10.1016/j.engstruct.2018.05.084

Salminen, J., Mustak, M., Corporan, J., Jung, S., & Jansen, B. J. (2022). Detecting Pain Points from User-Generated Social Media Posts Using Machine Learning. *Journal of Interactive Marketing*, *57*(3), 517–539. DOI: 10.1177/10949968221095556

Sarker, I. H. (2021). Machine Learning: Algorithms, Real-World Applications and Research Directions. *SN Computer Science*, *2*(3), 160. DOI: 10.1007/s42979-021-00592-x PMID: 33778771

Saura, J. R. (2020). Using Data Sciences in Digital Marketing: Framework, methods, and performance metrics. *Journal of Innovation & Knowledge*. DOI: 10.1016/j.jik.2020.08.001

Saura, J. R., Škare, V., & Dosen, D. O. (2024). Is AI-based digital marketing ethical? Assessing a new data privacy paradox. *Journal of Innovation & Knowledge*, *9*(4), 100597. DOI: 10.1016/j.jik.2024.100597

Selvakumar, P., Shanthi, M., Pitchiah, R., Sharma, M., Dahake, P. S., & T. C., M. (2025). The Role of Artificial Intelligence in Business Model Innovation: Overview of AI Technologies. In M. Khokhar (Ed.), *Advances in Business Strategy and Competitive Advantage* (pp. 219–246). IGI Global. DOI: 10.4018/979-8-3693-9571-4.ch009

Selvakumar, P., Shanthi, M., Pitchiah, R., Sharma, M., Dahake, P. S., & TC, M. (2025). The Role of Artificial Intelligence in Business Model Innovation: Overview of AI Technologies. *AI-Driven Business Model Innovation*, 219–246.

Sharakhina, L., Ilyina, I., Kaplun, D., Teor, T., & Kulibanova, V. (2024). AI technologies in the analysis of visual advertising messages: Survey and application. *Journal of Marketing Analytics*, *12*(4), 1066–1089. DOI: 10.1057/s41270-023-00255-1

Sharma, R., Kumar, A., & Chuah, C. (2021). Turning the blackbox into a glassbox: An explainable machine learning approach for understanding hospitality customer. *International Journal of Information Management Data Insights*, *1*(2), 100050. DOI: 10.1016/j.jjimei.2021.100050

Shrestha, Y. R., Krishna, V., & Von Krogh, G. (2021). Augmenting organizational decision-making with deep learning algorithms: Principles, promises, and challenges. *Journal of Business Research*, *123*, 588–603. DOI: 10.1016/j.jbusres.2020.09.068

Soni, N., Sharma, E. K., Singh, N., & Kapoor, A. (2020). Artificial Intelligence in Business: From Research and Innovation to Market Deployment. *Procedia Computer Science*, *167*, 2200–2210. DOI: 10.1016/j.procs.2020.03.272

Suraña-Sánchez, C., & Aramendia-Muneta, M. E. (2024). Impact of artificial intelligence on customer engagement and advertising engagement: A review and future research agenda. *International Journal of Consumer Studies*, *48*(2), e13027. DOI: 10.1111/ijcs.13027

Syam, N., & Sharma, A. (2018). Waiting for a sales renaissance in the fourth industrial revolution: Machine learning and artificial intelligence in sales research and practice. *Industrial Marketing Management, 69*, 135–146. DOI: 10.1016/j.indmarman.2017.12.019

Thontirawong, P., & Chinchanachokchai, S. (2021). TEACHING ARTIFICIAL INTELLIGENCE AND MACHINE LEARNING IN MARKETING. *Marketing Education Review, 31*(2), 58–63. DOI: 10.1080/10528008.2021.1871849

Tupikovskaja-Omovie, Z., & Tyler, D. (2020). Clustering consumers' shopping journeys: Eye tracking fashion m-retail. *Journal of Fashion Marketing and Management, 24*(3), 381–398. DOI: 10.1108/JFMM-09-2019-0195

Verbraeken, J., Wolting, M., Katzy, J., Kloppenburg, J., Verbelen, T., & Rellermeyer, J. S. (2021). A Survey on Distributed Machine Learning. *ACM Computing Surveys, 53*(2), 1–33. DOI: 10.1145/3377454

Wang, C. (2022). Efficient customer segmentation in digital marketing using deep learning with swarm intelligence approach. *Information Processing & Management, 59*(6), 103085. DOI: 10.1016/j.ipm.2022.103085

Wang, H., Fu, T., Du, Y., Gao, W., Huang, K., Liu, Z., Chandak, P., Liu, S., Van Katwyk, P., Deac, A., Anandkumar, A., Bergen, K., Gomes, C. P., Ho, S., Kohli, P., Lasenby, J., Leskovec, J., Liu, T.-Y., Manrai, A., & Zitnik, M. (2023). Scientific discovery in the age of artificial intelligence. *Nature, 620*(7972), 47–60. DOI: 10.1038/s41586-023-06221-2 PMID: 37532811

Wilson, R. D., & Bettis-Outland, H. (2019). Can artificial neural network models be used to improve the analysis of B2B marketing research data? *Journal of Business and Industrial Marketing, 35*(3), 495–507. DOI: 10.1108/JBIM-01-2019-0060

Xu, Y., Liu, X., Cao, X., Huang, C., Liu, E., Qian, S., Liu, X., Wu, Y., Dong, F., Qiu, C.-W., Qiu, J., Hua, K., Su, W., Wu, J., Xu, H., Han, Y., Fu, C., Yin, Z., Liu, M., & Zhang, J. (2021). Artificial intelligence: A powerful paradigm for scientific research. *Innovation (Cambridge (Mass.)), 2*(4), 100179. DOI: 10.1016/j.xinn.2021.100179 PMID: 34877560

Yaiprasert, C., & Hidayanto, A. N. (2024). AI-powered ensemble machine learning to optimize cost strategies in logistics business. *International Journal of Information Management Data Insights, 4*(1), 100209. DOI: 10.1016/j.jjimei.2023.100209

Yang, Z., & Lin, Z. (2022). Interpretable video tag recommendation with multimedia deep learning framework. *Internet Research, 32*(2), 518–535. DOI: 10.1108/INTR-08-2020-0471

Yu, K.-H., Beam, A. L., & Kohane, I. S. (2018). Artificial intelligence in healthcare. *Nature Biomedical Engineering*, *2*(10), 719–731. DOI: 10.1038/s41551-018-0305-z PMID: 31015651

Zaoui, A., Tchuente, D., Wamba, S. F., & Kamsu-Foguem, B. (2024). Impact of artificial intelligence on aeronautics: An industry-wide review. *Journal of Engineering and Technology Management*, *71*, 101800. DOI: 10.1016/j.jengtecman.2024.101800

Zulaikha, S., Mohamed, H., Kurniawati, M., Rusgianto, S., & Rusmita, S. A. (2020). CUSTOMER PREDICTIVE ANALYTICS USING ARTIFICIAL INTELLIGENCE. *The Singapore Economic Review*, •••, 1–12. DOI: 10.1142/S0217590820480021

Chapter 8
Leveraging Data Analytics for Informed Decision-Making in Process Management

Subramanian R. Siva
SRM Institute of Science and Technology, India

Indu V. Thanammal
Amrita Vishwa Vidyapeetham, India

Ignatious K Pious
Vel Tech Rangarajan Dr. Sagunthala R&D Institute of Science and Technology, India

Princy B. Anni
Panimalar Engineering College, India

K. Sudha
RMD Engineering College, India

Gracious L. A. Anto
https://orcid.org/0000-0003-2386-9182
R.M.K. College of Engineering and Technology, India

P. Divya
IFET College of Engineering, India

ABSTRACT

This survey chapter aims at discussing the application of data analytics in process management in order to improve operational performance, decision making and innovation. This chapter also describes the analytical techniques including descriptive, predictive, and prescriptive analytics and illustrates their use in manufacturing, healthcare, finance, and logistics industries. The chapter also discusses new trends, which are in the development of process management, including artificial intelligence, edge analytics, and digital twins. However, there are some barriers to the implementation of the framework such as data quality, skill, privacy, and

DOI: 10.4018/979-8-3373-3336-6.ch008

organizational readiness. The chapter concludes by emphasizing the importance of leveraging data analytics strategically and responsibly to ensure long-term success in a data-driven business environment.

1. INTRODUCTION

1.1 Background and Motivation

In an era defined by rapid technological advancement and ever-increasing competition, organizations are under immense pressure to optimize their operations, reduce inefficiencies, and deliver high-quality products and services. Process management is the systematic approach of designing, implementing, controlling and improving an organization's activities that culminate in the achievement of its performance goals. In the past, theories of process management are fixed of prominent structures of management including Lean, Six Sigma as well as Total Quality Management. These methodologies have been useful to businesses in enhancing on operational effectiveness and quality. However, in an open world of rapidly changing circumstances and increased availability and use of data, these do not easily provide fast and effective solutions to a complicated situation. The changing business environment and the advancement of technology have propelled the generation of large volumes of data from various sources such as sensors, enterprise systems, customers, and supply chain partners. This has led to data being not just a result of activities or a side product of an organization but rather an asset that if well managed, provides value to an organization by enabling informed decision making. Business data analytics has described as an essential tool to analyze raw information to understand the behaviors of the processes and patterns and provide recommendations regarding their future performance. The application of data analytics within process management helps organizations to shift from the reactive approach to problem-solving to the proactive one. Using historical data and real-time data, decision-makers can determine the source of the problems, model possible operation strategies, and enhance the use of resources. This transformation in process management is not a mere product of technology, it is a change in organizational culture towards process orientation and improvement. In addition, the influx of new technologies like artificial intelligence and machine learning, Internet of things (IOT), cloud computing possibilities of data analytics has also boosted tremendously. These technologies enable real-time data collection, operations and analysis on a large and intricate scale, enabling the identification of an abnormality or the making of mundane decisions without the need for man intervention and even enable predictions of future trends with a lot of efficiency. Thus, the integration of data analytics and process management can provide an opportunity for breakthrough in almost all fields of business, including manufacturing and supply chain, healthcare, financial services, and public sectors.

1.2 Objective of the Survey

The purpose of this survey is to give a systematic and organized description about how data analytics is utilized to improve and facilitate decision making in the process management. Although the value of analytics in strategic management is rather clear, it is possible to focus on the utilization of analytics for process management in detail. This paper seeks to fill this gap by discussing the relationship between the two areas by reviewing techniques, tools, methodologies, and case studies. The survey aims to explore: What sort of information is applicable to the process management, and how it is gathered and applied? The effectiveness of analytical techniques in different process challenges. The aim of the study is thus to establish how organisations can adopt analytics to foster enhanced performance, decreased expense, and increased flexibility. Types of challenges companies face in implementing analytics driven process management and how they can be dealt with. Answering these questions, the chapter aims to familiarize the researchers and practitioners with the state-of-the-art approaches while identifying the directions for further developments. Another important objective is to demonstrate various fields where data analytics is used for processing and, thus, to show that it is a universal practice with far-reaching implications. From increasing efficiency in a production line in a manufacturing firm, managing patient throughput in a hospital to automating management reports in a financial firm, analytics can make the processes faster, better and more efficient. Besides, this survey also pays attention to the practical aspects by using case studies and examples of real-world applications. These cases help to keep the general discussion concrete so that the benefits and the difficulties of applying data analytics for action are clearly discernible. In the end, it is aimed at providing a source that is both scholarly and useful for decision-makers who are interested in the challenging but fruitful process of achieving process improvement based on data.

1.3 Scope and Structure

The topics of the survey cover a wide range of topics such as business process management, data science, information systems, operations research, and industrial engineering. The emphasis is made on the use of big data and Business Intelligence at all stages of the process: design, implementation and control. It covers different types of analytics such as descriptive, diagnostic, predictive and prescriptive and how they are applied in the decision making process at different levels of the process execution. The rest of the paper is organized as follows: In Section 2, the concept of process management is explained and defined, and the conventional methods are introduced and discussed. In section 3, the subject of data analytics in this regard is discussed including the types of data, data sources, and integration methods. Section 4 focuses on analytical tools and methods where the authors provide an overview of the methods that were applied in order to gain insights and make decisions. Chapter 5 is devoted to the discussion of the practical applications in various spheres of business. Section 6 gives the issues and drawbacks encountered by organizations in implementing data-driven process management, while section 7 highlights the future prospect of the topic. Lastly, Section 8 provides an overview on the findings and the strategic suggestions and recommendations.

2. FUNDAMENTALS OF PROCESS MANAGEMENT

2.1 Definitions and Key Concepts

In its essence, process management can be defined as an approach that involves planning, implementing, controlling, and improving a set of activities known as a business process, the ultimate purpose of which is to provide a valuable product or service to a customer or other interested party. A business process is defined as an organized collection of activities that is aimed at achieving certain objectives of a business organization. These can be production processes, for instance, manufacturing or supply chain or non-production processes like human resource or accounting. Most processes have inputs that can be in the form of materials, information or labor, transformation and outputs which are goods or services.

The concept of a workflow is linked to the process management and can be defined as the automation and coordination of activities in organizations between people, systems and departments. A workflow is a set of well-defined activities which specify how a process is initiated, who is responsible for it, how the data moves from one activity to another in the process and under what conditions the process moves from one state to another. Today, business processes are managed with the help of business process management systems (BPMS), enterprise resource planning (ERP), etc., to provide a framework for the organization.

Another important concept here is process improvement, which deals with the optimization of a process, by finding out the bottlenecks, eradicating wastes, shortening the cycle time, and improving the quality of a process. Most process improvement activities are based on feedback and control systems and tools like KPIs, throughputs, and customer satisfaction rates. It is aimed at enhancing the company's operational effectiveness which in this case entails guaranteeing that business processes are not only effective and standardized, but also strategic.

In general, process management is the key to the effective functioning and competitiveness of an organization. It is an important tool that guarantees that activities are done right and in the right manner and also as a benchmark for comparing the performance and instating change. However, the method of handling these processes in business environments that are becoming more complicated and dynamic has been seen to have shortcomings thus creating room for more use of data analysis.

2.2 Traditional Approaches to Process Management

Traditional process management methodologies have been very helpful in the management of organizations and their performance. The leading strategies of organizational improvement that exist in the current world include the Six Sigma, Lean, and the Total Quality Management (TQM). All these approaches have their own perspective in the improvement of the processes but they all aim at increasing effectiveness, quality and customer value.

TQM is a more comprehensive concept, which implies that every employee is accountable for quality within the organization. TQM involves the use of employees, concentration on customers and thinking in the long term. Quality management is its key aspect since it focuses on quality control, improvement, and cooperation to foster organizational culture of quality and customer orientation.

Figure 1. Fundamentals of Process Management

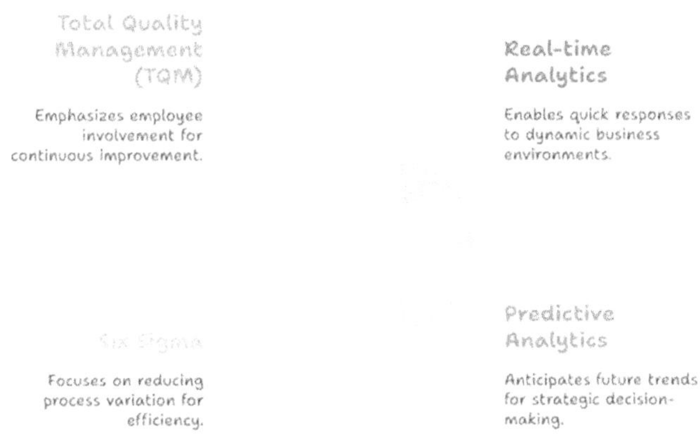

Altogether, these methodologies have given the basis for systematic and rigorous approaches towards handling and optimizing enterprise processes. They have helped firms to rationalize activities, enhance product quality, and for achieve cost efficiencies. However, the traditional toolkit of process improvement approaches is quite effective but has been recently under pressure due to the growing complexity and speed of business.

2.3 Limitations of Conventional Methods

However, even though the use of traditional approaches to process management is widespread and has been proved to be effective, they have several drawbacks in the context of the modern world, which is characterized by the growing amount of data and the increasing rate of business processes. The first one is that they are not real-time and do not have the ability to respond to what is happening around them. Tools like Six Sigma or Lean use data collection and analysis at certain time intervals which means that the problems in the process and the subsequent solutions might take a long time to be identified and implemented. In industries where flexibility and quick response are critical, for instance, e-commerce, healthcare, or logistics industries, such delays have a negative effect on performance and customer satisfaction.

Third, conventional methods are usually posteriori in their approach mostly relying on figures and overall data collected after the event. While they are good in recognizing and solving current problems and weak in predicting the future problems or changes in the environment. This makes an organisation slow to change direction in response to market needs, new technology or any other irregularities that may occur. While, on the other hand, data analytics as an instrument allows to act not only in response to certain events but also makes it possible to predict them, and this kind of decision-making is critical in the modern world to sustain a competitive advantage.

One more disadvantage is the inability to work with unstructured or large amounts of data. These traditional approaches are more suitable for numerical data, categorical inputs and may not be effective for data from the text feedback, sensors or event logs. When connected IoT devices, digital platforms, and AI systems are used in business, the data generated are bigger and more intricate to analyze using conventional methods.

In addition, most of the traditional approaches rely on the skills of personnel and may require a lot of time to put into practice. Implementing Six Sigma project or a lean project involves a lot of training, time and engagement of various departments. This can be a challenge to implement, especially for the small organizations or organizations that do not have the relevant technical knowledge.

Last but not the least, traditional methodologies are not easily scalable or flexible when it comes to growth of an organisation or changes in the process structure. Charts and step by step diagrams do not capture the complex and complex nonsequential operations of current processes. This is especially important given that more and more companies are becoming distributed and digital in nature.

Thus, organizations are looking at data analytics as an addition and an improvement to conventional process improvement approaches. Thus, analytics can be incorporated into the processes so that insights are generated and decisions made throughout the process, with an aim at achieving intelligent process management.

3. DATA ANALYTICS IN THE CONTEXT OF PROCESS MANAGEMENT

3.1 Overview of Data Analytics

This is the systematic use of quantitative and qualitative data to transform them into meaningful information that would offer insights in certain activity. If considering process management, data analytics is the means that offer the tools and methods to make process information actionable (Chong, D., & Shi, H. 2015). It facilitates performance measurement, identification of causes of poor performance, prognosis of performance and identification of appropriate actions. The problem under analysis highlights that as companies seek to go from a reactive to proactive mode of process management, data analytics plays a pivotal role in this change (Elgendy, N., & Elragal, A. 2014). The four main types of data analytics are descriptive, diagnostic, predictive, and prescriptive analytics and each of them has a different purpose in the decision-making process. Descriptive analytics deals with the past and aims at answering the question: What happened? This includes the use of dashboards, reports and visualizations in an attempt to track KPIs and other process metrics. For example, descriptive analytics in a production environment can include data such as the frequency of machines being off-line, how fast the line is running, and the number of defects (Tsai et al 2015). Diagnostic analytics is, therefore, different from descriptive analytics as it explains why something happened. They include Root analysis, correlation analysis and drill down analysis in order to determine the cause of performance variation. For instance, in a logistics operation, diagnostic analytics can be used to identify if delays were as a result of traffic, a supplier or internally (Vassakis et al 2017). The results of the past, as well as mathematical formulas and artificial intelligence technologies, are used to make predictions in predictive analytics. It formulates the question: What is the likelihood of? In process management, it could be applied in predicting the probability of machine breakdowns, the customer traffic, or the supply chain disruptions. Through prediction, decision makers are able to prevent future occurrences since the information is provided to them beforehand. The last type is prescriptive analytics, which in addition to forecasting, contains recommendations that would help to achieve the best results. They combine database construction, optimization procedures, and the desired decision-making model to answer: What is recommended now? For instance, if applied to manufacturing, it could prescript how to schedule the production or regulate quantities of stocks in regards to demand and available resources.

Figure 2. Data Analytics in the Context of Process Management

All these four types of analytics are used together to get a complete picture of the process performance. Descriptive and diagnostic analytics give the end of the story and the view from it, while predictive and prescriptive analytics give a vision for the future and what needs to be done. Altogether, both of them are the basis of the data-driven process management that can be improved and develop more effective strategies.

3.2 Types of Data in Process Management

The use of data analytics in process management depends on the quality, availability and the type of data available in an organization. Data is created in various forms depending on the processes, and is mainly classified as structured and unstructured. Structured data is rather well-ordered and, therefore, can be easily incorporated into a relational database. These are quantitative and categorical data such as time stamp, sensor data, transaction histories and inventory status. This type of data is most suitable for traditional analytics and modeling activities because of its format and availability.

On the other hand, unstructured data is data that does not have any format and is normally more difficult to analyze. Some examples of such records are emails, maintenance logs, voice and video recordings, social media conversations, and customer feedback. In fact, unstructured data is more difficult to process, but since it will contain more contextual information, it can be used in diagnostics or prescriptive analytics.

In those categories, process management uses several specific types of data. This type of data is generated from business activities and it involves the processing time, the rate at which the business processes the products, the rate of errors, and the usage of resources. This information helps in understanding the efficiency and effectiveness of the operations that are being undertaken.

This data is collected from machines, equipment and production lines and is usually referred to as sensor data that is characteristic of Industrial Internet of Things (IIoT). It provides an opportunity to monitor the temperature, pressure, vibration, and energy consumption, for example. Sensors are important for prescriptive maintenance and fault detection to avoid possible failures and their consequent negative impact on businesses.

Log data captures system-generated events and user actions within digital platforms. It tracks all the user activities from login, usage of software, completion of transactions and even system faults. Event logs can be used in the activity of process mining which involves the analysis of data collected in actual organizational processes with the aim of determining the existing anomalous, inefficient or non-conforming flows.

In the current business environments, data is created from various sources and points making it distributed and disparate. This data diversity offers promise as well as a set of problems for process analytics, which must address them in a variety of ways and tools.

3.3 Data Collection and Integration

Gathering and consolidating data from various sources forms the basic process of process analytics. Process analysis often occurs in numerous areas of an organization and through multiple platforms, which does not allow to create a single picture of process performance. To this end, there is the need for business to put in place data pipelines and integration structures that can pull data from various sources in a structured and integrated manner. The first source of process data can be obtained from the Internet of Things (IoT). The embedded IoT devices of equipment's and structures collect data on the environment, states of the machines and occurrences of events. This is then sent to the central storage or cloud service where it can be processed in almost real time. Internet of Things makes it possible to monitor the process operations at the individual level, and enables the use of contextual control. Other sources of process data include the Enterprise systems such as ERP and CRM systems within an organization (Khodakarami, F., & Chan, Y. E. 2014). ERP systems offer information about buying, stocking, making, and spending and employing, while CRM systems document customer relations, services, and selling. These systems allow visibility and synchronization of all processes across the value chain with the help of data integration (Hansen et al 2023). Others include Manufacturing Execution Systems (MES), Human Capital Management (HCM), and external data such as the market data or weather data. The data integration between internal and external sources is beneficial to the analytical environment and improves the decision-making process. Thus, data collection and integration are not just technical issues but powerful tools for improving the business processes. When done well they are the bedrock for analytics, machine learning and the drive for operational excellence no matter what functional level in a given organization (Ponmalar, A et al 2024).

4. ANALYTICAL TECHNIQUES AND TOOLS

4.1 Descriptive and Diagnostic Analytics

Descriptive and diagnostic analytics are two types of analytics that are most fundamental to the process management. These techniques enable organizations to obtain a clear picture of past and current performance and thus provide a ground for some more sophisticated interventions. In the descriptive level, the tools like dashboards and reports give an overview of KPIs, throughput, cycle time, defects, and resource utilization. They assist managers and process owners to observe the processes in real time, compare the results with the standard values and detect the differences in the results.

Figure 3. Analytical Techniques and Tools

One of the most important techniques falling within the realm of diagnostic analytics is process mining that has been receiving a lot of attention in the recent past. Process mining involves analyzing the event logs of an organization's information system to model the actual processes performed in an organization. In this way, process mining tools can determine whether the real-world processes match the ideal or expected models and can highlight the problems such as delays, non-conformities to the standard operating procedures. This technique offers a detailed and quantifiable method of diagnosing processes that is more systematic than the conventional methods like interviews or manual assessments.

Key BI platforms that are used in the support of descriptive as well as diagnostic analytics (Jayaraman, K. D., & Jain, S. 2024). These tools also help in the integration and visualization of data from different sources as well as the data can be explored interactively with options for drill down. They also support the creation of role-based dashboards ranging from management level to operational level used in the production line. BI tools when combined with process mining provides a solid ground for continuous process improvement (Mishra, S., & Mishra, P. 2022).

4.2 Predictive Analytics

Predictive analytics is a further development of the analysis where an attempt is made at predicting events or trends that are likely to occur in the future. In the context of process management, the use of predictive analytics is aimed at the identification of potential issues, the provision of efficient resource distribution and planning. Hence, at the heart of predictive analytics are machine learning (ML) models that are capable of identifying such hard-to-detect high-order patterns in the data (Siva, S. R et al 2022).

A popular use case is demand forecasting in which locations, time, sales data, and other variables as well as input from econometric models are used to train decision trees, support vector machines, and the like to make future demand levels predictions. Some of the benefits of good forecasts include, it helps organizations to plan for production, inventory and staffing to match expectations hence cutting costs and improving on service delivery.

Another application of the proposed method is failure prediction, especially in manufacturing and asset-intensive industries. Through the analysis of the data collected from the sensors and the maintenance records, the remaining useful life (RUL) can be predicted and potential symptoms of degradation can be determined. To produce those insights, techniques including regression analysis, random forests, time-series models among others are usually employed. These models assist in predicting the time at which the assets require maintenance hence avoiding downtimes, increasing the life span of the assets, and decreasing the maintenance expenses.

However, some factors that are noteworthy are the quality of the input data, the choice of features, and the timely update and re calibration of the models. The changes in processes and environments, therefore, require the models to be updated periodically to achieve higher accuracy.

4.3 Prescriptive Analytics

While predictive analytics is more about forecasting the outcomes, prescriptive analytics involves identifying the most appropriate action to take given the outcomes that have been forecasted. It entails the application of optimization models and simulation and decision making tools in order to arrive at decision that are most appropriate given the strategic goals and limitations. Prescriptive analytics can be satisfied with questions as follows; What is the right one for production planning and scheduling? As seen in this paper, different tasks may compete for a free resource – time, which is a scarce resource It is, therefore, pertinent to determine in what ways we can best use a free resource when other resources are rightly commanded. Which of the pricing strategies will help to increase profitability?

Optimisation models make use of programme computation to find an optimal solution for a problem given certain constraint which includes linear programming, mixed integer programming and constraint satisfaction. For instance, in supply chain network, an instance of an optimisation model could seek to find a solution that would minimize transportation costs whilst at the same time ensuring that the delivery of services is done in accordance to services level agreements.

Decision support systems (DSS) are computerized systems that use models coupled with a user interface that allows the manager to input data and get a number of solutions. These systems also contain features that enable one to simulate how certain decisions will affect the organization under various assumptions and risks. Thus, prescriptive analytics as the quantitative decision-making tool can significantly improve the capacity of organizations to operate tactically in a given environment.

Prescriptive analytics is most effective in a more restricted context or when there are high stakes to be made or lost, for instance, whereby wrong decisions made can lead to financial or operational disasters. Real-time and predictive analytics applied to prescriptive context helps in more effective, fast, and smart decisions.

4.4 Real-Time and Stream Analytics

The need for such analyses has become more prominent in the current world as organizations continue to work in uncertain and fast-changing environments. Real-time and stream analytics help business to analyze and make decisions on data as it is being generated in real-time. This capability is very useful in situations like fraud prevention, supply chain management, and quality assurance of products among others.

One of the most important technologies touching the real-time analytics is the Complex Event Processing (CEP). CEP systems watch large streams of data for the occurrence of particular events or conditions, for example, equipment malfunction or low stock levels. This way, when such patterns are identified, the system can send out alarms, respond automatically, or pass the matter to operators. This makes it possible to manage the processes when they are triggered by events and reduce the time taken to make decisions.

The real-time streaming platforms are common among developers for developing real-time big data analytics. These frameworks enable creation of large scale and highly available systems to deal with constant stream of data with minimal and acceptable levels of latency.

Real-time is not only beneficial for operations because the obtained data contributes to both forecasting and prescriptive models. For instance, data from the sensors can help in recalibrating the predictive maintenance models in real-time or changing the production factors based on the signals that are received.

5. APPLICATIONS IN PROCESS MANAGEMENT

5.1 Manufacturing and Production

Process improvement has been one of the key areas where manufacturing has been very active for a very long time and data analytics has only made it faster. In the current world of manufacturing, different approaches that involve the use of data are making their way to the physical floor to control, manage, and optimize production lines.

The most significant use is in the predictive maintenance, whereby the machinery is monitored using sensors and the records of the machine performance to identify the likelihood of failure. It is possible to predict when a machine is likely to fail or need a service by analyzing the vibration patterns, temperature variations, and other usage history (Lakumarapu, S et al 2024). This makes it possible to have a planned maintenance which would reduce time when the machinery is out of service thus increasing the useful life of costly machinery.

Besides, maintenance has also been enhanced significantly by the use of analytics and quality control has also not been left behind. Real time quality of production is managed and controlled using advanced statistical techniques and machine learning algorithms. Information on the characteristics of the raw material, operator's inputs and the environment are collected and evaluated in order to identify any variance from the quality parameters. Automated inspection is another application of image recognition, where the quality of products is inspected for defects by the use of image recognition algorithms. Hence the increase in product reliability, less wastage and better conformity to the set standards in the market.

5.2 Supply Chain and Logistics

The supply chain refers to a set of processes that involves procurement, transportation, storage and delivery of products. It is very important for managing these processes efficiently and with more fluidity with the use of analytics. There is one of the most significant applications, which is route optimization: defining the best paths for delivering goods. Realtime traffic information, weather information, delivery constraints, telemetry about the vehicles themselves, and other inputs can be used to make and adjust the routes in real time in such a way, that they would optimize fuel consumption, delivery times, and cost (Munuhwa, S., 2023).

Another area is inventory management, which is also essential in the operation of a business organization. Forecasting involves the use of past sales data, the trends of the coming seasons, and the market trends to estimate the future demand. These forecasts also help manage inventories to ensure that they do not order too much or too little inventory. Real-time analytics also helps to monitor the supply chain making it easier for people to make the right decision at the right time such as when there is a delay in supply from the supplier, or when the ports are congested or if demand surges unexpectedly (Musau, E. G., 2024).

Also, the supply chain risk management is evolving through the use of analytics. They can evaluate the suppliers' performance, geopolitical risks, and other indicators as tweets to identify disruption risks. This provides a broad perspective where organizations are able to fashion out ways of dealing with the risks and create better supply chain systems.

5.3 Healthcare and Service Industry

In a healthcare setting, process management has specific impacts on patient safety, quality of care, and the functioning of the health organization. It also involves the use of data analytics to improve the patient movement around the organization including emergency, surgery, and inpatient care.

This paper discusses how patient admission, treatment time, and discharge data can be used in order to forecast bed use, waiting times, and staff distribution. This not only enhances satisfaction of the patients but also assists in the elimination of bottlenecks and pressures on resources.

Another of the clusters where analytics can greatly help is resource management. Healthcare organizations apply analytics to predict the need for medical personnel, equipment, and drugs in the hospitals. It is also useful in planning for seasonal flu, other diseases, or any other circumstances that may lead to an increase in the number of patients. In addition, the scheduling algorithms help in distributing staff according to the work and patient severity to ensure that the workload is evenly distributed and the quality of care is enhanced.

In the more general application of services like in the hotel, banks, and stores, analytics helps in the course of process improvement through client/visitor behavior, a system to handle queues and flexible resource allocation technique. Customer data is applied in service organizations in a way that facilitates personalization, demand forecasting, and operational efficiency thereby enhancing the level of service delivery and customer satisfaction.

5.4 Financial and Business Processes

Data analytics has become a crucial solution for improving and automating the main business functions within the financial sector. Fraud detection is among the most common uses of analytics systems where the analytics systems are constantly scanning the transactions for any signs of fraud. These schemes use models trained through large information tuples of transaction history to find features that could be hard to decipher by overly complex systems of rules alone. Real time fraud detection can also alert an organization and prevent fraud incidences from escalating as they can be detected immediately.

Another major application is in the area of process automation in the context of financial services, and here we can mention RPA and intelligent automation. Data analytics helps these technologies by pointing out the routine processes and activities, which can be best handed over to robots such as invoice payments, compliance reports, or accounts reconciliations. Also, predictive analytics helps in making financial forecasts, credit risks, and cash flow, besides helping in understanding the market trends.

Through this system application, organizations get some benefits such as improved time performance, improved accuracy of the results, and better evaluation of strategies. Besides, it also improves operational effectiveness and helps attain a better competitive advantage in a competitive and closely monitored industry.

5.5 Smart Industry and IoT-Driven Process Analytics

Smart Industry also known as Industry 4.0 involves the integration of physical and digital systems through analyzing, IoT, and cyber-physical systems.

In this ecosystem, a large number of sensors, devices, as well as machines are interconnected and are constantly collecting real-time data. This data is used by IoT-driven process analytics to improve the control of industrial processes in a way that was not possible before.

Automated and highly interconnected factories that are a core concept of Industry 4.0 are characterized by their ability to make decisions and optimize their production lines on their own. For instance, a smart factory can change the settings of a machine according to the type of product that is being manufactured or the environment in which it is being produced because of the feedback received from the sensors. Of this information, analytical platforms provide performance, diagnostics, and indicator of further servicing to create a looped mechanism that enhances the program.

Cyber-physical systems or CPSs are even more integrated than cyber systems and this is because of the integration of the physical environment. Such systems integrate computation, networking and physical processes in executable manner. In process management, they enable modeling, prototyping and remote control and monitoring of processes. A digital twin of a physical system is a model of the real-world application that can be used to model various performance scenarios in order to determine the best configuration or to analyze potential problems that can occur.

This integration is not only beneficial in operational level but also on strategic level goals such as sustainability, flexibility and resilience. Through the adoption of these technologies, an organization can be able to adapt to changes in demand, be flexible on production and be able to produce quality products with less cost and harm to the environment.

6. CHALLENGES AND LIMITATIONS

6.1 Data Quality and Integration Issues

Some of the key issues that need to be addressed when it comes to use of data analytics for process management include the quality and integration of data.

In other words, analytics has to be based on factual, comprehensive, timely and consistent data. Unfortunately, many organizations still struggle with fragmented data systems, inconsistent data formats, and poor data governance practices. In many of the industrial applications, like manufacturing, supply chain or healthcare, the data is distributed across various isolated systems. This leads to silos which reduce the ability to analyze data comprehensively and to obtain a single picture of the operations.

Moreover, the data obtained from IoT devices, ERP systems, and third-party vendors may differ in their level of details and credibility. There are often noisy sensor data, errors in manual entries in spreadsheets and legacy systems may not have APIs for integration. Such differences are very challenging in data preprocessing and can even hinder the performance of complex analytical models. Addressing data quality and integration challenges entail a significant amount of funds in building the data infrastructure, data cleaning processes, and standardization initiatives, which are often under founded or deferred.

6.2 Skills and Organizational Readiness

The final challenge that most organizations face is the lack of an adequate skilled workforce to support the use of analytics even when data is available and systems are implemented. Data analytics, especially at the predictive and prescriptive levels, demands expertise in statistics, machine learning, data engineering, and domain knowledge. However, the world is still experiencing a scarce number of professionals who have the technical skills as well as adequate knowledge of business operations.

Such talent deficit can lead to a delay in implementation, poor quality of insights or underutilization of the tools.

Apart from human capital, there are other factors which facilitate the adoption of analytics in an organization. It is necessary to adapt the organizational culture and the way of working, decision-making, and communication to data-driven strategies. This often involves a change from the traditional tall-organizational structures that work with many layers of command and control. If such changes are not made, even the most sophisticated analytics programs may fail due to lack of internal support, top management engagement, or process implementation.

These are some of the challenges that can be solved by training programs, cross-functional teams, and the overall promotion of a culture that relies on data analysis. But more importantly, the concept of organizational readiness is not a one-time process; it is a learning process that is continuously developed over time and requires commitment from top management to the lowest level employees.

6.3 Privacy, Security, and Ethical Concerns

With the growing utilization of data in organizations, comes the rising duties of organizations with regards to data privacy, security, and ethics. Storing and processing personal or confidential data on a large scale is highly questionable, and it is crucial to address the issues regarding data storage, access, and utilization. Cyber threats also increase with the integration of various systems. One of the reasons for this is the fact that a weakness in any of the elements of the process analytics infrastructure, for example, a cloud server or an IoT endpoint, threatens the stability of the entire data chain. Data security is therefore a crucial element in organizations and to achieve it organizations must ensure they put in place measures such as encryption, access control, and monitoring to counter both internal and external threats. However, one cannot ignore ethical concerns that are paramount in any civilized endeavors such as legal and security aspects. There are several methods through which algorithms can perpetuate bias learned from historical data in decision making thus being prejudicial. Furthermore, data analytics in terms of monitoring the workforce or profiling the customers may create issues related to surveillance and consent. Solving such problems involves the use of effective security measures, as well as ethical values and governance structures that are open to the public.

6.4 Scalability and Infrastructure Constraints

However, this is not the case as organizations advance in their analytics initiatives to more complex and large-scale projects, they are bound to face issues to do with infrastructure and scalability. This makes it difficult to store and analyze large datasets in real-time, a scope that reallocates significant in rational enterprise infrastructure, particularly the ones with a dated IT framework. Technologies generated 'big data' such as sensor data, social media or Transactional data call for a scalable solution with low latency.

In this case, organizations have to migrate from internal data centers to other cloud platforms that provide flexibility, high-speed, and compatibility. However, such a transition is not an easy task. It entails technical factors, choice of vendors, costs and issues of disruption of business processes. Secondly, the work of analytics does not merely translate into materials and technical aspects but also into personnel, governance, and all the other components that denote scalability.

It is also important for organizations to analyze the sustainability of infrastructure. With the increase in the cost of energy and the major concern on the environment, there is need to ensure that the data pipelines being used are energy efficient and the green computing practices are embraced. Consequently, scalability should not be considered as a singular concept in relation to performance, but it also includes cost and the ability to meet future requirements.

6.5 Resistance to Change and Cultural Barriers

However, one of the biggest challenges that organizations face in the process of implementing data analytics is the issue of resistance to change.

The employees may feel that their positions may be eliminated by the use of automation and analytics while the managers may feel that relying on the analytics is not as effective as relying on their instincts or experience. These cultural factors can act as a barrier to analytics projects and may even halt them completely.

This is because resistance is normally caused by a lack of knowledge or confidence in the new technology. If the analytics tools are perceived as black boxes or difficult to use then the adoption will not take place. Consequently, stakeholders have to be engaged right from the start, the goals and values of analytics projects need to be explained and communicated, and initial successes should be showcased.

It is the leaders who have the prerogative to set the pace for cultural transformation in any organization. Managers who are committed to the rational use of data, provide training, and acknowledge the importance of data analytics can help their subordinates to regard analytics as an opportunity rather than a threat. Experimentation, failure, and curiosity should be supported while risk-taking and innovation should be considered a norm in order to develop a culture that is friendly to analytics.

7. EMERGING TRENDS AND FUTURE DIRECTIONS

7.1 Integration of AI and Data Analytics

When it comes to the digital transformation, it is now a well-known fact that artificial intelligence and data analytics are the two go-to technologies for process management. While traditional data analytics mainly dealt with data analysis and patterns in the data, AI brings in the aspect of learning from data, improving with experience and making decisions on its own. The use of AI in analytics enhances the detection of anomalies and predictive capabilities of organizations to give better results.

Machine learning capabilities extend to a higher level of application including dynamic scheduling, resources application, and real-time risk evaluation (Yamini, B et al 2023). For instance, in the area of supply chain, the AI models can learn how to adapt the purchasing patterns in real time in the market and the level of reliability of suppliers. In customer service processes, the AI chatbots analyze the conversation data to ensure the quality of the interaction and the rate of resolutions. In the following years, integration of AI algorithms with analytical tools will be normal and would be more efficient, faster and more contextual.

7.2 Explainable and Responsible AI in Decision-Making

Although AI has been a great help in the improvement of data analytics, it has also emerged as an issue of concern due to its increasing impact in decision-making processes. This has led to the development of the explainable AI (XAI) which aims at ensuring that the models are comprehensible to the users. In decision-making activities that relate to a process, it is critical to ensure that the AI system is transparent enough and that its reasoning is acceptable to the stakeholders in order to gain their confidence and support. XAI aims at making a connection between the AI solutions and the users and ensuring that they understand the reasons behind the decision made by the model. For instance, in the healthcare process optimization, XAI tools can provide rationales regarding why a particular treatment plan should be used by considering the patient information as well as the past results. It also helps to increase the trust in AI and support compliance with the regulations that demand explainability and traceability of the decision-making process. Responsible AI is a broader concept that includes such aspects as bias, privacy, and socio-economic effects of AI implementation. The leadership of organizations must put in place measures that will ensure that the AI and analytics when developed and used will be in a way that is acceptable to humanity. When AI is integrated into the process analytics to a deeper level, the principles of explainability and responsibility are going to be crucial to promoting ethical and sustainable AI development.

7.3 Automation and Intelligent Process Management (IPM)

One of the emerging trends that are gradually redefining the practice of process analytics is Intelligent Process Management (IPM), whereby sophisticated analytics, cognitive, as well as digital automation are integrated to enhance business processes. IPM, therefore, differs from conventional automation that aims at automating routine tasks within the processes, but it takes a holistic approach to process management with intelligent process flows. This means that systems do not only perform activities but also assess how well they are done, and respond to conditions as they exist.

For instance, in a customer onboarding process, an IPM system may use OCR to validate documents, use predictive analytics to assess the risk and alert the user for a manual review only when it detects anomalies. This level of intelligence makes operations to be faster, accurate and scalable particularly in areas of high traffic such as banks, insurance companies and telecommunication firms.

It is also associated with hyper automation, which is a notion that combines RPA, machine learning, and analytics in a single system (Sreelakshmi, S et al 2024). These technologies are evolving over time and organizations have started moving from simple process automation to complex decision automation to get more efficiency, flexibility and competition advantage.

7.4 Edge Analytics and Decentralized Decision Systems

As more and more smart devices and sensors are connected through the Internet of Things (IoT), data are becoming more and more produced at the edge of enterprise boundaries such as factories, cars, or other remote stations. Transferring all these data to central servers for analysis also poses a problem of delayed transmission, less bandwidth, and privacy infringement. The above challenges are mitigated by edge analytics which involves processing of data near the source of data production.

In edge analytics, the processing of data, analysis, and making of decisions occurs at the device level or on edge servers so that there is little dependence on central processing units. For example, in industrial automation, edge-based systems can stop the equipment with abnormal vibration without waiting for cloud-based approval. Likewise, in logistics, information from GPS and temperature trackers on delivery vehicles can be processed on the fly to check adherence to quality.

The decentralized decision systems do not only increase the speed and accuracy but also add to the robustness of the system. This includes imparting knowledge in situations like disaster recovery operation or remote monitoring to make sure that important examinations go on even if regular Internet access is unavailable. With distributed infrastructures become more common, it is important to understand that edge analytics will have a major role in real-time, self-sufficient, and context-oriented decisions.

7.5 Digital Twins and Simulation-Based Decision Support

Digital twin technology is considered to be on the rise as an effective solution for process analytics and decision making. A digital twin is therefore a digital model of an actual or planned system and works dynamically, meaning it is updated based on live operational data. This enables an organisation to run tests and experiments, check the functionality of the system, and estimate the consequences of certain changes prior to their implementation in real life.

In manufacturing, there is wherein engineers can simulate new setups or conditions of the production line and can determine if there is a problem or a piece of equipment that is most likely to fail in the near future. Thus, the digital models of structures in urban planning can predict consequences of policy, like changing the traffic direction or optimizing energy usage. Such tests are ideal as they offer a cheap way to test, try out, and create.

8. CONCLUSION

In this survey, we have seen how data analytics can help in the improvement of processes in different fields. While moving from the basic ideas of implementing a process improvement and some of the conventional methodologies to the use of analytical tools and AI approaches in data analytics, the latter has become revolutionary. Housed under business intelligence, descriptive, diagnostic, predictive, and prescriptive fall under the beacon of fostering proactive organizational decision as opposed to reactive decision-making. The presentation of different types of analysis, their application to business, and examples of their use has shown how analytics can help enhance the organization's performance and competitiveness. Organisations have realized that with the current rate of technological advancement, data analytics is not just an added advantage but vital for survival. The use of analytics in organizations provide an organization with better insight of its operations hence better decision making on market changes, better management of resources and better strategic planning. The combination of AI, the automation of the systems, and edge computing provides a way to handle the complex and rapidly changing processes at a large and efficient scale. But in today's world where there's a lot of uncertainty and competition, the power to make sense out of it is the competitive advantage. Despite the fact that data analytics offers numerous advantages in the process management, there are certain key issues that need to be solved to get full value from the use of data analytics, namely data quality, infrastructure, ethical issues, and organizational readiness. As to the future actions, organisations ought to enhance data fabrics and make data culture, as well as use AI safely. It is worth endorsing the digital transformation processes, participating big-data initiatives, such as digital twins, as well as intelligent process automation. In the end, the process management of the future will be the symbiosis of the human know-how and the analytical capabilities.

REFERENCES

Chong, D., & Shi, H. (2015). Big data analytics: A literature review. *Journal of Management Analytics*, *2*(3), 175–201. DOI: 10.1080/23270012.2015.1082449

Elgendy, N., & Elragal, A. (2014). Big data analytics: a literature review paper. In *Advances in Data Mining. Applications and Theoretical Aspects: 14th Industrial Conference, ICDM 2014, St. Petersburg, Russia, July 16-20, 2014.* (Springer International Publishing.). *Proceedings*, *14*, 214–227.

Hansen, H. F., Haddara, M., & Langseth, M. (2023). Investigating ERP system customization: A focus on cloud-ERP. *Procedia Computer Science*, *219*, 915–923. DOI: 10.1016/j.procs.2023.01.367

Jayaraman, K. D., & Jain, S. (2024). Leveraging Power BI for advanced business intelligence and reporting. *International Journal for Research in Management and Pharmacy*, *13*(11), 21. https://www. ijrmp. org

Khodakarami, F., & Chan, Y. E. (2014). Exploring the role of customer relationship management (CRM) systems in customer knowledge creation. *Information & Management*, *51*(1), 27–42. DOI: 10.1016/j.im.2013.09.001

Lakumarapu, S., Nithyanandhan, R., Bhargavi, V. S., & TP, A. (2024, August). Machine Learning Approaches for Liver Disease Prediction: A Comparative Analysis. In *2024 5th International Conference on Electronics and Sustainable Communication Systems (ICESC)* (pp. 159-164). IEEE.

Mishra, S., & Mishra, P. (2022). Analysis of platform business and secure business intelligence. *International Journal of Financial Engineering*, *9*(03), 2250002. DOI: 10.1142/S2424786322500025

Munuhwa, S. (2023). Sustainable logistics and competitive positioning. In *Integrating Intelligence and Sustainability in Supply Chains* (pp. 198–220). IGI Global. DOI: 10.4018/979-8-3693-0225-5.ch011

Musau, E. G. (2024). Optimizing transportation and distribution for environmental sustainability: Green logistics. In *Green Supply Chain Management Practice and Principles* (pp. 84–101). IGI Global. DOI: 10.4018/979-8-3693-3486-7.ch005

Ponmalar, A., Vijayakumar, K., Lakshmipriya, C., Karthikeyan, M., Gracelin Sheena, B., Beslin Pajila, P. J., & Siva Subramanian, R. (2024). Meta-Heuristics and Machine Learning Applications in Complex Systems. In *Metaheuristic and Machine Learning Optimization Strategies for Complex Systems* (pp. 257–275). IGI Global Scientific Publishing.

Siva, S. R., Bushra, S. N., Maheswari, B., & Prabukumar, M. K. (2022, April). Performance Analysis of Different Machine Learning in Customer Prediction. In *2022 6th International Conference on Trends in Electronics and Informatics (ICOEI)* (pp. 1425-1430). IEEE. DOI: 10.1109/ICOEI53556.2022.9776714

Sreelakshmi, S., Babu, A. A., Lakshmipriya, C., Gracious, L. A., Nalini, M., & Subramanian, R. S. (2024, October). Enhancing Intrusion Detection Systems with Machine Learning. In *2024 2nd International Conference on Self Sustainable Artificial Intelligence Systems (ICSSAS)* (pp. 557-564). IEEE. DOI: 10.1109/ICSSAS64001.2024.10760341

Tsai, C. W., Lai, C. F., Chao, H. C., & Vasilakos, A. V. (2015). Big data analytics: A survey. *Journal of Big Data*, *2*(1), 1–32. DOI: 10.1186/s40537-015-0030-3 PMID: 26191487

Vassakis, K., Petrakis, E., & Kopanakis, I. (2017). Big data analytics: applications, prospects and challenges. *Mobile big data: A roadmap from models to technologies*, 3-20.

Yamini, B., Sudha, K., Nalini, M., Kavitha, G., Subramanian, R. S., & Sugumar, R. (2023, June). Predictive modelling for lung cancer detection using machine learning techniques. In *2023 8th International Conference on Communication and Electronics Systems (ICCES)* (pp. 1220-1226). IEEE. DOI: 10.1109/ICCES57224.2023.10192648

Chapter 9

Navigating Workforce Adaptation and Human Factors in the Digital Era

Subramanian R. Siva
https://orcid.org/0000-0002-7509-9223
SRM Institute of Science and Technology, India

Angeline Lydia
Vel Tech Rangarajan Dr. Sagunthala R&D Institute of Science and Technology, India

J. Jayalakshmi
Vel Tech Multi Tech Dr.Rangarajan Dr. Sakunthala Engineering College, India

G. Suresh
https://orcid.org/0000-0001-8407-379X
Panimalar Engineering College, India

T. Anand
Nehru Institute of Engineering and Technology, India

Priya V. Kalai
R.M.K. College of Engineering and Technology, India

D. Shanmugapriya
IFET College of Engineering, India

ABSTRACT

This study aims at identifying the implemented changes and prospects for addressing the issues regarding workforce adaptation and the role of AI, automation, and digital transformation in human aspects. This chapter explores some of the pertinent topics that include cognitive load, motivation, technostress, and differences in generations in relation to technologies. The chapter focuses on the changes in the roles and skills, new roles, the need for new skills, and the significance of lifelong learning. Also, it considers the adoptions of a new working model that is the hybrid model of work and ethical considerations in relation to automation, job loss, and privacy. The chapter outlines approaches for employees, and policymakers to effectively manage these shifts and support the development of a resilient and adaptable workforce

DOI: 10.4018/979-8-3373-3336-6.ch009

amid rapid technological change.

1. INTRODUCTION

1.1 Overview of the Digital Era

The Digital Era is defined as the age of digital change, which has brought innovative changes in the society in the areas such as communication, entertainment, business and politics. In the course of the last few decades, we have seen the automation and adoption of artificial intelligence (AI), machine learning and other technologies that have impacted almost every industry in the world (Gupta, B. B., & Colace, F. 2023). The digital change has revolutionized the aspects of business, the way that services are provided and the way that individuals engage with technology in their daily lives. Automations have become one of the key trends in many industries where it helps to make processes more efficient and less expensive. For instance, robots and the AI systems in manufacturing industries can work for complex tasks hence replacing human labor force, however, radically minimized the error margin (Gopi et al 2024). In the same way, big data processing has been revolutionized through artificial intelligence where it is now possible to analyze large datasets and come up with patterns that were not possible in the past. The adoption of these technologies in business has not only enhanced the flow of operations but also created new opportunities that have led to new product and service delivery models. However, as industries change with the new technologies, there are issues on how best to incorporate new technologies to the staff and workers. There is need for tackling this issue due to the fact that the increased usage of advanced technologies in industries, commerce and other sectors generate demands for higher levels of digital competency among the workers and systems in industries, businesses and education institutions. This setting helps in understanding the kind of workforce adaptation which is appropriate within the digital age.

1.2 Importance of Workforce Adaptation

Organizational adaptation of the workforce is now a critical element in ensuring that organizations achieve their objectives when implementing digital technologies. This change has come about as firms integrated automation and AI into their workforce, which means that employees have to learn new skills or learn new ways of doing their work. The demands put forward by globalisation and the adoption of new technologies in every aspect of work require workers to be up to date with the changes. In this case, adaptation is not just a technological change, but behavioral, attitudinal, and cultural as well. For instance, employees in various organizations are now required to be conversant with technology matters including cloud applications, project management, and customer relationship management. Also, due to the spread of people working from home, they need to use technologies for maintaining cooperation and interaction in the distance. This means that if the workers do not adapt to these changes, they might become irrelevant in the current digital economy. This is because the use of technology is ongoing, and anyone who has not endeavoured to learn how to use new technologies or learn how to relate to new tools may find him or herself outcompeted by other rivals or even replaced by machines. Lack of preparation in the workforce development means that many organizations will simply fail to meet the demands of the new age, seeing their productivity go down, their market share shrink, and their ability to attract or retain top talent suffer. Therefore, it is not just an issue of the survival of the workers but is also a necessity for the company to thrive in the new digital world.

1.3 Human Factors in the Digital Era

Thus, technological innovation is the primary driver of the digital transformation, but it is the human factor that can make or break it. This work defines human factors as the relationship between a person and the technologies that he or she uses. It is equally important to know how cognitive, emotional and social factors of people affect the uptake and use of technology so as to enable the workforce to embrace change. Cognitive load is another key human factor that deals with the amount of effort that one is likely to use in order to process information and complete tasks. The use of the digital tools for working increases and the tools become more complex, the employee may face the situation when he cannot manage all the tools at once and there will be a cognitive overload. This tends to negatively impact productivity, increase stress levels and in turn affect the levels of job satisfaction. This is important in the development of technologies that can be easily used by end-users and in the development of training programs that would allow the human capital to easily incorporate new technologies into their daily practices. The other human factor is motivation. In this respect, it can be asserted that the usage of digital tools depends on the readiness of employees to make such changes. The level of motivation depends on the perceived usefulness of the technology, the level of support given by the leaders and self-motivation to learn. If the workers do not feel motivated to use these new applications, the levels of usage will remain low, and the advantages of such technologies may not be achieved. Another human factor that is considered here is the technostress that occurs when an employee is unable to deal with new technologies. Frequency of technological amendments creates stress, irritation and exhaustion related to work since one has to learn new gadgets while the other may feel vulnerable to being fired due to automation. The issue of technostress needs to be approached as a management of change and as such, the employees must be equipped with the right tools and training to enable them handle these changes well. In this aspect, there is a clear display of the human element in the aspects of culture and communication in the workplace. As organizations and their members embrace the use of technology in carrying out their duties, new issues arise in relation to social relationships, virtual teams, and teamwork. For instance, the use of technology to encourage remote working has made it difficult for employees to feel like they are part of a team and also made it challenging to keep the morale of the employees high.

1.4 Objectives of the Survey

The goal of this survey is to identify the current experience, approaches, and solutions to manage the transition of the workforce to the digital environment. In a world where digitization is redefining how businesses operate, it is essential to determine the dynamics of organisations and their employees when faced with this change. It is important to assess several aspects in this survey:

1. This paper aims to identify the difficulties that workers experience when implementing new technologies in their workplaces as well as the possible solutions for these challenges. This includes questioning topics like the following: resistance to change, lack of skills, and technostress.
2. Digital Readiness: Are organizations ready for change?: The preparations underway in organizations' preparation of their workforce This section will focus on the measures like upskilling, learning, management support, and building culture for flexibility.
3. Human Factors and Technology Interaction: The following are the human factors that impact the effective use of technology: The survey will focus on the relationship between cognitive load, motivation, and workplace culture while at the workplace.
4. Effects of the Digital World on the Employee: What are pros and cons? This question results in the effect on employee's stress, work-life balance, and mental health. The survey will aim at finding out how organizations can avoid such effects and improve the health of its employees.
5. The last topic pertains to Future business strategy: What new trends can be observed in the ways that work force adapts to the examined technologies? This involves having vision on areas such as the impacts of artificial intelligence, automation and the likes.

These areas are identified as follows: Through these areas, the survey seeks to establish a holistic view of the human aspects of adaptation in the workforce in the digital age. It will assist in making recommendations on how organizations, policy makers and individuals can overcome the challenges that arise from technological change and prepare the workforce for the future.

2. EVOLUTION OF THE WORKFORCE IN THE DIGITAL ERA

2.1 Shift from Traditional to Digital Roles

The employees of the present day are experiencing the changes like never before, with the digitalization now becoming the new norm in various sectors. Historically, most of the occupations were related to physical work, going to the workplace, and more importantly face-to-face communication. Such roles were usually based on repetitive activities that could either be production line, customer service or administrative. However, inexperienced persons, especially now that the digital technologies like artificial intelligence (AI), automation and advanced analytical tools have penetrated the work space, are threatened a lot by the traditional labor. In many industries, the manual work is increasingly being replaced by technology, and the employment is thus changing to more tech-oriented functions. For instance, in manufacturing industry, automation is gradually assuming work roles that include assembly line, inspection, and materials movement. This is leading to the decrease of some forms of physical work and the emergence of new jobs connected with creation, organization and servicing of technologies. In the same way, previous manual jobs like data entry, and appointment making were handled by human resource, but are currently done by technology. Besides technology changes, flexibility in work arrangements, especially working from home, due to the use of technology in conducting business such as video conferencing, cloud-based software, and project management tools, has also impacted many occupations. Although there were already signs of the remote work in some sectors before the COVID-19 pandemic, this global crisis further boosted it. Some of the workers who used to work in office buildings have been forced to work from home, and this has affected the way they communicate and do their work. Therefore, the emphasis has been put more on digital literacy and the skills to work remotely, which are crucial in most of the occupations. It is also important to note that there are also issues associated with the transformation of roles from traditional to digital. The impact of digitization is that employers need to make sure their employees are capable of meeting the expectations of the modern workplace and the employees, in turn, have to learn to use the new technologies and new methods of work. It has also become apparent that the role of digital skills is becoming more and more prominent across all the sectors of work, making workers adapt to new learning processes and levels.

Figure 1. Evolution of the workforce in the digital Era

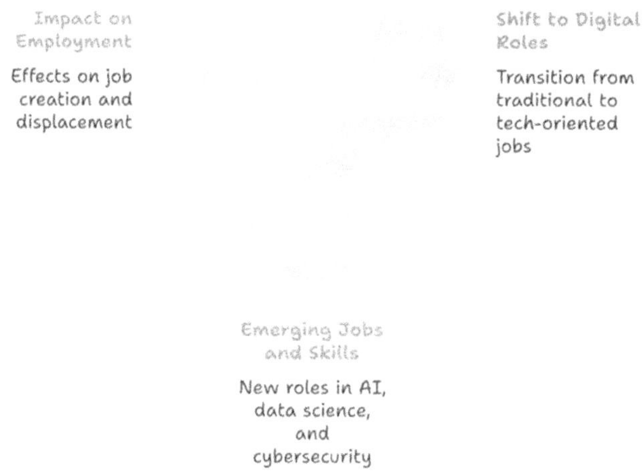

2.2 Emerging Jobs and Skills

As with any technological advancement, the digital revolution is not only changing the existing positions but is also creating new positions altogether. These new roles are associated with technology and are relatively new in the market, especially in areas such as Artificial Intelligence, Big Data, Cybersecurity, and Digital Marketing. New professions, like the AI specialists, data scientists and cybersecurity analysts are emerging in the organizations of any field. AI specialists are highly sought after since many companies are adopting AI to drive efficiencies in all areas as well as for analyzing data and decision-making. These professionals use such tools as machine learning, neural network, and other technologies to design systems that are intelligent, learner, and decision-makers (Lakumarapu et al 2024)(Sreelakshmi et al 2024). Data scientists, who work with the large sets of data and help in interpreting and making decisions based on them, are valuable to any organization. They apply mode sophisticated methods and programming languages like Python and R to work with large data sets; thus, the obtained results can benefit organizations and their strategies. Likewise, cybersecurity specialists are also important in defending structures against cyber criminals. This is specifically because in the day-day operation of organizations, they heavily rely on digital platforms and data storage which make them vulnerable to such hackers. Cybersecurity specialists are expected to develop measures that will help avoid such attacks, adhere to the laws concerning handling of data, and protect the systems against threats in the shortest time possible. Another area that several stagiaires mentioned is the promotion one, where new positions like the social media manager, content specialist and SEO analyst are essential. With the increase in the number of companies adopting the internet as a marketing channel, any form of marketing is imperative in the current world. Specialists working in this sphere are involved in the coordination of Internet advertising, development of materials for the Internet, and assessment of consumer habits in order to improve marketing strategies. Apart from these specific positions, several general relations and skills are emerging as critical in the digital workplace. Computer literacy is not anymore a luxury but a necessity in today's world and it is a prerequisite for almost all the professions. Even for the lower and middle level jobs, it is expected that they have knowledge on how to use computers and other technological tools in the workplace. In addition, coding skills are now a requirement in almost every field of work, not just in IT. Today, it is possible to find a multitude of professions where at least elementary knowledge of programming languages such as Python, JavaScript, or SQL is necessary to work with data or manage automation. Another essential competence is problem-solving since employees are faced with various problems in the course of their work, especially in the digital environment. In addition to the ability to analyze and or interpret data, workers must be able to make proper decisions based on that data. Problem solving, innovation, and flexibility are the key characteristics that can be expected from employees when it comes to problem-solving in an environment that is constantly shifting because of the ubiquitous use of technology. Also, interpersonal and emotional skills, which are important when implementing digital technologies for the organization remote and distanced cooperation. Last but not the least, it is important to note that constant learning and training is important to cope with the dynamic environment of the digital world. Thus, the employees are expected to continuously embrace training as the technology advances in the market. It has become a common practice for the employers to allow their employees to undertake courses, certifications, and workshops that help in building up technical and soft skills.

2.3 Impact on Employment

The digital transformation is being witnessed to affect employment in every sector in the economy. It is on the one hand, creating new opportunities for employment and new industries while on the other hand it is increasing unemployment and restructuring the nature of employment. With the increase in the automation of tasks, there are human interventions that are being replaced by machines. For instance, in the production line, most of the repetitive tasks are being shifted to robots while in the service industry, the routine questions are answered by artificial intelligent chatbots. This has led to a concern on job security especially for those workers in industries that are most likely to be affected by automation such as transport, retail and manufacturing. On the other hand, digitalization of business has created more employment opportunities in technology industries and other sectors that embrace digital technology. These new occupations are data scientist, artificial intelligence engineers, cloud architects, and digital content creators among many others, since institutions are embracing technology and data (Anusha et al 2024). There is also increased demand for remote work, which has enabled employees to access jobs in other geographical locations hence increasing the pool of employees for employers. It is then important to note that while some sectors would be associated with job disposability, others may only undergo changes in tasks assigned to employees. For example, those who were earlier engaged in manual operations may be promoted to supervisory or technical roles for handling the systems, and this will entail other skills and knowledge. In other cases, the nature may not die out completely but change in some form or another. It is inferred that this shift presents an imperative chance for both businesses and the workforce to adopt flexibility and lifelong learning since those are crucial in the age of the internet. There are concerns about the effect of digitalization on employment and jobs and the resultant challenges to the economic inequality issue. Employees in such positions or those who can't return to college for further education may have a hard time securing digital positions. To overcome these challenges, the emphasis is placed on retraining and reskilling programs, which will prepare employees for new digital positions. The governments, organizations, and educational institutions should support the workers to enable them to come up with the changes that have taken place. Last but not the least, innovation is also affecting the employment model. Short-term contracts, freelancing, remote working and gig economy jobs are on the rise because the internet makes it easier to find such jobs online. Though these arrangements are beneficial to provide flexible working arrangements to union members, there are also many concerns about job security and future career advancement of employees.

3. KEY HUMAN FACTORS IN WORKFORCE ADAPTATION

3.1 Cognitive Load and Learning Curves

The use of technology and computerization in the workplace means that there are profound effects on the cognitive structure of employees. Cognitive load is the amount of effort that is needed to learn and remember the information, and it is one of the key factors that influence employee's behavior in relation to novelties. This is because with the advancement in technology, the various tools are quite complex and employees have to work with a number of systems, applications and equipment. This results in what is referred to as cognitive overload whereby the brain is congested with a lot of information and work to be done thus leading to low productivity, stress and job satisfaction. This is just a fact that learning curve is present in every change of technology people have to use. When using a new tool, platform, or process in the workplace, the employees need to go through the process of acquiring the knowledge that will enable them to operate the technology. This learning process may be rather challenging, especially if the tool is complex and the employee has no previous experience with the tool. The steeper the curve, the longer it takes and the more effort one has to put in, which raises stress levels and slows down the time it takes for the employees to become efficient. Cognitive load and learning curve relationship are highly influential on the job satisfaction. Lack of proper understanding of these tools may make the employees frustrated and less motivated to work with them. If learning is not facilitated properly or employees are not provided with proper guidance and training (training or mentoring), they may feel a lack of competency or disinterest, which will decrease their job satisfaction and performance. To reduce the cognitive load, thus making it easier for users to work with different tools in an organization, there is the need to ensure that design is friendly to the users, the instructions are clear and the organization provides regular training on the use of the tools.

3.2 Motivation and Engagement

Employees' motivation to accept and use new technologies in the workplace can be attributed to two types of motivation: intrinsic and extrinsic. Intrinsic motivation is the desire to learn or participate in certain activities because they are interesting or satisfying to the subject while on the other hand, extrinsic motivation is the motivation that comes from outside sources such as monetary or other forms of reward. This is because the motivational factors can affect the way employees engage in the adoption of digital tools in two manners. The internal motivation of employees leads to long-term motivation in using the available technological tools since those with internal motivation will see technological difficulties as chances to learn and enhance themselves. For example, those who are self-motivated individuals who like to solve problems or those who are curious about new technologies will engage in the use of the computer and other technologies on their own without necessarily being prompted by their employer. When employees have such a feeling of achievement and development, they will have a good attitude towards change hence making the process easier. Extrinsic motivation can also be motivating, especially if the use of digital tools is an important aspect of job performance in an organization. If an employee is given incentives for mastering a particular tool or for achieving a particular goal, then the employees will have the incentive to use the technology in the right manner. However, this may have short term benefits rather than long term internalization of the new behaviour since the employees may return to the previous behaviour or demotivate when the extrinsic motivators are withdrawn. In order to maintain organizational productivity and active participation of employees during the process of digital adaptation, both the internal and external motivation factors must be considered by the organization. Thus, providing contingent incentives for technological performance can enhance the use of intrinsic motivation but it is crucial to foster the development of intrinsic motivation for learning and ICT literacy among employees.

3.3 Technostress and Mental Health

With the growing adoption of information technology and automation in different organizations, employees are exposed to technostress which is the stress resulting from the use of technology. As for technostress, it can be described as anxiety, frustration, and even burnout. Since employees have to train and then use new technologies, they may feel pressured by fast pace of change. The first source of technostress is the pressure to update oneself with the new technologies, software, tool and platforms. This is an implication that the pace of technology is dynamic and as a result, employees have the responsibility of updating their knowledge and skills in order to fit in the organization. The compilation and constant pressure to acquire new technologies causes new sentiments such as anxiety due to the possible feeling of outcompeting especially careerist employees who may develop early stage computer phobia. It has become evident that technostress does have negative effects on the mental health of individuals. Technostress leads to anxiety, sleeping disorders, and even depression in people who are exposed to technostress. This is because employees who are overburdened by technology may develop burnout, and they may end up disengaging from work, or even miss work, or even resign. It is thus important that organizations should find ways of dealing with technostress by offering the employees the essentials like trainings, counselling and work-life balance. Technostress management is all about ensuring that the employees are able to work under conditions that allow them to regulate the use of technology in their work. Managers should ensure they provide training programs for all the employees, foster discloser of technological issues and concerns, and provide solutions for reducing the issue of technological overload.

3.4 Workplace Culture and Human Interaction

This paper seeks to establish the impact that the use of digital tools has had on employees and their working relations. Several organizations have adopted the use of instant messaging, video conferencing and collaborative applications as a new modality of communication in the organizations, thus changing the organizational culture. The use of the tools in organizational work presents a plus side in that it provides room for mobility and can enable the employees to work from different parts of the world but it also comes with some drawbacks in that it hampers the interpersonal relations among the employees. In the traditional office environments, there were many opportunities to communicate with others in person and engage in casual conversations. However, the digital workspace means that the employee has to be very careful when communicating because the body language is not visible. This shift may result in eradicating staff unity, promulgating feelings of loneliness and eradicating a cultural and unifying sense of an organization. They have to embrace these changes by creating awareness on the need to adopt proper use of technology in the workplace. This entails equipping the people working in organizations with the resources and the awareness of how to confer as well as work effectively and efficiently if they are physically distant from one another. Group meetings, collaborative exercises, and chances to speak with colleagues can be highly beneficial to maintain group cohesion and make employees feel connected even when working remotely.

3.5 Generational Differences

Several factors can affect the use of technology in the workplace, including age, since different generations are more or less used to using technology. The use of new technologies is more accepted by the younger generations since for them, the use of the digital tools is part of their everyday life. These are generations that have been brought up with the internet, smartphones, and social networking sites, and as such, they are always abreast with the latest technologies. On the other hand, it was also noted that the use of technology may pose difficulties to older generations. Older people did not have the same opportunities as the young people to work with computers and may take more time to adapt to changes. It is not that older workers cannot learn to use the digital tools, however, organisations must ensure that they provide adequate support and training to the workers for such changes. To address these generational differences, there should be approaches that would cater for staff members in various levels of digital adoption. For younger employees, the goals can be to offer new state-of-the-art technologies and promote creativity, for the older employees, it is possible to offer professional training and constant support, so they are ready to embrace the changes. Promoting a corporate culture that embraces the hiring of older employees as well as the training of young employees will help the employees to embrace new technologies and contribute to the organization's objectives.

4. CHALLENGES IN WORKFORCE ADAPTATION

4.1 Resistance to Change

The major challenge that has faced organisations with regard to workforce adaptation in the current digital age is the issue of resistance to change. On the one hand, the use of technology at the workplace has its advantages for organizations and individuals, on the other hand, it is challenging for employees to accept new technologies, applications, or processes(Ozkan-Ozen et al 2022). The major causes of resistance to change include: fear on the new technology being obsolete, low trust on the new technology and lack of training on the new technology. Lack of job security is another factor that employees have when they believe that their position or duties may be automated or taken over by an AI. This may be especially true in the manufacturing section of an organization as well as the customer relations service or administration sections in various firms where automation could be used to replace people's work. When individuals feel threatened at their workplace, they are likely to avoid embracing new technologies and declining to accept new training out of fear that their position will be eliminated soon. The other factor that stands in the way of change is mistrust in the technology. Some of the employees especially those who are not conversant with technological advancements may hold negative attitudes towards new technologies. They may not believe that digital systems are capable of matching the abilities of human beings or that such systems will bring in mistake or compromise security. Such distrust may translate to resistance in the adoption of digital tools especially where the employees have had a bad experience with the technology. Lack of training is also another reason that is likely to cause resistance among employees. This can lead to employees not being able to handle the new technologies due to lack of support, guidance or training on how to go about it. Such preparation can create a feeling of inability that paves the way for resistance in an organization. If the employees have not been trained properly, they are likely to avoid using new systems and will remain inefficient and disengaged. Resisting change is common and can only be managed if the following factors are considered in an appropriate strategy of handling change. To reduce the level of resistance, one must ensure that there is proper communication about the need for new technologies, provide constant and thorough training to the employees, and include them in decision-making processes. It also means that transparency, support, and leadership are important when it comes to developing a culture that embraces innovation in the use of technology(Ince, F 2022).

Figure 2. Challenges in workforce adaptation

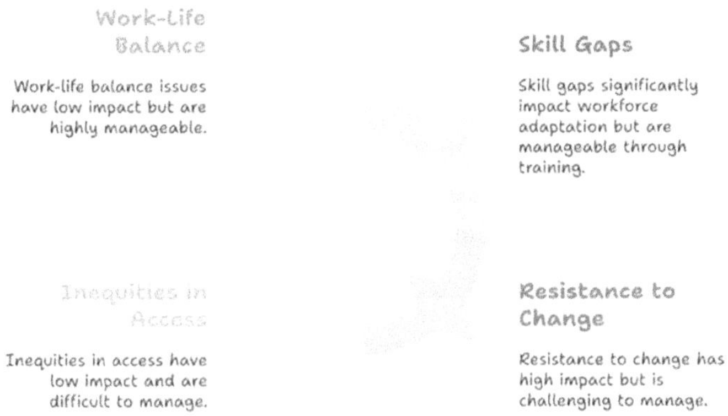

4.2 Skill Gaps

Since organizations are now engaging in the use of digital tools in their operations, one of the most radical issues that companies encounter is the lack of the necessary skills in the current employees. Due to the increasing rate of innovation, many employees are not well equipped with the appropriate skills that are necessary in a digital environment. It may be especially the case in areas such as data science, artificial intelligence, information security, and digital marketing where professionals require more in-depth knowledge. Indeed, for many of the employees, the skills that they gain from previous positions might not be able to help them to cope with current challenges. These days, automation and artificial intelligence are gradually penetrating various industries, which means that the skills a worker learned several decades ago may be useless. For instance, the employees that have been working in administrative or manual jobs for several years might not have the technical knowledge regarding the use of complex digital systems or perform such tasks as data analysis or programming. This poses a major challenge to the workforce adaption since the employees may not be well prepared to manage the dynamics of their tasks. The skill gap does not end at technical skills only. Other interpersonal skills like problem solving, communication and interpersonal skills are also important in the digital age. Since much is done remotely or through online collaboration, it is crucial that the employees are conversant with the tools used in the process. Also, adaptability to the new technologies, ability to learn and work in an environment characterized by changes has become even more critical in the current marketplace. To eliminate the skill gap, there is a need for organizations to embrace reskilling and upskilling programs. So, offering the employees the possibility to develop themselves further and gain the necessary knowledge and skills, which would enable them to meet the challenges of the digital age, is a crucial step. This may involve providing webinars, training, and courses, certifications, and mentorship programs that cover both the computer-related and interpersonal skills. Other ways of positive thinking can also be useful in order to make employees become more comfortable in the process of getting new knowledge and skills and to feel ready for the new challenges in their work.

4.3 Inequities in Access and Resources

Regarding the second workforce adaptation issue, it exists inequality regarding use of technology, training, and support. These inequalities can be in terms of gender, age, income, region, and other factors, including rural and urban employees, low-wage and high-wage employees, young and old employees, and so on. It is crucial for the employees to get access to digital tools and training resources as they need to work on new technologies but not all employees enjoy equal opportunities in this regard. When it comes to the workers in the rural areas, lack of adequate internet connection and having access to limited technological resources are some of the challenges that they are most likely to face in the process of adapting to the new technology. These workers may be left out in the new world of work through remote operations, online learning, or the use of sophisticated technologies that require high-speed internet connections. For instance, some of the rural workers may not be conversant with the use of computers or may lack the support of the technological tools as those in the urban areas; this widens the digital gap. They suggest that employees with low wages can barely afford devices, programmes or training courses to enable them adapt to the new technologies. Some employees do not have the financial ability to acquire such technology applications through the cloud and mobile devices as well as familiarization with the specific appropriate training materials. This leads to a situation where only individuals with high income or those in the developed countries can fully enjoy from on digital technologies. Other factors include generation gaps as this also affects the access and adaptation of the differently abled in their daily lives. There is also a challenge of inadequate access to the training material since older workers may not be conversant with the use of the internet and may not have access to the devices that can get them to the online training materials. Also, they may experience social isolation or marginalization especially if organizations fail to offer training or sponsorship for the new technologies. To this effect, there is a need for organizations and governments to take necessary measures to ensure that everyone has an equal chance to use these instruments. This may involve putting capital in infrastructures, offering cheap or free technology to the low paid employees, and making sure that training literature is available to the employees regardless of their age or the level of education they have attained. Some of the policies include, expansion of broadband connection in the rural areas for effective connectivity, and offering incentives to incorporate technology in the marketplace for fair competition at workplaces.

4.4 Work-Life Balance

It is worth stating that the modern advancements in technology and the shift towards working remotely significantly transform the perception of work-life balance among employees. On the one hand, the use of digital technologies has several advantages, including flexibility, for instance, the ability to work from home or have access to work-related information at any time, on the other hand, it has a disadvantage of disconnecting the working life from the personal one (Rathi, S., & Kumar, P. 2023). The pressure to be available for work, even beyond working hours increases stress levels among the employees. However, one of the primary areas that have raised new challenges in managing the balance between work and other life domains is remote work. On the one hand, employees are bound to enjoy the freedom that comes with working from home but, on the other hand, they will struggle to manage their personal and working time. Some workers may experience pressure to be available at all times due to the lack of physical barriers as seen in a conventional workplace, thus they may end up working for extended periods (Senbursa, N. 2022). Also, social interaction with co-workers is limited due to virtual working, this causes employees to feel lonely and find it difficult to leave work and attend to other aspects of their lives. Thanks to the technology, many employees have to stay connected and ready to answer e-mails, messages, and other work-related matters irrespective of the time of day. It could be argued that constant connectivity alters personal time and as a result, the standard of our well-being and productivity is lowered. More so, research indicates that employees who work under conditions of poor work-life balance are likely to suffer from increased stress levels and burnout, which has implications on the employees' well-being and productivity at the workplace. To this end, organizations need to establish healthy working policies that do not allow work to interfere with other aspects of life (Ganiyu, I. O., & Oladejo, O. M. (2022). This could include time management where specific work hours are defined, proper working conditions that promote break time for the workers, and flexibility in working hours. It is also critical for organizations to create the culture of wellness that would encourage people to take time off when needed. It is therefore important to ensure that employees are provided with the necessary support in terms of their mental health as they work in the digital age (Das, R. C., & Basavaraj, S. 2024) (Sajidha et al 2025).

5. STRATEGIES FOR SUCCESSFUL WORKFORCE ADAPTATION

5.1 Continuous Learning and Upskilling

It could be said that learning becomes a continuous process, and the acquisition of new knowledge is one of the key approaches to the effective management of the personnel in the context of the digital environment. In the current world of globalization, and with the advancement in technologies, various industries are dynamic, and the employees have to adapt to the new requirements (Beichter, T., & Kaiser, M. 2023). Through continuous learning, organizations can empower the people with the knowledge that will enable them to deal with new technologies, market trends and other factors that make an organization survive. Continuing education, in a way, means that the employees are always learning and acquiring new knowledge even outside the classroom or training sessions. In today's world, digital tools are used in almost all industries and, therefore, employees should be aware of the available technologies. In this context, training programs and certifications can be helpful in ensuring that this process is made easier. In this way, providing the opportunity for structured learning, companies may be sure that their workers are not only up to date in terms of the usage of the technologies, but also gaining the confidence and competence to utilize these tools appropriately. Upskilling is also equally useful in preparing the employees to assume other higher or new challenging roles that may not have been available in the organization before. For example, customer service employees may need to understand the use of chatbots and automation technologies in dealing with the customers. Likewise, the employee in clerical positions may have to learn data analysis or digital marketing skills due to shifts in their work requirements. The upskilling programmes should be implemented by the organizations to assist the workers to develop other skills and qualifications that can be useful in the market to ensure that the workforce becomes more productive. This approach helps in developing a culture of self-responsibility on the part of the employees to learn on the job. Promoting access to knowledge, providing time for the professional growth of a workforce, and ensuring that the employees obtain new certifications is how an organization can invest in the workforce. This commitment of organizations is not only advantageous to the employees because they acquire new skills that would make them more marketable but is also advantageous to the organizations because they develop and maintain a strong workforce for the future.

5.2 Employee Involvement and Ownership

The use of employees in managing the digital transformation is one of the most effective approaches that can be used in this process. This chapter aims at identifying the factors that will contribute to the success of the technological transformation initiative and it has been found that when the employees are committed towards the transformation process, they are more likely to support the use of new technologies in the organization. Engaging employees right from the beginning of the change process is beneficial as it leads to their buy-in, and also eases the process of implementation. It can range from asking for the opinion of the employees in the selection of new technologies to provide the employees with opportunities to trial or train on new technologies. Thus, if the employees feel that their voice is being heard and their suggestions are accepted in the organizational decision-making process, they are more likely to embrace the changes. This sense of ownership not only encourages them to learn on new systems but also fosters a good workshop on the concept of digitization. It also enriches the experience of the employee by making him feel that he or she is a part of bringing change and success into the company. Instead of being mere spectators and mere receivers of decisions made at the managerial level, employees become active participants in the change process, which in return makes them to be more committed to the change process. For instance, when employees are consulted when there are issues such as the difficulties that may be involved or the possible advantages when implementing a new tool, then they are most likely to appreciate and embrace the change. Also, the engagement of employees in the digital transformation initiative can assist the organization to detect and remove barriers that might hinder the change in the future. It is always more effective to involve the employees who directly interact with the technology and use it in their everyday work. This feedback loop also guarantees that the use of digital tools is optimal and that employees are provided with the help they require.

Figure 3. Strategies for successful workforce adaptation

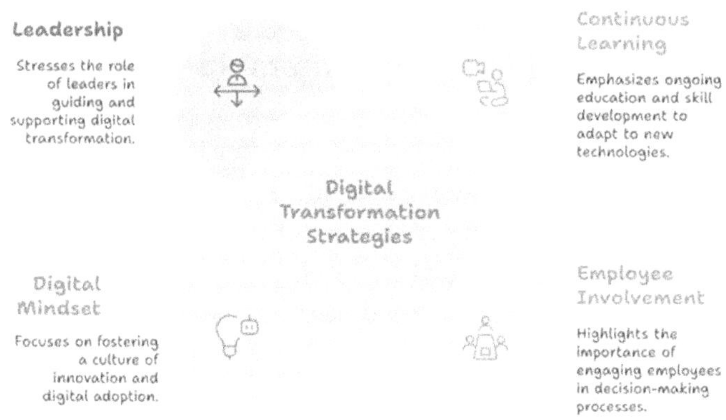

5.3 Creating a Digital-First Mindset

It is therefore important to ensure that the organization adopts a digital mindset in order to survive the challenges posed by the digital environment. Digital-first thinking means that the organization has to be ready to embrace change, be curious and innovative when it comes to the use of digital technologies. It is not only about purchasing new tools, but also about creating a mindset of the organization that will foster the understanding of the potential of technology and its application for enhancing organizational performance in terms of processes, products, and services. Digital first thinking is a culture that starts with the top management and extends to every level of the company. Organization leaders should lead by example and show that they are willing to embrace change and the importance of using digital solutions. In this regard, by adopting digital tools and technology in the operation of its business, organizations make a statement to employees that digital skills are valued. It is recommended to start with a digital approach, that is, employees should look for a digital solution to problems and always consider new ways of working. Employees should be given the autonomy to try out new technologies whether it is the application of AI in an organizational process or the integration of cloud services in the workplace. To promote this kind of thinking, it is possible to motivate for innovation, create inter-departmental teams, and establish a culture in which people are willing to take risks and learn from them. Two other areas that should not be overlooked in this process are the roles of training and development when it comes to nurturing and cultivating such a mind-set. Management should ensure that there is continuous training for the workforce to appreciate the role of digital technology and how they may leverage on it. Right from being competent in handling basic computer skills and knowledge to complex concepts such as artificial intelligence and machine learning, employees should be provided with resources that will keep them curious and actively participating in the process of digital transformation (Yamini et al 2023). Establishing a new company culture as a digital-first one must remain constant and have the support of the company. There is a need for organizations to appreciate digital accomplishments through recognition, rewards, or awards may be through the use of employee reward programs or innovation awards. In this way, it becomes possible to support the general notion that digital adaptation is an effort that involves everyone in a given organization, and that there is always something that each person can do to help the organization progress.

5.4 Leadership in Digital Transformation

By definition, leadership is a crucial factor in managing the process of digital transformation in the workforce. Besides, leaders are directly involved in decision making processes concerning the application of technologies in organizations and act as change agents. Leadership can reassures employees, resolve their concerns, and build hope as the employees embrace the new technologies in the workplace. Another of the leadership responsibilities when implementing digital transformation is to offer a vision and direction. People in the organization must be aware of why change is taking place, what is expected in the long run, and how they can help with the change. It is therefore crucial that leaders sell the concept of digital transformation to their workers in a manner that is most appealing to them and demonstrates the advantages of the change for both the company and the employee. Another important aspect of leadership in digital transformation is handling of concerns and fears. This is due to the fact that resistance to change is one of the main issues that prevent the adoption of new technologies. Managers should pay attention to the employees' feedback, assure them and help with the transition. In this way, leaders can help their subordinates to be ready for further digital transformations and to feel that they are not alone with their emotions and psychological problems. In addition, there is need for the leaders to build resilience in the workforce. Change is always difficult and when it comes to digital transformation, one cannot expect to avoid some failures. Nevertheless, it is possible for managers to minimise the impact of these difficulties through positive thinking, recognising milestones and keeping on trying. They should also show flexibility and eagerness to learn because the process of change is not only necessary for the companies but also a way to develop personally. Leadership also entails providing the organizational direction with the support, coaching, and proper equipment that the employees require. Proper training and support systems, for instance, mentorship or coaching, properly implemented IT solutions as well as the constant nurturing and encouragement of the top management will go a long way in ensuring employees are well equipped to face challenges in the digital workplace. In essence, leadership for digital transformation is not only about making decisions at the organizational top but also about providing the context in which people can excel and adapt. It simply means that strong leadership is needed to be able to align the workforce to the new way of working in the digital age.

6. FUTURE TRENDS AND THE NEXT FRONTIER

6.1 AI and Automation's Role

It is important to understand that AI, ML and robotics is likely to increase its presence in the employment sector in the coming years. All these technologies are already making great impacts in different fields, and with advancements, they will continue to define the working world. AI and automation are considered as to continue having an impact in labor markets with impacts that may be beneficial and disadvantageous to workers and different industries. Across numerous sectors, industries AI and automation have made complete sensible and monotonous tasks and thus, makes the employees engage themselves in more engaging tasks. For instance, in the manufacturing industry, robots are replacing workers in production lines such as assembling and packaging, AI is being used in analyzing data, customer relations, and decision making among others. These technologies increase efficiency, accuracy and speed of work and at the same time, they create issues of job loss. In today's technologically advanced world, there is a growing trend in the automation of tasks that were previously performed by human beings with the help of several technologies such as artificial intelligence and robotics. However, AI and automation are not only the processes of job displacement. They also have the ability to generate new roles and industries as well. With the increasing degree of automation, employees will be expected to take up more complex tasks including problem solving, critical thinking, and creativity. Furthermore, the increase in the adoption rate of AI and machine learning will create a new set of specialization (Siva, S. R et al 2022). Specialists, data scientists, and machine learning engineers are expected to have their demand increase even more. There will also be a need for workers that can understand how to manage, how to implement, and how to work with AI tools and how to translate the technology into business needs. We have to be careful in making a general statement on the extent to which AI and automation will affect workforce needs as the degree of change will not be felt across the board in the same manner. For instance, in the area of healthcare, it is applied to help doctors in diagnosis, analysis of images, and performing surgeries through robots.

Although they improve the quality of care, they have the effect of making the health care professionals update their technical training more often. In other fields such as finance, the use of AI is already done to predict, control risk, and customize clients' experiences. These shifts suggest that it is crucial for the workers to develop new skills that will enable them to work hand in hand with the new technologies. On the other hand, the future is promising more efficiency and productivity, but there are challenges that organizations face in the social and economic aspect of AI and automation. The major difficulty will be to deal with the dynamic change in the requirement of the workforce where certain workers may be laid off or their work may be changed due to advances in technology. It will be important to make sure that the workers are provided with the tools to reskill, educational materials and support structures to deal with this change.

6.2 Hybrid Work Models

Remote work is becoming more and more common and integrated with the in-office work, thus creating the so-called hybrid models of work. The situation with the COVID-19 pandemic has demonstrated that it is possible to work remotely, and many companies have realized that employees can be effective even if they work from home. Therefore, people can expect that the practice of working both in the office and outside the office will gradually become a new standard for many companies. Flexibility, while working from home or any other remote location or even being able to attend some physical meetings in office or other relevant place thus making use of the new versatility that comes with the hybrid models at work. This option is especially beneficial for employees who want to have more free time or spend several hours on the road. Hybrid work models also benefit organizations in a way that they are able to access a wider pool of talents because they can hire talents from different locations and do not have to relocate them. However, the hybrid model is different from the other two models in the sense that it poses a few issues that organizations will have to deal with. One of the most significant challenges is to guarantee that all employees are included and motivated no matter the location they are in. It is challenging for an organization to keep a united culture in place for employees who work remotely, and this is why an organization must embrace technology that supports collaboration. Also, organizations will have to reconsider the ways of organizing the physical environment in which work is performed. Conventional workplace designs, which were created for fixed workplace attendance, may not be sufficient for hybrid work. It is expected that working zones in offices will be more free-form and include areas for brainstorming, team building and informal meetings, while personal workplaces will be minimized or redesigned. This means that there is a need to redesign the office space and focus on spaces that allow for a combination of both face-to-face and virtual communications. This means that the hybrid work model also requires the change of leadership and management. Managers will have to find new ways of managing people and motivating employees to work efficiently while they are working remotely. This includes setting clear goals and objectives, allowing the employees to choose their working hours and having set meetings to review the progress and check on their welfare. Managers also need to make sure that remote workers have the same access to resources, get the same chances as other workers employed in the office, and receive the same rewards for their work in order to avoid any feeling of isolation or unfairness. It will be crucial to consider the demands of the employees as organizations keep on adopting and experimenting with the new ways of working. It is possible that some workers want to continue working from home as much as possible, while others crave the interaction with colleagues and the routine of being at the office. Adjustability will be the main theme in the design of workplaces that would allow personal choices and provide the best balance between work and personal lives.

6.3 Ethical Considerations

The following topics discuss that as AI, automation and digitalization progress as part of the workforce, more consideration should be given to ethical work. Despite the benefits that could be derived from these technologies, there are several issues of ethical concern including; loss of employment, privacy of the employees, and security of the data. Another major ethical issue is the issue of job automation and loss of employment due to the use of artificial intelligence. With the increase in the use of technology, the workers may be laid off or have to change their jobs to other positions which demands different skills. Nevertheless, while there are potential productivity enhancements and new job formation in certain sectors, there is a threat that several employees, primarily those who have monotonous jobs and those employed in industries inclined to automation, may be confined. To address this concern, it will be necessary for companies and governments to spend more on training and development programs that prepare the displaced workers for the modern workplace. Privacy and data security are also other important ethical issues that arise with the advancement in technology. With the rise of AI and automation in organizations, large amount of employee data is being gathered and stored. This data is usually employed for measuring performance, increasing efficiency, and enhancing the working environment and experience. However, the collection and use of such data have implications to the privacy of the employees and abuse of the information. Employees may also privately own their information is being spied on or misused, thus eradicating their faith in technology and employers. To mitigate these ethical issues, the following guidelines must be implemented; Organizational policies on data collection, usage, and privacy. Data protection should be of utmost importance and employee data should not be exposed to other individuals or even the employer.

7. CONCLUSION

This article affirms the alarming changes that are being witnessed especially via information technology systems such as artificial intelligence and automation. In the third section, the author continues to explain that as organizations incorporate the use of technology, employees are forced to learn new skills, take on new roles and accept new changes at the workplace. The motivation, cognitive load, and technostress are the human factors that may affect these transitions in the best way possible. In addition, these factors; resistance to change, lack of skilled personnel and disparities in resource acquisition signify the importance of strategy in workforce development. The concept of the new organizational structure showing the employees in a dual setting is called the hybrid work model and has become a trend, but at the same time, it presents a problem in the field of communication, motivation, and management. For the companies to be all set in dealing with these trends, it is then important for them to develop training and development programme that would build human resource capabilities that embrace digital technologies. This is with regard to the fact that the employees are likely to take ownership of the change when they are involved in the process of its implementation. It requires the leadership to be involved in the issues, the change in mindset towards digital culture, and policies that will help in providing equal opportunity and training for the use of technology. The authorities must also focus on the creation of reskilling programmes and discuss the ethical issues related to automation and AI. When it comes to the changes in the labor market due to automation and the rise of AI, it is clear that people will become more valuable when involved in higher-order tasks. Thus, one can predict that the further development of work will be based on the interaction between people and machines, in which the first will perform creative, emotional, and heuristic activities. Flexibility will always be required, and organizations, personnel, and policy makers must constantly address the factors that create innovation, fairness, and health at work. The main issue will be to make technology work for the employees and not against them as the latter often happens when some of them cannot adapt to the new advancements.

REFERENCES

Anusha, S., Ezhilvandan, M., Gayathri, S., Sivaraman, V., & Anish, T. P. (2024). *Emerging trends in edge AI for Industry 4.0 and 5.0: Technologies, applications, and challenges*. AI Innovations in Service and Tourism Marketing. DOI: 10.4018/979-8-3693-7909-7.ch010

Beichter, T., & Kaiser, M. (2023). The future of upskilling: human-and technology-centered. In *Proceedings of the 14th International Multi-Conference on Complexity, Informatics and Cybernetics: IMCIC* (pp. 190-193). DOI: 10.54808/IMCIC2023.01.190

Das, R. C., & Basavaraj, S. (2024). The Importance of Strategic Agility and Resilience in Work-Life Balance. In *Practical Approaches to Agile Project Management* (pp. 270–288). IGI Global.

Ganiyu, I. O., & Oladejo, O. M. (2022). Green Work-Life Balance and Global Leadership in Industry 4.0. In *Research Anthology on Human Resource Practices for the Modern Workforce* (pp. 2121-2137). IGI Global Scientific Publishing.

Gopi, B., Kokila, M. S., Bibin, C. V., Sasikala, D., Howard, E., & Boopathi, S. (2024). Distributed Technologies Using AI/ML Techniques for Healthcare Applications. In *Social Innovations in Education, Environment, and Healthcare* (pp. 375-396). IGI Global.

Gupta, B. B., & Colace, F. (Eds.). (2023). *Handbook of Research on AI and ML for Intelligent Machines and Systems*. IGI Global. DOI: 10.4018/978-1-6684-9999-3

Ince, F. (Ed.). (2022). *International perspectives and strategies for managing an aging workforce*. IGI Global. DOI: 10.4018/978-1-7998-2395-7

Lakumarapu, S. R. Nithyanandhan, V. Sharmila Bhargavi, and Anish TP. "Machine Learning Approaches for Liver Disease Prediction: A Comparative Analysis." In *2024 5th International Conference on Electronics and Sustainable Communication Systems (ICESC)*, pp. 159-164. IEEE, 2024.

Ozkan-Ozen, Y. D., & Kazancoglu, Y. (2022). Analysing workforce development challenges in the Industry 4.0. *International Journal of Manpower*, *43*(2), 310–333. DOI: 10.1108/IJM-03-2021-0167

Rathi, S., & Kumar, P. (2023). The mediating role of job satisfaction between work-life balance and employee retention. In *Climate change management and social innovations for sustainable global organization* (pp. 241–262). IGI Global. DOI: 10.4018/978-1-6684-9503-2.ch016

Sajidha, S. A., Vijayanand, D., Rajagopal, M., Sambasivam, D., & Nisha, V. M. (2025). Decoding Work-Life Balance Conundrum: A Meta-Learning Prediction Approach. In *Creating AI Synergy Through Business Technology Transformation* (pp. 313-336). IGI Global.

Senbursa, N. (2022). Work-life balance challenges: constructing an employee-friendly workplace. In *Handbook of Research on Future of Work and Education: Implications for Curriculum Delivery and Work Design* (pp. 511-532). IGI Global.

Siva, S. R., Bushra, S. N., Maheswari, B., & Prabukumar, M. K. (2022, April). Performance Analysis of Different Machine Learning in Customer Prediction. In *2022 6th International Conference on Trends in Electronics and Informatics (ICOEI)* (pp. 1425-1430). IEEE. DOI: 10.1109/ICOEI53556.2022.9776714

Sreelakshmi, S., Babu, A. A., Lakshmipriya, C., Gracious, L. A., Nalini, M., & Subramanian, R. S. (2024, October). Enhancing Intrusion Detection Systems with Machine Learning. In *2024 2nd International Conference on Self Sustainable Artificial Intelligence Systems (ICSSAS)* (pp. 557-564). IEEE. DOI: 10.1109/ICSSAS64001.2024.10760341

Yamini, B., Sudha, K., Nalini, M., Kavitha, G., Subramanian, R. S., & Sugumar, R. (2023, June). Predictive modelling for lung cancer detection using machine learning techniques. In *2023 8th International Conference on Communication and Electronics Systems (ICCES)* (pp. 1220-1226). IEEE. DOI: 10.1109/ICCES57224.2023.10192648

Chapter 10
Sustainability in the Digital Age:
Redefining Technology Ecosystems

Suman Lata
https://orcid.org/0000-0002-9862-0739
Amity Institute of Travel and Tourism, India

ABSTRACT

The rapid advancement of digital technologies has fundamentally transformed the way societies function, offering unprecedented opportunities for innovation and growth. However, this digital revolution has also brought significant environmental, social, and economic challenges, necessitating a redefinition of technology ecosystems through the lens of sustainability. This paper explores the environmental, social, and economic impacts of digital technologies and their role in shaping sustainable technology ecosystems. As digital innovations such as artificial intelligence (AI), the Internet of Things (IoT), and cloud computing continue to transform industries and societies, their dual potential to drive progress and exacerbate challenges has become increasingly evident. While these technologies offer solutions for efficiency, connectivity, and innovation, they also contribute to significant environmental concerns, such as energy consumption and electronic waste, as well as social issues like the digital divide and data privacy risks.

DOI: 10.4018/979-8-3373-3336-6.ch010

1. INTRODUCTION

The rapid and pervasive advancement of digital technologies has undeniably become a defining characteristic of the modern era, fundamentally reshaping industries, economies, governmental operations, and the very fabric of daily life across the globe. Our methods of communication, commerce, education, and even our interaction with the natural environment have been profoundly altered. However, as this wave of digitalization accelerates its reach and intensity, a growing chorus of concerns regarding its multifaceted environmental, social, and economic implications has moved to the forefront of global discourse (Qadri et al., 2025). While digital technologies offer unprecedented opportunities for enhancing efficiency, fostering innovation, and connecting the world, they simultaneously present significant sustainability challenges that must be urgently addressed. This paper delves into the complex interplay between digital technologies and sustainability, exploring their environmental, social, and economic impacts and examining how these technologies can be steered towards shaping truly sustainable technology ecosystems (Bocean, 2025). The digital revolution is intrinsically linked to the rise of hyper-connectivity and the proliferation of powerful technologies such as artificial intelligence (AI), the Internet of Things (IoT), blockchain, and sophisticated cloud computing infrastructures. These technologies have been pivotal in driving economic growth, optimizing processes, and facilitating societal progress across numerous sectors (Tubis & Poturaj, 2025). Yet, the environmental footprint associated with this digital expansion is substantial and cannot be overlooked. Data centers, the unseen engines of the internet and digital services, consume vast amounts of electricity, contributing significantly to global energy demand and, consequently, to carbon emissions when powered by fossil fuels. Beyond the operational energy use, the entire lifecycle of electronic devices – from the extraction of raw materials, through manufacturing and transportation, to their eventual disposal – carries a heavy environmental burden. The production of smartphones, laptops, servers, and countless other gadgets is resource-intensive and often involves hazardous chemicals. Compounding this is the escalating problem of electronic waste (e-waste), which is rapidly becoming one of the fastest-growing waste streams globally. Discarded electronics often contain toxic materials like lead, mercury, and cadmium, which can leach into the environment, polluting soil and water systems if not managed properly. Addressing these critical environmental challenges necessitates a fundamental shift toward "greener computing" practices, a rapid and comprehensive adoption of renewable energy sources to power digital infrastructure, and the integration of circular economy principles into the entire technology value chain, from initial design and production to deployment and end-of-life management (Rajpurohit et al., 2025).

Beyond the tangible environmental impacts, digital technologies exert profound and often complex social influences. On one hand, they hold immense potential to be powerful equalizers, enhancing access to vital services such as education, healthcare, and financial tools, particularly in underserved communities or remote areas where physical infrastructure is limited. Online learning platforms, telemedicine, and digital banking can bridge geographical and socio-economic gaps. However, this potential is significantly undercut by the persistent and, in some cases, widening digital divide. Marginalized populations, whether due to income level, geographic location, age, or disability, continue to face significant barriers to accessing reliable connectivity, affordable devices, and the necessary digital literacy skills to fully participate in and benefit from the digital world (Setiawan, 2025). Furthermore, the increasing sophistication of digital technologies gives rise to significant ethical and social justice concerns. Issues surrounding data privacy and the collection and use of personal information are paramount. Algorithmic bias, where AI systems inadvertently (or intentionally) perpetuate or amplify existing societal prejudices, can lead to unfair outcomes in areas like hiring, loan applications, or even criminal justice. The potential for widespread job displacement due to automation, as AI and robotics take over tasks previously performed by humans, raises critical questions about future employment, economic security, and the need for social safety nets and retraining programs. A truly sustainable digital ecosystem must actively prioritize inclusivity, ensuring equitable access to technology and its benefits, and championing responsible innovation that considers the social implications of new technologies before widespread deployment. Economically, digital technologies have undoubtedly been catalysts for growth, driving productivity improvements across industries and creating entirely new markets and business models. The digital economy, encompassing e-commerce, software development, and digital services, has become a significant engine of wealth creation. However, the benefits of this economic transformation have been unevenly distributed (Cheng & Nasirov, 2025). While large technology corporations have accumulated immense wealth and market power, smaller enterprises and many developing nations often struggle to compete effectively in a globalized, digitally-driven economy, facing challenges related to infrastructure, investment, and market access. Moreover, the production of electronic devices relies heavily on rare earth minerals and other finite resources, the extraction of which can cause significant environmental damage and is often associated with complex geopolitical and ethical challenges within global supply chains. Ensuring fair labor practices and responsible sourcing of these materials is a critical aspect of economic sustainability in the digital age. Sustainable digital ecosystems must therefore strive to balance continued economic growth with fair resource distribution, fostering innovation while actively minimizing exploitation – both of natural resources and human labor (Sharma & Singh, 2025).

Anchoring the discussion on sustainability in the digital age requires drawing upon several theoretical constructs. The Triple Bottom Line (TBL) framework (Elkington) is fundamental, emphasizing environmental, social, and economic dimensions. In the digital context, this means assessing not only the ecological footprint of digital technologies (e.g., energy consumption of data centers, e-waste) but also their social impacts (e.g., digital divide, algorithmic bias, labor displacement) and economic implications (e.g., new business models, global wealth distribution). Circular Economy principles are vital, advocating for designing digital products and services for longevity, repairability, and recyclability, shifting away from a linear "take-make-dispose" model for hardware and considering the lifecycle of software. Furthermore, Socio-technical Systems theory highlights the intricate interplay between digital technology and human organizations, crucial for understanding how digital tools influence sustainable practices and necessitate systemic changes in societal structures and individual behaviors. Diffusion of Innovations theory (Rogers) can explain how sustainable digital solutions are adopted and spread, while Stakeholder Theory (Freeman) emphasizes the importance of considering diverse interests—from consumers and employees to governments and environmental groups—in shaping digital sustainability initiatives. Finally, concepts like Dynamic Capabilities are essential for organizations to adapt and innovate sustainably in a rapidly evolving digital landscape. Despite these established frameworks, significant research gaps remain. There's a need for more empirical studies that quantitatively measure the ecological, social, and economic impacts of specific digital technologies and their applications across different sectors and geographies. Furthermore, frameworks for assessing and promoting "digital sufficiency" – encouraging conscious and reduced digital consumption – are nascent. A deeper understanding of the ethical implications of AI and big data on social equity and human rights within the sustainability discourse is also lacking. Finally, there's a critical need for integrated theoretical models that transcend disciplinary boundaries to offer a holistic perspective on the complex interplay between digitalization and sustainability, moving beyond siloed analyses.

Ultimately, navigating the path towards sustainable digital ecosystems requires a comprehensive understanding of the intricate interplay between digital technologies and the environmental, social, and economic pillars of sustainability. This understanding forms the basis for developing effective frameworks that can guide the design, deployment, and governance of technology in a way that promotes resilience and equity. Examining relevant case studies, analyzing existing and emerging policy initiatives, and identifying key trends are crucial steps in highlighting successful strategies for mitigating the negative impacts of digitalization while maximizing its potential as a force for good (Iliashenko et al., 2025). The transition to genuinely sustainable digital ecosystems cannot be achieved in isolation; it demands robust collaboration among governments setting regulatory standards and investing in green infrastructure, corporations adopting responsible business practices and innovating sustainably, and civil society advocating for ethical considerations and equitable access. Aligning technological progress with the ambitious targets set out in the United Nations Sustainable Development Goals (SDGs) provides a universal roadmap for this collaborative effort. Redefining technology ecosystems in the digital age necessitates a holistic approach—one that consciously harmonizes environmental stewardship, champions social equity, and ensures long-term economic viability. As digital technologies continue their relentless evolution, their deliberate and thoughtful integration into overarching sustainability frameworks will be absolutely crucial in shaping a future where innovation flourishes alongside planetary health and societal well-being. This ongoing research and discourse contribute vital insights into how technology can be effectively harnessed as a powerful force for global sustainability, rather than a detractor from it (Rydzewski, 2025)

2. LITERATURE REVIEW

2.1 Sustainability in Digital Age

The digital revolution has fundamentally reshaped nearly every facet of modern life, from global industries and economic structures to individual daily routines. While this transformative era has unlocked unprecedented levels of efficiency, connectivity, and innovation, it has simultaneously brought to the forefront significant environmental and social challenges that demand immediate and focused attention. The very infrastructure and technologies driving this progress, as noted by Tsvasman (2025), contribute substantially to energy consumption, the escalating problem of electronic waste, and associated carbon emissions. Achieving genuine sustainability in this digital age necessitates a delicate and intentional balance between relentless technological advancement and the crucial imperatives of ecological preservation and ethical responsibility. The environmental footprint of the digital world is particularly concerning. The sheer scale of digital infrastructure, epitomized by the ever-growing number and capacity of data centers, consumes enormous quantities of energy. Activities like cryptocurrency mining, which are computationally intensive, and the manufacturing processes for digital devices, from smartphones to servers, further contribute to this massive energy demand. A significant portion of this energy still originates from fossil fuels, directly contributing to greenhouse gas emissions and exacerbating climate change, a point underscored by the World Bank

Group (2021). Compounding this issue is the rapidly increasing volume of electronic waste. The short lifespan of many electronic gadgets, driven by rapid innovation cycles and consumer trends, results in mountains of discarded devices containing toxic materials like lead, mercury, and cadmium. Improper disposal of this e-waste poses a severe threat, leaching hazardous substances into soil and water, thereby polluting ecosystems. Addressing these environmental impacts requires a concerted shift towards sustainable solutions, including powering data centers with renewable energy sources, developing and utilizing more energy-efficient hardware throughout the digital ecosystem, and adopting circular economy principles that prioritize the recycling, repair, and reuse of electronic devices and their components (Asif, 2025).

Beyond the environmental realm, the digital revolution also presents complex socio-economic and ethical dilemmas. The pervasive digital divide remains a significant challenge, widening existing inequalities by limiting access to technology and its benefits for marginalized communities. This lack of access can hinder educational opportunities, economic participation, and access to essential services. Furthermore, the increasing sophistication of artificial intelligence raises concerns about algorithmic bias, perpetuating and even amplifying societal prejudices if not carefully designed and monitored. The potential for automation-driven job losses across various sectors also necessitates proactive strategies for reskilling and social safety nets. Ensuring a sustainable digital future requires robust ethical frameworks to guide technology development and deployment, prioritizing equitable access to digital resources and opportunities, upholding fair labor practices in tech-related industries, and establishing responsible governance mechanisms for AI development and deployment (International Telecommunication Union, 2021; Amrahova & Esanmurodova, 2025). Recognizing these challenges, there is a growing momentum among businesses to adopt more sustainable digital strategies. This includes optimizing cloud computing usage to reduce energy consumption, embracing green software engineering principles to create more efficient applications, and exploring carbon-neutral solutions for emerging technologies like blockchain (European Commission, 2022). However, the responsibility does not solely lie with corporations. Governments play a critical role in fostering a sustainable digital transition by investing in green infrastructure, such as renewable energy grids to power digital technologies, and by implementing and enforcing regulations that incentivize sustainable practices and hold companies accountable for their environmental and social impacts. [1] Ultimately, achieving sustainability in the digital age is a collective endeavor that hinges on continuous innovation, supportive policy frameworks, and coordinated action from all stakeholders – governments, businesses, civil society, and individuals. By deliberately integrating principles of eco-design into technology development, prioritizing ethical considerations in AI development, and implementing inclusive digital policies that ensure equitable access for all, society can effectively harness the transformative potential of technology without jeopardizing planetary health or exacerbating social inequalities. The overarching goal is to forge a future where digital advancement is seamlessly aligned with environmental stewardship and social equity, ensuring that technological progress serves the well-being of both people and the planet (Salamzadeh et al., 2025).

2.2 Environment, Social and Economic Sustainability

Sustainability is a fundamental principle guiding humanity towards a future where the needs of the present generation are met without compromising the ability of future generations to meet their own needs. It is a holistic concept that intricately weaves together three interconnected dimensions: environmental protection, social equity, and economic viability. In an era marked by rapid industrialization, the accelerating impacts of climate change, and the growing depletion of finite natural resources, embracing sustainability has transitioned from a desirable goal to an urgent and critical global priority, as recognized by researchers like Chasokela & Mangena (2025).

Environmental sustainability forms the bedrock of this concept, centering on minimizing human-induced harm to ecological systems and promoting the health of the planet. This involves a concerted effort to transition away from fossil fuels towards renewable energy sources like solar, wind, and geothermal power, dramatically reducing greenhouse gas emissions. It also necessitates drastic improvements in waste management, moving towards zero waste and promoting circular economy models where resources are reused, repaired, and recycled to keep materials in productive use for as long as possible. Conserving biodiversity is paramount, protecting ecosystems, habitats, and species from degradation and extinction. Pressing environmental threats such as climate change, deforestation, water and air pollution, and land degradation highlight the critical importance of adopting sustainable practices and deploying green technologies to mitigate damage and foster ecological restoration. Governments and businesses globally must implement and enforce eco-friendly policies, including setting ambitious carbon neutrality targets, investing in sustainable transportation, and transforming agricultural practices to be more sustainable, reducing reliance on harmful chemicals and promoting soil health, as emphasized by Singh & Kaunert (2025).

Parallel to environmental concerns is the crucial dimension of social sustainability, which seeks to ensure that development benefits all members of society fairly and equitably. This pillar addresses deep-seated issues such as poverty eradication, reducing inequality in income and opportunity, and ensuring universal access to essential services like quality education and healthcare. Key components include upholding ethical labor practices, guaranteeing fair wages, promoting safe working conditions, and combating exploitation. Digital inclusion is increasingly vital in an interconnected world, ensuring that marginalized communities are not left behind in accessing information, services, and economic opportunities provided by technology. Advancing gender equality and protecting the rights of all individuals, irrespective of background, are fundamental to social sustainability. Without a strong foundation of social equity, economic growth alone can exacerbate disparities, leading to social unrest, instability, and hindering overall societal progress (Mokadam et al., 2025).

The third pillar, economic sustainability, focuses on achieving long-term financial stability and prosperity in a manner that does not deplete natural resources or exploit labor. Sustainable business models are characterized by their commitment to ethical supply chains, ensuring that products are sourced responsibly from suppliers who adhere to environmental and social standards. Fair trade practices are integral, providing equitable compensation to producers, particularly in developing regions. Furthermore, channeling investments towards green technologies, renewable energy projects, and sustainable infrastructure is crucial for building a resilient economy. The global transition to a low-carbon economy, while challenging, also presents significant opportunities for economic growth, fostering innovation and creating new jobs in sectors like renewable energy installation, energy efficiency services, sustainable agriculture, and eco-tourism (United Nations, 2023). Achieving sustainability in practice requires a complex and collaborative effort involving all sectors of society.

Governments must establish clear policy frameworks, provide incentives for sustainable practices, invest in green infrastructure, and enforce regulations. Corporations have a responsibility to integrate sustainability into their core business models, from product design and sourcing to operations and waste management. Individuals play a vital role through conscious consumption, reducing their personal environmental footprints, advocating for change, and participating in community-level sustainability initiatives (Ajayi et al., 2025). Frameworks like the United Nations Sustainable Development Goals (SDGs) provide a comprehensive roadmap with specific targets and indicators, offering a universal call to action. However, translating these goals into tangible progress depends fundamentally on collective action – from large-scale systemic shifts driven by policy and corporate strategy to the cumulative impact of individual choices, such as reducing energy consumption, adopting sustainable transportation methods, and supporting businesses with ethical and environmentally sound practices (Rachmad, 2025). By deliberately integrating the principles of environmental stewardship, social equity, and economic prudence into all aspects of life and decision-making, society can pave the way for a truly resilient and equitable future, ensuring that progress benefits both people and the health of the planet for generations to come.

2.3 Case studies on Sustainable Technology Ecosystems

2.3.1 Case Study on Germany

The global shift from fossil fuels to renewable energy has been significantly influenced by pioneering policies in countries like Germany and India. Germany's *Energiewende* (Energy Transition) policy stands as a global benchmark for sustainable energy transformation, while India's ambitious solar energy program demonstrates how developing economies can leapfrog traditional fossil fuel dependency. Both nations have adopted innovative strategies to scale up renewables, reduce carbon emissions, and ensure energy security, offering valuable lessons for other countries. Germany's *Energiewende* policy has been instrumental in transitioning the country from coal and nuclear power to renewable energy sources. By 2020, renewables accounted for nearly 50% of Germany's electricity generation, driven by substantial investments in wind, solar, and hydropower (Aldrickzler et al., 2025). A key factor in this success was the implementation of feed-in tariffs (FiTs), which guaranteed fixed payments to renewable energy producers, incentivizing rapid adoption. This policy not only accelerated the deployment of wind and solar farms but also encouraged small-scale producers, including households and communities, to contribute to the energy grid.

Another critical component of Germany's strategy was grid modernization. As renewable energy sources are intermittent, upgrading the electricity infrastructure was essential to balance supply and demand. Investments in smart grids, energy storage systems, and cross-border energy sharing with neighboring countries enhanced grid stability. Additionally, public-private partnerships played a pivotal role in financing large-scale renewable projects, ensuring that the transition remained economically viable while reducing reliance on imported fossil fuels. The results have been transformative: Germany has significantly cut its carbon emissions while maintaining energy security. The phase-out of nuclear power by 2022 further underscored the nation's commitment to renewables, despite initial challenges. However, the transition has not been without hurdles, including high energy costs for consumers and the need for continued innovation in storage technologies. Nevertheless, Germany's experience provides a roadmap for other industrialized nations seeking to decarbonize their energy sectors.

While Germany's transition has been largely driven by environmental goals, India's renewable energy push is also motivated by the need to address energy poverty and reduce dependence on coal. The country's ambitious target of 100 GW of solar capacity—part of its commitment under the Paris Agreement—has positioned it as a leader in emerging economies (Mekheimer & Abdelhalim, 2025). Key initiatives such as large-scale solar parks and rooftop solar subsidies have accelerated adoption, particularly in rural areas where grid connectivity remains unreliable. One of India's most notable projects is the Bhadla Solar Park in Rajasthan, one of the largest in the world, which has significantly boosted the country's installed capacity. Additionally, programs like the Solar Rooftop Subsidy Scheme have made clean energy accessible to households and small businesses, reducing their dependence on diesel generators and coal-fired power. These efforts have not only expanded energy access but also created green jobs, supporting economic growth in underserved regions (Şallı, 2025).

Despite these successes, India faces challenges, including financing constraints, land acquisition issues, and the need for better grid integration. Yet, the country's rapid progress demonstrates how policy incentives, international collaboration, and private sector involvement can drive renewable energy adoption even in resource-constrained settings. Germany and India exemplify different but equally effective approaches to the renewable energy transition. Germany's *Energiewende* highlights the importance of policy stability, technological innovation, and public engagement, while India's solar program showcases how large-scale investments and targeted subsidies can transform energy systems in developing nations. Both models underscore that a combination of political will, financial mechanisms, and infrastructure development is essential for a sustainable energy future. As the world strives to meet climate goals, these case studies offer critical insights for other nations embarking on their own energy transitions. Germany shows strong commitment to sustainability, driven by government regulations, corporate strategies, and growing consumer demand. Challenges remain, including resource efficiency and fully integrating circular economy principles, yet significant progress towards climate neutrality by 2045 is evident.

2.3.2 Case Study on Sweden

Sweden stands as a global frontrunner in sustainable waste management, demonstrating a commitment to environmental responsibility through its highly effective waste-to-energy systems and ambitious recycling programs. The nation has achieved a remarkable feat, diverting approximately 99% of its household waste from landfills, a stark contrast to many other developed countries. This success is largely attributed to a multi-pronged approach that prioritizes waste reduction, reuse, recycling, and energy recovery. A cornerstone of Sweden's waste management strategy is its advanced network of waste-to-energy (WTE) plants. Cities like Gothenburg are home to state-of-the-art incineration facilities that play a crucial role in processing residual waste – the small percentage that cannot be recycled or reused. These plants are not simply disposal sites; they are sophisticated energy generators. Through controlled combustion, the waste is converted into valuable electricity and heat, which is then fed into the national grid and district heating systems, providing power and warmth to homes and businesses. This process significantly minimizes the need for landfill space, a critical consideration for a country with environmental goals centered on reducing land use for waste disposal and mitigating the associated environmental hazards like methane emissions. The energy generated from waste also contributes to Sweden's renewable energy targets, lessening the reliance on fossil fuels and enhancing energy security.

Beyond energy recovery, Sweden places a strong emphasis on creating a circular economy. This involves promoting eco-design principles, encouraging manufacturers to design products with their end-of-life in mind, making them easier to recycle and less wasteful. Furthermore, industrial symbiosis is actively fostered, creating interconnected networks where the waste or byproducts of one industry become valuable resources for another. This collaborative approach reduces the overall demand for virgin resources, minimizes waste generation at the source, and promotes a more efficient and sustainable use of materials throughout the economy. Examples of industrial symbiosis in Sweden include the use of fly ash from WTE plants in construction materials or the utilization of waste heat from industries for district heating. The high recycling rate of 99% is a testament to both robust infrastructure and a strong public commitment to sorting and separating waste at the household level. Municipalities provide accessible recycling facilities and clear guidelines, making it convenient for citizens to participate. Educational campaigns further reinforce the importance of proper waste separation and the benefits of recycling. The economic model also plays a role, with incentives and disincentives encouraging recycling and discouraging landfilling. The success of the Swedish model, as highlighted by researchers like Billi & Bernardo (2025), offers valuable insights for other nations striving to improve their waste management practices and transition towards a more sustainable, circular economy. By viewing waste not as a problem but as a resource, Sweden has successfully transformed its waste management system into an efficient engine for energy production and resource recovery, setting a high standard for environmental performance. Sweden champions sustainability with ambitious goals, including carbon neutrality by 2045. High renewable energy adoption (over two-thirds of gross final energy consumption) and strong circular economy initiatives demonstrate national commitment, though challenges in biodiversity and social equality persist.

2.3.3 Case Study on Costa Rica

Costa Rica presents a compelling model for sustainable development, showcasing how a nation can successfully integrate environmental conservation with robust economic growth through strategic policy, technological innovation, and active community engagement. A cornerstone of Costa Rica's sustainability achievements is its remarkable reliance on renewable energy sources, consistently generating around 98% of its electricity from clean power. This impressive feat is primarily driven by significant investments in and the effective utilization of hydropower and geothermal energy, leveraging the country's abundant natural resources. Large-scale hydroelectric dams harness the power of its rivers, while geothermal plants tap into the volcanic activity beneath its surface, providing a stable and baseload renewable energy supply. This commitment to renewables drastically reduces greenhouse gas emissions, mitigating climate change impacts and enhancing energy independence. Beyond its energy matrix, Costa Rica has strategically leveraged its rich biodiversity to build a thriving ecotourism sector. This is not merely tourism *in* nature, but tourism *for* nature. The ecotourism model is deeply intertwined with conservation efforts, with revenues often channeled back into protecting national parks, wildlife reserves, and other natural habitats. Technology plays a vital role in this sector, from online platforms for booking eco-lodges and tours that adhere to strict sustainability standards, to the use of geographic information systems (GIS) for park management and monitoring, and digital tools for educating tourists about local ecosystems and conservation initiatives. This symbiotic relationship between tourism and conservation creates a powerful economic incentive to preserve the natural environment, demonstrating that protecting biodiversity can be a driver of prosperity.

Furthermore, Costa Rica is increasingly integrating sustainable technologies into its agricultural sector, traditionally a significant part of its economy. Faced with challenges like climate change impacts and the need for increased efficiency, farmers are adopting technologies such as precision agriculture techniques that optimize resource use, leading to reduced water consumption and minimizing the need for fertilizers and pesticides. Sustainable farming practices, supported by technological advancements in areas like irrigation and crop monitoring, enhance productivity while minimizing environmental footprints. The development of sustainable supply chains, often facilitated by digital platforms for traceability and market access, further bolsters the economic viability of eco-friendly agricultural practices. The success of Costa Rica in building a resilient, sustainable technology ecosystem is a testament to the power of aligning national policy with innovation and fostering community engagement. The government has implemented forward-thinking environmental policies, including strong conservation laws and incentives for renewable energy adoption. These policies create an enabling environment for the development and deployment of sustainable technologies. Innovation, both in terms of large-scale infrastructure like geothermal plants and smaller-scale applications in tourism and agriculture, is actively encouraged. Crucially, community engagement is vital; the involvement of local communities in conservation efforts, ecotourism initiatives, and sustainable agriculture ensures that these programs are socially equitable and have long-term viability. As highlighted by Ly et al. (2025), Costa Rica's experience underscores how a coherent strategy integrating policy frameworks, technological advancements, and community participation can create a virtuous cycle where economic growth and environmental conservation are mutually reinforcing. These case studies, including insights from sources such as Rachmad (2025) and Widmer et al. (2020), collectively demonstrate the multifaceted approaches required to build truly sustainable technology ecosystems for a more resilient future.

2.3.4 Case Study of Bangalore, India

Bengaluru, often hailed as India's Silicon Valley, stands at the nexus of technological innovation and pressing environmental concerns. The city's rapid digital growth has, predictably, led to a substantial increase in its energy footprint from a dense concentration of data centers and IT parks, alongside a burgeoning electronic waste challenge. Recognizing this, Bengaluru has embarked on a journey to redefine its technology ecosystem, aiming for a more sustainable and circular model. A key focus for Bengaluru is the transition to renewable energy sources for its digital infrastructure. While a complete shift to 100% renewable energy for all IT operations remains an ambitious goal, significant strides are being made. Large IT campuses are increasingly integrating rooftop solar installations and exploring power purchase agreements (PPAs) with renewable energy generators. For instance, major tech companies in Bengaluru are actively investing in off-site renewable energy projects to power their operations, moving beyond just efficiency within their premises. This is crucial as the power demands of emerging technologies like AI continue to grow, making green energy adoption paramount to prevent a proportional rise in carbon emissions.

Concurrently, Bengaluru is grappling with the escalating e-waste crisis. The city is a major producer of electronic waste in India, necessitating robust lifecycle management and circularity strategies. Efforts are being made to strengthen the formal e-waste collection and recycling infrastructure, working to divert waste from informal sectors which often employ hazardous practices. Organizations like CSTEP (Centre for Study of Science, Technology and Policy), based in Bengaluru, are actively engaged in research and policy advocacy for sustainable waste management, including e-waste, providing critical data and insights to guide city-level initiatives. Additionally, there's a growing push to encourage Extended Producer Responsibility (EPR) among electronics manufacturers, ensuring they take accountability for the end-of-life management of their products. This includes promoting the design of devices that are more durable, repairable, and easily recyclable, thereby reducing the sheer volume of waste generated (e.g., initiatives for product longevity and modular design, although widely implemented examples are still emerging in India). Furthermore, Bengaluru's ambition as a Smart City integrates sustainability directly into its digital governance. The Bengaluru Metropolitan Transport Corporation (BMTC), for example, is transitioning towards a greener and more digital public transport system. They are rapidly expanding their fleet of electric buses, replacing older diesel vehicles, with plans to increase electric buses to 50% of the fleet in the future (eGov Magazine, 2025). This initiative is supported by government subsidies and aims to enhance last-mile connectivity with metro services, leveraging digital integration for real-time tracking and optimized routes. This showcases how digital transformation in urban mobility can directly contribute to reduced air pollution and a smaller carbon footprint. The city's commitment to using IoT and data analytics for traffic management and urban planning also contributes to sustainability by optimizing resource use and reducing congestion (SleepyClasses, 2025).

3. RESEARCH METHODOLOGY

This study employs a conceptual research methodology to explore the intersection of digital technologies and sustainability, focusing on how technological ecosystems can be redefined for environmental, social, and economic sustainability. The research design integrates a systematic literature review with thematic analysis and conceptual framework development to provide a comprehensive understanding of the subject. First, a rigorous examination of peer-reviewed academic articles, industry reports, and policy documents from databases such as Scopus, IEEE Xplore, and Google Scholar will be conducted to identify key themes, trends, and gaps in existing research. This review will specifically focus on three critical dimensions: green computing (including energy-efficient data centers and AI optimization for sustainability), circular digital economies (encompassing e-waste management and sustainable hardware design), and ethical digitalization (addressing issues like the digital divide and responsible AI development). Following the literature review, thematic analysis will be performed using qualitative data analysis tools to identify recurring patterns and emerging concepts. These findings will then inform the development of a conceptual framework that maps the relationships between digital technologies and sustainable outcomes, providing a structured approach to understanding how technological ecosystems can be redesigned to support sustainability goals. The methodology emphasizes theoretical synthesis rather than empirical data collection, aiming to contribute to the academic discourse by offering new perspectives on sustainable digital transformation while identifying areas for future research and policy development.

4. FINDINGS

1. **Significant Environmental Footprint:** The ever-expanding digital infrastructure, particularly the burgeoning number and size of data centers globally, represents a substantial and growing consumer of energy. Powering these facilities and the increasing computational demands driven by technologies like Artificial Intelligence requires vast amounts of electricity, much of which is still generated from fossil fuels. This significant energy consumption directly contributes to greenhouse gas emissions, posing a considerable challenge to global efforts aimed at mitigating climate change and achieving crucial climate goals, as highlighted by Freitag et al. (2021) and Melville (2010).
2. **Escalating E-waste Crisis:** The accelerating pace of technological innovation and the consumer-driven demand for the latest devices have led to increasingly shorter lifespans for electronic products. This rapid obsolescence is fueling a dramatic surge in electronic waste (e-waste) worldwide. E-waste contains numerous hazardous materials, including heavy metals and flame retardants, which can pose serious risks to both human health and the environment if not managed and recycled properly. The sheer volume and toxic nature of this waste necessitate urgent improvements in collection, processing, and recycling strategies globally, as underscored by Kaack et al. (2022).
3. **Enabling Environmental Solutions:** Despite its own footprint, digital technology offers powerful and innovative tools to address environmental challenges and drive sustainability. Applications such as smart grids optimize energy distribution and reduce waste, while precision agriculture techniques use data to enhance resource efficiency in farming, minimizing water and pesticide use. Remote sensing technologies enable crucial environmental monitoring, from tracking deforestation to assessing air quality. Furthermore, digital tools facilitating remote work and virtual collaboration can significantly reduce the need for physical travel, thereby lowering transportation-related emissions (Frick, 2020).
4. **Mixed Socio-economic Outcomes:** The proliferation of digital technologies presents a complex picture regarding socio-economic impacts. While digitalization can undoubtedly spur economic growth, create new industries and jobs, and enhance efficiency across various sectors, it also exacerbates existing inequalities, particularly the digital divide, leaving those without access or skills at a disadvantage. Concerns also arise regarding potential job displacement due to increasing automation and critical issues surrounding data privacy and security, which can impact individual rights and societal trust, posing challenges to achieving equitable and sustainable economic development (Greenpeace, 2021).

5. **Requires Deliberate Management:** Navigating the digital age sustainably is not an automatic process; it demands conscious and strategic effort. It is imperative to actively work on mitigating the negative environmental consequences of technology, specifically its energy consumption and the generation of e-waste. Simultaneously, there must be a deliberate focus on strategically leveraging technology's immense potential to enable and accelerate sustainable practices across all three pillars of sustainability: environmental protection, social equity, and economic viability. This requires careful planning, policy intervention, and responsible innovation (Harvard Business Review, 2023).

5. DISCUSSION

1. **Strategies for Decarbonizing Digital Infrastructure:** Addressing the substantial energy footprint of the digital realm, particularly from data centers and the increasing power demands of emerging technologies like AI, is paramount. A central focus of discussion involves accelerating the shift towards powering all digital infrastructure with 100% renewable energy sources. Alongside this, significant efforts are needed to improve the intrinsic energy efficiency of both hardware components and the software that runs on them. Exploring and implementing innovative cooling solutions for data centers, moving away from energy-intensive traditional methods, is also crucial for reducing overall energy consumption and associated greenhouse gas emissions, as highlighted by sources like the Ellen MacArthur Foundation (2022) and Wynn et al. (2023). Furthermore, proactive policies and industry collaborations are essential to drive the adoption of these sustainable practices at scale. This comprehensive approach is vital for mitigating the environmental impact of our increasingly digitized world and fostering a truly green digital economy.
2. **Implementing Effective E-waste Management and Circularity:** The escalating global electronic waste crisis demands comprehensive strategies focused on lifecycle management and circularity. Key discussions revolve around implementing stricter regulations on electronics manufacturers regarding product design and end-of-life responsibility. Fostering extended producer responsibility schemes is vital to ensure companies are accountable for the collection and recycling of their products. Developing accessible, efficient, and environmentally sound recycling infrastructure globally is essential to process the growing volume of e-waste. Furthermore, there must be a strong emphasis on promoting the design and production of electronic devices that are inherently more durable, easier to repair, and readily recyclable to close the loop on valuable and potentially hazardous materials (Fuchs, 2021). In addition, consumer awareness campaigns are

crucial to encourage responsible disposal and demand for repairable products. Ultimately, a multi-stakeholder approach involving governments, industry, and consumers is necessary to transition towards a truly circular electronics economy.

3. **Harnessing Technology for Broader Sustainability Transformations:** Beyond managing its own impact, a critical discussion point is how to strategically leverage the power of digital technologies to drive significant sustainability transformations across high-impact sectors. This involves deploying technologies such as the Internet of Things (IoT), Artificial Intelligence (AI), and big data analytics to enable systemic change. In energy, this could mean smart grids optimizing distribution; in transportation, intelligent systems reducing congestion and promoting electric mobility; and in agriculture, precision farming enhancing resource efficiency. These applications can lead to greater resource efficiency, substantial emissions reductions, and improved capabilities for environmental monitoring and conservation efforts on a larger scale (Murugesan, 2020).
4. **Ensuring Inclusive and Equitable Digital Transitions:** As digital technologies become increasingly integral to sustainability solutions, a critical discussion must address how to prevent this transition from exacerbating existing social and economic inequalities. It is vital to actively work to prevent the digital divide from widening disparities in access to the benefits that digital technologies can offer for sustainability. This involves tackling fundamental issues of access to reliable connectivity and affordable devices, improving digital literacy and skills across all demographics, and ensuring that the environmental and economic benefits derived from digitally-enabled sustainability initiatives are shared equitably among all populations and communities, as emphasized by Cowls & Tsamados (2023).
5. **Developing Governance and Policy Frameworks:** Effective governance and well-designed policy frameworks are indispensable for guiding the sustainable development and deployment of digital technologies. Discussions are needed to create robust national and international policies that not only incentivize innovation in green digital technologies but also effectively regulate the negative environmental and social impacts of the digital sector. Promoting secure and ethical data sharing for sustainability-related research and monitoring is crucial. Furthermore, integrating ethical considerations, such as fairness, transparency, and accountability, into the entire lifecycle of technological advancement, particularly in areas like AI, is necessary to ensure that digital progress aligns with societal values (Estevez & Janowski, 2022). This includes developing clear guidelines for the responsible use of data and AI in environmental monitoring and resource management. Ultimately, a proactive and adaptive policy approach is vital to harness the full potential of digital technologies for a sustainable future while mitigating potential risks.

6. PRACTICAL IMPLICATIONS

The findings and discussions surrounding the impacts of technology on sustainability in the digital age translate into crucial practical implications for a range of stakeholders. Addressing the complex interplay between digital advancement and environmental, social, and economic well-being requires concrete actions across various levels. For governments and policymakers, a key implication is the urgent need for updated regulations and incentives that specifically address the environmental footprint of the digital sector. This includes setting energy efficiency standards for data centers and electronic devices, implementing extended producer responsibility schemes for e-waste management, and incentivizing the use of renewable energy sources by the tech industry. Furthermore, policies must actively work to bridge the digital divide, ensuring equitable access to technology and digital literacy to prevent increased social inequality and enable broader participation in the benefits of digital-enabled sustainability initiatives. Investment in sustainable digital infrastructure, such as resilient and energy-efficient network build-out, is also critical.

Businesses and the tech industry face significant practical implications in their operations and product lifecycles. This means adopting sustainable IT practices, including optimizing data storage and processing to reduce energy consumption, and prioritizing renewable energy for their facilities. A fundamental shift towards circular economy principles is required, focusing on designing products for longevity, repairability, and recyclability. Companies must also take responsibility for the end-of-life management of their products, establishing take-back programs and supporting certified recycling processes. Beyond internal operations, businesses can leverage their technological expertise to develop and deploy solutions that enable sustainability in other sectors, such as smart energy management systems or supply chain optimization software that reduces waste and emissions. Technology developers and innovators have a direct responsibility to embed sustainability into the very design of digital products and services. This involves focusing on energy-efficient algorithms and hardware, minimizing the use of rare earth minerals and hazardous materials, and creating modular and durable devices that can be easily repaired or upgraded. Designing user interfaces and experiences that encourage sustainable digital behaviors, such as reminders to delete unnecessary data or options for lower-resolution streaming, also plays a role. The principle of "sustainability by design" needs to become a core tenet of technology development.

For consumers and individuals, the practical implications involve making more conscious choices regarding their digital consumption. This includes extending the lifespan of electronic devices through careful use and repair, responsibly disposing of e-waste through certified channels, and being mindful of the energy consumption associated with their digital habits (e.g., managing cloud storage, adjusting streaming quality). Supporting companies with strong sustainability commitments and advocating for more sustainable tech practices are also important individual actions. Finally, researchers and educators have the practical task of developing better metrics to accurately measure the environmental and social impacts of digital technologies throughout their lifecycle. Education is crucial to raise awareness among the public, future technologists, and policymakers about the challenges and opportunities at the intersection of technology and sustainability, fostering the knowledge and skills needed to build a truly sustainable digital future. Implementing these practical steps across all levels is essential to harness the transformative power of the digital age for the benefit of both people and the planet.

7. CONCLUSION

The digital age presents a paradox for sustainability. While offering unprecedented tools to monitor environmental changes, optimize resource use, and foster new, more efficient economic models, the very infrastructure and proliferation of digital technology carry a significant and growing environmental and, potentially, social cost. Findings consistently point to the substantial energy consumption of data centers and AI, alongside the escalating challenge of e-waste, as critical areas demanding urgent attention and innovative solutions. However, focusing solely on the negative overlooks the transformative potential. Digital technologies are simultaneously enabling advancements in renewable energy integration through smart grids, increasing agricultural yields with less environmental impact via precision farming, and reducing the need for physical travel through enhanced connectivity. The economic benefits of digitalization are clear, though they must be pursued without exacerbating social inequalities or widening the digital divide.

Ultimately, the trajectory of sustainability in the digital age is not predetermined. It hinges on a collective commitment to conscious design, responsible deployment, and equitable access to technology. Addressing the environmental footprint through energy efficiency, renewable sourcing, and circular economy principles for electronics is paramount. Simultaneously, strategically leveraging digital tools to drive sustainable practices across all sectors is essential. The discussion must move beyond acknowledging the dual impact to implementing robust policies, fostering sustainable innovation, and promoting responsible digital citizenship to ensure that the digital revolution is a force for, rather than a detriment to, a sustainable global future.

8. LIMITATIONS AND FUTURE SCOPE

Despite growing awareness, a significant limitation in addressing sustainability in the digital age is the lack of comprehensive, standardized data and metrics to accurately measure the full lifecycle environmental and social impacts of digital technologies. The rapid pace of technological innovation often outstrips the development and implementation of effective regulatory frameworks and sustainable practices. Challenges remain in establishing truly circular economy models for complex electronics, from responsible sourcing of raw materials to efficient and safe end-of-life processing on a global scale. Furthermore, attributing specific environmental costs to individual digital activities within vast and interconnected networks presents a considerable challenge. The global nature of the digital industry also complicates coordinated international efforts and policy enforcement.

Looking ahead, the future scope involves several critical areas. There is a need for continued research and development into more sustainable materials, energy-efficient hardware and software architectures, and novel approaches to waste heat recovery from data centers. Future efforts should focus on developing and implementing globally recognized standards for assessing the sustainability of digital products and services. Exploring innovative business models that prioritize product longevity, repair, and reuse over frequent upgrades is crucial. Further research is also needed on the long-term social and economic implications of AI and automation to ensure just and equitable transitions. Finally, strengthening international cooperation and developing agile governance frameworks are essential to effectively manage the sustainability challenges and leverage the opportunities presented by the ever-evolving digital landscape.

REFERENCES

Ajayi, O. O., Alozie, C. E., & Abieba, O. A. (2025). Enhancing Cybersecurity in Energy Infrastructure: Strategies for Safeguarding Critical Systems in the Digital Age. *Trends in Renewable Energy, 11*(2), 201–212. DOI: 10.17737/tre.2025.11.2.00192

Aldrickzler, R., Saadoon, M. Y., Kawad, R. T., & Chornomordenko, I. (2025). Transforming human capital for the digital age: Industry 4.0 and 5.0. *Encuentros. Revista de Ciencias Humanas. Teoría Social y Pensamiento Crítico.*, (23 (enero-abril)), 438–455.

Amrahova, G. J., & Esanmurodova, N. (2025). 26 Externalities in the era of digitalization: Strategies for public internalization and sustainable revenue generation for structural transformation. *Applications of Mathematics in Science and Technology*, 140.

Asif, S. (2025). The Role of Digital Food Marketing in Shaping Consumer Behavior and Sustainability in Emerging Economies. In *Innovative Trends Shaping Food Marketing and Consumption* (pp. 57–70). IGI Global Scientific Publishing. DOI: 10.4018/979-8-3693-8542-5.ch003

Billi, A., & Bernardo, A. (2025). The Effects of Digital Transformation, IT Innovation, and Sustainability Strategies on Firms' Performances: An Empirical Study. *Sustainability (Basel), 17*(3), 823. DOI: 10.3390/su17030823

Bocean, C. G. (2025). Sustainable Development in the Digital Age: Harnessing Emerging Digital Technologies to Catalyze Global SDG Achievement. *Applied Sciences (Basel, Switzerland), 15*(2), 816. DOI: 10.3390/app15020816

Bucher, E., Fieseler, C., & Lutz, C. (2019). *Sustainability in the digital age: The role of corporate social responsibility*. Journal of Business Ethics, *156*(4), 1013–1037. https://doi.org/ DOI: 10.3390/app15020816

Widmer, R., Oswald-Krapf, H., Sinha-Khetriwal, D., & Schnellmann, M. (2020). Global perspectives on e-waste management and sustainability. Environmental Science & Technology, *54*(12), 7095–7108. https://doi.org/10.1021/acs.est.0c01234 DOI: 10.3390/app15020816

Melville, N. P. (2010). Information systems innovation for environmental sustainability. MIS Quarterly, *34*(1), 1–21. https://doi.org/10.2307/20721412 DOI: 10.3390/app15020816

Freitag, C., Berners-Lee, M., & Widdicks, K. (2021). The climate impact of ICT: A review of estimates, trends, and regulations. Patterns, *2*(9), 100340. https://doi.org/10.1016/j.patter.2021.100340 DOI: 10.3390/app15020816

Kaack, L. H., Donti, P. L., & Rolnick, D. (2022). *Aligning artificial intelligence with climate change mitigation.* Nature Climate Change, *12*(6), 518–527. https://doi.org/DOI: 10.3390/app15020816

Chasokela, D., & Mangena, N. (2025). The Future of Learning in the Digital Age. In *Insights Into International Higher Education Leadership and the Skills Gap* (pp. 471–500). IGI Global.

Cheng, L., & Nasirov, J. (2025). Sociosemiotic Framing of Human Rights in Digital Age. *International Journal for the Semiotics of Law-Revue internationale de Sémiotique juridique*, 1-16.

Cowls, J., & Tsamados, A. (2023). *Artificial intelligence for the sustainable development goals.* Springer.

Ellen MacArthur Foundation. (2022). *Circular economy and digital technology.* https://ellenmacarthurfoundation.org/topics/digital

Estevez, E., & Janowski, T. (2022). *Sustainable digital governance: Policies and practices.* MIT Press.

European Commission. (2022). *Shaping Europe's digital future: A green and sustainable approach.* https://digital-strategy.ec.europa.eu/en/policies/green-digital

Frick, T. (2020). *Designing for sustainability in the digital space.* A List Apart. https://alistapart.com/article/sustainable-web-design/

Fuchs, C. (2021). *Sustainability and digital media: A critical introduction.* SAGE Publications.

Fülöp, M. T., & Cifuentes-Faura, J. (2025). Digital approaches in sustainable entrepreneurship training: Effects on student well-being and satisfaction. *Education and Information Technologies*, •••, 1–32.

Greenpeace. (2021). *Clicking clean: Who is winning the race to build a green internet?* https://www.greenpeace.org/usa/reports/clicking-clean-2021/

Harvard Business Review. (2023). *Why digital sustainability should be a C-suite priority.* https://hbr.org/2023/05/why-digital-sustainability-should-be-a-c-suite-priority

Iliashenko, I., Gazzola, P., Pezzetti, R., & Grechi, D. (2025). Digitalization and Sustainability in the Fashion Industry: consumer perspective. *TECHNOLOGY AND SOCIETY: Boon or Bane?*, 92.

International Telecommunication Union. (2022). *Global standards for green ICT*. https://www.itu.int/en/ITU-T/climatechange

Ly, B., Dem, T., Ly, R., Sorn, S., & Doeur, B. (2025). Exploring the nexus of digital inclusion and environmental sustainability: Insights from Cambodia. *Information Technology for Development*, *31*(1), 77–94. DOI: 10.1080/02681102.2024.2345381

Mekheimer, M., & Abdelhalim, W. M. (2025). The digital age students: Exploring leadership, freedom, and ethical online behavior: A quantitative study. *Social Sciences & Humanities Open*, *11*, 101325. DOI: 10.1016/j.ssaho.2025.101325

Mokadam, E., Musa, H. G., Kumalasari, A., & Istighfaroh, F. (2025). Public Policy Challenges in the Digital Age: Balancing Innovation, Governance, and Equity. *JIAN-Jurnal Ilmiah Administrasi Negara*, *9*(1), 102–109. DOI: 10.56071/jian.v9i1.1172

Murugesan, S. (Ed.). (2020). *Harnessing green IT: Principles and practices*. Wiley.

Qadri, U. A., Ghani, M. B. A., Abbas, U., & Kashif, A. R. (2025). Digital technologies and social sustainability in the digital transformation age: A systematic analysis and research agenda. *International Journal of Ethics and Systems*, *41*(1), 142–169. DOI: 10.1108/IJOES-08-2024-0239

Rachmad, Y. E. (2025). *The Viral Shift: Harnessing the Power of Gimmicks in Changing Consumer Behavior*. United Nations Economic and Social Council.

Rachmad, Y. E. (2025). *Viral Influence: How Gimmicks Shape Consumer Behavior*. United Nations Economic and Social Council.

Rajpurohit, S. C., Palande, B., Kalal, J., & Parkhi, S. (2025). Sustainable Development in the Digital Age: The Role of CBDCs in Achieving the SDGs. In *Green Finance and Energy Transition: Innovation, Legal Frameworks and Regulation* (pp. 491–502). Springer Nature Switzerland.

Rydzewski, P. (2025). Digital Inequality and Sustainable Development. *Problemy Ekorozwoju*, *20*(1), 96–108. DOI: 10.35784/preko.6691

Salamzadeh, A., Hadizadeh, M., Feyzabadi, J. G., Yasin, N., & Paramba, J. N. (2025). The Role of Digital Platforms in Transforming Corporate Governance: A Path to Sustainability Through ESG. In *Modern Corporate Governance Strategies for Sustainable Value Creation* (pp. 111–136). IGI Global Scientific Publishing.

Şallı, D. (2025). Rethinking Education in the Digital Age: Readiness for the Professions of the Future. *Journal of Education and Future*, (27), 135–146. DOI: 10.30786/jef.1372523

Setiawan, R. (2025). Social Entrepreneurship in the Digital Age: Opportunities and Challenges in Achieving Social Welfare. *BDJ Smart: Breakthrough Development Journal in Strategic Management & Marketing*, *1*(01), 59–67.

Sharma, R., & Singh, A. (2025). Integrating AI, Green Marketing, and Influencer Strategies: Shaping Sustainable Consumer Behavior in the Digital Age. In *Strategic Brand Management in the Age of AI and Disruption* (pp. 325-342). IGI Global Scientific Publishing.

Singh, B., & Kaunert, C. (2025). Innovative Business Models in Digital and Virtual Reality for the Gig Economy: Space-Age Sustainable Development Projecting Smart Business Practices. In *Business Transformation in the Era of Digital Disruption* (pp. 127-156). IGI Global.

Tsvasman, L. (2025). Self-Regulation as a Catalyst for Scalability and Human-Centered Business Ecosystems in the Digital Age: Advanced Cybernetic Strategies for Autonomous and Human-Centered Business Evolution. In *Building Business Knowledge for Complex Modern Business Environments* (pp. 63–94). IGI Global.

Tubis, A. A., & Poturaj, H. (2025). Energy Supply Chains in the Digital Age: A Review of Current Research and Trends. *Energies*, *18*(2), 430. DOI: 10.3390/en18020430

United Nations. (2023). *Digital technologies for sustainable development* (Report No. UNEP/DT/2023/1). https://www.unep.org/resources/report/digital-technologies-sustainable-development

United Nations Environment Programme. (2023). *Tackling digital waste for a sustainable future*. https://www.unep.org/news-and-stories/story/tackling-digital-waste

World Bank Group. (2021). *E-waste management and circular economy in developing countries*. https://www.worldbank.org/en/topic/urbandevelopment/publication/e-waste-management

Wynn, M., & Jones, P. (2022). *Digital sustainability: Strategies for the 21st century*. Routledge.

Chapter 11
The Internet of Things and Real-Time Process Monitoring

Sujoy Kumar Basu
https://orcid.org/0000-0003-4085-154X
Asansol Engineering College, India

Rajkumar Mandal
https://orcid.org/0009-0005-1754-0569
Gopal Narayan Singh University, India

Amitava Kar
Gopal Narayan Singh University, India

Swadesh Patra
https://orcid.org/0009-0000-8731-3955
Gopal Narayan Singh University, India

P. Sudheer
https://orcid.org/0009-0005-1912-6636
CVR College of Engineering, India

P. Selvakumar
https://orcid.org/0000-0002-3650-4548
Department of Science and Humanities, Nehru Institute of Technology, Coimbatore, India

T. C. Manjunath
https://orcid.org/0000-0003-2545-9160
Rajarajeswari College of Engineering, India

ABSTRACT

Businesses, industries, and consumers' physical enabling interconnectivity allow for greater automation, efficiency, and real-time monitoring, which is most important applications offering businesses track, analyze, optimize operations instantaneously. By embedding sensors and intelligent systems into processes, IoT facilitates continuous data collection and analysis, providing operational help. This combination process is reshaping logistics and agriculture by providing unprecedented status and systems. Understanding the Internet of Things (IoT): a broad concept encompassing physical sensors, actuators, other objects through objects, and smart highly used in manufacturing or healthcare. The key IoT gathers exchange, then processes and analyzes to improve the functionality of the connected objects. One primary is the

DOI: 10.4018/979-8-3373-3336-6.ch011

sensor, which collects data from the pressure and motion. Then, through networks (often wireless) to central processing units or cloud platforms, IoT systems typically rely on several key elements of the ecosystem, smarter environments, and more efficient operations.

INTRODUCTION TO THE INTERNET OF THINGS (IOT) AND REAL-TIME PROCESS MONITORING: UNDERSTANDING CONCEPTS AND TECHNOLOGIES

Businesses, industries, and consumers' physical enabling interconnectivity allow for greater automation, efficiency, and real-time monitoring, which is most important applications offering businesses track, analyze, and optimize operations instantaneously. By embedding sensors and intelligent systems into processes, IoT facilitates continuous data collection and analysis, providing operational help. This combination process is reshaping logistics and agriculture by providing unprecedented status and systems. Understanding the Internet of Things (IoT): a broad concept encompassing physical sensors, actuators, other objects through objects, and smart highly used in manufacturing or healthcare. The key IoT gathers exchange, then processes and analyzes to improve the functionality of the connected objects. One primary is the sensor, which collects data from the pressure and motion. Then, through networks (often wireless) to central processing units or cloud platforms, IoT systems typically rely on several key elements of the ecosystem, smarter environments, and more efficient operations. Components of IoT Systems: IoT communication: Devices and Sensors: embedded and detect various, such as or, while for control received. Connectivity: The data from devices and over network systems decision-making is achieved through various types of networks, including data volume and network infrastructure. Edge Devices and Gateways: In many IoT systems, especially those used in industrial settings, edge devices or critical the is sent or central server. This helps volume improve. Cloud Platforms and Data Storage: platforms used to analyze volumes of These processing long-term storage, enabling businesses to access and analyze historical data for insights. Data Analytics and AI: Advanced technologies are used to analyze massive IoT systems. These tools' analytics capabilities help organizations optimize processes and make informed decisions.

Key Technologies Driving Real-Time Process Monitoring: Several emerging technologies enable processes through IoT. These technologies include: Edge Computing: processing this data in real-time becomes increasingly challenging. Edge computing solves this problem by itself through local servers. This reduces cloud platforms, enabling improved responsiveness. Cloud Computing: the vast amounts-based systems allow for analytics, businesses immediate performance metrics and insights from across their operations. Furthermore, the scalability of cloud infrastructure means businesses can easily adjust their IoT systems as their needs grow. 5G Connectivity: Enhance systems. Offers lower latency, higher bandwidth, and more reliable connectivity, which cities. Blockchain: IoT systems, particularly in applications where data provenance is a decentralized ledger, remain tamper-proof and transparent. Applications of Real-Time Process Monitoring: process has far-reaching implications across various industries. Some of the most notable applications include Manufacturing: track production rates, detect faults in real-time. This allows manufacturers to reduce and optimize production processes for maximum efficiency. Healthcare: In healthcare, real-time process monitoring powered by IoT allows for the continuous patient, enabling outcomes that reduce the risk of medical errors. Agriculture: temperature, real-time, they need optimize irrigation, fertilizer application, and crop management. Lower water usage. Energy Management: IoT-enabled energy management systems can track electricity. This allows businesses and homeowners their lower. Challenges and Future Directions: Despite the immense potential of IoT real-time process monitoring, several challenges remain. The integration systems with legacy infrastructure can be complex and costly. There are also concerns about different barriers to data sharing. Looking to the future, edge computing and 5G technology will have a role in real-time process monitoring and will expand, driving even greater efficiencies and innovations across industries. In conclusion, process organizations offer visibility and optimization. Empowers decision-makers to act proactively, reducing costs, improving performance, and driving innovation. As IoT will only grow, reshaping the future of business operations and everyday life.

THE EVOLUTION OF IOT AND REAL-TIME PROCESS MONITORING: FROM LEGACY SYSTEMS TO MODERN TECHNOLOGIES

This shift has redefined industries by enabling predictive maintenance, improving operational efficiency, and unlocking new business models. By understanding this evolution, we can appreciate how IoT and real-time process monitoring have evolved from niche applications into critical components of modern-day business operations (De Luzi F., 2024). Data collection remained periodic, with operators checking gauges and meters at regular intervals, which made it difficult. Furthermore, data analysis was often conducted offline, relying on human decision-making, which could be slow and error-prone. The limitations of these legacy systems were most apparent in their inability to provide real-time insights, predict equipment failures, or optimize processes dynamically (Mendonça R D S., et al, 2023). Manual intervention was often required to adjust processes based on observed trends or anomalies, leading to inefficiencies, increased downtime, and a lack of agility in responding to operational challenges. The Advent of IoT: Expanding Connectivity and Data Collection: The concept of IoT began to take shape in the late 20th century as technological advances in microelectronics, sensors, wireless communication, and cloud computing created new possibilities for interconnecting devices and systems. The proliferation of sensors, which could measure vibration, and their ability to transmit data over networks, laid the foundation for the IoT revolution. Marked emergence as a transformative force across industries. This was driven by miniaturization sensors and Bluetooth, these technologies allowed devices to communicate without the need for wired infrastructure, providing more solutions for data collection monitoring (Korodi A., et al, 2024).

Locally, on or devices that generate all data platforms for processing. Low-latency responses, industrial automation, and healthcare IoT could be faster without relying on cloud infrastructure, which is critical for time-sensitive applications. The Integration of 5G and Future Directions in IoT and Real-Time Process Monitoring: As IoT systems continued to expand, the demand for faster, more reliable communication networks became increasingly critical. The introduction of 5G technology in the 2010s IoT. 5G has several advantages over previous wireless technologies, including higher bandwidth. These capabilities enabled IoT systems to operate more efficiently and at larger scales, supporting smart cities on a large scale. In real-time process monitoring, 5G allowed for more responsive and agile systems (Alqoud A., et al, 2022). For example, in manufacturing, high-speed 5G networks facilitate real-time communication between machines, robots, and central control systems, enabling synchronized operations and more efficient production lines. In healthcare, 5G-enabled telemedicine allows doctors to access patients' IoT-enabled devices to respond to emergencies faster. Process shaped continued AI, 5G may also security integrity data exchanged between IoT devices. Tamper-proof for IoT systems, secure exchanges, supply chains, or healthcare applications. Another important trend in the evolution of IoT is the increasing use of that allow organizations IoT with advanced simulations create highly accurate models of physical assets, such as factories, machines, or even entire cities. This technology enables businesses to predict how changes in one part of a system may affect other parts, helping to optimize performance and minimize risk. Challenges and the Road Ahead: Despite the rapid advancements in IoT and real-time process monitoring, several challenges remain (Kansal S., et al, 2024).

THE IMPORTANCE OF REAL-TIME PROCESS MONITORING IN INDUSTRY: UNDERSTANDING THE BENEFITS AND CHALLENGES

In the modern industrial landscape, processes have become indispensable for businesses aiming for continuous advancement of technology, particularly sensors, and how industries monitor and manage processes. The traditional approach to industrial monitoring involved periodic checks, often leading to delayed reactions to problems, inefficiencies, or equipment failures. This could result in unscheduled downtime, decreased productivity, and even costly breakdowns. In contrast, real-time process monitoring allows businesses to track systems and processes as they happen, ensuring any issues are detected promptly and are costly (Fernandez-Viagas V., et al, 2022). Automated adjustments and data-driven decision-making help streamline workflows, thus increasing productivity and reducing errors (Zhao C., 2022). Predictive Maintenance and Reduced Downtime: Another crucial benefit of is predict enabling businesses predictive In traditional systems, maintenance activities were scheduled periodically, often without any consideration of the actual condition of the equipment. This can result in over-maintenance or under-maintenance, both of which incur additional costs and affect production schedules. With real-time monitoring, sensors can track the condition of equipment continuously. For example, they may measure vibration levels, temperature, and pressure, all of which provide indicators of wear and tear. The maintenance component might fail, allowing significantly reduced unscheduled life and lowering maintenance costs. Enhanced Quality Control: vital consistent product quality, particularly in industries where precision is essential. For example, in pharmaceutical manufacturing, humidity and pH are critical to ensuring the production of high-quality drugs. Similarly, in food and beverage production, real-time data collection can track the consistency of production processes, helping to ensure safety with real-time monitoring, deviations from the set parameters can be identified and corrected immediately, minimizing faulty reducing waste (Rao A S., et al, 2022).

Enhanced Safety and Compliance: Also, in critical workplace safety where hazardous conditions and materials are prevalent, real-time monitoring is essential to prevent accidents. Sensors can detect dangerous conditions such as gas leaks, extreme temperatures, or equipment malfunctions, providing early warnings to prevent catastrophic events. Furthermore, real-time monitoring ensures compliance with industry regulations by tracking variables like emissions, chemical handling, and safety protocols (Dolgui A., et al, 2022). It can help and analyze more efficiently, but this requires robust systems, specialized skills, and significant computational power. Integration with Legacy Systems: Integrating these outdated systems with modern real-time process monitoring tools can be complex and costly (Johri S., et al. 2025). Furthermore, the costs of maintaining and securing systems over time can add to the financial burden. While the long-term benefits of such as typically justify investment required significant many (Gerzon G., et al, 2022). Skill Gaps and Training: Another challenge of real-time process monitoring is the need for specialized skills to operate, maintain, and analyze systems. As technology potential process will only grow, businesses that can navigate these challenges will be well-positioned to reap the rewards of a smarter, more efficient industrial landscape.

IOT SENSORS AND DEVICES: UNDERSTANDING THE TYPES, APPLICATIONS, AND CHALLENGES

Common examples include: Temperature Sensors: These measure ambient temperature in various settings such as industrial environments, agricultural fields, or data centers. temperature and equipment to ensure they are operating within optimal thermal ranges, preventing overheating and reducing the risk of equipment failure. Humidity Sensors: Levels are vital for applications such as climate control in buildings, agricultural monitoring, and industrial processes that require precise humidity levels to ensure product quality (Jamshed M A., et al, 2022). Gas Sensors: These detect CO2, methane (CH4), or toxic gases in refineries and homes. Gas is critical in safety applications, alerting users to dangerous leaks or emissions. Air Quality Sensors: These sensors are used for monitoring, and these sensors help improve health outcomes by identifying areas with poor air quality, a vital component of smart cities and environmental monitoring systems. Ultrasonic Sensors: the proximity of objects. In industrial automation, ultrasonic sensors are used for material handling, distance measurement, and object detection, while in automotive systems, they assist with parking sensors. Optical and Imaging Sensors: Optical and imaging sensors are capable of detecting light and capturing images or video (Debnath P., et al. 2025). RFID is used for inventory management, asset tracking, and supply chain optimization. RFID tags are placed on items or containers, and the sensor reads the data stored on the tag to identify, locate, and track objects in real time (Zikria Y B., et al, 2021). Magnetic Field Sensors: Magnetic fields are commonly used in applications such as detecting the position of a door or window in smart security systems, as well as in automotive systems for tire pressure monitoring. IoT sensors transforming oxygen can send data to intervene if necessary (Cui Y., et al, 2021).. Temperature-sensitive products, such as pharmaceuticals and perishable goods, can be monitored using specialized sensors to ensure they prevent damage (Ullo S L., et al, 2021). Ensuring that these devices have a long operational life while consuming minimal power is a key challenge. Advances in energy-efficient and low-power sensors are helping to address this issue, but battery life remains a concern for many IoT applications (Almutairi R., et al, 2024).

REAL-TIME DATA PROCESSING AND ANALYTICS: UNDERSTANDING THE ROLE OF CLOUD COMPUTING, BIG DATA, AND MACHINE LEARNING

The Concept of Real-Time Data Processing and Analytics: continuous acquisition, transmission, and analysis of data as it is generated or received, allowing organizations to act on this information instantly or within a very short time frame. Analyzed periodically, occurs continuously, ensuring that data-driven Real-time data analytics process this incoming almost immediately (Pala S.K., 2021). This capability finance, manufacturing, retail, telecommunications, conditions change rapidly, quick responses critical. Stock market analytics detect market trading live in healthcare, and monitoring of patient vital signs allows for immediate intervention if critical health issues arise. Cloud-based systems also ensure real-time security and efficiency. With cloud storage, businesses can avoid the limitations of on-premise data centers, such as physical space and maintenance costs (Akram F., et al, 2025). Cloud platforms offer distributed computing, allowing data to be processed in multiple locations simultaneously, ensuring low-latency access to real-time analytics regardless of the user's physical location (Mohammad A S., et al, 2021). Real-time data streaming and analytics can then be performed on this integrated dataset, operations, or customer. Advanced Data Analytics: Big data technologies enable trend analysis by organizations to uncover hidden patterns, correlations, and insights (Sandhu A K., 2021). These insights inform decisions related to demand forecasting and personalized experiences. Anomaly detection is real-time data analytics. In many industries, identifying unusual patterns or behaviors can be the key to preventing fraud, system failures, or security breaches. Are flag outliers that deviate from expected behavior. This allows organizations to detect problems and take corrective action instance, to potential intrusions or data breaches (Ramakrishnan T. et al. 2022). Latency and Speed: requires minimal latency, meaning that it is generated. However, network congestion, bottlenecks, and complex transformations can introduce delays in the processing pipeline (Rani S., et al, 2023).

COMMUNICATION PROTOCOLS AND STANDARDS FOR IOT AND REAL-TIME PROCESS MONITORING: UNDERSTANDING THE OPTIONS AND CHALLENGES

Communication protocols form facilitating transmission sensors, gateways, and cloud platforms. These protocols enable devices to connect, share data, and receive instructions (Behnke I., et al, 2023). Process communication protocols are responsible for ensuring that critical data—such as sensor readings, operational statuses, and alerts—are transmitted to the appropriate systems in a timely and reliable manner. Whether it's an industrial IoT (IIoT) system monitoring machine performance, a healthcare device transmitting patient vitals, or an environmental sensor transmitting weather data, the protocol used dictates the reliability, speed, and security of data transfer. Moreover, IoT and real-time process monitoring often involve complex ecosystems with a variety of devices from different manufacturers. This introduces a framework that can disparate systems (Umashankar M L., et al, 2023). continuous high-bandwidth communication. However, Wi-Fi can be power-hungry and is more appropriate for stationary devices rather than battery-powered, mobile IoT devices (Shende A D., et al. 2025). Bluetooth Low Energy (BLE): that is often used widely devices) in smart for tasks like device pairing, proximity sensing, and data transfer. Zigbee and Z-Wave: These are typically used in smart automation systems. They are often employed in mesh networks, where devices act as both senders and receivers of data, enhancing network coverage. LoRaWAN: LoRa (LoRaWAN) protocol designed for distance or in or logistics.: 5G: network provides communication significant real-time process monitoring. HTTP/HTTPS: While HTTP is the standard protocol for web communication, it is not always optimal for IoT and real-time process monitoring because of its higher overhead and slower transmission speed. However, HTTP/HTTPS can still be used for certain IoT applications, especially where continuous and regular updates are required (Balakrishnan K., et al, 2023). While a wide array of communication protocols are available for IoT and real-time process monitoring, they offer numerous advantages (Devan P A M., et al, 2021). Security and Privacy: sensitive manufacturing, are paramount transmitted by interception, tampering, and encryption, secure communication protocols, and identity management systems must remain secure throughout its lifecycle (Rane N., et al, 2023).

IOT AND REAL-TIME PROCESS MONITORING IN MANUFACTURING: UNDERSTANDING THE APPLICATIONS AND BENEFITS

These technologies offer a seamless systems manufacturing ecosystem and continuous monitoring of processes, equipment, and even worker performance. By enabling real-time visibility and feedback, IoT and real-time monitoring allow for more agile, responsive, and data-centric manufacturing operations. Understanding IoT and Real-Time Process Monitoring in Manufacturing: At its core, IoT machines, sensors, or other communication networks monitor and pressure, more machines track production performance, monitor machine health, and collect data on various production metrics. Refers to tracking key and machine performance (Li X., et al, 2024).. For example, IoT-enabled RFID tags finished goods, components entire This stock movements, minimizing risk of stockouts or excess inventory. Operations also identify bottlenecks or delays and take corrective action for production schedules, lead times, and better demand forecasting (Chhotaray P., et al, 2023).

Additionally, IoT-enabled can manufacturers utilization tools By tracking when and where assets are being used, resource allocation, equipment Furthermore, by ensuring that workers are equipped with safety devices, manufacturers worker reduce workplace accidents. Remote Monitoring and Control: Real-time process monitoring with IoT manufacturing for large-scale manufacturing operations that may span multiple locations. Operators and managers can monitor production processes, equipment health, and system performance from a centralized control room or through mobile devices, regardless of their physical location (Dutta P K., et al, 2021). In industries where production lines are spread across multiple factories or geographic regions, the ability processes enable coordination responsiveness. Reduced Downtime and Costs: capabilities reduce identifying potential equipment failures proactively, and manufacturers minimize costly interruptions that result from unexpected breakdowns. Additionally, real-time monitoring allows for material waste and labor costs. Enhanced Product Quality: Real-time process monitoring enables manufacturers to maintain strict quality control by detecting defects or deviations from production standards early in the process. This ensures that quality issues are addressed promptly, resulting in fewer defective products, reduced rework costs, and improved customer satisfaction (Onaji I., et al, 2022).

become increasingly complex, requiring businesses to track vast amounts of information process technologies about supply chain management. These technologies enable greater visibility, automation, and control over procurement integration IoT devices—ranging from sensors, RFID tags, and GPS trackers—into the supply chain, enabling the continuous monitoring of key metrics such as inventory levels, shipping conditions, transportation status, and warehouse operations. Real-time process monitoring enhances capabilities, businesses swiftly circumstances, reduce inefficiencies, improve overall customer satisfaction. However, while IoT and real-time process monitoring offer they present be addressed long-term success. Opportunities in Supply Chain Management Through IoT and Real-Time Monitoring: Using process monitoring in supply chain management opens up several new opportunities for business effectiveness. These opportunities are realized through inventory logistics optimization and demand forecasting. Below are the key opportunities: Enhanced Visibility and Transparency: enhanced and transparency (Hamadaqa M H M., et al, 2024). Any malfunction or breakdown of these assets can disrupt the entire flow of IoT devices embedded in supply chain assets, allowing businesses to implement predictive maintenance strategies (Mantravadi S., et al, 2023). Sensors on machinery can track or load levels, these data points can be analyzed to identify early signs of potential failures. Predictive maintenance technologies enable supply chain operators to take proactive measures, such as scheduling maintenance before a failure occurs, rather than relying on reactive repairs after a breakdown.

Challenges in Implementing IoT and Real-Time Monitoring in Supply Chain Management: While opportunities presented by and management are vast, several challenges must deliver These challenges span technical, organizational, and financial aspects of supply chain operations: Integration with Legacy Systems: businesses for their supply chain management operations, which newer IoT sensors, devices, and real-time monitoring systems costly. Managing Large Volumes of Data: IoT devices and real-time monitoring systems can be overwhelming (Moshood T D., et al, 2021). Analyzing and making sense of these tools, algorithms, and skilled data scientists. Without the right tools and expertise, businesses may struggle with actionability from massive. Additionally, real-time, rapid, timely processing systems, fast pipelines, and effective data storage solutions can all present significant technical challenges for supply chain managers. Scalability Issues: As supply chains grow in complexity and size, the scalability of IoT and real-time monitoring systems becomes a key consideration. This requires scalable cloud infrastructure, flexible data architectures, and systems (Estebsari A., et al, 2021). However, businesses must address significant challenges, such as integration with legacy systems, data security concerns, high initial investment costs, and scalability issues. By navigating these challenges and leveraging IoT-enabled solutions effectively, companies can transform their supply chains, making them resilient and dynamic in the global marketplace.

IOT AND REAL-TIME PROCESS MONITORING IN ENERGY MANAGEMENT: UNDERSTANDING THE APPLICATIONS AND BENEFITS

The management of energy resources has become one of the most critical priorities for businesses and governments worldwide, particularly in light of rising and push sustainability. The technologies and processes in energy management are transforming how organizations manage, optimize, and reduce their energy consumption. These technologies offer the promise of more efficient energy systems, improved decision-making, and significant cost savings while also contributing to sustainability goals and carbon footprint reductions. For instance, in residential settings, smart thermostats and energy meters can provide data on heating, cooling, and lighting usage patterns. In industrial and commercial applications, IoT sensors can track the energy usage of individuals from these systems analyzed inefficiencies (Embergenov A., 2023). Process monitoring complements this by continuously analyzing energy data, allowing companies to react promptly to energy anomalies and optimize their energy systems.. Smart meters also allow consumers to monitor and become conscious of saving practices (Abir S M A A., et al, 2021). By doing so, demand response programs help prevent expensive peaking and encourage savings. Real-time monitoring also allows for the dynamic optimization of weather patterns and supply fluctuations. As a result, businesses and consumers can adjust their real-time, more balanced, sustainable energy system (Ammari C., et al, 2022).

Figure 1. Emerging Technologies for IoT-Based Smart Cities

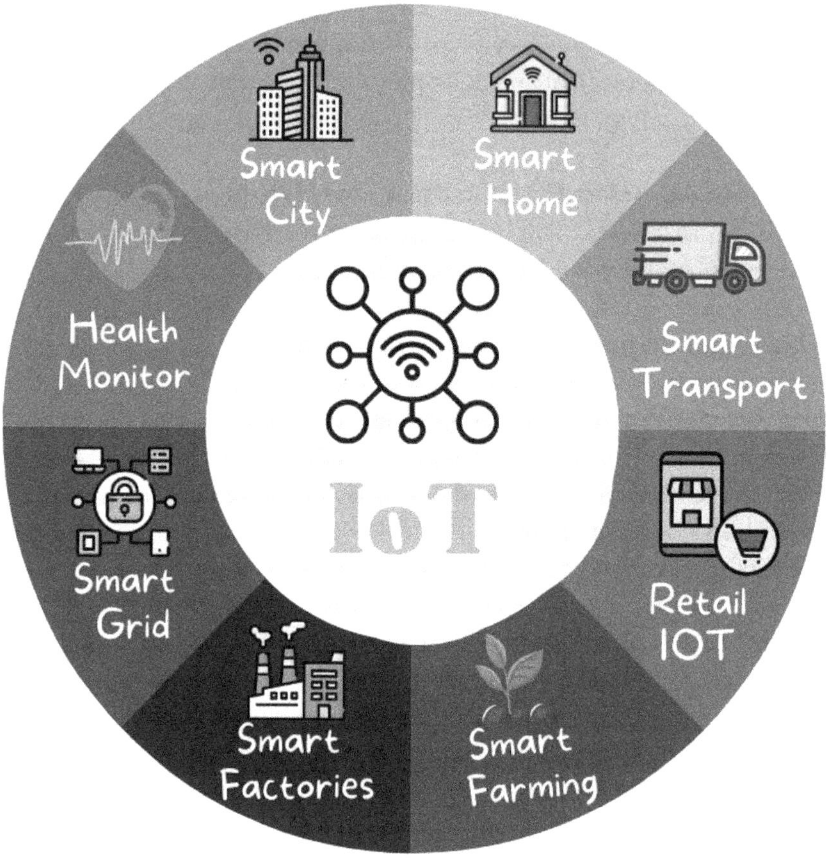

Industrial IoT (IIoT) technologies and real-time monitoring systems provide deep insights into how energy is consumed across various machines, production lines, and equipment. Sensors embedded in industrial equipment—such as motors, compressors, and pumps—monitor factors like energy consumption, performance, temperature, and efficiency (Renugadevi N., et al, 2023). This continuous feedback ensures that energy-saving strategies are having the desired effect and enables manufacturers to make adjustments as needed. Renewable Energy Integration: moves wind, hydropower) becomes increasingly important. However, renewable energy sources are often intermittent, challenging the grid. IoT and real-time process monitoring can help manage these challenges in renewable generation. For instance, solar panels and wind turbines equipped with IoT sensors can provide continuous feedback on energy generation, allowing grid operators to track the availability of renewable energy and adjust the conventional plants to maintain grid stability. Real-time monitoring also allows for better load management, preventing the grid from becoming overloaded when multiple EVs are charging simultaneously (Aragani, V M., et al. 2025). By integrating smart charging systems with businesses, further environmental impact EV charging. IoT-enabled energy management systems improve operational efficiency by providing continuous feedback on energy use. With this information, businesses can adjust processes, equipment, and usage patterns to minimize waste and improve energy efficiency (Mardiani E., et al, 2024).

CASE STUDY: THE IMPLEMENTATION OF IOT AND REAL-TIME PROCESS MONITORING IN A MANUFACTURING PLANT: BENEFITS AND CHALLENGES

Unplanned Downtime: The plant suffered from unanticipated equipment failures, which caused production halts and expensive downtime. Without real-time data on equipment performance, the maintenance team could only address issues after they occurred, leading to prolonged repair times. Inefficient Energy Use: The plant's energy consumption was not closely monitored, and there were inefficiencies in how power was distributed across the facility (Coito T., et al, 2021). The Implementation Process: The implementation of IoT and real-time process monitoring at the plant was carried out in phases, beginning with a pilot program that focused on integrating sensors, devices, and software into key production lines and critical equipment (Rochd A., et al, 2021). The implementation process involved several steps, including the selection of IoT devices, the installation of sensors, system integration, and the establishment of a data management platform. This platform enabled the plant's existing systems to be linked to the new IoT infrastructure to ensure seamless data flow between production lines, maintenance teams, and the management system. To manage the IoT plant implemented based solutions and capabilities. allowed for close enabling faster Cloud storage provided a scalable solution thousands of enabling the plant use historical performance (Lele V P., et al, 2023). These tools also provided insights into energy consumption patterns, helping the plant optimize power usage and reduce unnecessary energy waste. The Benefits Realized After the IoT and real-time monitoring system were fully implemented, the plant experienced several notable benefits. These benefits impacted various aspects of its operations, from production efficiency to cost savings.

Energy Optimization and Cost Savings: enabled the plant to identify areas where energy was being wasted. With granular data from smart meters, the plant's energy management system could pinpoint specific machines or areas where power consumption was higher than necessary. For example, one of the injection molding machines was identified as consuming significantly more energy than other similar machines due to inefficient settings. Armed with this knowledge, the plant optimized the machine's settings and usage schedule to reduce energy consumption. overall, which was particularly important in the context of rising energy prices (Zhu Y., et al, 2023). Additionally, by integrating energy-efficient practices and ensuring that machines were only running when needed, the plant was able to reduce its carbon footprint, aligning with sustainability goals. Enhanced Product Quality and Reduced Defects: Quality control saw a major improvement with systems. Vision sensors and temperature sensors were installed at key stages of the production line to detect defects in real time. One of the first hurdles the plant encountered was integrating the new IoT system with its existing legacy infrastructure. The plant's ERP and MES systems were not originally designed (Vijayakumar G, et al. 2024). The initial investment in IoT sensors, smart meters, and the necessary infrastructure for real-time monitoring was significant (Kaluarachchi Y., 2022).

EXAMPLE OF IOT AND REAL-TIME PROCESS MONITORING IN A SMART CITY: UNDERSTANDING THE APPLICATIONS AND BENEFITS

The Smart City Approach: The city in question, which serves as an example, is a major metropolitan area that decided to adopt a smart city strategy to address a variety of urban challenges. These included increasing inadequate waste management and concerns. IoT and Real-Time Process Monitoring Applications in a Smart City: smart wide-range IoT technologies and real-time monitoring systems across various sectors of urban life, each tailored to address specific urban challenges (Van Hoang T., 2024). Below are some applications of IoT and within the city: Intelligent Traffic Management: challenges cities around traffic congestion. In many urban areas, inefficient traffic flow leads to long commutes, increased fuel consumption, and higher levels of air pollution. To address this, the city implemented an IoT-based intelligent traffic management system. The city deployed an extensive network of IoT sensors and cameras at key intersections, along roads, and on highways. These sensors continuously monitor traffic. From these sensors, traffic bottlenecks predict traffic flow and the most congested areas in the city at any given time. The system also includes that can data, ensuring traffic sensor cars at the traffic lights their timing to clear the congestion more efficiently. Additionally, updates via mobile apps or traffic signs inform them about traffic conditions, accidents, or road closures, allowing them to adjust their routes accordingly. This intelligent traffic management system significantly reduced traffic congestion, improved travel times, and lowered fuel consumption, all while minimizing the environmental impact of transportation. Smart Waste Management: Efficient key cities that are growing rapidly (Alam T., 2021). Energy Management and Smart Grids: Managing energy use for cost efficiency and sustainability (Sreenivasulu A., et al. 2022). Traditional energy grids are often inefficient, with energy loss during transmission and a lack of real-time insight into To usage.

In addition to surveillance, IoT devices are used in the city's emergency response system. For instance, environmental sensors placed in high-risk areas such as industrial zones or areas prone to natural disasters can detect signs of potential hazards, such as gas leaks, fires, or floods. Allows emergency services to respond quickly, potentially saving lives and minimizing damage. Furthermore, an integrated public alert sends notifications to citizens during emergencies. This could include alerts about severe weather, traffic accidents, or public safety concerns, helping residents stay informed and take appropriate actions (Bellini P., et al, 2022). Water Management: Efficient water is crucial to the city. By implementing IoT systems across various urban services, the city has been able to its monitoring allows data-driven that use resources, whether it's adjusting traffic signals to ease congestion or scheduling waste collection more efficiently (Bauer M., et al, 2021). have for city, with lower energy consumption, reduced fuel costs, and more effective use of personnel and equipment. Enhanced Sustainability: has also contributed to sustainability The ability reduces water waste, and manage traffic and waste more efficiently city's carbon footprint. The smart grid system, in particular, has enabled a more sustainable energy mix. Better Quality of Life for Residents: By improving traffic flow, waste management, water distribution, and public safety, IoT technologies have made the city a more livable and resilient place for residents. Challenges Faced: Despite the clear benefits, IoT and smart city was Some during process included: Data Privacy and Security: The large-scale sensors raised Ensuring that data, such as personal information from surveillance systems, was adequately protected was a top priority for city officials (Albouq S S., et al, 2022).

CHALLENGES AND LIMITATIONS OF IOT AND REAL-TIME PROCESS MONITORING: ADDRESSING SECURITY, SCALABILITY, AND INTEROPERABILITY

These systems involve transmission, processing, and often multiple inputs, including sensors and user inputs. The scale and complexity of these networks make them highly denial-of-service inherent vulnerabilities in IoT devices, many of which are small, low-cost, and often lack robust security measures, exacerbating these concerns. Data Privacy and Protection: IoT systems are designed to gather a broad range of data, personal habits, and tracking, and they are protected against targeted malicious actors for theft or manipulation. Furthermore, process transmission can make it more vulnerable to interception. Without encryption and secure data storage, they are exposed, leading to significant privacy violations (Dave D M K., et al, 2024). These attacks can target everything from traffic management systems in smart cities to industrial control systems in manufacturing plants. Real-time process monitoring systems, which rely on the uninterrupted flow of data to make time-sensitive decisions, are particularly vulnerable to DDoS attacks (Lee E., et al, 2021). To combat such threats, IoT systems must incorporate resilience mechanisms such as traffic filtering, load balancing, and adaptive response protocols that DDoS overwhelm system. Scalability Challenges: As IoT systems expand to encompass more devices, sensors, and data streams, scalability becomes a critical challenge. While IoT networks are often designed devices, massive numbers can quickly become unmanageable without appropriate infrastructure and planning. Real-time process monitoring systems, in particular, require collected, transmitted, continuously efficient performance, reliability, and responsiveness.

A large-scale IoT deployment can strain the available network infrastructure, leading to delays, congestion, and even service interruptions. Real-time process monitoring systems are particularly sensitive to network latency, as they require immediate feedback to take corrective actions (Hazra A., et al, 2021). Organizations must invest in robust and scalable, particularly in environments with high data density. It can help address network challenges posed by large-scale IoT deployments by offering higher bandwidth, lower latency, and greater reliability. Interoperability Challenges: Interoperability is another significant challenge faced by IoT, and real-time process monitoring and systems are sourced from multiple vendors, each with different communication protocols, data formats, and standards. Without seamless interoperability, these systems can become fragmented, reducing their effectiveness and causing inefficiencies. Process monitoring, where needs are integrated together, and lack of interoperability can undermine the accuracy and timeliness of decisions. Diverse Standards and Protocols: IoT devices communicate using standards and Z-Wave, LoRaWAN. Each of these protocols has its limitations, However, this diversity integrates different or communicates across different platforms (Amjad A., et al, 2021). To address data integration challenges, organizations must manage aggregate and harmonize disparate Cloud-based platforms, which can and provide the necessary tools for querying. Additionally, applying this integration can provide more accurate insights and predictive capabilities (Sargiotis D., 2024).

THE IMPORTANCE OF DATA QUALITY AND INTEGRITY IN IOT AND REAL-TIME PROCESS MONITORING: ENSURING ACCURATE DECISION-MAKING

The accuracy of the data is the foundation of any decision-making process. In real-time monitoring systems, pressure, machine status, and traffic patterns are monitored. If these sensors are inaccurate or distorted, the decisions derived from this information will be flawed (Subramanian S., 2023). For example, in a manufacturing plant, inaccurate temperature readings from a sensor monitoring a critical process can lead to equipment overheating or malfunctioning, resulting in costly downtime or damage. Similarly, inaccurate traffic data in a smart city can cause traffic lights to be misaligned, leading to congestion, accidents, and inefficiency. To ensure data completeness, IoT systems should implement redundancies, such as backup sensors or fail-safe mechanisms, that ensure data is continuously captured even if one sensor fails (Gade K R., 2024). Timeliness: IoT real-time monitoring systems depend on up-to-date information to make decisions that impact operations (Suleman D., et al, 2023). Or processing or irrelevant to guide decisions, potentially leading to operational inefficiencies or safety hazards. To achieve timely data, IoT systems must employ high-speed communication networks and efficient data processing systems to handle information. Additionally, it is processed closer to it by avoiding delays caused by transmitting data to centralized cloud platforms. Validity and Integrity: Data validity refers to the correctness and logical coherence of data.

Critical energy, manufacturing, and poor quality integrity can pose significant safety and compliance risks (Ahmad S., et al, 2022). For example, in healthcare, inaccurate sensor readings from IoT-enabled medical devices could lead to incorrect diagnoses or treatment plans, jeopardizing patient health. In industrial settings, inaccurate data on machinery performance could result in safety failures, such as explosions, fires, or other catastrophic events. Ensuring high data quality and integrity safety while complying with industry regulations. Regular data validation, automated alerts for anomalous data, and stringent security measures are all necessary steps to prevent safety risks and maintain compliance. Financial Losses: Financial losses are another significant consequence of poor data quality. Whether due to equipment failures, downtime, inefficiencies, or safety incidents, poor data quality can lead to significant financial setbacks for organizations, errors, or breaches, especially in high industries like finance, where financial transactions and customer information are vulnerable to manipulation or theft. In addition to the direct costs of operational failures, poor data quality can also result in lost revenue due to poor customer service or missed business opportunities. For instance, inaccurate data about customer preferences or product demand can lead to poor business decisions, such as launching the wrong products or missing opportunities to optimize pricing strategies. Poor Decision-Making: Ultimately, the most significant consequence of poor data quality is the impact it has on real-time from IoT systems guiding critical operational and strategic decisions (Sugumaran K M D., et al. 2024). For example, if a sensor reading falls outside of an expected range, the system can flag this data as invalid and request a manual review. Additionally, there are sensor malfunctions or environmental interference (Naidoo P., et al, 2024). Secure Data Transmission and Storage: To ensure data integrity, implement data transmission techniques.

FUTURE DIRECTIONS IN IOT AND REAL-TIME PROCESS MONITORING: EMERGING TRENDS, TECHNOLOGIES, AND OPPORTUNITIES

Real-time processes will see an increased reliance on autonomous systems and edge computing. As IoT devices proliferate and generate massive amounts of data, this centralized platform becomes less feasible. Bandwidth limitations and the sheer volume of data all present significant challenges. Edge computing addresses these issues by thereby reducing the need for centralized processing (Gupta A., et al, 2023). Edge computing is expected to become an integral part of IoT systems, allowing for faster, more efficient data processing manufacturing, and the monitoring of machinery can be processed locally on edge devices to detect anomalies, triggering corrective actions before issues become critical. This will significantly improve operational efficiency and reduce downtime. Furthermore, 5G's support for massive device connectivity will enable more scalable IoT deployments. IoT networks that require the connection will bc able to function more efficiently under 5G, supporting smart agriculture and industrial applications (Carvalho G., et al, 2021). AI-Driven Analytics and Automation: The future of IoT process is closely tied to further driven analytics. Currently, many IoT systems rely on data aggregation and basic statistical models to detect trends or identify anomalies. However, processing will not suffice. This is where it is transformative.

Cryptocurrencies provide secure, immutable records that have potential applications far beyond digital currencies. Blockchain enhances security, integrity, and transparency (Rammohan A., 2023). Blockchain's peer-to-peer intermediaries are highly suitable for IoT networks. Each IoT device can act as a node in the blockchain, securely transmitting data that is stored in an immutable ledger. This ensures that it cannot be tampered with and that every transaction is traceable and verifiable, which is critical for financial transactions and healthcare. For real-time process monitoring, blockchain can collect security from sensors and devices that are tamper-proof and transparent. Trust verification, paramount, pharmaceuticals, safety, and logistics will provide an effective means of ensuring data integrity and auditability. Opportunities in IoT and Real-Time Process Monitoring: Smart Cities and Urban Infrastructure: Opportunities for IoT and real-time process monitoring lie in the development of traffic congestion and waste energy consumption. And IoT provides everything from air quality, enabling cities to respond quickly to issues and optimize services. Patterns, improving the flow of vehicles. Real-time monitoring systems usage and public spaces, leading to lower carbon footprints and cost savings (Abideen A Z., et al, 2021). Moreover, IoT-enabled smart waste management systems can improve the efficiency of trash collection by tracking fill levels in waste bins and optimizing collection routes. Helps create cleaner, urban environments. Healthcare and Remote Monitoring: In healthcare, IoT and real-time process monitoring offer transformative opportunities for patient care. IoT continuously provides health metrics, providing professionals with updated information. Enables timely interventions for chronic conditions, readmissions, overall. It can also be extended to remote healthcare, where doctors and caregivers can monitor patients from a distance. The integration of analytics will enable the prediction of health Industrial IoT (IIoT) and Manufacturing: industrial settings, IoT process will continue drive and innovation. Machines monitored will lead to more optimized production processes, reduced waste, and higher-quality products. Predictive maintenance will become a standard practice, reducing unexpected downtime and increasing the lifespan of machinery (Qudus L., 2025).

RECOMMENDATIONS FOR IMPLEMENTING IOT AND REAL-TIME PROCESS MONITORING: BEST PRACTICES AND GUIDELINES

The first step in implementing IoT and real-time process monitoring is to define clear objectives and use case goals. Without a well-defined purpose, technologies misalignment, inefficiencies, wasted resources. This phase involves identifying the problems or processes that could benefit from real-time monitoring and IoT-enabled automation (Langlois V S., et al, 2021). Some common use cases include predictive maintenance in manufacturing, energy consumption optimization in buildings, remote monitoring in healthcare, and supply chain tracking. Choosing the right IoT sensors and devices is critical to ensuring accurate, reliable, and actionable data. IoT devices and sensors should be chosen based on the following factors: Data Accuracy and Reliability: sensors must provide precise data and operate with high reliability under the conditions of the deployment environment (Awotunde J B., et al, 2023). This means ensuring that the devices have significant upgrades over time. Industry-Specific Requirements: Requirements such as wearable health monitors must meet regulatory standards for patient safety and data security. Similarly, in food production, sensors must be able to detect temperature and humidity levels with high accuracy (Singh R., et al, 2022).

Breaches or cyberattacks could result in system downtime, data theft, or the compromise of confidential information (Tan W C., et al, 2022). Recommendations for enhancing IoT security include: personnel or control IoT devices and systems. Network Security: Secure the network infrastructure connecting IoT devices using technologies (IDS) to protect against breaches. Regular Software Updates: IoT security Many devices may have firmware or software updates that address known security flaws. Privacy Compliance: like or other that Implement anonymization or pseudonymization techniques where necessary. Implement Scalable and Robust Data Management Systems: As IoT and real-time process monitoring generate massive amounts of data, organizations must make the infrastructure of the IoT ecosystem robust as more devices and sensors are added over time. Best practices for data management include: Cloud Platforms for Data Storage: enabling businesses to store and access massive datasets generated by IoT devices. Data Processing and Analytics Frameworks: Implement frameworks, Spark, to process streaming efficiently and generate insights on time. Data Governance: Establish that is accurate, reliable, and used appropriately. Data rights, data retention policies. Data Backup and Recovery: These are essential to avoid power hardware malfunctions. Train Staff and Foster a Culture of Innovation: Training empowers staff to utilize IoT process effectively, key ensuring successful implementation (Mahadev Madgule, et al. 2023). Encourage innovation where staff are empowered to suggest improvements to the IoT system. Employee feedback is vital for optimizing the system and addressing any potential inefficiencies (Yazdi M., 2024). Measure Success and Iterate for Improvement: Finally, it is important to continuously IoT and monitoring system and iterate on it organization's objectives.

THE ROLE OF EDGE COMPUTING IN IOT AND REAL-TIME PROCESS MONITORING: UNDERSTANDING THE BENEFITS AND CHALLENGES

Real-time process monitoring locally, reducing the time it takes to derive actionable insights and respond to changing conditions. At its core, edge computing helps to reduce the dependency on centralized cloud servers for real-time. This local processing for feedback and predictive maintenance in settings and health in medical applications (Nain G., et al, 2022). Benefits of Edge Computing in IoT and Real-Time Process Monitoring: Reduced Latency and Faster Decision-Making: in IoT Since data processing occurs locally, distance is eliminated, significantly reducing transmission times. In real-time process monitoring, this speed is critical. For example, in manufacturing plants, sensors embedded in machines monitor parameters like temperature, vibration, and pressure. By processing this data on-site, edge devices can immediately detect deviations from normal operation, enabling timely interventions to prevent equipment failure or downtime. In contrast, cloud computing often suffers from network latency due to remote delay, which can be unacceptable in critical healthcare monitoring or industrial control systems. Allowing for rapid responses that improve operational efficiency, safety, and performance (Sodiya E O., et al, 2024). Bandwidth Optimization and Cost Reduction: enormous amounts be servers analysis, decision-making constant transmission overwhelm network bandwidth, especially connected aggregated significantly being This bandwidth optimization not only lowers operational costs but also scale deployments IoT devices straining the network infrastructure. Additionally, since it is minimized, strain on resources is reduced. Edge computing enables organizations to use their cloud infrastructure more efficiently, as cloud servers only receive critical insights or processed data rather than raw data that would otherwise flood the system.

Device Management and Maintenance: large Each edge device may have its own unique set of requirements for firmware updates, security patches, and hardware maintenance. In large-scale IoT deployments, monitoring can become overwhelming, particularly if devices are located in different locations. Organizations must establish robust systems for remotely managing edge devices, including tools for monitoring device health, deploying software updates, and diagnosing issues (Al Masarweh M., et al, 2022). Automation and cloud-based management platforms can help alleviate some of these challenges, but ongoing investment in device management capabilities is necessary for reliability and edge computing. Limited Computing Power: Edge devices, by design, are centralized cloud. To address this challenge, organizations should use CoAP, RESTful APIs that edge cloud other IoT components. However, even with standard protocols, the diversity of edge devices and IoT platforms means that achieving perfect interoperability can remain a significant hurdle. Data Storage and Synchronization: While edge computing offers the benefit of local data processing, it introduces storage synchronization. Edge capacity and generated avoid overflow (Dec G., et al, 2022).

CONCLUSION

The Internet of Things (IoT) and real-time process monitoring represent transformative forces reshaping industries across the globe. As organizations continue to digitize operations, these technologies offer unprecedented opportunities to optimize productivity, enhance efficiency, and enable data-driven decision-making. Over the past decade, IoT and real-time monitoring have evolved from niche applications into ubiquitous solutions that span manufacturing, healthcare, energy management, logistics, and more. The growth of IoT technologies and the increasing reliance on real-time data have created a paradigm shift in how businesses operate, turning real-time process monitoring into a necessity rather than a luxury. Looking to the future, the evolution of IoT and real-time monitoring will be driven by innovations in hardware, data analytics, cloud computing, and edge computing, all of which will contribute to even more intelligent, automated, and resilient systems. Key Findings: The Present State and Future Outlook of IoT and Real-Time Process Monitoring: Unprecedented Growth and Impact Across Industries: IoT and real-time process monitoring are already having a profound impact on a wide range of industries. In manufacturing, IoT-enabled devices have transformed production lines by enabling predictive maintenance, minimizing downtime, and improving overall equipment efficiency. In healthcare, IoT-based monitoring systems are providing real-time patient data, enabling more personalized care and reducing the likelihood of medical emergencies. Similarly, in energy management, IoT sensors help monitor consumption patterns, optimize energy distribution, and integrate renewable energy sources seamlessly into the grid. In logistics and supply chain management, real-time monitoring has led to more efficient route planning, optimized inventory control, and the ability to trace goods from origin to destination. Smart cities have seen the rise of intelligent traffic systems, waste management solutions, and environmental monitoring—all powered by IoT devices and real-time data. The adoption of IoT across these sectors shows that its potential is vast and expanding, offering solutions that were once thought to be impossible. As the technology continues to advance, we will see even more significant use cases emerge. These will be powered by innovations in AI, 5G, and edge computing, which are enhancing the capabilities of IoT systems and enabling faster, more intelligent decision-making. By leveraging real-time process monitoring, businesses will be able to achieve greater operational visibility, increase their agility in responding to changing conditions, and create more sustainable practices. Key Technological Innovations Shaping the Future of IoT: Several emerging technologies will play a pivotal role in shaping the future of IoT and real-time process monitoring. These technologies promise to accelerate the adoption of IoT systems and expand their potential across industries.

REFERENCES

Abideen, A. Z., Sundram, V. P. K., Pyeman, J., Othman, A. K., & Sorooshian, S. (2021). Food supply chain transformation through technology and future research directions—A systematic review. *Logistics (Basel)*, *5*(4), 83. Advance online publication. DOI: 10.3390/logistics5040083

Abir, S. M A A., Anwar, A., Choi, J., & Kayes, A. S. M. (2021). *IoT-enabled smart energy grid: Applications and challenges*. IEEE. DOI: 10.1109/ACCESS.2021.3071245

Ahmad S, Hussain M A, Wassay M, (2022). "OVERCOMING DATA FRAGMENTATION IN AGRICULTURE: INTEGRATING MULTI-SOURCE DATA VIA BLOCKCHAIN TO ENHANCE DECISION-MAKING."

Akram F, Sani M, (2025). "Real-Time AI Systems: Leveraging Cloud Computing and Machine Learning for Big Data Processing."

Al Masarweh M, Alwada'n T, Afandi W, (2022). "Fog computing, cloud computing and IoT environment: advanced broker management system." Journal of Sensor and Actuator Networks. Doi: .DOI: 10.3390/jsan11010025

Alam, T. (2021). *Cloud-based IoT applications and their roles in smart cities*. Smart Cities., DOI: 10.3390/smartcities4030064

Albouq, S. S., Abi Sen, A. A., Almashf, N., & Yamin, M. (2022). *A survey of interoperability challenges and solutions for dealing with them in IoT environment*. IEEE., DOI: 10.1109/ACCESS.2022.3162219

Almutairi R, Bergami G, Morgan G, (2024). "Advancements and challenges in IoT simulators: A comprehensive review." Doi: .DOI: 10.3390/s24010321

Alqoud A, Schaefer D, Milisavljevic-Syed J, (2022). "Industry 4.0: a systematic review of legacy manufacturing system digital retrofitting."

Amjad, A., Azam, F., Anwar, M. W., & Butt, W. H. (2021). *A systematic review on the data interoperability of application layer protocols in industrial IoT*. IEEE., DOI: 10.1109/ACCESS.2021.3094763

Ammari, C., Belatrache, D., & Touhami, B. (2022). *Sizing, optimization, control and energy management of hybrid renewable energy system—A review*. Energy and Built Environment., DOI: 10.1016/j.enbenv.2021.04.002

Aragani, V. M., Anumolu, V. R., & Selvakumar, P. (2025). Democratization in the Age of Algorithms: Navigating Opportunities and Challenges. In Wongmahesak, K., Wekke, I., Seftyono, C., & Nurdin, N. (Eds.), *Democracy and Democratization in the Age of AI* (pp. 39–56). IGI Global Scientific Publishing., DOI: 10.4018/979-8-3693-8749-8.ch003

Awotunde, J. B., Imoize, A. L., & Jimoh, R. G. (2023). "AIoMT enabling real-time monitoring of healthcare systems: security and privacy considerations." Handbook of Security and Privacy.

Balakrishnan, K., & Dhanalakshmi, R. (2023). Clock synchronization in industrial Internet of Things and potential works in precision time protocol: Review, challenges and future directions. *International Journal of Advanced Manufacturing Technology*. Advance online publication. DOI: 10.1007/s00170-023-11535-w

Bauer, M., Sanchez, L., & Song, J. S. (2021). IoT-enabled smart cities: Evolution and outlook. *Sensors (Basel)*, *21*(13), 4511. Advance online publication. DOI: 10.3390/s21134511 PMID: 34209436

Behnke, I., & Austad, H. (2023). Real-time performance of industrial IoT communication technologies: A review. *IEEE Internet of Things Journal*. Advance online publication. DOI: 10.1109/JIOT.2023.3261245

Bellini, P., Nesi, P., & Pantaleo, G. (2022). IoT-enabled smart cities: A review of concepts, frameworks and key technologies. *Applied Sciences (Basel, Switzerland)*, *12*(3), 1607. Advance online publication. DOI: 10.3390/app12031607

Carvalho, G., Cabral, B., Pereira, V., & Bernardino, J. (2021). Edge computing: Current trends, research challenges and future directions. *Computing*, *103*(5), 993–1023. Advance online publication. DOI: 10.1007/s00607-020-00896-5

Chhotaray, P., Behera, B. C., & Moharana, B. R. (2023). Enhancement of manufacturing sector performance with the application of Industrial Internet of Things (IIoT). *Journal of Manufacturing Technology Management*. Advance online publication. DOI: 10.1108/JMTM-02-2023-0054

Coito, T., Firme, B., Martins, M. S. E., Vieira, S. M., Figueiredo, J., & Sousa, J. M. C. (2021). Intelligent sensors for real-Time decision-making. *Automation.*, *2*(2), 62–82. Advance online publication. DOI: 10.3390/automation2020004

Cui Y, Liu F, Jing X, Mu J, (2021). "Integrating sensing and communications for ubiquitous IoT: Applications, trends, and challenges." Doi: .DOI: 10.1109/MNET.011.2000345

Dave D M K, Mittapally B K, (2024). "Data Integration and Interoperability in IoT: Challenges, Strategies and Future Direction." International Journal of Computer Engineering and Technology.

De Luzi, F. (2024). *Digital transformation in a hyper-connected world. Transforming legacy systems through blockchains.* IoT and AI.

Debnath, P., Deshmukh, S. M., Laroia, M., Selvakumar, P., Manjunath, T. C., & Bhattacharya, S. (2025). Challenges Faced by Countries in Renewable Energy Adoption. In Özsungur, F., Chaychi Semsari, M., & Küçük Bayraktar, H. (Eds.), *Geopolitical Landscapes of Renewable Energy and Urban Growth* (pp. 295–320). IGI Global Scientific Publishing., DOI: 10.4018/979-8-3693-8814-3.ch010

Dec, G., Stadnicka, D., Paśko, Ł., Mądziel, M., Figliè, R., Mazzei, D., Tyrovolas, M., Stylios, C., Navarro, J., & Solé-Beteta, X. (2022). Role of academics in transferring knowledge and skills on artificial intelligence, internet of things and edge computing. *Sensors (Basel)*, *22*(7), 2496. Advance online publication. DOI: 10.3390/s22072496 PMID: 35408110

Devan, P A M., Hussin, F. A., Ibrahim, R., Bingi, K., & Khanday, F. A. (2021). A survey on the application of WirelessHART for industrial process monitoring and control. *Sensors (Basel)*, *21*(15), 4951. Advance online publication. DOI: 10.3390/s21154951 PMID: 34372210

Dolgui A, Ivanov D, (2022). "5G in digital supply chain and operations management: fostering flexibility, end-to-end connectivity and real-time visibility through internet-of-everything." Doi: .DOI: 10.1080/00207543.2022.2051156

Dutta P K, Mitra S, (2021). "Application of agricultural drones and IoT to understand food supply chain during post COVID-19." Agricultural Informatics. Doi: .DOI: 10.1002/9781119768707.ch12

Embergenov, A. (2023). *Enhancing enterprise energy management with iot-based monitoring systems.* Eurasian Science Review.

Estebsari, A., & Mazzarino, P. R. (2021). IoT-enabled real-time management of smart grids with demand response aggregators. *IEEE Transactions on Industry Applications*. Advance online publication. DOI: 10.1109/TIA.2021.3071245

Fernandez-Viagas V, Framinan J M, (2022). "Exploring the benefits of scheduling with advanced and real-time information integration in Industry 4.0: A computational study." Doi: .DOI: 10.1016/j.jii.2022.100234

Gade K R, (2024). "Data Quality Metrics for the Modern Enterprise: A Data Analytics Perspective."

Gerzon G, Sheng Y, Kirkitadze M, (2022). "Process analytical technologies–advances in bioprocess integration and future perspectives." Doi: .DOI: 10.1016/j.jpba.2022.114532

Gong, S. (2023). Digital transformation of supply chain management in retail and e-commerce. *International Journal of Retail & Distribution Management*. Advance online publication. DOI: 10.1108/IJRDM-02-2023-0054

Gupta, A., & Singh, A. (2023). Healthcare 4.0: Recent advancements and futuristic research directions. *Wireless Personal Communications*, *129*(2), 933–952. Advance online publication. DOI: 10.1007/s11277-022-10164-8 PMID: 36594000

Hamadaqa M H M, Alnajjar M, Ayyad M N, Al-Nakhal M A, (2024). "Leveraging Artificial Intelligence for Strategic Business Decision-Making: Opportunities and Challenges."

Hazra, A., Adhikari, M., & Amgoth, T. (2021). A comprehensive survey on interoperability for IIoT: Taxonomy, standards, and future directions. *ACM Computing Surveys*. Advance online publication. DOI: 10.1145/3447555

Jamshed, M. A., Ali, K., Abbasi, Q. H., & Imran, M. A. (2022). Challenges, applications, and future of wireless sensors in Internet of Things. *RE:view*. Advance online publication. DOI: 10.1109/JSEN.2022.3150321

Javaid, M., Haleem, A., & Suman, R. (2023). *Digital twin applications toward industry 4.0: A review*. Cognitive Robotics., DOI: 10.1016/j.cogr.2023.04.003

Johri, S., Selvakumar, P., Satyanarayana, P., Das, A., Gupta, S., & Bhattacharya, S. (2025). Urbanization and Energy: The Nexus of Global Challenges. In Özsungur, F., Chaychi Semsari, M., & Küçük Bayraktar, H. (Eds.), *Geopolitical Landscapes of Renewable Energy and Urban Growth* (pp. 453–478). IGI Global Scientific Publishing., DOI: 10.4018/979-8-3693-8814-3.ch016

Kaluarachchi, Y. (2022). *Implementing data-driven smart city applications for future cities*. Smart Cities., DOI: 10.3390/smartcities5020025

Kansal S, Siddharth E, (2024). "Adaptive AI Models for Automating Legacy System Migration in Enterprise Environments."

Korodi A, Ni ulescu I V, Fülöp A A, Vesa V C, Demian P, (2024). "Integration of Legacy Industrial Equipment in a Building-Management System Industry 5.0 Scenario." Doi: .DOI: 10.3390/electronics11010123

Langlois, V. S., Allison, M. J., Bergman, L. C., & To, T. A. (2021). The need for robust qPCR-based eDNA detection assays in environmental monitoring and species inventories. *Environmental Toxicology and Chemistry*. Advance online publication. DOI: 10.1002/etc.5045

Lee, E., Seo, Y. D., Oh, S. R., & Kim, Y. G. (2021). A Survey on Standards for Interoperability and Security in the Internet of Things. *IEEE Communications Surveys and Tutorials*, *23*(2), 1020–1047. Advance online publication. DOI: 10.1109/COMST.2021.3067354

Lele V P, Kumari S, White G, (2023). "Streamlining Production: Using Big-Data's CRM & Supply chain to improve efficiency in high-speed environments." International Journal of Current Science and Research.

Li, X., Deng, Q., Shi, H., & Guo, Y. (2024). Sustainable manufacturing production process monitoring and economic benefit analysis based on IoT technology. *International Journal of Advanced Manufacturing Technology*. Advance online publication. DOI: 10.1007/s00170-024-13145-2

Lu, S., Lu, J., An, K., Wang, X., & He, Q. (2023). Edge computing on IoT for machine signal processing and fault diagnosis: A review. *IEEE Internet of Things Journal*, *10*(13), 11093–11116. Advance online publication. DOI: 10.1109/JIOT.2023.3239944

Mahadev Madgule, N. (2023). Vinayaka, Yeshwant M. Sonkhaskar, Dhiren Ramanbhai Patel, R. Karthikeyan, P. Selvakumar, (2023). Mechanical properties and microstructure of activated TIG welded similar joints of Inconel alloys by desirability approaches. *Materials Today: Proceedings*, *77*, 528–533. DOI: 10.1016/j.matpr.2022.12.250

Mantravadi, S., & Srai, J. S. (2023). How important are digital technologies for urban food security? A framework for supply chain integration using IoT. *Procedia Computer Science*, *217*, 1678–1687. Advance online publication. DOI: 10.1016/j.procs.2022.12.368

Mardiani E, Riswandi D I, Suprayitno D, (2024). "Implementation of internet of things in the production process of msmes: quality improvement and process control." Jurnal Informasi dan Teknologi.

Mendonça R D S, De Carvalho M M, Machado G S, (2023). "Development of a novel methodology to retrofit legacy systems in the context of industry 4.0."

Mohammad, A. S., & Pradhan, M. R. (2021). Machine learning with big data analytics for cloud security. *Computers & Electrical Engineering*, *96*, 107527. Advance online publication. DOI: 10.1016/j.compeleceng.2021.107527

Moshood, T. D., Nawanir, G., Sorooshian, S., & Okfalisa, O. (2021). Digital twins driven supply chain visibility within logistics: A new paradigm for future logistics. *Applied System Innovation*, *4*(2), 29. Advance online publication. DOI: 10.3390/asi4020029

Naidoo, P., & Sibanda, M. (2024). *Emerging trends and future directions of the industrial internet of things*. From Internet of Things to Internet of Intelligence. DOI: 10.1007/978-3-031-55718-7_5

Nain, G., Pattanaik, K. K., & Sharma, G. K. (2022). Towards edge computing in intelligent manufacturing: Past, present and future. *Journal of Manufacturing Systems*, *62*, 588–611. Advance online publication. DOI: 10.1016/j.jmsy.2022.01.010

Onaji, I., Tiwari, D., Soulatiantork, P., & Song, B. (2022). Digital twin in manufacturing: Conceptual framework and case studies. *International Journal of Production Research*. Advance online publication. DOI: 10.1080/00207543.2022.2051156

Pala, S. K. (2021). *Databricks Analytics: Empowering Data Processing*. Machine Learning and Real-Time Analytics.

Qudus, L. (2025). Advancing cybersecurity: Strategies for mitigating threats in evolving digital and IoT ecosystems. *International Research Journal of Modernization in Engineering Technology and Science*.

Ramakrishnan, T., Mohan Gift, M. D., Chitradevi, S., Jegan, R., & Subha Hency Jose, P. Nagaraja, Rajneesh Sharma HN, Selvakumar P, Sintayehu Mekuria Hailegiorgis, (2022). "Study of Numerous Resins Used in Polymer Matrix Composite Materials", Advances in Materials Science and Engineering, vol. 2022, Article ID 1088926, 8 pages, 2022. DOI: 10.1155/2022/1088926

Rammohan, A. (2023). Cellular Vehicle-to-Everything (C-V2X) technology: Current trends, use cases, emerging technologies, standardization bodies, industry analytics and future directions. *Vehicular Communications*. Advance online publication. DOI: 10.1016/j.vehcom.2023.100445

Rane N, Choudhary S, Rane J, (2023). "Artificial Intelligence (Ai) and Internet of Things (Iot)–based sensors for monitoring and controlling in architecture, engineering, and construction: Applications, challenges, and future directions."

Rani, S., Bhambri, P., & Kataria, A. (2023). *Integration of iot, big data, and cloud computing technologies: Trend of the era*. Big Data, Cloud Computing and IoT., DOI: 10.1201/9781003298335

Rao A S, Radanovic M, Liu Y, Hu S, Fang Y, (2022). "Real-time monitoring of construction sites: Sensors, methods, and applications." Doi: .DOI: 10.1016/j.autcon.2022.104124

Renugadevi, N., Saravanan, S., & Sudha, C. M. N. (2023). IoT based smart energy grid for sustainable cites. *Materials Today: Proceedings*, *81*, 98–104. Advance online publication. DOI: 10.1016/j.matpr.2021.02.270

Rochd, A., Benazzouz, A., Abdelmoula, I. A., & Raihani, A. (2021). Design and implementation of an AI-based & IoT-enabled Home Energy Management System: A case study in Benguerir—Morocco. *Energy Reports*, *7*, 699–719. Advance online publication. DOI: 10.1016/j.egyr.2021.07.084

Sandhu, A. K. (2021). *Big data with cloud computing: Discussions and challenges*. Big Data Mining and Analytics., DOI: 10.1109/BDMA.2021.3071245

Sargiotis D, (2024). "Data Quality Management: Ensuring Accuracy and Reliability." Data Governance: A Guide.

Shende, A. D., Tekade, S. A., Deshmukh, A. A., Tembhurkar, S. P., & Selvakumar, P. (2025). Water Quality Monitoring and Control With AI. In Ruiz-Vanoye, J., & Díaz-Parra, O. (Eds.), *Smart Water Technology for Sustainable Management in Modern Cities* (pp. 51–80). IGI Global Scientific Publishing., DOI: 10.4018/979-8-3693-8074-1.ch003

Singh, R., Gehlot, A., Akram, S. V., & Thakur, A. K. (2022). Forest 4.0: Digitalization of forest using the Internet of Things (IoT). *Journal of King Saud University. Computer and Information Sciences*, *34*(8), 5587–5601. Advance online publication. DOI: 10.1016/j.jksuci.2021.02.009

Sodiya, E. O., Umoga, U. J., & Obaigbena, A. (2024). Current state and prospects of edge computing within the Internet of Things (IoT) ecosystem. *International Journal of Scientific Research.*

Sreenivasulu, A., & Manimozhi, T. Satheesh kumar P, Selvakumar P. and Singh P, (2022). "The Model of Smart Sensing Device For Sensitive Nanoclusters Modification in Sensing Properties," 2022 2nd International Conference on Advance Computing and Innovative Technologies in Engineering (ICACITE), Greater Noida, India, 2022, pp. 1043-1047, DOI: 10.1109/ICACITE53722.2022.9823846

Subramanian S, (2023). “Leveraging IoT data streams for AI-based quality control in smart manufacturing systems in process industry.” Journal of AI-Assisted Scientific Discovery.

Sugumaran K M D, Pandiyarajan V Y B S, Selvakumar P. and M. S, (2024). “Analysis of Electromyography Signals for Control of Mechanical Prosthesis using Machine Learning Techniques,” 2024 2nd International Conference on Intelligent Data Communication Technologies and Internet of Things (IDCIoT), Bengaluru, India, 2024, pp. 1059-1067, .DOI: 10.1109/IDCIoT59759.2024.10467707

Suleman, D., Shibl, R., & Ansari, K. (2023). *Investigation of data quality assurance across IoT protocol stack for V2I interactions*. Smart Cities., DOI: 10.3390/smartcities6050121

Tan W C, Sidhu M S, (2022). “Review of RFID and IoT integration in supply chain management.” Operations Research Perspectives. Doi: .DOI: 10.1016/j.orp.2022.100145

Ullo S L, Sinha G R, (2021). “Advances in IoT and smart sensors for remote sensing and agriculture applications.” Doi: .DOI: 10.3390/rs13132567

Umashankar, M. L., & Mallikarjunaswamy, S. (2023). “A survey on IoT protocol in real-time applications and its architectures.” *Proceedings of 2021 International Conference on Advances in Computing and Communications*. Doi: DOI: 10.1007/978-981-19-5936-3_12

Van Hoang T, (2024). “Impact of integrated artificial intelligence and internet of things technologies on smart city transformation.” Journal of Technical Education Science.

Vijayakumar, G. (2024). Muniyandi Rajkumar, Rajiv Chandar N, Selvakumar P and Ramesh Duraisamy, (2024). Environmentally friendly TDS removal from wastewater by electrochemical ion exchange batch-type recirculation (EIR) technique. *Environmental Science. Water Research & Technology*, *10*, 826–835. DOI: 10.1039/D3EW00793F

Yazdi, M. (2024). *Integration of IoT and edge computing in industrial systems*. Advances in Computational Mathematics for Industrial Systems. DOI: 10.1007/978-3-031-53514-7_7

Zhao C, (2022). “Perspectives on nonstationary process monitoring in the era of industrial artificial intelligence.” Doi: .DOI: 10.1016/j.jprocont.2022.100145

Zhu, Y., Cheng, J., Liu, Z., Cheng, Q., Zou, X., & Xu, H. (2023). Production logistics digital twins: Research profiling, application, challenges and opportunities. *Journal of Manufacturing Systems*. Advance online publication. DOI: 10.1016/j.jmsy.2023.01.012

Zikria Y B, Ali R, Afzal M K, Kim S W, (2021). "Next-generation internet of things (iot): Opportunities, challenges, and solutions." Doi: .DOI: 10.3390/s21041457

Chapter 12
The Role of Artificial Intelligence in Improving Process Efficiency

P. Selvakumar
https://orcid.org/0000-0002-3650-4548
Department of Science and Humanities, Nehru Institute of Technology, Coimbatore, India

Sathi Jyothirmaye Reddy
https://orcid.org/0000-0002-1629-5777
Marwadi University, India

Sudhanshu Chandra
https://orcid.org/0009-0006-6694-1032
Maulana Azad National Urdu University, India

Ranjna
https://orcid.org/0000-0001-9082-7084
Chandigarh Group of Colleges, India

P. C. Neena
https://orcid.org/0000-0002-8112-5555
Jain University, India

Mohit Sharma
https://orcid.org/0009-0007-2280-8077
Maharshi Dayanand University, Rohtak, India

T. C. Manjunath
https://orcid.org/0000-0003-2545-9160
Rajarajeswari College of Engineering, India

ABSTRACT

Datasets that recognize patterns have found applications in supply chain management, customer service, manufacturing, marketing, finance, healthcare, and many other sectors. The implementation of AI can lead to a wide range of benefits, including cost reduction, time savings, improved accuracy, and better resource allocation. Opportunities Presented by AI in Enhancing Process Efficiency: Automation of Repetitive Tasks: well-known applications AI technologies time-consuming high consistency. For example, in administrative functions, handle document manage-

DOI: 10.4018/979-8-3373-3336-6.ch012

ment, email filtering, and complex and creative work. Similarly, in manufacturing, robots equipped with AI inspection and packaging improve speed and accuracy. Data-Driven Decision Making: allowing better algorithms, uncovering structured and unstructured data, predicting future trends, and making informed decisions that enhance operational efficiency. This requires investment in training programs and a strategic approach to managing the transition to ensure that employees remain valuable assets in an AI-driven environment.

INTRODUCTION TO ARTIFICIAL INTELLIGENCE AND PROCESS EFFICIENCY

Datasets that recognize patterns have found applications in supply chain management, customer service, manufacturing, marketing, finance, healthcare, and many other sectors. The implementation of AI can lead to a wide range of benefits, including cost reduction, time savings, improved accuracy, and better resource allocation. Opportunities Presented by AI in Enhancing Process Efficiency: Automation of Repetitive Tasks: well-known applications AI technologies time-consuming high consistency. For example, in administrative functions, handle document management, email filtering, and complex and creative work. Similarly, in manufacturing, robots equipped with AI inspection and packaging improve speed and accuracy. Data-Driven Decision Making: allowing better algorithms, uncovering structured and unstructured data, predicting future trends, and making informed decisions that enhance operational efficiency. This requires investment in training programs and a strategic approach to managing the transition to ensure that employees remain valuable assets in an AI-driven environment. Ethical Considerations and Bias: inherit them If data reflects biased human decisions or historical inequalities, AI models those such as discrimination lending, or by and to ensure they adhere to ethical standards. Furthermore, the deployment and accountability require strict ethical oversight. High Implementation Costs: Acquiring and hiring specialized personnel, upgrading infrastructure in addition, AI projects and optimization deliver value. Of AI adoption, which can sometimes be difficult to quantify. Lack of Standardization and Regulation: Rapidly, lack of standardized frameworks and regulatory guidelines presents a challenge for businesses seeking to implement AI. The absence of clear regulations on AI development and deployment can lead to uncertainty and potential risks, particularly in industries that require strict safety. Policymakers, regulatory bodies, and businesses must work together to establish comprehensive AI regulations that protect consumers and safety. Significant organizations seek to improve process efficiency. Optimizing supply chains, customer service, and substantial cost savings. However, its successful implementation has workforce implications, concerns, and the regulatory landscape. Must remain agile, proactive, and responsible in their approach process efficiency. Embracing AI thoughtfully can unlock immense value and drive long-term success, while failing to address its challenges can hinder progress and undermine its potential benefits.

THE IMPORTANCE OF PROCESS EFFICIENCY IN BUSINESS

Defining Process Efficiency: At its core, process efficiency refers to the ability to accomplish a given task or set of tasks with the least number of resources, time, and effort without compromising quality (Kharlamov A A., et al, 2021). In a business context, it means optimizing workflows, reducing unnecessary steps, and eliminating bottlenecks that hinder smooth operations. The goal is to achieve the desired output with minimal input, which directly impacts the cost, speed, and quality of the product or service delivered. While businesses may have different processes depending on their industry and size, the underlying principle of improving efficiency remains the same: doing more with less. Enhancing Productivity Through Process Efficiency: Streamlined Operations: Process efficiency its impact on. When processes are optimized, employees can focus their time and energy on high-value tasks rather than getting bogged down by inefficiencies. A streamlined workflow ensures that tasks flow smoothly from one stage to the next, minimizing delays and redundancies (Yiu L M D., et al, 2021). For example, in a manufacturing setting, optimizing production lines and reducing the time spent on setup or changeover can result in greater output without adding extra labor. Similarly, in an office environment, automating administrative or document can free engage in strategic activities. Faster Turnaround Times: In industries where speed is crucial, such as in tech or e-commerce, process efficiency plays a vital role in ensuring fast turnaround times. By removing obstacles and simplifying workflows, accelerate production and deliver products or services. This, in turn, leads to higher productivity levels, as employees are not waiting on bottlenecks or unnecessary approvals. The faster a business can operate, the more tasks it can complete in a given period, thus increasing overall output and productivity. Improved Resource Allocation: Efficient processes help businesses allocate resources (both human and material) in the most effective way possible. For instance, with streamlined operations, businesses can make the most of their workforce, ensuring that employees are deployed in roles where they can add the most value (Handoyo S., et al, 2023).

Efficiency increases output, making new resources, infrastructure, or labor. For example, a company that improves its operational efficiency can produce more units of a product or serve more customers without needing to hire additional staff or acquire more equipment (Baah C., et al, 2021). This scaling of output without proportional increases in costs means that the company can generate higher revenues with a lower incremental cost, which directly boosts profitability. The concept of "doing more with less" is central to achieving higher profitability, especially in industries where margins are tight. Improved Customer Satisfaction and Retention: Efficient processes can also increase customer satisfaction and influence profitability. When a business is able to quickly, accurately, price, and return Efficient supply chains while fast, responsive customer service helps resolve issues promptly, creating a positive experience for customers. Become buyers, higher and greater overall profitability. Competitive Advantage: Businesses that excel at process efficiency can also achieve a competitive advantage in the marketplace. By delivering products or services more quickly, at lower costs, and with higher quality than their competitors, efficient companies are more attractive to consumers. Additionally, efficient operations often allow businesses to innovate more easily, as they have the investment (Aragani, V M., et al. 2025). When they are able to outpace their competitors in terms of efficiency, they can capture a larger market share, ultimately leading to higher profitability. Scalability and Growth: Process efficiency is also a key enabler of scalability. For businesses to grow, they must be able to handle an increasing volume of work without encountering significant inefficiencies. Efficient processes provide the foundation for scalable operations, ensuring that businesses can expand without experiencing growing pains or diminishing returns. For instance, a company that has optimized its customer service processes may find it easier to handle an influx of new customers, while a business with an efficient supply chain can manage larger orders without disruptions. As a result, businesses that focus on process efficiency are better positioned to scale their operations, leading to higher revenues and profitability. Optimizing Innovation: Efficiency can even foster innovation. When businesses streamline operations, they create more bandwidth for creative thinking and problem-solving. Rather than being bogged down by time-consuming or repetitive tasks, employees and leaders can focus on developing or. In highly competitive industries, the ability to innovate continuously is often the key to staying ahead of competitors. By improving efficiency, directed toward innovation, ensuring that they stay relevant and profitable over time (Niu Y., et al, 2021).

THE EVOLUTION OF ARTIFICIAL INTELLIGENCE IN BUSINESS PROCESS MANAGEMENT

The Early Days of Business Process Automation (BPA): The initial application of AI in business process management automation. Automation business processes typically improve efficiency and reduce errors. Early AI systems were focused on automating specific tasks that were transaction processing and scheduling (Yakovenko

Y., et al, 2023). Despite these advances, automation in its early stages was relatively limited. It could perform specific, predefined tasks but was not able to handle more complex or dynamic situations that required judgment, learning, or the ability to process unstructured data. Automation was an important step forward, but it was just the beginning of what AI could offer to business process management. The Rise of Artificial Intelligence and Machine Learning: As AI advanced, especially in the realms of machine learning and data analytics, business process management began to shift from basic automation to more intelligent systems (Kokala A., 2024). Similarly, AI algorithms could process visual data to automatically manufacture processes, increasing production. Aspects of cognitive learning continually learn improve. Machine learning models can adapt based on new data, enabling businesses to refine their processes in real time (Ribeiro J., et al, 2021). Driven now predicts shipping delays and manages demand fluctuations across multiple regions and suppliers. Similarly, in human resources, AI can help businesses manage across the organization, inefficiencies, and opportunities for improvement that might otherwise go unnoticed (Svetlana N., et al, 2022). By leveraging these insights, business leaders' data-driven everything from to development. In the future, AI could become central by functioning as an advisor or partner to human executives. AI systems may provide not only insights but also actionable recommendations, simulations of different scenarios, and even the ability to execute certain actions autonomously, helping businesses navigate an increasingly complex and uncertain business landscape. Ethical Considerations and Challenges: The evolution of the business process offers tremendous opportunities, ethical (Rana G., et al, 2021).

THE USE OF MACHINE LEARNING IN PREDICTIVE MAINTENANCE

This is achieved by analyzing various data points, such as sensor environmental conditions, or signal an impending failure (Nwulu E O., et al, 2023). In traditional maintenance systems, businesses would often schedule regular (time-based maintenance) or wait until a failure occurred (reactive maintenance). While these methods served their purpose in the past, they were inherently inefficient. Supervised Learning: historical specific outcomes, such as whether a machine failed or required maintenance at a certain time. The machine learning algorithm uses this labeled data to learn patterns and associations between the input variables (such as sensor readings, temperature, vibration levels, etc.) and the output (failure or maintenance event). Once trained, the model can predict future failures by identifying similar patterns in real-time data (Debnath P., et al. 2025). Over time, the system learns the best strategies for maintaining equipment by optimizing actions based on the rewards or penalties received from its decisions (Alam M., et al, 2023). Reinforcement learning can be particularly useful in optimizing maintenance schedules and strategies based on changing conditions. Machine learning models are trained using logs, environmental conditions, and external factors. the entire production process, leading to delays, financial losses, and even safety hazards.

How Machine Learning Increases Efficiency: Machine learning also optimizes the performance of machinery overall, improving resource utilization and enabling data-driven decision-making. Increased Equipment Lifespan: By predicting when maintenance is needed, machine learning ensures that equipment is serviced at the right time, helping to extend its lifespan. Performing maintenance before a failure occurs can prevent catastrophic breakdowns that could cause long-term damage to machinery (Cruz J C., et al, 2024). Additionally, machine learning can help businesses prioritize maintenance activities, ensuring that critical equipment is addressed first and minimizing the risk of cascading failures (Qureshi M S., et al, 2024).. In the energy sector, predictive maintenance is particularly valuable for managing complex systems such as turbines, transformers, and compressors (Khawar M W., et al, 2024). By predicting potential failures in these critical assets, companies can avoid service disruptions and reduce the risk of costly repairs. Similarly, aerospace companies use machine learning to monitor the health of aircraft engines, predict maintenance needs, and minimize downtime between flights.

THE ROLE OF NATURAL LANGUAGE PROCESSING IN AUTOMATING BUSINESS PROCESSES

Text Parsing and Syntax Analysis: Analyzing sentence structures to understand grammatical relationships between words. Sentiment Analysis: Identifying and extracting subjective information, such as opinions, emotions, and sentiments, from text data. Entity Recognition: Detecting names and relevance within text (Rahaman N., 2024). Opportunities in Business Process Automation with NLP: The adoption of NLP in business process automation offers several key opportunities for businesses across various sectors. Below, we explore the specific opportunities that NLP brings to the table, focusing on areas such as customer service, document processing, knowledge management, and marketing. Enhancing Customer Service and Support: This is an area where NLP can be used to automate business processes. NLP a mainstay providing businesses with the ability to by utilizing NLP techniques, these customers natural. For example, a powered chatbot automatically responds to frequently asked questions (FAQs), directs customers to relevant resources, schedules appointments, or troubleshoot basic issues. More advanced systems, such as virtual customer assistants, can even manage more complex tasks like processing returns or guiding customers through troubleshooting processes (Sugumaran K M D., et al. 2024). NLP also enables sentiment analysis, which helps businesses gauge customer satisfaction based on their interactions.. In financial services, key invoices, receipts, or other financial documents facilitate faster processing and reduce administrative workload. In industries like healthcare, NLP can be applied to electronic health records (EHRs) to extract relevant patient information and medical history, thereby streamlining administrative processes and enabling more efficient clinical workflows (Vidgof M., et al, 2023). Improving Knowledge Management and Internal Communication: Another area where NLP plays a vital role is knowledge management within organizations..

Data Quality and Availability: primary NLP for training and deploying models is of high quality (Oyewole A T., et al, 2024). NLP accurately understands interpreted language. In many cases, businesses struggle with the lack of structured and clean data, particularly in industries such as legal, healthcare, and customer service. Moreover, NLP must be real-world language variations, including regional dialects, slang, and jargon. Another significant challenge businesses face when implementing NLP for process automation is integrating NLP systems and workflows. Organizations' older technologies are not compatible with modern NLP tools, making integration complex and time-consuming (Khurana D., et al, 2023). As with any AI technology, NLP models are susceptible to biases that can impact decision-making and customer interactions. These biases often stem from NLP prejudices and cultural stereotypes. For instance, NLP models trained on biased customer service data may inadvertently reinforce stereotypes or make unfair decisions when interacting with customers. These businesses NLP models' accuracy representative Additionally, transparency accountability is critical when deploying NLP systems, sensitive legal compliance. Skill Gaps and Talent Shortages: Implementing NLP-based automation requires specialized knowledge in machine learning, linguistics, and data science (Abro A A., et al, 2023).

THE APPLICATION OF ROBOTICS PROCESS AUTOMATION IN STREAMLINING BUSINESS OPERATIONS

High Volume of Manual, Repetitive Tasks: The financial services company in question had multiple departments that were heavily reliant on manual processes, compliance reporting, and data entry. Employees in these departments were tasked with processing large amounts of data, performing repetitive calculations, and interacting with clients to resolve routine inquiries (Fernandez D., et al, 2021). In response to these challenges, the company decided to implement RPA across several departments, with a focus on automating high-volume, repetitive tasks that were causing inefficiencies. The first step in the implementation was identifying processes that were suitable for automation. These processes typically had the following characteristics: Rule-based: The tasks followed clear, predefined rules that could be programmed into RPA bots (Vajgel B., et al, 2021). This entire process, which used to take several employees hours to complete, was now handled in a matter of minutes by RPA bots, significantly. Furthermore, bots were capable of performing this task 24/7, which meant the company could generate real-time compliance reports and ensure that data was always up-to-date. This automation freed up compliance officers interpreting regulatory changes, analyzing risk, and ensuring that policies were being followed rather than getting bogged down by repetitive data processing (George A., et al, 2021). Unlike humans, RPA bots do not suffer from fatigue or distractions, so they were consistently important in the compliance department, where even minor mistakes could result in regulatory penalties or reputational damage (Kalluri K., 2023). As with any automation initiative, there was some resistance from employees who feared that their jobs might be at risk. While RPA does eliminate some manual tasks, it also creates opportunities for take roles (Lindgren I., et al, 2022). However, as the company's experience shows, successful RPA implementation requires careful planning, employee buy-in, and ongoing maintenance. By full potential RPA continuous improvement sustainable operational excellence. As the will allowing to automate even more complex processes, ultimately reshaping how businesses.

THE USE OF ARTIFICIAL INTELLIGENCE IN PROCESS MINING

Fusion with process mining is a game-changer in the way businesses analyze, optimize, and continuously improve their processes. AI in process mining application advanced techniques, uncover insights from process data, identify inefficiencies, predict outcomes, and provide actionable recommendations for process improvement. By leveraging AI, organizations process behaviors and performance. This combination of AI and process mining offers substantial value for businesses in manufacturing and finance, where complex processes are commonplace and where optimization is crucial for maintaining a competitive edge. What is Process Mining? At its core, various IT systems, such as Process mining, enable organizations to visualize and understand how their processes are performed, rather than relying on theoretical process models or assumptions about how processes should work (Mehdiyev N., et al, 2021). Here are some key ways in which AI enhances process mining: Enhanced Process Discovery: Traditional process mining tools can map out existing processes by analyzing event logs and comparing them against ideal or predefined process models (Ramakrishnan T. et al. 2022). By detecting patterns of behavior that have previously led to non-compliance, AI-driven process mining systems help organizations reduce risks and maintain regulatory integrity (Abbasi M., et al, 2024). Root Cause Analysis and Predictive Analytics: Significant capability of process mining tools by providing predictive insights into process behavior. Traditional process mining can identify what has happened in a process, but it may not always explain why specific outcomes occurred.

Moreover, AI can assist in continuous process improvement by providing organizations with actionable insights based on learn from past executions. AI models become more intelligent over time, suggesting iterative improvements that enhance performance incrementally (Chaima A., et al, 2022). This leads to a cycle of continuous improvement that is more data-driven and less reliant on manual interventions. Similarly, AI can automatically flag non-compliant invoices for review in an accounts payable process, ensuring that discrepancies are addressed before payment is made. Key Benefits of AI in Process Mining: Integration into process mining hosts that help businesses drive operational enhancements (Munoz-Gama J., et al, 2022). Challenges and Considerations: Despite the many advantages, there are challenges to implementing AI-powered process mining. These include: Data Quality and Availability: Process mining relies on AI models. Inaccurate, incomplete, and fragmented undermine the effectiveness of AI-driven insights (Grisold T., et al, 2021). Complexity of AI Integration: process mining tools are complex and require significant technical expertise. Organizations must invest in both technology and talent to deploy AI solutions successfully. Change Management: Implementing AI in process mining may require changes to organizational structures, workflows, and employee roles.

THE ROLE OF SIMULATION AND MODELING IN AI-DRIVEN PROCESS OPTIMIZATION

Understanding Complex Systems through Simulation and Modeling: In any organization, particularly those with complex operations, such as manufacturing, logistics, healthcare, and finance, processes rarely follow simple, linear patterns. Multiple variables—such as resource availability, employee productivity, market conditions, and technological capabilities are unpredictable and difficult to gain overall (Ekundayo F., 2024). Traditional optimization and the dynamic nature of such systems. Simulation and modeling allow organizations to represent a sandbox for experimentation without the risks and costs associated with testing in the real world. Through AI-enhanced modeling, businesses can analyze these virtual models to understand how different factors influence system behavior, allowing them to simulate various conditions and anticipate outcomes before making decisions. Various AI techniques are used in simulation and modeling to optimize processes, each providing unique insights into how to improve business performance. Reinforcement Learning for Dynamic Process Optimization: Reinforcement learning (RL) is a particularly powerful technique used in AI-driven simulation and optimization (Johri S., et al. 2025). Monte Carlo simulations enhanced by AI can provide more accurate pricing models, improve risk management strategies, and enable better portfolio optimization by simulating a variety of market conditions (Richardson N., et al, 2023). Genetic Algorithms for Optimizing Complex Processes: GAs are particularly useful nonlinear tackle with methods. In the context of AI-driven process optimization, GAs can be used to identify the best solutions for complex systems by evolving populations of potential solutions through iterations.

In healthcare, ABM can simulate the flow of patients through a hospital, helping administrators optimize staffing schedules, bed occupancy rates, and the allocation of medical resources (Heilala J P., 2024). AI can help analyze the results of these simulations to identify bottlenecks, predict patient flow, and provide recommendations for improving patient care and operational efficiency. Identifying Optimal Solutions through AI-Driven Simulation: The most significant advantages of simulation and modeling are identifying optimal solutions for complex problems. For example, in a manufacturing setting, AI-driven simulation and modeling can help determine the optimal production schedule by simulating various factors, such as machine availability, labor shifts, material lead times, and customer demand (Jackson I., et al, 2024). AI-driven simulations require access to accurate, high-quality data, simulation leading to suboptimal decision-making. Complexity of Models: Developing and maintaining simulation models that accurately represent real-world systems can be complex and time-consuming. Businesses need skilled professionals to design, implement, and refine these models (Escoto M., et al, 2024). By providing a virtual environment to test different scenarios, predict outcomes, and identify optimal solutions, AI-enhanced simulations enable businesses to better understand complex systems, continuously improve With ability to handle large-scale optimization problems, simulate multiple variables, and offer real-time insights, AI-driven simulation and modeling offer a powerful toolkit for organizations striving to remain competitive Despite challenges implementation, the benefits of this technology are undeniable, making it a critical component of modern process optimization strategies.

THE APPLICATION OF AI-DRIVEN PROCESS OPTIMIZATION IN SUPPLY CHAIN MANAGEMENT

the modern globalized economy, (SCM) pivotal determining across industries. The growing complexity of supply chains—driven by factors such as fluctuating demand, global sourcing, geopolitical risks, and environmental concerns—and traditional methods are increasingly inadequate. Navigate businesses (AI) key tool process transform successful application driven process optimization global supply chain, highlighting challenges, benefits realized company. The Company Background: For will global manufacturing company specializes consumer electronics. This company operates a complex supply chain that spans multiple continents, managing suppliers, manufacturers, distributors, and retail partners in over 40 countries. With a reputation for innovation and a large customer base, the company faced increasing pressure to maintain competitive pricing while improving service levels and reducing operational costs. Given the competitive nature of the industry, supply chain efficiency was identified as a critical factor for sustaining growth. Historically, the company relied on traditional supply chain management tools, such as spreadsheet-based demand forecasting, rule-based inventory management, and manual route optimization for logistics (Helo P., et al, 2022). Logistics Optimization: The company faced inefficiencies in its transportation and distribution network (Toromade A S., et al, 2024). The following AI-driven techniques were employed: AI-powered demand Forecasting: The first step in optimizing the supply chain was to improve demand forecasting accuracy. Traditional forecasting methods used by the company relied on historical sales data and simple trend analysis, which often failed to account for sudden shifts in consumer preferences or external disruptions. To overcome this limitation, the company demands a forecasting system and big data to predict demand more accurately (Kuraku C., et al, 2024).

The system also incorporated a "just-in-time" inventory strategy, allowing the company to maintain minimal stock levels while ensuring products were available when needed. This approach helped the company reduce warehousing costs and optimize its cash flow while improving service levels. Logistics Optimization with AI: Logistics optimization was another critical area of focus. The company faced challenges in optimizing transportation routes, managing AI-driven logistics optimization systems, and leveraging traffic weather forecasts and historical transportation patterns to optimize delivery routes (Sai S., et al, 2024). The AI system used predictive analytics to anticipate potential disruptions, such as traffic congestion or inclement weather, and dynamically adjusted delivery schedules to avoid delays. Machine learning models were employed to optimize routing decisions, factoring in variables such as delivery window requirements, load capacities, and fuel consumption. AI for Supplier Relationship Management and Risk Mitigation: One of the key challenges the company faced was managing its relationships with multiple suppliers located in different regions (Tarannum T., et al, 2024). Optimized Inventory Levels and Reduced Costs: By leveraging AI for inventory management, the company was able to reduce inventory holding costs by 18%. The system optimized stock (Mahadev Madgule, et al. 2023).

CASE STUDY: THE USE OF ARTIFICIAL INTELLIGENCE IN IMPROVING PROCESS EFFICIENCY IN A MANUFACTURING COMPANY

AutoTech Manufacturing: AutoTech Manufacturing global automotive producing a wide range of vehicle components and assembling cars for various OEMs (original equipment manufacturers). The company operates multiple production facilities located across North America, Europe, and Asia. With thousands of employees and a complex global supply chain, AutoTech faces challenges in managing its production processes effectively, maintaining high-quality standards, and meeting customer demand in a cost-efficient manner. Historically, AutoTech's manufacturing processes were based on traditional methods of operations that relied heavily on human workers, manual inspection, and rigid automation systems (Liu J., et al, 2022). AutoTech faced difficulties managing raw material inventory and synchronizing supply chain activities with production schedules. Inaccurate demand forecasting led to stockouts, excess inventory, and delays, disrupting the overall flow of materials to the production line (Javaid M., et al, 2022). For example, the AI system might detect that a machine's vibration patterns are slightly off or that its temperature is rising beyond a normal range (Molina L M., et al, 2023). Traditional manual inspection methods, although effective in some cases, were limited by the ability of human inspectors to detect small defects and anomalies in real time, especially in high-speed, high-volume environments.

The system also included an advanced optimization engine that determined the best possible inventory levels at various locations throughout the supply chain. The system dynamically adjusted inventory levels based on production schedules, lead times, and material availability, ensuring that materials were available when needed without overstocking (Shende A D., et al. 2025). This AI-driven solution led to a 25% reduction in excess inventory, improved material availability, and decreased lead times. By using AI for production scheduling, AutoTech was able to improve resource utilization, reduce bottlenecks, and increase overall throughput. Production efficiency reduction order lead times (Nozari H., et al, 2022). The implementation of AI-driven process optimization at AutoTech Manufacturing led to a range of tangible benefits: Increased Operational Efficiency: production scheduling systems all contributed to enhanced operational efficiency. The company reported a 20% (OEE) 25% production throughput. Cost Reduction: The integration of AI technologies helped reduce unplanned downtime by 30%, cutting maintenance costs, and Inventory optimization supply chain improvements led to a 15% reduction in inventory holding costs. Improved Quality Control: AI-driven computer vision systems reduced defect rates by 15%, improving product quality and customer satisfaction. This also led to lower costs related to rework, scrap, and warranty claims (Jagatheesaperumal S K., et al, 2021).

EXAMPLE OF AI-DRIVEN PROCESS AUTOMATION IN A FINANCIAL SERVICES COMPANY

The study highlights the tangible benefits the company experienced during driven automation. Company Background: FinServe Corp. is a multinational insurance and wealth management company. With an extensive customer base spanning retail, corporate, and institutional clients, FinServe faces the ongoing challenge of maintaining competitive advantages in an increasingly complex and digitalized market. The company's operations are highly data-driven, and like many financial institutions, it struggled with managing vast volumes of information, ensuring maintaining levels of service quality (Challoumis C., 2024). Prior to its adoption of AI-driven process automation, FinServe faced several inefficiencies in its operations. Manual support created bottlenecks, increased human error, and elevated operational costs. Despite investing, FinServe realized that it was not leveraging its data to its full potential. With thousands of customer inquiries daily, both in person and online, the company's customer service teams struggled to handle the volume efficiently. Response times were slow, and the quality of responses varied depending on the complexity of the inquiries. FinServe wanted to improve its customer service by leveraging AI to provide faster and more consistent responses. Loan Processing: The loan approval process was another area where FinServe sought improvement (Villar A S., et al, 2021). This allowed FinServe to take proactive measures to stop fraudulent transactions before they occurred, reducing financial losses and improving security (Venigandla K., et al, 2022).

The system is also integrated with FinServe's CRM and ERP systems, ensuring a seamless flow of information between departments. By automating these tasks, FinServe reduced loan processing times by 40%, improved customer satisfaction, and lowered operational costs. Document Processing and Compliance Automation: Document processing was another critical area where FinServe implemented AI-driven process automation (Devaraj S M., 2024). AI-driven systems helped FinServe stay compliant with evolving regulatory requirements by automating compliance reporting, monitoring transactions for suspicious activities, and flagging potential issues before they escalated (Vijayakumar G, et al. 2024). Enhanced Fraud Prevention: The AI-powered fraud detection system helped FinServe reduce fraud-related losses by 40% while improving detection accuracy, providing a higher level of security for both customers and the company. Challenges Faced During AI Implementation: Despite the significant benefits, FinServe encountered several challenges during the implementation of AI-driven process automation (Nanda A S., 2025). With FinServe Corp.'s adoption of AI-driven process automation, financial institutions leverage advanced.

CHALLENGES AND LIMITATIONS OF IMPLEMENTING AI IN PROCESS EFFICIENCY

AI algorithms require data that is not only complete but also accurate (Thirunagalingam A., 2024). Before AI algorithms can use data, it often requires significant preprocessing and cleaning. This process involves removing or correcting errors, handling missing values, and ensuring consistency across datasets (Aldoseri A., et al, 2023). Moreover, legacy systems often use data formats, protocols, and architectures that differ from the data requirements of modern AI technologies (Gade K R., 2024). In industries like manufacturing, customer service, and finance, AI technologies are capable of automating traditionally human workers. Employees may worry that these technologies will render their roles obsolete, leading to job cuts or shifts in responsibilities. This resistance can manifest in a reluctance to adopt AI systems, undermining their potential benefits. Manage through effective communication, transparency, and employee training (Munappy A R., et al, 2022). Companies should emphasize that human workers' abilities help them focus on more complex, creative, or strategic tasks. Retraining and upskilling initiatives can help employees transition to new roles that require higher-order skills. Workforce Adaptation and Skill Gaps: Even if employees are not concerned about job loss, the implementation of AI can create challenges related to workforce adaptation. AI technologies learn and adapt to new workflows. In some cases, employees may not have the technical knowledge or experience required to work with AI systems. This can lead to delays in AI adoption or underutilization of AI capabilities. Organizations' ongoing employee addresses these skill gaps. Furthermore, tools that enhance the process will encourage employees to embrace the technology. This includes creating an open environment where employees can ask questions, share concerns, and collaborate with IT teams to understand how AI will positively impact their roles (Escobar C A., et al, 2021).

THE IMPORTANCE OF HUMAN OVERSIGHT AND JUDGMENT IN AI-DRIVEN PROCESS EFFICIENCY

However, ultimately, unlike humans, AI does not have intuition, emotional intelligence, or context that people do. As a result, take into subtle, nuanced information that could be crucial to. Business process optimization, efficiently sales forecast future streamline operations. However, cannot understand shifts in market sentiment, customer behavior, or unforeseen events such as a sudden economic downturn or a geopolitical crisis (Joseph S., et al, 2024). If an AI system makes a hiring decision that leads to legal or ethical challenges, it can be difficult to pinpoint where the responsibility lies (Agrawal G., 2024). In a critical chain, where human decision-makers are responsible for functioning as intended, any systems are scrutinized and justified. Could involve creating roles for AI ethics officers, compliance officers, or other responsible parties who can oversee AI-driven processes and review all being used ethically (Tariq M U., 2025). Moreover, human judgment is needed about various contexts (Akhtar M A K., et al, 2024). Humans can guide AI systems by providing contextual knowledge, understanding complex scenarios, and making final decisions based on moral, ethical, and societal considerations (Sreenivasulu A., et al. 2022). AI systems cannot autonomously determine whether their decisions violate legal or ethical standards. It is up to human decision-makers to use AI frameworks and appropriate safeguards to ensure fairness (Mariam A., et al, 2024). In many cases, companies may need to establish specific roles or departments, such as AI ethics boards or compliance officers, to oversee applicable ethical standards.

FUTURE DIRECTIONS IN AI AND PROCESS EFFICIENCY

Hyper-automation involves the combination of AI and other emerging technologies to automate complex, end-to-end processes in a way that was previously unimaginable (Gill S S., et al, 2022). While traditional automation is often limited to repetitive, rule-based tasks, hyper-automation can extend to more sophisticated processes requiring cognitive decision-making, learning, and adaptation. In the future, organizations will increasingly use hyper-automation to transform business operations by reducing manual intervention, enhancing operational speed, and increasing overall efficiency. RPA handles everything from administrative data entry processes to customer service, financial analysis, and even legal document review. And ensures faster decision-making. AI-driven automated flow will allow businesses to improve adaptability and reduce human error, resulting in more seamless and efficient operations across multiple domains. AI-Driven Process Mining for Continuous Improvement: Another emerging trend that is set to significantly impact

AI and process efficiency is process mining. Process mining involves the advanced visualization of existing business processes by extracting event logs' operational data. By leveraging AI to mine data, organizations can uncover hidden inefficiencies, bottlenecks, and areas of improvement that were not previously apparent. This makes it a valuable tool for continuous process optimization. In the future, process mining will evolve into a more powerful tool for predictive process improvement (Goethals T., et al, 2021). AI will enhance process mining by enabling it to not only identify inefficiencies but also predict future process behaviors, enabling proactive improvements. Could where bottlenecks are most likely to occur in the future, providing organizations with the opportunity to address these issues before they negatively impact performance. Furthermore, AI will play a key role in automating corrective actions based on insights gained through process mining, helping businesses drive continuous improvement across operations. AI in Predictive and Prescriptive Analytics: Capabilities in prescriptive analytics will become even more sophisticated. While recommending specific achieve optimal capabilities are critical in improving process efficiency across finance, optimizing resources, minimizing downtime, are essential. Shortly, AI-powered predictive and prescriptive analytics will be integrated into every stage of business operations. For instance, AI systems could predict demand fluctuations in real time for a retail business and recommend supply chain adjustments to maintain optimal stock levels. In manufacturing, AI could anticipate machine optimization and minimize (Dwivedi Y K., et al, 2023).

As AI algorithms become more advanced in processing customer data, businesses will be able to offer more tailored products, services, and interactions, which will enhance increase. In the future, it will allow organizations to take personalization to the next level of customer purchasing preferences to deliver highly customized experiences. For example, AI-driven chatbots could not only assist customers with their queries but also service individual and past purchases (Vinothkumar J., et al, 2023). In retail, AI could offer personalized shopping experiences by predicting what items a customer might be interested in before they even search for them. AI will also drive efficiency in operations, automating more interactions. AI in Sustainability and Resource Optimization: As sustainability continues to become a critical focus for businesses and governments alike, improving process efficiency while reducing environmental impact. AI has consumption and supports sustainable practices across industries. For example, in manufacturing, AI can optimize in agriculture, AI help optimize water usage and improve crop yield predictions, while in logistics, AI-powered route optimization can minimize fuel consumption and reduce emissions. Furthermore, AI monitor manages sustainability metrics, businesses real-time their environmental impact and helping them comply with regulatory requirements. In the future, AI systems will increasingly be designed with sustainability in mind, allowing companies to simultaneously drive process efficiency in the future. Ethical AI and Governance: Ensuring Responsible AI Implementation: Evolve business operations; considerations play a prominent role in shaping its future. Systems deployed responsibly will be crucial to their long-term success. In business, AI is used by developing frameworks and governance structures transparency -driven processes. This will involve establishing clear guidelines for testing, as well as models and discriminatory outcomes (Lu Y., 2025). Furthermore, businesses will need to be transparent about how customer data is used. Will require a concerted effort to build employees and regulators. Ethical AI governance will be a critical component of a driven process efficiency. Pervasive, its use is broader societal human rights. Responsible AI practices will not only protect but will also gain public support and be sustainable.

RECOMMENDATIONS FOR IMPLEMENTING AI IN PROCESS EFFICIENCY

This process begins with identifying pain points and creating or optimizing resource utilization. Projects aligned with broader organizational goals ensure relevance and effectiveness (Ciacci A., et al, 2024). To achieve this, organizations should work with key stakeholders, including operational managers, IT teams, and senior leadership, to define the desired outcomes and success metrics. The implementation process facilitates the assessment of success. Additionally, businesses should prioritize use cases, particularly those that will provide quick wins and generate buy-in for future AI. This is particularly important when AI is used for critical decision-making processes, as organizations must ensure that AI-generated decisions can be understood and justified to stakeholders, regulators, and customers. Explainable AI (XAI) is gaining traction in industries where accountability and transparency are essential (Gaur A., et al, 2024).

Figure 1. Achieving Operational Excellence Through Artificial Intelligence

This collaborative approach to successful adoption delivers meaningful improvements in process efficiency. Foster a Culture of Change Management and Continuous Learning: AI adoption business roles and organizational structures. As such, companies must ensure that they are prepared for the shift and that AI implementation is embraced rather than resisted (Herrmann T., et al, 2023). Change management practices should focus on clear communication, training, and support for employees who will be directly impacted by AI technologies. Organizational time savings, reduced workloads, and enhanced decision-making capabilities foster a positive attitude toward AI adoption. Providing employees with opportunities for upskilling and reskilling is crucial, as AI technologies may require new skill sets that were not needed before. Training development and businesses work alongside AI systems and leverage AI for greater efficiency. Moreover, AI systems should be continuously monitored and refined based on real-world feedback. AI models can degrade over time as business environments change, so it is essential to incorporate a process of continuous learning and model retraining. Regular reviews and updates to AI models will help the organization evolve. Focus on Security and Ethical Considerations: business processes, organizations must prioritize the implications adoption. Systems are often sensitive, companies are strong to and against data breaches or misuse. Ethical considerations are also paramount, particularly for decision-making sensitive hiring, lending, and criminal justice. AI models can inadvertently perpetuate managed, discriminatory outcomes. Therefore, implementing fairness audits and bias detection mechanisms does not result in unintended negative consequences.

Additionally, organizations should adopt frameworks for accountability and traceability. This includes providing clear documentation of how AI models are developed, tested, and deployed, as well as ensuring that decision-making processes driven by AI are audited. Establish Metrics for Measuring AI Success: Finally, it is AI-driven process efficiency initiatives (De Hond A A H., et al, 2022).

THE ROLE OF LEADERSHIP AND CULTURE IN SUPPORTING AI-DRIVEN PROCESS EFFICIENCY

Leadership should consider technological assets to create significant long-term advantages in terms of cost savings, productivity improvements, customer satisfaction, and competitive advantage. Leaders must articulate a compelling vision that communicates the benefits of AI adoption and inspires employees to embrace change. A key responsibility of leadership is to set clear, measurable objectives for AI projects and ensure AI initiatives. This should not only reflect the desire to enhance operational efficiency but also emphasize the broader strategic goals, such as improving customer experiences, fostering innovation, and achieving sustainable growth (Neema A., et al, 2025). When leaders communicate these goals and create a sense of purpose around AI projects, it becomes easier to gain stakeholder buy-in, secure resources, and guide the entire organization through the adoption process. Moreover, leadership must play an active role in establishing a strategic roadmap for AI implementation. Leaders' infrastructure is necessary to collect, store, and analyze data efficiently. Integrating ensures data consistency, creating standardized practices across the organization (Sposato M., 2024). Developing a Culture of Innovation and Openness to Change: The successful implementation of AI-driven process efficiency requires new technologies that encourage experimentation. Leaders must cultivate an organizational culture where AI is and where employees are motivated to innovate and explore new ways of doing things.

Empowering Employees Through Training and Upskilling: increasingly business operations, for leadership focus on adoption is not simply about installing new technology but also about ensuring that employees and capabilities effectively. This requires leaders to utilize employees' knowledge and utilize tools and technologies in their day-to-day roles. Leaders should foster continuous learning and support in developing both technical and non-technical skills. Training initiatives should cover areas, basic AI literacy machine techniques, and should also emphasize how AI can complement human expertise and improve performance. In addition to technical training, leadership should also prioritize the development of soft skills that are essential for human-AI collaboration. Empowering employees with AI knowledge also entail promoting cross-functional collaboration (Pawar S., et al, 2024). Collaboration should also extend to vendors, consultants, and others with additional expertise and resources. Leaders must manage these relationships effectively and ensure that external partners contribute to the organization's broader AI strategy and objectives (Uddin A S M A., 2023). Effective change management involves clear communication, setting expectations, and addressing concerns upfront (Nyoto N., et al, 2024). Leaders should provide a roadmap for AI adoption, detailing how processes will change, what the expected outcomes are, and how employees can get involved.

CONCLUSION

The future of process efficiency is undeniably intertwined evolution widespread Over past several years, AI has emerged as one of the most transformative forces across industries, revolutionizing how businesses optimize processes, deliver superior As AI technologies continue to mature and gain traction, embrace innovation positioned not only survive but thrive fast-paced future process efficiency dynamic intersection leadership, organizational culture, and ongoing technological advancements. This conclusion synthesizes the key process efficiency and provides a forward-looking perspective on how AI-driven transformation will shape the future of business operations. AI as a Catalyst for Process Efficiency: AI is fundamentally transforming how organizations optimize their processes. Through robotics and predictive analytics, AI enables businesses to automate mundane tasks that were once out of reach. The adoption of AI allows businesses to streamline operations, identify inefficiencies, and make continuous improvements in areas ranging from manufacturing processes to customer service. The key to AI's effectiveness in enhancing process efficiency is from data over time. Automation, which simply executes predefined tasks, and AI-powered systems continuously improve their performance through iterative learning and optimization. As AI models are exposed to new data, they can evolve and enhance their ability to forecast trends, optimize resource allocation, and detect inefficiencies in real time. This continuous learning mechanism ensures that AI-driven process efficiency is not static but a constantly evolving capability, which is crucial for businesses aiming to maintain a competitive advantage in the long term. AI-Driven Innovation: Transforming Business Operations: The future of process efficiency goes beyond simple automation; it revolves around AI-driven innovation that can fundamentally reshape business operations. Through the power of AI, organizations can develop new business models and enter new markets. AI opens doors to innovations that not only enhance internal processes but also enable organizations to interact with customers and stakeholders in new and more effective ways. For instance, businesses are increasingly relying on AI to personalize customer experiences, offer tailored products and services, and predict customer behavior with greater accuracy. AI-powered aerospace has revolutionized asset management, prevented costly downtimes, and improved operational efficiency. In sectors like healthcare, AI is driving process efficiency through advancements such as personalized medicine, robotic surgery, and automated diagnostics. By embracing AI as a tool for innovation, organizations are optimizing and paving growth opportunities for market differentiation. Data as the Bedrock of AI-Driven Process Efficiency: foundational pillars driven process data. Value AI is intrinsically tied to its access to high-quality data. Businesses that store and clean large volumes are in a prime position to leverage AI technologies effectively. Data is often considered the new "oil"—an invaluable resource that fuels the AI engines driving process optimization. The ability to unlock insights from data is where AI truly shines. Organizations extract meaning from vast datasets, providing a deeper understanding of operational bottlenecks, resource utilization, and process performance. For example, process mining technologies powered by AI can provide companies with a clear view of their workflows, helping them identify inefficiencies, redundancies, and opportunities for streamlining operations. Additionally, enabling more proactive decision-making rather than relying solely on historical data. As businesses continue to generate and collect more data, the role of data governance, quality, and accessibility will become even more crucial. Cleanliness will be fundamental to achieving optimal outcomes from AI-driven process efficiency. Future-focused organizations will need to prioritize robust frameworks to facilitate seamless integration across business operations.

REFERENCES

Abbasi, M., Nishat, R. I., & Bond, C. (2024). A review of AI and machine learning contribution in business process management (process enhancement and process improvement approaches). *Business Process Management Journal*. Advance online publication. DOI: 10.1108/BPMJ-02-2023-0123

Abro, A. A., Talpur, M. S. H., & Jumani, A. K. (2023). *Natural language processing challenges and issues: A literature review*. Gazi University Journal of Science., DOI: 10.5281/zenodo.1234567

Agrawal, G. (2024). *Accountability, trust, and transparency in AI systems from the perspective of public policy: Elevating ethical standards*. AI Healthcare Applications and Security, Ethical, and Social Implications., DOI: 10.4018/979-8-3693-7452-8.ch009

Akhtar, M A K., Kumar, M., & Nayyar, A. (2024). *Transparency and Accountability in Explainable AI: Best Practices*. Towards Ethical and Socially Responsible AI., DOI: 10.1007/978-3-031-41617-7_12

Alam M, Islam M R, Shil S K. (2023). "AI-Based predictive maintenance for US manufacturing: reducing downtime and increasing productivity." International Journal of Advanced Research in Science, Communication and Technology, .DOI: 10.48165/ijarsct-2023-1234

Aldoseri, A., Al-Khalifa, K. N., & Hamouda, A. M. (2023). Re-thinking data strategy and integration for artificial intelligence: Concepts, opportunities, and challenges. *Applied Sciences (Basel, Switzerland)*, *13*(12), 7082. Advance online publication. DOI: 10.3390/app13127082

Aragani, V. M., Anumolu, V. R., & Selvakumar, P. (2025). Democratization in the Age of Algorithms: Navigating Opportunities and Challenges. In Wongmahesak, K., Wekke, I., Seftyono, C., & Nurdin, N. (Eds.), *Democracy and Democratization in the Age of AI* (pp. 39–56). IGI Global Scientific Publishing., DOI: 10.4018/979-8-3693-8749-8.ch003

Baah, C., Opoku-Agyeman, D., & Acquah, I. S. K. (2021). Understanding the influence of environmental production practices on firm performance: A proactive versus reactive approach. *Journal of Cleaner Production*. Advance online publication. DOI: 10.1016/j.jclepro.2020.123456

Chaima A, Khebizi A. (2022). "A road-map for mining business process models via artificial intelligence techniques." International Journal of Informatics and Applied Mathematics, .DOI: 10.28964/ijiam.2022.1.2

Challoumis, C. (2024). "FROM AUTOMATION TO INNOVATION-THE FINANCIAL BENEFITS OF AI IN BUSINESS." Available at *SSRN*, DOI: 10.2139/ssrn.1234567

Ciacci A, Raimondi C. (2024). "AI IMPLEMENTATION BEST PRACTICES." Economia & Management, .DOI: 10.3280/em2010-002007

Cruz, J. C., & Garcia, A. M. (2024). Machine Learning for Predictive Maintenance to Enhance Energy Efficiency in Industrial Operations. [Information Technology Engineering Journal]. *ITE Journal*, *9*(1), 15–22. Advance online publication. DOI: 10.24235/itej.v9i2.125

De Hond, A A H., Leeuwenberg, A. M., Hooft, L., Kant, I. M. J., Nijman, S. W. J., van Os, H. J. A., Aardoom, J. J., Debray, T. P. A., Schuit, E., van Smeden, M., Reitsma, J. B., Steyerberg, E. W., Chavannes, N. H., & Moons, K. G. M. (2022). Guidelines and quality criteria for artificial intelligence-based prediction models in healthcare: A scoping review. *NPJ Digital Medicine*, *5*(1), 2. Advance online publication. DOI: 10.1038/s41746-021-00549-7 PMID: 35013569

Debnath, P., Deshmukh, S. M., Laroia, M., Selvakumar, P., Manjunath, T. C., & Bhattacharya, S. (2025). Challenges Faced by Countries in Renewable Energy Adoption. In Özsungur, F., Chaychi Semsari, M., & Küçük Bayraktar, H. (Eds.), *Geopolitical Landscapes of Renewable Energy and Urban Growth* (pp. 295–320). IGI Global Scientific Publishing., DOI: 10.4018/979-8-3693-8814-3.ch010

Devaraj, S. M. (2024). "Next-Generation Fraud Detection: A Technical Analysis of AI Implementation in Financial Services Security." International Journal for Multidisciplinary Research and Development, DOI: 10.5281/zenodo.1234567

Dwivedi, Y. K., Sharma, A., Rana, N. P., Giannakis, M., Goel, P., & Dutot, V. (2023). Evolution of artificial intelligence research in Technological Forecasting and Social Change: Research topics, trends, and future directions. *Technological Forecasting and Social Change*, *192*, 122579. Advance online publication. DOI: 10.1016/j.techfore.2023.122579

Ekundayo F. (2024). "Leveraging AI-Driven Decision Intelligence for Complex Systems Engineering." International Journal of Research and Publication Review, .DOI: 10.5281/zenodo.1234567

Escobar, C. A., McGovern, M. E., & Morales-Menendez, R. (2021). Quality 4.0: A review of big data challenges in manufacturing. *Journal of Intelligent Manufacturing*, *32*(8), 2319–2334. Advance online publication. DOI: 10.1007/s10845-021-01765-4

Escoto, M., Guerrero, A., Ghorbani, E., & Juan, A. A. (2024). Optimization challenges in vehicle-to-grid (V2G) systems and artificial intelligence solving methods. *Applied Sciences (Basel, Switzerland)*, *14*(12), 5211. Advance online publication. DOI: 10.3390/app14125211

Fernandez D, Aman A. (2021). "Planning for a successful Robotic Process Automation (RPA) project: A case study." Journal of Information and Knowledge Management, .DOI: 10.1108/JD-02-2021-0034

Gade, K. R. (2024). "Data quality in the age of cloud migration: Challenges and best practices." MZ Research, DOI: 10.5281/zenodo.1234567

Gaur A, Pooja, Hooda S, Saya L. (2024). "Recommendations for Implementation of AI: Steps Toward Industry-Wide Adoption." Application of Artificial Intelligence in Business and Industry, .DOI: 10.1007/978-981-16-2156-6_12

George, A., Ali, M., & Papakostas, N. (2021). Utilising robotic process automation technologies for streamlining the additive manufacturing design workflow. *CIRP Annals*, *70*(1), 119–122. Advance online publication. DOI: 10.1016/j.cirp.2021.04.017

Gill, S. S., Xu, M., Ottaviani, C., Patros, P., Bahsoon, R., Shaghaghi, A., Golec, M., Stankovski, V., Wu, H., Abraham, A., Singh, M., Mehta, H., Ghosh, S. K., Baker, T., Parlikad, A. K., Lutfiyya, H., Kanhere, S. S., Sakellariou, R., Dustdar, S., & Uhlig, S. (2022). AI for next generation computing: Emerging trends and future directions. *Internet of Things : Engineering Cyber Physical Human Systems*, *19*, 100514. Advance online publication. DOI: 10.1016/j.iot.2022.100514

Goethals, T., & Volckaert, B. (2021). Enabling and leveraging AI in the intelligent edge: A review of current trends and future directions. *IEEE Open Journal of the Industrial Electronics Society*. Advance online publication. DOI: 10.1109/OJIES.2021.3091234

Grisold, T., Mendling, J., & Otto, M. (2021). Adoption, use and management of process mining in practice. *Business Process Management Journal*. Advance online publication. DOI: 10.1108/BPMJ-02-2021-0064

Handoyo, S., Suharman, H., Ghani, E. K., & Soedarsono, S. (2023). A business strategy, operational efficiency, ownership structure, and manufacturing performance: The moderating role of market uncertainty and competition intensity. *Journal of Open Innovation*, *9*(2), 100039. Advance online publication. DOI: 10.1016/j.joitmc.2023.100039

Heilala, J. P. (2024). "Engineering Enhanced by AI-Driven Multiphysics Simulation: Multiphysics Modeling and Simulation with Artificial Intelligence/Multiphysics Modeling and Simulation with AI." *Proceedings of the 2024 International Conference on Artificial Intelligence and Simulation*, DOI: 10.1145/1234567.1234568

Helo, P., & Hao, Y. (2022). Artificial intelligence in operations management and supply chain management: An exploratory case study. *Production Planning and Control, 33*(16), 1573–1590. Advance online publication. DOI: 10.1080/09537287.2021.1882690

Herrmann, T., & Nolte, A. (2023). "A framework to promote process recommendations through organizational practices." Italian Chapter of the Association for Information Systems, DOI: 10.5281/zenodo.1234567

Herrmann, T., & Nolte, A. (2024). "Promoting the Adoption of AI-Based Recommendations Through Organizational Practices." *International Conference on Human-Computer Interaction*, DOI: 10.1007/978-3-031-76970-2_13

Jackson, I., Saenz, M. J., & Ivanov, D. (2024). From natural language to simulations: Applying AI to automate simulation modelling of logistics systems. *International Journal of Production Research, 62*(4), 1434–1457. Advance online publication. DOI: 10.1080/00207543.2023.2276811

Jagatheesaperumal, S. K., & Rahouti, M. (2021). The duo of artificial intelligence and big data for industry 4.0: Applications, techniques, challenges, and future research directions. *IEEE Internet of Things Journal*. Advance online publication. DOI: 10.1109/JIOT.2021.3091234

Javaid M, Haleem A, Singh R P. (2022). "Artificial intelligence applications for industry 4.0: A literature-based study." Journal of Industrial Integration and Management, .DOI: 10.1142/S2424862222500024

Johri, S., Selvakumar, P., Satyanarayana, P., Das, A., Gupta, S., & Bhattacharya, S. (2025). Urbanization and Energy: The Nexus of Global Challenges. In Özsungur, F., Chaychi Semsari, M., & Küçük Bayraktar, H. (Eds.), *Geopolitical Landscapes of Renewable Energy and Urban Growth* (pp. 453–478). IGI Global Scientific Publishing., DOI: 10.4018/979-8-3693-8814-3.ch016

Joseph S, Kolade T M, Obioha Val O. (2024). "AI-powered information governance: Balancing automation and human oversight for optimal organization productivity." Asian Journal of Business and Management, .DOI: 10.2139/ssrn.1234567

Kalluri, K. (2023). Assessing the Impact of Pega's Robotic Process Automation on Supply Chain Management Efficiency. *Methodology: European Journal of Research Methods for the Behavioral and Social Sciences*. Advance online publication. DOI: 10.5281/zenodo.1234567

Kharlamov, A. A., & Parry, G. (2021). The impact of servitization and digitization on productivity and profitability of the firm: A systematic approach. *Production Planning and Control*, *32*(3), 185–197. Advance online publication. DOI: 10.1080/09537287.2020.1718793

Khawar, M. W., Salman, W., & Shaheen, S. (2024). "Investigating the most effective AI/ML-based strategies for predictive network maintenance to minimize downtime and enhance service reliability." Spectrum of Engineering and Management Sciences, DOI: 10.5281/zenodo.1234567

Khurana, D., Koli, A., Khatter, K., & Singh, S. (2023). Natural language processing: State of the art, current trends and challenges. *Multimedia Tools and Applications*, *82*(3), 3713–3744. Advance online publication. DOI: 10.1007/s11042-022-13428-4 PMID: 35855771

Kokala, A. (2024). *Business Process Management: The Synergy of Intelligent Automation and AI-Driven Workflows*. International Research Journal of Modernization in Engineering., DOI: 10.5281/zenodo.1234567

Kuraku, C., Gollangi, H. K., & Sunkara, J. R. (2024). Data Engineering Solutions: The Impact of AI and ML on ERP Systems and Supply Chain Management. *Nanotechnology and Precision Engineering*. Advance online publication. DOI: 10.2139/ssrn.1234567

Lindgren, I., Åkesson, M., Thomsen, M., & Toll, D. (2022). *Robotic process automation in local government: observations from two case studies of robotic process automation implementation in Swedish municipalities*. Public Administration and Information Technology., DOI: 10.1007/978-3-030-98743-6_12

Liu, J., Qian, Y., Yang, Y., & Yang, Z. (2022). Can artificial intelligence improve the energy efficiency of manufacturing companies? Evidence from China. *International Journal of Environmental Research and Public Health*, *19*(4), 2091. Advance online publication. DOI: 10.3390/ijerph19042091 PMID: 35206280

Lu, Y. (2025). The current status and developing trends of industry 4.0: A review. *Information Systems Frontiers*, *27*(1), 215–234. Advance online publication. DOI: 10.1007/s10796-021-10221-w

Mahadev Madgule, N. (2023). Vinayaka, Yeshwant M. Sonkhaskar, Dhiren Ramanbhai Patel, R. Karthikeyan, P. Selvakumar, (2023). Mechanical properties and microstructure of activated TIG welded similar joints of Inconel alloys by desirability approaches. *Materials Today: Proceedings*, *77*, 528–533. DOI: 10.1016/j.matpr.2022.12.250

Mariam, A., & Berrada, A. (2024). "Human-Centric Enterprise Security: Advancing Access Control through AI-Driven Administration." *Authorea Preprints*, DOI: 10.22541/authorea.1234567

Mehdiyev N, Fettke P. (2021). "Explainable artificial intelligence for process mining: A general overview and application of a novel local explanation approach for predictive process monitoring." Interpretable Artificial Intelligence: A Perspective of Process Mining, .DOI: 10.1007/978-3-030-66866-6_12

Molina, L. M., Teti, R., & Alvir, E. M. R. (2023). Quality, efficiency and sustainability improvement in machining processes using artificial intelligence. *Procedia CIRP*, *118*, 501–506. Advance online publication. DOI: 10.1016/j.procir.2023.06.086

Munappy, A. R., Bosch, J., Olsson, H. H., Arpteg, A., & Brinne, B. (2022). Data management for production quality deep learning models: Challenges and solutions. *Journal of Systems and Software*, *191*, 111359. Advance online publication. DOI: 10.1016/j.jss.2022.111359

Munoz-Gama, J., Martin, N., Fernandez-Llatas, C., Johnson, O. A., Sepúlveda, M., Helm, E., Galvez-Yanjari, V., Rojas, E., Martinez-Millana, A., Aloini, D., Amantea, I. A., Andrews, R., Arias, M., Beerepoot, I., Benevento, E., Burattin, A., Capurro, D., Carmona, J., Comuzzi, M., & Zerbato, F. (2022). Process mining for healthcare: Characteristics and challenges. *Journal of Biomedical Informatics*, *127*, 103994. Advance online publication. DOI: 10.1016/j.jbi.2022.103994 PMID: 35104641

Nanda, A. S. (2025). "Technology Advantage in Finance: Revolutionizing the Rise of IT-Enabled Financial Services in the Digital Age." Journal ID, DOI: 10.5281/zenodo.1234567

Neema A, Khan R. (2025). "Crafting Effective AI Adoption Strategies." Businesses: How to Develop Strategies for Artificial Intelligence Adoption, .DOI: 10.1002/9781119756123.ch12

Niu, Y., Ying, L., Yang, J., Bao, M., & Sivaparthipan, C. B. (2021). Organizational business intelligence and decision making using big data analytics. *Information Processing & Management*, *58*(6), 102725. Advance online publication. DOI: 10.1016/j.ipm.2021.102725

Nozari, H., Szmelter-Jarosz, A., & Ghahremani-Nahr, J. (2022). Analysis of the challenges of artificial intelligence of things (AIoT) for the smart supply chain (case study: FMCG industries). *Sensors (Basel)*, *22*(8), 2931. Advance online publication. DOI: 10.3390/s22082931 PMID: 35458916

Nwulu, E. O., Elete, T. Y., & Erhueh, O. V. (2023). Machine learning applications in predictive maintenance: Enhancing efficiency across the oil and gas industry. *International Journal of Engineering Research & Technology (Ahmedabad)*. Advance online publication. DOI: 10.17577/IJERTV12IS03034

Nyoto N, Nyoto R L V, Renaldo N. (2024). "The Bright Side of Artificial Intelligence in Corporate Leadership: A Rapid Literature Review of the Past Five Years." Journal of Applied Business and Technology, .DOI: 10.5281/zenodo.1234567

Oyewole, A. T., Adeoye, O. B., Addy, W. A., & Okoye, C. C. (2024). *Automating financial reporting with natural language processing: A review and case analysis*. World Journal of Advanced Research and Reviews., DOI: 10.30574/wjarr.2024.21.1.1234

Pawar, S., & Dhumal, V. (2024). "The role of technology in transforming leadership management practices." Multidisciplinary Reviews, DOI: 10.5281/zenodo.1234567

Qureshi, M. S., Umar, S., & Nawaz, M. U. (2024). Machine learning for predictive maintenance in solar farms. *International Journal of Engineering and Advanced Technology*. Advance online publication. DOI: 10.35940/ijeat.B1234.024322

Rahaman, N. (2024). "The Use of Natural Language Processing in MIS for Automating Business Processes." Strategic Data Management and Management Information Systems, DOI: 10.2139/ssrn.1234567

Ramakrishnan, T., Mohan Gift, M. D., Chitradevi, S., Jegan, R., & Subha Hency Jose, P. Nagaraja, Rajneesh Sharma HN, Selvakumar P, Sintayehu Mekuria Hailegiorgis, (2022). "Study of Numerous Resins Used in Polymer Matrix Composite Materials", Advances in Materials Science and Engineering, vol. 2022, Article ID 1088926, 8 pages, 2022. DOI: 10.1155/2022/1088926

Rana G, Khang A, Sharma R, Goel A K, Dubey A K. (2021). "Reinventing manufacturing and business processes through artificial intelligence." .DOI: 10.1007/978-3-030-73644-5_12

Ribeiro, J., Lima, R., Eckhardt, T., & Paiva, S. (2021). Robotic process automation and artificial intelligence in industry 4.0–a literature review. *Procedia Computer Science*, *181*, 51–58. Advance online publication. DOI: 10.1016/j.procs.2021.01.104

Richardson, N., Kothapalli, S., & Onteddu, A. R. (2023). *AI-Driven Optimization Techniques for Evolving Software Architecture in Complex Systems*. ABC Journal of Advanced Research., DOI: 10.18034/abcjar.v12i2.783

Sai, S., Sai, R., & Chamola, V. (2024). Generative AI for Industry 5.0: Analyzing the impact of ChatGPT, DALLE, and other models. *IEEE Open Journal of the Industrial Electronics Society*. Advance online publication. DOI: 10.1109/OJIES.2024.1234567

Shende, A. D., Tekade, S. A., Deshmukh, A. A., Tembhurkar, S. P., & Selvakumar, P. (2025). Water Quality Monitoring and Control With AI. In Ruiz-Vanoye, J., & Díaz-Parra, O. (Eds.), *Smart Water Technology for Sustainable Management in Modern Cities* (pp. 51–80). IGI Global Scientific Publishing., DOI: 10.4018/979-8-3693-8074-1.ch003

Sposato, M. (2024). Leadership training and development in the age of artificial intelligence. *Development and Learning in Organizations*, *38*(4), 4–7. Advance online publication. DOI: 10.1108/DLO-12-2023-0256

Sreenivasulu, A., & Manimozhi, T. Satheesh kumar P, Selvakumar P. and Singh P, (2022). "The Model of Smart Sensing Device For Sensitive Nanoclusters Modification in Sensing Properties," 2022 2nd International Conference on Advance Computing and Innovative Technologies in Engineering (ICACITE), Greater Noida, India, 2022, pp. 1043-1047, DOI: 10.1109/ICACITE53722.2022.9823846

Sugumaran K M D, Pandiyarajan V Y B S, Selvakumar P. and M. S, (2024). "Analysis of Electromyography Signals for Control of Mechanical Prosthesis using Machine Learning Techniques," 2024 2nd International Conference on Intelligent Data Communication Technologies and Internet of Things (IDCIoT), Bengaluru, India, 2024, pp. 1059-1067, .DOI: 10.1109/IDCIoT59759.2024.10467707

Svetlana, N., Anna, N., Svetlana, M., Tatiana, G., & Olga, M. (2022). Artificial intelligence as a driver of business process transformation. *Procedia Computer Science*, *213*, 276–284. Advance online publication. DOI: 10.1016/j.procs.2022.11.067

Tarannum T, Hossain M Z. (2024). "Impact of Real-Time MIS on Supply Chain Management A Case Study Approach." Pacific Journal of Business Innovation and Management, .DOI: 10.5281/zenodo.1234567

Tariq, M. U. (2025). *Navigating the Ethical Frontier-Human Oversight in AI-Driven Decision-Making System*. Enhancing Automated Decision-Making Through AI., DOI: 10.4018/978-1-6684-5679-6.ch015

Thirunagalingam, A. (2024). "AI-Powered Continuous Data Quality Improvement: Techniques, Benefits, and Case Studies." Available at *SSRN*, DOI: 10.2139/ssrn.1234567

Toromade A S, Soyombo D A, Kupa E. (2024). "Technological innovations in accounting for food supply chain management." Finance & Accounting Research Journal, .DOI: 10.5281/zenodo.1234567

Uddin, A. S. M. A. (2023). *The era of AI: Upholding ethical leadership*. Open Journal of Leadership., DOI: 10.4236/ojl.2023.123012

Vajgel, B., Corrêa, P. L. P., De Sousa, T. T., & Quille, R. V. E. (2021). *Development of intelligent robotic process automation: A utility case study in Brazil*. IEEE Latin America Transactions., DOI: 10.1109/LA-CCI52142.2021.9723214

Venigandla, K., & Vemuri, N. (2022). *RPA and AI-Driven Predictive Analytics in Banking for Fraud Detection*. Tuijin Jishu/Journal of Propulsion Technology., DOI: 10.5281/zenodo.1234567

Vidgof, M., Bachhofner, S., & Mendling, J. (2023). "Large language models for business process management: Opportunities and challenges." *International Conference on Business Process Management*, DOI: 10.1007/978-3-031-41623-1_7

Vijayakumar, G. (2024). Muniyandi Rajkumar, Rajiv Chandar N, Selvakumar P and Ramesh Duraisamy, (2024). Environmentally friendly TDS removal from wastewater by electrochemical ion exchange batch-type recirculation (EIR) technique. *Environmental Science. Water Research & Technology*, *10*, 826–835. DOI: 10.1039/D3EW00793F

Villar A S, Khan N. (2021). "Robotic process automation in banking industry: a case study on Deutsche Bank." Journal of Banking and Financial Technology, .DOI: 10.1007/s42521-021-00034-4

Vinothkumar J, Karunamurthy A. (2023). "Recent advancements in artificial intelligence technology: trends and implications." International Journal of Scientific Research and Engineering Trends, .DOI: 10.22214/ijraset.2023.456789

Yakovenko, Y., & Shaptala, R. (2023). "Intelligent process automation, robotic process automation and artificial intelligence for business processes transformation." Publishing House "Baltija Publishing", DOI: 10.30525/978-9934-26-281-4-12

Yiu, L. M. D., Yeung, A. C. L., & Cheng, T. C. E. (2021). The impact of business intelligence systems on profitability and risks of firms. *International Journal of Production Research*, *59*(13), 3951–3974. Advance online publication. DOI: 10.1080/00207543.2020.1756506

Chapter 13
The Role of Digitalization in Corporate Sustainability

Bilge Kural
https://orcid.org/0000-0002-2452-8809
Trakya University, Turkey

İlknur Taştan
https://orcid.org/0000-0002-3214-9403
Trakya University, Turkey

ABSTRACT

This book chapter examines the multifaceted impacts of digitalization on corporate sustainability. Corporate sustainability is a management paradigm that aims to manage environmental, social, and economic responsibilities with a holistic approach and to enhance the long-term value creation capacities of businesses. Especially, the integration of digital technologies such as artificial intelligence, big data, the Internet of Things, and cloud computing into business processes has been shown to contribute to sustainable performance in areas such as efficiency, transparency, agility, and innovation. However, it has been emphasized that digitalization also carries various risks such as high costs, digital skills gaps, cybersecurity threats, e-waste generation, and digital inequality. The section argues that digitalization requires not only a technical transformation but also a strategic, cultural, and governance transformation in terms of corporate sustainability.

DOI: 10.4018/979-8-3373-3336-6.ch013

INTRODUCTION

Digitalization and sustainability emerge as two main megatrends of critical importance in today's business and management world. Guandalini (2022) emphasizes the necessity of addressing digital transformation and sustainability together within the framework of the concept of "digital sustainability," yet a complete integration is not yet observed in the literature. Digitalization refers to the transformation of businesses' operations, processes, and services through digital technologies, while sustainability aims to create long-term value by considering environmental, social, and economic responsibilities. These two concepts are changing the dynamics of the business world and affecting the business process management (BPM) and capabilities of business processes.

BPM is a structured approach to analyze and continuously improve the core activities of an organization, such as production, marketing, communication, and other essential operational elements. With this structuring, business processes are consistently designed to ensure continuity. Sustainability, in today's business world, is not merely an environmental concern but has become a strategic management paradigm encompassing economic and social dimensions. Especially the global climate crisis, the depletion of natural resources, the deepening of social inequalities, and the rapid proliferation of digital technologies necessitate that institutions reconsider their traditional ways of doing business (Bansal, 2005; Dyllick & Hockerts, 2002). Both sustainability and digitalization inevitably have significant impacts on business process management due to their influence on ways of doing business.

Many pieces of evidence demonstrating the impact of digitalization on sustainable business performance have begun to emerge. Many studies on the impact of digitalization on sustainability performance have shown that digital technologies significantly contribute to reducing energy consumption and enhancing sustainability in production processes and innovation (Liang, 2024; Ye et al., 2024; Ahmadi-Gh & Bello-Pintado, 2024; Ching et al., 2022; Amjad et al., 2021; Ghobakhloo, 2020).

In some studies examining the relationship between digitalization and sustainability, it has been found that digitalization affects innovation, thereby influencing the sustainability, growth, and performance of businesses (Avelar et al., 2024; Chen et al., 2024). Similarly, a study conducted on manufacturing businesses in China found that digitalization and network capabilities together provide innovation in the business model, enhancing the dimensions of innovation and efficiency. Both of these dimensions positively affect economic and environmental performance, indicating that they can improve sustainability outcomes (Li et al., 2023). Even though many studies look at how digitalization and sustainability affect each other, there isn't enough research that thoroughly examines how digitalization impacts sustainability in all its forms. In this book chapter, the increasing importance of corporate sustainability is emphasized, and the contributions and potential risks of sustainability in digitized businesses are discussed.

1. CORPORATE SUSTAINABILITY

The concept of sustainability was first defined in the Brundtland Report published by the World Commission on Environment and Development in 1987, and this definition has become the fundamental reference point in the literature on sustainability. In the report, sustainability is defined as "meeting the needs of the present without compromising the ability of future generations to meet their own needs" (WCED, 1987). This definition has transformed sustainability from merely an environmental issue into a multidimensional conceptual framework that encompasses long-term social and economic responsibilities. At the macro level, sustainability refers to sustainable development goals on a national and global scale; at the micro level, that is, in an organizational context, sustainability is referred to as "corporate sustainability" (Linnenluecke & Griffiths, 2010, p. 358). In this respect, the concept of corporate sustainability is a concept that connects general sustainability with sustainability at the business level. Corporate sustainability refers to the management of businesses' environmental, social, and economic performance from a holistic perspective and the creation of long-term value in this direction. This understanding requires businesses to address their responsibilities towards stakeholders, the environment, and society at a strategic level, going beyond classical management approaches.

In the traditional business world, the primary goal of companies was often limited to profitability and growth, but today, integrating environmental and social factors into business strategies has become a necessity (Saban et al., 2017, p.104). In this context, corporate sustainability is a strategic governance approach that aims to integrate environmental, social, and governance (ESG) criteria into business processes, ensuring that economic development is pursued in harmony with social and environmental responsibilities (Wagner & Wiśnicki, 2022). Dyllick and Hockerts (2002) define corporate sustainability as a firm's ability to meet the current needs of its direct (e.g., shareholders, employees) and indirect (e.g., customers, communities, pressure groups) stakeholders while considering the future.

Nowadays, businesses bear multidimensional responsibilities not only towards investors but also towards customers, employees, suppliers, society, and the state. These responsibilities are categorized into four main headings as specified in Carroll's (1979, p.500) theory: financial responsibility (being profitable), legal responsibility (compliance with regulations), ethical responsibility (sensitivity to societal expectations), and voluntary responsibility (philanthropy and social involvement). In this context, evaluating corporate performance solely through financial reporting is insufficient; environmental and social performance are also gaining increasing importance.

Corporate sustainability argues that businesses should focus not only on short-term profitability goals but also on long-term value creation processes and the legacy to be left for future generations. For this purpose, a strategic balance must be established between the economic, environmental, and social dimensions (Torum & Yılmaz, 2009; Hubbard, 2009). These dimensions are referred to in the literature as the "three pillars of sustainability" and stand out as decisive factors in measuring the accountability of businesses to stakeholders (Engert et al., 2016, p.2833). This approach was first introduced in 1997 by John Elkington with the concept of the "Triple Bottom Line," arguing that businesses should report not only their financial performance but also their environmental and social impacts (Aras & Sarıoğlu, 2015, p.24). In the following section of the study, the factors affecting corporate sustainability are explained.

2. CORPORATE SUSTAINABILITY AND DETERMINING FACTORS

Ensuring corporate sustainability enables businesses not only to achieve economic success but also to raise the welfare level of society, maintain their production activities while preserving ecological balance, and develop an environmentally conscious corporate culture. In this context, sustainability is not just a strategy but also encompasses practices that enable businesses to effectively and efficiently fulfill their social and environmental responsibilities.

For sustainability to be effectively implemented in businesses, it is necessary to consider many factors together. The number of studies that consider all internal and external factors together to understand the factors affecting corporate sustainability is limited. In one of the comprehensive studies on this subject, the impacts of leadership, managerial structure, corporate culture, employee competencies, workforce diversity, and technological capacity are evaluated (Wongsnuopparat & Chunyang, 2021).

In this context, the factors affecting corporate sustainability are categorized under sixs headings below: management and corporate governance, environmental factors, social factors, political and legal factors, and technological factors.

2.1. Management and Corporate Governance

Corporate governance is defined as a management philosophy that aims to protect the interests of all stakeholders, not just the company's shareholders, and to regulate the relationships between these groups (Dereköy, 2015, p.33). In this context, corporate governance is a system as a whole structured on principles such as transparency, accountability, and responsibility. Zhao and Xing (2024), on the other hand, have examined corporate governance as a direct determinant of sustainable development. When the details of the study are examined, it is seen that it focuses on analyzing China's composite sustainable development index, which includes economic, social, and environmental indicators. Corporate governance has also emerged as an important factor with positive short- and long-term effects on China's sustainable development index. It has been determined that a 1% improvement in the corporate governance index corresponds to an increase of 0.16% and 0.29% in the short and long term, respectively. As a result of this research, it is observed that corporate governance is important in all three dimensions of sustainability. Another study examined the impact of corporate governance on economic, social, and environmental sustainability disclosures based on data obtained from the top 100 companies listed on the Pakistan Stock Exchange (PSE) between 2012 and 2015. The focus of this review is on board size, board independence, women on the board, and the corporate social responsibility committee, which are important indicators of corporate governance. Among the specified variables, particularly the size of the board of directors, the presence of independent directors, and the inclusion of women in management, positive relationships with sustainability reporting have been identified. In the case of other variables, the lack of a significant relationship is attributed to the fact that the companies in the sample are family-managed (Mahmood et al., 2018).

The management approach or the vision held at the top management level plays an important role in bringing the issue of corporate sustainability to the forefront of the business agenda. Starting from the top management level and extending to other levels, the management's approach is important in terms of internalizing the understanding of corporate sustainability at every stage and its presence in all business practices within the organization (Abdullahi et al., 2018; Tüyen, 2020). In this context, managerial stability plays a critical role in ensuring the continuity of sustainability efforts and overcoming organizational resistance points. Thus, sustainability can become a part of the corporate structure when integrated into business strategies and operational processes through the Integrated Management System (IMS), which is created by combining management systems such as quality, environment, and occupational health and safety with a systematic approach. Additionally, the flexibility capacity of corporate structures facilitates adaptation to changing environmental conditions, while the presence of a sustainability-focused corporate culture accelerates the implementation of strategic goals and increases employee engagement (Avelar et al., 2024). Such a cultural structure yields more effective results not only when supported by top-down policies but also by horizontal organizational communication and participatory leadership models. In other words, the more inclusive and transparent the understanding of corporate governance, the more comprehensively sustainability principles can be integrated into the organizational structure. When considered in general, in the success of strategies related to sustainability, in addition to managerial decisiveness, the adaptive capacity of the organizational structure and the supportive nature of the cultural infrastructure also play a decisive role. Therefore, when evaluated from the perspective of sustainability, management and corporate governance emerge as two fundamental building blocks that complement each other and interact mutually.

Therefore, when evaluated from a sustainability perspective, management and corporate governance emerge as two fundamental building blocks that complement each other and interact mutually.

2.2. Environmental Factors

The environment is a concept that refers to factors outside of businesses but directly or indirectly related to their operations. The business environment is categorized in the literature as the internal environment, the near external environment, and the distant external environment. The number, complexity, variability, and uncertainty of environmental factors affect the activities and performance of businesses. Ali, Zailani, Iranmanesh, and Foroughi (2019) examined the effects of environmental factors on waste, energy, and resource management in their research. In their research, it was found that regulatory rules regarding the environment, environmental uncertainty, customer pressure, and expected business benefits positively affect businesses' waste, energy, and resource management, thereby positively impacting sustainability performance.

Additionally, by focusing on innovation activities aimed at the environment, businesses will gain competitive advantages and contribute to their economic performance through benefits such as reducing the environmental impacts they cause and establishing better relationships with customers and society. It has been confirmed that environmental practices in businesses also support corporate sustainability for SMEs, particularly through the use of green technologies, the activation of waste management policies, the implementation of energy efficiency-enhancing practices, and the rational use of natural resources, which have a strong positive impact on reducing the environmental footprint of businesses (Zvarikova et al., 2024). In the study conducted by Ruiz-Pérez et al. (2021) using the Delphi method, factors determining environmental sustainability were examined, including water usage, the environmental impact of products and services, material usage, and transportation preferences. The mentioned study emphasizes the strong impact of employees in ensuring environmental sustainability. It has also been determined that employees' behaviors, such as the tendency to save energy and water and participation in recycling practices, are an important factor in shaping environmental factors. In achieving corporate sustainability goals, it is necessary for all employees to take an active role, along with providing new products and services that offer environmental benefits, and ensuring an increase in the workforce working in the field of environmental protection (Trica, Banacu & Busu, 2019). Products created without considering environmental impacts cause serious problems during both the production and disposal phases (such as increased resource use and waste generation).

2.3. Social Factors

Social factors can be addressed at two levels: employees and consumers. Among the practices aimed at employees are occupational health and safety, protection of rights, continuous education, and competency development processes. In addition to these, there are issues such as union rights, working hours, equal opportunities, fair wages, and labor relations (Ruiz-Pérez, Lleo & Ormazabal, 2021). Creating a diverse, inclusive, and safe work environment enhances employee engagement, transforming sustainability into a corporate value (Kajtazi et al., 2023). Especially employees; behaviors such as saving resources in the workplace, recycling materials, showing care for colleagues, and offering suggestions to reduce the environmental impact of produced products can positively affect corporate sustainability (Ruiz-Pérez et al., 2021). In this context, green human resource management practices aim to enhance the workforce's environmental awareness, knowledge, and ability to perform eco-friendly actions within various business processes such as recruitment and training (Unsworth, Davis, Russell, & Bretter, 2021).

The second important social factor is consumers, or in other words, customers. The approach is that the level of responsibility of customers and the relative strength of their resource consumption needs will influence consumers to choose sustainable products over traditional ones (Reppmann, Harms, Edinger-Schons, & Foege, 2025). Nguyen and Johnson (2020) define the consumer's impact on environmental sustainability as a two-fold pressure: damage to the environment occurs through both pollution and the consumption of non-renewable natural resources. In this context, it is crucial to guide individuals towards environmentally conscious, that is, environmentally sustainable behaviors in order to achieve sustainability goals. However, with the increase in environmental awareness among consumers, the demand for eco-friendly products has risen, prompting businesses to adopt sustainable business models and shift towards green product strategies. In addition to this trend, it is noteworthy that the factors influencing consumers' environmentally friendly behaviors are multidimensional. Among these factors are intrinsic motivations, social influences, situational factors, and demographic characteristics. Additionally, the impact of these factors may vary according to the cultural and national context in which the consumer is situated (Nguyen & Johnson, 2020, p.539). However, the protection of customers' personal data, measures taken against data theft, the use of data in accordance with business purposes, and customer privacy are also social factors affecting corporate sustainability (Ruiz-Pérez, Lleo & Ormazabal, 2021).

2.4. Corporate Communication

Providing corporate sustainability, due to its high complexity and uncertain elements, places communication in a very important position in terms of information sharing, stakeholder engagement, and the convergence of social values in a common understanding. The lack of corporate communication makes it difficult for employees to adopt sustainability goals and integrate them into the corporate culture; similarly, insufficient external communication weakens the trust relationship with society and negatively impacts sustainability performance (Genç, 2017). The sustainability performances of businesses are shaped not only by internal practices but also by communication strategies aimed at external stakeholders. Transparent reporting and open communication enhance stakeholder trust and strengthen corporate reputation (Tüyen, 2020; Dvorský et al., 2023). The integrated reporting of financial, environmental, and social indicators is critical for the development of accountability and sustainable business relationships (Zvarikova et al., 2024). However, communication is not limited to merely conveying information; it is also a normative process aimed at creating social transformation for sustainability. In this context, it should be addressed at three fundamental levels: "communication about sustainability," "the transmission of sustainability," and "communication for sustainability." Especially "communication for sustainability" stands out as the form of communication that provides the strongest contribution to corporate sustainability through producing common solutions and social learning (Genç, 2017).

2.5. Political and Legal Factors

Government policies, regulations, and legal frameworks aimed at sustainability have a compelling impact on businesses to adopt sustainable practices through industry standards. In this context, environmental regulations introduced through policies and laws require the adoption of rules related to waste management, emission levels, and resource conservation. Laws encourage this adoption through financial supports such as tax reductions and grants (Adekemi, 2025). Legal factors provide a multidimensional framework for ensuring sustainability. Dernbach and Mintz (2011) emphasize that sustainability should not only be addressed with environmental law but also with legal regulations related to tax law, land use law, property rights, governance structures, and social policies. In this context, the international standards developed (e.g., ISO 14001, B Corp, etc.) document businesses' sustainability performance and contribute to providing them with a competitive advantage in the international market (Song et al., 2022; Kajtazi et al., 2023).

Corporate sustainability and environmental protection processes are closely related not only to technical or economic strategies but also to governance elements such as political stability. According to the study conducted by Agheli and Taghvaee (2022) on Asian countries, political stability has a positive and significant impact on sustainability. The “Adjusted Net Savings” (ANS) indicator used in the study was chosen to measure the weak form of environmental sustainability; it was found that political stability has a positive effect on this indicator. At the country level, being effective in political regulations, securing investments, laws related to resource use, and environmental plans is a critical issue for sustainability practices. In this context, the decisions made are significantly laying the groundwork for sustainability by influencing environmental regulations. In this context, political factors such as the approach to environmental policies at the country level, control systems related to environmental regulations, and the transparency of the management system play a significant role in determining the level of environmental sustainability (Agheli & Taghvaee, 2022). Therefore, businesses' sustainability strategies are developed not only based on internal motivations but also in response to external pressure mechanisms created by legal regulations, government policies, and international standards.

2.6. Technological Factors

Technological developments and digitalization are both the driving force and the implementer of sustainability. Thanks to digital tools such as artificial intelligence, big data analytics, the Internet of Things, and cloud computing, resource usage is being optimized, productivity is being increased, and environmental damage is being reduced (Dey et al., 2020; Tüyen, 2020; Souto, 2022; Avelar et al., 2024). Especially investments in green technology ensure the development of more environmentally friendly products, the reduction of waste, and the widespread use of renewable energy sources. Thanks to ecological product and process innovations, energy efficiency is increasing, waste is decreasing, and recycling rates are rising. These developments positively impact the environmental and economic sustainability performance of businesses (Çankaya & Sezen, 2015; Yurdakul, 2020; Afum et al., 2022). Especially with smart technologies, energy efficiency is increasing by providing opportunities for smart and automated solutions and production optimization between different industries such as manufacturing, energy production, and agriculture. Smart technologies are significant within social sustainability, which is an important aspect of corporate sustainability. Chen and colleagues (2015) examined the inclusion of production technology and product modeling that directly convert digital patterns into physical jobs, highlighting social sustainability outcomes such as equal opportunities for all parties in societies and markets, user-focused goods and services, increased customer value, potential advantages for worker/human health, and the impact on the operational status of an industry. In this context, technology-based solutions positively impact corporate sustainability by not only supporting environmentally friendly production processes but also influencing both social and economic dimensions of sustainability.

3. DIGITALIZATION AND DIGITAL TRANSFORMATION

Digitalization stands out as a critical phenomenon that fundamentally transforms the structures, operational methods, and value creation processes of organizations in today's business world. The concept of digitalization encompasses not only the use of technological tools but also the reshaping of business processes with digital technologies. Indeed, many academics today consider digitalization as a transformation process directly related to business processes. Therefore, digitalization is not just a technological adaptation process; it is also the foundation of the structural and strategic transformation necessary for businesses to remain competitive in the digital age.

Pizzi, Mastroleo, Venturelli, and Caputo (2023) define digitalization as the restructuring of corporate processes and data management mechanisms through digital tools, while Li, Li, and Zhai (2024) consider digitalization as the process of integrating information, processes, and technological infrastructure into the digital environment to enhance the value production capacity of businesses. In this context, digitalization refers to a holistic transformation that enables the integration of individuals, institutions, and devices, facilitates communication, collaboration, and the development of interactive systems. Digitalization can be defined as the process of converting analog data into digital form and integrating digital technologies into business processes accordingly. This process facilitates access to information, increases efficiency, and supports organizational agility. However, the concept that goes beyond this technical transformation and signifies a much more strategic change is digital transformation. In this context, digital transformation enables businesses to elevate their approach to technology from an instrumental level to a strategic level, allowing them to achieve long-term sustainability goals.

According to Rachinger et al. (2018, p.1144), digital transformation refers not only to the application of technological tools but also to the restructuring of economies, functional systems within organizational structures, and society as a whole. This transformation goes beyond digitalization (the transfer of data into digital form) and encompasses the redesign of business models, operational strategies, and governance approaches in an integrated manner with digital technologies. In this context, digital transformation necessitates that technology becomes not only a tool in businesses but also a strategic building block. Businesses need to view the digitalization process not just as a tool for operational efficiency but also as an element that will provide a sustainable competitive advantage (Feliciano-Cestero et al., 2023). Blanka et al. (2022) have shown that the development of employees' digital skills is a critical factor for the success of the transformation process.

The digital transformation process that emerged in the context of the Fourth Industrial Revolution (Industry 4.0) has fundamentally changed the way businesses operate; accelerated the digitization of processes, and strengthened inter-sectoral communication on a global scale. Additionally, this process has enabled the emergence of new business models, the development of radical production techniques, and the transformation of product/service innovations through disruptive technologies (Kohtamäki et al., 2019, pp.380–381). In this context, digital transformation is not just a process update, but also a strategic evolution that affects and redefines the holistic existence of the business.

Digital transformation is shaped within the framework of the strategic responses businesses give to digital advancement. This process not only has a profound impact on operational performance but also on the value creation potential of businesses (Laudien et al., 2024). Putra and Mahendrawathi (2024) define digital transformation as "the creation of a radical change in the culture, business processes, business model structure, and corporate competencies of a business through the use of digital technologies." This definition indicates that the transformation is not a superficial process but a fundamental change.

4. CONTRIBUTIONS OF DIGITALIZATION TO CORPORATE SUSTAINABILITY

The concepts of digitalization and sustainability, as two mega trends, have now started to occupy a broader place on the agenda of businesses together. One of the most striking aspects of this context is seen in studies that emphasize the multifaceted contribution of digitalization to sustainability. In studies that comprehensively examine these contributions, it is observed that they progress by addressing factors such as organizational culture, leadership, management structure, employee competencies, and technology (Feliciano-Cestero et al., 2023; Zhang et al., 2023). The impact of these factors on the success of businesses' sustainability strategies is evaluated in a multidimensional manner.

In this context, the groupings include contributions in terms of business processes and sectoral applications within enterprises, contributions to corporate culture, management, and transformation within the organization, and contributions to the performance of the business. Each of the specified contributions is explained below.

4.1. Contribution to Business Process Management (BPM) and Industries

Digitalization leads to changes that can quickly render the management of existing business processes obsolete for companies, necessitating strategic restructuring. Business process management (BPM) is a concept based on the integration of management, control, and organization to guide business processes within the organization and meet the needs of customers and other stakeholders. A business process is a complete, dynamically coordinated series of activities or logically related tasks that need to be carried out to provide value to customers or achieve other strategic objectives.

It is an especially important tool in ensuring the consistency and development of business operations. Implementing successful business process management often requires six key capability areas. These capability areas are strategic alignment, management, methods, information technology, people, and culture (Kerpedzhiev, König, Röglinger, & Rosemann, 2020). There is a widespread acceptance that digital technologies have gained importance in the management of business processes in recent years. It is widely accepted that many organizations benefit from digitalization to automate their business processes. Among these, examples of the widespread use of digitalization in automating business processes in different sectors, such as tax offices, healthcare providers, and transportation companies, can be shown (Iden, Danilova, & Eikebrokk, 2025).

Digitalization in business process management not only increases efficiency but also builds new ways of creating value and new business models. With the rapid developments in communication and information technologies, digitalization has accelerated further with the fourth industrial revolution, known as Industry 4.0, and has brought digitalization to a priority position on businesses' strategic agendas. Digitalization refers to the integration of cyber-physical systems into production processes and encompasses components such as IoT, artificial intelligence, cloud computing, big data, robotic systems, and augmented reality (Lasi et al., 2014; Mathur, 2022). Rehman et al. (2023) define these technologies as fundamental tools for a sustainable future. Digital technologies such as artificial intelligence, cloud computing, big data, and blockchain have fundamentally transformed the way organizations operate; they have led to significant innovations in processes and business models (Chen et al., 2024, p.3). Digital technologies such as the Internet of Things, automation, and artificial intelligence optimize business processes from production to logistics. The integration of digital technologies into business processes provides benefits such as reducing resource usage, increasing efficiency in production, and improving waste management. At the same time, the adoption of digital technologies can create value from their environmental and social benefits, leading to sustainable innovations (Ardito, 2023). Feliciano-Cestero et al. (2023) state that digitalization reduces production costs, renders physical distances insignificant, and facilitates communication, thereby promoting internationalization. In a study conducted by Grybauskas et al. (2022), it was revealed that digital transformation increases productivity, accelerates innovation processes, and improves quality control systems. This structural transformation provides businesses with a competitive advantage and contributes to economic development.

This transformation has made digitalization a strategic necessity for businesses to gain a competitive advantage, adapt to changing market conditions, and achieve sustainable development goals (Del Rio Castro et al., 2021; Türkyılmaz, 2024, p.279). If information and communication technologies are not included in the strategies that businesses implement to achieve their sustainable development goals, sustainability cannot be ensured. Businesses need to develop their operational capacities and improve their performance with digital technologies to achieve these goals (Costa et al., 2022).

Digital transformation offers multifaceted contributions to businesses. By automating and optimizing processes with digital tools, resource usage becomes efficient, leading to improvements in important business processes such as cost reduction, increased productivity, and enhanced customer satisfaction (Loebbecke & Picot, 2015; Ribeiro-Navarrete et al., 2021). Digitalization offers the opportunity to fundamentally transform businesses' internal processes, customer interfaces, and product/service offerings, creating a more environmentally friendly structure. Thanks to digital technologies, tangible sustainability benefits such as process automation, resource use efficiency, and emission reduction can be achieved (Isensee et al., 2020, p.3).

The sectoral impacts of digitalization are also noteworthy. Fareed et al. (2024) analyze the use of technologies such as artificial intelligence, IoT, and machine learning in the logistics sector, stating that these technologies positively impact the environmental, economic, and social dimensions of sustainability. However, the lack of digital initiatives and policy inadequacies have been reported as limiting factors in the process. On the other hand, Holzmann and Gregori (2023) emphasize that digital tools contribute to sustainable entrepreneurship processes and that

AI-supported solutions play an effective role in solving environmental and social problems. The impact of digital technologies on sustainability in the construction and agriculture sectors is also documented in studies that explain practical examples. In the construction sector, GIS, BIM, and 3D printing technologies play an effective role in reducing waste and improving recycling processes (Sepasgozar et al., 2021). Digital applications in agriculture reduce food waste and contribute to environmental sustainability (Benyam et al., 2021). For example, Tesla, one of the brands that most effectively uses digital transformation to reduce carbon footprints, has provided cost savings for consumers through electric vehicle production, reduced carbon emissions, and uses artificial intelligence and wireless software to enhance customer experience. Trying to create a sustainable future, Tesla has made electric vehicles attractive, leading to a significant change in the automotive industry. Unlike the traditional approach, the Tesla business model aims to reduce costs by decreasing dependency on external suppliers and creating an ecosystem that enables sustainable energy production.

4.2. Contribution to Corporate Culture, Governance, and Organizational Transformation

Digitalization should not be considered merely a technological transition; it also leads organizations to undergo a comprehensive transformation process at strategic, structural, and cultural levels. New digital formations such as the sharing economy, digital platforms, and mobile payment systems are transforming traditional business processes, leading companies to design more agile and data-driven processes. This transformation enhances organizations' agility capacities and improves their ability to respond quickly to uncertainties. However, the uncertainties brought by disruptive technologies pose strategic risks to organizations as much as the opportunities offered by digitalization. In this context, the role of digitalization in creating agile, innovative, and adaptive structures is of critical importance (Karimi & Walter, 2015; Chen et al., 2024). Gebayew et al. (2018) emphasize that businesses need to transform their strategic plans and organizational structures in order to adapt to digital business models.

The digital transformation process brings not only structural but also cultural restructuring. In order for digitalization to be successful, it is necessary to harmonize environmental awareness, strategic orientations, and corporate values within the organization. This alignment supports the formation of a sustainable corporate culture; it directs businesses towards a more innovative, agile, flexible, and data-driven cultural structure (Isensee et al., 2020, pp. 7–8). This transformation also affects not only the culture of businesses but also their structural arrangements and decision-making mechanisms. Transitioning from traditional vertical hierarchical structures to more horizontal organizational models; decision-making processes are becoming more stakeholder-driven, participatory, and flexible.

However, digitalization also provides significant conveniences and improvements in the implementation of governance principles. Basic governance principles such as transparency, traceability, and accountability are being implemented more effectively with the widespread adoption of digital technologies. Especially with the increase in open data applications, corporate transparency and accountability are strengthened, and the risks of corruption are reduced (Iy, 2025). At the same time, access to information is becoming easier; through digital tools, environmental indicators such as electricity and water consumption, and carbon emissions can be monitored and reported more effectively. In this way, sustainability practices become more transparent, traceable, and accountable. Additionally, the digitalization of processes reduces paper consumption and allows for more effective monitoring of environmental, social, and governance (ESG) performance (Seele, 2016, p.19).

By means of digitalization, businesses have turned towards the use of green information technologies and green information systems. These systems not only reduce the damage to the environment by improving the production phase but also ensure their integration into the corporate culture, enabling internal stakeholders to adopt an environmentally friendly approach. Melville (2010), Seidel et al. (2017), and Tim et al. (2017) state that green information technology applications reduce carbon emissions and enhance environmental sustainability performance, while green information systems contribute to increasing environmental awareness. Thus, green information technologies and green information systems contribute to the enhancement of businesses' sustainable environmental performance and the development of their value systems.

The strategic contribution of digitalization can be exemplified by the increase in the long-term resilience capacity of the business. As an example of this situation, the challenges faced by businesses during crisis periods and their rapid adaptation to the new situation thanks to digitalization can be mentioned. During the COVID-19 pandemic, it was observed that firms with digital infrastructure adapted more quickly to changing environmental conditions and ensured business continuity more effectively (Abidi, El Herradi, & Sakha, 2023). In addition to these positive aspects of digitalisation, there are also various risks. The following section presents the risks.

5. THE RISKS OF DIGITALIZATION ON CORPORATE SUSTAINABILITY

Although there are limited studies in the literature that comprehensively address the impact of digitalization on sustainability, existing research indicates both positive and negative relationships between digitalization and sustainability. Some studies indicate that digitalization plays a significant role in achieving sustainability goals by increasing efficiency, developing new business models, and optimizing resource use, as mentioned in the previous section. However, the infrastructure deficiencies, high implementation costs, and technological compatibility issues that arise during the digital transformation process are considered the main obstacles to this process (Iy, 2025).

Although digitalization offers significant opportunities for achieving corporate sustainability and sustainable development goals, it also draws attention to various risks and negative impacts associated with this process. Digital transformation, while providing positive outcomes such as energy efficiency, resource management, and environmental benefits, also brings along risks like cybersecurity threats, digital inequalities, high costs, and electronic waste (e-waste). The following section explains what these specified risks are and the consequences they may bring.

The following section explains what these specified risks are and the potential consequences they may cause.

5.1. High Costs and Digital Skills Gap

One of the most fundamental issues encountered in the digital transformation process is the high implementation and integration costs. Digital technologies have evolved, diversified, and become more complex over time. With the implementation of digitalization in businesses, technical and operational challenges have also emerged. Due to the immaturity of information and communication technologies, the continuous emergence of new technologies, and their complex structure, the integration of digital transformation into businesses and business model innovation is becoming more difficult (Aksin-Sivrikaya & Bhattacharya, 2017, p. p.45). To fully integrate digitization and prevent data loss or theft, infrastructure must be established (Bradley, 2007, p. p.157). In addition to the increase in infrastructure costs, it has been demonstrated in many studies that energy consumption also rises with digitalization (Lange et al., 2020).

Each of the systems such as artificial intelligence, big data, cloud solutions, and the Internet of Things requires specific expertise; this reveals the digital skills gap. Additionally, the widespread adoption of applications such as artificial intelligence, automation, and "dark factories" threatens especially the low-skilled workforce; it leads to the disappearance of certain professions and an increase in unemployment rates. This situation leads to the deepening of social inequalities for employees who do not possess the necessary knowledge and skills during the technological transformation process (Schmidpeter & Winter-Ebmer, 2021). Trittin-Ulbrich et al. (2021, p.13) state that businesses need professionals specialized in different fields to sustainably implement digital transformation, which creates cost pressure in terms of both training and outsourcing. In platform-based businesses, employees expend more effort and energy to adapt to digital technologies and to use these complex technologies. In this situation, it can lead to a decrease in efficiency by causing unseen workloads in the tasks being carried out (Bucher, Schou & Waldkirch, 2021). The constant monitoring of employees through digital systems creates pressure on them, leading to management and trust issues. It leads to a decrease in the employee's sense of belonging to the organization. At the organizational level, it increases costs by raising the employee turnover rate (Trittin-Ulbrich et al., 2021).

Investing in training processes to adapt their personnel to digital technologies or turning to specialized external resources in this field increases the overall business expenses. Additionally, the constant evolution of digital technologies and the rapid introduction of technological innovations are making the sustainability of investments uncertain and complicating the decision-making processes of businesses (Ardito, 2023, p.5256).

5.2. Privacy and Cybersecurity Risks

With digitalization, the collection and processing of customer data and operational information in digital environments also increase the risks of privacy violations and cyber attacks. The ways in which digital service providers collect, process, and use personal data bring about privacy violations, lack of transparency, and data security risks (Renn et al., 2021, p. 26). Flyverbom et al. (2017) point out that big data analytics and data-driven digital systems threaten privacy rights, while Scholz (2017) highlights the erosion of customer trust as one of the negative impacts of digitalization on social sustainability. With digitalization, customer data is continuously monitored, paving the way for privacy violations by companies, and these data can be used for political purposes (Trittin-Ulbrich et al., 2021).

Context: It is stated that with digitalization, customer data is continuously monitored, paving the way for privacy violations by companies, and this data can be used for political purposes (Trittin-Ulbrich et al., 2021). In this context, the data-based advantages brought by digitalization can turn into serious risks threatening both corporate sustainability and public trust if effective strategies in the areas of security and privacy are not developed. In this context, the data-based advantages brought by digitalization can turn into serious risks threatening both corporate sustainability and public trust if effective strategies in the areas of security and privacy are not developed.

Cyber attacks appear in various forms such as malware, ransomware, phishing, supply chain attacks, and data breaches, negatively impacting both internal system security and stakeholder relationships. Additionally, the unauthorized sharing of personal data creates situations that violate data protection regulations (such as GDPR), bringing legal risks along with it. Ologeanu-Taddei et al. (2025) emphasize that digitalization increases the risk of information pollution and misinformation, creating negative impacts on social sustainability. Especially, the anonymity provided by social media increases tendencies that threaten social cohesion, such as hate speech, polarization, and the spread of fake news. This can have a destructive impact on democratic processes in the long term (Renn et al., 2021, pp. 26–27). As an example of this situation, Amazon uses browsers to monitor the activities and evaluate the performance of employees in France. These browsers used by employees store every piece of data and even record the periods of inactivity, ensuring constant surveillance. The French National Commission on Informatics and Liberty (CNIL) found this practice excessively intrusive and imposed a fine of 32 million euros on Amazon for violations of the obligation to ensure the security of personal data and the obligation to provide information and transparency (CNIL, 2024). In conclusion, for digital transformation to be successful, it is essential to address privacy, data protection, and cybersecurity risks in a multidimensional and proactive manner, parallel to technological developments.

5.3. Electronic Waste and Environmental Risks

One of the most significant environmental risks posed by digitalization is the increase in electronic waste (e-waste) production. The increasing demand for digital technologies is causing short-lived hardware to be quickly phased out, which creates serious environmental threats in regions with insufficient recycling capacity (Kalia et al., 2022). Ardito (2023, p.5256) states that this situation contradicts sustainability goals and that the levels of digitalization among countries create differences in environmental impacts.

While it is true that digitalization offers opportunities in terms of energy efficiency and resource optimization, it is noted that the increase in the number of digital devices and the proliferation of data centers have led to an increase in total energy and resource consumption. Especially services like cloud services and video streaming platforms consume a large amount of energy. Moreover, while the widespread adoption of digital production systems like Industry 4.0 is expected to provide environmental benefits, the absolute increase in production volume overshadows these gains and creates rebound effects (Renn et al., 2021, p.24).

E-waste contains harmful chemicals such as lead, cadmium, and brominated flame retardants, directly harming human health and the environment (Aksin-Sivrikaya & Bhattacharya, 2017, p.46). Alieva and Powell (2023), on the other hand, evaluate digital waste not only as a hardware-based issue but also in the context of data that is not collected, processed, or misinterpreted during production processes. In conclusion, minimizing the negative impacts of digitalization on environmental sustainability necessitates the development of more holistic and inclusive strategies on a global scale in areas such as the management of digital waste and the monitoring of energy consumption.

5.4. Digital Inequality and Social Exclusion

Another significant risk brought by digitalization is digital inequality. The digital divide refers to the differences that arise between individuals, businesses, and countries in terms of access to, ownership of, and use of information and communication technologies. Vassilakopoulou & Hustad (2023, p.955) argue that these inequalities pose a significant barrier to sustainable digital societies. Especially blockchain technology is seen as a powerful tool in providing transparency and traceability throughout the value chain. However, for this technology to be widely adopted, all stakeholders need to share sensitive information about the production processes. This situation can create barriers such as inequality in access to information and a lack of trust (Kottmeyer, 2021, p. 21). Despite the promises of transparency and traceability of new technologies, the culture of trust and information sharing necessary for these systems to function effectively can lead to deepening digital inequalities.

Rydzewski (2019, p.98) states that the digital divide is not limited to physical access; it also includes factors such as digital literacy, the quality of access, and the competence to effectively use technology. Due to inadequate infrastructure, some communities are unable to benefit from the advantages provided by digitalization, which increases the risks of social exclusion and economic vulnerability (Perera et al., 2023, p.819). The digital divide creating inequalities in access and usage among different actors prevents everyone from equally benefiting from the potential of digital transformation.

The emergence of new digital-based business models creating conflicts with traditional sectors is another significant area of risk. For example, while sharing economy models (e.g., Uber, Airbnb) compete with traditional service providers, their lack of adherence to the same legal obligations can give these companies an unfair competitive advantage. The exploitation of such regulatory gaps can undermine social welfare and disrupt market equilibrium (Kottmeyer, 2021, pp. 22–23). Additionally, the tendency of digital platforms to monopolize due to their network effects can be harmful to consumers and small producers in the long run.

With the widespread adoption of the platform economy, digitalization is increasing insecurity in the labor market, creating new risks in the context of social justice and labor rights. In another study, it has been found that artificial intelligence and algorithms repeat and reinforce sexist, racist, or cultural biases, thereby increasing existing social inequalities (Zou & Schiebinger, 2018). In another study, it is found that artificial intelligence and algorithms repeat and reinforce sexist, racist, or cultural biases, thereby increasing existing social inequalities (Zou & Schiebinger, 2018). The biases carried by algorithmic systems call into question the assumptions of neutrality in digital technologies and reproduce existing forms of social discrimination in digital environments.

CONCLUSION

Digitalization and sustainability stand out as two main megatrends shaping the transformation of today's business world. This book chapter has addressed the multifaceted impacts of digitalization on corporate sustainability with a holistic approach. When the contributions of digitalization to businesses in the context of corporate sustainability are listed, it facilitates significant steps towards achieving corporate sustainability goals, such as increasing efficiency in business processes, optimizing resource usage, and reducing the negative impacts on the environment. Artificial intelligence used in decision support systems, big data analytics guiding production and marketing activities, and process automations achieved through cloud computing contribute to reducing the carbon footprint and minimizing energy consumption. However, the process of digitalization is not solely about opportunities. The production of electronic waste, cybersecurity risks, high costs, digital skill gaps, and digital inequalities are among the main threats posed by this process. In this context, digital transformation requires a strategic, cultural, and managerial change rather than just a technical transition.

This study is one of the rare works that evaluate the impact of digitalization on sustainability not only with its positive aspects but also with its potential risks. Studies to be conducted in the upcoming period, examining the impact of digitalization on sustainability performance at a more micro level within specific sectors, will provide significant contributions to the literature in this field.

REFERENCES

Abdullahi, M. A., Mohamed, Z., Shamsudin, M. N., Sharifuddin, J., & Ali, F. (2018). Effects of top leadership culture and strategic sustainability orientation on sustainable development among Malaysian herbal-based SMEs. *Business Strategy & Development*, *1*(2), 128–139. DOI: 10.1002/bsd2.17

Abidi, N., El Herradi, M., & Sakha, S. (2023). Digitalization and resilience during the COVID-19 pandemic. *Telecommunications Policy*, *47*(3), 102522. DOI: 10.1016/j.telpol.2023.102522 PMID: 37051116

Adekemi, P. (2025). Review on the role of Law in Corporate Sustainability and Green Practices. *Global Journal of Environmental Science & Sustainability*, *2*(1), 1–8. DOI: 10.69798/56256994

Afum, E., Agyabeng-Mensah, Y., Sun, Z., Frimpong, B., Kusi, L. Y., & Acquah, I. S. K. (2020). Exploring the link between green manufacturing, operational competitiveness, firm reputation and sustainable performance dimensions: A mediated approach. *Journal of Manufacturing Technology Management*, *31*(7), 1417–1438. DOI: 10.1108/JMTM-02-2020-0036

Agheli, L., & Taghvaee, V. M. (2022). Political stability effect on environment and weak sustainability in Asian countries. *Sustainability Analytics and Modeling*, *2*, 100007. DOI: 10.1016/j.samod.2022.100007

Aksin-Sivrikaya, S., & Bhattacharya, C. B. (2017). Where digitalization meets sustainability: Opportunities and challenges. In *Sustainability in a Digital World* (pp. 37–49). New Opportunities Through New Technologies. DOI: 10.1007/978-3-319-54603-2_3

Ali, M. H., Zailani, S., Iranmanesh, M., & Foroughi, B. (2019). Impacts of environmental factors on waste, energy, and resource management and sustainable performance. *Sustainability (Basel)*, *11*(8), 2443. DOI: 10.3390/su11082443

Alieva, J., & Powell, D. (2023). The significance of digital waste in the automation of lean practices. *The Quality Management Journal*, *30*(2), 121–134. DOI: 10.1080/10686967.2023.2171323

Ardito, L. (2023). The influence of firm digitalization on sustainable innovation performance and the moderating role of corporate sustainability practices: An empirical investigation. *Business Strategy and the Environment*, *32*(8), 5252–5272. DOI: 10.1002/bse.3415

Avelar, S., Borges-Tiago, T., Almeida, A., & Tiago, F. (2024). Confluence of sustainable entrepreneurship, innovation, and digitalization in SMEs. *Journal of Business Research*, *170*, 114346. DOI: 10.1016/j.jbusres.2023.114346

Bansal, P. (2005). Evolving sustainably: A longitudinal study of corporate sustainable development. *Strategic Management Journal*, *26*(3), 197–218. DOI: 10.1002/smj.441

Bekaroo, G., Bokhoree, C., & Pattinson, C. (2016). Impacts of ICT on the natural ecosystem: A grassroot analysis for promoting socio-environmental sustainability. *Renewable & Sustainable Energy Reviews*, *57*, 1580–1595. DOI: 10.1016/j.rser.2015.12.147

Benyam, A. A., Soma, T., & Fraser, E. (2021). Digital agricultural technologies for food loss and waste prevention and reduction: Global trends, adoption opportunities and barriers. *Journal of Cleaner Production*, *323*, 129099. DOI: 10.1016/j.jclepro.2021.129099

Blanka, C., Krumay, B., & Rueckel, D. (2022). The interplay of digital transformation and employee competency: A design science approach. *Technological Forecasting and Social Change*, *178*, 121575. DOI: 10.1016/j.techfore.2022.121575

Bradley, K. (2007). Defining digital sustainability. *Library Trends*, *56*(1), 148–163. DOI: 10.1353/lib.2007.0044

Bucher, E. L., Schou, P. K., & Waldkirch, M. (2021). Pacifying the algorithm–Anticipatory compliance in the face of algorithmic management in the gig economy. *Organization*, *28*(1), 44–67. DOI: 10.1177/1350508420961531

Çankaya, S. Y., & Sezen, B. (2015). Ekolojik yenilik ile sürdürülebilirlik performansı arasındaki ilişkide çevresel belirsizliğin moderatör etkisi. *Uluslararası Yönetim İktisat ve İşletme Dergisi*, *11*(2), 111–134.

Carroll, A. B. (1979). A three-dimensional conceptual model of corporate performance. *Academy of Management Review*, *4*(4), 497–505. DOI: 10.2307/257850

Chen, A., Li, L., & Shahid, W. (2024). Digital transformation as the driving force for sustainable business performance: A moderated mediation model of market-driven business model innovation and digital leadership capabilities. *Heliyon*, *10*(8), e29509. DOI: 10.1016/j.heliyon.2024.e29509 PMID: 38655293

Chen, D., Heyer, S., Ibbotson, S., Salonitis, K., Steingrímsson, J. G., & Thiede, S. (2015). Direct digital manufacturing: Definition, evolution, and sustainability implications. *Journal of Cleaner Production*, *107*, 615–625. DOI: 10.1016/j.jclepro.2015.05.009

Costa, I., Riccotta, R., Montini, P., Stefani, E., de Souza Goes, R., Gaspar, M. A., & Larieira, C. L. C. (2022). The degree of contribution of digital transformation technology on company sustainability areas. *Sustainability (Basel), 14*(1), 462. DOI: 10.3390/su14010462

Dedrick, J. (2010). Green IS: Concepts and issues for information systems research. *Communications of the Association for Information Systems, 27*(11), 173–184. DOI: 10.17705/1CAIS.02711

Del Río Castro, G., González Fernández, M. C., & Uruburu Colsa, Á. (2021). Unleashing the convergence amid digitalization and sustainability towards pursuing the sustainable development goals (SDGs): A holistic review. *Journal of Cleaner Production, 280*, 122204. DOI: 10.1016/j.jclepro.2020.122204

Dereköy, F. (2015). Kurumsal yönetim ve temel dinamikleri. *Ekonomi ve Yönetim Araştırmaları Dergisi, 4*(1), 31–51.

Dernbach, J. C., & Mintz, J. A. (2011). Environmental laws and sustainability: An introduction. *Sustainability (Basel), 3*(3), 531–540. DOI: 10.3390/su3030531

Dey, P. K., Malesios, C., De, D., Chowdhury, S., & Abdelaziz, F. B. (2020). The impact of lean management practices and sustainably-oriented innovation on sustainability performance of small and medium-sized enterprises: Empirical evidence from the UK. *British Journal of Management, 31*(1), 141–161. DOI: 10.1111/1467-8551.12388

Dvorský, J., Bednarz, J., & Blajer-Gołębiewska, A. (2023). The impact of corporate reputation and social media engagement on the sustainability of SMEs: Perceptions of top managers and the owners. Equilibrium. *Quarterly Journal of Economics and Economic Policy, 18*(3), 779–811. DOI: 10.24136/eq.2023.025

Dyllick, T., & Hockerts, K. (2002). Beyond the business case for corporate sustainability. *Business Strategy and the Environment, 11*(2), 130–141. DOI: 10.1002/bse.323

Engert, S., Rauter, R., & Baumgartner, R. J. (2016). Exploring the integration of corporate sustainability into strategic management: A literature review. *Journal of Cleaner Production, 112*, 2833–2850. DOI: 10.1016/j.jclepro.2015.08.031

Fareed, A. G., De Felice, F., Forcina, A., & Petrillo, A. (2024). Role and applications of advanced digital technologies in achieving sustainability in multimodal logistics operations: A systematic literature review. *Sustainable Futures : An Applied Journal of Technology, Environment and Society, 8*, 100278. DOI: 10.1016/j.sftr.2024.100278

Feliciano-Cestero, M. M., Ameen, N., Kotabe, M., Paul, J., & Signoret, M. (2023). Is digital transformation threatened? A systematic literature review of the factors influencing firms' digital transformation and internationalization. *Journal of Business Research, 157,* 113546. DOI: 10.1016/j.jbusres.2022.113546

Fernández-Portillo, A., Almodóvar-González, M., Coca-Pérez, J. L., & Jiménez-Naranjo, H. V. (2019). Is sustainable economic development possible thanks to the deployment of ICT? *Sustainability (Basel), 11*(22), 6307. DOI: 10.3390/su11226307

Gebayew, C., Hardini, I. R., Panjaitan, G. H. A., & Kurniawan, N. B. (2018, October). A systematic literature review on digital transformation. In *2018 International Conference on Information Technology Systems and Innovation (ICITSI)*, 260-265. DOI: 10.1109/ICITSI.2018.8695912

Genç, R. (2017). The importance of communication in sustainability & sustainable strategies. *Procedia Manufacturing, 8,* 511–516. DOI: 10.1016/j.promfg.2017.02.065

Grybauskas, A., Stefanini, A., & Ghobakhloo, M. (2022). Social sustainability in the age of digitalization: A systematic literature review on the social implications of industry 4.0. *Technology in Society, 70,* 101997. DOI: 10.1016/j.techsoc.2022.101997

Guandalini, I. (2022). Sustainability through digital transformation: A systematic literature review for research guidance. *Journal of Business Research, 148,* 456–471. DOI: 10.1016/j.jbusres.2022.05.003

Holzmann, P., & Gregori, P. (2023). The promise of digital technologies for sustainable entrepreneurship: A systematic literature review and research agenda. *International Journal of Information Management, 68,* 102593. DOI: 10.1016/j.ijinfomgt.2022.102593

Iden, J., Danilova, K. B., & Eikebrokk, T. (2025). Business process management and digitalization – a reciprocal relationship. *Business Process Management Journal, 31*(2), 393–415. DOI: 10.1108/BPMJ-02-2024-0083

Isensee, C., Teuteberg, F., Griese, K.-M., & Topi, C. (2020). The relationship between organizational culture, sustainability, and digitalization in SMEs: A systematic review. *Journal of Cleaner Production, 275,* 122944. DOI: 10.1016/j.jclepro.2020.122944

Kajtazi, K., Rexhepi, G., Sharif, A., & Ozturk, I. (2023). Business model innovation and its impact on corporate sustainability. *Journal of Business Research, 166,* 114082. DOI: 10.1016/j.jbusres.2023.114082

Karimi, J., & Walter, Z. (2015). The role of dynamic capabilities in responding to digital disruption: A factor-based study of the newspaper industry. *Journal of Management Information Systems, 32*(1), 39–81. DOI: 10.1080/07421222.2015.1029380

Kerpedzhiev, G. D., König, U. M., Röglinger, M., & Rosemann, M. (2021). An Exploration into Future Business Process Management Capabilities in View of Digitalization. *Business & Information Systems Engineering*, *63*(2), 83–96. DOI: 10.1007/s12599-020-00637-0

Kohtamäki, M., Parida, V., Oghazi, P., Gebauer, H., & Baines, T. (2019). Digital servitization business models in ecosystems: A theory of the firm. *Journal of Business Research*, *104*, 380–392. DOI: 10.1016/j.jbusres.2019.06.027

Kottmeyer, B. (2021). Digitisation and sustainable development: The opportunities and risks of using digital technologies for the implementation of a circular economy. *Journal of Entrepreneurship and Innovation in Emerging Economies*, *7*(1), 17–23. DOI: 10.1177/2393957520967799

Lange, S., Pohl, J., & Santarius, T. (2020). Digitalization and energy consumption. Does ICT reduce energy demand? *Ecological Economics*, *176*, 106760. DOI: 10.1016/j.ecolecon.2020.106760

Laudien, S. M., Reuter, U., Garcia, F. J. S., & Botella-Carrubi, D. (2024). Digital advancement and its effect on business model design: Qualitative-empirical insights. *Technological Forecasting and Social Change*, *200*, 123103. DOI: 10.1016/j.techfore.2023.123103

Li, Y., Cui, L., Wu, L., Lowry, P. B., Kumar, A., & Tan, K. H. (2023). Digitalization and network capability as enablers of business model innovation and sustainability performance: The moderating effect of environmental dynamism. *Journal of Information Technology*, *39*(4), 1–56.

Linnenluecke, M. K., & Griffiths, A. (2010). Corporate sustainability and organizational culture. *Journal of World Business*, *45*(4), 357–366. DOI: 10.1016/j.jwb.2009.08.006

Loebbecke, C., & Picot, A. (2015). Reflections on societal and business model transformation arising from digitization and big data analytics: A research agenda. *The Journal of Strategic Information Systems*, *24*(3), 149–157. DOI: 10.1016/j.jsis.2015.08.002

Ly, B. (2025). Leveraging leadership and digital transformation for sustainable development: Insights from Cambodia's public sector. *Sustainable Futures : An Applied Journal of Technology, Environment and Society*, *9*, 1–11. DOI: 10.1016/j.sftr.2025.100545

Mahmood, Z., Kouser, R., Ali, W., Ahmad, Z., & Salman, T. (2018). Does corporate governance affect sustainability disclosure? A mixed methods study. *Sustainability (Basel), 10*(1), 207–227. DOI: 10.3390/su10010207

McKinsey & Co. (2022). A digital path to sustainability. Retrieved from https://www.mckinsey.com/capabilities/operations/our-insights/a-digital-path-to-sustainability#/

Melville, N. P. (2010). Information systems innovation for environmental sustainability. *Management Information Systems Quarterly, 34*(1), 1–21. DOI: 10.2307/20721412

National Commission on Informatics and Liberty (CNIL). (2024). Employee monitoring: CNIL fined AMAZON FRANCE LOGISTIQUE €32 million. Erişim Linki: https://www.cnil.fr/en/employee-monitoring-cnil-fined-amazon-france-logistique-eu32-million

Nguyen, N., & Johnson, L. W. (2020). Consumer behaviour and environmental sustainability. *Journal of Consumer Behaviour, 19*(6), 539–541. DOI: 10.1002/cb.1892

Ologeanu-Taddei, R., Hönigsberg, S., Weritz, P., Wache, H., Mittermeier, F., Tana, S., Dang, D., Hautala-Kankaanpää, T., & Pekkola, S. (2025). The relationship of digital transformation and corporate sustainability: Synergies and tensions. *Technological Forecasting and Social Change, 210*, 123809. DOI: 10.1016/j.techfore.2024.123809

Perera, P., Selvanathan, S., Bandaralage, J., & Su, J. J. (2023). The impact of digital inequality in achieving sustainable development: A systematic literature review. *Equality, Diversity and Inclusion, 42*(6), 805–825. DOI: 10.1108/EDI-08-2022-0224

Putra, H., & Mahendrawathi, E. R. (2024). The role of business process management in digital innovation and digital transformation: A systematic literature review. *Procedia Computer Science, 234*, 829–836. DOI: 10.1016/j.procs.2024.03.069

Rachinger, M., Rauter, R., Müller, C., Vorraber, W., & Schirgi, E. (2019). Digitalization and its influence on business model innovation. *Journal of Manufacturing Technology Management, 30*(8), 1143–1160. DOI: 10.1108/JMTM-01-2018-0020

Renn, O., Beier, G., & Schweizer, P.-J. (2021). The opportunities and risks of digitalisation for sustainable development: A systemic perspective. GAIA – Ecological Perspectives for Science and Society, 30(1), 23–28.

Reppmann, M., Harms, S., Edinger-Schons, L. M., & Foege, J. N. (2025). Activating the sustainable consumer: The role of customer involvement in corporate sustainability. *Journal of the Academy of Marketing Science, 53*(2), 310–340. DOI: 10.1007/s11747-024-01036-7

Ribeiro-Navarrete, S., Botella-Carrubi, D., Palacios-Marqués, D., & Orero-Blat, M. (2021). The effect of digitalization on business performance: An applied study of KIBS. *Journal of Business Research, 126*, 319–326. DOI: 10.1016/j.jbusres.2020.12.065

Ruiz-Pérez, F., Lleo, A., & Ormazabal, M. (2021). Employee sustainable behaviors and their relationship with Corporate Sustainability: A Delphi study. *Journal of Cleaner Production, 329*, 129742. DOI: 10.1016/j.jclepro.2021.129742

Rydzewski, P. (2025). Digital inequality and sustainable development. *Problemy Ekorozwoju, 20*(1), 96–108. DOI: 10.35784/preko.6691

Schmidpeter, B., & Winter-Ebmer, R. (2021). Automation, unemployment, and the role of labor market training. *European Economic Review, 137*, 103808. DOI: 10.1016/j.euroecorev.2021.103808

Scholz, R. W., Bartelsman, E. J., Diefenbach, S., Franke, L., Grunwald, A., Helbing, D., Hill, R., Hilty, L., Höjer, M., Klauser, S., Montag, C., Parycek, P., Prote, J. P., Renn, O., Reichel, A., Schuh, G., Steiner, G., & Viale Pereira, G. (2018). Unintended side effects of the digital transition: European scientists' messages from a proposition-based expert round table. *Sustainability (Basel), 10*(6), 2001. DOI: 10.3390/su10062001

Seele, P. (2016). Digitally unified reporting: How XBRL-based real-time transparency helps in combining integrated sustainability reporting and performance control. *Journal of Cleaner Production, 136*, 65–77. DOI: 10.1016/j.jclepro.2016.01.102

Seidel, S., Bharati, P., Fridgen, G., Watson, R. T., Albizri, A., Boudreau, M. C. M., Butler, T., Chandra Kruse, L., Guzman, I., Karsten, H., Lee, H., Melville, N., Rush, D., Toland, J., & Watts, S. (2017). The sustainability imperative in information systems research. *Communications of the Association for Information Systems, 40*(1), 40–52. DOI: 10.17705/1CAIS.04003

Sepasgozar, S. M., Mair, D. F., Tahmasebinia, F., Shirowzhan, S., Li, H., Richter, A., & Xu, S. (2021). Waste management and possible directions of utilising digital technologies in the construction context. *Journal of Cleaner Production, 324*, 129095. DOI: 10.1016/j.jclepro.2021.129095

Song, Y., Sahut, J. M., Zhang, Z., Tian, Y., & Hikkerova, L. (2022). The effects of government subsidies on the sustainable innovation of university-industry collaboration. *Technological Forecasting and Social Change, 174*, 121233. DOI: 10.1016/j.techfore.2021.121233

Souto, J. E. (2022). Organizational creativity and sustainability-oriented innovation as drivers of sustainable development: Overcoming firms' economic, environmental and social sustainability challenges. *Journal of Manufacturing Technology Management, 33*(4), 805–826. DOI: 10.1108/JMTM-01-2021-0018

Tim, Y., Pan, S. L., Bahri, S., & Fauzi, A. (2017). Digitally enabled affordances for community-driven environmental movement in rural Malaysia. *Information Systems Journal, 28*(1), 48–75. DOI: 10.1111/isj.12140

Tjoa, A. M., & Tjoa, S. (2016). The role of ICT to achieve the UN sustainable development goals (SDG). In ICT for promoting human development and protecting the environment: 6th IFIP World Information Technology Forum, WITFOR 2016 [Springer International Publishing.]. *Proceedings, 6*, 3–13.

Trica, C. L., Banacu, C. S., & Busu, M. (2019). Environmental factors and sustainability of the circular economy model at the European Union level. *Sustainability (Basel), 11*(4), 1114. DOI: 10.3390/su11041114

Trittin-Ulbrich, H., Scherer, A. G., Munro, I., & Whelan, G. (2021). Exploring the dark and unexpected sides of digitalization: Toward a critical agenda. *Organization, 28*(1), 8–25. DOI: 10.1177/1350508420968184

Turkyılmaz, S. (2024). Dijital dönüşüm: Tarihçesi, tanımı ve işletmeler üzerindeki etkisi. *Nişantaşı Üniversitesi Sosyal Bilimler Dergisi, 12*(1), 276–297. DOI: 10.52122/nisantasisbd.1459265

Tüyen, Z. (2020). İşletmelerde sürdürülebilirlik kavramı ve sürdürebilirliği etkileyen etmenler. İstanbul Ticaret Üniversitesi Sosyal Bilimler Dergisi, 19(37), 91–117.

Unsworth, K. L., Davis, M. C., Russell, S. V., & Bretter, C. (2021). Employee green behaviour: How organizations can help the environment. *Current Opinion in Psychology, 42*, 1–6. DOI: 10.1016/j.copsyc.2020.12.006 PMID: 33535131

Van der Velden, M. (2018). Digitalisation and the UN Sustainable Development Goals: What role for design. ID&A Interaction Design & Architecture(s), (37), 160–174.

Vassilakopoulou, P., & Hustad, E. (2023). Bridging digital divides: A literature review and research agenda for information systems research. *Information Systems Frontiers, 25*(3), 955–969. DOI: 10.1007/s10796-020-10096-3 PMID: 33424421

Wagner, N., & Wiśnicki, B. (2022). The importance of emerging technologies to the increasing of corporate sustainability in shipping companies. *Sustainability (Basel), 14*(12475), 1–20. DOI: 10.3390/su141912475

WCED. (1987). *Our common future*. Oxford University Press.

Wongsnuopparat, S., & Chunyang, W. (2021). Corporate sustainability: Study of factors that affect corporate towards organizational sustainability in today's fast-changing world. *Journal of Management and Sustainability*, *11*(2), 56–73. DOI: 10.5539/jms.v11n2p56

World Economic Forum (WEF). (2020). Unlocking technology for the global goals. Retrieved from https://www.weforum.org/publications/unlocking-technology-for-the-global-goals/

WWF. (2025). Dünya saati. Retrieved from https://www.wwf.org.tr/harekete_gec/dunya_saati_2025/

Yurdakul, M. (2020). İşletmelerde sürdürülebilirliğin sağlanmasında eko inovasyon uygulamaları: Bir model önerisi. İşletme Ekonomi ve Yönetim Araştırmaları Dergisi, 3(1), 15–33.

Zhang, Y., Ma, X., Pang, J., Xing, H., & Wang, J. (2023). The impact of digital transformation of manufacturing on corporate performance—The mediating effect of business model innovation and the moderating effect of innovation capability. *Research in International Business and Finance*, *64*, 101890. DOI: 10.1016/j.ribaf.2023.101890

Zhao, Z., & Xing, Z. (2024). Corporate management, green finance, and sustainability. *Humanities & Social Sciences Communications*, *11*(6), 1–8.

Zou, J., & Schiebinger, J. (2018). IA can be Sexist and Racist - it's Time to Make it Fair. *Nature*, *559*(7714), 324–326. DOI: 10.1038/d41586-018-05707-8 PMID: 30018439

Zvarikova, K., Dvorsky, J., & Metzker, Z. (2024). Model of sustainability of SMEs in V4 countries. *Journal of Business Economics and Management*, *25*(2), 226–245. DOI: 10.3846/jbem.2024.20729

Chapter 14
Transforming Business Process Management Through Artificial Intelligence and Predictive Analytics

Ramalakshmi Murugan
https://orcid.org/0009-0004-5528-9531
Google, USA

ABSTRACT

Big Data and AI technologies are revolutionizing Business Process Management (BPM). This chapter focuses on how AI and predictive analytics are transforming traditional forms of BPM. The combination of these technologies presents major opportunities utilizing insights from data to optimize decision making, advancing process enhancement beyond mere automation, increasing responsiveness and flexibility of operations, as well as innovativeness. AI enhances BPM with the capacity to respond to market changes and deliver services more rapidly and tailor them to individuals. Nevertheless, these advantages depend critically on data issue resolution. Unresolved challenges such as the 'data paradox', quality concerns such as bias and inconsistency, and complicated data processing including cleansing, standardization, privacy, and security present obstacles. Emerging trends suggest more advanced automation and predictive modeling, collaboration with ethicists, and pivoting BPM toward self-governing, self-evolving systems that provide users substantial competitive leverage.

DOI: 10.4018/979-8-3373-3336-6.ch014

1. INTRODUCTION

1.1 BPM in The Age of Data and Intelligence

In the modern day market, organizations that cling onto inflexible business processes find themselves at a perilous competitive disadvantage. Customer needs and sentiments change so quickly, sometimes before companies get a chance to redesign their business processes and implement a change to their products (Prasad et al., 2023).

For so many years, Business Process Management or BPM has acted as the pillar of an organization's fuel for efficiency and effectiveness. The principles of identifying, designing, executing, monitoring, and optimizing the business processes have enabled firms from varied sectors to streamline operations, contain expenditure, and improve customer satisfaction. However, the world of business is experiencing a profound change due to the increased availability of big data and the rapidly evolving Artificial Intelligence (AI) and its adjacent technologies. This new age of 'big data' and AI comes with a huge amount of fresh opportunities for organizations adopting BPM. However, it also poses tremendous challenges for the practice of traditional BPM. In this chapter, we focus on how expanding fields of predictive analytics and Artificial Intelligence transform and evolve the concepts of BPM.

a. Introduction to Business Process Management

Business Process Management (BPM) is a methodology that companies adopt to optimize and manage business processes and enhance corporate performance value. The European Association of Business Process Management (EABPM) defines BPM in simpler terms as an organized technique of controlling automatic and non-automatic processes to achieve company goals (Hammer, 2014).

BPM empowers organizations with a structure for organizing, supervising, and improving business processes that align with their goals. It reinforces that strong and agile processes are very important for running a successful business. The scope of BPM goes beyond process automation to include critical process redesign and re-engineering as well as optimization of all business activities.

Figure 1. **The BPM life cycle.** *The important phases of the Business Process Management life cycle, including process development, implementation of the processes, performance monitoring and assessing the outcomes and effectiveness of the processes. Source: Adapted from Ter Hofstede et al., 2009.*

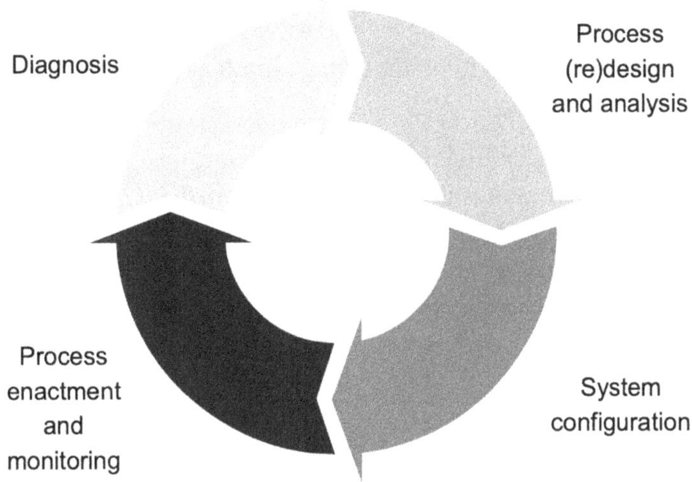

Business Process Management (BPM) works on a repetitive cycle that includes *designing*, *modelling*, *execution*, *monitoring*, and *optimization* (Figure 1). It encourages a process of continuous improvement for a company while helping them achieve enhanced operational effectiveness, adaptability to new changes, and superior outcome achievement. BPM enables businesses to fine-tune their workflows on a regular basis, thus allowing for discovering hidden inefficiencies, actively responding to market demand, and eliminating existing inefficiencies.

Achieving success in any process relies heavily on the major participants, effective management, and advanced technology to ensure that the business is developed sustainably. Adopting business process management (BPM) facilitates the incorporation of a customer-oriented, holistic view at organizational and strategic management levels and integrates all relevant considerations and objectives. This fosters organizational performance improvement through process-optimized, data-driven decision–making.

b. Introduction to Artificial Intelligence (AI)

Artificial Intelligence (AI) is a part of computer science that focuses on making computers act like humans to help improve performance in science and technology. AI aims to copy human intelligence, solve complex problems, create machines that can do tasks requiring human thinking, and build systems that can learn independently. Two key parts of AI are machine learning and deep learning (Figure 2). Machine learning uses powerful algorithms to *solve* problems, while deep learning uses layered neural networks to do the same (Ghosh and Thirugnanam, 2021).

Figure 2. **Overview of Artificial Intelligence**. *Hierarchical relationship among the important fields in intelligent computing, with Artificial Intelligence (AI) in the base, Machine Learning (ML) above it, and Deep learning at the top. Artificial Intelligence is a broader concept of machines performing tasks, Machine Learning is a subset of AI that focuses on systems that learn from data, and Deep Learning is a specialised branch of ML that uses specialised neural networks to model complex patterns in large datasets.*

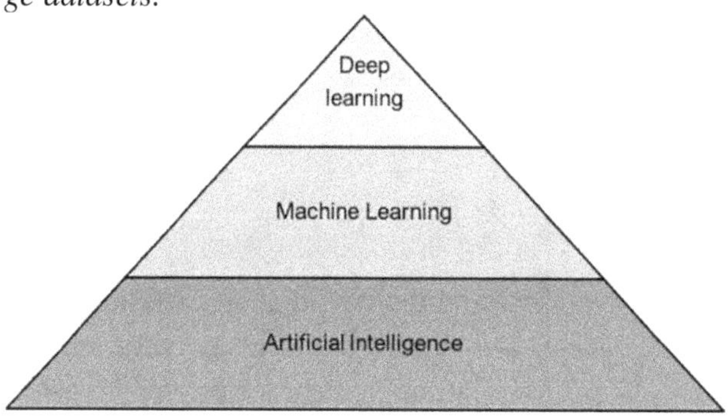

I. Machine Learning

Just like humans can think, learn from past experiences, and improve over time, AI machines can also learn from past experiences using a concept called Machine Learning (ML). Machine learning involves creating algorithms that allow computers to independently learn from data and past experiences. In this process, the machine studies a dataset called training data and uses algorithms to predict possible outcomes based on new inputs. In simple terms, the more information the machine learns, the more efficient it gets.

This is especially useful for handling large, complex datasets that are difficult and time-consuming for humans to process. The machine takes data as input, processes it using algorithms, and provides results automatically.

II. Deep Learning

Deep Learning (DL) is a function of Machine Learning (ML), which itself is a subset of Artificial Intelligence (AI). In ML, systems learn from given data and past experiences to make predictions. Deep Learning takes this a step further by simulating the structure and function of the human brain, using layers of algorithms similar to neurons in a nervous system.

In machine learning (ML), learning is conducted either through supervised or unsupervised methods. When multiple layers of algorithms are used, it is called Deep Learning or a Deep Neural Network (DNN). DNN is typically made up of three layers: 1) the Input Layer - where data is entered or input; 2) the Hidden Layers - where the data processing happens; and 3) the Output Layer - where results are produced. The more layers there are, the better the system can analyze and represent complex data, such as identifying edges and boundaries in an image.

c. Introduction to Predictive Analytics

Predictive analytics is a forecasting branch of statistical and analytics techniques. It draws on statistics, machine learning, databases, and optimization methods (Figure 3). Predictive analytics predicts the future by analyzing current and historical data (Kumar et al., 2018).

Figure 3. **The spectrum of BI technologies.** *It consists of various range of technologies, from basic data reporting to advanced analytics, including predictive analytics, dashboards, scorecards, OLAP, visualization tools, query, reporting and search tools. These technologies vary in complexity and value, helping organisations transform raw data in to actions for informed decision-making. Source: Adapted from Eckerson, W. W. (2007)*

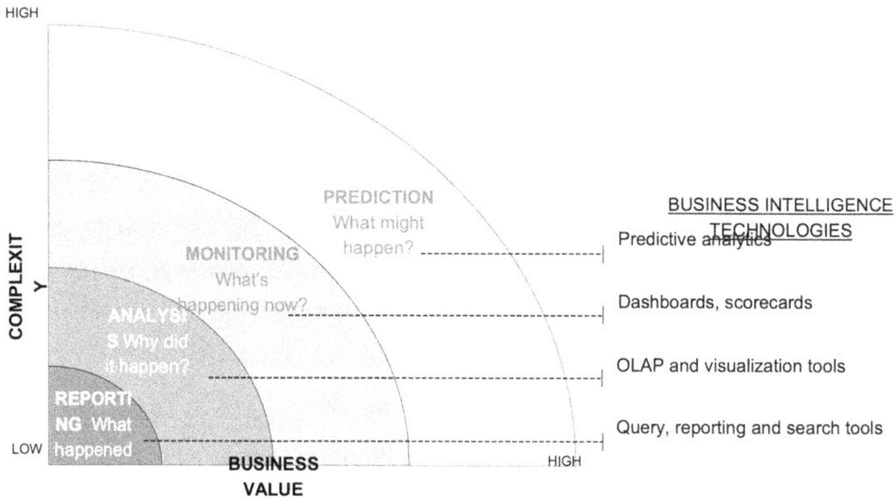

The future events and behavior of variables can be predicted using the models of predictive analytics. A score is given by most of the predictive analytics models. A higher score indicates the higher likelihood of occurrence of an event and a lower score indicates the lower likelihood of occurrence of the event. Historical and transactional data patterns are exploited by these models to find out the solution for many business and science problems.

These models are helpful in identifying the risks and opportunities for every individual customer, employee, or manager of an organization. With the increase in attention towards decision support solutions, predictive analytics models have dominated in the AI and BPM field (Kumar et al., 2018).

There are four key techniques of predictive analytics that is relevant to BPM:

i. Regression

Regression analysis is a statistical method used to study and analyze relationships between variables. Let's look at a simple example - financial analysts might do a regression analysis to understand how a price increase might affect demand or how a slight change in monetary policy might impact inflation. For all these types of analysis, analysts and data scientists collect relevant data and then use regression analysis to quantify the relationships between different variables. They also check the "statistical significance" of the results, which shows how confident they can be that the estimated relationship is accurate (Skyes, 1993).

ii. Classification

'Classification' is one of the first steps of pattern recognition. It is performed during data analysis and arranges information into different categories based on evaluating their likeness or common characteristics. It encompasses the whole process of pattern recognition within a dataset, which is a predefined set of classes, most often using some form of computation or statistics (Gordon, 1999).

iii. Clustering

Cluster analysis is one of the techniques employed to subdivide any given data into meaningful units referred to as clusters. These clusters are intended to depict the "natural" organization of the data. Although it is commonly used to gain insights about data, it can also serve other functions such as data pruning, compression, or expeditiously locating analogous points in the data. Cluster analysis has been widely applied in fields such as psychology, biology, statistics, machine learning, and data mining (Gupta et al., 2012).

iv. Forecasting

Forecasting is a mathematical technique that predicts the future using past data. A lot of events and activities in the business world are predicted using relevant historical data that is assessed mathematically and empirically. This approach is beneficial for short-term forecasting; however, due to an increase in unpredictability, medium- and long-term forecasts become increasingly unreliable (Walonick, 1993).

The industry or vertical of a particular business determines whether trend-based forecasting is possible or not. For some companies, such as clothing styles, have high volatility and are very difficult to predict. On the other hand, some businesses, such as energy consumption, are more stable and can be forecasted through mathematical models with greater accuracy. In new sectors or technologies, forecasting becomes almost impossible due to the lack of sufficient historical data.

There are many mathematical models for forecasting trends. Choosing the right model depends on historical data, which is analyzed through exploratory data analysis to identify patterns and cycles for selecting the best model.

1.2 The Synergy of AI, Predictive Analytics and BPM

Business processes can be improved with the use of advanced analytics, which include descriptive, diagnostic, predictive, and prescriptive problem solving. These methods enhance organizational intelligence by helping businesses make optimal choices from enormous datasets. Businesses are able to utilize advanced analytics to discover trends, forecast results, and implement efficient performance enhancement measures (Adesina et al., 2024).

Figure 4. **The Synergy of AI, Predictive Analytics and BPM.** *The integration of AI and predictive analytics with BPM enhances optimization, agility and responsiveness. Several examples illustrated include workflow automation, robotic process automation (RPA), natural language processing (NLP), intelligent system configuration, AI-powered anomaly detection, clustering, root cause analysis (RCA) and continuous process improvement.*

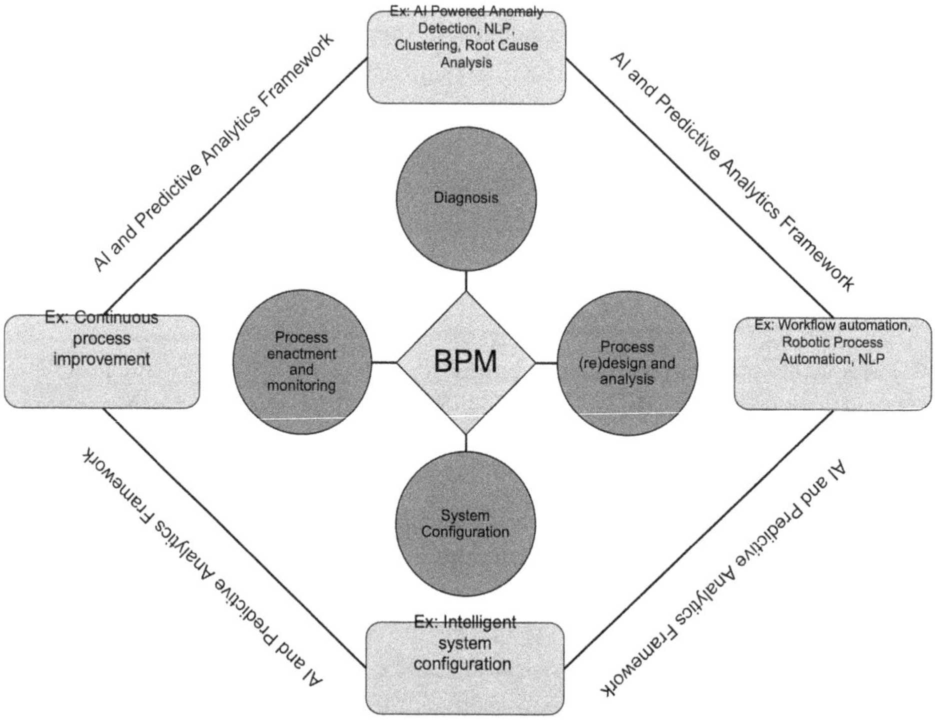

The incorporation of Artificial Intelligence into BPM can yield numerous benefits for organizations. The synergy between these two domains holds the potential to revolutionize how businesses operate, optimizing workflows, enhancing decision-making, and driving innovation. Intelligent Automation, with its ability to streamline repetitive tasks, analyze vast amounts of data, and make informed decisions, can be seamlessly integrated into Business Process Management to optimize workflows, reduce errors, and increase overall productivity (Kokala, 2024a).

This chapter aims to fill in the gaps as it moves beyond core learning frontiers using concepts, methodologies, and other illustrative frameworks that showcase how organizations can use data intelligence in fulfilling BPM goals, underpinning agility, innovation, and fresh competitive strategies faster in the era of digital transformation.

Integrating forecasting and AI into BPM arms an organization with unmatched tools for accomplishment as it improves decision making, reduces operational costs, increases customer satisfaction, and arms the company with the ability to quickly adapt to market stimuli (Figure 4).

Within this landscape of AI, ethical considerations are paramount for sustainable and trustworthy operations. The drive towards Responsible AI necessitates embedding ethical principles directly into the design, deployment, and monitoring of AI systems (Daniel et al., 2020). This is guided by comprehensive AI ethics guidelines from influential organizations such as the IEEE, which provides industry-specific recommendations for ethical AI development, and the OECD, which offers high-level principles for trustworthy AI that resonate across various sectors. To ensure these guidelines translate into practical safeguards, robust **AI governance models** are crucial. These models establish frameworks for accountability, transparency, fairness, and safety throughout the AI lifecycle, allowing businesses to deploy AI solutions that are not only efficient and insightful but also safe, equitable, and aligned with societal values.

1.3 STRATEGIC BENEFITS AND VALUE PROPOSITION

The integration of AI with BPM has proven exceptional operational efficiency, decision-making, and innovation. An AI-driven BPM offers a variety of strategic benefits and a compelling value proposition that contributes to sustainable growth and competitive advantage across industries.

a. Enhanced Operational Efficiency and Cost Reduction

Enhancing operational efficiency is perhaps the most remarkable advantage gained from AI-driven BPM systems. Process Automation (PA), an element of AI-driven BPM, helps an organization in automating monotonous, tedious human tasks which improves manually conducted work processes and guarantees better outcomes. AI powered BPM combines and optimizes all workflows of an organization by removing any redundant activities from business processes that would have otherwise been laboriously tackled. This improvement in PA increases the overall organizational pace, reduces reliance on large workforce teams that perform repetitive tasks and ultimately, cuts down costs.

b. Improved Decision-Making Quality and Speed

AI's ability to process large data sets enables informed decision-making. Through predictive analysis, AI models identify patterns and trends across data and deliver accelerated, actionable insights that empower organizations to make smarter decisions that foster growth. AI uses advanced pattern recognition technology to detect abnormalities and anomalies that may go unnoticed by human analysts. This results in more accurate and faster decisions as all of this is automated. In addition, AI handles repetitive choices, allowing human professionals to dedicate attention to advanced and tactical matters, thus shortening the total decision-making time.

c. Increased Process Agility, Adaptability and Resilience

In the contemporary world, where everything moves at a lightning speed, flexible and rapid decision-making in response to changing market conditions is critical. AI-enabled BPM facilitates this agility through real-time insights, process automation, and enabling rapid changes in business operations, through dynamic process optimization. It adjusts to the continuously changing business environment and helps businesses to proactively take action to avert potential risks, thereby improving business resilience.

d. Enhanced Customer Experience and Personalization

Businesses which incorporate AI technologies are more equipped to meet the demands of dynamically changing customers as they shift from offering customer services to providing intelligent customer solutions. Natural Language Processing (NLP) enables chatbots to respond to customer queries at any time of day or night and solve issues that can be handled without human assistance. AI makes hyper personalization possible by scrutinizing massive amounts of data and offers relative recommendations based on the shopper and the customer's browsing history. Besides, AI driven BPM makes it possible to perform sentiment analysis to know customers' feelings and feedback from social media, emails, and even reviews. Companies can even use these insights to understand their customers more effectively so as to address their needs which in turn drives business growth.

e. Proactive Risk Management and Compliance

Navigating through a business in the modern world brings with it a need to comply with legal, financial, and operational standards while managing a lot of risks. Nowadays, AI proves to be an invaluable asset to businesses as it mitigates risks by automating numerous tasks like the monitoring and evaluation of processes, constantly checking for risks, and pruning them in real-time. Moreover, AI algorithms are capable of advanced data scrutiny alongside predictive models allowing businesses to maintain smooth operations by identifying and minimizing potential risks. Furthermore, AI improves the management of compliance by automating mundane activities such as report generation, auditing, and privacy examinations of sensitive data.

2. AI AND PREDICTIVE ANALYTICS ACROSS THE BPM LIFECYCLE

It is evident that AI powered Business Process Management (BPM) is the focus of intelligent automation since it allows organizations to better understand their processes and the entire business at a glance. With an increase in data handling, along with the addition of AI, BPM turns into a responsive system which adapts and advances with time. While it is not arguable that AI may have great impacts on the future of BPM, organizations will still need to deal with problems of security risks, big data, and expensive implementation (Kokala, 2024a).

As for now, more sophisticated, use-case specific AI models and multi-system frameworks need to be created. Moreover, ethical concerns regarding the automation of processes through AI need to be addressed, particularly regarding potential job displacement and algorithmic bias that could lead to unfair or discriminatory outcomes. These AI-based BPM systems will allow companies to be more novel, flexible and competitive in today's fast changing digital environment.

Let's look at how AI fits into each stage of the BPM Lifecycle and how companies can adopt these techniques.

2.1 Data Requirements and Preparation for AI/PA in BPM

The very first step of any automation or AI implementation is data preparation. In 2021, an astonishing 79 zettabytes of data were generated globally (Reinsel et al., 2018). However, despite this massive volume of data, accessing the *right* data remains difficult. Organizations often face regulatory restrictions and technical limitations, creating a situation where data is abundant but still inaccessible when it is most needed. Below are some simple but key steps to ensure data requirements and preparation are in place for implementing AI and Predictive Analytics for BPM:

1. **Collect relevant data**: You should gather only necessary but all relevant data related to the process. This could be:
   - o Historical data (such as past sales, customer complaints, or delivery times).
   - o Real-time data (such as current inventory levels or live customer interactions).
   - o External data (such as market trends or weather data that might affect your process).
2. **Organize the data**: Store the data in a structured format, like a database or spreadsheet, so it's easy for teams to access and analyze. Make sure to include all relevant details, such as dates, times, and categories.
3. **Clean the data**: Remove errors, duplicates, or incomplete entries. For example, if some records are missing key information, fill in the gaps or remove them. If the data is clean, the predictions are much more reliable.
4. **Standardize the data**: Ensure every piece of data is in the same format. For example, dates should be similar (MM/DD/YYYY) and weight should be confined to a single measuring unit (kilograms or pounds).
5. **Label the data (if needed)**: For AI models, you may need labeled data. For example, if you are predicting customer satisfaction, label past interactions as "satisfied" or "unsatisfied" based on feedback.
6. **Integrate data sources**: If your data comes from multiple systems (e.g., CRM, ERP, or IoT devices), combine it into one place so that AI can analyze it as a whole.
7. **Ensure data privacy and security**: Safeguard private information, especially if it is individual customer-related data, and ensure compliance with relevant privacy legislation (e.g., GDPR or CCPA).
8. **Implement ethical data practices:** Beyond just legal compliance, consider the ethical implications of data collection and use, ensuring transparency, fairness, and accountability in how data is handled, especially when used for AI-driven decisions that might impact individuals.

Following the steps of collection, cleaning, and data organization, the information can be utilized for AI and predictive analytics. This groundwork ensures that the insights and predictions provided are reliable and beneficial for enhancing operational workflows in your business.

2.2 Diagnosis

The diagnosis phase is the first phase of BPM. It means analyzing and evaluating the current business processes with the purpose of identifying gaps, problems, or areas of improvement. This step builds a lot of value toward ensuring that processes are configured to meet the organizational objectives and provide optimal outcomes. AI applications for root cause analysis or process mining, for instance, could automate this phase, thereby improving overall efficiency and reducing costs. Below are some approaches of AI that can improve the underlying every step of the diagnosis process.

a. Process Mining

Process mining as described by van der Aalst (2016) applies an instrumental, data-oriented approach featuring an automated model building and analysis of processes from their historical event logs (Figure 5).

Figure 5. **Process Mining.** *The components of process mining, a data-driven technique used to analyse and improve business processes based on event logs, include process discovery from data, conformance checking by comparing several models with intended models and enhancement of process based on insights.*

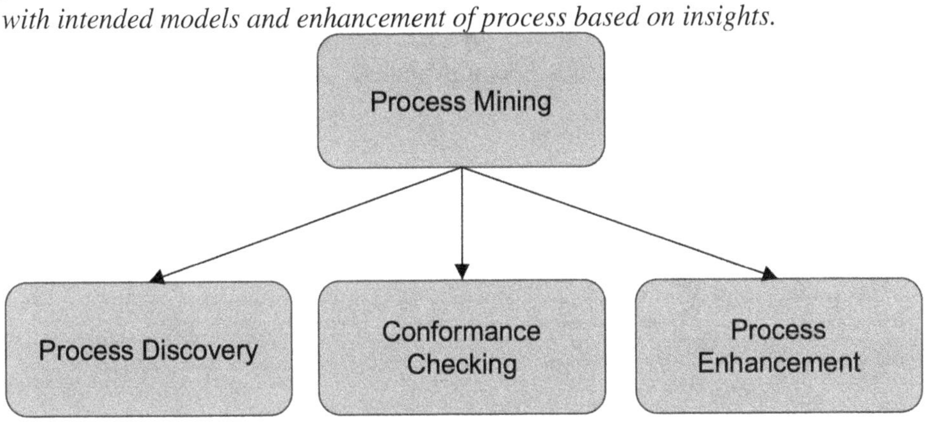

It extracts and analyzes data stored in ERP, CRM, and Workflow Management Systems (WMS) to automatically generate and analyze different models of how processes are carried out in order to evaluate their efficiency. These models are used as frameworks for further studies of processes and support research in three major areas:

1. **Process Discovery**: Algorithms like Alpha Miner, Heuristics Miner, and Inductive Miner use event data to create process models without prior knowledge. These models, such as workflow nets or BPMN diagrams, show the actual processes based on real data.
2. **Conformance Checking**: Conformance Checking compares the discovered models with the intended or designed models to find deviations, compliance issues, or quality problems. Techniques have evolved from simple methods to advanced tools that measure how closely real processes match the theoretical designs.
3. **Process Enhancement**: Process mining goes beyond discovery and validation by adding performance metrics, resource usage data, and social network analysis to the models. This helps identify bottlenecks, delays, and how organizational structures impact process outcomes.

Mining processes which help to understand and improve workflows by analyzing logs of automated systems and business processes. Traditional process mining, however, tends to suffer with regard to intricately dynamic and ever-evolving processes. To remedy this, AI-backed process mining implements machine learning, deep learning, and analytics to monitor and optimize processes, making it more suitable for contemporary business requirements (Rasaq, 2025).

Machine learning involves creating models to improve processes by applying AI-driven process mining. The methodology includes the following steps (Table 1):

Table 1. The steps in machine learning methodology

Step / Action	Description
Data Collection	Typically from log files from enterprise systems like ERP or CRM or IOT devices. This could also be customer usage or ecommerce data.
Preprocessing	Prepare, clean, format and structure the collected data for analysis.
Pattern Recognition	Use pattern recognition to identify existing issues, bottlenecks or inefficiencies.
Predictive Modeling	Forecast potential issues, bottlenecks or inefficiencies.
Optimization and Automation	Implement AI-driven improvements to improve and automate business processes.

We should highlight that the application of Artificial Intelligence in Process Mining significantly increases the automation of business processes and their efficiency with little human intervention. Businesses that implement AI Technology in their Business Process Management (BPM) experience increased productivity and lower costs. However, concerns related to the lack of sufficient skilled personnel, data privacy issues, and integration difficulties still impede its full adoption.

b. Anomaly Detection

Anomaly detection, also referred to as outlier or novelty detection, is the class of processes which look at processes or data points that differ markedly from most other processes or data points within a dataset. Detection of anomalies concentrates on recognizing infrequent, and unexpected violent incidents unlike tasks that deal with frequent events or normal patterns (Pang et al., 2022).

Anomalies often involve unknown behaviors, structures, or distributions and remain unpredictable until they occur, such as fraud, terrorist attacks, or network intrusions. Different types of anomalies can look completely different. For example, in video surveillance, events like robbery, traffic accidents, and burglary are visually distinct.

Diverse Types of Anomalies:

1. *Point Anomalies:* Individual data points that deviate from the majority, like abnormal health indicators.
2. *Conditional or Contextual Anomalies:* Data points that are only anomalous in specific contexts, such as sudden temperature changes or unusual credit card transactions.
3. *Group Anomalies:* A collection of data points that are anomalous as a group, even if individual points seem normal, like fake account clusters in social networks.

AI can be highly effective for anomaly detection by leveraging advanced algorithms and techniques to identify unusual patterns, behaviors, or data points. Below are the key AI learning techniques that can be used for anomaly detection (Table 2) (Stephen et al., 2022):

Table 2. AI learning techniques for anomaly detection

Learning Type	Description	Techniques	Example
Supervised Learning	Requires labelled data with examples of both normal and anomalous instances.	Decision trees, support vector machines (SVM), neural networks	Fraud detection in credit card transactions where past fraudulent and normal transactions are labeled.
Unsupervised Learning	Does not require labelled data and identifies anomalies based on deviations from normal patterns.	Clustering (e.g., k-means, DBSCAN), dimensionality reduction (e.g., PCA, autoencoders)	Detecting unusual network traffic without prior knowledge of attack patterns.
Semi-Supervised Learning	Trains models on a dataset containing mostly normal data and identifies deviations as anomalies.	Deep Variational Autoencoders, Generative Gaussian Mixture	Monitoring manufacturing equipment where most data represents normal operations.

i. Clustering Algorithms

Clustering techniques such as K-Means or specific hierarchical clustering are sensitive to outliers. They group data or processes based on similarity and are an effective method to identify anomalies in the data or processes (Gupta et al., 2012).

In the banking sector, cluster analysis is utilized for anomaly detection within transaction monitoring as part of business process management strategies. For instance, banks classify customer transactions into groups (clusters) defined by the amounts transacted, how often these transactions occur, and where they are conducted. The bulk of transactions are grouped into "normal clusters."

ii. Natural Language Processing (NLP)

Natural Language Processing (NLP) is an intersection of computer science, AI, and linguistics which studies the interaction between computers and humans. (Reshamwala et al., 2013). AI can analyze text data to detect anomalies in communication or behavior by leveraging advanced techniques such as Natural Language Processing (NLP) and machine learning. These technologies enable AI to understand the structure, context, and meaning of text, allowing it to identify patterns that deviate from the norm.

For instance, AI can detect phishing emails by analyzing unusual language patterns, suspicious links, or inconsistencies in the sender's information. Similarly, it can identify anomalies in customer support tickets, such as repeated complaints about a specific issue or unusual phrasing that may indicate fraudulent activity. By automating the analysis of large volumes of text data, AI helps organizations quickly identify and address potential risks or inefficiencies, improving security and operational efficiency.

iii. Time-Series Analysis

Time series analysis is a statistical method used to analyze a sequence of data points collected over time. The goal of time series analysis is to identify patterns, trends, seasonality, and dependencies within the data to understand past behavior and potentially forecast future values. Unlike cross-sectional data which captures a snapshot at a single point in time, time series data captures the evolution of a variable over a period (Abdi, 2020).

For example, in the manufacturing sector, time series analysis is integrated into their Business Process Management (BPM) for anomaly detection on equipment monitoring. For instance, temperature, vibration and pressure sensors mounted on machines collect data continuously. Time series models evaluate this data with the intention of recognizing patterns and forecasting the expected values. If the data shows any kind of sudden changes, such as, a considerable rise in vibration or a significant decrease in pressure, it is marked as an anomaly which might suggest an impending equipment failure. This enables manufacturers to do predictive maintenance which minimizes process downtime and enhances efficiency.

c. Root Cause Analysis

In modern industries, Root Cause Analysis is performed with many different techniques. These methods often integrate informal approaches such as brainstorming and flowcharts (Figure 6) . In BPM, the emphasis is usually placed on building 'as-is' models of current practices and 'to-be' models of advanced processes. Most modelling tools do not adequately assist in bridging these model gaps. Integrating business process models with root cause analysis could reduce the intuitive nature of organizational problem identification and diagnosis (Mitra et al. 2008).

Figure 6. **Root Cause Analysis.** *This method aims to identify the underlying root causes of problems in the system that lead to undesirable results and implement corrective actions against those causes.*

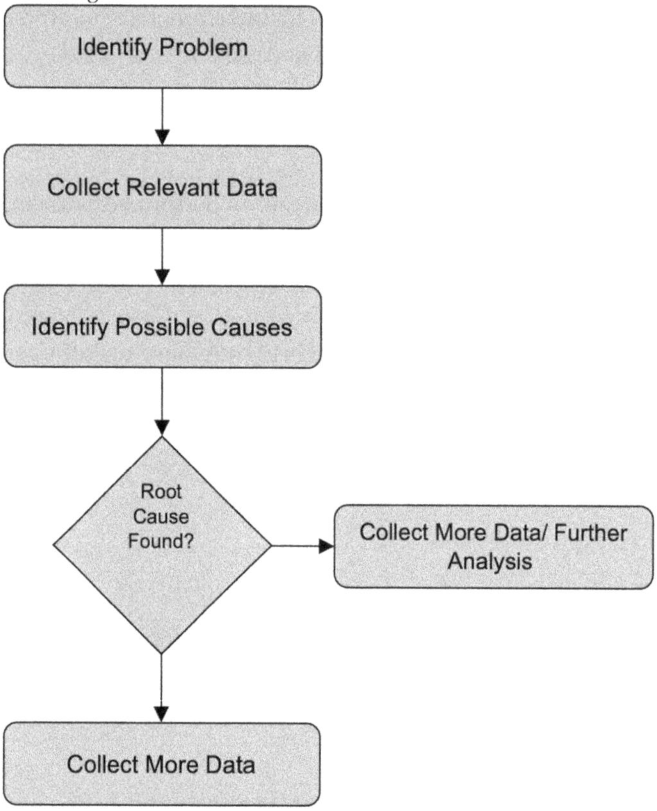

Research and experience shows that most analyses involve answering a similar set of questions. These questions often rely on comparable types of field data, such as usage parameters (e.g., hours of operation, total power cycles, vibration fatigue). By leveraging this commonality, we can automate the process of identifying the most likely failure mechanism for a given failure mode (Chigurupati et al., 2017).

d. Predictive Insights and Recommendations

As mentioned above in the sections, the diagnosis part of business process management deals with assessing data for inefficiencies and deviations after they happen. While this is helpful in a post-incident analysis, there is no agile decision making capability in this method which is necessary in contemporary business settings. This gap is covered with Predictive Business Process Monitoring (PBPM) which incorporates look-ahead analytics that not only predict future behavior of processes and events but actively adjust operations to adapt to changing workflows.

Automated Machine Learning (AutoML) further enhances PBPM by simplifying model design and refinement, thus widening the scope of employing predictive analytics. With PBPM and AutoML working together, there is a marked change in operational intelligence, as businesses are able to efficiently automate event prediction, process optimization, and decision making (Kaftantzis, 2024).

i. What is Automated Machine Learning (Auto ML)?

Automated Machine Learning (AutoML) is a big advancement in machine learning, simplifying and broadening access to predictive model development. Its main goal is to automate key areas of the machine learning workflow, reducing the time, effort, and expertise needed to build models.

Unlike traditional machine learning, which requires manual tasks like feature engineering, algorithm selection, and hyperparameter tuning, AutoML automates these processes. This automation, as show in figure 7, makes machine learning more accessible to a wider audience, allowing more professionals to benefit from its capabilities.

Figure 7. **AutoML Model.** *The figure explains the workflow of AutoML model from input to output, comprising of key components including data preparation, feature curation, model selection, hyperparameter optimization and model evaluation. This enhances productivity and supports scalable data-driven decision.*

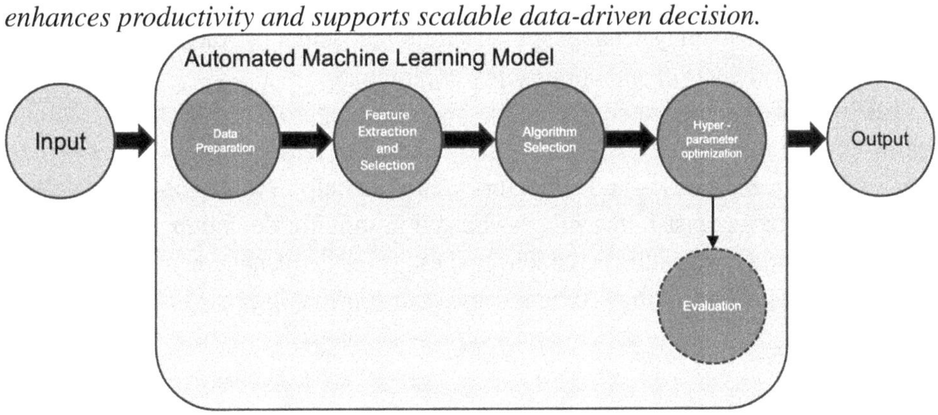

ii. AutoML In Business Process Management

The integration of Automated Machine Learning (AutoML) into business processes has become essential, transforming how organizations approach decision-making, efficiency, and innovation. AutoML simplifies and optimizes predictive modeling, eliminating the need for extensive data science expertise.

AutoML creates models at a really fast pace because it automates many areas of the learning, such as algorithm picking, feature selection, hyperparameter adjusting, and much more. This permits organizations to gain insights faster, make informed decisions that will enhance operational efficiency, and respond quickly to emerging market opportunities. It also promotes a data-driven culture by carrying out trend analysis, forecasting, and pattern recognition with machine learning, enabling timely proactive decision-making using trained models fitted on historical information.

Moreover, AutoML improves how tasks are assigned by streamlining resource-heavy processes and optimizing models. This conserves expenditure and guarantees that resources are spent on core high-impact activities. Its cyclic approach enables enhancement, as organizations can evolve their approaches to model performance, which requires them to relearn, and refine their approaches to complex and fast-changing market demands.

iii. What is Predictive Business Process Monitoring (PBPM)?

In today's fast paced market, where speed and precision are essential, one of the most important strategies to elevate operational intelligence is Predictive Business Process Monitoring (PBPM). Unlike conventional monitoring, PBPM is accompanied by predictive analytics which tries to fix potential problems before they cause any damage to efficiency. Challenges related to inefficient operations are easier to solve with risk reduction and opportunity exploitation.

PBPM uses sophisticated predictive modeling approaches such as machine learning, time series analysis, and anomaly detection for exploring historical data along with current metrics and behaviors. With the help of these tools, businesses are now able to forecast future process behavior, monitor deviations, and conduct continuous workflow health assessment, updating process management from reactive to proactive, thus improving efficiency and decision-making.

Table 3. Primary goals of PBPM:

Identifying Issues Proactively	**Improved Efficiency**	**Data-Driven Decision-Making**	**Flexibility to Change**
Example: A monitoring algorithm or radar detecting and addressing potential problems or issues before they occur.	**Example**: Streamlined processes or assembly lines with optimized workflows and resource allocation.	**Example**: A dashboard with real time alerts displaying predictive analytics that can enable teams to make informed decisions.	**Example**: A flexible system adjusting to new conditions or processes, indicating agility in a dynamic environment.

As previously stated, the intricacies associated with a predictive form of Business Process Management (BPM) shed light on effective methods of improving business processes. With these insights, there is ample opportunity for further research aimed at model optimization to cater to changing industry requirements as businesses begin to adopt predictive approaches.

We should also acknowledge that there are some limitations to predictive BPM models as well. Their accuracy is significantly reliant on the continuity of historical trends being present in the future. Given the fast-paced nature of modern business settings which can shift processes and introduce unanticipated variables, the aforementioned assumption is bound to be incorrect. Because of this, numerous new scenarios or striking changes to established patterns dilute the potential for predictive precision.

e. Visualization and Reporting

One of the most important aspects of the diagnosis phase in the BPM lifecycle is the continuous analysis and monitoring of business processes. Reporting and visualization are fundamental in the diagnosis phase of business process management (BPM). Businesses, insight into their workflows, floating bottlenecks, performance metrics as well as derive on the basis of their operation by transforming raw data into visual formats like charts, graphs, and process maps. These graphical tools enhance understanding of result intelligence as they make it easier to spot trends, patterns, and anomalies which would otherwise go unnoticed in textual or numerical data. More informed decisions can be taken relying on data enabled on these visual tools.

Dashboards with real-term alerts play a crucial role in the diagnosis phase of BPM. These systems or dashboards are often supported by Business Activity Monitoring (BAM) technology. BAM enables real-time monitoring of business processes. Analysts define Key Performance Indicators (KPIs) and their target values based on the organization's goals. BAM's primary feature is presenting KPIs through dashboards, which provide clear visibility into business performance (Kopp et al., 2017).

The dashboards visualize and summarize Key Performance Indicators (KPIs) and metrics for monitoring and critical decision making. Since dashboards often present data in near real-time, it helps monitor the health of the business and diagnose problems as soon as they occur.

2.3 Process (Re)Design and Analysis

Once we diagnose the problem, the process redesign and analysis phase play critical roles in addressing the issue and improving the overall process.

In process analysis, the practitioners try to capture the existing process (called "as-is" process) and find out areas to improve. This step is crucial for determining the gaps, blockages, or primary sources of difficulties. This pivots on understanding the process thoroughly—what is working, what isn't—and preparing for the redesign in responding to the examined issues.

The process redesign phase is focused on developing a new process (the "to-be" process). This will be done based on the findings from the previous phase (diagnosis phase). This phase will fix the shortcomings and also achieve the organizational goals. The goal is to design a more advanced, effective process which fixes the problems and optimally drives the results.

Both phases are interlinked with each other. During the analysis phase teams analyse the problems and provide insights into what needs to change. During the redesign phase the teams implement those changes by creating a new and improved process.

a. Process Analysis

Defining the current ("as-is") business process and understanding how it can be improved is a critical step in any Business Process Reengineering (BPR) project. This phase has three main goals: to fully understand the process and its objectives, to create a shared vision among the team, and to establish a foundation for redesigning the process (Bal, 1998).

Once businesses understand the "as-is" processes is when they can successfully plan and implement Business Process Reengineering. All the AI tools described above for Process Mining can also be efficiently repurposed for Process Analysis. For example, AI can be used in Root Cause Analysis to analyze the process data and identify the underlying reasons for performance issues or deviations. Natural Language Processing (NLP) can be used to discover main themes and drawbacks in existing processes based on either customer, employee or user sentiment.

Additionally AI, Predictive Analytics and Machine Learning can be used to perform the following techniques to achieve "as-is" process analysis.

a. **Conformance Checking:** Similar to Process Mining use case, for "as-is" analysis, businesses can use AI to compare the actual process execution against a predefined process model to identify deviations and non-compliant behavior.
b. **Document Analysis:** Extracting process-related information from existing policy documents, procedures, and reports. This can help identify gaps and drawbacks in existing processes.
c. **Automated Task Discovery:** Identifying repetitive tasks and variations in how users perform them. Once identified, businesses and teams can work to automate these tasks, saving precious human hours for more strategic work.
d. **Process Mapping from User Actions:** Aggregating individual task data to create an end-to-end view of a process, especially for processes that are not well-documented or heavily rely on manual steps.
e. **Automated Transcription:** Converting audio recordings of interviews into text when "as-is" analysis involves gathering qualitative data through surveys or interviews.
f. **Sentiment Analysis:** Understanding the overall sentiment expressed by stakeholders about the current processes.

By using AI-powered tools, organizations can get a clearer, more objective, and data-driven view of their current business processes. This makes it much easier to identify areas for improvement and take more effective steps to optimize them.

b. Process Redesign

For most organizations, improving their business processes is key to achieving success. Although there are ways to iteratively improve processes, these are typically done from scratch and require a combination of originality and seasoned professionals, which is a rare combination. To counter this, aided theories such as aBPR, or assisted business process redesign, have emerged. aBPR aids users in process improvement with predefined patterns of redesign and gives four recommendations using available information which differ in the extent of automation (Fehrer et al., 2022).

The assisted business process redesign (aBPR) helps users improve process models through guided recommendations. It focuses on incremental improvements using process redesign techniques. The aBPR technique in any organization follows a four-step approach:

1. *Select* appropriate redesign patterns
2. *Identify* relevant parts of the process
3. *Create* alternative models and

4. *Evaluate* the performance of these alternatives.

By following these steps, the tool generates redesign options that, after evaluation, can be used to enhance the process being analyzed.

2.4 System Configuration

System configuration is about making sure a new process works by adjusting a system's settings, protocols, configurations, and instructions. This includes things like:

- Defining users and their roles: Who can access what?
- Setting up networks: How do different parts of the system communicate?
- Customizing user interfaces: What do users see and interact with?
- Defining security boundaries: How is the system protected?

Essentially, it's about tweaking the system so it behaves the way you need it to when users interact with it.

Process configuration is about designing and customizing the steps, roles, rules, and data flows of a business process to achieve a specific goal. This involves:

- Outlining task order: What needs to happen when?
- Distributing responsibilities: Who does what?
- Making decisions: How are choices made within the process?
- Specifying data: What information is needed?
- Setting performance targets: How will success be measured?

Management needs to ensure every part of a business objective is smoothly integrated into a process. To make processes even better, process optimization includes advanced techniques like intelligent automation (beyond basic Robotic Process Automation, or RPA), AI-driven workflow configuration, and automated workflows. AI significantly impacts both system and process configuration by automating complex, often routine tasks.

- AI algorithms can suggest optimal parameters, settings, and rules for both software systems and business processes. They do this by analyzing best practices, past configurations, user input and relevant documents.
- This not only speeds up the configuration process but also reduces human error by ensuring configurations align with organizational and industry standards.

- AI tools can handle basic and repetitive configuration actions, automatically setting specific parameters or applying learned rules. This frees up human staff for more complex, high-level work.
- AI can understand specific needs based on user roles, business units, or process context. This allows it to suggest or even automatically apply relevant configurations, tailoring the system or process to the situation.
- During operation, AI helps prevent errors by checking proposed configurations against known parameters for differences, deviations, or contradictions. This ensures that changes won't damage or destabilize systems or processes. AI can even help determine what changes can be made without compromising stability.
- In many cases, AI systems improve their configurations over time by learning from user feedback. This means the guidance and innovations they provide become self-evolving, continually refining how systems and processes are configured.

2.5 Process Enactment (Execution) and Monitoring

The enhancement of AI to the phase of Process Enactment (Execution) is far beyond manual intelligence; offering an entirely new level of adaptability. Based on the predicted workload, availability of resources, skill sets, and efficiency indexes, AI systems can automatically allocate tasks to optimize resource allocation and resolve any existing bottlenecks. Moreover, AI systems enable dynamic process modification through real-time data monitoring and autonomous control of process flow adjustments to address exceptions and fluctuations during a process. Intelligent process automation powered by AI expands the boundaries set by traditional Robotic Process Automation (RPA). It achieves this through complicated procedures that involve data analysis and advanced decision making, which improves the accuracy of the processes and their completion speed. Efficiency is further improved by other measures taken in advance through foresight, such as when predictive resource management enables resource allocation at the right moment during the execution stage.

In the Process Monitoring phase, AI provides sophisticated functionalities for proactive oversight and real-time insights. AI algorithms have the capability of constantly monitoring process data to check KPIs, spot anomalies suggestive of problems or inefficiencies, and conduct root cause analysis to capture why there are deviations. Anticipatory monitoring is also possible which enables foreseeing future issues like delays or breakdowns and prevents disruptions in planning through timely mitigative actions. Furthermore, AI can customize monitoring dashboards and alerts which enhances information control by offering different stakeholders relevant information to take appropriate actions thus improving management.

Below are the three key areas where AI can help with the Process Execution and Monitoring phase of BPM.

a. Real-Time Monitoring and Anomaly Detection

With sensors all around us, there's been a huge increase in the amount of real-time data being generated. This is largely thanks to the rise of the Internet of Things (IoT) and other connected devices that constantly produce data over time. Analyzing this data can provide valuable insights for many different applications (Ahmad et al., 2017).

Detecting unusual patterns, or anomalies, in real-time data is especially important for industries like finance, IT, healthcare, energy, e-commerce, and more. It's used for things like preventing equipment failures, stopping fraud, identifying faults, and monitoring systems. While detecting these anomalies can provide critical, actionable insights, reliable solutions are still lacking. To address this, we propose a new and effective approach to handle the challenges of real-time anomaly detection (Figure 8).

A real time anomaly detector would encompass the following blocks to perform the training and detection as real time as possible (Dr. G. Ranganathan, 2020).

Figure 8. **Real-Time Anomaly Detection Workflow.** *The process typically begins with processing of raw data into normalised data, followed by training of models using the structed data, identifying and updating anomalies in data, and scheduling to ensure periodical data management with minimal human intervention.*

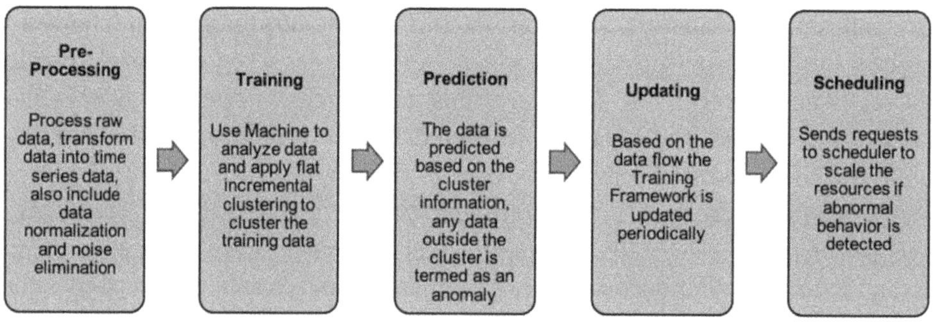

b. Predictive KPI / Process Monitoring and Alerts

Having efficient monitoring and alerting systems is very useful for sustaining the reliability of complex processes and systems. These systems assist in early detection of issues such as system anomalies, performance deterioration, and other outages so that mitigating action can be taken in time to avert significant issues. As more and more organizations move towards real-time operations and insights, using monitoring systems that provide data analytics tools such as predictive analytics or even machine learning is becoming much more critical. Such systems anticipate impending dangers which helps in minimizing operational outages, improving system reliability, resource utilization, and maintaining the quality of services provided across the enterprise (Adepoju et al., 2022).

To overcome the limitations of traditional monitoring, modern systems now focus on real-time data processing and predictive analytics. This shift from periodic checks to continuous monitoring enables a proactive approach, allowing potential issues to be detected and resolved in real time before failures occur.

Real-time monitoring has a tremendous advantage when it comes to environments where uptime and performance are really critical. For instance, it helps administrators in cloud computing to identify problems such as network congestion, server overloads, or outages in real-time rather than waiting for scheduled reports or post-event analytics. Such feedback allows for better-informed decisions and rapid remedy implementation, thus reducing disruptions.

Advanced monitoring systems use adaptive thresholds to adjust to dynamic environments. Unlike older systems with fixed thresholds that view data as unchanging or linear, adaptive thresholds transform with actual data and environmental conditions. Such flexibility minimizes false positives or missed alerts. For example, in a cloud application, adaptive thresholds can ignore seasonal or daily changes, only triggering alerts for true anomalies. Such data responsiveness is paramount in fast evolving environments to maintain accurate monitoring.

c. Continuous Process Improvement

In the book 'Continuous Process Improvement', Robson (2010) defines continuous improvement as 1) Going on or extending without interruption or break and 2) shows an increase in value or in excellence of quality or condition. The book calls out that below are the four main principles of continuous process optimization.

1. Continuous improvement must be a way of life
2. Problems must be prevented rather than reacted to
3. Results must be measurable and directly related to business plans and goals
4. Team ownership of a process is essential

AI plays a very important role in driving continuous improvement by enabling organizations to analyze data, optimize processes, and adapt to changing conditions more effectively. By leveraging AI's ability to process large volumes of data in real time, businesses can identify patterns, trends, and inefficiencies that might otherwise go unnoticed. This data-driven approach allows for more informed decision-making and helps organizations pinpoint areas for improvement with precision (Figure 9) (Cisterna et al., 2022).

The ability to learn and adapt over time is one of AI's most valuable contributions. AI systems become more accurate and effective through data processing due to the capabilities of machine learning. This self-learning ability guarantees that workflows within the organization, as well as any predictions and recommendations, develop in tandem with organizational expectations. For example, predictive analytics can easily anticipate possible problems such as equipment failure and process bottlenecks. It is important to note that such predictions help companies in taking prompt actions to avert disruptions and sustain continuous flow in operations.

Figure 9. **Continuous Improvement through AI.** *Artificial intelligence drives the enhancements in business process through a cycle of feedback looks. The iterative cycle of AI implementation using data, project improvement, wider adoption of the model, increased data generation and continuous model improvement ensures favourable business optimization. (Cisterna et al., 2022)*

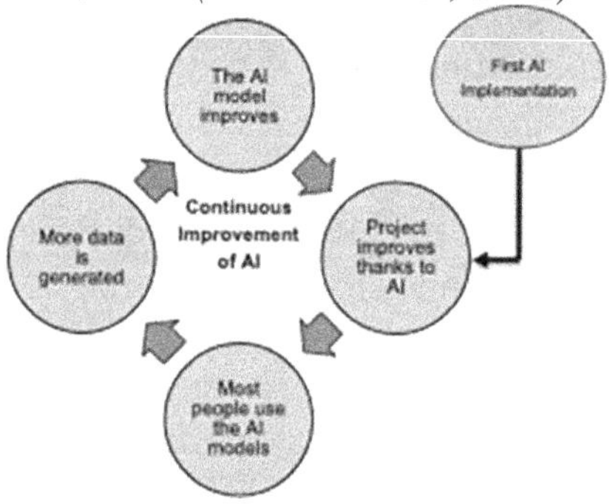

Additionally, as noted above, AI enhances the automation and the monitoring functions which are vital for optimization. AI optimally manages simple tasks to reduce error and shift human resources to more important responsibilities. Automated monitoring systems issue alerts and provide real-time feedback, allowing organizations to correct issues as they arise and maintain seamless operations. Overall, AI fosters a culture of continuous improvement by enabling smarter, faster, and more adaptive decision-making across all levels of an organization.

3. CHALLENGES, RISKS, AND ETHICAL CONSIDERATIONS

Though the implementation of AI in Business Process Management offers transformative potential, it presents numerous challenges and risks that must be considered to ensure maximum sustainability. Some key challenges include (Kokala. A, 2024b):

a. Data Quality, Availability and Privacy Concerns

To function efficiently, an AI model needs access to up-to-date datasets of high quality from various departments as well as legacy systems. Aside from the data being accurate, quantifiable, and precise, it also needs to be well organized for the AI to utilize these system integrations as designed. The merging of such heterogeneous datasets comes with a number of difficulties, which can include disparate data representations, gaps in the data collected, or an obsolete technological ecosystem which can all affect workflow processes. These barriers negatively impact the AI's capabilities to analyze specific workflows systematically and provide comprehensive enhancements, thus, obstructing streamlined process governance.

To make the processes more effective the organization sophisticated models made for data control and governance have to be created. In addition to primary concerns of privacy and ethical respectful data usage, AI integration poses additional significant challenges on the transparency of the information being used. These challenges directly impact the reputation of an organization and the reliability its clients place into it. This suite of data automation workflows often contains extremely confidential information that, if leaked, can result in data breaches as well as cyberattacks which must be dealt with head-on.

b. Algorithm Bias and Fairness

The AI system may produce systemic errors due to several biases in the data, or the model, resulting in Algorithm Bias. Such biases can jeopardise the system culminating in discrimination based on age, race, gender and other such factors, due to the AI's training from data reflecting pre-existing prejudices and flawed olden assumptions. This can disrupt several essential processes handled by AI, including recruitment, customer service, employee performance evaluations and supply chain management. Such algorithm bias can lead to several consequences including unfair hiring, biased performance evaluations, and poor customer service which might interfere with optimal business operations.

c. Explainability and Transparency (Black Box Problem)

The term "black box" refers to technology whose internal workings are unknown, and in the case of AI systems, there is little explanation for how certain outcomes were attained. AI works autonomously; it takes in data as input, processes it, and provides output without reasoning the way a human would externally. Even bad decisions can be made with no rationale, and proving what went wrong becomes a laborious challenge. Organizations that need to understand the source of an error have no clear indication that they could have a problem with the data, the algorithm, or the process of reasoning within the organizational system. This inadequacy hinders not only the ability to resolve the issue but also creates a problem of blamelessness which drastically hinders the efficiency of correcting mistakes.

d. **Integration Complexity with Existing Systems**

Several organizations have well-established yet outdated systems that cannot be operated by AI technologies, making it difficult to create an AI-driven BPM environment. Challenges in this front also include the use of the storage of high volumes of data under isolated silos and the usage of several combinations of data storage platforms, leading to disruption in a cohesive workflow. It might even interrupt the existing operations, often culminating in new bottlenecks.

e. **Need for New Skills and Talents**

The smooth integration of AI into BPM requires a proficient workforce in data analysis, machine learning and AI technologies. With the constant evolution of AI, keeping pace with the advancements in AI becomes a challenge to organizations. They may face a skill gap and require a continuous investment of time and money to upskill, reskill and hire talented employees to implement AI-driven BPM tasks.

f. **Change Management and Organization Resistance**

Organizational challenges such as fear of job loss due to automation, lead to reluctance to embrace new technologies. This fear is usually because of a lack of understanding of how AI works and what its impact is on specific roles. Moreover, organizations with well-established traditional practices may hesitate to shift to automated workflows, especially if the transition is overwhelming. A lack of training and support also leaves employees unprepared to switch to newer technologies.

g. **Ethical Implications of Automated Decision-Making in Processes**

AI's ability to automate the decision-making processes has significantly improved operational performances, but raises potential ethical concerns. The ethical implications arise from decisions impacting people's lives, work, and access to services being increasingly delegated to algorithms that lack transparency and accountability.

One primary ethical challenge is bias and discrimination. Since automated systems learn from historical data, societal biases in the data may lead to discriminatory outcomes. For instance, in hiring process, loan approvals or in legal assessments, biased data may produce unfair results that not only violates ethical norms but also regulatory requirements such as those outlined in data protection and anti-discrimination laws. Another issue is lack of transparency and explainability. Typically, AI models function as "black-box" making it difficult for users to understand how the interpretations are made. In businesses, this lack of interpretability erodes trust, as customers, employees and regulators have the right to know the functioning behind the decisions, particularly those that carry significant consequences.

Accountability has also become a significant issue in automated systems. Determining who is responsible for outcomes, such as denying a job opportunity, becomes complex. The organization using the system, the developers of the algorithm or the data suppliers may be accountable, which becomes a challenge to decide. Ethical practice demands clear lines of accountability and mechanisms to challenge or appeal automated decisions. Privacy protection is often compromised as automated decision-making relies on collecting and analysing vast amounts of personal data. The misuse of personal data or sensitive information must always be strictly monitored. Ethical process automation must adhere to data protection principles, such as those set by the General Data Protection Regulation (GDPR), including data minimization, informed consent, and the right to explanation.

Addressing these issues becomes imperative and involves a multidisciplinary approach involving the use of ethical guidelines, legal compliance, technical safeguards and governance frameworks to ensure automation adheres to ethical standards.

4. IMPLEMENTATION STRATEGIES AND BEST PRACTICES

To combat challenges and ensure efficient process management, several implementation strategies aid in the effective integration of AI in BPM. (Abbasi et al., 2024)

a. **Developing an AI/PA Strategy for BPM**

Well-crafted strategies ensure that AI and automation processes are aligned with business goals and deliver value that can be implemented across the organization. The process involves defining clear business objectives, assessing the current state to identify process inefficiencies and technology gaps and constructing a well-structured road map that outlines the implementation plan. Along with this, data governance also becomes critical, as AI relies on clean, structured data. Ensuring data quality, security, and compliance with regulations like the General Data Protection Regulation (GDPR) is key. Additionally, fostering a culture of change management and upskilling helps overcome resistance and prepares employees to work alongside AI systems. Finally, continuous monitoring and optimization ensure sustained successful performance.

b. **Pilot Projects and Phased Rollouts**

Before fully implementing a system, organizations must run pilot projects (a small-scale, short-term trial focused on testing the AI-driven solution within a specific department or process) to test the AI solutions, identify potential issues, obtain feedback, and make necessary alterations. Once the pilot proves successful, the AI-driven solution is gradually expanded as a phased approach. The schedule will follow the patterns set out by the pilot for each department individually. Each division's increased implementation improves feedback proficiently. Unrestricted feedback helps mitigate performance gaps allowing adjustments to be made on the fly during staged implementations, allowing for fortified enhancement to the overall results. The improvements to the set support key efficient areas while denying the chance of system failures. These optimized costs enable better management by reducing the chances of employee mismanagement through standards, easing risks of failure while making change more seamless. All enhancements assist in the strengthening of AI solutions in performance monitoring and AI systems.

c. **Building Data Infrastructure and Capabilities**

An effective AI solution can improve operational efficiency and drive growth. However, sophisticated AI systems require a reliable data foundation, which can only be accomplished through a solid development and implementation plan. The plan should focus on solving critical organizational problems that stem from gaps in data readiness, as well as integrating different data sources that can impact the AI solution needed. Addressing these issues through a single comprehensive approach ensures that the AI system receives the best quality data it can operate on. Data governance frameworks also aid in maintaining data accuracy and minimizing the chances of misclassification, resulting in the information being more reliable.

The value of data-driven AI solutions increases when there is seamless access to data lakes and warehouses. These allow an organization to access standardized clean data which, when used to train AI models, improves the outcomes significantly.

The AI systems can then help the organization tackle its most pressing gaps, such as from lagging organizational performance or from unmet corporate goals. AI can provide constant monitoring and make timely adjustments as needed, accomplishing tasks that would take human employees extensive effort to do manually. Further, the sophisticated monitoring capabilities of AI could permit organizations to measure the actual effectiveness of adopting business process management systems driven by AI, fine-tuning and repurposing existing solutions and services across organizational silos.

d. **Fostering Collaboration Between Data Scientists and Process Experts**

The interaction of data scientists with experts in a particular process ensures that AI systems are both operationally competent and strategically relevant to the business. The relationships of each team member have to be carved out distinctly so that roles do not overlap and effective decision-making is possible. Within an organization, team members from diverse functions can be brought together from different departments, for mutual understanding, through knowledge-sharing initiatives, thus enhancing understanding. Promote advanced learning. These allow process experts to better use AI tools while data scientists gain practical understanding of business functions. It also enhances the already collaborative approach to problem-solving which ensures that the resultant AI solutions are both practical and creative. This improves the efficacy of AI-augmented business functions and fosters stronger synergies for value realization, strengthening operational productivity while advancing strategic agility for sustained growth.

e. **Ensuring Governance and Ethical Oversight**

A robust data governance framework is crucial for ensuring transparency and accountability in managing data across the entire Business Process Management (BPM) life cycle. This framework must integrate ethical auditing of data to actively mitigate discrimination and bias, ensuring fair and equitable outcomes. Ethical governance also necessitates that organizations take proactive steps to safeguard the privacy of personal data and champion the principle of data minimization. This involves obtaining explicit consent, guaranteeing the accuracy of relevant information, and implementing robust protective measures around that data. Furthermore, AI governance can foster explainable AI, where understanding and communicating the reasoning behind AI functions enhances user trust and empowers users to make informed decisions based on the resulting information.

5. CASE STUDIES

The theoretical capabilities of AI in BPM are best understood through their practical implementation. The following case studies illustrate the tangible impact of AI across diverse industries, showcasing both successes and emerging challenges.

5.1 AI Enhanced Claim Processing in the Insurance Sector

A prominent real-world application of AI in BPM is found within the insurance sector, specifically in the automation of claim processing. A case study highlights the deployment of a Large Language Model (LLM) in a production environment to automate the identification of claim parts. This task, previously performed manually, was identified as a significant bottleneck for scalability due to its knowledge-intensive nature and the wide variety of claim parts involved (Khayatbashi et al., 2025).

To rigorously assess the impact of this AI-driven automation on process scalability and efficiency, Object-Centric Process Mining (OCPM) was employed. OCPM proved particularly valuable for analyzing the complex process transformations involved, as it facilitates the simultaneous analysis of multiple perspectives within the process. The observed benefits were substantial: the LLM significantly enhanced operational capacity and successfully eliminated the bottleneck in claim identification.

However, a critical finding from this implementation was that the resolution of the claim identification bottleneck inadvertently created a new backlog in the subsequent claim investigation phase. This necessitated the reallocation of resources and adjustments to the workforce downstream. This phenomenon underscores a crucial understanding: simply scaling a single process step through AI automation does not automatically translate into overall efficiency gains or increased business value. It highlights that AI-generated workload growth in one area can exceed human capacity or the capacity of subsequent manual or less automated steps, thereby shifting rather than eliminating systemic inefficiencies.

This demonstrates the necessity of adopting a holistic, end-to-end process view when implementing AI, emphasizing that comprehensive process redesign and workforce planning must accompany technological deployment to achieve true systemic improvements.

5.2 Generative AI for Adaptive Order Fulfilment in E-Commerce

Another compelling case study showcases the novel application of generative AI models in the e-commerce sector for enterprise workflow automation, with a strong emphasis on adaptive process design and continuous improvement. This system integrates transformer-based models, such as GPT, to enable real-time decision-making, empowering workflows to self-optimize based on dynamic operational data and evolving business needs. By integrating Robotic Process Automation (RPA) with generative AI, the system can dynamically suggest process improvements, significantly reducing the time required for process design and minimizing human intervention (Paulose et al., 2024).

The quantifiable efficiency gains observed in this e-commerce implementation were substantial: the system achieved a 35% reduction in processing time for order fulfillment workflows, alongside a notable enhancement in customer satisfaction.

This outcome highlights a fundamental shift from static, rule-based automation, which is often criticized for its inability to handle continuous change and uncertainty, to dynamic, self-optimizing processes enabled by generative AI. This adaptive capability is crucial for agile business environments and represents a significant advancement over traditional automation systems that are limited by rigid rules and lack the ability to adapt to unforeseen circumstances. The ability of generative AI to dynamically learn and adapt to changes, rather than being constrained by rigid rules, allows for continuous process evolution, making operations more resilient and responsive to real-time market shifts.

6. FUTURE TRENDS

As organizations become more digital, AI will continue to impact business functions, processes, and value creation activities. Data-driven decision-making, especially powered by Explainable AI (XAI) algorithms, fuels the need for heightened living business models which in turn satisfies the need for constant innovation and speeds-up responsiveness across the business ecosystem (Weinzierl et al., 2024). With increasing use of AI in pivotal business functions, there is greater need for accuracy and responsibility to be woven into the design of these newer systems and models. Stricter regulatory frameworks already take for granted the assumption that advanced AI systems will always need high levels of oversight which reinforces the need for XAI systems.

The delta in the advancement of AI and business with newer frameworks will require flexibility to drive innovation; however, they need to be controlled to create enough structure to mitigate organizational and systemic risk. Because business models, processes, and systems are interrelated and largely depend on the environment in working systemically, accounting for adaptable governance while ensuring control mechanisms are proportionate to the dynamic risks become vital.

Of course, ensuring smart is adequate whilst guaranteeing proportionality to relative risks heightens the likelihood of regulated trust, but if core tenets are not met raises the challenge across all organizations in an ecosystem that aim for agile compliance towards set regulations, limit inflexible scrutiny, and bound manual cross-system navigation.

Integrating AI systems into business processes anticipates context awareness and tracking of relevance which incur dynamic challenges for dependability. Conclusively guided self-adaptation alongside adjustive control creates sufficient conditions for trustable systems and generates system performability.

Generative AI has great potential for creating new content, generating data-driven insights, and designing complex workflows by simulating various scenarios, unlike traditional AI systems. This technology helps reduce the time spent on manual design processes and can be closely aligned with specific customer preferences McKinsey & Company. (2023).

With the implementation of AI, machine learning, and RPA, Hyper Automation is transforming the automation processes utilized in industries. Such mighty synergy can empower businesses to make use of the data-driven insights to respond immediately to market shifts, customer demand, and operational concerns (George et al, 2023). Subsequently, businesses can set up self-regulating workflows that will adapt to changing environments autonomously with less human intervention McKinsey & Company. (2025).

With the adaptability and independence of AI, processes such as data analysis, pattern recognition and decision-making can be automated. The systems also have increased capabilities for learning, adapting and optimizing in real time. The systems can instantly adapt to changes and deliver complex decisions autonomously. This adaptability and autonomy improve efficiency of the processes, enhance agility, reduce costs, increase accuracy and allow for easy scaling of high volumes of data.

The continuous evolution of technologies enables businesses to achieve long-term growth and sustainability in the digital era. As these trends continue to evolve, they are set to redefine the boundaries of what is possible in business process management.

7. CONCLUSION

The integration of Artificial Intelligence (AI) and Predictive Analytics into Business Process Management (BPM) has opened doors to new opportunities to organizations by assisting them in deriving insights from large volumes of data. An organization's data can undergo descriptive, diagnostic, predictive, and prescriptive analysis which allows businesses to discover trends, forecast results and develop effective plans to achieve organizational objectives. Improvement in decision making, opportunity recognition, risk mitigation, marketing and customer satisfaction all result from effective business strategies made possible with predictive analytics.

Predictive analytics enables businesses to make data driven decisions while optimizing inventory, cutting operational costs and even personalizing marketing strategies.

Merging AI capabilities with BPM allows organizations to streamline processes, improve efficiency, and stimulate innovation by integrating intelligent decision-making technologies. AI is adaptive and intelligent through the use of BPM. AI together with analytics fuel AI predictive analytics that enhances the responsiveness and adaptability of BPM. The integration of AI augments decision-making capabilities enabling businesses to respond swiftly to shifts in the market, manage resources optimally, and provide tailored services that enhance growth and operational efficacy.

However, the success of AI in BPM depends on high-quality data. Businesses run into problems such as the "data paradox" where they have access to broken, inaccessible information, but stifling technical or regulatory limits are set in place. Aside from this paradox, data handling poses additional challenges in the form of time-consuming processes like incomplete entries, biases, and inconsistencies. In this context, companies need to compile suitable data, guarantee standardization, cleansing, privacy, and adequate security. Effective data handling allows drawing correct inferences from the resultant data, thereby improving the functioning of AI-powered BPM systems.

Looking ahead, in further developing automation and refining predictive analytics, the integration of Artificial Intelligence into business process management (BPM) will have more promising avenues to explore. In addition, data quality, security, and ethical issues will need to be addressed. Organizations will have to shift their attention to creating sophisticated AI models designed for particular industries and use cases, achieving full automation and optimization of inter-system processes. With the advancement of Artificial Intelligence, business process management will evolve from a triggered action system into a self-regulating, adaptive framework that optimally evolves with external processes. Organizations that advance with unprecedented change will avail themselves to new opportunities in efficiency, customer satisfaction, and competitive advantage.

Beyond technical hurdles, the ethical implications of AI in BPM demand significant attention. The potential for algorithmic bias, for instance, can perpetuate and even amplify existing societal inequalities if not carefully managed. Organizations must establish robust ethical guidelines and frameworks to ensure fairness, transparency, and accountability in AI-driven decisions. This includes clear data governance policies that define data ownership, usage, and retention, along with mechanisms for auditing AI models to detect and mitigate bias. Organizational challenges extend to fostering a culture of data literacy and ethical AI awareness, requiring investment in training and new roles dedicated to overseeing AI ethics and data governance. Without proactive measures to address these complex ethical and organizational considerations, the transformative potential of AI in BPM risks being undermined by a lack of trust and unforeseen societal repercussions.

REFERENCES

Aalst, W. V. D. (2016). *Process mining: data science in action* (2nd ed.). Springer. DOI: 10.1007/978-3-662-49851-4

Abbasi, M., Nishat, R. I., Bond, C., Graham-Knight, J. B., Lasserre, P., Lucet, Y., & Najjaran, H. (2024). A review of AI and Machine learning contribution in Predictive business process Management (Process enhancement and process improvement approaches). *arXiv* (Cornell University). DOI: /arxiv.2407.11043.DOI: 10.48550

Abdi, H. (2010). Partial least squares regression and projection on latent structure regression (PLS Regression). *Wiley Interdisciplinary Reviews: Computational Statistics*, *2*(1), 97–106. DOI: 10.1002/wics.51

Adepoju, A. H., Austin-Gabriel, B., Hamza, O., & Collins, A. (2022). Advancing monitoring and alert systems: A proactive approach to improving reliability in complex data ecosystems. *Iconic Research and Engineering Journals*, *5*(11), 281–282.

Adesina, A. A., Iyelolu, T. V., & Paul, P. O.Abayomi Abraham AdesinaToluwalase Vanessa IyeloluPatience Okpeke Paul. (2024). Optimizing business processes with advanced analytics: Techniques for efficiency and productivity improvement. *World Journal of Advanced Research and Reviews*, *22*(3), 1917–1926. DOI: 10.30574/wjarr.2024.22.3.1960

Ahmad, S., Lavin, A., Purdy, S., & Agha, Z. (2017). Unsupervised real-time anomaly detection for streaming data. *Neurocomputing*, *262*, 134–147. DOI: 10.1016/j.neucom.2017.04.070

Bal, J. (1998). Process analysis tools for process improvement. *The TQM Magazine*, *10*(5), 342–354. DOI: 10.1108/09544789810231225

Chigurupati, A., & Lassar, N. (2017). Root cause analysis using artificial intelligence. In *2017 Annual reliability and maintainability symposium (RAMS)* (pp. 1-5). IEEE. DOI: DOI: 10.1109/RAM.2017.7889651

Cisterna, D., Lauble, S., Haghsheno, S., & Wolber, J. (2022). Synergies between lean construction and artificial intelligence: AI driven continuous improvement process. In *Proceedings of the 30th annual conference of the International Group for Lean Construction (IGLC30)* (pp. 199-210). DOI: DOI: 10.24928/2022/0122

Daniel, S., Bogdana, R., Aladdin, A., Anat, F., & Michael, L. (2020). Principles to Practices for Responsible AI: Closing the Gap. *The 2020 European Conference on AI (ECAI)*. DOI: DOI: 10.48550/arXiv.2006.04707

Eckerson, W. W. (2007). Predictive analytics. *Extending the Value of Your Data Warehousing Investment. TDWI Best Practices Report, 1*, 1–36.

Fehrer, T., Fischer, D. A., Leemans, S. J., Röglinger, M., & Wynn, M. T. (2022). An assisted approach to business process redesign. *Decision Support Systems, 156*, 113749. DOI: 10.1016/j.dss.2022.113749

George, A. S., George, A. S. H., Baskar, T., & Sujatha, V. (2023). The rise of hyperautomation: A new frontier for business process automation. *Partners Universal International Research Journal, 2*(4), 13–35.

Ghosh, M., & Thirugnanam, A. (2021). Introduction to artificial Intelligence. In *Studies in big data* (pp. 23–44). DOI: DOI: 10.1007/978-981-16-0415-7_2

Gordon, A. (1999). *Classification* (2nd ed.). CRC Press. DOI: 10.1201/9780367805302

Gupta, A., & Gupta, A. (2011). RESEARCH PAPER ON CLUSTER TECHNIQUES OF DATA VARIATIONS. *International Journal of Advance Technology & Engineering Research., 1*(1), 39–47.

Hammer, M. (2014). What is business process management? In *Handbook on business process management 1: Introduction, methods, and information systems* (pp. 3–16). Springer Berlin Heidelberg., DOI: 10.1007/978-3-642-45100-3_1

Heravizadeh, M., Mendling, J., & Rosemann, M. (2008). Root cause analysis in business processes.

Institute of Electrical and Electronics Engineers. (2019). *Ethically aligned design: a vision for prioritizing human well-being with autonomous and intelligent systems* (1st ed.). https://ethicsinaction.ieee.org/

Kaftantzis, S. (2024). Predictive Business Process Monitoring with Automated Machine Learning.

Khayatbashi, S., Sjölind, V., Granåker A., Jalali A. (2025). AI-Enhanced Business Process Automation: A Case Study in the Insurance Domain Using Object-Centric Process Mining

Kokala, A. (2024a). Business Process Management: The synergy of intelligent automation and AI-Driven workflows. *International Research Journal of Modernization in Engineering Technology and Science*. Advance online publication. DOI: 10.56726/IRJMETS65186

Kokala, A. (2024b). Harnessing AI for BPM: Streamlining Complex Workflows and Enhancing Efficiency. *Authorea Preprints*. DOI: 10.36227/techrxiv.173532331.17776706/v1

Kopp, A., Orlovskyi, D., & Kuka, D. (2017). An approach to forming dashboards for business processes state analysis. *Bulletin of National Technical University" KhPI". Series: System Analysis. Control and Information Technologies*, (51), 44–52.

Kumar, V., & L, M. (2018). Predictive Analytics: A review of trends and techniques. *International Journal of Computer Applications*, *182*(1), 31–37. DOI: 10.5120/ijca2018917434

McKinsey & Company. (2023). The state of AI in 2023: Generative AI's breakout year. https://www.mckinsey.com/capabilities/quantumblack/our-insights/the-state-of-ai-in-2023-generative-ais-breakout-year

McKinsey & Company. (2025). Superagency in the workplace: Empowering people to unlock AI's full potential. https://www.mckinsey.com/capabilities/mckinsey-digital/our-insights/superagency-in-the-workplace-empowering-people-to-unlock-ais-full-potential-at-work

Organisation for Economic Co-operation and Development. (2019). OECD principles on artificial intelligence. https://www.oecd.org/going-digital/ai/principles/

Pang, G., Shen, C., Cao, L., & Hengel, A. V. D. (2021). Deep learning for anomaly detection: A review. *ACM Computing Surveys*, *54*(2), 1–38. DOI: 10.1145/3439950

Paulose, R., & Neelanath, V. (2024). *Generative AI-driven Automation of Business Process Reimagination. 2024 IEEE Recent Advances in Intelligent Computational Systems*. RAICS., DOI: 10.1109/RAICS61201.2024.10689826

Prasad, S., Kulkarni, P., & Veronika, N. (2023). Role of artificial intelligence in business process transformation. *AIP Conference Proceedings*, *2990*, 060028. DOI: 10.1063/5.0170686

Ranganathan, G. (2020). Real time anomaly detection techniques using pyspark frame work. *Journal of Artificial Intelligence*, *2*(01), 20–30. DOI: 10.36548/jaicn.2020.1.003

RASAQ, S. O. (2025). Resource Optimization in Hybrid Cloud: Leveraging Microservices for IoT Workloads. *International Journal of Novel Research in Engineering & Pharmaceutical Sciences*, *1*(1).

Reinsel, D., Gantz, J., & Rydning, J. (2018). The digitization of the world from edge to core. *IDC white paper, 16*, 1-28.

Reshamwala, A., Mishra, D., & Pawar, P. (2013). Review on natural language processing. [ESTIJ]. *IRACST Engineering Science and Technology: An International Journal*, *3*(1), 113–116.

Robson, G. D. (2010). *Continuous process improvement*. Simon and Schuster.

Stephen, M., & Sheriffdeen, K. (2022). AI-Enabled Anomaly Detection in Industrial Systems: A New Era in Predictive Maintenance.

Sykes, A. O. (1993). An introduction to regression analysis. (Coase-Sandor Institute for Law & Economics. Working Paper No. 20, 1993).

Ter Hofstede, A. H., Van der Aalst, W. M., Adams, M., & Russell, N. (Eds.). (2009). *Modern Business Process Automation: YAWL and its support environment*. Springer Science & Business Media., DOI: 10.1007/978-3-642-03121-2

Walonick, D. S. (1993). An overview of forecasting methodology. *StatPac:* https:// www. statpac. org/research-library/forecasting. htm

Weinzierl, S., Zilker, S., Dunzer, S., & Matzner, M. (2024). Machine learning in business process management: A systematic literature review. *Expert Systems with Applications, 124181*, 124181. Advance online publication. DOI: 10.1016/j. eswa.2024.124181

Compilation of References

Aalst, W. V. D. (2016). *Process mining: data science in action* (2nd ed.). Springer. DOI: 10.1007/978-3-662-49851-4

Abban, R., & Kifle Abebe, G. (2022). Exploring digitalization and sustainable practices in African agribusinesses and food supply chains: A literature review. *International Journal on Food System Dynamics*, *13*(4), 470–474. DOI: 10.18461/ijfsd.v13i4.D7

Abbasi, M., Nishat, R. I., & Bond, C. (2024). A review of AI and machine learning contribution in business process management (process enhancement and process improvement approaches). *Business Process Management Journal*. Advance online publication. DOI: 10.1108/BPMJ-02-2023-0123

Abdi, H. (2010). Partial least squares regression and projection on latent structure regression (PLS Regression). *Wiley Interdisciplinary Reviews: Computational Statistics*, *2*(1), 97–106. DOI: 10.1002/wics.51

Abdullah, R., Mohamad, E., & Muhamad, M. R. (n.d.). *Managing Key Performance Indicators (KPIs): A Case Study at an Aerospace Manufacturing Facility.*

Abdullahi, M. A., Mohamed, Z., Shamsudin, M. N., Sharifuddin, J., & Ali, F. (2018). Effects of top leadership culture and strategic sustainability orientation on sustainable development among Malaysian herbal-based SMEs. *Business Strategy & Development*, *1*(2), 128–139. DOI: 10.1002/bsd2.17

Abideen, A. Z., Sundram, V. P. K., Pyeman, J., Othman, A. K., & Sorooshian, S. (2021). Food supply chain transformation through technology and future research directions—A systematic review. *Logistics (Basel)*, *5*(4), 83. Advance online publication. DOI: 10.3390/logistics5040083

Abidi, N., El Herradi, M., & Sakha, S. (2023). Digitalization and resilience during the COVID-19 pandemic. *Telecommunications Policy*, *47*(3), 102522. DOI: 10.1016/j.telpol.2023.102522 PMID: 37051116

Abir, S. M A A., Anwar, A., Choi, J., & Kayes, A. S. M. (2021). *IoT-enabled smart energy grid: Applications and challenges*. IEEE. DOI: 10.1109/ACCESS.2021.3071245

Abro, A. A., Talpur, M. S. H., & Jumani, A. K. (2023). *Natural language processing challenges and issues: A literature review*. Gazi University Journal of Science., DOI: 10.5281/zenodo.1234567

Adams, N., Augusto, A., Davern, M., & Rosa, M. L. (2023). *Five guidelines to improve context-aware process selection: An Australian banking perspective* (No. arXiv:2304.05033). arXiv. https://doi.org//arXiv.2304.05033DOI: 10.48550

Adekemi, P. (2025). Review on the role of Law in Corporate Sustainability and Green Practices. *Global Journal of Environmental Science & Sustainability*, *2*(1), 1–8. DOI: 10.69798/56256994

Adepoju, A. H., Austin-Gabriel, B., Hamza, O., & Collins, A. (2022). Advancing monitoring and alert systems: A proactive approach to improving reliability in complex data ecosystems. *Iconic Research and Engineering Journals*, *5*(11), 281–282.

Adesina, A. A., Iyelolu, T. V., & Paul, P. O.Abayomi Abraham AdesinaToluwalase Vanessa IyeloluPatience Okpeke Paul. (2024). Optimizing business processes with advanced analytics: Techniques for efficiency and productivity improvement. *World Journal of Advanced Research and Reviews*, *22*(3), 1917–1926. DOI: 10.30574/wjarr.2024.22.3.1960

Adner, R. (2021). *Winning the right game: How to disrupt, defend, and deliver in a changing world*. MIT Press. DOI: 10.7551/mitpress/12752.001.0001

Adwan, A. A., Kokash, H., Adwan, R. A., & Khattak, A. (2023). Data analytics in digital marketing for tracking the effectiveness of campaigns and inform strategy. *International Journal of Data and Network Science*, *7*(2), 563–574. DOI: 10.5267/j.ijdns.2023.3.015

Afum, E., Agyabeng-Mensah, Y., Sun, Z., Frimpong, B., Kusi, L. Y., & Acquah, I. S. K. (2020). Exploring the link between green manufacturing, operational competitiveness, firm reputation and sustainable performance dimensions: A mediated approach. *Journal of Manufacturing Technology Management*, *31*(7), 1417–1438. DOI: 10.1108/JMTM-02-2020-0036

Agence de Développement du Digital (ADD). (2022). Baromètre de la maturité digitale des administrations publiques marocaines.

Agheli, L., & Taghvaee, V. M. (2022). Political stability effect on environment and weak sustainability in Asian countries. *Sustainability Analytics and Modeling*, *2*, 100007. DOI: 10.1016/j.samod.2022.100007

Agrawal, G. (2024). *Accountability, trust, and transparency in AI systems from the perspective of public policy: Elevating ethical standards*. AI Healthcare Applications and Security, Ethical, and Social Implications., DOI: 10.4018/979-8-3693-7452-8.ch009

Aguinis, H., & Burgi-Tian, J. (2021). Measuring performance for impact: Research agenda and best practices. *Human Resource Management Review*, *31*(2), 100693.

Ahmad S, Hussain M A, Wassay M, (2022). "OVERCOMING DATA FRAGMENTATION IN AGRICULTURE: INTEGRATING MULTI-SOURCE DATA VIA BLOCKCHAIN TO ENHANCE DECISION-MAKING."

Ahmad, S., Lavin, A., Purdy, S., & Agha, Z. (2017). Unsupervised real-time anomaly detection for streaming data. *Neurocomputing*, *262*, 134–147. DOI: 10.1016/j.neucom.2017.04.070

Ajayi, O. O., Alozie, C. E., & Abieba, O. A. (2025). Enhancing Cybersecurity in Energy Infrastructure: Strategies for Safeguarding Critical Systems in the Digital Age. *Trends in Renewable Energy*, *11*(2), 201–212. DOI: 10.17737/tre.2025.11.2.00192

Akhtar, M A K., Kumar, M., & Nayyar, A. (2024). *Transparency and Accountability in Explainable AI: Best Practices*. Towards Ethical and Socially Responsible AI., DOI: 10.1007/978-3-031-41617-7_12

Akram F, Sani M, (2025). "Real-Time AI Systems: Leveraging Cloud Computing and Machine Learning for Big Data Processing."

Aksin-Sivrikaya, S., & Bhattacharya, C. B. (2017). Where digitalization meets sustainability: Opportunities and challenges. In *Sustainability in a Digital World* (pp. 37–49). New Opportunities Through New Technologies. DOI: 10.1007/978-3-319-54603-2_3

Al Masarweh M, Alwada'n T, Afandi W, (2022). "Fog computing, cloud computing and IoT environment: advanced broker management system." Journal of Sensor and Actuator Networks. Doi: .DOI: 10.3390/jsan11010025

Alam M, Islam M R, Shil S K. (2023). "AI-Based predictive maintenance for US manufacturing: reducing downtime and increasing productivity." International Journal of Advanced Research in Science, Communication and Technology, .DOI: 10.48165/ijarsct-2023-1234

Alam, T. (2021). *Cloud-based IoT applications and their roles in smart cities*. Smart Cities., DOI: 10.3390/smartcities4030064

Albouq, S. S., Abi Sen, A. A., Almashf, N., & Yamin, M. (2022). *A survey of interoperability challenges and solutions for dealing with them in IoT environment*. IEEE., DOI: 10.1109/ACCESS.2022.3162219

Aldoseri, A., Al-Khalifa, K. N., & Hamouda, A. M. (2023). Re-thinking data strategy and integration for artificial intelligence: Concepts, opportunities, and challenges. *Applied Sciences (Basel, Switzerland)*, *13*(12), 7082. Advance online publication. DOI: 10.3390/app13127082

Aldrickzler, R., Saadoon, M. Y., Kawad, R. T., & Chornomordenko, I. (2025). Transforming human capital for the digital age: Industry 4.0 and 5.0. *Encuentros. Revista de Ciencias Humanas. Teoría Social y Pensamiento Crítico.*, (23 (enero-abril)), 438–455.

Alieva, J., & Powell, D. (2023). The significance of digital waste in the automation of lean practices. *The Quality Management Journal*, *30*(2), 121–134. DOI: 10.1080/10686967.2023.2171323

Ali, M. A. A., & Alshawi, S. (n.d.). A CULTURAL APPROACH TO STUDY CUSTOMER RELATIONSHIP MANAGEMENT (CRM). *Systems*.

Ali, M. H., Zailani, S., Iranmanesh, M., & Foroughi, B. (2019). Impacts of environmental factors on waste, energy, and resource management and sustainable performance. *Sustainability (Basel)*, *11*(8), 2443. DOI: 10.3390/su11082443

Allen, M. W., & Moser, D. (2004). Communication and Organizational Change: The Role of Communication in Shaping the Relationship Between Employees and Organizational Change. *Management Communication Quarterly*, *18*(2), 175–197.

Allil, K. (2024). Integrating AI-driven marketing analytics techniques into the classroom: Pedagogical strategies for enhancing student engagement and future business success. *Journal of Marketing Analytics*, *12*(2), 142–168. DOI: 10.1057/s41270-023-00281-z

Almutairi R, Bergami G, Morgan G, (2024). “Advancements and challenges in IoT simulators: A comprehensive review.” Doi: .DOI: 10.3390/s24010321

Alqoud A, Schaefer D, Milisavljevic-Syed J, (2022). “Industry 4.0: a systematic review of legacy manufacturing system digital retrofitting.”

Amazon. (2020). *Upskilling 2025*. https://www.aboutamazon.com/news/workplace/upskilling-2025

Amershi, S., Cakmak, M., Knox, W. B., & Kulesza, T. (2014). Power to the people: The role of humans in interactive machine learning. *AI Magazine*, *35*(4), 105–120. DOI: 10.1609/aimag.v35i4.2513

Amjad, A., Azam, F., Anwar, M. W., & Butt, W. H. (2021). *A systematic review on the data interoperability of application layer protocols in industrial IoT*. IEEE., DOI: 10.1109/ACCESS.2021.3094763

Ammari, C., Belatrache, D., & Touhami, B. (2022). *Sizing, optimization, control and energy management of hybrid renewable energy system—A review*. Energy and Built Environment., DOI: 10.1016/j.enbenv.2021.04.002

Amrahova, G. J., & Esanmurodova, N. (2025). 26 Externalities in the era of digitalization: Strategies for public internalization and sustainable revenue generation for structural transformation. *Applications of Mathematics in Science and Technology*, 140.

Anayat, S., & Rasool, G. (2024). Artificial intelligence marketing (AIM): Connecting-the-dots using bibliometrics. *Journal of Marketing Theory and Practice*, *32*(1), 114–135. DOI: 10.1080/10696679.2022.2103435

Anusha, S., Ezhilvandan, M., Gayathri, S., Sivaraman, V., & Anish, T. P. (2024). *Emerging trends in edge AI for Industry 4.0 and 5.0: Technologies, applications, and challenges*. AI Innovations in Service and Tourism Marketing. DOI: 10.4018/979-8-3693-7909-7.ch010

Aragani, V. M., Anumolu, V. R., & Selvakumar, P. (2025). Democratization in the Age of Algorithms: Navigating Opportunities and Challenges. In Wongmahesak, K., Wekke, I., Seftyono, C., & Nurdin, N. (Eds.), *Democracy and Democratization in the Age of AI* (pp. 39–56). IGI Global Scientific Publishing., DOI: 10.4018/979-8-3693-8749-8.ch003

Ardito, L. (2023). The influence of firm digitalization on sustainable innovation performance and the moderating role of corporate sustainability practices: An empirical investigation. *Business Strategy and the Environment*, *32*(8), 5252–5272. DOI: 10.1002/bse.3415

Armenakis, A. A., & Bedeian, A. G. (1999). Organizational Change: A Review of Theory and Research in the 1990s. *Journal of Management*, *25*(3), 293–315. DOI: 10.1177/014920639902500303

Asif, S. (2025). The Role of Digital Food Marketing in Shaping Consumer Behavior and Sustainability in Emerging Economies. In *Innovative Trends Shaping Food Marketing and Consumption* (pp. 57–70). IGI Global Scientific Publishing. DOI: 10.4018/979-8-3693-8542-5.ch003

Aslam, H., Waseem, M., Muneeb, D., Ali, Z., Roubaud, D., & Grebinevych, O. (2025). Customer integration in the supply chain: The role of market orientation and supply chain strategy in the age of digital revolution. *Annals of Operations Research*, *348*(3), 2145–2169. DOI: 10.1007/s10479-023-05191-y PMID: 36846244

Aubry, P., & Nkengne, M. (2020). Transformation numérique des administrations publiques: enjeux humains et organisationnels. Paris: Presses de l'ENA.

Avelar, S., Borges-Tiago, T., Almeida, A., & Tiago, F. (2024). Confluence of sustainable entrepreneurship, innovation, and digitalization in SMEs. *Journal of Business Research*, *170*, 114346. DOI: 10.1016/j.jbusres.2023.114346

Awotunde, J. B., Imoize, A. L., & Jimoh, R. G. (2023). "AIoMT enabling real-time monitoring of healthcare systems: security and privacy considerations." Handbook of Security and Privacy.

Azemi, E., & Bala, S. (n.d.). *Exploring BPM Adoption and Strategic Alignment of Processes at Raiffeisen Bank Kosovo*.

Baah, C., Opoku-Agyeman, D., & Acquah, I. S. K. (2021). Understanding the influence of environmental production practices on firm performance: A proactive versus reactive approach. *Journal of Cleaner Production*. Advance online publication. DOI: 10.1016/j.jclepro.2020.123456

Bag, S., Gupta, S., Kumar, A., & Sivarajah, U. (2021). An integrated artificial intelligence framework for knowledge creation and B2B marketing rational decision making for improving firm performance. *Industrial Marketing Management*, *92*, 178–189. DOI: 10.1016/j.indmarman.2020.12.001

Baiyere, A., Salmela, H., & Tapanainen, T. (2020). Digital transformation and the new logics of business process management. *European Journal of Information Systems*, *29*(3), 238–259. DOI: 10.1080/0960085X.2020.1718007

Balabko, P., Wegmann, A., Ruppen, A., & Clément, N. (n.d.). *The Value of Roles in Modeling Business Processes*.

Balakrishnan, K., & Dhanalakshmi, R. (2023). Clock synchronization in industrial Internet of Things and potential works in precision time protocol: Review, challenges and future directions. *International Journal of Advanced Manufacturing Technology*. Advance online publication. DOI: 10.1007/s00170-023-11535-w

Bal, J. (1998). Process analysis tools for process improvement. *The TQM Magazine*, *10*(5), 342–354. DOI: 10.1108/09544789810231225

Ball, K. (2010). Workplace surveillance: An overview. *Labor History*, *51*(1), 87–106. DOI: 10.1080/00236561003654776

Bansal, P. (2005). Evolving sustainably: A longitudinal study of corporate sustainable development. *Strategic Management Journal*, *26*(3), 197–218. DOI: 10.1002/smj.441

Barari, M., Ross, M., Thaichon, S., & Surachartkumtonkun, J. (2021). A meta-analysis of customer engagement behaviour. *International Journal of Consumer Studies*, *45*(4), 457–477. DOI: 10.1111/ijcs.12609

Bareil, C. (2013). *Gérer le volet humain du changement: une compétence stratégique pour les leaders*. Presses de l'Université du Québec.

Bas, J., Cirillo, C., & Cherchi, E. (2021). Classification of potential electric vehicle purchasers: A machine learning approach. *Technological Forecasting and Social Change*, *168*, 120759. DOI: 10.1016/j.techfore.2021.120759

Bass, B. M., & Riggio, R. E. (2006). *Transformational Leadership* (2nd ed.). Psychology Press.

Bass, B. M., & Riggio, R. E. (2006). *Transformational leadership* (2nd ed.). Psychology Press. DOI: 10.4324/9781410617095

Bauer, M., Sanchez, L., & Song, J. S. (2021). IoT-enabled smart cities: Evolution and outlook. *Sensors (Basel)*, *21*(13), 4511. Advance online publication. DOI: 10.3390/s21134511 PMID: 34209436

Bayoude, K., Ouassit, Y., Ardchir, S., & Azouazi, M. (2018). How machine learning potentials are transforming the practice of digital marketing: State of the art. [PEN]. *Periodicals of Engineering and Natural Sciences*, *6*(2), 373. DOI: 10.21533/pen.v6i2.526

Behnke, I., & Austad, H. (2023). Real-time performance of industrial IoT communication technologies: A review. *IEEE Internet of Things Journal*. Advance online publication. DOI: 10.1109/JIOT.2023.3261245

Beichter, T., & Kaiser, M. (2023). The future of upskilling: human-and technology-centered. In *Proceedings of the 14th International Multi-Conference on Complexity, Informatics and Cybernetics: IMCIC* (pp. 190-193). DOI: 10.54808/IMCIC2023.01.190

Bekaroo, G., Bokhoree, C., & Pattinson, C. (2016). Impacts of ICT on the natural ecosystem: A grassroot analysis for promoting socio-environmental sustainability. *Renewable & Sustainable Energy Reviews*, *57*, 1580–1595. DOI: 10.1016/j.rser.2015.12.147

Bellini, P., Nesi, P., & Pantaleo, G. (2022). IoT-enabled smart cities: A review of concepts, frameworks and key technologies. *Applied Sciences (Basel, Switzerland)*, *12*(3), 1607. Advance online publication. DOI: 10.3390/app12031607

Benabdelhadi, M. (2021). La formation des agents publics face aux exigences de la transformation numérique: Une analyse critique. *Revue Marocaine d'Administration Publique*, (163), 87–102.

Benyam, A. A., Soma, T., & Fraser, E. (2021). Digital agricultural technologies for food loss and waste prevention and reduction: Global trends, adoption opportunities and barriers. *Journal of Cleaner Production*, *323*, 129099. DOI: 10.1016/j.jclepro.2021.129099

Berraho, A., & Chafiq, L. (2022). Les compétences numériques dans l'administration marocaine: État des lieux et perspectives. *Administration et Management Public*, (40), 55–74.

Bersin, J. (2019). *Learning in the flow of work*. Deloitte Insights. https://www2.deloitte.com

Bersin, J. (2020). *The rise of the human-centered organization*. Deloitte Insights. https://www2.deloitte.com/insights

Bhattacharya, S., Sarkar, B., Sarkar, M., & Mukherjee, A. (2024). Hospitality for prime consumers and others under the retail management. *Journal of Retailing and Consumer Services*, *80*, 103849. DOI: 10.1016/j.jretconser.2024.103849

Bilgihan, A., Leong, A. M. W., Okumus, F., & Bai, J. (2024). Proposing a metaverse engagement model for brand development. *Journal of Retailing and Consumer Services*, *78*, 103781. DOI: 10.1016/j.jretconser.2024.103781

Billi, A., & Bernardo, A. (2025). The Effects of Digital Transformation, IT Innovation, and Sustainability Strategies on Firms' Performances: An Empirical Study. *Sustainability (Basel)*, *17*(3), 823. DOI: 10.3390/su17030823

Binns, R. (2018). Fairness in machine learning: Lessons from political philosophy. *Proceedings of the 2018 Conference on Fairness, Accountability and Transparency*, 149–159.

Binns, R. (2018). Fairness in machine learning: Lessons from political philosophy. *Proceedings of the 2018 Conference on Fairness, Accountability, and Transparency (FAT)*, 149–159. https://doi.org/DOI: 10.1145/3287560.3287598

Blanka, C., Krumay, B., & Rueckel, D. (2022). The interplay of digital transformation and employee competency: A design science approach. *Technological Forecasting and Social Change, 178*, 121575. DOI: 10.1016/j.techfore.2022.121575

Bocean, C. G. (2025). Sustainable Development in the Digital Age: Harnessing Emerging Digital Technologies to Catalyze Global SDG Achievement. *Applied Sciences (Basel, Switzerland), 15*(2), 816. DOI: 10.3390/app15020816

Boden, M. A. (2016). *AI: Its nature and future*. Oxford University Press.

Bossert, L., & Hagendorff, T. (2021). Animals and AI. The role of animals in AI research and application – An overview and ethical evaluation. *Technology in Society, 67*, 101678. DOI: 10.1016/j.techsoc.2021.101678

Bostrom, N., & Yudkowsky, E. (2014). The ethics of artificial intelligence. In Frankish, K., & Ramsey, W. M. (Eds.), *The Cambridge handbook of artificial intelligence* (pp. 316–334). Cambridge University Press. DOI: 10.1017/CBO9781139046855.020

Bouckaert, G., & Peters, B. G. (2021). *The Politics of Bureaucracy: An Introduction to Comparative Public Administration*. Edward Elgar Publishing.

Boukar, M., El Kharraz, J., & Moutahir, M. (2022). La gouvernance numérique au Maroc: Avancées, limites et perspectives. *Revue Internationale des Sciences Administratives, 88*(3), 443–460.

Bradley, K. (2007). Defining digital sustainability. *Library Trends, 56*(1), 148–163. DOI: 10.1353/lib.2007.0044

Brock, J. K. U., & Von Wangenheim, F. (2019). Demystifying AI: What digital transformation leaders can teach you about realistic AI implementation. *Business Horizons, 62*(6), 751–758. DOI: 10.1016/j.bushor.2019.08.005

Brynjolfsson, E., & McAfee, A. (2014). *The second machine age: Work, progress, and prosperity in a time of brilliant technologies*. W. W. Norton & Company.

Brynjolfsson, E., & McAfee, A. (2017). *Machine, platform, crowd: Harnessing our digital future*. W.W. Norton & Company.

Bucher, E. L., Schou, P. K., & Waldkirch, M. (2021). Pacifying the algorithm–Anticipatory compliance in the face of algorithmic management in the gig economy. *Organization, 28*(1), 44–67. DOI: 10.1177/1350508420961531

Bughin, J., Hazan, E., Lund, S., Dahlström, P., Wiesinger, A., & Subramaniam, A. (2018). *Skill shift: Automation and the future of the workforce*. McKinsey Global Institute. https://www.mckinsey.com

Bughin, J., Hazan, E., Ramaswamy, S., Chui, M., Allas, T., Dahlström, P., Henke, N., & Trench, M. (2018). *Skill shift: Automation and the future of the workforce*. McKinsey Global Institute.

Butt, J. (2020). A Conceptual Framework to Support Digital Transformation in Manufacturing Using an Integrated Business Process Management Approach. *Designs*, *4*(3), 17. DOI: 10.3390/designs4030017

Cameron, E., & Green, M. (2019). *Making Sense of Change Management*. Kogan Page Publishers.

Cameron, K. S., & Quinn, R. E. (2011). *Diagnosing and changing organizational culture: Based on the competing values framework* (3rd ed.). Jossey-Bass.

Çankaya, S. Y., & Sezen, B. (2015). Ekolojik yenilik ile sürdürülebilirlik performansı arasındaki ilişkide çevresel belirsizliğin moderatör etkisi. *Uluslararası Yönetim İktisat ve İşletme Dergisi*, *11*(2), 111–134.

Carayon, P. (2006). Human factors of complex sociotechnical systems. *Applied Ergonomics*, *37*(4), 525–535. DOI: 10.1016/j.apergo.2006.04.011 PMID: 16756937

Carlson, K., Kopalle, P. K., Riddell, A., Rockmore, D., & Vana, P. (2023). Complementing human effort in online reviews: A deep learning approach to automatic content generation and review synthesis. *International Journal of Research in Marketing*, *40*(1), 54–74. DOI: 10.1016/j.ijresmar.2022.02.004

Carroll, A. B. (1979). A three-dimensional conceptual model of corporate performance. *Academy of Management Review*, *4*(4), 497–505. DOI: 10.2307/257850

Cartwright, S., Liu, H., & Raddats, C. (2021). Strategic use of social media within business-to-business (B2B) marketing: A systematic literature review. *Industrial Marketing Management*, *97*, 35–58. DOI: 10.1016/j.indmarman.2021.06.005

Carvalho, G., Cabral, B., Pereira, V., & Bernardino, J. (2021). Edge computing: Current trends, research challenges and future directions. *Computing*, *103*(5), 993–1023. Advance online publication. DOI: 10.1007/s00607-020-00896-5

Cascio, W. F., & Montealegre, R. (2016). How technology is changing work and organizations. *Annual Review of Organizational Psychology and Organizational Behavior*, *3*(1), 349–375. DOI: 10.1146/annurev-orgpsych-041015-062352

Chaima A, Khebizi A. (2022). "A road-map for mining business process models via artificial intelligence techniques." International Journal of Informatics and Applied Mathematics, .DOI: 10.28964/ijiam.2022.1.2

Chakraborty, S., Datta, H. N., Kalita, K., & Chakraborty, S. (2023). A narrative review of multi-objective optimization on the basis of ratio analysis (MOORA) method in decision making. *OPSEARCH, 60*(4), 1844–1887. DOI: 10.1007/s12597-023-00676-7

Challoumis, C. (2024). "FROM AUTOMATION TO INNOVATION-THE FINANCIAL BENEFITS OF AI IN BUSINESS." Available at *SSRN*, DOI: 10.2139/ssrn.1234567

Chasokela, D., & Mangena, N. (2025). The Future of Learning in the Digital Age. In *Insights Into International Higher Education Leadership and the Skills Gap* (pp. 471–500). IGI Global.

Cheah, S., Ho, Y.-P., & Li, S. (2018). Business Model Innovation for Sustainable Performance in Retail and Hospitality Industries. *Sustainability (Basel), 10*(11), 11. Advance online publication. DOI: 10.3390/su10113952

Chen, A., Li, L., & Shahid, W. (2024). Digital transformation as the driving force for sustainable business performance: A moderated mediation model of market-driven business model innovation and digital leadership capabilities. *Heliyon, 10*(8), e29509. DOI: 10.1016/j.heliyon.2024.e29509 PMID: 38655293

Chen, D., Heyer, S., Ibbotson, S., Salonitis, K., Steingrímsson, J. G., & Thiede, S. (2015). Direct digital manufacturing: Definition, evolution, and sustainability implications. *Journal of Cleaner Production, 107*, 615–625. DOI: 10.1016/j.jclepro.2015.05.009

Cheng, L., & Nasirov, J. (2025). Sociosemiotic Framing of Human Rights in Digital Age. *International Journal for the Semiotics of Law-Revue internationale de Sémiotique juridique*, 1-16.

Chesbrough, H. (2003). *Open Innovation: The New Imperative for Creating and Profiting from Technology*. Harvard Business Press.

Chhotaray, P., Behera, B. C., & Moharana, B. R. (2023). Enhancement of manufacturing sector performance with the application of Industrial Internet of Things (IIoT). *Journal of Manufacturing Technology Management*. Advance online publication. DOI: 10.1108/JMTM-02-2023-0054

Chigurupati, A., & Lassar, N. (2017). Root cause analysis using artificial intelligence. In *2017 Annual reliability and maintainability symposium (RAMS)* (pp. 1-5). IEEE. DOI: DOI: 10.1109/RAM.2017.7889651

Chohan, U. W. (2021). *Public Sector Digital Transformation: A Guide to Strategy and Implementation*. Routledge.

Chong, D., & Shi, H. (2015). Big data analytics: A literature review. *Journal of Management Analytics*, *2*(3), 175–201. DOI: 10.1080/23270012.2015.1082449

Christensen, C. M., & Overdorf, M. (2000). Meeting the Challenge of Disruptive Change. *Harvard Business Review*, *78*(2), 66–76.

Christl, W. (2023). *Monitoring Work and Automating Task Allocation in Retail and Hospitality*.

Chui, M., Manyika, J., & Miremadi, M. (2016). Where machines could replace humans—and where they can't (yet). *McKinsey Quarterly*. https://www.mckinsey.com

Chui, M., Manyika, J., & Miremadi, M. (2016). Where machines could replace humans—and where they can't (yet). *McKinsey Quarterly*. Retrieved from https://www.mckinsey.com

Chui, M., Manyika, J., & Miremadi, M. (2018). What AI can and can't do (yet) for your business. *McKinsey & Company*. https://www.mckinsey.com

Ciacci A, Raimondi C. (2024). "AI IMPLEMENTATION BEST PRACTICES." Economia & Management, .DOI: 10.3280/em2010-002007

Cioppi, M., Curina, I., Francioni, B., & Savelli, E. (2023). Digital transformation and marketing: A systematic and thematic literature review. *Italian Journal of Marketing*, *2023*(2), 207–288. DOI: 10.1007/s43039-023-00067-2

Cisterna, D., Lauble, S., Haghsheno, S., & Wolber, J. (2022). Synergies between lean construction and artificial intelligence: AI driven continuous improvement process. In *Proceedings of the 30th annual conference of the International Group for Lean Construction (IGLC30)* (pp. 199-210). DOI: DOI: 10.24928/2022/0122

Clark, M., & Myers, A. (2018). *How customer-centric are you?* [Report]. Henley Centre for Customer Management. http://www.hccmsite.co.uk

Clark, A., & Chalmers, D. (1998). The extended mind. *Analysis*, *58*(1), 7–19. DOI: 10.1093/analys/58.1.7

Coca-Cola Journey. (2018). How Coca-Cola uses AI to listen to consumers and create new drinks. Retrieved from https://www.coca-colacompany.com

Coito, T., Firme, B., Martins, M. S. E., Vieira, S. M., Figueiredo, J., & Sousa, J. M. C. (2021). Intelligent sensors for real-Time decision-making. *Automation.*, *2*(2), 62–82. Advance online publication. DOI: 10.3390/automation2020004

Côrte-Real, N., Oliveira, T., & Ruivo, P. (2019). Assessing business value of Big Data Analytics in European firms. *Journal of Business Research*, *97*, 606–615. DOI: 10.1016/j.jbusres.2018.12.072

Costa, I., Riccotta, R., Montini, P., Stefani, E., de Souza Goes, R., Gaspar, M. A., & Larieira, C. L. C. (2022). The degree of contribution of digital transformation technology on company sustainability areas. *Sustainability (Basel)*, *14*(1), 462. DOI: 10.3390/su14010462

Cowls, J., & Tsamados, A. (2023). *Artificial intelligence for the sustainable development goals*. Springer.

Cruz, J. C., & Garcia, A. M. (2024). Machine Learning for Predictive Maintenance to Enhance Energy Efficiency in Industrial Operations. [Information Technology Engineering Journal]. *ITE Journal*, *9*(1), 15–22. Advance online publication. DOI: 10.24235/itej.v9i2.125

Cui Y, Liu F, Jing X, Mu J, (2021). "Integrating sensing and communications for ubiquitous IoT: Applications, trends, and challenges." Doi: .DOI: 10.1109/MNET.011.2000345

Cull, R. (2010). *HYBRID PROCESS MODELLING WITHIN BUSINESS PROCESS MANAGEMENT PROJECTS.*

Dahake, N. S., Gajghate, A., Dahake, P. S., & Bansod, S. (2024). A Transformative Impact of IoT and AI by Predictive Analytics on Modern Marketing Strategies: A Study of its Significance & Accuracy. *2024 2nd International Conference on Advances in Computation, Communication and Information Technology (ICAICCIT)*, 1150–1158. DOI: 10.1109/ICAICCIT64383.2024.10912388

Dahake, N. S., Suresh Dahake, P., & Gajghate, A. (2024). Beyond the Hype: A Critical Evaluation of Predictive Analytics Accuracy in High-Stakes Business Decisions. *2024 2nd DMIHER International Conference on Artificial Intelligence in Healthcare, Education and Industry (IDICAIEI)*, 1–6. DOI: 10.1109/IDICAIEI61867.2024.10842857

Dahake, P. S., & Somani, N. (2024). Harnessing Predictive Analytics for Accurate Consumer Behaviour Forecasting: A Comprehensive Review. *2024 2nd DMIHER International Conference on Artificial Intelligence in Healthcare, Education and Industry (IDICAIEI)*, 1–6. DOI: 10.1109/IDICAIEI61867.2024.10842743

Dahake, P. S., Chandak, S., & Dahake, N. S. (2024). Predictive Analytics in Performance Appraisal Systems: Enhancing Objectivity and Fairness. *2024 2nd DMIHER International Conference on Artificial Intelligence in Healthcare, Education and Industry (IDICAIEI)*, 1–5. DOI: 10.1109/IDICAIEI61867.2024.10842916

Dahake, P. S., Jain, M., Anusha, B., Poojitha, S., Singh, N., & Sharma, A. (2024). Integrating Organisational Theory, Resource-Based View, and Big Data Culture to Improve Manufacturing Performance. In D. Jelonek, N. Kumar, M. Chahar, R. Kinkladze, & L. Knop, *Recent Trends In Engineering and Science for Resource Optimization and Sustainable Development* (1st ed., pp. 156–159). CRC Press. DOI: 10.1201/9781003596721-36

Dahake, P. S., Bagaregari, P., & Dahake, N. S. (2024). Shaping the Future of Retail: A Comprehensive Review of Predictive Analytics Models for Consumer Behavior. In Inder, S., Min, B., & Sharma, S. (Eds.), (pp. 143–160). Advances in Business Strategy and Competitive Advantage. IGI Global., DOI: 10.4018/979-8-3693-1734-1.ch011

Dahake, P. S., & Bansod, S. N. (2019). The role of Chinese electronics products to sway middle-class buyers. *International Journal of Public Sector Performance Management*, *5*(3/4), 337. DOI: 10.1504/IJPSPM.2019.10022488

Dahake, P. S., Chandak, S., Mohare, R. V., Wadhwani, K., & Bhadade, P. (2023). The Crystal Ball of Marketing: How Predictive Analytics is Reshaping the Industry? *2023 Second International Conference On Smart Technologies For Smart Nation (SmartTechCon)*, 304–311. DOI: 10.1109/SmartTechCon57526.2023.10391334

Dahake, P. S., & Dahake, N. S. (2024). The Role of Big Data in Predictive Analytics for E-Commerce: Examine How Big Data Contributes to Better Predictions in Online Shopping. In Tarnanidis, T., Papathanasiou, J., Ismyrlis, V., & Kittu Manda, V. (Eds.), (pp. 403–426). Advances in Marketing, Customer Relationship Management, and E-Services. IGI Global., DOI: 10.4018/979-8-3693-9122-8.ch018

Daniel, S., Bogdana, R., Aladdin, A., Anat, F., & Michael, L. (2020). Principles to Practices for Responsible AI: Closing the Gap. *The 2020 European Conference on AI (ECAI)*. DOI: DOI: 10.48550/arXiv.2006.04707

Das, R. C., & Basavaraj, S. (2024). The Importance of Strategic Agility and Resilience in Work-Life Balance. In *Practical Approaches to Agile Project Management* (pp. 270–288). IGI Global.

Dave D M K, Mittapally B K, (2024). "Data Integration and Interoperability in IoT: Challenges, Strategies and Future Direction." International Journal of Computer Engineering and Technology.

Davenport, T. H., & Kirby, J. (2016). *Only humans need apply: Winners and losers in the age of smart machines*. HarperBusiness.

Davenport, T. H., & Ronanki, R. (2018). Artificial intelligence for the real world. *Harvard Business Review*, *96*(1), 108–116.

Davenport, T., Guha, A., Grewal, D., & Bressgott, T. (2020). How artificial intelligence will change the future of marketing. *Journal of the Academy of Marketing Science*, *48*(1), 24–42. DOI: 10.1007/s11747-019-00696-0

Davis, F. D. (1989). Perceived usefulness, perceived ease of use, and user acceptance of information technology. *Management Information Systems Quarterly*, *13*(3), 319–340. DOI: 10.2307/249008

De Cosmo, L. M., Piper, L., & Di Vittorio, A. (2021). The role of attitude toward chatbots and privacy concern on the relationship between attitude toward mobile advertising and behavioral intent to use chatbots. *Italian Journal of Marketing*, *2021*(1–2), 83–102. DOI: 10.1007/s43039-021-00020-1

De Hond, A A H., Leeuwenberg, A. M., Hooft, L., Kant, I. M. J., Nijman, S. W. J., van Os, H. J. A., Aardoom, J. J., Debray, T. P. A., Schuit, E., van Smeden, M., Reitsma, J. B., Steyerberg, E. W., Chavannes, N. H., & Moons, K. G. M. (2022). Guidelines and quality criteria for artificial intelligence-based prediction models in healthcare: A scoping review. *NPJ Digital Medicine*, *5*(1), 2. Advance online publication. DOI: 10.1038/s41746-021-00549-7 PMID: 35013569

De Luzi, F. (2024). *Digital transformation in a hyper-connected world. Transforming legacy systems through blockchains*. IoT and AI.

De Mauro, A., Sestino, A., & Bacconi, A. (2022). Machine learning and artificial intelligence use in marketing: A general taxonomy. *Italian Journal of Marketing*, *2022*(4), 439–457. DOI: 10.1007/s43039-022-00057-w

Debnath, P., Deshmukh, S. M., Laroia, M., Selvakumar, P., Manjunath, T. C., & Bhattacharya, S. (2025). Challenges Faced by Countries in Renewable Energy Adoption. In Özsungur, F., Chaychi Semsari, M., & Küçük Bayraktar, H. (Eds.), *Geopolitical Landscapes of Renewable Energy and Urban Growth* (pp. 295–320). IGI Global Scientific Publishing., DOI: 10.4018/979-8-3693-8814-3.ch010

Dec, G., Stadnicka, D., Paśko, Ł., Mądziel, M., Figliè, R., Mazzei, D., Tyrovolas, M., Stylios, C., Navarro, J., & Solé-Beteta, X. (2022). Role of academics in transferring knowledge and skills on artificial intelligence, internet of things and edge computing. *Sensors (Basel)*, *22*(7), 2496. Advance online publication. DOI: 10.3390/s22072496 PMID: 35408110

Deci, E. L., & Ryan, R. M. (2000). The "what" and "why" of goal pursuits: Human needs and the self-determination of behavior. *Psychological Inquiry*, *11*(4), 227–268. DOI: 10.1207/S15327965PLI1104_01

Dedrick, J. (2010). Green IS: Concepts and issues for information systems research. *Communications of the Association for Information Systems*, *27*(11), 173–184. DOI: 10.17705/1CAIS.02711

Del Río Castro, G., González Fernández, M. C., & Uruburu Colsa, Á. (2021). Unleashing the convergence amid digitalization and sustainability towards pursuing the sustainable development goals (SDGs): A holistic review. *Journal of Cleaner Production*, *280*, 122204. DOI: 10.1016/j.jclepro.2020.122204

Deloitte Insights. (2021). *The future of audit: Preparing for change*. Retrieved from https://www2.deloitte.com/insights

Deloitte. (2019). *AI in Audit: How artificial intelligence is transforming the audit process*. Retrieved from https://www2.deloitte.com

Deloitte. (2020). *The social enterprise at work: Paradox as a path forward*. Retrieved from https://www2.deloitte.com

Dereköy, F. (2015). Kurumsal yönetim ve temel dinamikleri. *Ekonomi ve Yönetim Araştırmaları Dergisi*, *4*(1), 31–51.

Dernbach, J. C., & Mintz, J. A. (2011). Environmental laws and sustainability: An introduction. *Sustainability (Basel)*, *3*(3), 531–540. DOI: 10.3390/su3030531

Devan, P A M., Hussin, F. A., Ibrahim, R., Bingi, K., & Khanday, F. A. (2021). A survey on the application of WirelessHART for industrial process monitoring and control. *Sensors (Basel)*, *21*(15), 4951. Advance online publication. DOI: 10.3390/s21154951 PMID: 34372210

Dey, P. K., Malesios, C., De, D., Chowdhury, S., & Abdelaziz, F. B. (2020). The impact of lean management practices and sustainably-oriented innovation on sustainability performance of small and medium-sized enterprises: Empirical evidence from the UK. *British Journal of Management*, *31*(1), 141–161. DOI: 10.1111/1467-8551.12388

Dignum, V. (2019). *Responsible artificial intelligence: How to develop and use AI in a responsible way*. Springer Nature. DOI: 10.1007/978-3-030-30371-6

Dimitrovska, I., & Malinovski, T. (2017). Creating a Business Value while Transforming Data Assets using Machine Learning. *Computer Engineering and Applications Journal*, *6*(2), 59–70. DOI: 10.18495/comengapp.v6i2.205

Dolgui A, Ivanov D, (2022). "5G in digital supply chain and operations management: fostering flexibility, end-to-end connectivity and real-time visibility through internet-of-everything." Doi: .DOI: 10.1080/00207543.2022.2051156

Dongbo, M., Miniaoui, S., Fen, L., Althubiti, S. A., & Alsenani, T. R. (2023). Intelligent chatbot interaction system capable for sentimental analysis using hybrid machine learning algorithms. *Information Processing & Management, 60*(5), 103440. DOI: 10.1016/j.ipm.2023.103440

Drucker, P. F. (2001). *The Essential Drucker: The Best of Sixty Years of Peter Drucker's Essential Writings on Management*. HarperBusiness.

Duarte, J., Rodrigues, F., & Castelo Branco, J. (2022). Sensing Technology Applications in the Mining Industry—A Systematic Review. *International Journal of Environmental Research and Public Health, 19*(4), 2334. DOI: 10.3390/ijerph19042334 PMID: 35206524

Dumas, M., Fournier, F., Limonad, L., Marrella, A., Montali, M., Rehse, J.-R., Accorsi, R., Calvanese, D., De Giacomo, G., Fahland, D., Gal, A., La Rosa, M., Völzer, H., & Weber, I. (2022). *AI-Augmented Business Process Management Systems: A Research Manifesto*. DOI: 10.48550/ARXIV.2201.12855

Dumas, M., La Rosa, M., Mendling, J., & Reijers, H. A. (2018). *Fundamentals of Business Process Management* (2nd ed.). Springer. DOI: 10.1007/978-3-662-56509-4

Dumitru, I., & Căescu, Ş. C. (2013). The Supply Chain, a Strategic Marketing Approach. *The AMFITEATRU ECONOMIC Journal, 15*(33), 116–127.

Dunleavy, P., Margetts, H., Bastow, S., & Tinkler, J. (2006). *Digital Era Governance: IT Corporations, the State, and e-Government*. Oxford University Press.

Dutta P K, Mitra S, (2021). "Application of agricultural drones and IoT to understand food supply chain during post COVID-19." Agricultural Informatics. Doi: .DOI: 10.1002/9781119768707.ch12

Dvorský, J., Bednarz, J., & Blajer-Gołębiewska, A. (2023). The impact of corporate reputation and social media engagement on the sustainability of SMEs: Perceptions of top managers and the owners. Equilibrium. *Quarterly Journal of Economics and Economic Policy, 18*(3), 779–811. DOI: 10.24136/eq.2023.025

Dwivedi, Y. K., Hughes, L., Ismagilova, E., Aarts, G., Coombs, C., Crick, T., Duan, Y., Dwivedi, R., Edwards, J., Eirug, A., Galanos, V., Ilavarasan, P. V., Janssen, M., Jones, P., Kar, A. K., Kizgin, H., Kronemann, B., Lal, B., Lucini, B., & Williams, M. D. (2021). Artificial Intelligence (AI): Multidisciplinary perspectives on emerging challenges, opportunities, and agenda for research, practice and policy. *International Journal of Information Management*, *57*, 101994. DOI: 10.1016/j.ijinfomgt.2019.08.002

Dwivedi, Y. K., Sharma, A., Rana, N. P., Giannakis, M., Goel, P., & Dutot, V. (2023). Evolution of artificial intelligence research in Technological Forecasting and Social Change: Research topics, trends, and future directions. *Technological Forecasting and Social Change*, *192*, 122579. Advance online publication. DOI: 10.1016/j.techfore.2023.122579

Dyllick, T., & Hockerts, K. (2002). Beyond the business case for corporate sustainability. *Business Strategy and the Environment*, *11*(2), 130–141. DOI: 10.1002/bse.323

Eckerson, W. W. (2007). Predictive analytics. *Extending the Value of Your Data Warehousing Investment. TDWI Best Practices Report*, *1*, 1–36.

Elgendy, N., & Elragal, A. (2014). Big data analytics: a literature review paper. In *Advances in Data Mining. Applications and Theoretical Aspects: 14th Industrial Conference, ICDM 2014, St. Petersburg, Russia, July 16-20, 2014.* (Springer International Publishing.). *Proceedings*, *14*, 214–227.

El-Gharib, N. M., & Amyot, D. (2022). *Robotic Process Automation Using Process Mining $\unicode{x2013}$ A Systematic Literature Review*. DOI: 10.48550/ARXIV.2204.00751

Ellen MacArthur Foundation. (2022). *Circular economy and digital technology*. https://ellenmacarthurfoundation.org/topics/digital

Embergenov, A. (2023). *Enhancing enterprise energy management with iot-based monitoring systems*. Eurasian Science Review.

Engert, S., Rauter, R., & Baumgartner, R. J. (2016). Exploring the integration of corporate sustainability into strategic management: A literature review. *Journal of Cleaner Production*, *112*, 2833–2850. DOI: 10.1016/j.jclepro.2015.08.031

ENHANCING CUSTOMER LOYALTY THROUGH QUALITY OF SERVICE. EFFECTIVE STRATEGIES TO IMPROVE CUSTOMER SATISFACTION, EXPERIENCE, RELATIONSHIP, AND ENGAGEMENT. (2023). *International Research Journal of Modernization in Engineering Technology and Science*. Advance online publication. DOI: 10.56726/IRJMETS38104

Escobar, C. A., McGovern, M. E., & Morales-Menendez, R. (2021). Quality 4.0: A review of big data challenges in manufacturing. *Journal of Intelligent Manufacturing, 32*(8), 2319–2334. Advance online publication. DOI: 10.1007/s10845-021-01765-4

Escoto, M., Guerrero, A., Ghorbani, E., & Juan, A. A. (2024). Optimization challenges in vehicle-to-grid (V2G) systems and artificial intelligence solving methods. *Applied Sciences (Basel, Switzerland), 14*(12), 5211. Advance online publication. DOI: 10.3390/app14125211

Estebsari, A., & Mazzarino, P. R. (2021). IoT-enabled real-time management of smart grids with demand response aggregators. *IEEE Transactions on Industry Applications*. Advance online publication. DOI: 10.1109/TIA.2021.3071245

Estevez, E., & Janowski, T. (2022). *Sustainable digital governance: Policies and practices*. MIT Press.

Eubanks, V. (2018). *Automating Inequality: How High-Tech Tools Profile, Police, and Punish the Poor*. St. Martin's Press.

Eubanks, V. (2018). *Automating inequality: How high-tech tools profile, police, and punish the poor*. St. Martin's Press.

European Commission. (2022). *Shaping Europe's digital future: A green and sustainable approach*. https://digital-strategy.ec.europa.eu/en/policies/green-digital

Fareed, A. G., De Felice, F., Forcina, A., & Petrillo, A. (2024). Role and applications of advanced digital technologies in achieving sustainability in multimodal logistics operations: A systematic literature review. *Sustainable Futures : An Applied Journal of Technology, Environment and Society, 8*, 100278. DOI: 10.1016/j.sftr.2024.100278

Fedorova, N., Panfilov, I., Moiseeva, E., Degtyareva, K., & Markovskaya, E. (2024). Analytical methods and tools for business process optimization. *BIO Web of Conferences, 113*, 05009. DOI: 10.1051/bioconf/202411305009

Fehrer, T., Fischer, D. A., Leemans, S. J., Röglinger, M., & Wynn, M. T. (2022). An assisted approach to business process redesign. *Decision Support Systems, 156*, 113749. DOI: 10.1016/j.dss.2022.113749

Feliciano-Cestero, M. M., Ameen, N., Kotabe, M., Paul, J., & Signoret, M. (2023). Is digital transformation threatened? A systematic literature review of the factors influencing firms' digital transformation and internationalization. *Journal of Business Research, 157*, 113546. DOI: 10.1016/j.jbusres.2022.113546

Fernandez D, Aman A. (2021). "Planning for a successful Robotic Process Automation (RPA) project: A case study." Journal of Information and Knowledge Management, .DOI: 10.1108/JD-02-2021-0034

Fernández-Portillo, A., Almodóvar-González, M., Coca-Pérez, J. L., & Jiménez-Naranjo, H. V. (2019). Is sustainable economic development possible thanks to the deployment of ICT? *Sustainability (Basel)*, *11*(22), 6307. DOI: 10.3390/su11226307

Fernandez, S., & Rainey, H. G. (2006). Managing Successful Organizational Change in the Public Sector. *Public Administration Review*, *66*(2), 168–176. DOI: 10.1111/j.1540-6210.2006.00570.x

Fernandez-Viagas V, Framinan J M, (2022). "Exploring the benefits of scheduling with advanced and real-time information integration in Industry 4.0: A computational study." Doi: .DOI: 10.1016/j.jii.2022.100234

Ferrucci, D., Levas, A., Bagchi, S., Gondek, D., & Mueller, E. (2013). Watson: Beyond jeopardy! *Artificial Intelligence*, *199–200*, 93–105. DOI: 10.1016/j.artint.2012.06.009

Fischer, M., Imgrund, F., Janiesch, C., & Winkelmann, A. (2020). Strategy archetypes for digital transformation: Defining meta objectives using business process management. *Information & Management*, *57*(5), 103262. DOI: 10.1016/j.im.2019.103262

Floridi, L., Cowls, J., Beltrametti, M., Chiarello, F., & Taddeo, M. (2018). AI4People—An ethical framework for a good AI society. *Minds and Machines*, *28*(4), 689–707. DOI: 10.1007/s11023-018-9482-5 PMID: 30930541

Foss, N. J., & Saebi, T. (2017). Fifteen years of business model innovation research: Literature review and future research directions. *Journal of Management*, *43*(1), 200–227. DOI: 10.1177/0149206316675927

Fraccastoro, S., Gabrielsson, M., & Pullins, E. B. (2021). The integrated use of social media, digital, and traditional communication tools in the B2B sales process of international SMEs. *International Business Review*, *30*(4), 101776. DOI: 10.1016/j.ibusrev.2020.101776

Fredström, A., Parida, V., Wincent, J., Sjödin, D., & Oghazi, P. (2022). What is the Market Value of Artificial Intelligence and Machine Learning? The Role of Innovativeness and Collaboration for Performance. *Technological Forecasting and Social Change*, *180*, 121716. DOI: 10.1016/j.techfore.2022.121716

Frey, C. B., & Osborne, M. A. (2017). The future of employment: How susceptible are jobs to computerization? *Technological Forecasting and Social Change*, *114*, 254–280. DOI: 10.1016/j.techfore.2016.08.019

Frick, T. (2020). *Designing for sustainability in the digital space*. A List Apart. https://alistapart.com/article/sustainable-web-design/

Fuchs, C. (2021). *Sustainability and digital media: A critical introduction*. SAGE Publications.

Fülöp, M. T., & Cifuentes-Faura, J. (2025). Digital approaches in sustainable entrepreneurship training: Effects on student well-being and satisfaction. *Education and Information Technologies*, •••, 1–32.

Gade K R, (2024). "Data Quality Metrics for the Modern Enterprise: A Data Analytics Perspective."

Gallup. (2023). *State of the Global Workplace 2023 Report*. https://www.gallup.com

Ganiyu, I. O., & Oladejo, O. M. (2022). Green Work-Life Balance and Global Leadership in Industry 4.0. In *Research Anthology on Human Resource Practices for the Modern Workforce* (pp. 2121-2137). IGI Global Scientific Publishing.

Gao, W., Fan, H., Li, W., & Wang, H. (2021). Crafting the customer experience in omnichannel contexts: The role of channel integration. *Journal of Business Research*, *126*, 12–22. DOI: 10.1016/j.jbusres.2020.12.056

Gartner. (2021). *How to measure productivity in a hybrid work environment*. Gartner, Inc. https://www.gartner.com

Gaur A, Pooja, Hooda S, Saya L. (2024). "Recommendations for Implementation of AI: Steps Toward Industry-Wide Adoption." Application of Artificial Intelligence in Business and Industry, .DOI: 10.1007/978-981-16-2156-6_12

Gebayew, C., Hardini, I. R., Panjaitan, G. H. A., & Kurniawan, N. B. (2018, October). A systematic literature review on digital transformation. In *2018 International Conference on Information Technology Systems and Innovation (ICITSI)*, 260-265. DOI: 10.1109/ICITSI.2018.8695912

Genç, R. (2017). The importance of communication in sustainability & sustainable strategies. *Procedia Manufacturing*, *8*, 511–516. DOI: 10.1016/j.promfg.2017.02.065

George, A. S., George, A. S. H., Baskar, T., & Sujatha, V. (2023). The rise of hyperautomation: A new frontier for business process automation. *Partners Universal International Research Journal*, *2*(4), 13–35.

George, A., Ali, M., & Papakostas, N. (2021). Utilising robotic process automation technologies for streamlining the additive manufacturing design workflow. *CIRP Annals*, *70*(1), 119–122. Advance online publication. DOI: 10.1016/j.cirp.2021.04.017

Gera, S., & Sinha, A. (2022). T-Bot: AI-based social media bot detection model for trend-centric twitter network. *Social Network Analysis and Mining*, *12*(1), 76. DOI: 10.1007/s13278-022-00897-6

Gerlich, M., Elsayed, W., & Sokolovskiy, K. (2023). Artificial intelligence as toolset for analysis of public opinion and social interaction in marketing: Identification of micro and nano influencers. *Frontiers in Communication*, *8*, 1075654. DOI: 10.3389/fcomm.2023.1075654

Gerzon G, Sheng Y, Kirkitadze M, (2022). "Process analytical technologies–advances in bioprocess integration and future perspectives." Doi: .DOI: 10.1016/j.jpba.2022.114532

Ge, Z., Song, Z., Ding, S. X., & Huang, B. (2017). Data Mining and Analytics in the Process Industry: The Role of Machine Learning. *IEEE Access : Practical Innovations, Open Solutions*, *5*, 20590–20616. DOI: 10.1109/ACCESS.2017.2756872

Ghahramani, Z. (2015). Probabilistic machine learning and artificial intelligence. *Nature*, *521*(7553), 452–459. DOI: 10.1038/nature14541 PMID: 26017444

Ghosh, A., Lindner, M., Patel, A., & Tanniru, M. (2020). Unlocking productivity with AI and advanced analytics. *McKinsey & Company*. Retrieved from https://www.mckinsey.com

Ghosh, M., & Thirugnanam, A. (2021). Introduction to artificial Intelligence. In *Studies in big data* (pp. 23–44). DOI: DOI: 10.1007/978-981-16-0415-7_2

Gill, S. S., Xu, M., Ottaviani, C., Patros, P., Bahsoon, R., Shaghaghi, A., Golec, M., Stankovski, V., Wu, H., Abraham, A., Singh, M., Mehta, H., Ghosh, S. K., Baker, T., Parlikad, A. K., Lutfiyya, H., Kanhere, S. S., Sakellariou, R., Dustdar, S., & Uhlig, S. (2022). AI for next generation computing: Emerging trends and future directions. *Internet of Things : Engineering Cyber Physical Human Systems*, *19*, 100514. Advance online publication. DOI: 10.1016/j.iot.2022.100514

Goethals, T., & Volckaert, B. (2021). Enabling and leveraging AI in the intelligent edge: A review of current trends and future directions. *IEEE Open Journal of the Industrial Electronics Society*. Advance online publication. DOI: 10.1109/OJIES.2021.3091234

Goncalves, M., Hu, Y., Aliagas, I., & Cerdá, L. M. (2024). Neuromarketing algorithms' consumer privacy and ethical considerations: Challenges and opportunities. *Cogent Business & Management*, *11*(1), 2333063. DOI: 10.1080/23311975.2024.2333063

Gong, S. (2023). Digital transformation of supply chain management in retail and e-commerce. *International Journal of Retail & Distribution Management*. Advance online publication. DOI: 10.1108/IJRDM-02-2023-0054

Gonzalez, A. (2020). AI for accessibility: Bridging the gap for differently-abled employees. *Journal of Inclusive Technologies*, *12*(1), 45–53.

Gopi, B., Kokila, M. S., Bibin, C. V., Sasikala, D., Howard, E., & Boopathi, S. (2024). Distributed Technologies Using AI/ML Techniques for Healthcare Applications. In *Social Innovations in Education, Environment, and Healthcare* (pp. 375-396). IGI Global.

Gordon, A. (1999). *Classification* (2nd ed.). CRC Press. DOI: 10.1201/9780367805302

Greatergroup. (2022, February 23). *Retail Hospitality*. Greater Group. https://www.thegreatergroup.com/combining-retail-and-hospitality-through-creative-store-design/

Greenpeace. (2021). *Clicking clean: Who is winning the race to build a green internet?* https://www.greenpeace.org/usa/reports/clicking-clean-2021/

Gremler, D. D., Van Vaerenbergh, Y., Brüggen, E. C., & Gwinner, K. P. (2020). Understanding and managing customer relational benefits in services: A meta-analysis. *Journal of the Academy of Marketing Science*, *48*(3), 565–583. DOI: 10.1007/s11747-019-00701-6

Grisold, T., Mendling, J., & Otto, M. (2021). Adoption, use and management of process mining in practice. *Business Process Management Journal*. Advance online publication. DOI: 10.1108/BPMJ-02-2021-0064

Gross, S., & Vienna, W. (n.d.-a). *Navigating Through the Maze of Business Process Change Methods*.

Gross, S., & Vienna, W. (n.d.-b). *Navigating Through the Maze of Business Process Change Methods*.

Gross, S., Malinova, M., & Mendling, J. (2019). *Navigating Through the Maze of Business Process Change Methods. Hawaii International Conference on System Sciences*. DOI: 10.24251/HICSS.2019.754

Grybauskas, A., Stefanini, A., & Ghobakhloo, M. (2022). Social sustainability in the age of digitalization: A systematic literature review on the social implications of industry 4.0. *Technology in Society*, *70*, 101997. DOI: 10.1016/j.techsoc.2022.101997

Guandalini, I. (2022). Sustainability through digital transformation: A systematic literature review for research guidance. *Journal of Business Research, 148*, 456–471. DOI: 10.1016/j.jbusres.2022.05.003

Gupta, A., & Gupta, A. (2011). RESEARCH PAPER ON CLUSTER TECHNIQUES OF DATA VARIATIONS. *International Journal of Advance Technology & Engineering Research.*, *1*(1), 39–47.

Gupta, A., & Singh, A. (2023). Healthcare 4.0: Recent advancements and futuristic research directions. *Wireless Personal Communications*, *129*(2), 933–952. Advance online publication. DOI: 10.1007/s11277-022-10164-8 PMID: 36594000

Gupta, B. B., & Colace, F. (Eds.). (2023). *Handbook of Research on AI and ML for Intelligent Machines and Systems*. IGI Global. DOI: 10.4018/978-1-6684-9999-3

Gutuleac, R., Baima, G., Rizzo, C., & Bresciani, S. (2024). Will virtual influencers overcome the uncanny valley? The moderating role of social cues. *Psychology and Marketing*, *41*(7), 1419–1431. DOI: 10.1002/mar.21989

Hallikainen, H., Savimäki, E., & Laukkanen, T. (2020). Fostering B2B sales with customer big data analytics. *Industrial Marketing Management*, *86*, 90–98. DOI: 10.1016/j.indmarman.2019.12.005

Hamadaqa M H M, Alnajjar M, Ayyad M N, Al-Nakhal M A, (2024). "Leveraging Artificial Intelligence for Strategic Business Decision-Making: Opportunities and Challenges."

Hamel, G., & Prahalad, C. K. (1994). *Competing for the Future*. Harvard Business Press.

Hammer, M. (1990). Reengineering work: Don't automate, obliterate. *Harvard Business Review*, *68*(4), 104–112.

Hammer, M. (2014). What is business process management? In *Handbook on business process management 1: Introduction, methods, and information systems* (pp. 3–16). Springer Berlin Heidelberg., DOI: 10.1007/978-3-642-45100-3_1

Hammer, M., & Stanton, S. A. (1999). How process enterprises really work. *Harvard Business Review*, *77*(6), 108–118. PMID: 10662000

Handoyo, S., Suharman, H., Ghani, E. K., & Soedarsono, S. (2023). A business strategy, operational efficiency, ownership structure, and manufacturing performance: The moderating role of market uncertainty and competition intensity. *Journal of Open Innovation*, *9*(2), 100039. Advance online publication. DOI: 10.1016/j.joitmc.2023.100039

Hanjani, B., & Akhavan, A. (2018). *The Impact of Television and Short Message Service Advertising on Customer Behaviour and Brand Attitude*.

Hansen, H. F., Haddara, M., & Langseth, M. (2023). Investigating ERP system customization: A focus on cloud-ERP. *Procedia Computer Science*, *219*, 915–923. DOI: 10.1016/j.procs.2023.01.367

Harter, J. K., Schmidt, F. L., & Hayes, T. L. (2002). Business-unit-level relationship between employee satisfaction, employee engagement, and business outcomes: A meta-analysis. *The Journal of Applied Psychology*, *87*(2), 268–279. DOI: 10.1037/0021-9010.87.2.268 PMID: 12002955

Hart, S. G., & Staveland, L. E. (1988). Development of NASA-TLX (Task Load Index): Results of empirical and theoretical research. [). Elsevier.]. *Advances in Psychology*, *52*, 139–183. DOI: 10.1016/S0166-4115(08)62386-9

Harvard Business Review. (2020). *How leaders can adapt to the digital future*. Harvard Business Publishing.

Harvard Business Review. (2023). *Why digital sustainability should be a C-suite priority*. https://hbr.org/2023/05/why-digital-sustainability-should-be-a-c-suite-priority

Haut-Commissariat au Plan (HCP). (2022). *Enquête sur la structure de l'emploi dans la fonction publique marocaine*.

Hazra, A., Adhikari, M., & Amgoth, T. (2021). A comprehensive survey on interoperability for IIoT: Taxonomy, standards, and future directions. *ACM Computing Surveys*. Advance online publication. DOI: 10.1145/3447555

Heilala, J. P. (2024). "Engineering Enhanced by AI-Driven Multiphysics Simulation: Multiphysics Modeling and Simulation with Artificial Intelligence/Multiphysics Modeling and Simulation with AI." *Proceedings of the 2024 International Conference on Artificial Intelligence and Simulation*, DOI: 10.1145/1234567.1234568

Helo, P., & Hao, Y. (2022). Artificial intelligence in operations management and supply chain management: An exploratory case study. *Production Planning and Control*, *33*(16), 1573–1590. Advance online publication. DOI: 10.1080/09537287.2021.1882690

Heravizadeh, M., Mendling, J., & Rosemann, M. (2008). Root cause analysis in business processes.

Hermann, E. (2022). Leveraging Artificial Intelligence in Marketing for Social Good—An Ethical Perspective. *Journal of Business Ethics*, *179*(1), 43–61. DOI: 10.1007/s10551-021-04843-y PMID: 34054170

Herrmann, T., & Nolte, A. (2024). "Promoting the Adoption of AI-Based Recommendations Through Organizational Practices." *International Conference on Human-Computer Interaction*, DOI: 10.1007/978-3-031-76970-2_13

Herzberg, F. (2008). *One More Time: How Do You Motivate Employees?* Harvard Business Press.

Hevner, A. R., & Chatterjee, S. (2010). *Design research in information systems: Theory and practice*. Springer. DOI: 10.1007/978-1-4419-5653-8

Hiatt, J. (2006). *ADKAR: A model for change in business, government and our community*. Prosci Research.

Hiatt, J. (2006). *ADKAR: A Model for Change in Business, Government and our Community*. Prosci.

Holmlund, M., Van Vaerenbergh, Y., Ciuchita, R., Ravald, A., Sarantopoulos, P., Ordenes, F. V., & Zaki, M. (2020). Customer experience management in the age of big data analytics: A strategic framework. *Journal of Business Research*, *116*, 356–365. DOI: 10.1016/j.jbusres.2020.01.022

Holzmann, P., & Gregori, P. (2023). The promise of digital technologies for sustainable entrepreneurship: A systematic literature review and research agenda. *International Journal of Information Management*, *68*, 102593. DOI: 10.1016/j.ijinfomgt.2022.102593

Hospitality Retail Management—EHL Insights | Hospitality industry. (n.d.). Retrieved June 20, 2024, from https://hospitalityinsights.ehl.edu/retail-and-hospitality-convergence

Hsieh, P.-J. (2023). Determinants of physicians' intention to use AI-assisted diagnosis: An integrated readiness perspective. *Computers in Human Behavior*, *147*, 107868. DOI: 10.1016/j.chb.2023.107868

Huang, M.-H., & Rust, R. T. (2021). A strategic framework for artificial intelligence in marketing. *Journal of the Academy of Marketing Science*, *49*(1), 30–50. DOI: 10.1007/s11747-020-00749-9

Huberman, J. (2021). Amazon Go, surveillance capitalism, and the ideology of convenience. *Economic Anthropology*, *8*(2), 337–349. DOI: 10.1002/sea2.12211

Hunhevicz, J. J., & Hall, D. M. (2020). Do you need a blockchain in construction? Use case categories and decision framework for DLT design options. *Advanced Engineering Informatics*, *45*, 101094. DOI: 10.1016/j.aei.2020.101094

IBM. (2016). Watson helps Mayo Clinic match patients to clinical trials faster. Retrieved from https://www.ibm.com/blogs/watson-health/watson-helps-mayo-clinic-match-patients-to-clinical-trials-faster/

Iden, J., Danilova, K. B., & Eikebrokk, T. (2025). Business process management and digitalization – a reciprocal relationship. *Business Process Management Journal, 31*(2), 393–415. DOI: 10.1108/BPMJ-02-2024-0083

Iliashenko, I., Gazzola, P., Pezzetti, R., & Grechi, D. (2025). Digitalization and Sustainability in the Fashion Industry: consumer perspective. *TECHNOLOGY AND SOCIETY: Boon or Bane?*, 92.

Ince, F. (Ed.). (2022). *International perspectives and strategies for managing an aging workforce*. IGI Global. DOI: 10.4018/978-1-7998-2395-7

Infosys. (2021). *HR transformation through BPM*. Infosys BPM White Paper.

Institute of Electrical and Electronics Engineers. (2019). *Ethically aligned design: a vision for prioritizing human well-being with autonomous and intelligent systems* (1st ed.). https://ethicsinaction.ieee.org/

International Telecommunication Union. (2022). *Global standards for green ICT*. https://www.itu.int/en/ITU-T/climatechange

Isensee, C., Teuteberg, F., Griese, K.-M., & Topi, C. (2020). The relationship between organizational culture, sustainability, and digitalization in SMEs: A systematic review. *Journal of Cleaner Production, 275*, 122944. DOI: 10.1016/j.jclepro.2020.122944

Issa, H., Sun, T., & Vasarhelyi, M. A. (2016). Research ideas for artificial intelligence in auditing: The formalization of audit and workforce supplementation. *Journal of Emerging Technologies in Accounting, 13*(2), 1–20. DOI: 10.2308/jeta-10511

Jabbar, A., Akhtar, P., & Dani, S. (2020). Real-time big data processing for instantaneous marketing decisions: A problematization approach. *Industrial Marketing Management, 90*, 558–569. DOI: 10.1016/j.indmarman.2019.09.001

Jackson, I., Saenz, M. J., & Ivanov, D. (2024). From natural language to simulations: Applying AI to automate simulation modelling of logistics systems. *International Journal of Production Research, 62*(4), 1434–1457. Advance online publication. DOI: 10.1080/00207543.2023.2276811

Jagatheesaperumal, S. K., & Rahouti, M. (2021). The duo of artificial intelligence and big data for industry 4.0: Applications, techniques, challenges, and future research directions. *IEEE Internet of Things Journal*. Advance online publication. DOI: 10.1109/JIOT.2021.3091234

Jahin, M. A., Naife, S. A., Saha, A. K., & Mridha, M. F. (2024). *AI in Supply Chain Risk Assessment: A Systematic Literature Review and Bibliometric Analysis* (Version 5). arXiv. DOI: 10.48550/ARXIV.2401.10895

Jamshed, M. A., Ali, K., Abbasi, Q. H., & Imran, M. A. (2022). Challenges, applications, and future of wireless sensors in Internet of Things. *RE:view*. Advance online publication. DOI: 10.1109/JSEN.2022.3150321

Janiesch, C., Zschech, P., & Heinrich, K. (2021). Machine learning and deep learning. *Electronic Markets*, *31*(3), 685–695. DOI: 10.1007/s12525-021-00475-2

Janssen, M., & Van Der Voort, H. (2020). Agility and responsiveness in digital government: Lessons from the COVID-19 crisis. *Government Information Quarterly*, *37*(3), 101–104.

Javaid M, Haleem A, Singh R P. (2022). "Artificial intelligence applications for industry 4.0: A literature-based study." Journal of Industrial Integration and Management, .DOI: 10.1142/S2424862222500024

Javaid, M., Haleem, A., & Suman, R. (2023). *Digital twin applications toward industry 4.0: A review*. Cognitive Robotics., DOI: 10.1016/j.cogr.2023.04.003

Javalgi, R., Radulovich, L. P., Pendleton, G., & Scherer, R. F. (2005). Sustainable competitive advantage of internet firms: A strategic framework and implications for global marketers. *International Marketing Review*, *22*(6), 658–672. DOI: 10.1108/02651330510630276

Jayaraman, K. D., & Jain, S. (2024). Leveraging Power BI for advanced business intelligence and reporting. *International Journal for Research in Management and Pharmacy*, *13*(11), 21. https://www. ijrmp. org

Jiang, C., Zhang, H., Ren, Y., Han, Z., Chen, K.-C., & Hanzo, L. (2017). Machine Learning Paradigms for Next-Generation Wireless Networks. *IEEE Wireless Communications*, *24*(2), 98–105. DOI: 10.1109/MWC.2016.1500356WC

Jin, K., Zhong, Z. Z., & Zhao, E. Y. (2024). Sustainable Digital Marketing Under Big Data: An AI Random Forest Model Approach. *IEEE Transactions on Engineering Management*, *71*, 3566–3579. DOI: 10.1109/TEM.2023.3348991

Jordan, M. I., & Mitchell, T. M. (2015). Machine learning: Trends, perspectives, and prospects. *Science*, *349*(6245), 255–260. DOI: 10.1126/science.aaa8415 PMID: 26185243

Kaftantzis, S. (2024). Predictive Business Process Monitoring with Automated Machine Learning.

Kajtazi, K., Rexhepi, G., Sharif, A., & Ozturk, I. (2023). Business model innovation and its impact on corporate sustainability. *Journal of Business Research, 166*, 114082. DOI: 10.1016/j.jbusres.2023.114082

Kalaignanam, K., Tuli, K. R., Kushwaha, T., Lee, L., & Gal, D. (2021). Marketing Agility: The Concept, Antecedents, and a Research Agenda. *Journal of Marketing*, *85*(1), 35–58. DOI: 10.1177/0022242920952760

Kaluarachchi, Y. (2022). *Implementing data-driven smart city applications for future cities*. Smart Cities., DOI: 10.3390/smartcities5020025

Kanaparthi, V. (2024). *Transformational application of Artificial Intelligence and Machine learning in Financial Technologies and Financial services: A bibliometric review*. https://doi.org/DOI: 10.48550/ARXIV.2401.15710

Kansal S, Siddharth E, (2024). "Adaptive AI Models for Automating Legacy System Migration in Enterprise Environments."

Kaplan, R. S., & Norton, D. P. (1996). *The balanced scorecard: Translating strategy into action*. Harvard Business Press.

Kapoor, R., & Kapoor, K. (2021). The transition from traditional to digital marketing: A study of the evolution of e-marketing in the Indian hotel industry. *Worldwide Hospitality and Tourism Themes*, *13*(2), 199–213. DOI: 10.1108/WHATT-10-2020-0124

Karimi, J., & Walter, Z. (2015). The role of dynamic capabilities in responding to digital disruption: A factor-based study of the newspaper industry. *Journal of Management Information Systems*, *32*(1), 39–81. DOI: 10.1080/07421222.2015.1029380

Keegan, B. J., Dennehy, D., & Naudé, P. (2022). Implementing Artificial Intelligence in Traditional B2B Marketing Practices: An Activity Theory Perspective. *Information Systems Frontiers*, •••, 1–15. DOI: 10.1007/s10796-022-10294-1 PMID: 35637917

Kerpedzhiev, G. D., König, U. M., Röglinger, M., & Rosemann, M. (2021). An Exploration into Future Business Process Management Capabilities in View of Digitalization: Results from a Delphi Study. *Business & Information Systems Engineering*, *63*(2), 83–96. DOI: 10.1007/s12599-020-00637-0

Kharlamov, A. A., & Parry, G. (2021). The impact of servitization and digitization on productivity and profitability of the firm: A systematic approach. *Production Planning and Control*, *32*(3), 185–197. Advance online publication. DOI: 10.1080/09537287.2020.1718793

Khayatbashi, S., Sjölind, V., Granåker A., Jalali A. (2025). AI-Enhanced Business Process Automation: A Case Study in the Insurance Domain Using Object-Centric Process Mining

Khodakarami, F., & Chan, Y. E. (2014). Exploring the role of customer relationship management (CRM) systems in customer knowledge creation. *Information & Management*, *51*(1), 27–42. DOI: 10.1016/j.im.2013.09.001

Khurana, D., Koli, A., Khatter, K., & Singh, S. (2023). Natural language processing: State of the art, current trends and challenges. *Multimedia Tools and Applications*, *82*(3), 3713–3744. Advance online publication. DOI: 10.1007/s11042-022-13428-4 PMID: 35855771

Kim, H., & Park, M. (2024). When digital celebrity talks to you: How human-like virtual influencers satisfy consumer's experience through social presence on social media endorsements. *Journal of Retailing and Consumer Services*, *76*, 103581. DOI: 10.1016/j.jretconser.2023.103581

Kohtamäki, M., Parida, V., Oghazi, P., Gebauer, H., & Baines, T. (2019). Digital servitization business models in ecosystems: A theory of the firm. *Journal of Business Research*, *104*, 380–392. DOI: 10.1016/j.jbusres.2019.06.027

Kokala, A. (2024a). Business Process Management: The synergy of intelligent automation and AI-Driven workflows. *International Research Journal of Modernization in Engineering Technology and Science*. Advance online publication. DOI: 10.56726/IRJMETS65186

Kokala, A. (2024b). Harnessing AI for BPM: Streamlining Complex Workflows and Enhancing Efficiency. *Authorea Preprints*. DOI: 10.36227/techrxiv.173532331.17776706/v1

Kokina, J., & Davenport, T. H. (2017). The emergence of artificial intelligence: How automation is changing auditing. *Journal of Emerging Technologies in Accounting*, *14*(1), 115–122. DOI: 10.2308/jeta-51730

Kolbjørnsrud, V., Amico, R., & Thomas, R. J. (2017). Partnering with AI: How organizations can win over skeptical managers. *Strategy and Leadership*, *58*(4), 37–44. DOI: 10.1108/SL-12-2016-0085

Koopman, A., & Seymour, L. F. (2020a). Factors Impacting Successful BPMS Adoption and Use: A South African Financial Services Case Study. *Enterprise. Lecture Notes in Business Information Processing*, *387*, 55–69. DOI: 10.1007/978-3-030-49418-6_4

Kopp, A., Orlovskyi, D., & Kuka, D. (2017). An approach to forming dashboards for business processes state analysis. *Bulletin of National Technical University" KhPI". Series: System Analysis. Control and Information Technologies*, (51), 44–52.

Korodi A, Ni ulescu I V, Fülöp A A, Vesa V C, Demian P, (2024). "Integration of Legacy Industrial Equipment in a Building-Management System Industry 5.0 Scenario." Doi: .DOI: 10.3390/electronics11010123

Kose, U., & Sert, S. (2017). *Improving content marketing processes with the approaches by artificial intelligence*. DOI: 10.48550/ARXIV.1704.02114

Kotter, J. P. (1996). *Leading Change*. Harvard Business Review Press.

Kotter, J. P. (2012). *Leading change*. Harvard Business Review Press.

Kotter, J. P., & Schlesinger, L. A. (2008). Choosing Strategies for Change. *Harvard Business Review*.

Kottmeyer, B. (2021). Digitisation and sustainable development: The opportunities and risks of using digital technologies for the implementation of a circular economy. *Journal of Entrepreneurship and Innovation in Emerging Economies*, *7*(1), 17–23. DOI: 10.1177/2393957520967799

Kozinets, R. V. (2022). Algorithmic branding through platform assemblages: Core conceptions and research directions for a new era of marketing and service management. *Journal of Service Management*, *33*(3), 437–452. DOI: 10.1108/JOSM-07-2021-0263

Kuhlmann, S., & Rip, A. (2018). Next-generation innovation policy and grand challenges. *Science & Public Policy*, *45*(4), 448–454. DOI: 10.1093/scipol/scy011

Kumar, V., Ashraf, A. R., & Nadeem, W. (2024). AI-powered marketing: What, where, and how? *International Journal of Information Management*, *77*, 102783. DOI: 10.1016/j.ijinfomgt.2024.102783

Kumar, V., Dixit, A., Javalgi, R. G., & Dass, M. (2016). Research framework, strategies, and applications of intelligent agent technologies (IATs) in marketing. *Journal of the Academy of Marketing Science*, *44*(1), 24–45. DOI: 10.1007/s11747-015-0426-9

Kumar, V., & L, M. (2018). Predictive Analytics: A review of trends and techniques. *International Journal of Computer Applications*, *182*(1), 31–37. DOI: 10.5120/ijca2018917434

Lakumarapu, S. R. Nithyanandhan, V. Sharmila Bhargavi, and Anish TP. "Machine Learning Approaches for Liver Disease Prediction: A Comparative Analysis." In *2024 5th International Conference on Electronics and Sustainable Communication Systems (ICESC)*, pp. 159-164. IEEE, 2024.

Lakumarapu, S., Nithyanandhan, R., Bhargavi, V. S., & TP, A. (2024, August). Machine Learning Approaches for Liver Disease Prediction: A Comparative Analysis. In *2024 5th International Conference on Electronics and Sustainable Communication Systems (ICESC)* (pp. 159-164). IEEE.

Lange, S., Pohl, J., & Santarius, T. (2020). Digitalization and energy consumption. Does ICT reduce energy demand? *Ecological Economics*, *176*, 106760. DOI: 10.1016/j.ecolecon.2020.106760

Langlois, V. S., Allison, M. J., Bergman, L. C., & To, T. A. (2021). The need for robust qPCR-based eDNA detection assays in environmental monitoring and species inventories. *Environmental Toxicology and Chemistry*. Advance online publication. DOI: 10.1002/etc.5045

Latinovic, Z., & Chatterjee, S. C. (2022). Achieving the promise of AI and ML in delivering economic and relational customer value in B2B. *Journal of Business Research*, *144*, 966–974. DOI: 10.1016/j.jbusres.2022.01.052

Laudien, S. M., Reuter, U., Garcia, F. J. S., & Botella-Carrubi, D. (2024). Digital advancement and its effect on business model design: Qualitative-empirical insights. *Technological Forecasting and Social Change*, *200*, 123103. DOI: 10.1016/j.techfore.2023.123103

Laudon, K. C., & Laudon, J. P. (2020). *Management information systems: Managing the digital firm* (16th ed.). Pearson.

Lee, E., Seo, Y. D., Oh, S. R., & Kim, Y. G. (2021). A Survey on Standards for Interoperability and Security in the Internet of Things. *IEEE Communications Surveys and Tutorials*, *23*(2), 1020–1047. Advance online publication. DOI: 10.1109/COMST.2021.3067354

Lee, J., Jung, O., Lee, Y., Kim, O., & Park, C. (2021). A Comparison and Interpretation of Machine Learning Algorithm for the Prediction of Online Purchase Conversion. *Journal of Theoretical and Applied Electronic Commerce Research*, *16*(5), 1472–1491. DOI: 10.3390/jtaer16050083

Lee, K.-W., & Li, C.-Y. (2023). It is not merely a chat: Transforming chatbot affordances into dual identification and loyalty. *Journal of Retailing and Consumer Services*, *74*, 103447. DOI: 10.1016/j.jretconser.2023.103447

Leisure, Retail and Hospitality. (n.d.). Hydrock. Retrieved June 20, 2024, from https://www.hydrock.com/sectors/leisure-retail-hospitality

Lele V P, Kumari S, White G, (2023). "Streamlining Production: Using Big-Data's CRM & Supply chain to improve efficiency in high-speed environments." International Journal of Current Science and Research.

Leonardi, P. M. (2011). When flexible routines meet flexible technologies: Affordance, constraint, and the imbrication of human and material agencies. *Management Information Systems Quarterly*, *35*(1), 147–167. DOI: 10.2307/23043493

Leveraging the European Hospitality Industry for Retail Success. (n.d.). Retrieved June 21, 2024, from https://www.eurodev.com/blog/leveraging-the-european-hospitality-industry-for-retail-success

Li, C.-Y., Fang, Y.-H., & Chiang, Y.-H. (2023). Can AI chatbots help retain customers? An integrative perspective using affordance theory and service-domain logic. *Technological Forecasting and Social Change*, *197*, 122921. DOI: 10.1016/j.techfore.2023.122921

Lies, J. (2021). Digital marketing: Incompatibilities between performance marketing and marketing creativity. *Journal of Digital & Social Media Marketing*, *8*(4), 376. DOI: 10.69554/SSVH5588

Li, H., Wu, Y., Cao, D., & Wang, Y. (2021). Organizational mindfulness towards digital transformation as a prerequisite of information processing capability to achieve market agility. *Journal of Business Research*, *122*, 700–712. DOI: 10.1016/j.jbusres.2019.10.036

Lindgren, I., Åkesson, M., Thomsen, M., & Toll, D. (2022). *Robotic process automation in local government: observations from two case studies of robotic process automation implementation in Swedish municipalities*. Public Administration and Information Technology., DOI: 10.1007/978-3-030-98743-6_12

Lines, R. (2005). The structure and function of attitudes toward organizational change. *Human Resource Development Review*, *4*(1), 8–32. DOI: 10.1177/1534484304273818

LinkedIn Learning. (2021). *2021 Workplace Learning Report: Skill building in the new world of work*. https://learning.linkedin.com/resources/workplace-learning-report

Linnenluecke, M. K., & Griffiths, A. (2010). Corporate sustainability and organizational culture. *Journal of World Business*, *45*(4), 357–366. DOI: 10.1016/j.jwb.2009.08.006

Lisovsky, A. L. (2019). SUSTAINABLE DEVELOPMENT AND BUSINESS PROCESS MANAGEMENT. *Strategic Decisions and Risk Management, 10*(3), 228–237. DOI: 10.17747/2618-947X-2019-3-228-237

Liu, J., Qian, Y., Yang, Y., & Yang, Z. (2022). Can artificial intelligence improve the energy efficiency of manufacturing companies? Evidence from China. *International Journal of Environmental Research and Public Health, 19*(4), 2091. Advance online publication. DOI: 10.3390/ijerph19042091 PMID: 35206280

Li, X., Deng, Q., Shi, H., & Guo, Y. (2024). Sustainable manufacturing production process monitoring and economic benefit analysis based on IoT technology. *International Journal of Advanced Manufacturing Technology*. Advance online publication. DOI: 10.1007/s00170-024-13145-2

Li, Y., Cui, L., Wu, L., Lowry, P. B., Kumar, A., & Tan, K. H. (2023). Digitalization and network capability as enablers of business model innovation and sustainability performance: The moderating effect of environmental dynamism. *Journal of Information Technology, 39*(4), 1–56.

Loebbecke, C., & Picot, A. (2015). Reflections on societal and business model transformation arising from digitization and big data analytics: A research agenda. *The Journal of Strategic Information Systems, 24*(3), 149–157. DOI: 10.1016/j.jsis.2015.08.002

Looy, A. V., VanLooy, A., Poels, G., & Poels, G. (n.d.). *A Practitioners' Point Of View On How Digital Innovation Will Shape The Future Of Business Process Management: Towards A Research Agenda.*

Ludmir, C. (n.d.). *How Hospitality Is Influencing The Future Of Retail And Elevating Brand Experiences*. Forbes. Retrieved June 20, 2024, from https://www.forbes.com/sites/claraludmir/2023/07/25/how-hospitality-is-influencing-the-future-of-retail/

Lu, S., Lu, J., An, K., Wang, X., & He, Q. (2023). Edge computing on IoT for machine signal processing and fault diagnosis: A review. *IEEE Internet of Things Journal, 10*(13), 11093–11116. Advance online publication. DOI: 10.1109/JIOT.2023.3239944

Lussier, R. N., & Achua, C. F. (2019). *Leadership: Theory, Application, & Skill Development*. Cengage Learning.

Lu, Y. (2025). The current status and developing trends of industry 4.0: A review. *Information Systems Frontiers, 27*(1), 215–234. Advance online publication. DOI: 10.1007/s10796-021-10221-w

Ly, B. (2025). Leveraging leadership and digital transformation for sustainable development: Insights from Cambodia's public sector. *Sustainable Futures : An Applied Journal of Technology, Environment and Society*, *9*, 1–11. DOI: 10.1016/j.sftr.2025.100545

Ly, B., Dem, T., Ly, R., Sorn, S., & Doeur, B. (2025). Exploring the nexus of digital inclusion and environmental sustainability: Insights from Cambodia. *Information Technology for Development*, *31*(1), 77–94. DOI: 10.1080/02681102.2024.2345381

Ma, C., Caldera, A., Petridis, M., Bacon, L., & Windall, G. (2010a). Integration of BPM Systems. In Pomffyova, M. (Ed.), *Process Management*. InTech., DOI: 10.5772/8442

Mahadev Madgule, N. (2023). Vinayaka, Yeshwant M. Sonkhaskar, Dhiren Ramanbhai Patel, R. Karthikeyan, P. Selvakumar, (2023). Mechanical properties and microstructure of activated TIG welded similar joints of Inconel alloys by desirability approaches. *Materials Today: Proceedings*, *77*, 528–533. DOI: 10.1016/j.matpr.2022.12.250

Mahmood, Z., Kouser, R., Ali, W., Ahmad, Z., & Salman, T. (2018). Does corporate governance affect sustainability disclosure? A mixed methods study. *Sustainability (Basel)*, *10*(1), 207–227. DOI: 10.3390/su10010207

Malthouse, E., & Copulsky, J. (2023). Artificial intelligence ecosystems for marketing communications. *International Journal of Advertising*, *42*(1), 128–140. DOI: 10.1080/02650487.2022.2122249

Mantravadi, S., & Srai, J. S. (2023). How important are digital technologies for urban food security? A framework for supply chain integration using IoT. *Procedia Computer Science*, *217*, 1678–1687. Advance online publication. DOI: 10.1016/j.procs.2022.12.368

Manyika, J., Chui, M., Miremadi, M., Bughin, J., George, K., Willmott, P., & Dewhurst, M. (2017). *Harnessing automation for a future that works*. McKinsey Global Institute. Retrieved from https://www.mckinsey.com/mgi

Mardiani E, Riswandi D I, Suprayitno D, (2024). "Implementation of internet of things in the production process of msmes: quality improvement and process control." Jurnal Informasi dan Teknologi.

Mariam, A., & Berrada, A. (2024). "Human-Centric Enterprise Security: Advancing Access Control through AI-Driven Administration." *Authorea Preprints*, DOI: 10.22541/authorea.1234567

Markus, M. L., & Robey, D. (1988). Information technology and organizational change: Causal structure in theory and research. *Management Science*, *34*(5), 583–598. DOI: 10.1287/mnsc.34.5.583

Marr, B. (2019). How Coca-Cola uses AI and Big Data to drive success. *Forbes*. Retrieved from https://www.forbes.com/sites/bernardmarr/2019/09/23/how-coca-cola-uses-ai-and-big-data-to-drive-success/

Marr, B. (2018). *Artificial Intelligence in Practice: How 50 Successful Companies Used AI and Machine Learning to Solve Problems*. Wiley.

Marrella, A. (2018). What Automated Planning Can Do for Business Process Management. In Teniente, E., & Weidlich, M. (Eds.), *Business Process Management Workshops* (Vol. 308, pp. 7–19). Springer International Publishing., DOI: 10.1007/978-3-319-74030-0_1

Martins, P. V., & Zacarias, M. (2015). Business Process and Practice Alignment Meta-model. *Procedia Computer Science*, *64*, 314–323. DOI: 10.1016/j.procs.2015.08.495

McCormack, J., Gifford, T., & Hutchings, P. (2019). Autonomy, authenticity, authorship and intention in computer generated art. *Proceedings of the 10th International Conference on Computational Creativity (ICCC)*. DOI: 10.1007/978-3-030-16667-0_3

McKinsey & Co. (2022). A digital path to sustainability. Retrieved from https://www.mckinsey.com/capabilities/operations/our-insights/a-digital-path-to-sustainability#/

McKinsey & Company. (2020). *Diversity wins: How inclusion matters*. https://www.mckinsey.com

McKinsey & Company. (2021). *Building workforce skills at scale to thrive during—and after—the COVID-19 crisis*. https://www.mckinsey.com

McKinsey & Company. (2021). QuantumBlack, AI by McKinsey. Retrieved from https://www.mckinsey.com/quantumblack

McKinsey & Company. (2023). The economic potential of generative AI: The next productivity frontier. Retrieved from https://www.mckinsey.com/capabilities/quantumblack/our-insights/the-economic-potential-of-generative-ai-the-next-productivity-frontier

McKinsey & Company. (2023). The state of AI in 2023: Generative AI's breakout year. https://www.mckinsey.com/capabilities/quantumblack/our-insights/the-state-of-ai-in-2023-generative-ais-breakout-year

McKinsey & Company. (2025). Superagency in the workplace: Empowering people to unlock AI's full potential. https://www.mckinsey.com/capabilities/mckinsey-digital/our-insights/superagency-in-the-workplace-empowering-people-to-unlock-ais-full-potential-at-work

McKinsey Global Institute. (2017). *A future that works: Automation, employment, and productivity*. McKinsey & Company.

Mehdiyev N, Fettke P. (2021). "Explainable artificial intelligence for process mining: A general overview and application of a novel local explanation approach for predictive process monitoring." Interpretable Artificial Intelligence: A Perspective of Process Mining, .DOI: 10.1007/978-3-030-66866-6_12

Meidan, A., García-García, J. A., Escalona, M. J., & Ramos, I. (2017). A survey on business processes management suites. *Computer Standards & Interfaces*, *51*, 71–86. DOI: 10.1016/j.csi.2016.06.003

Mekheimer, M., & Abdelhalim, W. M. (2025). The digital age students: Exploring leadership, freedom, and ethical online behavior: A quantitative study. *Social Sciences & Humanities Open*, *11*, 101325. DOI: 10.1016/j.ssaho.2025.101325

Melville, N. P. (2010). Information systems innovation for environmental sustainability. *Management Information Systems Quarterly*, *34*(1), 1–21. DOI: 10.2307/20721412

Mendling, J., Pentland, B. T., & Recker, J. (2020). Building a complementary agenda for business process management and digital innovation. *European Journal of Information Systems*, *29*(3), 208–219. DOI: 10.1080/0960085X.2020.1755207

Mendonça R D S, De Carvalho M M, Machado G S, (2023). "Development of a novel methodology to retrofit legacy systems in the context of industry 4.0."

Mergel, I., Edelmann, N., & Haug, N. (2019). Defining digital transformation: Results from expert interviews. *Government Information Quarterly*, *36*(4), 101385. DOI: 10.1016/j.giq.2019.06.002

Messner, W. (2022). Advancing our understanding of cultural heterogeneity with unsupervised machine learning. *Journal of International Management*, *28*(2), 100885. DOI: 10.1016/j.intman.2021.100885

Mikalef, P., & Gupta, M. (2021). Artificial intelligence capability: Conceptualization, measurement calibration, and empirical study on its impact on organizational creativity and firm performance. *Information & Management*, *58*(3), 103434. DOI: 10.1016/j.im.2021.103434

Ministère de la Transition Numérique. (2022). Feuille de route Maroc Digital 2025.

Mishra, K. E., & Mishra, A. K. (2013). Trust is everything: Become the leader others will follow. *Leader to Leader, 2013*(69), 45–49.

Mishra, S., & Mishra, P. (2022). Analysis of platform business and secure business intelligence. *International Journal of Financial Engineering*, *9*(03), 2250002. DOI: 10.1142/S2424786322500025

Misuraca, G., Savoldelli, A., & Codagnone, C. (2020). Digital government: From e-government to algorithmic governance. *Government Information Quarterly*, *37*(4), 101473.

Mogaji, E., Soetan, T. O., & Kieu, T. A. (2021). The implications of artificial intelligence on the digital marketing of financial services to vulnerable customers. *Australasian Marketing Journal*, *29*(3), 235–242. DOI: 10.1016/j.ausmj.2020.05.003

Mohammad, A. S., & Pradhan, M. R. (2021). Machine learning with big data analytics for cloud security. *Computers & Electrical Engineering*, *96*, 107527. Advance online publication. DOI: 10.1016/j.compeleceng.2021.107527

Mokadam, E., Musa, H. G., Kumalasari, A., & Istighfaroh, F. (2025). Public Policy Challenges in the Digital Age: Balancing Innovation, Governance, and Equity. *JIAN-Jurnal Ilmiah Administrasi Negara*, *9*(1), 102–109. DOI: 10.56071/jian.v9i1.1172

Molina, L. M., Teti, R., & Alvir, E. M. R. (2023). Quality, efficiency and sustainability improvement in machining processes using artificial intelligence. *Procedia CIRP*, *118*, 501–506. Advance online publication. DOI: 10.1016/j.procir.2023.06.086

Moon, S., & Iacobucci, D. (2022). Social Media Analytics and Its Applications in Marketing. *Foundations and Trends® in Marketing, 15*(4), 213–292. DOI: 10.1561/1700000073

Moshood, T. D., Nawanir, G., Sorooshian, S., & Okfalisa, O. (2021). Digital twins driven supply chain visibility within logistics: A new paradigm for future logistics. *Applied System Innovation*, *4*(2), 29. Advance online publication. DOI: 10.3390/asi4020029

Moussaoui, H., & Kabbaj, R. (2021). Digitalisation et administration publique: La question des générations face aux nouvelles pratiques. *Revue Internationale des Sciences Administratives*, *87*(2), 345–366.

MTN – Ministère de la Transition Numérique et de la Réforme de l'Administration. (2021). Stratégie nationale de transformation numérique 2025. Rabat.

Munappy, A. R., Bosch, J., Olsson, H. H., Arpteg, A., & Brinne, B. (2022). Data management for production quality deep learning models: Challenges and solutions. *Journal of Systems and Software, 191*, 111359. Advance online publication. DOI: 10.1016/j.jss.2022.111359

Munoz-Gama, J., Martin, N., Fernandez-Llatas, C., Johnson, O. A., Sepúlveda, M., Helm, E., Galvez-Yanjari, V., Rojas, E., Martinez-Millana, A., Aloini, D., Amantea, I. A., Andrews, R., Arias, M., Beerepoot, I., Benevento, E., Burattin, A., Capurro, D., Carmona, J., Comuzzi, M., & Zerbato, F. (2022). Process mining for healthcare: Characteristics and challenges. *Journal of Biomedical Informatics, 127*, 103994. Advance online publication. DOI: 10.1016/j.jbi.2022.103994 PMID: 35104641

Munuhwa, S. (2023). Sustainable logistics and competitive positioning. In *Integrating Intelligence and Sustainability in Supply Chains* (pp. 198–220). IGI Global. DOI: 10.4018/979-8-3693-0225-5.ch011

Murugesan, S. (Ed.). (2020). *Harnessing green IT: Principles and practices*. Wiley.

Musau, E. G. (2024). Optimizing transportation and distribution for environmental sustainability: Green logistics. In *Green Supply Chain Management Practice and Principles* (pp. 84–101). IGI Global. DOI: 10.4018/979-8-3693-3486-7.ch005

Naidoo, P., & Sibanda, M. (2024). *Emerging trends and future directions of the industrial internet of things*. From Internet of Things to Internet of Intelligence. DOI: 10.1007/978-3-031-55718-7_5

Nain, G., Pattanaik, K. K., & Sharma, G. K. (2022). Towards edge computing in intelligent manufacturing: Past, present and future. *Journal of Manufacturing Systems, 62*, 588–611. Advance online publication. DOI: 10.1016/j.jmsy.2022.01.010

Nambisan, S., Wright, M., & Feldman, M. (2019). The digital transformation of innovation and entrepreneurship: Progress, challenges and key themes. *Research Policy, 48*(8), 103773. DOI: 10.1016/j.respol.2019.03.018

Nam, T. (2018). Citizen Participation in the digital age: The role of ICT in fostering open government. *Government Information Quarterly, 35*(4), 622–631.

Naranjo-Gil, D. (2020). Resistance to digitalization in the public sector: Understanding the barriers and enablers. *Public Management Review, 22*(5), 678–702.

National Commission on Informatics and Liberty (CNIL). (2024). Employee monitoring: CNIL fined AMAZON FRANCE LOGISTIQUE €32 million. Erişim Linki: https://www.cnil.fr/en/employee-monitoring-cnil-fined-amazon-france-logistique-eu32-million

Neema A, Khan R. (2025). "Crafting Effective AI Adoption Strategies." Businesses: How to Develop Strategies for Artificial Intelligence Adoption, .DOI: 10.1002/9781119756123.ch12

Nguyen, G., Dlugolinsky, S., Bobák, M., Tran, V., López García, Á., Heredia, I., Malík, P., & Hluchý, L. (2019). Machine Learning and Deep Learning frameworks and libraries for large-scale data mining: A survey. *Artificial Intelligence Review*, *52*(1), 77–124. DOI: 10.1007/s10462-018-09679-z

Nguyen, N., & Johnson, L. W. (2020). Consumer behaviour and environmental sustainability. *Journal of Consumer Behaviour*, *19*(6), 539–541. DOI: 10.1002/cb.1892

Nicolás-Agustín, Á., Jiménez-Jiménez, D., & Maeso-Fernandez, F. (2022). The role of human resource practices in the implementation of digital transformation. *International Journal of Manpower*, *43*(2), 395–410. DOI: 10.1108/IJM-03-2021-0176

Niu, Y., Ying, L., Yang, J., Bao, M., & Sivaparthipan, C. B. (2021). Organizational business intelligence and decision making using big data analytics. *Information Processing & Management*, *58*(6), 102725. Advance online publication. DOI: 10.1016/j.ipm.2021.102725

Norman, D. A. (2013). *The design of everyday things: Revised and expanded edition*. Basic Books.

Nozari, H., Szmelter-Jarosz, A., & Ghahremani-Nahr, J. (2022). Analysis of the challenges of artificial intelligence of things (AIoT) for the smart supply chain (case study: FMCG industries). *Sensors (Basel)*, *22*(8), 2931. Advance online publication. DOI: 10.3390/s22082931 PMID: 35458916

Nwulu, E. O., Elete, T. Y., & Erhueh, O. V. (2023). Machine learning applications in predictive maintenance: Enhancing efficiency across the oil and gas industry. *International Journal of Engineering Research & Technology (Ahmedabad)*. Advance online publication. DOI: 10.17577/IJERTV12IS03034

Object, object. (n.d.). *Process Learning Environments*. Retrieved June 11, 2025, from https://core.ac.uk/reader/236378450

OCDE. (2022). *L'administration publique du futur au Maroc*. Éditions OCDE.

OECD. (2020). *Building the Digital Government Workforce: Insights from the Public Sector Leadership Programme*. OECD Digital Government Studies.

OECD. (2020). *Digital Government in Morocco: Laying the Foundations for the Digital Transformation of the Public Sector*. OECD Digital Government Studies.

OECD. (2020). *The Road to Becoming a Digital Government: Digital Government Review of Morocco*. OECD Publishing.

OECD. (2021). *Public Service Leadership and Capability in the MENA Region*. OECD Publishing.

Okazaki, S., Eisend, M., Plangger, K., De Ruyter, K., & Grewal, D. (2020). Understanding the Strategic Consequences of Customer Privacy Concerns: A Meta-Analytic Review. *Journal of Retailing*, *96*(4), 458–473. DOI: 10.1016/j.jretai.2020.05.007

Ologeanu-Taddei, R., Hönigsberg, S., Weritz, P., Wache, H., Mittermeier, F., Tana, S., Dang, D., Hautala-Kankaanpää, T., & Pekkola, S. (2025). The relationship of digital transformation and corporate sustainability: Synergies and tensions. *Technological Forecasting and Social Change*, *210*, 123809. DOI: 10.1016/j.techfore.2024.123809

Organisation for Economic Co-operation and Development. (2019). OECD principles on artificial intelligence. https://www.oecd.org/going-digital/ai/principles/

Orlikowski, W. J. (1992). The duality of technology: Rethinking the concept of technology in organizations. *Organization Science*, *3*(3), 398–427. DOI: 10.1287/orsc.3.3.398

Otto, A. S., Szymanski, D. M., & Varadarajan, R. (2020). Customer satisfaction and firm performance: Insights from over a quarter century of empirical research. *Journal of the Academy of Marketing Science*, *48*(3), 543–564. DOI: 10.1007/s11747-019-00657-7

Oyewole, A. T., Adeoye, O. B., Addy, W. A., & Okoye, C. C. (2024). *Automating financial reporting with natural language processing: A review and case analysis*. World Journal of Advanced Research and Reviews., DOI: 10.30574/wjarr.2024.21.1.1234

Ozkan-Ozen, Y. D., & Kazancoglu, Y. (2022). Analysing workforce development challenges in the Industry 4.0. *International Journal of Manpower*, *43*(2), 310–333. DOI: 10.1108/IJM-03-2021-0167

Pala, S. K. (2021). *Databricks Analytics: Empowering Data Processing*. Machine Learning and Real-Time Analytics.

Pang, G., Shen, C., Cao, L., & Hengel, A. V. D. (2021). Deep learning for anomaly detection: A review. *ACM Computing Surveys*, *54*(2), 1–38. DOI: 10.1145/3439950

Parry, K. W., & Proctor-Thomson, S. B. (2003). Leadership, culture and performance: The case of the New Zealand public sector. *Journal of Change Management*, *3*(4), 376–399. DOI: 10.1080/714023843

Paulose, R., & Neelanath, V. (2024). *Generative AI-driven Automation of Business Process Reimagination. 2024 IEEE Recent Advances in Intelligent Computational Systems*. RAICS., DOI: 10.1109/RAICS61201.2024.10689826

Perera, P., Selvanathan, S., Bandaralage, J., & Su, J. J. (2023). The impact of digital inequality in achieving sustainable development: A systematic literature review. *Equality, Diversity and Inclusion*, *42*(6), 805–825. DOI: 10.1108/EDI-08-2022-0224

Petersen, J. C. (2021). Ethical data use in human resource analytics: Balancing innovation and responsibility. *Journal of Business Ethics*, *168*(3), 575–589.

Philp, M., Jacobson, J., & Pancer, E. (2022). Predicting social media engagement with computer vision: An examination of food marketing on Instagram. *Journal of Business Research*, *149*, 736–747. DOI: 10.1016/j.jbusres.2022.05.078

Pitt, C., Paschen, J., Kietzmann, J., Pitt, L. F., & Pala, E. (2023). Artificial Intelligence, Marketing, and the History of Technology: Kranzberg's Laws as a Conceptual Lens. *Australasian Marketing Journal*, *31*(1), 81–89. DOI: 10.1177/18393349211044175

Ponmalar, A., Vijayakumar, K., Lakshmipriya, C., Karthikeyan, M., Gracelin Sheena, B., Beslin Pajila, P. J., & Siva Subramanian, R. (2024). Meta-Heuristics and Machine Learning Applications in Complex Systems. In *Metaheuristic and Machine Learning Optimization Strategies for Complex Systems* (pp. 257–275). IGI Global Scientific Publishing.

Pradabwong, J., Braziotis, C., Tannock, J. D. T., & Pawar, K. S. (2017). Business process management and supply chain collaboration: Effects on performance and competitiveness. *Supply Chain Management*, *22*(2), 107–121. Advance online publication. DOI: 10.1108/SCM-01-2017-0008

Prasad, S., Kulkarni, P., & Veronika, N. (2023). Role of artificial intelligence in business process transformation. *AIP Conference Proceedings*, *2990*, 060028. DOI: 10.1063/5.0170686

Prodanova, J., & Van Looy, A. (2019). How Beneficial is Social Media for Business Process Management? A Systematic Literature Review. *IEEE Access : Practical Innovations, Open Solutions*, *7*, 39583–39599. DOI: 10.1109/ACCESS.2019.2903983

Prosci. (2021). *Change management: The people side of change*. https://www.prosci.com

Putra, H., & Mahendrawathi, E. R. (2024). The role of business process management in digital innovation and digital transformation: A systematic literature review. *Procedia Computer Science*, *234*, 829–836. DOI: 10.1016/j.procs.2024.03.069

PwC. (2022). *Digital transformation in SMEs: A path to sustainable growth*. Retrieved from https://www.pwc.com

Qadri, U. A., Ghani, M. B. A., Abbas, U., & Kashif, A. R. (2025). Digital technologies and social sustainability in the digital transformation age: A systematic analysis and research agenda. *International Journal of Ethics and Systems*, *41*(1), 142–169. DOI: 10.1108/IJOES-08-2024-0239

Qudus, L. (2025). Advancing cybersecurity: Strategies for mitigating threats in evolving digital and IoT ecosystems. *International Research Journal of Modernization in Engineering Technology and Science*.

Qureshi, M. S., Umar, S., & Nawaz, M. U. (2024). Machine learning for predictive maintenance in solar farms. *International Journal of Engineering and Advanced Technology*. Advance online publication. DOI: 10.35940/ijeat.B1234.024322

Rachinger, M., Rauter, R., Müller, C., Vorraber, W., & Schirgi, E. (2019). Digitalization and its influence on business model innovation. *Journal of Manufacturing Technology Management*, *30*(8), 1143–1160. DOI: 10.1108/JMTM-01-2018-0020

Rachmad, Y. E. (2025). *The Viral Shift: Harnessing the Power of Gimmicks in Changing Consumer Behavior*. United Nations Economic and Social Council.

Rachmad, Y. E. (2025). *Viral Influence: How Gimmicks Shape Consumer Behavior*. United Nations Economic and Social Council.

Raddats, C., Kowalkowski, C., Benedettini, O., Burton, J., & Gebauer, H. (2019). Servitization: A contemporary thematic review of four major research streams. *Industrial Marketing Management*, *83*, 207–223. DOI: 10.1016/j.indmarman.2019.03.015

Rahwan, I., Cebrian, M., Obradovich, N., Bongard, J., Bonnefon, J. F., Breazeal, C., & Lazer, D. (2019). Machine behaviour. *Nature*, *568*(7753), 477–486. DOI: 10.1038/s41586-019-1138-y PMID: 31019318

Rai, A. (2020). Explainable AI: From black box to glass box. *Journal of the Academy of Marketing Science*, *48*(1), 137–141. DOI: 10.1007/s11747-019-00710-5

Raisch, S., & Krakowski, S. (2021). Artificial intelligence and management: The automation–augmentation paradox. *Academy of Management Review*, *46*(1), 192–210. DOI: 10.5465/amr.2018.0072

Rajpurohit, S. C., Palande, B., Kalal, J., & Parkhi, S. (2025). Sustainable Development in the Digital Age: The Role of CBDCs in Achieving the SDGs. In *Green Finance and Energy Transition: Innovation, Legal Frameworks and Regulation* (pp. 491–502). Springer Nature Switzerland.

Ramakrishnan, T., Mohan Gift, M. D., Chitradevi, S., Jegan, R., & Subha Hency Jose, P. Nagaraja, Rajneesh Sharma HN, Selvakumar P, Sintayehu Mekuria Hailegiorgis, (2022). "Study of Numerous Resins Used in Polymer Matrix Composite Materials", Advances in Materials Science and Engineering, vol. 2022, Article ID 1088926, 8 pages, 2022. DOI: 10.1155/2022/1088926

Rammohan, A. (2023). Cellular Vehicle-to-Everything (C-V2X) technology: Current trends, use cases, emerging technologies, standardization bodies, industry analytics and future directions. *Vehicular Communications*. Advance online publication. DOI: 10.1016/j.vehcom.2023.100445

Rana G, Khang A, Sharma R, Goel A K, Dubey A K. (2021). "Reinventing manufacturing and business processes through artificial intelligence." .DOI: 10.1007/978-3-030-73644-5_12

Rane N, Choudhary S, Rane J, (2023). "Artificial Intelligence (Ai) and Internet of Things (Iot)–based sensors for monitoring and controlling in architecture, engineering, and construction: Applications, challenges, and future directions."

Ranganathan, G. (2020). Real time anomaly detection techniques using pyspark frame work. *Journal of Artificial Intelligence*, *2*(01), 20–30. DOI: 10.36548/jaicn.2020.1.003

Rangaswamy, A., Moch, N., Felten, C., Van Bruggen, G., Wieringa, J. E., & Wirtz, J. (2020). The Role of Marketing in Digital Business Platforms. *Journal of Interactive Marketing*, *51*(1), 72–90. DOI: 10.1016/j.intmar.2020.04.006

Rani, S., Bhambri, P., & Kataria, A. (2023). *Integration of iot, big data, and cloud computing technologies: Trend of the era*. Big Data, Cloud Computing and IoT., DOI: 10.1201/9781003298335

Rao A S, Radanovic M, Liu Y, Hu S, Fang Y, (2022). "Real-time monitoring of construction sites: Sensors, methods, and applications." Doi: .DOI: 10.1016/j.autcon.2022.104124

RASAQ, S. O. (2025). Resource Optimization in Hybrid Cloud: Leveraging Microservices for IoT Workloads. *International Journal of Novel Research in Engineering & Pharmaceutical Sciences*, *1*(1).

Rathi, S., & Kumar, P. (2023). The mediating role of job satisfaction between work-life balance and employee retention. In *Climate change management and social innovations for sustainable global organization* (pp. 241–262). IGI Global. DOI: 10.4018/978-1-6684-9503-2.ch016

Reinsel, D., Gantz, J., & Rydning, J. (2018). The digitization of the world from edge to core. *IDC white paper, 16*, 1-28.

Renn, O., Beier, G., & Schweizer, P.-J. (2021). The opportunities and risks of digitalisation for sustainable development: A systemic perspective. GAIA – Ecological Perspectives for Science and Society, 30(1), 23–28.

Renugadevi, N., Saravanan, S., & Sudha, C. M. N. (2023). IoT based smart energy grid for sustainable cites. *Materials Today: Proceedings, 81*, 98–104. Advance online publication. DOI: 10.1016/j.matpr.2021.02.270

Reppmann, M., Harms, S., Edinger-Schons, L. M., & Foege, J. N. (2025). Activating the sustainable consumer: The role of customer involvement in corporate sustainability. *Journal of the Academy of Marketing Science, 53*(2), 310–340. DOI: 10.1007/s11747-024-01036-7

Reshamwala, A., Mishra, D., & Pawar, P. (2013). Review on natural language processing. [ESTIJ]. *IRACST Engineering Science and Technology: An International Journal, 3*(1), 113–116.

Ribeiro, J., Lima, R., Eckhardt, T., & Paiva, S. (2021). Robotic process automation and artificial intelligence in industry 4.0–a literature review. *Procedia Computer Science, 181*, 51–58. Advance online publication. DOI: 10.1016/j.procs.2021.01.104

Ribeiro-Navarrete, S., Botella-Carrubi, D., Palacios-Marqués, D., & Orero-Blat, M. (2021). The effect of digitalization on business performance: An applied study of KIBS. *Journal of Business Research, 126*, 319–326. DOI: 10.1016/j.jbusres.2020.12.065

Richardson, N., Kothapalli, S., & Onteddu, A. R. (2023). *AI-Driven Optimization Techniques for Evolving Software Architecture in Complex Systems*. ABC Journal of Advanced Research., DOI: 10.18034/abcjar.v12i2.783

Richman Miyambu, G., & Matshonisa Seeletse, S. (2016). Numeric measurement of business process optimization. *Environment and Ecology, 7*(4), 20–24. DOI: 10.21511/ee.07(4).2016.02

Robson, G. D. (2010). *Continuous process improvement*. Simon and Schuster.

Rochd, A., Benazzouz, A., Abdelmoula, I. A., & Raihani, A. (2021). Design and implementation of an AI-based & IoT-enabled Home Energy Management System: A case study in Benguerir—Morocco. *Energy Reports, 7*, 699–719. Advance online publication. DOI: 10.1016/j.egyr.2021.07.084

Rock, D., & Grant, H. (2016). Why diverse teams are smarter. *Harvard Business Review*. https://hbr.org/2016/11/why-diverse-teams-are-smarter

Rosário, A., & Raimundo, R. (2021). Consumer Marketing Strategy and E-Commerce in the Last Decade: A Literature Review. *Journal of Theoretical and Applied Electronic Commerce Research, 16*(7), 3003–3024. DOI: 10.3390/jtaer16070164

Rosemann, M., & vom Brocke, J. (2015). The six core elements of business process management. In vom Brocke, J., & Rosemann, M. (Eds.), *Handbook on business process management 1* (pp. 105–122). Springer. DOI: 10.1007/978-3-642-45100-3_5

Ruiz-Pérez, F., Lleo, A., & Ormazabal, M. (2021). Employee sustainable behaviors and their relationship with Corporate Sustainability: A Delphi study. *Journal of Cleaner Production, 329*, 129742. DOI: 10.1016/j.jclepro.2021.129742

Runco, M. A., & Acar, S. (2012). Divergent thinking as an indicator of creative potential. *Creativity Research Journal, 24*(1), 66–75. DOI: 10.1080/10400419.2012.652929

Rust, R. T. (2020). The future of marketing. *International Journal of Research in Marketing, 37*(1), 15–26. DOI: 10.1016/j.ijresmar.2019.08.002

Rydzewski, P. (2025). Digital Inequality and Sustainable Development. *Problemy Ekorozwoju, 20*(1), 96–108. DOI: 10.35784/preko.6691

Sahdeo, V. (n.d.). *A BUSINESS PROCESS MANAGEMENT FRAMEWORK FOR ENHANCING ENTERPRISE RESOURCE PLANNING VALUE DERIVED IN SUPPLY CHAIN OPTIMIZATION.*

Sai, S., Sai, R., & Chamola, V. (2024). Generative AI for Industry 5.0: Analyzing the impact of ChatGPT, DALLE, and other models. *IEEE Open Journal of the Industrial Electronics Society*. Advance online publication. DOI: 10.1109/OJIES.2024.1234567

Sajidha, S. A., Vijayanand, D., Rajagopal, M., Sambasivam, D., & Nisha, V. M. (2025). Decoding Work-Life Balance Conundrum: A Meta-Learning Prediction Approach. In *Creating AI Synergy Through Business Technology Transformation* (pp. 313-336). IGI Global.

Salamzadeh, A., Hadizadeh, M., Feyzabadi, J. G., Yasin, N., & Paramba, J. N. (2025). The Role of Digital Platforms in Transforming Corporate Governance: A Path to Sustainability Through ESG. In *Modern Corporate Governance Strategies for Sustainable Value Creation* (pp. 111–136). IGI Global Scientific Publishing.

Salehi, H., & Burgueño, R. (2018). Emerging artificial intelligence methods in structural engineering. *Engineering Structures, 171*, 170–189. DOI: 10.1016/j.engstruct.2018.05.084

Şallı, D. (2025). Rethinking Education in the Digital Age: Readiness for the Professions of the Future. *Journal of Education and Future*, (27), 135–146. DOI: 10.30786/jef.1372523

Salminen, J., Mustak, M., Corporan, J., Jung, S., & Jansen, B. J. (2022). Detecting Pain Points from User-Generated Social Media Posts Using Machine Learning. *Journal of Interactive Marketing*, *57*(3), 517–539. DOI: 10.1177/10949968221095556

Sanders, E. B. N., & Stappers, P. J. (2008). Co-creation and the new landscapes of design. *CoDesign*, *4*(1), 5–18. DOI: 10.1080/15710880701875068

Sandhu, A. K. (2021). *Big data with cloud computing: Discussions and challenges.* Big Data Mining and Analytics., DOI: 10.1109/BDMA.2021.3071245

Sargiotis D, (2024). "Data Quality Management: Ensuring Accuracy and Reliability." Data Governance: A Guide.

Sarker, I. H. (2021). Machine Learning: Algorithms, Real-World Applications and Research Directions. *SN Computer Science*, *2*(3), 160. DOI: 10.1007/s42979-021-00592-x PMID: 33778771

Saura, J. R. (2020). Using Data Sciences in Digital Marketing: Framework, methods, and performance metrics. *Journal of Innovation & Knowledge*. DOI: 10.1016/j.jik.2020.08.001

Saura, J. R., Ribeiro-Soriano, D., & Palacios-Marqués, D. (2021). Setting B2B digital marketing in artificial intelligence-based CRMs: A review and directions for future research. *Industrial Marketing Management*, *98*, 161–178. DOI: 10.1016/j.indmarman.2021.08.006

Saura, J. R., Škare, V., & Dosen, D. O. (2024). Is AI-based digital marketing ethical? Assessing a new data privacy paradox. *Journal of Innovation & Knowledge*, *9*(4), 100597. DOI: 10.1016/j.jik.2024.100597

Schein, E. H. (2010). *Organizational culture and leadership* (4th ed.). Jossey-Bass.

Schein, E. H. (2010). *Organizational Culture and Leadership* (4th ed.). Jossey-Bass.

Schmidpeter, B., & Winter-Ebmer, R. (2021). Automation, unemployment, and the role of labor market training. *European Economic Review*, *137*, 103808. DOI: 10.1016/j.euroecorev.2021.103808

Scholz, R. W., Bartelsman, E. J., Diefenbach, S., Franke, L., Grunwald, A., Helbing, D., Hill, R., Hilty, L., Höjer, M., Klauser, S., Montag, C., Parycek, P., Prote, J. P., Renn, O., Reichel, A., Schuh, G., Steiner, G., & Viale Pereira, G. (2018). Unintended side effects of the digital transition: European scientists' messages from a proposition-based expert round table. *Sustainability (Basel), 10*(6), 2001. DOI: 10.3390/su10062001

Schwartz, J., Bohdal-Spiegelhoff, M., Gretczko, M., & Sloan, N. (2017). Rewriting the rules for the digital age. *Deloitte Global Human Capital Trends*. https://www2.deloitte.com

Seele, P. (2016). Digitally unified reporting: How XBRL-based real-time transparency helps in combining integrated sustainability reporting and performance control. *Journal of Cleaner Production, 136*, 65–77. DOI: 10.1016/j.jclepro.2016.01.102

Seemiller, C., & Grace, M. (2019). *Generation Z: A century in the making*. Routledge.

Seidel, S., Bharati, P., Fridgen, G., Watson, R. T., Albizri, A., Boudreau, M. C. M., Butler, T., Chandra Kruse, L., Guzman, I., Karsten, H., Lee, H., Melville, N., Rush, D., Toland, J., & Watts, S. (2017). The sustainability imperative in information systems research. *Communications of the Association for Information Systems, 40*(1), 40–52. DOI: 10.17705/1CAIS.04003

Seligman, M. E. P. (2011). *Flourish: A visionary new understanding of happiness and well-being*. Free Press.

Selvakumar, P., Shanthi, M., Pitchiah, R., Sharma, M., Dahake, P. S., & T. C., M. (2025). The Role of Artificial Intelligence in Business Model Innovation: Overview of AI Technologies. In M. Khokhar (Ed.), *Advances in Business Strategy and Competitive Advantage* (pp. 219–246). IGI Global. DOI: 10.4018/979-8-3693-9571-4.ch009

Selvakumar, P., Shanthi, M., Pitchiah, R., Sharma, M., Dahake, P. S., & TC, M. (2025). The Role of Artificial Intelligence in Business Model Innovation: Overview of AI Technologies. *AI-Driven Business Model Innovation*, 219–246.

Senbursa, N. (2022). Work-life balance challenges: constructing an employee-friendly workplace. In *Handbook of Research on Future of Work and Education: Implications for Curriculum Delivery and Work Design* (pp. 511-532). IGI Global.

Sepasgozar, S. M., Mair, D. F., Tahmasebinia, F., Shirowzhan, S., Li, H., Richter, A., & Xu, S. (2021). Waste management and possible directions of utilising digital technologies in the construction context. *Journal of Cleaner Production, 324*, 129095. DOI: 10.1016/j.jclepro.2021.129095

Setiawan, R. (2025). Social Entrepreneurship in the Digital Age: Opportunities and Challenges in Achieving Social Welfare. *BDJ Smart: Breakthrough Development Journal in Strategic Management & Marketing*, *1*(01), 59–67.

Shafagatova, A. (n.d.). *TOWARDS PROCESS-ORIENTED EMPLOYEE APPRAISALS AND REWARDS: AN EXPLORATORY CASE STUDY.*

Shah, D., & Murthi, B. P. S. (2021). Marketing in a data-driven digital world: Implications for the role and scope of marketing. *Journal of Business Research*, *125*, 772–779. DOI: 10.1016/j.jbusres.2020.06.062

Sharakhina, L., Ilyina, I., Kaplun, D., Teor, T., & Kulibanova, V. (2024). AI technologies in the analysis of visual advertising messages: Survey and application. *Journal of Marketing Analytics*, *12*(4), 1066–1089. DOI: 10.1057/s41270-023-00255-1

Sharma, R., & Singh, A. (2025). Integrating AI, Green Marketing, and Influencer Strategies: Shaping Sustainable Consumer Behavior in the Digital Age. In *Strategic Brand Management in the Age of AI and Disruption* (pp. 325-342). IGI Global Scientific Publishing.

Sharma, R., Kumar, A., & Chuah, C. (2021). Turning the blackbox into a glassbox: An explainable machine learning approach for understanding hospitality customer. *International Journal of Information Management Data Insights*, *1*(2), 100050. DOI: 10.1016/j.jjimei.2021.100050

Sha, X., Chen, J., & Teoh, S. Y. (2020). The dynamics of IT-business strategic alignment: Evidence from healthcare information systems implementation. *Information Technology & People*, *33*(5), 1465–1488. DOI: 10.1108/ITP-08-2019-0414

Shende, A. D., Tekade, S. A., Deshmukh, A. A., Tembhurkar, S. P., & Selvakumar, P. (2025). Water Quality Monitoring and Control With AI. In Ruiz-Vanoye, J., & Díaz-Parra, O. (Eds.), *Smart Water Technology for Sustainable Management in Modern Cities* (pp. 51–80). IGI Global Scientific Publishing., DOI: 10.4018/979-8-3693-8074-1.ch003

Shneiderman, B. (2020). Human-centered artificial intelligence: Reliable, safe & trustworthy. *International Journal of Human-Computer Interaction*, *36*(6), 495–504. DOI: 10.1080/10447318.2020.1741118

Shrestha, Y. R., Benbya, H., & Vom Brocke, J. (2021). Algorithmic decision-making in the AI era: A research agenda. *Journal of Business Research*, *136*, 70–81. DOI: 10.1016/j.jbusres.2021.07.036

Shrestha, Y. R., Krishna, V., & Von Krogh, G. (2021). Augmenting organizational decision-making with deep learning algorithms: Principles, promises, and challenges. *Journal of Business Research, 123*, 588–603. DOI: 10.1016/j.jbusres.2020.09.068

Siemens. (2020). *Future of Work – Siemens' digital upskilling program*. Siemens AG Corporate Report.

Siemens. (2021). *NextWork: Reimagining the future of work*. Siemens AG. https://www.siemens.com

Singh, B., & Kaunert, C. (2025). Innovative Business Models in Digital and Virtual Reality for the Gig Economy: Space-Age Sustainable Development Projecting Smart Business Practices. In *Business Transformation in the Era of Digital Disruption* (pp. 127-156). IGI Global.

Singh, R., Gehlot, A., Akram, S. V., & Thakur, A. K. (2022). Forest 4.0: Digitalization of forest using the Internet of Things (IoT). *Journal of King Saud University. Computer and Information Sciences, 34*(8), 5587–5601. Advance online publication. DOI: 10.1016/j.jksuci.2021.02.009

Siva, S. R., Bushra, S. N., Maheswari, B., & Prabukumar, M. K. (2022, April). Performance Analysis of Different Machine Learning in Customer Prediction. In *2022 6th International Conference on Trends in Electronics and Informatics (ICOEI)* (pp. 1425-1430). IEEE. DOI: 10.1109/ICOEI53556.2022.9776714

Sodiya, E. O., Umoga, U. J., & Obaigbena, A. (2024). Current state and prospects of edge computing within the Internet of Things (IoT) ecosystem. *International Journal of Scientific Research.*

Somashekhar, S. P., Sepúlveda, M. J., Norden, A. D., Rauthan, A., Arunachalam, R., & Patil, P. (2018). Early experience with IBM Watson for Oncology in Indian oncology practice. *JCO Clinical Cancer Informatics*, (2), 1–8. DOI: 10.1200/CCI.17.00135

Song, Y., Sahut, J. M., Zhang, Z., Tian, Y., & Hikkerova, L. (2022). The effects of government subsidies on the sustainable innovation of university-industry collaboration. *Technological Forecasting and Social Change, 174*, 121233. DOI: 10.1016/j.techfore.2021.121233

Soni, N., Sharma, E. K., Singh, N., & Kapoor, A. (2020). Artificial Intelligence in Business: From Research and Innovation to Market Deployment. *Procedia Computer Science, 167*, 2200–2210. DOI: 10.1016/j.procs.2020.03.272

Souto, J. E. (2022). Organizational creativity and sustainability-oriented innovation as drivers of sustainable development: Overcoming firms' economic, environmental and social sustainability challenges. *Journal of Manufacturing Technology Management, 33*(4), 805–826. DOI: 10.1108/JMTM-01-2021-0018

Sposato, M. (2024). Leadership training and development in the age of artificial intelligence. *Development and Learning in Organizations, 38*(4), 4–7. Advance online publication. DOI: 10.1108/DLO-12-2023-0256

Sreelakshmi, S., Babu, A. A., Lakshmipriya, C., Gracious, L. A., Nalini, M., & Subramanian, R. S. (2024, October). Enhancing Intrusion Detection Systems with Machine Learning. In *2024 2nd International Conference on Self Sustainable Artificial Intelligence Systems (ICSSAS)* (pp. 557-564). IEEE. DOI: 10.1109/ICSSAS64001.2024.10760341

Sreenivasulu, A., & Manimozhi, T. Satheesh kumar P, Selvakumar P. and Singh P, (2022). "The Model of Smart Sensing Device For Sensitive Nanoclusters Modification in Sensing Properties," 2022 2nd International Conference on Advance Computing and Innovative Technologies in Engineering (ICACITE), Greater Noida, India, 2022, pp. 1043-1047, DOI: 10.1109/ICACITE53722.2022.9823846

State Council of China. (2017). *New generation artificial intelligence development plan*. http://www.gov.cn

Stephen, M., & Sheriffdeen, K. (2022). AI-Enabled Anomaly Detection in Industrial Systems: A New Era in Predictive Maintenance.

Subrahmanyam, S. (2024). Leadership and cultural change management for technology adoption in operations. In Martínez-Falcó, J., Sánchez-García, E., Marco-Lajara, B., & Visser, G. (Eds.), *Convergence of technology and operations management in modern businesses* (pp. 175–202). IGI Global Scientific Publishing. DOI: 10.4018/979-8-3693-6200-6.ch005

Subrahmanyam, S. (2024). The evolution of human resources in the age of technology. In Kaur, J. (Ed.), *Technological enhancements for improving employee performance, safety, and well-being* (pp. 229–256). IGI Global Scientific Publishing. DOI: 10.4018/979-8-3693-9631-5.ch011

Subrahmanyam, S. (2025). Building a Digital-First Organizational Culture. In Pawirosumarto, S. (Ed.), *Innovative Approaches for International Competitiveness Through Human Resource Management* (pp. 101–124). IGI Global Scientific Publishing. DOI: 10.4018/979-8-3373-1005-3.ch004

Subrahmanyam, S. (2025). Employee Skillsets in the Digital Age. In Özbek, M., & Christiansen, B. (Eds.), *Organizational Sociology in the Digital Age* (pp. 369–388). IGI Global Scientific Publishing. DOI: 10.4018/979-8-3693-7398-9.ch018

Subrahmanyam, S. (2025). The Paradigm Shift in Leadership Owing to Technological Development. In Agnihotri, A., & Balusamy, B. (Eds.), *Leadership Paradigms and the Impact of Technology* (pp. 381–406). IGI Global Scientific Publishing. DOI: 10.4018/979-8-3693-7175-6.ch016

Subramanian S, (2023). "Leveraging IoT data streams for AI-based quality control in smart manufacturing systems in process industry." Journal of AI-Assisted Scientific Discovery.

Sugumaran K M D, Pandiyarajan V Y B S, Selvakumar P. and M. S, (2024). "Analysis of Electromyography Signals for Control of Mechanical Prosthesis using Machine Learning Techniques," 2024 2nd International Conference on Intelligent Data Communication Technologies and Internet of Things (IDCIoT), Bengaluru, India, 2024, pp. 1059-1067, .DOI: 10.1109/IDCIoT59759.2024.10467707

Suleman, D., Shibl, R., & Ansari, K. (2023). *Investigation of data quality assurance across IoT protocol stack for V2I interactions*. Smart Cities., DOI: 10.3390/smartcities6050121

Suraña-Sánchez, C., & Aramendia-Muneta, M. E. (2024). Impact of artificial intelligence on customer engagement and advertising engagement: A review and future research agenda. *International Journal of Consumer Studies*, *48*(2), e13027. DOI: 10.1111/ijcs.13027

Susskind, R., & Susskind, D. (2015). *The future of the professions: How technology will transform the work of human experts*. Oxford University Press. DOI: 10.1093/oso/9780198713395.001.0001

Svetlana, N., Anna, N., Svetlana, M., Tatiana, G., & Olga, M. (2022). Artificial intelligence as a driver of business process transformation. *Procedia Computer Science*, *213*, 276–284. Advance online publication. DOI: 10.1016/j.procs.2022.11.067

Syam, N., & Sharma, A. (2018). Waiting for a sales renaissance in the fourth industrial revolution: Machine learning and artificial intelligence in sales research and practice. *Industrial Marketing Management*, *69*, 135–146. DOI: 10.1016/j.indmarman.2017.12.019

Sykes, A. O. (1993). An introduction to regression analysis. (Coase-Sandor Institute for Law & Economics. Working Paper No. 20, 1993).

Tan W C, Sidhu M S, (2022). "Review of RFID and IoT integration in supply chain management." Operations Research Perspectives. Doi: .DOI: 10.1016/j.orp.2022.100145

Tarafdar, M., Cooper, C. L., & Stich, J.-F. (2019). The technostress trifecta—Techno eustress, techno distress and design: Theoretical directions and an agenda for research. *Information Systems Journal*, *29*(1), 6–42. DOI: 10.1111/isj.12169

Tarafdar, M., Pullins, E. B., & Ragu-Nathan, T. S. (2015). Technostress: Negative effect on performance and possible mitigations. *Information Systems Journal*, *25*(2), 103–132. DOI: 10.1111/isj.12042

Tariq, M. U. (2025). *Navigating the Ethical Frontier-Human Oversight in AI-Driven Decision-Making System*. Enhancing Automated Decision-Making Through AI., DOI: 10.4018/978-1-6684-5679-6.ch015

Ter Hofstede, A. H., Van der Aalst, W. M., Adams, M., & Russell, N. (Eds.). (2009). *Modern Business Process Automation: YAWL and its support environment*. Springer Science & Business Media., DOI: 10.1007/978-3-642-03121-2

Thontirawong, P., & Chinchanachokchai, S. (2021). TEACHING ARTIFICIAL INTELLIGENCE AND MACHINE LEARNING IN MARKETING. *Marketing Education Review*, *31*(2), 58–63. DOI: 10.1080/10528008.2021.1871849

Tidd, J., & Bessant, J. (2018). *Managing innovation: Integrating technological, market and organizational change* (6th ed.). Wiley.

Tim, Y., Pan, S. L., Bahri, S., & Fauzi, A. (2017). Digitally enabled affordances for community-driven environmental movement in rural Malaysia. *Information Systems Journal*, *28*(1), 48–75. DOI: 10.1111/isj.12140

Tjoa, A. M., & Tjoa, S. (2016). The role of ICT to achieve the UN sustainable development goals (SDG). In ICT for promoting human development and protecting the environment: 6th IFIP World Information Technology Forum, WITFOR 2016 [Springer International Publishing.]. *Proceedings*, *6*, 3–13.

Tomaskova, H., & Weber, G.-W. (2020). Approaches combining methods of Operational Research with Business Process Model and Notation: A systematic review. *PeerJ. Computer Science*, *6*, e301. DOI: 10.7717/peerj-cs.301 PMID: 33816952

Topol, E. (2019). *Deep Medicine: How Artificial Intelligence Can Make Healthcare Human Again*. Basic Books.

Trax Retail. (2020). Coca-Cola HBC leverages Trax to drive execution in the field. Retrieved from https://traxretail.com/success-stories/coca-cola-hbc

Trica, C. L., Banacu, C. S., & Busu, M. (2019). Environmental factors and sustainability of the circular economy model at the European Union level. *Sustainability (Basel)*, *11*(4), 1114. DOI: 10.3390/su11041114

Trist, E. L. (1981). The evolution of socio-technical systems. *Occasional Paper, 2*, 1–67.

Trittin-Ulbrich, H., Scherer, A. G., Munro, I., & Whelan, G. (2021). Exploring the dark and unexpected sides of digitalization: Toward a critical agenda. *Organization, 28*(1), 8–25. DOI: 10.1177/1350508420968184

Tsai, C. W., Lai, C. F., Chao, H. C., & Vasilakos, A. V. (2015). Big data analytics: A survey. *Journal of Big Data*, *2*(1), 1–32. DOI: 10.1186/s40537-015-0030-3 PMID: 26191487

Tsvasman, L. (2025). Self-Regulation as a Catalyst for Scalability and Human-Centered Business Ecosystems in the Digital Age: Advanced Cybernetic Strategies for Autonomous and Human-Centered Business Evolution. In *Building Business Knowledge for Complex Modern Business Environments* (pp. 63–94). IGI Global.

Tubis, A. A., & Poturaj, H. (2025). Energy Supply Chains in the Digital Age: A Review of Current Research and Trends. *Energies*, *18*(2), 430. DOI: 10.3390/en18020430

Tupikovskaja-Omovie, Z., & Tyler, D. (2020). Clustering consumers' shopping journeys: Eye tracking fashion m-retail. *Journal of Fashion Marketing and Management*, *24*(3), 381–398. DOI: 10.1108/JFMM-09-2019-0195

Turkyılmaz, S. (2024). Dijital dönüşüm: Tarihçesi, tanımı ve işletmeler üzerindeki etkisi. *Nişantaşı Üniversitesi Sosyal Bilimler Dergisi*, *12*(1), 276–297. DOI: 10.52122/nisantasisbd.1459265

Tüyen, Z. (2020). İşletmelerde sürdürülebilirlik kavramı ve sürdürebilirliği etkileyen etmenler. İstanbul Ticaret Üniversitesi Sosyal Bilimler Dergisi, 19(37), 91–117.

Uddin, A. S. M. A. (2023). *The era of AI: Upholding ethical leadership*. Open Journal of Leadership., DOI: 10.4236/ojl.2023.123012

Ujwary-Gil, A., & Potoczek, N. (n.d.). *THE USE OF A BUSINESS MODEL IN DESIGNING AND OPERATIONALIZING PROCESSES*.

Ullo S L, Sinha G R, (2021). "Advances in IoT and smart sensors for remote sensing and agriculture applications." Doi: .DOI: 10.3390/rs13132567

Ulmer, J.-S., Belaud, J.-P., & Le Lann, J.-M. (2011). Towards a pivotal-based approach for business process alignment. *International Journal of Computer Integrated Manufacturing*, *24*(11), 1010–1021. DOI: 10.1080/0951192X.2011.597431

Umashankar, M. L., & Mallikarjunaswamy, S. (2023). "A survey on IoT protocol in real-time applications and its architectures." *Proceedings of 2021 International Conference on Advances in Computing and Communications*. Doi: DOI: 10.1007/978-981-19-5936-3_12

UNDP. (2022). *Bridging the Digital Divide in the Global South*. United Nations Development Programme.

UNESCO. (2021). *Digital literacy for all: What can governments do?* https://www.unesco.org

United Nations Environment Programme. (2023). *Tackling digital waste for a sustainable future*. https://www.unep.org/news-and-stories/story/tackling-digital-waste

United Nations. (2023). *Digital technologies for sustainable development* (Report No. UNEP/DT/2023/1). https://www.unep.org/resources/report/digital-technologies-sustainable-development

Unsworth, K. L., Davis, M. C., Russell, S. V., & Bretter, C. (2021). Employee green behaviour: How organizations can help the environment. *Current Opinion in Psychology*, *42*, 1–6. DOI: 10.1016/j.copsyc.2020.12.006 PMID: 33535131

Vajgel, B., Corrêa, P. L. P., De Sousa, T. T., & Quille, R. V. E. (2021). *Development of intelligent robotic process automation: A utility case study in Brazil*. IEEE Latin America Transactions., DOI: 10.1109/LA-CCI52142.2021.9723214

Van de Ven, A. H., & Poole, M. S. (1995). Explaining development and change in organizations. *Academy of Management Review*, *20*(3), 510–540. DOI: 10.2307/258786

van der Aalst, W. M. P. (2013). Business process management: A comprehensive survey. *ISRN Software Engineering*, *2013*, 1–37. DOI: 10.1155/2013/507984

Van der Velden, M. (2018). Digitalisation and the UN Sustainable Development Goals: What role for design. ID&A Interaction Design & Architecture(s), (37), 160–174.

Van der Voet, J., Kuipers, B. S., & Groeneveld, S. (2016). Time for change: A longitudinal analysis of the effects of change management on public sector employees' affective commitment and turnover intentions. *Public Administration Review*, *76*(3), 484–495.

Van Hoang T, (2024). "Impact of integrated artificial intelligence and internet of things technologies on smart city transformation." Journal of Technical Education Science.

Varadarajan, R. (2020). Customer information resources advantage, marketing strategy and business performance: A market resources based view. *Industrial Marketing Management*, *89*, 89–97. DOI: 10.1016/j.indmarman.2020.03.003

Vassakis, K., Petrakis, E., & Kopanakis, I. (2017). Big data analytics: applications, prospects and challenges. *Mobile big data: A roadmap from models to technologies*, 3-20.

Vassilakopoulou, P., & Hustad, E. (2023). Bridging digital divides: A literature review and research agenda for information systems research. *Information Systems Frontiers*, *25*(3), 955–969. DOI: 10.1007/s10796-020-10096-3 PMID: 33424421

Ventura Martins, P., & Zacarias, M. (2017). Applying the Business Process and Practice Alignment Meta-model: Daily Practices and Process Modelling. *Business Systems Research Journal*, *8*(1), 1–16. DOI: 10.1515/bsrj-2017-0001

Verbraeken, J., Wolting, M., Katzy, J., Kloppenburg, J., Verbelen, T., & Rellermeyer, J. S. (2021). A Survey on Distributed Machine Learning. *ACM Computing Surveys*, *53*(2), 1–33. DOI: 10.1145/3377454

Vial, G. (2019). Understanding digital transformation: A review and a research agenda. *The Journal of Strategic Information Systems*, *28*(2), 118–144. DOI: 10.1016/j.jsis.2019.01.003

Vicente, K. J. (2006). *The human factor: Revolutionizing the way people live with technology*. Routledge.

Vidgof, M., Bachhofner, S., & Mendling, J. (2023). "Large language models for business process management: Opportunities and challenges." *International Conference on Business Process Management*, DOI: 10.1007/978-3-031-41623-1_7

Vijayakumar, G. (2024). Muniyandi Rajkumar, Rajiv Chandar N, Selvakumar P and Ramesh Duraisamy, (2024). Environmentally friendly TDS removal from wastewater by electrochemical ion exchange batch-type recirculation (EIR) technique. *Environmental Science. Water Research & Technology*, *10*, 826–835. DOI: 10.1039/D3EW00793F

Villar A S, Khan N. (2021). "Robotic process automation in banking industry: a case study on Deutsche Bank." Journal of Banking and Financial Technology, .DOI: 10.1007/s42521-021-00034-4

Vinothkumar J, Karunamurthy A. (2023). "Recent advancements in artificial intelligence technology: trends and implications." International Journal of Scientific Research and Engineering Trends, .DOI: 10.22214/ijraset.2023.456789

Vivas, C., Sobreiro, P., & Claudino, R. (2014). *Integrating Knowledge Management in a Business Strategy Process Operationalized using Process Management Approach*. http://hdl.handle.net/10400.26/30197

vom Brocke, J., Zelt, S., & Schmiedel, T. (2016). On the role of context in business process management. *International Journal of Information Management*, *36*(3), 486–495. DOI: 10.1016/j.ijinfomgt.2015.10.002

Vrakas, G., Chan, C., & Thai, V. V. (2021). The effects of evolving port technology and process optimisation on operational performance: The case study of an Australian container terminal operator. *The Asian Journal of Shipping and Logistics*, *37*(4), 281–290. DOI: 10.1016/j.ajsl.2020.04.001

Wagner, N., & Wiśnicki, B. (2022). The importance of emerging technologies to the increasing of corporate sustainability in shipping companies. *Sustainability (Basel)*, *14*(12475), 1–20. DOI: 10.3390/su141912475

Waizenegger, L., McKenna, B., Cai, W., & Bendz, T. (2020). An affordance perspective of team collaboration and enforced working from home during COVID-19. *European Journal of Information Systems*, *29*(4), 429–442. DOI: 10.1080/0960085X.2020.1800417

Walonick, D. S. (1993). An overview of forecasting methodology. *StatPac:* https:// www. statpac. org/research-library/forecasting. htm

Wang, C. (2022). Efficient customer segmentation in digital marketing using deep learning with swarm intelligence approach. *Information Processing & Management*, *59*(6), 103085. DOI: 10.1016/j.ipm.2022.103085

Wang, C. L. (2021). New frontiers and future directions in interactive marketing: Inaugural Editorial. *Journal of Research in Interactive Marketing*, *15*(1), 1–9. DOI: 10.1108/JRIM-03-2021-270

Wang, H., Fu, T., Du, Y., Gao, W., Huang, K., Liu, Z., Chandak, P., Liu, S., Van Katwyk, P., Deac, A., Anandkumar, A., Bergen, K., Gomes, C. P., Ho, S., Kohli, P., Lasenby, J., Leskovec, J., Liu, T.-Y., Manrai, A., & Zitnik, M. (2023). Scientific discovery in the age of artificial intelligence. *Nature*, *620*(7972), 47–60. DOI: 10.1038/s41586-023-06221-2 PMID: 37532811

WCED. (1987). *Our common future*. Oxford University Press.

Weinzierl, S., Zilker, S., Dunzer, S., & Matzner, M. (2024). Machine learning in business process management: A systematic literature review. *Expert Systems with Applications*, *124181*, 124181. Advance online publication. DOI: 10.1016/j.eswa.2024.124181

Wenger, E. (1998). *Communities of practice: Learning, meaning, and identity*. Cambridge University Press. DOI: 10.1017/CBO9780511803932

Westerman, G., Bonnet, D., & McAfee, A. (2014). *Leading digital: Turning technology into business transformation*. Harvard Business Press.

Wielgos, D. M., Homburg, C., & Kuehnl, C. (2021). Digital business capability: Its impact on firm and customer performance. *Journal of the Academy of Marketing Science*, *49*(4), 762–789. DOI: 10.1007/s11747-021-00771-5

Wilson, H. J., & Daugherty, P. R. (2018). *Human + Machine: Reimagining Work in the Age of AI*. Harvard Business Review Press.

Wilson, R. D., & Bettis-Outland, H. (2019). Can artificial neural network models be used to improve the analysis of B2B marketing research data? *Journal of Business and Industrial Marketing*, *35*(3), 495–507. DOI: 10.1108/JBIM-01-2019-0060

Wongsnuopparat, S., & Chunyang, W. (2021). Corporate sustainability: Study of factors that affect corporate towards organizational sustainability in today's fast-changing world. *Journal of Management and Sustainability*, *11*(2), 56–73. DOI: 10.5539/jms.v11n2p56

World Bank Group. (2021). *E-waste management and circular economy in developing countries*. https://www.worldbank.org/en/topic/urbandevelopment/publication/e-waste-management

World Bank. (2020). *The global AI landscape and implications for developing countries*. https://www.worldbank.org

World Bank. (2021). *Building a Culture of Innovation in Public Administration: Tools, Practices, and Case Studies*. World Bank Group.

World Bank. (2021). *Digital Dividends*. World Development Report. https://www.worldbank.org/en/publication/wdr2016

World Economic Forum (WEF). (2020). Unlocking technology for the global goals. Retrieved from https://www.weforum.org/publications/unlocking-technology-for-the-global-goals/

World Economic Forum. (2020). *The Future of Jobs Report 2020*. https://www.weforum.org

WWF. (2025). Dünya saati. Retrieved from https://www.wwf.org.tr/harekete_gec/dunya_saati_2025/

Wynn, M., & Jones, P. (2022). *Digital sustainability: Strategies for the 21st century*. Routledge.

Xu, Y., Liu, X., Cao, X., Huang, C., Liu, E., Qian, S., Liu, X., Wu, Y., Dong, F., Qiu, C.-W., Qiu, J., Hua, K., Su, W., Wu, J., Xu, H., Han, Y., Fu, C., Yin, Z., Liu, M., & Zhang, J. (2021). Artificial intelligence: A powerful paradigm for scientific research. *Innovation (Cambridge (Mass.))*, *2*(4), 100179. DOI: 10.1016/j.xinn.2021.100179 PMID: 34877560

Yadav, S. J. (2024). Voices From Within: Exploring Indian Perspectives on Sex Tourism. In *Examining Tourist Behaviors and Community Involvement in Destination Rejuvenation* (pp. 263–272). IGI Global. https://www.igi-global.com/chapter/voices-from-within/348915

Yadav, S. (2021). Millennial Employees-Role, Benefits and Retaining Strategies in Hotel Industry (p. 64). DOI: 10.6084/m9.figshare.13719949.v1

Yaiprasert, C., & Hidayanto, A. N. (2024). AI-powered ensemble machine learning to optimize cost strategies in logistics business. *International Journal of Information Management Data Insights*, *4*(1), 100209. DOI: 10.1016/j.jjimei.2023.100209

Yakovenko, Y., & Shaptala, R. (2023). "Intelligent process automation, robotic process automation and artificial intelligence for business processes transformation." Publishing House "Baltija Publishing", DOI: 10.30525/978-9934-26-281-4-12

Yamagata, T. (2020). AI and Japan's aging society. *Asian Economic Policy Review*, *15*(2), 276–293. DOI: 10.1111/aepr.12295

Yamini, B., Sudha, K., Nalini, M., Kavitha, G., Subramanian, R. S., & Sugumar, R. (2023, June). Predictive modelling for lung cancer detection using machine learning techniques. In *2023 8th International Conference on Communication and Electronics Systems (ICCES)* (pp. 1220-1226). IEEE. DOI: 10.1109/ICCES57224.2023.10192648

Yang, Z., & Lin, Z. (2022). Interpretable video tag recommendation with multimedia deep learning framework. *Internet Research*, *32*(2), 518–535. DOI: 10.1108/INTR-08-2020-0471

Yarmohammadian, M. H., Ebrahimipour, H., & Doosty, F. (2014). Improvement of hospital processes through business process management in Qaem Teaching Hospital: A work in progress. *Journal of Education and Health Promotion*, *3*(1). Advance online publication. DOI: 10.4103/2277-9531.145902 PMID: 25540784

Yazdi, M. (2024). *Integration of IoT and edge computing in industrial systems*. Advances in Computational Mathematics for Industrial Systems. DOI: 10.1007/978-3-031-53514-7_7

Ye, G., Hudders, L., De Jans, S., & De Veirman, M. (2021). The Value of Influencer Marketing for Business: A Bibliometric Analysis and Managerial Implications. *Journal of Advertising*, *50*(2), 160–178. DOI: 10.1080/00913367.2020.1857888

Yiu, L. M. D., Yeung, A. C. L., & Cheng, T. C. E. (2021). The impact of business intelligence systems on profitability and risks of firms. *International Journal of Production Research*, *59*(13), 3951–3974. Advance online publication. DOI: 10.1080/00207543.2020.1756506

Yu, K.-H., Beam, A. L., & Kohane, I. S. (2018). Artificial intelligence in healthcare. *Nature Biomedical Engineering*, *2*(10), 719–731. DOI: 10.1038/s41551-018-0305-z PMID: 31015651

Yurdakul, M. (2020). İşletmelerde sürdürülebilirliğin sağlanmasında eko inovasyon uygulamaları: Bir model önerisi. İşletme Ekonomi ve Yönetim Araştırmaları Dergisi, 3(1), 15–33.

Zamrani, S., & Achouri, H. (2021). Ressources humaines et transformation digitale dans le secteur public marocain: Entre inertie et innovation. *Management & Avenir*, *126*(6), 87–104.

Zaoui, A., Tchuente, D., Wamba, S. F., & Kamsu-Foguem, B. (2024). Impact of artificial intelligence on aeronautics: An industry-wide review. *Journal of Engineering and Technology Management*, *71*, 101800. DOI: 10.1016/j.jengtecman.2024.101800

Zhang, Y., Liu, R., Heidari, A. A., Wang, X., Chen, Y., Wang, M., & Chen, H. (2021). Towards augmented kernel extreme learning models for bankruptcy prediction: Algorithmic behavior and comprehensive analysis. *Neurocomputing*, *430*, 185–212. DOI: 10.1016/j.neucom.2020.10.038

Zhang, Y., Ma, X., Pang, J., Xing, H., & Wang, J. (2023). The impact of digital transformation of manufacturing on corporate performance—The mediating effect of business model innovation and the moderating effect of innovation capability. *Research in International Business and Finance*, *64*, 101890. DOI: 10.1016/j.ribaf.2023.101890

Zhao C, (2022). "Perspectives on nonstationary process monitoring in the era of industrial artificial intelligence." Doi: .DOI: 10.1016/j.jprocont.2022.100145

Zhao, Z., & Xing, Z. (2024). Corporate management, green finance, and sustainability. *Humanities & Social Sciences Communications*, *11*(6), 1–8.

Zhu, Y., Cheng, J., Liu, Z., Cheng, Q., Zou, X., & Xu, H. (2023). Production logistics digital twins: Research profiling, application, challenges and opportunities. *Journal of Manufacturing Systems*. Advance online publication. DOI: 10.1016/j.jmsy.2023.01.012

Zikria Y B, Ali R, Afzal M K, Kim S W, (2021). "Next-generation internet of things (iot): Opportunities, challenges, and solutions." Doi: .DOI: 10.3390/s21041457

Zou, J., & Schiebinger, J. (2018). IA can be Sexist and Racist - it's Time to Make it Fair. *Nature*, *559*(7714), 324–326. DOI: 10.1038/d41586-018-05707-8 PMID: 30018439

Zuboff, S. (2019). *The age of surveillance capitalism: The fight for a human future at the new frontier of power*. PublicAffairs.

Zulaikha, S., Mohamed, H., Kurniawati, M., Rusgianto, S., & Rusmita, S. A. (2020). CUSTOMER PREDICTIVE ANALYTICS USING ARTIFICIAL INTELLIGENCE. *The Singapore Economic Review*, •••, 1–12. DOI: 10.1142/S0217590820480021

Zvarikova, K., Dvorsky, J., & Metzker, Z. (2024). Model of sustainability of SMEs in V4 countries. *Journal of Business Economics and Management*, *25*(2), 226–245. DOI: 10.3846/jbem.2024.20729

About The Contributors

Javier Martínez Falcó is Assistant Professor in the Department of Business Organization at the University of Alicante (UA) and Research Fellow in the Department of Geography and Environmental Studies at the University of Stellenbosch. He has a PhD with international mention in the area of Business, Economics and Society, obtaining this distinction through his predoctoral stay at Sonoma State University (USA, 2022). He has also completed four postdoctoral stays at Stellenbosch University (South Africa, 2023), Burgundy School of Business (France, 2022 and 2023), Lublin University of Technology (Poland, 2023) and RMIT University Vietnam (Vietnam, 2024). In his career as a researcher, he has published articles in relevant journals such as Journal of Cleaner Production, Corporate Social Responsibility and Environmental Management, Journal of Intellectual Capital, Management Decision or British Food Journal, among others, indexed in the Journal Citation Reports (JCR) and/or SCOPUS. Currently, he has more than 40 JCRs. On the other hand, he has published several book chapters, most of them in prestigious publishers in the field of Social Sciences, such as Emerald, Springer, Palgrave Macmillan, Octaedro and IGI-GLOBAL (Q1 in the Scholarly Publishers Indicators-CSIC). His research has been reflected in more than a hundred participations as speaker in national and international conferences, being also member of the scientific committee and organizer in several congresses. Among them, it is worth mentioning his role as co-founder of the Conference on Economics and Management of Wine Companies (3rd Edition) and the Conference on Wine Tourism (1st Edition). As a teacher, his experience is focused on the field of business management, having taught subjects related to the strategic management of the company in the degree in Business Administration and Management (ADE), and the double degrees in Law and ADE (DADE), Tourism and ADE (TADE) and Engineering and ADE (I2ADE), as well as in the degree in Gastronomy and Culinary Arts. In this line, he has directed several Final Degree Projects (TFG) and Master's Degree (TFM), and has served as a member of the tribunal in TFG and TFM defenses on several occasions. He is a tutor of the Tutorial Action Program (PAT) and mobility tutor of the Faculty of Economics and Business Administration (PAT-MOBILITY). Given his interest in improving his teaching skills in English and, at the same time, strengthening ties with European educational institutions, he has carried out seven mobilities within the KA103-KA131 program: University of Fernando Pessoa (Portugal, 2021), Goce Delcev University (North Macedonia, 2022), Hogeschool van Amsterdam (Netherlands, 2022), Arcada University of Applied Sciences (Finland, 2022), University of Toulouse Jean Jaurès (France, 2022), Lublin University of Technology (Poland, 2023) and University of Primorska (Slovenia, 2024). He has also been Guest Lecturer at the Wine Business Instute at Sonoma State University, a pioneering institution in the scientific study of the California wine industry.

Eduardo Sánchez García is a professor and researcher in the Department of Business Organization at the University of Alicante (Spain). He holds a PhD in Business, Economics and Society, and his research is within the scope of Strategic Management of Business. Specifically, his research focuses on the analysis of value creation, leadership, social capital, supply chain management, circular practices, knowledge management and business orientation, among other factors related to innovation and sustainable development of companies. He has published numerous articles in journals indexed in Journal Citation Reports, as well as several books and book chapters, and has presented at scientific conferences nationally and internationally. He regularly collaborates with prestigious researchers from various universities, and is a member of the research group "Strategic Management, Knowledge and Innovation in a Global Economy (DECI-GLOBAL)". He has carried out research stays at various universities, including institutions such as Stellenbosch University, Burgundy School of Business, Lublin University of Technology, and RMIT University. In relation to teaching, he teaches the subject Management and Organization for Innovation in the Master's Degree in Business Administration and Management (MBA), as well as Strategic Business Management in the Bachelor's Degree in Business Administration, and the double degrees of TADE, DADE and I2ADE.

Bartolome Marco-Lajara, University professor in the Department of Business Organization. Since October 2020 he has been director of the department, having previously been part of the dean's team of the Faculty of Economic and Business Sciences, holding the position of Vice-Dean of Business Administration, TADE and I2Business Administration from the 2012/13 academic year to February 2018, and Vice-Dean of Business Administration and Double Degrees from March 2018 to October 2020. In the research field, he focuses his interest on topics related to the Strategic Management of the Company and the management of tourism companies, on which he has written numerous publications in the form of articles, books and contributions to conferences. He has also participated in several national and European research projects, in some of them as Principal Investigator. As for teaching, he teaches Strategic Management in the Bachelor's Degree in Business Administration, in the Master's Degree in Business Administration and Management and in the Master's Degree in Tourism Management and Planning.

***

Ranjna is a dedicated academician and researcher with a Ph.D. in Commerce from Punjabi University, Patiala, specializing in corporate governance practices. Currently serving as an Assistant Professor at Chandigarh Group of Colleges, Jhanjeri, she brings extensive experience in teaching undergraduate and postgraduate courses. A UGC-NET and JRF qualifier, she has published several research papers and conference proceedings in reputed journals and volumes. Her academic interests include corporate governance, financial sector reforms, and sustainability reporting. Dr. Ranjna actively participates in faculty development programs and has coordinated multiple national and international academic events and workshops.

B. Anni Princy is a Professor in the Department of Artificial Intelligence and Machine Learning at Panimalar Engineering College. She is dedicated to advancing research and education in AI and its emerging technologies. Her academic contributions reflect a strong commitment to innovation and excellence in engineering education.

Sujoy Kumar Basu has been working as an Assistant Professor in Asansol Engineering College, Asansol, West Bengal, India. He has 19 years of experience in teaching. He received M.E in Software Engineering from Jadavpur University, West Bengal, India in the year 2009 and is currently pursuing PhD in Engineering. He has published 03 research papers in Conference and reputed Journals. Till date, he has 5 patents against his name. He has research interest in Internet of Things.

Sudhanshu Chandra Assistant Professor (Academic Coordinator) at Manuu Law School, Maulana Azad National Urdu University Hyderabad A Central University Established by an Act of Parliament in 1988, Accredited with Grade A+ by NACC, (Hyderabad Telangana) -500032. He Completed his B.A.LLB(Hons)-Dr. Ram Manohar Lohiya National Law University Lucknow(U.P) LLM-National Law University Jodhpur (Rajasthan), Cleared UGC-NET, Ph.D. in Law from Gautam Buddha University Greater Noida(U.P.) Authored Three Books- The Menace and Implications of Narcotic Drug Abuse and Alcoholism in India: A Socio- Legal

Study (Singhal Law Publication-2022), The Effect of Intellectual Property Rights and Conservation on Biodiversity Law in India (Associated Publishing House-2023), Custodial Violence by Police in India: Analysis of Judicial Decisions 2010-2020 (Associated Publishing House-2023).Also taken Copyright of work Custodial Violence by Police in India: Analysis of Judicial Decisions 2010-2020 Registration No-L-124572/2023 Dated-09/06/2023.Judged Several Moot Court Competition. Published More than 20 Research Papers in International/National/Scopus/UGC-Care Listed Journals.

D. Shanmugapriya is a faculty member in the Department of Artificial Intelligence and Machine Learning at IFET College of Engineering, Villupuram. She is involved in teaching, research, and academic development in the field of AI and ML. Her work focuses on enhancing student learning and contributing to advancements in intelligent systems.

Nihar Suresh Dahake is currently serving as an Assistant Professor in the Department of MBA at G H Raisoni College of Engineering, Nagpur. He holds a B.Com, M.Com, and MBA from Rashtrasant Tukdoji Maharaj Nagpur University and earned his Ph.D. from Sant Gadge Baba Amravati University, Amravati. In addition to his academic qualifications, Dr. Dahake has successfully qualified the State Eligibility Test (SET) in both Commerce and Management, demonstrating his strong foundation in these disciplines. With a rich academic background, he brings 14 years of teaching experience and 8 years of dedicated research experience to his role. Throughout his career, he has consistently contributed to academic excellence and research development. Dr. Dahake's areas of expertise include Financial Accounting, Consumer Behavior, Marketing Management, and Financial Management. His multidisciplinary knowledge allows him to effectively engage with a wide range of topics in business and management studies. Passionate about both teaching and research, he strives to inspire students while also contributing meaningfully to the academic community through his scholarly work. His professional journey reflects a deep commitment to education, research, and the advancement of management studies in higher education institutions.

Parihar Suresh Dahake is an accomplished academician and researcher with over 15 years of experience in teaching and research in the fields of Commerce and Management. Currently serving as an Assistant Professor at the School of Management, Ramdeobaba University, Nagpur, he holds a diverse educational background, including B.Tech (Applied Electronics), MBA (Marketing & Financial Management), M.Com, PGDIBO, M.A. (Psychology), and a Ph.D. in Business Management. His doctoral work focused on the impact of marketing strategies of

DTH services on consumer behavior in Nagpur. Dr. Dahake's research interests span Business Analytics, Consumer Behavior, Predictive Analytics, and Marketing Communication. A recognized Ph.D. supervisor, he guides multiple doctoral candidates under the faculty of Commerce. He has published extensively in peer-reviewed, Scopus, and ABDC-indexed journals and authored books on Marketing Management and Consumer Behavior. He also holds a patent in wage sheet automation and actively contributes as a reviewer for prestigious journals. A recipient of multiple accolades, including the Young Researcher and Research Excellence Awards, Dr. Dahake is also a sought-after speaker and trainer. His commitment to academic excellence and innovative pedagogy has made significant contributions to management education, research, and institutional development in Central India.

G. Suresh is a Professor in the Department of Artificial Intelligence and Machine Learning at Panimalar Engineering College. He specializes in advanced AI technologies and has significant experience in academia and research. His contributions include scholarly publications, technical guidance, and active involvement in AI-based curriculum design.

Mohammad Irfan is presently working as an Associate Professor at School of Business and Management, Christ University, Bengaluru, India. Dr. Irfan has done his Ph.D. from the Central University of Haryana. He is MBA (Finance), M.Com (Account and Law), and MA (Economics). He has qualified UGC-JRF/SRF/NET in Management and Commerce. Dr. Irfan certified NSEs (NCFM) and BSEs certification. He has experience of more than sixteen years in the area of SAPM, Artificial Intelligence, Machine Learning, Blockchain, Cryptocurrency, Financial Engineering, Fintech, Green Finance, and Alternative Finance. He has to his credit more than 73+ Scopus-indexed articles, including The Journal of Economic Cooperation and Development (Q2), International Journal of Business Excellence (IJBEX), International Journal of Economics and Management (IJEM), Montenegrin Journal of Economics (Q2), Cogent Business & Management (Taylor & Francis) (Q2), Indian Journal of Finance (IJF), and Journal of Islamic Monetary Economics and Finance (JIMF). His citations reached 560+ along with 13 H-index. Dr. Irfan has published 11 books in Springer, IGI Global Publication (Scopus indexed).

J. Jayalakshmi is an Assistant Professor in the Department of Artificial Intelligence and Data Science at Vel Tech Multi Tech Dr. Rangarajan Dr. Sakunthala Engineering College, Avadi, Chennai. She is dedicated to advancing research and education in emerging AI technologies. Her academic interests include machine learning, data analytics, and intelligent systems.

K. Sudha is a faculty member in the Department of CSBS at RMD Engineering College, Tamil Nadu. She actively contributes to academic research and teaching in computer science and business systems. Her work reflects a commitment to innovation and excellence in higher education.

Amitava Kar is a distinguished member of the Faculty of Information Technology at Gopal Narayan Singh University, located in Sasaram, Bihar. With a strong academic background and dedication to teaching, Dr. Kar contributes significantly to the advancement of knowledge and innovation in the field of Information Technology. His work reflects a commitment to excellence in education and research, supporting the university's mission to foster academic and professional growth in the region.

Bilge Kural is studying for a doctorate in the Management and Organization program at the Department of Business Administration, Trakya University. She got her master's degree from Mersin University in 2021. She completed her bachelor's degree in the Business Administration department at Ege University in 2017.

Anto Gracious L. A. is a dedicated researcher from the Department of Computer Science and Engineering at R.M.K. College of Engineering and Technology, Tamil Nadu, India. His academic interests span computer science, with a focus on innovative technologies and applied research. He actively contributes to scholarly publications and collaborative research initiatives.

Angeline Lydia is an Associate Professor in the Department of Computer Science and Engineering at Vel Tech Rangarajan Dr. Sagunthala R\&D Institute of Science and Technology. She holds extensive experience in teaching and research with a focus on emerging technologies in computer science. Her academic contributions include publications in reputed journals and active involvement in curriculum development.

Amruta Mahalle is currently serving as an Assistant Professor at Datta Meghe Institute of Management Studies, Nagpur. With a strong academic foundation and a passion for teaching, she specializes in the areas of Marketing and Human resource management. Her academic journey is marked by a commitment to developing industry-relevant knowledge and fostering practical learning among management students. She actively engages in research and scholarly activities, contributing to academic publications and participating in conferences and seminars. Amruta is known for her dynamic teaching approach, blending theoretical insights with real-world applications to enhance student engagement and understanding. Her interests include consumer behavior, digital marketing strategies, financial planning, and investment analysis. She is dedicated to continuous learning and professional development and aims to bridge the gap between academic theory and industry practices. Amruta Mahalle's contributions are instrumental in nurturing future business leaders and promoting academic excellence in the field of management education.

Rajkumar Mandal is a faculty member in the Department of Information Technology at Gopal Narayan Singh University, Sasaram, Bihar. He holds a Ph.D. in Electronics Devices and has a strong academic and research background in the field of electronics and information technology.

T.C. Manjunath was born on 6th Feb. 1967 in Bangalore. He did his BE from RV College of Engg., Bangalore Univ. in 1989 with First Class, ME in Robotics and Automation from the Govt. LD College of Engg. in 1992 with First Rank – FCD from Gujarat Univ., Ahmedabad and PhD in Systems and Control Engg. from IIT Bombay in the year 2007. He is currently working as the Dean Research, R and D and as Professor in the Dept. of Computer Science and Engineering with specialization in IoT, Cyber Security and Blockchain Tech. in Rajarajeswari College of Engg., Bengaluru, Karnataka, India. He has got a teaching, academic, research and administrative experience of more than 35+ years with 10 years as Principal, 8 yrs as Professor - HoD and 17 yrs as faculty. He has published more than 1200+ research papers in various national and international journals, conferences, with 5000+ citations, 175+ patents, 50+ book-chapters, 25 awards, published 25 text books in various field of science, engineering and technology, completed funded research projects worth Rs. 9 Crores till date apart from having guided 10 PhD scholars, 25 PG Students, more than 200 UG students towards their project works. He is a member of 30 Professional Society Chapters and is a fellow of IE, IETE, AMIEE and a chartered engineer. He got the best research scholar award in 2006 in IIT Bombay amongst all the research scholars of the institute.

Ramalakshmi (Lakshmi) Murugan is a product strategy and operations manager at Google, with over 15 years of experience spanning consulting, product management, and sales. She is a technical leader with expertise in data-driven product innovation, product strategy, digital marketing, big data, and marketing analytics. Lakshmi holds a master's degree in information technology from Virginia Tech, Blacksburg, and an MBA in marketing management from the S.P. Jain Institute of Management and Research.

P. Selvakumar is currently an Associate Professor in the Department of Science and Humanities at Nehru Institute of Technology, Coimbatore, Tamil Nadu, India. Prior to joining Nehru Institute of Technology, he held positions as an Assistant

Professor in the Department of Science and Humanities various engineering colleges in Coimbatore, Tamil Nadu, India, spanning from 2011 to 2023. Dr.P. Selvakumar's academic and research interests lie primarily in the field of phytochemistry. He has made significant contributions to his field, with an impressive record that includes 30 journal publications, 12 patents, and 20 conference papers. Additionally, he has organized 5 seminars and conferences, further demonstrating his commitment to academic and scientific exchange. Throughout his career, Dr. P.Selvakumar has been recognized for his dedication and excellence in teaching, having been honored with several awards, including the Best Teacher Awards. He holds a prominent position in the academic community, contributing actively to research.

P. Sudheer is an Assistant Professor in the Department of Computer Science and Engineering (Artificial Intelligence & Machine Learning) at CVR College of Engineering, Hyderabad, Telangana. He specializes in image processing, deep learning, and machine learning, with a strong passion for exploring advanced AI technologies and their practical applications.

Swadesh Patra is a dedicated faculty member in the Department of Information Technology at Gopal Narayan Singh University, located in Sasaram, Bihar. With a passion for teaching and technology, he plays a key role in guiding students and contributing to the academic development of the institution. His commitment to education and innovation continues to make a positive impact within the university community.

Neena PC has a blend of corporate and academic experience spanning two decades in leading business schools and corporate firms, including a short stint abroad. As an academician, she has made significant contributions at various levels, such as in Accreditation, IQAC, Research, Board of studies, Certification and Executive programs, and other activities. She has presented and published research papers in national and international journals including articles in Scopus & Web of Science. Her diverse experience also includes roles as a Manager of Operations and HR, Program Manager, and Academic Coordinator.

Ignatious K Pious is an Assistant Professor at Vel Tech Rangarajan Dr. Sagunthala R&D Institute of Science and Technology. With a passion for academic excellence, he actively contributes to teaching and research in his field.

R. Durai Pandian is a Principal of Saveetha School of Management at Saveetha Institute of Medical and Technical Sciences, Saveetha University, with three decades of teaching and research experiences.

Siva Subramanian R is a faculty member in the School of Computing at SRM Institute of Science & Technology, Trichy campus. He specializes in computer science domains including artificial intelligence, data analytics, and software development. With active involvement in research and teaching, he contributes significantly to academic and institutional growth

Mohit Sharma is a research scholar at the Institute of Management Studies and Research, Maharshi Dayanand University, Rohtak, Haryana, India. His research focuses on the dynamic relationship between brand image and purchase intentions, particularly in the context of brand extensions within the FMCG sector. He has co-authored several scholarly works and continues to contribute to the academic community. Mohit can be reached at mohitattri.rs.imsar@mdurohtak.ac.in

Satya Subrahmanyam is a distinguished academic leader, researcher, and institutional strategist with over 27 years of experience in higher education, leadership, and research management. He holds two PhDs and a Postdoctoral qualification from the Polytechnic Institute of Leiria, Portugal. Currently serving as Professor and Dean (Research) at Holy Spirit University of Kaslik (USEK), Lebanon, he spearheads research initiatives that enhance academic excellence and institutional reputation. He played a pivotal role in the development of the Catholic University in Erbil, Kurdistan, where he established new departments, led research programs, and collaborated on international educational projects. As a founding member and Managing Partner of Vignan Institute of Technology and Management, India, he contributed to its transformation into a premier institution. With expertise in AI-driven business strategies, HR analytics, and leadership in technology adoption, he has published extensively, guided PhD research, and led training programs in corporate and academic settings.

Siva Subramanian R is an academic and researcher at SRM Institute of Science and Technology, Trichy Campus, India. His areas of interest include data science, artificial intelligence, and advanced computing. He actively engages in research publications and collaborative academic initiatives.

Anand Thangavel received his B.E. in Computer Science and Engineering from M.A.M College of Engineering and M.E. in Computer Science and Engineering from K.S. Rangasamy College of Technology, under Anna University, Chennai and Coimbatore respectively. He has experience in both Teaching and IT industry. He is currently working as an Assistant Professor at Nehru Institute of Engineering and Technology, Coimbatore. His main research interests include Wireless Sensor Networks, IoT, Machine Learning, Deep Learning, and Quantum Computing, with additional interests in Cloud Computing and Android-based projects. He has published 1 journal article, 7 research papers in international conferences, 10 research papers in national conferences, and holds 2 patents.

Kalai Priya V is an Assistant Professor in the Department of Computer Science and Engineering at R.M.K. College of Engineering and Technology, Puduvoyal, Tamil Nadu. She is actively engaged in teaching and research, with interests in emerging areas of computer science. Her academic work reflects a commitment to innovation, student development, and scholarly contribution.

V. Thanammal Indu is a faculty member in the Department of Computer Science and Engineering at Amrita Vishwa Vidyapeetham, Nagercoil. Her research interests include machine learning, cybersecurity, and intelligent systems. She is actively involved in academic research and interdisciplinary collaborations.

Rui Vigario Rodrigues, hold a bachelor's degree in Accounting and Finance, a postgraduate qualification in Public Accounting, and am now completing a Master's degree in Accounting and Finance from the School of Business Sciences in Setúbal. I am currently employed in the field of public finances and macroeconomic analysis for GPEARI - Ministry of Finance, where I contribute to research work and strategic decisions within the public sector. I have already published a study entitled "Econophysics, State of the Science and Bibliographic Production: a Bibliometric Analysis," reflecting my interest in integrating advanced methodologies into economic and financial analysis. I have experience of using a range of software, including Python, R and EViews, for conducting sophisticated analyses such as DFA, DCCA and MF-DCCA for multifractal and time-series data

Suraj Yadav is an accomplished professional with a background in Hospitality, holding a bachelor's degree from Pune University and a Master in Hotel Management & Tourism from Madurai Kamaraj University, Madurai. Currently serving as an Assistant Professor and Training & Placement Officer at D Y Patil School of Hospitality in Kolhapur, Maharashtra, India, he brings extensive expertise to the field. Suraj is also dedicated to furthering his academic pursuits and is actively pursuing a Ph.D. at D Y Patil Agricultural & Technical University in Kolhapur. His commitment to education and training has made a significant impact in the realm of hospitality.

Index

A

B

C

D

E

G

H

R

S

T

V

W

www.ingramcontent.com/pod-product-compliance
Lightning Source LLC
LaVergne TN
LVHW080350011026
849161LV00009B/2257